Hi Hitler!

The Third Reich's legacy is in flux. For much of the postwar period, the Nazi era has been viewed moralistically as an exceptional period of history intrinsically different from all others. Since the turn of the millennium, however, this view has been challenged by a powerful wave of normalization. Gavriel D. Rosenfeld charts this important international trend by examining the shifting representation of the Nazi past in contemporary Western intellectual and cultural life. Focusing on works of historical scholarship, popular novels, counterfactual histories, feature films, and Internet websites, he identifies notable changes in the depiction of the Second World War, the Holocaust, and the figure of Adolf Hitler himself. By exploring the origins of these works and assessing the controversies they have sparked in the United States and Europe, *Hi Hitler!* offers a fascinating and timely analysis of the shifting status of the Nazi past in Western memory.

Gavriel D. Rosenfeld is Professor of History at Fairfield University.

Hi Hitler!

How the Nazi Past is Being Normalized in Contemporary Culture

Gavriel D. Rosenfeld

CAMBRIDGE
UNIVERSITY PRESS

University Printing House, Cambridge CB2 8BS, United Kingdom

Cambridge University Press is part of the University of Cambridge.

It furthers the University's mission by disseminating knowledge in the pursuit of education, learning and research at the highest international levels of excellence.

www.cambridge.org
Information on this title: www.cambridge.org/9781107423978

© Gavriel D. Rosenfeld 2015

First published 2015

Printed and bound in the United Kingdom by TJ International Ltd. Padstow Cornwall

A catalogue record for this publication is available from the British Library

Library of Congress Cataloguing in Publication data
Rosenfeld, Gavriel David, 1967–
Hi Hitler! : how the Nazi past is being normalized in contemporary culture / Gavriel D. Rosenfeld.
    pages cm
ISBN 978-1-107-07399-9 (hardback)
1. World War, 1939–1945 – Germany. 2. Hitler, Adolf, 1889–1945. 3. National socialism – History. 4. Holocaust, Jewish (1939–1945) – History and criticism. 5. Imaginary histories – History and criticism. 6. Alternative histories (Fiction) – History and criticism. 7. Collective memory. I. Title.
D757.R685 2014
943.086–dc23

2014024241

ISBN 978-1-107-07399-9 Hardback
ISBN 978-1-107-42397-8 Paperback

Cambridge University Press has no responsibility for the persistence or accuracy of URLs for external or third-party internet websites referred to in this publication, and does not guarantee that any content on such websites is, or will remain, accurate or appropriate.

CONTENTS

FIGURES

Cover: Heinrich Hoffmann's famous photograph of Hitler from 1927 has been satirized frequently on the Internet in the form of humorous image macros (or memes).

Figure Acknowledgments

Fig 1 Bavarian State Library, Munich; Fig 2. Reproduced with permission of Lizard2176; Fig 4. © KeepCalmAndPosters.com; Fig 5. © Ullsteinhaus Book Publishers GmbH; Fig 6. Creative Commons; Fig 7. © Simon & Schuster; Fig 8. © Penguin Books; Fig 9. © ullstein bild / The Granger Collection, NY; Fig 10. © Fred Stein Archive / Getty Images; Fig 11. © Corsair /Constable & Robinson; Fig 12. © MacMillan; Fig 13. © Faber and Faber; Fig 14. © Cinedigm; Fig 15. © Del Ray Books / Random House; Fig 16. © Bantam / Random House; Fig 17. © 2014 NBC Universal; Fig 18. © Atlantis Verlag; Fig 19. © Blind Spot Pictures; Fig 20. © Fischer, S. / Dieter

Kühn; Fig 21. © Edition Q / Wolfgang Brenner; Fig 22. © Cosmopol-Film; Fig 23. Reproduced with kind permission of HarperCollins; Fig 24. © Romaine Film Corp; Fig 25. © Cosmopol-Film; Fig 26. © AF archive / Alamy; Fig 27. © Alliance Atlantic Communications, Acquired by Eone Films; Fig 28. © AF archive / Alamy; Fig 29. © AAMPI Inc; Fig 30. © AF archive / Alamy; Fig 31. © Shiwago Film Co; Fig 32. © Moviestore collection Ltd / Alamy; Fig 33. © Constantin Film Production; Fig 34. © Assistentin Uwe Schott, X Filme Creative Pool GmbH; Fig 35. © Arte; Fig 36. © AF archive / Alamy; Fig 37. © Universal Pictures; Fig 38. © 2008–2011 Thirdreichlocations.com; all rights reserved; Fig 39. © Liste Anti-Sioniste; Fig 41. From: Walter Moers, "Der Bonker. Eine Tragikomödie in drei Akten." © Walter Moers/GFP. 2005; Fig 42. Reproduced with kind permission of HipsterHitler.com; Fig 43. Reproduced with kind permission of catsthatlooklikehitler.com; Fig 44.© D Legakis Photography; Fig 45. Creative Commons; Fig 46. © Quantum Foods (Pty) Ltd: (a subsidiary of Pioneer Foods (Pty) Ltd). Reproduced with kind permission.

ACKNOWLEDGMENTS

"What if" questions abound in this book, and the first involves the ironies of gratitude. Back in 2008, I submitted a newly completed journal article on the revisionist turn in recent World War II historiography to one of the leading publications in the historical profession, only to be told that its word count was more than twice the length permitted by the journal's submission rules. Daunted by the task of cutting so much material from the essay, I was unsure about whether to accept the editor's offer to edit it and resubmit. I soon declined, however, following a brief discussion with my father, who suggested that I keep the essay as is and incorporate it into a larger study on the memory of the Nazi past since the turn of the millennium. Inspired by his suggestion, I proceeded to expand my analysis to encompass a variety of related topics, all of which are included in the present volume. In retrospect, it is clear to me that had my article been accepted for publication, my book probably would never have come into existence. My acknowledgments thus begin with an ironic extension of thanks to the unnamed academic journal for validating the law of unintended consequences and facilitating my book's publication.

Fortunately, I also have more traditional expressions of gratitude to extend to friends and colleagues. I would like to thank Alvin H. Rosenfeld, Saul Friedlander, Alon Confino, and Catherine Epstein for reading portions of the manuscript and providing me with constructive feedback. Heartfelt thanks also go to Guy Saville, Brendan Dubois, Dirk Moses, Omer Bartov, and Jon Reffs for answering questions and providing me with material related to their work. I would additionally like to acknowledge academic colleagues who participated in conference panels in which I presented material from the book, including Michael Berkowitz, Doris Bergen, Eugene Sheppard, and Steve Zipperstein. I am especially grateful to my agent, Andrew Stuart, for helping to steer the book to publication. I would also like to communicate my profound gratitude to my editor at Cambridge University Press, Michael Watson, for many years of congenial collaboration on book projects past and present. Thanks also go to Kaiya Shang and Amanda George at Cambridge University Press for their skillful work in helping to secure permissions for the book's images, as well as to Laurence Marsh for his skilled copy-editing work and Joanna Breeze, for her help with the index. Robbin Crabtree, Fairfield University's Dean of the College of Arts and Sciences, also deserves thanks for generously helping to subsidize the book's images with the aid of supplemental funds. Lastly, I would like to thank members of my extended and immediate family. I owe special thanks to my sister-in-law, Miranda Banks, who several years ago alerted me to the existence of the "Hi Hitler!" meme, which she discovered lurking in one of her students' final exams. My wife, Erika Banks, by now needs no formulaic expressions of thanks for encouraging my research projects. She knows full well that my love and devotion to her lie well outside of the realm of history. My children, Julia and Benjamin, meanwhile, have become increasingly interested in all things historical as they have matured. Although they remain immersed in the world of the Internet and its incessant glorification of the present, their exposure to the many bizarre representations of Nazism on the World Wide Web (examples of which I confess to having told them about on many occasions), has stimulated their curiosity about the past. It is in the hope that they will continue to develop their interests in history that I dedicate this book to them.

INTRODUCTION

Originally mocked, subsequently feared, posthumously vilified, Adolf Hitler today is becoming normalized. Throughout the Western world, the Nazi dictator has long been regarded as the epitome of evil. But since the turn of the millennium, he has been increasingly transformed into a more ambiguous figure. Nowhere is this transformation clearer than on the Internet. Anyone who conducts a simple image search of Hitler on the World Wide Web will encounter an eclectic array of representations, ranging from archival photographs documenting the dictator's role in the Third Reich to digitally altered images that spoof him for laughs. The diversity of images is striking, but what is most notable is how the line separating them is beginning to blur. As discerning web users probably know, certain photographs of Hitler are now doing double duty, serving the purpose of both documentation and exploitation.

Consider Figure 1. Originally taken by Hitler's personal photographer, Heinrich Hoffmann, in his Munich studio in 1927, it is one of a famous series of photographs that portray the then struggling Nazi party leader meticulously practicing his oratorical choreography.[1] The photograph depicts Hitler in a pose of fanatical intensity, his fists clenched, his face contorted in an expression of fury about what we can only imagine was one of the countless grievances that fueled his political agenda. As a document of history, the photograph is significant for showing how Hitler methodically rehearsed what were widely thought to be "spontaneous" gestures, a fact that explains why the Nazi party leader, eager to protect his image as a "naturally" gifted

Figure 1. This photograph of Hitler, taken by his personal photographer Heinrich Hoffmann in 1927, was part of a larger series of photos in which the Nazi party leader rehearsed his "spontaneous" oratorical gestures for the camera.

orator, forbade the image – and the entire series of which it was part – from being shown to the German public during his lifetime.[2]

Hoffmann's photograph is not merely a document of history, however, but a document of memory thanks to its recent transformation on the Internet. More than eighty years after it was originally taken, Hoffmann's photo appeared on the popular website, Meme Generator, having been dramatically altered by the addition of a 1970s-style mirror ball over the Nazi dictator's head (Figure 2).[3] The mashup image, called "Disco Hitler," radically subverts the original photograph's intended purpose of portraying the Nazi leader as a passionate politician by satirically depicting him as a dexterous dancer. The transfiguration does not stop there, however. Meme Generator allows web users to add humorous captions to the digitally altered image, thereby transforming it into an "image macro."[4] The term may not be familiar to average readers, but image macros are a staple of contemporary Internet culture. Comprised of photographs with superimposed texts rendered in (by now ubiquitous) Impact font, image macros seek to make people laugh by juxtaposing images and texts in ironic, incongruous, or absurd combinations. Many such images have proliferated on Internet

Figure 2. "Disco Hitler" is one of the more popular image macros on the Internet that lampoons Hitler. Thousands of web users have added crudely humorous captions to the image on websites, such as Meme Generator. This particular caption is a German-themed pun on the well-known rap phrase, "Where My Bitches At?"

websites, forums, and imageboards in recent years – so much so, that image macros have risen to the status of Internet "memes," ideas that have spread virally and achieved iconic status on the World Wide Web. "Disco Hitler" is one of the more popular image macros of the Nazi dictator on the Internet, with nearly three thousand currently in existence on Meme Generator alone.[5] Although their captions appear in many different languages, all of them strive to be humorous, albeit in different ways. Some seek laughs by employing crude puns and occasional German words, for instance: "Disco Hitler Says Stalin Alive!" and "Wehrmacht Bitches At?" Others end up offending rather than amusing, as with the tasteless phrases: "I Said 'A Glass of Juice,' Not Gas the Jews!" and "Six Million! New High Score!" Still other captions veer toward the absurd, as with "I Did It for the Lulz."[6]

These and countless other versions of "Disco Hitler" are merely a tiny fraction of the myriad image macros that poke fun at the Nazi dictator on the Internet. An estimated 61,000 Hitler-related image macros are currently listed on Meme Generator and thousands more exist on competing meme-generating sites.[7] They include the

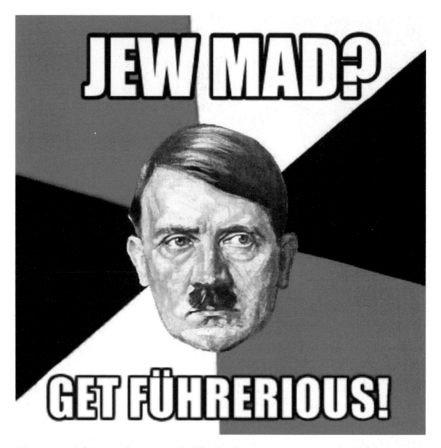

Figure 3. "Advice Hitler" is probably the best-known image macro of the Nazi dictator on the Internet. A take-off of the famous meme, Advice Dog, it depicts the Nazi dictator offering words of "advice," often in the form of groan-inducing puns.

ever-popular "Advice Hitler" (a knock-off of the famous "Advice Dog" meme), which features the Nazi dictator's disembodied head – set against the backdrop of a black, white, and red color wheel – dispensing words of bad "advice" (Figure 3). There is "Bedtime Hitler," depicting a pajama-clad Führer riding a toboggan across a night-time sky. There is "Chilling Hitler," which shows the dictator relaxing with a newspaper on a patio chair in Berchtesgaden.[8] There are even image macros of Hitler's head photoshopped onto the bodies of supermodels, pop singers, and rappers.[9] Like "Disco Hitler," all of these images have also been supplied with user-generated captions meant to elicit laughs.

Among the many captions that have accompanied these images, one of the most memorable is "Hi Hitler!" The phrase has appeared in

Figure 4. The "Hi Hitler" meme has found expression in many forms, such as this parody of the famous British poster from 1939, "Keep Calm and Carry On."

the "Disco Hitler" and "Advice Hitler" memes, as well as in other off-shoots, including parodies of the Pokemon character Pikachu; spoofs of vintage British posters ("Keep Calm and Hi Hitler" (Figure 4)); and photographs of sundry house pets.[10] At first glance, the phrase "Hi Hitler!" may seem banal. Read at the literal level, the phrase merely extends a greeting – a colloquial version of the word "hello" – to an image of the Nazi dictator. At a deeper level, however, the phrase contains a more satirical message. As even moderately informed web users know, the exclamation "Hi Hitler!" is a corruption of the infamous Nazi salutation, "Heil Hitler!" ("Hail Hitler"). This German slogan was originally coined in the early 1920s to buttress the cult of personality known as the "Führer myth."[11] In its more recent incarnation, however, the slogan's original meaning has been inverted. The substitution of the casual English word "hi" for the more grandiose German word "heil" punctures the Nazi salutation's pomposity and renders it laughable. The humorous effect is further enhanced by the ambiguity of whether or not the mangling of the original salutation is intentional. In all probability, the phrase "Hi Hitler!" has spread on the Internet due to the efforts of savvy web users who appreciate a good pun. Yet there is anecdotal evidence that certain people, ignorant of German, have mistaken the original German "heil" for the English "hi," and naively believe that "Hi Hitler" represents a historically authentic phrase. In reproducing and circulating it, therefore, they have added to its humor by unintentionally committing a malapropism.[12]

The phrase "Hi Hitler!" is notable not merely for being funny, however, but for symbolizing a new trend in the representation of Nazism. In an ironic turnabout – indeed, in what might be regarded as a bizarre form of deferred justice – the politician who insisted on maintaining complete control over his public image during his lifetime has, of late, been subjected to infinite forms of digital distortion. Thanks to the Internet, Hitler has been transformed into a meme in his own right.[13] Beyond appearing in countless image macros, he has starred in thousands of satirical movie and music videos; he has been featured in Web-based comic strips; he has been profiled in mock encyclopedia entries; he has even inspired online games. In light of this trend, the phrase "Hi Hitler!" can be interpreted as a gesture of welcome to a radically new view of the Nazi dictator – one that regards him as a symbol of humor instead of horror.

The increasingly comic representation of Hitler on the Internet is part of a larger shift currently underway in the memory of the Nazi past. Since the turn of the millennium, the traditional belief throughout much of the Western world that the Third Reich should be remembered from a moralistic perspective has been challenged by a powerful wave of normalization. This wave has manifested itself in many areas of contemporary intellectual and cultural life. It has appeared in sophisticated works of academic scholarship and journalism; in popular novels and short stories; in works of film and television; and, most prominently, on innumerable Internet websites. Whether aiming high or low, all of these works have transformed the Third Reich in different ways. Some have relativized it in order to minimize its historical distinctiveness. Others have universalized it in order to emphasize its alleged relevance for contemporary issues. Still others have aestheticized it through unconventional means of representation. The works comprising this trend have appeared in many different nations, whether in Europe, North America, or the non-Western world. They have reflected diverse motives, ranging from the political to the puerile. This diversity notwithstanding, the normalizing wave has generally focused on a single goal: overturning the perceived exceptionality of the Nazi era.

Memory and normalization

Overturning the sense of the past's exceptionality is one of several goals that define the broader phenomenon of normalization. Normalization is a relatively new concept that historians and other scholars have increasingly employed to understand how and why perceptions of the past shift over time.[14] The concept has been used in different ways: to explain how the past is represented in written history, how it takes shape in cultural memory, how it determines group identity, and even how it influences governmental policy. Regardless of the form it takes, normalization is defined by several basic features. At the most abstract level, it entails the replacement of difference with similarity. With respect to history and memory, for example, normalization involves a process through which a specific historical legacy comes to be viewed like any other. The legacy may involve a particular era, an event, a person, or a combination thereof. But for a given past to become normalized, it has to shed the features that set it apart from other pasts. The normalization of the past can also shape the formation of group identity, enabling nations and other collectively defined groups to perceive themselves as being similar to, instead of different from, others. Normalization can furthermore liberate national governments to embrace the same kind of "normal" domestic and foreign policies that are pursued by other nations. To be sure, the assertion that normalizing the past can have these effects is underpinned by certain assumptions: first, that certain pasts may some-how be "abnormal" in the first place; second, that there is an ultimate end point of "normality" towards which all pasts eventually proceed. These assumptions are far from being unproblematic. But no matter what one thinks of them, they are rooted in an undeniable fact: not all pasts are created equal. Some are less – and some are more – "normal" than others.

What determines whether or not a given past is perceived as normal? There is no simple answer to this question, partly due to the difficulty of defining the concept of normality in the first place. On the one hand, normality is typically associated with positive qualities – for example, being healthy, natural, and stable. At the same time, normality can be defined via negation, with reference to traits that are directly opposed to it, such as abnormality and deviance.[15] All of these qualities rest on standards that vary according to time and place, and so normality is ultimately a relative concept. At its core, though, normality is associ-ated with the condition of being typical, unexceptional, or average.

These observations help us determine whether or not a given past can be seen as "normal." Generally speaking, the normality of a specific historical legacy depends on its status within a nation's historical consciousness. Most eras of a nation's history, it is safe to say, are viewed with a sense of detachment, if not indifference. Ask ordinary Europeans about the reigns of most of their country's monarchs, ask Americans about the administrations of most of their presidents, and you will typically get a shrug of the shoulders. These "normal" eras receive little notice, as they are defined by the ordinary, the routine, and the run-of-the-mill. Other eras, by contrast, have a less normal status because of their disproportionate presence in popular consciousness. These eras are typically associated with pivotal events in a nation's history. These events may be positive ones that contribute to a nation's sense of self-esteem, such as successful revolutions or military triumphs. Or they may be negative ones – military defeats, political crimes, or other injustices – that are surrounded by trauma, guilt, and shame. Both types of events, whether positive or negative, usually have a strong emotional impact upon the people who experienced them and often their descendants as well. As a result, these particular historical legacies acquire a special status in memory.

More than anything else, they become viewed from a moralistic perspective. This perspective is underpinned by the conviction that the past should not merely be explained, but judged. It should be studied not only from a stance of dispassionate neutrality, but of ethical engagement. Above all, the past should be studied in such a way that its proper "lessons" are learned and preserved in memory. These lessons can be positive ones of emulation or negative ones of admonition; they can highlight accomplishments that should be repeated or errors that should be avoided. In both cases, the past is to be viewed didactically. This perspective is, in many ways, an admirable one that stems from noble motives. Yet it is prone to certain excesses. A moralistic perspective towards the past can foster distortions in historical consciousness. It can cloak the past with myths and taboos that are meant to reinforce its accepted "lessons" and prevent subsequent challenges to them. It can foster a dogmatic and ritualistic form of historical consciousness that can easily devolve into stale orthodoxy. And it can produce a view of the past that impedes, rather than promotes, genuine historical understanding.[16] To be sure, a moralistic view of history need not fall victim to these pitfalls. But being aware of their existence is necessary to prevent it from happening. In the end, it is far from clear when exactly a moralistic view of the past begins to obey the law of diminishing returns. One thing, though, is indisputable: it is the moralistic aura surrounding a given historical legacy that defines its exceptional status and keeps it from being considered "normal."

The fading of this sense of exceptionality, in turn, marks the phenomenon of normalization. Why, though, do perceptions of the past change? What forces shape the evolution of historical memory? In answering these questions, it is important to recognize that memory is not monolithic. Rarely does a single view of a specific historical legacy exist in a given society. Instead, there are multiple competing perspectives. Some are dominant, or "official," memories, defined by state support; others are "counter-memories," defined by popular dissent.[17] These competing memories exist in different forms. There is the "communicative memory" of historical events, meaning the oral preservation and transmission of eyewitness recollections of the past. And there is the "cultural memory" of historical events, referring to their subsequent representation in different cultural forms, whether film, literature, theater, art, or architecture.[18] These forms, finally, serve different social functions. Communicative memories are usually expressed and preserved in the private sphere; cultural memories typically have a more public presence. Taken together, all these forms of memory – official and counter, communicative and cultural, private and public – determine a society's historical consciousness. Their coexistence, however, is rarely static and evolves over time. The official memory that predominates in one era can easily be replaced by a dissenting counter-memory in another; communicative memories eventually yield to cultural memories; and recollections originally restricted to the sphere of private memory often become public.

These patterns of interaction are all involved in the process of normalization. To be sure, the process is far from simple. As with memory in general, normalization is not monolithic; it assumes different forms and develops in different ways according to different methods. To begin with, there is the phenomenon of organic normalization. This concept refers to the process in which the passing of time, the disappearance of older generations of people who personally experienced historical events, and the maturation of new generations bearing a less personal relationship to them, bring about a less morally oriented perspective towards the past. In this version of the phenomenon, normalization is a descriptive concept that denotes a natural, if not inevitable, process. It is a process, moreover, that offers an important corrective to some of moralism's pitfalls. Organic normalization can promote a shift from an emotionally charged view of the past to one that is more dispassionate; it can facilitate a turn away from subjective judgment to objective understanding.

Organic normalization is not alone, however. There are other, more prescriptive, versions of normalization that take a more active role in shaping the memory of the past. These versions assume different forms, but they all express a basic human desire for normality. The desire to feel normal, whether at the individual or group level, is a natural one that should be seen as entirely legitimate. Yet, because normality ultimately is an ideal, attaining it in practice can be difficult. Those who pursue it, therefore, often become impatient and employ various strategies to hasten its arrival. They may seek to relativize a specific historical legacy by minimizing its distinctiveness through comparisons to other historical events. They may attempt to universalize it by explaining its origins, and highlighting its relevance, in general rather than particular terms.[19] And they may try to aestheticize it by subjecting it to forms of representation that mute its moral dimensions. All three strategies differ in their methods, but they pursue the common goal of overturning the sense of the past's exceptionality.

This goal clearly underpins the strategy of relativization. Those who pursue this version of normalization are typically frustrated by the fact that a given past prevents them from establishing a normal identity. The problem, in their view, is that the past remains surrounded by a moralistic aura that makes it the object of excessive, if not obsessive, attention. This attention can assume both positive and negative forms. A triumphant historical event – say, a major military victory – may be excessively venerated in popular memory. A historical episode involving failure – an abortive revolution or a disastrous civil war – may be viewed with excessive shame. The attempt to relativize either one of these kinds of historical events, in turn, entails comparing it to other, allegedly similar, events in order to reduce its exceptionality, minimize its significance, and strip it of its moralistic aura. This is not to say that the proponents of relativization do not have moral agendas of their own. Those who seek to minimize the significance of a particular historical event often claim that they are doing so in the best interests of their country. Some, typically on the political right, contend that relativizing a shameful act of historical injustice can help restore a sense of national pride. Others, usually on the political left, insist that relativizing a major triumph can help temper a penchant for national hubris. These claims reveal that normalization is not incompatible with a moral sensibility. At the same time, by striving to undermine the moral aura of exceptionality that surrounds a given past, the supporters of relativization erode its specificity and contribute to its normalization.

Similar traits define the strategy of universalization. The supporters of this form of normalization also help erode the past's aura of exceptionality. Unlike the practitioners of relativization, however, they do so not to minimize the past's significance, but to expand its relevance. The supporters of universalization typically promote this goal in the process of pursuing larger analytical and political agendas. They often expand the past's relevance, for instance, in the process of explaining the origins of a given historical event (a major revolution, war, or case of genocide) with generalizing concepts that focus on the role of broader universal forces instead of particular historical circumstances. They also expand the past's relevance in the process of rhetorically invoking it to direct attention to other historical or contemporary events they deem to be important. Both kinds of comparison are entirely legitimate and can advance historical understanding. But they instrumentalize the past for broader purposes. The promoters of universalization commonly admit that their aim in invoking specific historical events is to raise awareness about, and ultimately ameliorate, present-day social, economic, and political problems. Like the practitioners of relativization, they are not averse to moralism. Nonetheless, their historical comparisons, by emphasizing similarity over difference, end up obscuring the moral aura of exceptionality that surrounds a given past. The more frequent (and exaggerated) such comparisons become, moreover, the less credibility they enjoy. As the past's relevance is inflated, its distinctiveness is diminished. The past's universalization, in short, can easily lead to its normalization.

The same is true of the strategy of aestheticization. It, too, is motivated by a sense of impatience with the past's exceptionality, specifically with the existence of morally grounded restrictions on how it can be aesthetically represented. Within Western intellectual and cultural life, it has long been believed that historical events should be depicted from a realistic perspective. In historiography, literature, and film, the use of realism reflects the prevailing desire to preserve the integrity of the historical record.[20] This desire has clear moral underpinnings. But it comes at the price of limiting artistic freedom. As a result, scholars, writers, artists, and filmmakers have often rebelled against realistic methods of representing the past and pursued more unconventional aesthetic methods of doing so, drawing on such genres as satire, fantasy, and counterfactual history. Regardless of the methods they have employed, however, the supporters of aestheticization have been less concerned with the moral dimensions of the past than the artistic challenges of representing it. As a result, they run the risk of sacrificing substance for superficiality. To be sure, those who end up aestheticizing the past often claim to be pursuing deeper moral agendas of their own. They may claim that humorous modes of representation demythologize historical villains and heroes; that imaginative modes of representation provide new insights into historical reality; and that counterfactual modes of representation help explain historical causality. They are not incorrect in making such claims, which contain more than a degree of truth. But while their aesthetically oriented approaches can help illuminate aspects of the past, they can easily become ends in themselves and overshadow the past's moral dimensions. Aestheticization, in short, also promotes normalization.

Taken together, these prescriptive forms of normalization share a common goal, but they often fall short of attaining it. More often than

not, they backfire and produce the exact opposite of what their supporters intend. They produce a dialectic of normalization, in which the
deliberate effort to normalize the past ends up underscoring its exceptionality.[21] This phenomenon has been visible in countless disputes over
contested historical legacies in recent years. It has been particularly
visible in efforts to relativize the past. Every time that individuals or
groups attempt to forcibly minimize the significance of a particular
historical legacy, they inspire resistance from opponents committed to
defending its singularity.[22] As views clash and controversy erupts, the
effort to direct attention away from the past ultimately draws attention
towards it. The same is true of efforts to universalize the past, albeit in
reverse. The more that a given historical legacy is invoked for present-
day comparative purposes, the more it sparks protests from critics who
claim that the past's relevance is being exaggerated and its singularity
effaced. These critics insist that the past should exist for its own sake and
not be instrumentalized. Some go so far as to combat what they see as the
inflation of memory by recommending a healthy dose of forgetting. In
the end, whether calling for more or less memory, the dialectical
responses to relativization and universalization end up keeping the past
in the public eye. This being the case, the very concept of prescriptive
normalization may be a contradiction in terms. In the same way that it is
impossible to "decree spontaneity," it may also be impossible to impose
normality upon the past.[23] So long as efforts to normalize it are perceived
as premature, forced, or driven by ulterior motives, they will be met with
resistance.

Only when competing memories are reconciled is there a
possibility of advancing the goal of normality. Indeed, for a past to be
truly normalized, it needs to be successfully "come to terms with" and
"mastered." These concepts, which derive from the German notion of
Vergangenheitsbewältigung, have increasingly been used to explain how
disputes over controversial historical legacies can potentially be
resolved.[24] Over the course of the last generation, scholars have examined how different countries have contended with divisive pasts and have
identified the measures needed to master them.[25] Most of these pasts
have involved the perpetration of an injustice by one group against
another and thus have been surrounded by legacies of guilt and suffering.
To come to terms with such a past, the injustice must be atoned for
through various measures. They may be legal, financial, symbolic, or
commemorative; they may entail trials of perpetrators, reparations to

victims, official apologies, or the creation of memorials and museums.[26] What is important is that these measures foster a willingness among contending parties – those representing perpetrators, victims, bystanders, and their descendants – to reconcile with one another and forge a mnemonic consensus. Only by going through this process can a controversial historical legacy ever have the hope of becoming normalized. As long as reconciliation does not happen, competing groups will remain trapped in a dialectic of normalization. The past will remain unmastered. Normality will remain a distant ideal.

Normalizing the Nazi past: 1945–2000

An absence of normality has long defined the memory of the Third Reich. Ever since the end of World War II, the Nazi era has widely been viewed as different from other periods of history. The main reason for its exceptional status is its notorious degree of criminality. In unleashing the Second World War and perpetrating the Holocaust, the Nazis committed unprecedented crimes. These crimes took place in the recent past, moreover, and thus still exist in communicative memory. For these reasons, the Nazi period has come to be viewed in most Western countries – whether on the winning or losing side of World War II – from a moralistic perspective. The essence of this perspective has long been defined by the phrase, "never again." These two words convey the simple moral message that posterity should heed the "lessons" of the Nazi dictatorship and make sure its disasters are never repeated.[27]

For most of the postwar period, this admonition was generally respected. Immediately after the war's end, the Nuremberg Trials signaled the Allies' commitment to bring Nazi war criminals to justice, while subsequent trials in the Federal Republic of Germany during the 1960s and 1970s revealed the West German government's recognition of its importance as well. Reparations payments by the Federal Republic to Israel in the 1950s showed an economic commitment to making moral absolution for the Nazi past. Symbolic and commemorative gestures in the form of memorials, museums, and ceremonial speeches reinforced this message throughout Europe and the United States. And countless cultural and intellectual works, including novels, poems, films, plays, and academic studies, wrestled directly with the Nazi era's moral implications. It took time, of course, for this confrontation to commence, and it did not unfold evenly in all areas of Western life. But it gradually accelerated as the postwar era progressed.

The confrontation reached its peak of intensity during the "memory boom" of the 1990s.[28] In the years between the end of the Cold War and the turn of the millennium, the legacy of the Third Reich – especially the Holocaust – became anchored in Western historical consciousness as never before. The end of the Cold War allowed buried memories from the Nazi era to be confronted throughout Europe. Reunified Germany for the first time accepted full responsibility for crimes perpetrated against Jews and other Europeans. The post-communist states of Eastern Europe, as well as various Western European nations, began to confront their own legacies of wartime collaboration. European and American political officials began to invoke Nazi era crimes as grounds for launching humanitarian military inter-ventions in places like Iraq and Yugoslavia. And Western governments officially worked to establish the Nazi genocide as a global symbol of moral admonition with the Declaration of the Stockholm International Forum on the Holocaust in 2000. By the turn of the millennium, in short, a broad consensus had been forged in support of remembering the Nazi past from a strong moral perspective.

This commitment to memory did not go unchallenged, however. During the same period, from 1945 up through the year 2000, counter-vailing efforts to normalize the Nazi past also appeared. These efforts surfaced sporadically at different times in different countries. They reflected different motives and assumed different forms. But they were linked by the desire to challenge the moralistic representation of the Nazi years as an era of historical exceptionality. During this period, these efforts failed to break the moralistic consensus on the Nazi past. But they eroded its strength and laid the groundwork for the more intense wave of normalization that commenced after the turn of the millennium.

Germany

The effort to normalize the Nazi past was most visible in Germany. After the end of World War II, many Germans had difficulty taking full responsibility for the Third Reich's criminal legacy. They were not averse to remembering the Nazi era as such, but their memories of it were "self-directed," rather than "other-directed"; they preferred to focus on their own suffering rather than that of the regime's millions of victims.[29] Not long after the war's end, Germans in both the eastern and western parts of the divided country strove to avoid a sense of guilt for the recent past by seeking to normalize it. In the communist German Democratic Republic (GDR), government officials universalized Nazism's significance by explaining it as the by-product of capitalism, the abolition of which after 1945 ostensibly absolved the new country of its recent crimes and granted it a clean bill of health. In the democratic Federal Republic of Germany (FRG), meanwhile, the conservative CDU government of Chancellor Konrad Adenauer pursued a strategy of relativizing the Nazis' crimes by offsetting them against the wartime and postwar suffering of the German people (whether due to Allied aerial bombing raids, expulsions from the east, or postwar "victors' justice").[30] This normalizing strategy defined both the communicative and cultural memories of many West Germans in the early postwar period. Indeed, it was widely seen as necessary for the Federal Republic's postwar reconstruction and democratization.[31]

Before long, however, the strategy sparked a backlash. By the 1960s, new social and political trends – epitomized by the rise of the "generation of 1968" and the turn to the political left – prompted increasing numbers of Germans in the Federal Republic to explore their elders' involvement in Nazi atrocities. The resumption of war crimes trials for ex-Nazis after the early 1960s (most notably, the Frankfurt Auschwitz Trials of 1963–65) and the revelation that major conservative politicians, such as CDU Chancellor Kurt Georg Kiesinger (1966–69), had been Nazi party members, disenchanted younger Germans and convinced them that their country's socio-economic order was latently fascist. Their ensuing effort to trace continuities between the Nazi past and the West German present represented an important development in German remembrance by reorienting its moral focus.[32] Rather than concentrating on German suffering, it now focused on German guilt. That said, the generation of 1968's approach to remembrance remained self-directed. It also tended to universalize the Nazi era's relevance by focusing on its global (mostly capitalist) roots instead of its specific German dimensions. This pattern only began to change in the 1970s. Beginning with SPD Chancellor Willy Brandt's symbolic decision to kneel down in front of the Warsaw Ghetto Heroes Monument while on a state visit to Poland in 1970 and accelerating after the broadcast of the American docudrama, *Holocaust*, on West German television in 1979, Germans slowly began to pay attention to the

new-found culture of contrition as a badge of normality. In short, by the year 2000, Germany had altered the political valence of normalization and appeared well on its way towards mastering its Nazi past.

Despite this important development, however, the country continued to display signs of abnormality due to the dialectic of normalization. Although German leaders made notable strides in integrating "other-directed" memories into official memory, ordinary Germans continued to have difficulty doing so in the realm of cultural memory. Conservative Germans, in particular, remained unable to deal with the topic that continued to prevent the achievement of full normality – the legacy of the Holocaust. Ever since Holocaust consciousness began to acquire a central place in German identity in the 1990s, conservative scholars, writers, and politicians tried to marginalize it through prescriptive strategies of normalization.[39] In the early and mid-1990s, for example, various political figures and scholars sought to relativize and universalize the Third Reich's crimes against the Jews by comparing them to those of the East German regime or attributing them to the amorphous concept of "modernity."[40] Later in the decade, public figures, such as the German writer, Martin Walser, condemned what he described as the instrumental use of the Holocaust as a "moral cudgel" to prevent Germans from attaining normality.[41] Not long thereafter, conservative politicians, such as Jürgen Möllemann and Martin Hohmann, tried to relativize Germany's reputation as a "nation of perpetrators" by explicitly calling for an end to the post-Holocaust taboo against criticizing Jews and the State of Israel.[42] Not surprisingly, these efforts backfired by sparking extended controversy that drew attention towards, instead of away from, the Nazi past. Yet, as would soon become clear, they were merely the beginning of a stronger wave of normalization that would arrive in Germany after the turn of the millennium.

Great Britain and the United States

Outside of Germany, the process of normalization followed a different trajectory. This was especially true in the nations that made up the Western alliance during World War II: Great Britain and the United States. In the years after 1945, the British resembled the Germans in regarding the Nazi period as an important part of their national identity. The obvious difference was that since the British were on the winning side of the war, they viewed the period from a triumphalistic, rather than a tragic, perspective. This perspective quickly became associated with the mythic idea of the "finest hour."[43] The core of this idea, which was immortalized by Prime Minister Winston Churchill in his famous speech to parliament on June 18, 1940, was that the British people had proved their strength of character by deciding, after the fall of France, to forgo a separate peace with the Nazis and fight them alone. Although the odds of victory were slim, the setback of Dunkirk painful, and the Battle of Britain traumatic, the British kept a stiff upper lip and emerged victorious, thereby helping save Western civilization from Nazi barbarism.[44] After 1945, this heroic and deeply moralistic view of the country's wartime actions became canonized in British intellectual, and cultural life, finding expression in countless works of history, film, theater, television, and art.[45] It was especially widespread in popular culture, which offered up endless Nazis – from the dastardly to the bumbling – as foils to the heroic Britons.[46]

At various junctures in the postwar period, however, this moralistic perspective was questioned by Britons intent on normalizing the memory of the war years. This British version of normalization differed from that which existed in Germany. It was driven not by the desire to avoid feelings of excessive guilt, but feelings of excessive pride. This self-critical reaction was rooted in the growing sense that Britain had become too self-satisfied about its wartime accomplishments. This sentiment surfaced in periods of national crisis, when present-day problems threatened to undermine Britain's historically based sense of self-esteem. In the 1960s and 1970s, for example, as the country was increasingly suffering from the effects of imperial decline and economic stagnation, various works of revisionist historiography, film, and literature challenged the finest hour myth by offering more critical portraits of the British and nuanced representations of the Germans.[47] These works, which mostly hailed from the political left, tended to universalize the Nazi era's significance by identifying the potential for fascism within Great Britain itself, thereby effacing the finest hour myth's clear moral lines between heroic Britons and evil Germans. This self-critical form of normalization declined in the 1980s, when Margaret Thatcher's Tory government revived the finest hour myth for nationalist purposes. In doing so, however, British conservatives, supported by segments of the media, promoted their own – highly self-serving – form of universalization. By constantly invoking the legacy of World War II in confronting present-day domestic and foreign crises, especially during the Falklands War of 1982, the British right effaced the Nazi era's historic specificity.[48]

Following the end of the Cold War and then throughout the 1990s, however, Britons once again embraced a self-critical form of normalization. The catalysts for this development were German and European unification, both of which were seen as threatening Britain with renewed decline.[49] In this period, growing numbers of Britons on the left and right became convinced that the country's obsession with the Nazis reflected a desire to live in the past and avoid dealing with contemporary challenges. This skepticism was articulated in new revisionist histories of the war years, as well as in comments in the mass media.[50] The reason Britons believed that the "war . . . must never . . . be allowed to end," as one journalist put it in 1999, was their fear of the emptiness that would exist without it. With British identity in flux in an era of multiculturalism, World War II was one of the few things that provide a source of national unity. As one observer declared: "We may no longer know who we are in this country, or where we're heading, but we know that we're not Nazis." Certain critics bemoaned this mindset, however, arguing that the excessive veneration of the war experience was a symptom of "our . . . present confusion." In order to avoid being "throttled" by the past, they demanded that Britain "embark on its own journey of normalisation" and pursue a more self-critical view of the nation's recent history.[51] By the turn of the millennium, growing numbers of Britons would do precisely that.

The same pattern held true in the United States. As in Great Britain, most Americans after 1945 viewed the history of the Third Reich from a strictly moralistic perspective. This was especially visible in American attitudes towards the Second World War. Most Americans adhered to a triumphalistic view of the conflict, believing their country's decision to fight against the Axis powers had been both wise and just. This belief was epitomized by the idea that World War II had been a "good war" waged against Nazi evil. This moralistic understanding of the Third Reich was enshrined during the early postwar years in countless works of academic scholarship, literature, theater, and film. It was further bolstered after the 1980s by the growth of Holocaust consciousness, which was institutionally anchored in educational curricula, the mass media, and memorials and museums.[52]

There were only sporadic challenges to this view of the Nazi era. As in Britain, periods of crisis in the United States brought forth dissenting views about the past and efforts to normalize it. During the 1960s and 1970s, for example, the Vietnam War, the Civil Rights movement, and economic recession fostered the production of revisionist histories of World War II that questioned the wisdom of the United States' entry into the conflict. These works relativized Nazism's evil by portraying it as a lesser threat than Soviet communism, which was depicted as triumphing after 1945 thanks to American interventionism.[53] There were also efforts to universalize the Nazi past. In the 1960s, individuals and groups on the political left began to invoke the crimes of the Third Reich to condemn American racism, sexism, and military intervention in Vietnam.[54] Later in the 1980s and 1990s, representatives of the political right invoked the Nazi era to condemn abortion, gun control, and other controversial social issues.[55] These efforts at normalization sparked controversy whenever they appeared. But, like the revisionist histories, they were unable to overturn the moralistic American consensus on the Nazi era. Indeed, during the administration of President Ronald Reagan in the 1980s, and especially in the decade after the end of the Cold War, renewed feelings of American triumphalism led to an upsurge of patriotic feeling about World War II. Since the turn of the millennium, however, the mood has changed. As in Great Britain, a renewed sense of crisis has generated a wave of pessimism in the United States that has accelerated the normalization of the Nazi past.

Eastern Europe, Israel, and beyond

Similar shifts in memory were visible in other countries prior to the year 2000. Among the nations of Eastern Europe, different approaches to normalization competed with one another. During the Cold War, most Eastern Bloc regimes took their marching orders from the Soviet Union and tendentiously explained the Third Reich as the by-product of capitalism. This view universalized the Nazi regime's significance by effacing its German origins, marginalizing its crimes against the Jews, and glossing over the willingness of Eastern European states to collaborate with it during the Second World War.[56] With the fall of communism in 1989, however, the state-imposed strategy of universalization was challenged by populist efforts at relativization. This new approach emerged in tandem with the effort of newly independent Eastern European nations to regain a normal sense of national identity by rewriting their national histories of the war years. Predictably, most Eastern Europeans were inclined to emphasize their victimization by the Nazis. At the same time, they felt pressure to follow the moralistic mandate established by the memory boom and atone for historical injustices they had perpetrated against others.[57] As a result, they could not avoid dealing with their own shameful episodes of wartime collaboration. As was shown by controversies that erupted in Poland (over the massacre at Jedwabne), Croatia (over the killings at Jasenovac and Bleiburg), and other Axis-affiliated nations, such as Hungary, Romania, and the Baltic states, Eastern Europeans found it very difficult to reconcile their legacies of victimization, collaboration, and perpetration.[58] In practice, however, most elected to relativize their responsibility for working with the Nazis by stressing how they had been victimized by them.

This strategy of normalization was less visible in nations with clearer legacies of victimization. In Israel, for example, the magnitude of Jewish suffering in the Holocaust meant that the Nazi past was not defined by comparable attempts at relativization. Yet, even in the Jewish State, memory was influenced by the dynamics of normalization. Ever since the early 1960s, Israeli political leaders framed the Holocaust in strongly moralistic terms as part of the effort to make it a central feature of the country's official memory and national identity, a trend epitomized by Prime Minister David Ben-Gurion's decision in 1960 to have SS officer Adolf Eichmann stand trial in Jerusalem for crimes against humanity and the Jewish people. Over time, however, the Israeli fixation on the Nazi genocide led to its gradual universalization. Both liberal and conservative Israelis employed Nazi analogies for political purposes. Among politicians, Labor and Likud leaders both compared Arab rulers – whether Egyptian ruler Gamal Abdel Nasser in the 1960s or PLO chief Yasser Arafat in the 1980s – to Hitler. Among ordinary Israelis, meanwhile, secular leftists were as likely as ultra-orthodox Haredim to make Nazi comparisons in attacking government policies at home or in occupied Palestinian territories.[59] By the 1990s, this universalized treatment of the Nazi past became so widespread that it inspired a skeptical backlash against remembrance altogether. The first intifada, the rise of post-Zionism, and the thaw in Arab–Israeli relations during the Oslo process led various Israeli observers to doubt whether the emphasis on Jewish victimization in the Holocaust had any political or moral utility whatsoever. Like certain British critics, they believed the time had come for Holocaust memory to assume a less central place in Israeli national life.

In order to achieve this, they pursued a revisionist approach to the Nazi genocide, reassessing the Zionist leadership's policies towards rescuing Jews during the war, questioning the Israeli state's treatment of survivors after 1945, and criticizing longstanding taboos – for example, against playing the music of Richard Wagner or translating controversial foreign works of Holocaust scholarship into Hebrew – in the effort to restore a sense of normality to the past.[60] Other Israelis insisted on preserving established patterns of remembrance, however, and so the result was endless debate and continuing abnormality.

The normalization of the Nazi past, finally, was also visible in parts of the non-Western world. In countries that were far removed from the European theater of World War II – in Asia, for example – the topic of the Third Reich understandably triggered fewer emotions and was less politically sensitive. There were thus comparatively few efforts to relativize or universalize its significance. At the same time, though, there were increasing attempts to aestheticize the Nazi past. Starting in the 1990s in parts of East and South Asia, Nazi iconography began turning up in various public forms. Images of Hitler, Nazi uniforms, swastika flags, and other insignia appeared in Taiwanese advertisements, Korean bar décor, Japanese manga comics, Thai T-shirts, and Indian pop songs.[61] This crass manipulation of the Nazi legacy had little political significance, as it was mostly meant to attract attention and generate profits. Yet it was far from harmless. The commercial exploitation of Nazi symbols removed them from their original historical context, marginalized their criminal purpose, and transformed them into empty signifiers. In short, the aestheticization of the Nazi past obscured its exceptionality and contributed to its further normalization.

Normalizing the Nazi past since the turn of the millennium

Since the year 2000, the process of normalization has only intensified. The effort to relativize, universalize, and aestheticize the Nazi past has manifested itself in many areas of contemporary intellectual and cultural life: in historiography, literature, film, television, and the Internet. It has been most visible in countries that were directly affected by the Nazi experience – Germany, Great Britain, the United States, and parts of Eastern Europe – but it has extended beyond them to other continents as well.

The global wave of normalization has been driven by various social, political and cultural factors. The first is organic normalization. With the arrival of the year 2000, the Third Reich symbolically receded even further into the past by retreating into a different century. This milestone underscored how the passing of time was inexorably transforming the memory of the Nazi era. By the turn of the millennium, the composition of Western society had become dramatically altered. The number of people in Europe or North America who were young adults at the time of the Third Reich – that is, those born at least in the 1920s – and had now entered old age were declining as a percentage of their countries' overall populations. At the same time, the number of young people without any personal experience of the Nazi era was growing ever larger. Both trends had an important impact on the memory of the Third Reich. As the older generation progressively disappeared, so too did their living memory of the Nazi years. The events that once stood in communicative memory were now passing into cultural memory. This development weakened older moralistic modes of representing the Nazi era. With fewer people alive to testify to the past's horrors, there was less resistance to the new and often unconventional methods chosen by young people to represent it. There was thus less resistance to the surging wave of normalization.

A second factor facilitating this process was the crisis-ridden nature of the post-9/11 world. Prior to this point, during the memory boom of the 1990s, the international climate was comparatively relaxed and afforded many nations the opportunity to confront long-neglected historical legacies of injustice. This was particularly true of the Nazi past, which was seen during this optimistic period as a reservoir of moral lessons that could foster reconciliation and mutual understanding among nations. Yet, in the wake of Al Qaeda's attacks against the United States in 2001, the ensuing wars in Afghanistan and Iraq, the intensifying strife between Israel and its Arab and Muslim neighbors, and the world financial crash of 2008, the context of global memory culture changed. The new atmosphere of crisis promoted a pessimistic mood that fostered a more partisan approach to the memory of the Nazi period. Increasingly, groups and individuals representing both the political left and the right relativized and universalized the Third Reich's significance in commenting on contemporary political events. Tendentious comparisons to Hitler and Nazism proliferated not only in political discourse, moreover, but in works of historiography, literature, and film. These comparisons were not without their own moral agendas; but in utilizing the past for present-day purposes, they diminished its distinctiveness.

A third contributing factor was the information revolution and the increasing influence of the Internet. During the 1980s and 1990s, the appearance of new digital technologies led to new ways of producing, accessing, and disseminating information. This development was punctuated after the middle of the 1990s with the arrival of the World Wide Web, which for the first time allowed mass access to the Internet. The Internet had many consequences for remembering as a cognitive process, but it had a specific impact on the memory of the Nazi era. Thanks to its global reach and anonymous, democratic character, the Internet allowed previously marginal views about the period – whether expressing hatred or humor – to be broadcast more widely than ever before. It also helped amplify existing efforts to relativize and universalize the Third Reich's significance. Most importantly, the Internet intensified the aestheticization of the Nazi past by enabling it to be represented in countless new, and previously unimaginable ways. Thanks to the advent of photo and video-editing software, an endless array of highly unconventional images of Hitler and the Nazi era was increasingly produced and disseminated around the world. In the process, they, too, helped undermine traditional, moralistic modes of remembrance.

The new wave of normalization, finally, was also promoted by the growing popularity of counterfactual thinking. In the last generation, the tendency to embrace speculative "what if?" questions has become increasingly common in Western culture. This trend has been visible in the growing popularity of alternate history as a sub-genre of historiography, as well as in the use of counterfactual reasoning in traditional fields of academic scholarship. The rise of this speculative kind of thought was promoted by broader trends before the turn of the millennium, such as the end of the Cold War, which discredited deterministic modes of thought; the rise of postmodernism, which blurred the distinction between history and fiction; and the information revolution, which gave rise to a new modes of virtual existence beyond conventional reality. As with the rise of the Internet, the growing popularity of counterfactual thinking had an important impact on the memory of Nazism. Speculative "what if?" questions about the Nazi era began to find expression not only in literary and cinematic works of alternate history, but in mainstream academic scholarship on World War II and the Holocaust, in contemporary films about Hitler, and on Internet websites. These narratives promoted new opportunities for normalizing the Nazi era. For by liberating people's imagination to contemplate events that never happened, they shifted attention away from the ethical questions that defined traditional narratives of the Nazi era towards the aesthetic challenges of representing the hypothetical. Especially as many counterfactual narratives exploited their "what if?" scenarios for laughs, they contributed to the aestheticization of the Nazi past.

Shaped by these factors, the current wave of normalization has become increasingly visible in different areas of Western intellectual and cultural life. The chapters that follow devote equal attention to both realms. The first half of the book focuses primarily on the subject of historiography. Chapter 1 examines the recent upsurge in revisionist historical studies of the Second World War. It begins with a brief survey of revisionist trends in Germany and Eastern Europe before focusing on the ways in which Anglo-American scholarship has challenged World War II's reputation as a "good war." Whether emanating from the political left or right, these revisionist studies – including works by Nicholson Baker, Niall Ferguson, and Norman Davies – have been shaped by the political climate of the post-9/11 world and have sought to relativize and universalize the Nazi era's significance. They have deliberately blurred the once clear moral lines between the wartime Allies and Axis in the effort to critique present-day Anglo-American foreign policy. In the process, they have sparked considerable criticism and controversy. Chapter 2 discusses the concurrent historiographical debate over the Holocaust's uniqueness. This debate, which began in the 1990s, has also been shaped by recent political events, whether the end of the Cold War or the American-led "war on terror." In the debate's latest phase, major new studies by scholars such as Donald Bloxham, Timothy Snyder, and A. Dirk Moses have subtly normalized the Nazi past by questioning the distinctiveness of the Third Reich's genocidal crimes. In the process, they, too, have sown discord. Chapter 3 concludes the focus on historiography by examining the growing use of counterfactual reasoning in Holocaust scholarship. Since the 1990s, scholars have asked many "what if?" questions pertaining to the Nazi genocide: Could Jews have done more to resist? Could bystanders have done more to help them? Would the Holocaust have happened without Hitler? Would Israel have been created without the Holocaust? The growing tendency to ask these and other counterfactual questions has many causes, but it generally reveals that there are no longer any limits – cognitive, moral, or aesthetic – to representing the Holocaust.

The book's second half shows how the new wave of normalization has shaped popular culture. Chapter 4 explores how counterfactual thinking has manifested itself in recent alternate histories of the Third Reich. Whether in the form of novels, short stories, films, or television programs, these new works – including major texts by writers such as Harry Turtledove, Dieter Kühn, Timur Vermes, and Michael Chabon – have explored a variety of subjects, such as the Nazis winning World War II, Hitler being assassinated, Hitler surviving World War II, and the Holocaust never taking place. In so doing, they have universalized and relativized the Nazi past in the service of political agendas related to the post-9/11 world. Chapter 5 identifies similar trends at work in recent films about the Nazi dictator. In contrast to prior motion pictures about the Führer, most of which moralistically portrayed him as a demon, recent films, including *Max, Downfall,* and *Mein Führer,* have depicted him in comparatively humanized fashion, often with jarringly humorous and counterfactual elements. This pattern of normalization through aestheticization, finally, defines the subject of Chapter 6, the representation of Nazism on the Internet. While the Internet offers much legitimate information about the history of the Third Reich, a considerable amount lacks any moral grounding. Some of it appears on neo-Nazi and other rightwing websites that seek to relativize the past. The majority, however, is visible on satirical sites that have aestheticized the Nazi legacy through humor. Sites such as Hipster Hitler and Cats That Look Like Hitler have promoted the rise of the Hitler Meme and nurtured the tendency to view the Nazi era from a comic perspective. Indeed, as seen in the countless video parodies and image macros of Hitler that have spread on YouTube and other websites, the Internet has produced what might be called a "Law of Ironic Hitlerization" that has removed the historical Hitler from any moral–historical context and turned him into an easy punch line. Given the Internet's increasingly important role in allowing people to spread information about the Nazi past, this aspect of normalization may prove the most lasting for the future development of memory.

Where the new wave of normalization is heading, how long it will last, what its ultimate effects will be, no one can say. But the book's conclusion suggests that the memory of the Nazi past will probably continue to be determined by dialectical forces. For the foreseeable future, remembrance will be shaped by the ongoing struggle between normality and morality.

1 A "GOOD WAR" NO MORE: THE NEW WORLD WAR II REVISIONISM

> The [Second World War] ... in Europe was dominated by two evil monsters, not by one ... Everyone who values the concept of liberty ... must admit that the [war's] outcome was at best ambiguous, that the victory of the West was only partial, and that the moral reputation of the Allied Coalition was severely tarnished. If, after considering all this they can still bring themselves to identify the West with the 'Good,' they are entitled to do so. But they can surely do it only with extensive reservations.[1]
>
> NORMAN DAVIES

Since the turn of the millennium, a major revisionist offensive has been launched against the longstanding belief that the Second World War in Europe was a "good war" waged against Nazi evil. The offensive has struck many of the countries that participated in the conflict. It has rolled through Germany, where attention has shifted from the Nazis' perpetration of unprecedented crimes against Jews and other Europeans to the suffering of German civilians at the hands of the Allies. It has also struck Eastern Europe, where Poles, Russians, and the citizens of the Baltic states have battled over claims that Joseph Stalin was just as responsible as Adolf Hitler for causing the war and committing comparable atrocities. But it has been in Great Britain and the United States where the revisionist trend has recently been the most apparent. As is shown by British historian Norman Davies's assertion above, growing numbers of Anglo-American historians and journalists have explicitly challenged World War II's reputation as a good war by re-evaluating its origins and consequences. Some of the revisionists have alleged that the conflict erupted not so much from aggressive German expansionism as reckless Allied interventionism. Others have decried the Allies' manner of waging war, arguing that their brutality differed little from that of the Nazis. Still others have counterfactually suggested that history would have turned out better if the Allies had abstained from fighting the war entirely.

The sudden appearance of these revisionist claims points to a shift in European and American views of the Nazi past. For most of the postwar period, the nations that participated in World War II embraced moralistic historical narratives that portrayed the Allies as the embodiment of good and the Nazis as the epitome of evil. By contrast, the new revisionist wave has blurred the lines between the behavior of the Allies and the Axis, lessening the virtue of the former and the infamy of the latter. In the process, the new revisionism has undermined the moral foundation upon which the good war narrative has long rested. This assault been driven by diverse motives, but its effect has been to advance the normalization of the Nazi past.

The good war consensus

The idea that World War II was a good war dates back to the early postwar period, when triumphalistic narratives about the conflict arose in the countries that comprised the wartime Allied powers. The citizens of Great Britain embraced the view that their decision to fight against the Nazis represented their "finest hour." The inhabitants of the Soviet Union adhered to the belief that the conflict against Germany represented a "Great Patriotic War." And the people of France accepted the "resistancialist" myth that they had valiantly liberated themselves from German rule.[2] Linking all of these narratives were several beliefs: that the Second World War in Europe had been deliberately unleashed by the Nazis; that the Allied campaign to defeat them had been part of a moral crusade; and that the Allies' ultimate victory had been critical for the survival of Western civilization. This consensus first took shape during the war itself, as part of the Allies' respective propaganda efforts in support of the conflict. It was further reinforced after 1945 at the Nuremberg Trials. And it was officially sanctioned by the Allies' respective postwar governments, all of which used it to buttress their postwar rule.[3] It was not only politicians, however, that supported the good war consensus. Scholars did so as well. Postwar historians in Great Britain,

France, and the Soviet Union all agreed – despite differences in focus and methodology – that the responsibility for the war lay squarely with the Nazis and that the Allies had been fully justified in intervening to stop them.[4]

All of these trends also held true in the United States, where the concept of the "good war" was first coined. Today, this signifier for the Second World War enjoys near canonical status. But it was long in coming. While the US's wartime allies adopted their own versions of the concept during or soon after World War II, Americans waited considerably longer before referring to the conflict as the "good war." This delay was not because Americans viewed the war any less positively than their European allies. American historians largely agreed that the Nazis were to blame for the conflict and that the US had been right to join the Allied cause.[5] This agreement notwithstanding, Americans lacked an iconic phrase for the war until the early 1980s. In 1984, however, they finally received one, courtesy of American writer Studs Terkel's Pulitzer Prize-winning book, *"The Good War": An Oral History of World War II*.[6] Terkel's book was a bestseller that resonated with many American readers. But the author did not deliberately set out to produce a paean to patriotism. Indeed, despite the book's seemingly triumphalistic title, Terkel originally meant the phrase, the "good war," to be viewed ambiguously (hence the title's quotation marks). This intended ambiguity notwithstanding, the phrase was quickly refashioned into a nostalgic concept. Like Great Britain's notion of the finest hour, the good war came to denote a heroic past that could compensate for a lackluster present. The concept gained traction at a time when President Ronald Reagan was trying to extricate the US out of a period of prolonged crisis, rooted in the traumas of Vietnam, the humiliations of Watergate, and the failures of the Carter years. These difficult events made the Second World War appear in a more flattering light and transformed it into an inspirational spur to present-day revival. The concept of the good war, indeed, symbolically functioned as the backward-looking counterpart to President Reagan's forward-looking claim (also coined in 1984) that it was "morning again in America." The concept's popularization represented a kind of wish fulfillment, an instance of trying to safeguard the future by ennobling the past.[7]

Fittingly, the belief that World War II had been a good war appeared to be vindicated by subsequent historical events, for with the fall of communism and the end of the Cold War in 1989–90, Americans increasingly came to view the Second World War as a harbinger of their country's ultimate postwar success. In the years that followed, the conflict was sanctified in American political and cultural life. Presidents George H. W. Bush and Bill Clinton each invoked the war's legacy to justify American military campaigns around the world, whether in Iraq or Yugoslavia. In American culture, meanwhile, the popularity of war-related books, such as Stephen Ambrose's *Band of Brothers* (1992) and Tom Brokaw's *The Greatest Generation* (1998), films such as Steven Spielberg's *Saving Private Ryan* (1998), and commemorative projects, such as the commissioning of the World War II memorial on the National Mall in Washington DC (1993–2004), confirmed the dominant place of the good war consensus in American historical memory. Indeed, before the turn of the millennium, the consensus appeared unshakeable.

The roots of revisionism

The good war consensus did not go entirely unchallenged, however. At various junctures between 1945 and the year 2000, dissenting voices questioned the upbeat narrative of the Second World War and tried to replace it with revisionist alternatives. Revisionist accounts of World War II appeared in various areas of Western intellectual and cultural life. They were most apparent in the realm of historiography, especially in the United States and Great Britain. But they also found expression in works of literature and film. Taken together, this intellectual and cultural output revealed that the good war consensus, while strong, was not unanimous.

The appearance of revisionist histories of World War II was inevitable. Ever since the establishment of the modern historical profession, historians have grouped themselves into competing orthodox and revisionist camps. The impulse to re-evaluate, reassess, and revise prevailing interpretations of the past has always been a hallmark of mainstream historical study.[8] For this reason, revisionism should be regarded as an entirely legitimate activity and should not be viewed pejoratively because of its misuse by right-wing extremists, who in recent years have appropriated the term in the effort to disguise their biased "scholarship."[9] Given the normativity of the revisionist impulse, scholarly works challenging the orthodox view of World War II predictably emerged in the decades after 1945. These works were diverse in focus and emanated from all wings of the political spectrum. But they tended to appear during periods of crisis when dissatisfaction with the present prompted a reassessment of the past.[10]

The first revisionist accounts of World War II appeared in the United States. Starting in the late 1940s and continuing into the 1950s, a noted group of historians, including Charles Beard, Harry Elmer Barnes, William Henry Chamberlin, and David Hoggan, published a series of studies challenging the good war consensus. These studies charged that the Allies were as guilty as Hitler for starting the war, had committed just as many crimes as the Nazis, and had succeeded only in making the world safe for communism.[11] This initial wave of revisionism emanated mostly from the political right and reflected the early postwar era's fierce anti-communist sentiment. Many of the revisionist scholars were former isolationists who were seeking to justify their wartime position by showing how American intervention had accomplished little, aside from sparking the Cold War. Thanks to their strident tone, the revisionist studies found a wide audience. Yet, they also met with fierce criticism. The widespread condemnation of their claims by the far more numerous supporters of the orthodox interventionist camp revealed that the revisionist movement enjoyed little support.[12]

By contrast, during the 1960s, revisionist accounts of the war gained a new measure of legitimacy and entered the mainstream. This shift followed the publication of eminent British historian, A. J. P. Taylor's famous book, *The Origins of the Second World War* (1961). Taylor's study challenged the good war consensus by asserting that World War II was less the result of Hitler's premeditated plans for military conquest than "diplomatic blunders" on both the Allied and German sides.[13] In submitting this thesis, Taylor implied that the war could have been avoided, a claim made explicit in subsequent studies by American scholars, Bruce M. Russett and Melvin Small, both of whom argued that the United States had never faced a serious threat from the Nazis and would have been better off staying out of the war completely.[14] These scholars' apparent endorsement of isolationism seemed to place them in the same camp as the conservative historians of the 1950s. Yet this resemblance was deceptive, for they all hailed from the political left. Their revisionism reflected a very different set of Cold War concerns, namely the belief that the crises of the 1960s and early 1970s – intensifying East–West tensions, the threat of nuclear proliferation, and the war in Vietnam – could be traced back to the mistaken decision of

Great Britain and the United States to enter the Second World War.[15] This argument, like that of the right-wing revisionists a decade earlier, also received a wide hearing among scholars and the general public. But its generally negative reception confirmed that it, too, was an exception to the larger historiographical rule.[16]

The same was true of the revisionist scholarship that appeared in the 1980s and 1990s. The works of this period differed from earlier studies by focusing less on the Second World War's origins than its conduct and consequences. Some, such as Paul Fussell's *Wartime* (1989) and Michael C. C. Adams's *The Best War Ever* (1994), emphasized the unglamorous reality of combat and critically examined its wartime and postwar whitewashing.[17] Others, such as James Bacque's *Other Losses* (1989), about the postwar deaths of German POWs under Allied control, and Alfred-Maurice de Zayas's *A Terrible Revenge* (1994), about the expulsion of ethnic Germans, polemically accused the Allies of having perpetrated war crimes comparable to those of the Nazis.[18] No common political agenda linked these studies, but they all sought to counter the nostalgic view of World War II that was emerging in the United States in the period around the end of the Cold War.[19] These texts, however, also met with a hostile reception.[20] A similar pattern existed at the same time in Great Britain. There, revisionist books by conservative scholars Correlli Barnett and John Charmley were attacked for claiming that British intervention in World War II had caused the country's postwar decline.[21] Similarly, revisionist studies by left-leaning writers, such as Clive Ponting and Madeleine Bunting, were criticized for attempting to subvert the finest hour myth.[22] In Anglo-American historiography, in short, prevailing views of the Second World War appeared to hold sway.

This reality was confirmed by revisionist works of literature and film. In the United States, Great Britain, and elsewhere, dissenting views about the good war found periodic literary and cinematic expression in the years after 1945. Early postwar novels by American writers who had served in World War II, such as Norman Mailer's *The Naked and the Dead* (1948), James Jones's *From Here to Eternity* (1951), and Joseph Heller's *Catch-22* (1961), portrayed the conflict unsentimentally as an event filled with savagery and suffering.[23] American films, such as *The Best Years of Our Lives* (1946) and *The Man in the Grey Flannel Suit* (1956), also focused on the darker sides of the war, especially its traumatizing impact on returning soldiers. In Great Britain, alternate histories focusing on a Nazi invasion and occupation of the country, such as Kevin Brownlow and Andrew Mollo's film, *It Happened Here* (1966) and Len Deighton's novel, *SS-GB* (1978), challenged the finest hour myth by imagining the British people willingly collaborating with their German occupiers. Even in communist Eastern Europe, films, such as Mikhail Kalatozov's *The Cranes Are Flying* (1957) and Andrzej Wajda's *Ashes and Diamonds* (1958), portrayed World War II in de-heroized terms, emphasizing its emotional toll on combatants and civilians alike.[24] All of these works were influential and found large audiences. But none of them posed a serious threat to the good war consensus. While they broke with official, romanticized views of the war, they never challenged its fundamental legitimacy. While they raised concerns about the war's human toll, they never questioned the necessity of defeating the Nazi enemy.[25] Finally, while they qualified as notable works in and of themselves, they were exceeded in number and prominence by works representing the orthodox triumphalist narrative.[26] On balance, while the revisionist impulse found intermittent expression in Western intellectual and cultural life between 1945 and 2000, it never threatened the orthodox view of the Second World War.

The new revisionism

Since the turn of the millennium, however, the revisionist challenge to the good war consensus has intensified. The new revisionist wave has hit much of the Western world, first striking Germany and the post-communist nations of Eastern Europe before arriving in Great Britain and North America. In all of these places, the wave has assumed intellectual as well as cultural forms, manifesting itself in new works of historical scholarship as well as literature, television, and commemorative projects involving holidays, museums, and memorials. This variation notwithstanding, the new revisionism has displayed common features in its arguments, goals, and impact. Its supporters have explicitly criticized the wartime behavior of the Allies – the Soviets, British, and Americans – by accusing them of perpetrating war crimes comparable to those of the Nazis; they have levied these accusations for political reasons related to the end of the Cold War and the onset of the "war on terror"; their claims have served to relativize the singularity of the Nazis' wartime crimes; and they have sparked controversy wherever they have appeared.

German revisionism

The new revisionism first arose in Germany. There, revisionists faced something of a unique situation, for the country's historiographical orthodoxy lacked the triumphalist tone that existed in Great Britain, the United States, and the Soviet Union. For obvious reasons, most Germans after 1945 did not regard World War II as a good war. Given their country's wartime devastation, they could not embrace a redemptive narrative about the conflict and instead self-critically probed their responsibility for it. This focus was visible in the postwar scholarship of German historians, which was devoted to examining the Nazi dictatorship's origins, its reasons for unleashing the war, and its role in perpetrating atrocities against enemy combatants and civilians.[27] This emphasis on the Nazi regime's crimes was a crucial part of the Federal Republic's effort to show the world that it had learned the proper lessons from the recent past. It further explained why German historians gave little attention to the suffering of German civilians, whether as a result of wartime bombings, flight, expulsion, rape, or imprisonment in POW camps.[28] Indeed, when certain conservative historians tried to direct attention to German suffering during the Historians' Debate in the mid-1980s, they were widely rebuked.[29] As long as the Federal Republic's neighbors remained uncertain about the country's democratic rehabilitation (and as long as uneasiness persisted about the prospect of national reunification), the topic of German victimization was viewed by moderate, center-left Germans as politically suspect and was confined to conservative and right-wing circles.[30]

Yet, while their focus on Nazi crimes prevented Germans from viewing World War II as a good war, they were still able to find a silver lining to it. Over the course of the postwar period, increasing numbers of Germans came to see the defeat of 1945 as a "liberation" that paved the way for the Federal Republic's postwar success.[31] This desire to find a positive legacy in the war was visible in numerous areas, whether the desire of the Federal German government (especially in the era of Chancellor Helmut Kohl) to be included in commemorative ceremonies organized by the victorious wartime Allies, the delivery of high-profile speeches by German politicians (most famously the parliamentary speech delivered by President Richard von Weizsäcker on May 8, 1985), or the creation of memorials commemorating wartime "liberation" in German cities.[32] The desire to view the war positively intensified after reunification in 1990, when the German government began to follow the precedent set by postwar American and British governments and cited the events of the Second World War – especially the Holocaust – as a means of justifying German military intervention in international crisis zones, such as Kosovo and Afghanistan.[33]

It was largely in reaction to this redemptive mindset that the new wave of German revisionism arose. Beginning slowly in the mid-1990s and continuing up until the present day, a series of commemorative projects, scholarly studies, and works of literature challenged the view that World War II had liberated the German people by shifting attention to how it brought them untold suffering. In 1995, on the fiftieth anniversary of the war's end, a coalition of conservative and right-leaning groups organized a high-profile campaign "Against Forgetting" in the German media that recast May 8, 1945 as a day of defeat instead of liberation, directing attention to the ways in which the German population had been victimized after the war's conclusion, especially in mass expulsions.[34] Several years later, a wave of books dealing with the Allied aerial destruction of German cities began to appear, including Hans-Erich Nossack's *Der Untergang* (1996), W. G. Sebald's *Luftkrieg und Literatur* (1999), Walter Kempowski's second volume of *Das Echolot* (2000), and Jörg Friedrich's *Der Brand* (2002) (Figure 5).[35] Other works focused on more specific wartime episodes. Günter Grass's best-selling novel, *Im Krebsgang* (2002), addressed the history and memory of the worst maritime disaster in recorded history, the sinking of the *Wilhelm Gustloff* cruise ship (together with its nearly 10,000 civilian passengers) by a Soviet submarine in January of 1945.[36] The subject of rape was tackled in the anonymous memoir, *Eine Frau in Berlin*, which was posthumously published in Germany to great acclaim in 2003.[37] The mass expulsion of ethnic Germans was addressed in a 1999 proposal to create a major museum, known as a Center Against Expulsions (*Zentrum gegen Vertreibungen*), in Berlin; and it was dramatized in several films (most notably, *Dresden* and *Die Flucht*) that aired on the German television networks ZDF and ARD in 2006–07.[38] Finally, the theme of German wartime victimization stood at the center of the recent blockbuster television miniseries, *Unsere Mütter, unsere Väter* (2013), which dramatized the suffering of ordinary Germans by portraying the war's traumatic impact on five young friends, who are forced to make difficult moral choices on the brutal eastern front.[39]

Figure 5. Jörg Friedrich's bestselling book, *Der Brand* (*The Fire*), appeared in 2002 and sparked controversy for its portrayal of German civilian suffering during Allied air raids.

The new revisionist works signaled an important shift in the German memory of World War II. By focusing on Germans as victims, they inevitably shifted attention towards the Allies as perpetrators. In the process, they blurred the line between Allied and Axis crimes and implicitly relativized German guilt for the Nazi era. Friedrich's jarring use of Holocaust terminology to refer to German air raid victims (he likened the transformation of German cellars during bombing raids to "crematoria") was a clear example of this trend, as was Sebald's description of the raids as an "act of extermination" (*Vernichtungsaktion*) – a phrase that echoed the language employed by the Nazis against the Jews.[40] Similarly, *Der Spiegel*'s invocation of Mohandas Gandhi's remark that, in firebombing Dresden, the Allies "defeated Hitler with [the methods of] Hitler" and the *Bild Zeitung*'s subsequent demand that the Queen of England "apologize" for the bombing of the Saxon city (just as German leaders had repeatedly apologized for their own misdeeds on previous occasions) further promoted this blurring process.[41] So, too, did the television films, *Dresden* and *Die Flucht*, both of which featured numerous scenes of Allied callousness, whether in the form of British Bomber Command officials bluntly telling their pilots to "bomb Dresden 'til it burns" or Soviet soldiers assaulting German civilians. A similar message was advanced by the supporters of the Center Against Expulsion, whose educational mission unavoidably cast attention upon the violent actions of Poles, Czechs, and other Eastern Europeans against the Germans at the war's end. Finally, *Unsere Mütter, unsere Väter* reinforced its narrative of German suffering with an unflattering portrait of Slavs, depicting Russians as marauding rapists and Poles as inveterate anti-Semites. All of these works, by dwelling on the harsh wartime and postwar policies that other nations imposed upon the Germans, served to reduce the exceptionality of Nazi criminality.

Significantly, the revisionist works received a positive response from many ordinary Germans. The books, films, and television programs on the Second World War were enormously popular, earning a wide readership and strong ratings from viewers.[42] They also received broad support from reviewers, who welcomed the confrontation with German suffering as the breaking of a "taboo." Historian Hans-Ulrich Wehler, commenting on the renewed interest in the expulsion of ethnic Germans in 1945, noted that the process of "recovering and quietly discussing a sunken piece of our collective history of suffering" was likely to have a "liberating effect."[43] Similarly, novelist Peter Schneider confidently affirmed that "the [Germans'] belated recollection of suffering ... in no sense arouses desires for revenge ... but opens their eyes to ... the destruction that the Nazi[s] ... brought upon other nations."[44] Commentators praised *Dresden* and *Die Flucht* for portraying the war's destruction realistically, rather than moralistically, thereby allowing viewers to empathetically experience the "hell" suffered by ordinary German civilians during the conflict.[45] Finally, various observers affirmed that *Unsere Mütter, unsere Väter's* unsparing portrait of the Second World War's brutality promised to advance intergenerational understanding between young people and their elders, who would be prompted, at long last, to discuss their war experiences before they passed away.[46]

These positive reactions partly reflected the belief that the revisionist wave was politically unthreatening. While many Germans had traditionally avoided the subject of German wartime suffering because of its traditional association with the far right, they now embraced it as part of an overdue confrontation with a neglected aspect of their nation's past. Many Germans were reassured by the fact that many of the prominent promoters of the wave hailed from the anti-Nazi left-liberal and centrist wings of the German political spectrum. Major authors such as Friedrich and Grass, for instance, had strong leftist political credentials, while the creative team responsible for the television dramas, *Dresden*, *Die Flucht*, and *Unsere Mütter, unsere Väter* (most notably producer Nico Hofmann and screenwriter Stefan Kolditz), also had liberal backgrounds and represented the centrist establishment associated with German public television.[47] The moderate backgrounds of these figures made it clear that their focus on German wartime suffering was not part of a right-wing agenda and helped convince liberally inclined Germans that the topic could be addressed without having adverse political consequences. Reinforcing this belief was the growing conviction that the German government had made great strides in acknowledging the Nazi regime's wartime crimes. Especially after Gerhard Schroeder's Red-Green coalition came to power in 1998 and openly highlighted Germany's responsibility for the Holocaust, many Germans became convinced that it was now politically acceptable to refocus attention on their compatriots' wartime suffering.[48]

The readiness of many Germans to accept the new revisionist wave also reflected the political climate of the post-9/11 world. Following the United States' invasion of Afghanistan and Iraq, there was a dramatic increase in anti-war sentiment among broad segments of the German public, especially on the center-left, which was deeply uncomfortable with the aggressive turn in American foreign policy. This sentiment explained some of the popularity of Sebald's, Friedrich's, and Grass's books. Their focus on the wartime travails of German civilians was often invoked by German pacifists in order to mobilize public sympathy for Iraqi civilians caught in the crossfire of the American military campaign against Saddam Hussein.[49] This connection was less visible in the response to the subsequent television dramas, but their popularity was also conditioned by the anti-war climate of the post-9/11 era. German support for the revisionist wave, in short, partly reflected the desire to universalize the Nazi past.

This fact notwithstanding, the revisionists ultimately accomplished the opposite of what they hoped to achieve. In keeping with the dialectic of normalization, their efforts elicited widespread opposition from critics committed to defending the Nazi past's singularity. Both within Germany and abroad, various observers worried that the Germans' sudden focus on their wartime suffering signaled a renewed desire to forget the Nazis' crimes. American and British readers of Sebald's and Friedrich's books for instance, charged that they established a "moral equivalency" between Allied and Axis behavior.[50] Eastern European (especially Czech and Polish) critics, together with Israeli commentators, attacked the proposed Center Against Expulsions for using the experience of German suffering to mitigate German wartime crimes against Slavs and Jews.[51] Critics of the films, Dresden and Die Flucht, attacked them as melodramatic narratives whose ostensible striving for balance ultimately "diminished the guilt of ordinary German citizens" by getting viewers to emotionally identify with their misfortune.[52] And reviewers of Unsere Mütter, unsere Väter complained that the film diminished the singularity of Germany's wartime misdeeds by blaming them not on Nazi ideology, but on the tragic ability of war "to bring out the worst in all of us."[53] Overall, both German and foreign critics worried that the revisionist wave threatened to undo the nation's progress in coming to terms with the Nazi past and restore a more conservative, self-exculpatory view typical of the early postwar period.[54]

In fact, critics' concerns about the new revisionism were not altogether unfounded. While it was partly motivated by the genuine desire for a more comprehensive view of the war years, the revisionist wave's popularity was also driven by the desire to normalize the Nazi past. This was clearly shown by the attempt of right-wing groups to exploit the legacy of German wartime suffering for nationalistic purposes. The effort of neo-Nazis in 2005 (as well as in subsequent years) to organize mass demonstrations in Dresden marking what they tendentiously called the "Bombing Holocaust," showed how German suffering could be deliberately used to relativize the Third Reich's crimes.[55] The desire to assert an equivalence between German and Jewish victimization was also confirmed by the widespread support of right-wing groups for the Center Against Expulsions, whose main promoter, CDU politician and leading figure in the nationalistic League of German Expellees, Erika Steinbach, pointedly called for the museum to be located "in historical and spatial proximity" to Germany's National Memorial to the Murdered Jews of Europe.[56] The fear that a right-wing agenda underpinned the attention to German suffering was further bolstered by the revelation that even some of its left-wing promoters had their own right-wing pasts, most notably Günter Grass, who confessed in 2006 about having served in the Waffen SS during the war.[57] Meanwhile, CDU Chancellor Angela Merkel's support for the Center Against Expulsions – and her government's subsequent approval of a smaller-scale "Exhibition, Documentation, and Information Center On Flight and Expulsion" in Berlin (to open in 2015) – showed the potential for centrist forces to make common cause with more conservative groups.[58]

In the end, the protests sparked by the new revisionism helped resist the effort to normalize the Nazi past, but they nevertheless revealed an important shift in German memory. Seventy-five years after the beginning of the Second World War, increasing numbers of Germans were showing themselves to be less interested in the conflict's origins than its conclusion. They were less interested in reflecting on their ancestors' role in supporting the ideology that sparked the war than on the suffering that it brought home to them. In short, they were less interested in reflecting on the aspects of the war that were particular to themselves – namely, their historical guilt – than on those that they shared with other Europeans, particularly the experience of victimization. To be sure, not all Germans who supported the new revisionism consciously shared these tendencies. But enough did to reveal that the movement was as devoted to forgetting as it was to remembering.

Eastern European revisionism

Similar controversies were sparked by revisionists in Eastern Europe. As in Germany, the new revisionism emerged in reaction to the dominant orthodox view of World War II, specifically the official Soviet portrayal of the conflict as the "Great Patriotic War." Throughout the Cold War, Eastern Europeans were told that World War II had resulted from the Nazi regime's attack against the Soviet Union in 1941; that the Nazis had perpetrated unprecedented atrocities against the Soviet population; and that the valiant Red Army was responsible for liberating the region from Nazi tyranny. Predictably, this narrative was challenged following the collapse of communism in the years 1989–91. Now, instead of explaining the war as the result of German aggression, revisionist voices in Poland, the Baltic states, and, to a lesser degree, even Russia itself, explained it as a result of Soviet duplicity. According to the new view, it was the Soviet Union's signing of the Molotov–Ribbentrop pact with Nazi Germany on August 23, 1939 that paved the way for the Nazi onslaught.[59] Eastern European revisionists did not merely reassess the war's origins, however, but also its conduct and consequences. Eager to overturn longstanding taboos and increase awareness of the war's ignored aspects, they devoted special attention to the many crimes perpetrated by the Soviets against Eastern Europeans during the conflict. In so doing, they discussed these crimes not in isolation but in comparison to those of the Nazis. The supporters of revisionism often moved to equate Stalinism with Nazism, going so far as to claim that the two totalitarian regimes were guilty of having perpetrated a "double genocide" during the war, not only against Jews but also the peoples of Eastern Europe. In short, Eastern European revisionists normalized the Nazi past by universalizing and relativizing its significance.

The revisionist agenda found expression in different forms, the most prominent being government-sponsored documents and pronouncements. Already in the late 1990s, many countries, including Latvia, Lithuania, and Estonia, established special historical commissions to investigate crimes committed during the war by both the Soviet and Nazi regimes.[60] After the turn of the millennium, these commissions published their findings in various official publications, many of which used the term "genocide" to describe the Soviets' arrest, deportation, and killing of Eastern Europeans.[61] A similar tendency was visible in other pan-European documents, most notably the "Prague Declaration on

European Conscience and Communism." Initiated by former Czech president Vaclav Havel and signed by a series of Eastern European politicians on June 3, 2008, the Prague Declaration sought to increase public awareness of communist crimes perpetrated during and after the Second World War. Significantly, the declaration condemned these crimes in specific comparison to Nazi atrocities. The declaration demanded, for example, that "[the] many crimes committed in the name of Communism should be assessed as crimes against humanity ... in the same way Nazi crimes were assessed by the Nuremberg Tribunal." Subsequent declarations by various EU institutions and signed by various member states, such as the Vilnius declaration in 2009, amplified the comparison, stating that the two "totalitarian regimes, Nazi and Stalinist, ... brought about genocide."[62]

The effort to equate communist and Nazi crimes was also visible in commemorative holidays, museums, and memorials. The Prague Declaration called for establishing August 23rd – the day of the Molotov–Ribbentrop Pact – as a "European Day of Remembrance for Victims of Stalinism and Nazism." The holiday's creation was justified by the claim that the victims of communist terror should be honored "in the same way Europe remembers the victims of the Holocaust on January 27th."[63] A similar equation of Nazi and Soviet crimes was visible in a range of Eastern European history museums. With the establishment of Lithuania's Museum of Genocide Victims in Vilnius (1992), Latvia's Museum of the Occupation in Riga (1993), Hungary's House of Terror in Budapest (2002), Estonia's Museum of Occupations in Tallinn (2003), and Ukraine's Lonsky Street Prison Museum in Lviv (2009), Eastern European states created institutions whose core exhibits gave equal weight to the double occupation regimes of the Soviets and Nazis (Figure 6). Finally, the desire to overturn the previous Soviet narrative of World War II was displayed in Estonia, Georgia, and Bulgaria, with the demolition, relocation, or desecration of Soviet-era war memorials that marked the Red Army's role in "liberating" various Eastern European peoples from Nazi rule.[64]

The motives behind this revisionist campaign varied. It was partly driven by the legitimate desire of Eastern Europeans to increase popular awareness of communist crimes, most of which had been suppressed during the Cold War. The fact that Eastern Europe experienced invasion and occupation by both Nazi Germany and the Soviet

Figure 6. The House of Terror Museum in Budapest opened in 2002 and chronicles the suffering of Hungarian civilians at the hands of both the Nazis and Soviets during and after World War II.

Union explained the popular desire to stress the similarities between them. It was equally understandable that revisionists employed the strategy – known to activists the world over – of garnering attention for their causes by drawing comparisons to the Holocaust. This particular brand of revisionism, however, had the effect of diminishing the Nazi genocide's singularity by universalizing its significance. A second type of revisionism, meanwhile, normalized the Holocaust more deliberately. Associated with Eastern European nationalist groups, this strategy challenged the Holocaust's singularity by striving to relativize it. Since gaining independence in 1989, many Eastern Europeans re-established a positive sense of national identity by defining themselves against the Soviet Union (and, after 1991, Russia). In this effort, they focused attention on their suffering at the hands of the Soviets during and after the war. The problem, however, was that Eastern Europeans were not only victims during World War II, but also perpetrators, having collaborated with the Nazis in the crimes of the Holocaust. Soon after the collapse of communism in 1989, Jewish organizations brought attention to this shameful history through a variety of educational initiatives and

appeals to Eastern European governments. In response, various nationalist groups tried to deflect this new attention by employing defensive
strategies, one of which was to claim that, like the Jews, Eastern
Europeans had also suffered "genocide" at the hands of the Soviets.[65]
The "double genocide" claim was intended to mask guilt for wartime
collaboration and minimize the Holocaust's significance. This rhetorical
strategy of evading responsibility for wartime misdeeds – in addition to
others, such as the failure of Eastern European states to bring aging war
criminals to justice, their willingness to rehabilitate and venerate wartime
fascist collaborators, and their toleration of SS veterans groups' reunions
and neo-Nazi marches – showed that the revisionist effort to equate
Stalinist and Nazi crimes was driven by a reluctance to come to terms
with the past.[66]

Predictably, the effort to reassess the origins and consequences
of World War II sparked controversy. Russian officials were especially
outraged by the revisionist campaign. Ever since the rise to power of
Vladimir Putin at the turn of the millennium, the Russian government
moved to reaffirm the idea of the Great Patriotic War in national
memory, insisting, as Putin did in 2005, that the war against Nazism
represented a "victory of good over evil."[67] As a result, Russian authorities responded harshly to instances of revisionism. In 2007, Putin
furiously criticized Estonia's demolition of a Soviet-era war memorial
in Tallinn, claiming that it disrespected Soviet sacrifices against the
Nazis.[68] Even more heated was the discord that ensued between
Russia and Poland on September 1, 2009 on the occasion of the 70th
anniversary of the war's eruption. Prior to the ceremonies marking the
Battle of Westerplatte in Gdansk, Poland's president, Lech Kaczynski,
adopted a revisionist position about the war's origins, accusing the
Soviet Union of "stabbing Poland in the back" by colluding with
Germany in its invasion of the country.[69] Putin responded by rejecting
the claim that the Molotov–Ribbentrop pact was responsible for the
war, claiming that, while the pact was "immoral," it was less important
than the Western Allies' appeasement of Hitler and their reluctance in
the late 1930s to ally with the Soviets against him.[70] Russia's president
Dmitry Medvedev added that it was "a flat-out lie" to say that the
Soviet Union was partly responsible for the war's outbreak and later
formed an official commission to draft a law "defend[ing] Russia
against ... those who would deny Soviet contribution to the victory
in World War II."[71]

Russia's sharp reaction to the revisionist wave reflected several considerations. At the most basic psychological level, it was difficult for the Russian government (or people) to think of their country as anything but a historical victim in the Second World War, given the death of some 27 million Soviet citizens following the Nazi invasion of 1941. Yet, political calculations also played an important role. In defending the idea of the Great Patriotic War, Russian authorities hoped to prevent Eastern European nationalists from using historical arguments to legitimize present-day political grievances against their country. They also sought to reinforce the prestige of the Russian army, whose reputation had taken a hit during its two brutal wars in Chechnya between 1994 and 2000.[72] For these strategic reasons, Russian officials were vigilant about rejecting any comparisons between the Soviet Union and the Third Reich. To defend against them, the state-supported Russian media went on the offensive in 2009 with a series of stories highlighting Eastern European collaboration with the Nazis.[73] The same year, the Russian parliament passed a bill "On Counteracting the Rehabilitation of Nazism, Nazi Criminals and Their Accomplices in New Independent States on the Territory of the Former USSR."[74] These efforts, all of which found support among Jewish groups, Holocaust historians, and other academics, sought to prevent Eastern European nationalists from evading guilt for wartime crimes.[75] At the same time, however, Russia did not use the Second World War's legacy only for defensive purposes. During the crisis over Ukraine in early 2014, Vladimir Putin and other Russian officials aggressively (and erroneously) attacked Ukrainian nationalist protesters at Kiev's Independence Square, or Maidan, as "fascists," "Nazis," and "anti-Semites" in the effort to discredit their rebellion against the Russian-backed government of Viktor Yanukovych. In so doing, Russian officials showed how the opposition to revisionism could produce its own distortions of memory.[76]

The result of this extended debate was ambiguous. On the one hand, the attempt of Eastern Europeans to revise the inherited view of World War II brought about a fuller and more balanced perspective on the conflict than had existed during the Cold War. At the same time, the means used to establish the new view relativized and universalized the Nazi past. This normalizing effect, to be sure, had limits. In keeping with the dialectic of normalization, the fierce response to the new revisionism ensured that the past remained the object of public interest.

Anglo-American revisionism

In contrast to the situation in Germany and Eastern Europe, the revisionist wave in England and the United States transpired less in the realm of political discourse than scholarship. This is not to say it was any less controversial. Around the turn of the millennium and accelerating thereafter, a slew of historical studies garnered headlines by offering revisionist assessments of the Second World War. Written by prominent historians and journalists, the revisionist literature was quite diverse. Some of the books focused on the war in Europe, while others included the Pacific theater. Some concentrated on the war's early years, while others covered the conflict's entirety. Finally, some broadened their analysis of the war by focusing on its aftermath and the ensuing era of Allied occupation, while others extended their view even further and historicized the war within the larger context of the twentieth century.

This diversity notwithstanding, the revisionist literature displayed many common features. First, the new works sought to replace the reigning black and white view of World War II as a conflict of good versus evil in favor of a grayer approach that blurred the distinctions between the Allies and the Axis. Second, in offering this critical view, the revisionist literature assumed one of two forms: a "hard" version that doubted the wisdom of fighting the war altogether and a "soft" version that condemned its means while accepting its ends. Third, both forms of revisionism were shaped by the growing disaffection with the geopolitical realities of the post-9/11 world. Many Anglo-American revisionists – both on the left and the right – opposed the United States' aggressive response to the attacks of September 11th and believed that the invasions of Afghanistan and Iraq discredited war as a tool of foreign policy. Having developed this belief as a result of present-day events, they applied it to the history of World War II, reassessing its origins and critiquing its consequences. Fourth, many revisionists added rhetorical power to their arguments by employing counterfactual modes of argumentation. Their narratives did not merely critique the course of the war, but speculated about how it might have turned out better. The inclusion of "what if?" scenarios revealed how fantasies and nightmares about the past persisted into the present. In all of these ways, the revisionist studies pointed to a growing willingness of Anglo-American scholars to normalize the Nazi past by relativizing and universalizing its significance. They did not do so unopposed, however, for they elicited sharp criticism and sparked extended controversy.

The hard revisionists

Among the most strident examples of Anglo-American revisionism were two books published in 2008: Nicholson Baker's *Human Smoke* and Patrick Buchanan's *Churchill, Hitler, and "The Unnecessary War."*[77] Despite emanating from completely different wings of the political spectrum, both studies challenged the notion that World War II was a good war and argued that it could have been avoided altogether. Had it been, both writers speculated, the course of history would have been dramatically improved.

Baker's *Human Smoke* (Figure 7) was an example of stealth historiography, in the sense that it masqueraded as a neutral chronicle of events while advancing a tendentious thesis. Baker laid out his narrative in strict chronological fashion, presenting what at first glance appeared to be a series of unrelated news stories in the United States, Europe, and Asia from the late nineteenth century up through the last date of its narrative, December 31, 1941. The text lacked an introduction alerting readers to Baker's agenda, though the book's afterword made it unmistakable. There, Baker explained that his goal in writing the volume was to determine, first of all, whether the Second World War had actually been a "good war" and, second, whether "waging it [had helped] ... anyone who needed help?" Baker did not explicitly answer this question, but his dedication of the book to "American and British pacifists" who tried "to stop the war from happening" revealed his desire to challenge the Allies' decision to become embroiled in the conflict in the first place.[78]

Throughout the book, Baker blurred the previously accepted line between the admirable Allies and evil Axis. He presented numerous news accounts that undermined Winston Churchill and Franklin D. Roosevelt's reputations as the heroic defenders of Western values. The accounts that Baker selected cast the two leaders in a variety of unflattering roles: as warmongers who went out of their way to seek a showdown against Germany and Japan instead of trying to defuse tensions via diplomacy; as plutocratic profiteers who sank enormous sums of money into the production of arms, including chemical and biological weapons, thereby enriching big business; as liberal hypocrites

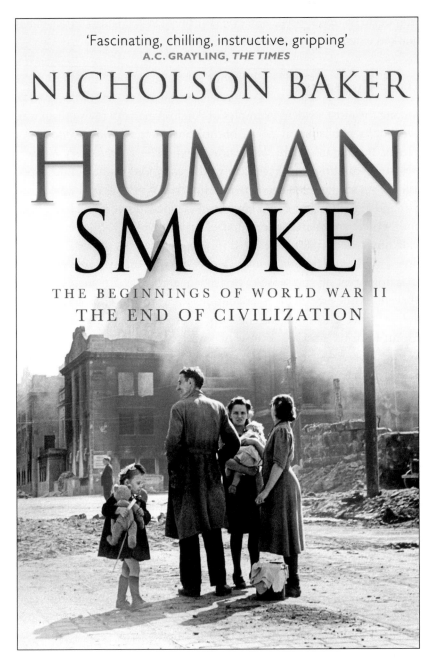

Figure 7. Nicholson Baker's book, *Human Smoke* (2008), challenged the idea that World War II was a "good war" by portraying the tremendous human suffering caused by the conflict.

who violated civil liberties at home while preaching them abroad; and as intolerant racists who uttered anti-Semitic slurs, locked up German Jewish exiles as enemy aliens, and refused sanctuary to Jews seeking refuge. This list of immoral behavior helped Baker make his point that the Western Allies were hardly innocent in regard to the outbreak of the Second World War.

Baker traced the origins of this immorality to broader forces that preceded the actual conflict. He began his narrative in the year 1892 with a news story describing Swedish explosives manufacturer Alfred Nobel naively predicting that his dynamite factories would bring an end to all war. He then described a host of other tragic events, paying particular attention to British colonial depredations in the Middle East. In so doing, Baker historicized World War II within the larger context of Western militarism and imperialism. He went on to note how these violent traditions overwhelmed the efforts of American and British pacifists to avert the coming carnage. By detailing how peace activists were ignored, derided, and arrested for their efforts, Baker indicted the Western Allies for the impending war.

Baker's ensuing discussion of Allied intervention showed that its main result was needless civilian suffering. The writer made his case in different ways, usually by describing the deaths of innocent civilians in military attacks. But he put an exclamation point on his argument by provocatively suggesting that Allied intervention was ultimately responsible for the war's worst atrocity, the Holocaust. To support this contention, Baker enlisted the words of Mohandas Gandhi, who in 1938 predicted that "if the Allies were to go to war against Germany," Hitler might respond with "'a general massacre of the Jews ...[as] his first answer to the declaration of ... hostilities.'"[79] Baker further embraced Gandhi's support for non-violence, quoting his recommendation, made after the Nazis overran Poland and France, that the only viable response was to "'fight Nazism without arms.'"[80] If only the Allies had chosen this pacifist response, Baker counterfactually mused, the Holocaust might have been averted. Indeed, had England not continued to fight against Germany in the summer and fall of 1940, the Nazis might have chosen to deport the Jews from Europe instead of murdering them. Baker pointed out that, following the fall of France, Nazi officials were busy making arrangements to deport the Jews of Europe by sea to Madagascar "as soon as ships could travel freely again – in other words, as soon as England made its peace with Germany and stopped blockading ocean traffic." There was a stumbling block for the operation, however, for "it was all contingent on peace with Churchill."[81] And the British Prime Minister, Baker regretfully noted, did not want peace. Because of Churchill's commitment to resisting the Nazis during the Battle of Britain, "the Madagascar Plan ... went away – ships full of deported Jews wouldn't be able to pass the blockade."[82]

The result of this stubborn resistance, Baker implied, was the Nazis' intensified persecution of the Jews. Baker pointed to numerous efforts by Hitler in the years 1939–41 to make peace with England, as well as remarks by the Führer that he had no quarrel with the United States. But because of Churchill and Roosevelt's determination to stand up to the Nazis, the war's continuation merely led to worse suffering. The Allied economic blockade against Germany, meant to starve its civilian population, only prompted the Germans to starve the Jews in the ghettos of Poland.[83] The Allied bombing campaign against German cities merely "'fed Hitler's wrath ... against [the Jews] and helped ... justify further Nazi atrocities against [them].'" Finally, with the formal entry of the United States into the war in December of 1941, Hitler decided to make good on his infamous January 30, 1939 prophecy that a world war would bring about the "annihilation of the Jewish race in Europe." Before long, the Nazi dictator proceeded to "make a clean sweep" of the Jews that ended with their "'annihiliation ...[as] the necessary consequence.'"[84] Hitler thus bore direct responsibility for the Holocaust. But the Allies, according to Baker, shared in it. Quoting Gandhi, the writer provocatively declared that in using force to fight against Hitler, the defenders of democracy were "doing the same work of destruction as the Germans." The Hindu leader, Baker concluded, was ultimately right in claiming that "Hitlerism and Churchillism are ... the same thing."[85]

In arguing that Hitler's murderous agenda was aided and abetted by the Allies, Baker implied that Nazism was hardly a singular form of evil. He instead portrayed it as the predictable by-product of modern forces – especially militarism and imperialism – that were also present in the Western democracies. There was thus little difference between the Axis and Allies. Baker largely advanced this conclusion for political reasons. Although known more for his fiction than his activism, the writer has long harbored left-wing and pacifist beliefs. He also displayed a distinctly presentist view of history. Baker was a fierce critic of the American invasion of Iraq and openly noted in a 2008 interview that the conflict influenced his revisionist portrayal of the Anglo-American decision to go to war in 1939–41.[86] Baker displayed a keen sense of self-awareness in making this admission. Yet, he was less aware of how his political outlook distorted his understanding of the Second World War's origins and consequences. His view that the war grew out of imperialist forces led him to grossly underestimate the role played by Nazi ideology. His misunderstanding of Nazi ideology, in turn, undermined the plausibility of his counterfactual claim that Allied non-intervention would have led history to turn out better. In fact, the opposite likely would have been the case. Had the British and Americans remained neutral in World War II, the Nazis would have arguably defeated the Soviet Union and gone on to pursue their ideological vision of a racial utopia in Eastern Europe. The result would have been even greater suffering for its Jewish and Slavic populations.[87] Baker's inability to appreciate this fact was partly explained by his self-described "ignorance" about the Second World War, which he confessed he "never really understood."[88] But it was ultimately a product of his political views, which led him to universalize the Nazi experience by explaining it as merely one of many examples of Western civilization's modern legacy of aggression and oppression.

A second book that sought to normalize the Nazi legacy was Patrick Buchanan's study, *Churchill, Hitler, and "The Unnecessary War."* As shown by its title, Buchanan's book agreed with Baker's claim that World War II was avoidable. Compared with *Human Smoke*, however, *Churchill, Hitler, and "The Unnecessary War"* submitted its case less in sadness than in anger. It was also far less innovative, being an example of what might be called derivative revisionism, relying exclusively on secondary sources produced by earlier American and British revisionist historians.[89] Buchanan, moreover, did not advance his position from a stance of left-wing pacifism but right-wing isolationism. These differences notwithstanding, Buchanan arrived at many of the same conclusions as Baker, declaring that Great Britain under the leadership of Neville Chamberlain and Winston Churchill chose an ill-advised policy of confrontation with Nazi Germany that caused the Second World War and all of its catastrophic consequences for Europe and Western civilization at large. If only Great Britain had chosen a policy of rapprochement with Nazi Germany, he counterfactually argued, history would have turned out vastly better.

Buchanan began his argument by asserting that Great Britain and France were primarily responsible for the war by foolishly guaranteeing the security of Poland. On March 31, 1939, Neville Chamberlain committed "the greatest blunder in British history" by committing the country to defending Poland's independence in the event of a German attack. The decision was ill advised for all kinds of reasons. First, there was little sense in democratic Great Britain defending a country that was "'every bit as undemocratic and anti-Semitic as Germany.'"[90] Second, the British decision to guarantee Polish security was "cynical," since they had neither the ability nor the intention to follow up on their promises.[91] Finally, the decision proved to be "fatal" because it emboldened the Polish government to resist Hitler's demand to surrender Danzig and prevented the diplomatic resolution of Polish–German differences. As Buchanan put it, Britain mistakenly gave "a war guarantee to a dictatorship it did not trust, in a part of Europe where it had no vital interests, committing itself to a war it could not win."[92]

Because Britain proceeded to declare war on Nazi Germany, a conflict that was originally limited in scope quickly escalated and spread across Europe. This catastrophic turn of events was needless, according to Buchanan, since Hitler did not want war with either England or France. Hitler would have been willing to give up all German claims in Western Europe in exchange for an alliance with England, but despite floating numerous peace initiatives to this effect, he was consistently rebuffed by Churchill.[93] Buchanan conceded that England's refusal to accept German mastery over Europe ensured Germany's ultimate defeat. But he insisted that the price was too high, for Churchill was only able to defeat Hitler by allying with "the greatest mass murderer of the century," Joseph Stalin.[94] In the end, "British diplomatic folly succeeded only in getting Western Europe overrun [by the Nazis] and making Eastern Europe safe for Stalinism."[95] Worse still was the fact that, in doing so, Britain made countless moral compromises, colluding with the Soviet Union in the expulsion of millions of ethnic Germans at the war's end, radically altering the borders of Poland, and forcing thousands of Soviet POWs to return home to certain doom in the gulags. To cap it all off, Britain ended the war bankrupt and soon lost its colonies and its Empire.[96] The long-term repercussions were even more massive. The Second World War "brought an end to centuries of Western rule, and advanced the death of . . .[Western] civilization" itself.[97]

If only Britain had refused to defend Poland, Buchanan speculated, history would have turned out better. "Had there been no war guarantee," he wrote, "Poland, isolated and friendless, might have done a deal over Danzig and spared six million dead ...[T]here would have been no British declaration of war on September 3, and there might have been no German invasion of France in May 1940, or ever."[98] Without the war guarantee, he continued,

> the Soviet Union would almost surely have borne the brunt of the blow that fell on France. The Red Army, ravaged by Stalin's purge of senior officers, might have collapsed. Bolshevism might have been crushed. Communism might have perished in 1940, instead of living on for fifty years and murdering tens of millions more in Russia, China, Korea, Vietnam, and Cuba. A Hitler-Stalin war might have been the only war in Europe in the 1940s. Tens of millions might never have died terrible deaths in the greatest war in all history.[99]

Buchanan even suggested that there would have been no Holocaust as we know it. "With no war in the west," he mused, "all the Jews of Norway, Denmark, Holland, Belgium, Luxembourg, France, Italy, Yugoslavia, and Greece might have survived."[100]

Like most fantasies about alternate pasts, Buchanan's was inspired by disaffection with the present. His narrative resembled Baker's in its disgust with American foreign policy under the presidency of George W. Bush. Buchanan has long been a proponent of limited American involvement in world affairs, as was visible in books such as *A Republic Not An Empire* (1999).[101] His isolationism deepened after 2001, however, when the United States' military response to the attacks of September 11th brought the country to the brink of what he believed was imperial collapse. For Buchanan, the strategy that had enabled the United States' rise to world power in the twentieth century – "avoiding entangling alliances, staying out of European wars, and not going 'abroad in search of monsters to destroy'" – was abandoned under Bush.[102] Buchanan saw multiple reasons for this trend, some of which dated back to the country's increasing hubris following the collapse of communism and the Cold War in 1989–90. But one of his chief explanations was the existence of a "Churchill cult" in the US. For Buchanan, the view that "Churchill was ... a peerless war leader ... whose life ... should be the model for every statesman" directly inspired Bush, who, not coincidentally, ordered a bust of the British leader to be "placed in his Oval Office."[103] The problem was that after 9/11, the Churchill cult "helped to persuade an untutored president that the liberation of Iraq from Saddam would be like the liberation of Europe from Hitler," when in reality, it was anything but.[104] In short, the "Churchill cult gave us our present calamity."[105] Only by challenging this cult, and the myths surrounding it – most notably the idea that "World War II was the 'Good War'" – would the United States be able to avoid following in the path of "imperial Britain in her plunge from power."[106]

Like Baker, Buchanan's political views led him to adopt an uncritical view of the Third Reich. He minimized Nazism's ideological fanaticism out of a belief that Soviet communism posed a greater danger to Western security.[107] Unlike the majority of historians who viewed Nazi Germany as an aggressively expansionistic state driven by a virulently racist ideology, Buchanan saw it as a comparatively benign power that never represented a threat to Anglo-American interests. Insisting that Hitler "subordinate[d] ideology to raison d'état," Buchanan portrayed Hitler as a reasonable statesman who was provoked by the Western powers to adopt more radical geopolitical goals than he otherwise would have.[108] Buchanan assumed, for example, that if Hitler had gotten Danzig, he would not have threatened the Poles any further. He claimed that the Nazi invasion of the Soviet Union was not about *Lebensraum* or eliminating the alleged Judeo-Bolshevik threat, but a strategic method of forcing Great Britain to agree to a separate peace with Nazi Germany.[109] He added that the Nazis never threatened the interests of the United States and never had the actual capacity to attack it. All of these claims, however, ignored historical evidence to the contrary. It overlooked the Nazis' ideologically driven creation of SS Einsatzgruppen units to assist the Wehrmacht in ethnically cleansing Poland and the Soviet Union; and it ignored Hitler's efforts to develop weapons systems (long-range bombers, missiles, and atomic weaponry) with the potential to threaten US interests if the nation did not act to eliminate them.[110] Buchanan's inability to grasp the singularity of Hitler's criminality, however, ultimately found its best expression in his treatment of the Holocaust. Like Baker, he failed to recognize that his fantasy scenario, in which the Western Allies remained neutral and allowed the Nazis to focus their attack against the Soviet Union, would have effectively consigned all of Eastern European Jewry to certain death. In short, Buchanan relativized the significance of the Holocaust and, in so doing, expressed a normalized view of Nazism.

The soft revisionists

Sharing many of the views, if not all the conclusions, of Baker and Buchanan were more moderate revisionist texts that also challenged the idea that World War II was a good war. One of the first was Canadian scholar Jacques Pauwels's book, *The Myth of the Good War: America in the Second World War* (2002).[111] Like Baker, Pauwels critiqued US intervention in World War II from a left-wing perspective. Drawing on a variety of leftist revisionist works, Pauwels challenged the view that the United States idealistically went to war against the Nazis to defend democracy and instead argued that American intervention was driven by the pursuit of "business interests, money, and profits."[112] This thesis reflected Pauwels's belief that American foreign policy had traditionally been dictated by a "power elite" of corporate behemoths intent on pursuing its class interests at the expense of larger political ideals. He claimed that this pattern was on full display in the period leading up to, as well as during, the Second World War, when the power elite abruptly shifted its political allegiances as the great power conflict was unfolding in Europe. Prior to 1939–40, Pauwels argued, the elite sympathized with the Nazis, believing that they could best defend capitalism against Soviet communism. Yet, while this pro-Nazi sentiment made America neutral in the first two years of the war, the power elite's shifting assessment of its class interests eventually changed the country's political calculations. When Hitler's plans for autarky threatened to shut American firms out of the German-controlled European market, the power elite recognized that it could make even greater profits by arming Great Britain through Lend-Lease, a policy that enabled them to boost their exports and lift the US economy out of the Depression.[113] In short, American intervention in World War II was less about the defense of democracy than the pursuit of economic self-interest.

Pauwels further undercut the good war consensus by showing how the motives behind American interventionism placed the US government in close proximity to the Third Reich itself. He denied that America's decision to fight against Germany was influenced by moral opposition to the racist Nazi regime, pointing to the pervasiveness of racism in American society, whether in the American army – whose leaders "were just as convinced as the Nazis of the superiority of the white race" – or in the popular support for the same "racist eugenic theories" that were sanctioned by the Nazi state.[114] He further claimed that the desire of American corporations, such as Ford and Texaco, to make profits through their German subsidiaries led them to provide the Wehrmacht with much-needed trucks and fuel, both of which helped in the Nazi invasion of Poland and the Soviet Union, thereby making the US an accessory to murder.[115] Finally, he argued that the Anglo-American bombing of Dresden was not driven by genuine military considerations, but by the political desire to "intimidate the Soviets" with a demonstration of Allied air power, hardly a justifiable reason for the "senseless slaughter" of what he claimed may have been a quarter of a million German civilians.[116] All of these points supported Pauwels's contention that the Americans "did not emerge [from the war] with clean hands."[117]

In reassessing America's wartime policies, Pauwels offered some of his critiques in counterfactual fashion. In musing that "if Hitler had attacked the Soviet Union . . . just one year earlier, he would . . . have been cheered by the American media," Pauwels underscored the power elite's traditional sympathy towards fascism and hostility towards communism.[118] Similarly, in asserting that "without certain kinds of synthetic fuel made available by US firms, Hitler 'would never have considered invading Poland,'" Pauwels portrayed the United States as a de facto Nazi collaborator and made it complicit in the war's eruption.[119] Finally, the historian stressed the United States' duplicitous behavior towards its Soviet Allies by hypothesizing that if Anglo-American forces "[had only] opened a second front in France in 1942 . . . their troops might. . .have penetrated much deeper into . . . Germany than would be the case in 1944 and 1945 . . .[thereby allowing them] the kind of advantage vis-à-vis the Soviets that they had sought to attain by *not* opening a second front."[120]

For Pauwels, the United States' bad faith relationship with the Soviets made it difficult to see World War II as a good war. After all, the conflict established the central paradigm for America's subsequent involvement in other ill-advised military adventures. Just as the American power elite was driven by economic considerations to ally with the Soviets against the Nazis, it was inspired by similar considerations (especially, the desire to maintain profits through high levels of military spending) to shed the alliance after 1945. This postwar policy of confrontation regrettably led to the four-decade East-West standoff known as the Cold War. Even after the Cold War came to end, Pauwels added, economic considerations continued to shape American policy, as the power elite justified the preservation of America's "colossal arsenal" by identifying "new Hitlers" to fight: Saddam Hussein, Slobodan Milosevic, and, after the attacks of 9/11, "the vague concept [of] . . . terrorism." For Pauwels, this development confirmed that US intervention in World War II inaugurated an era of "permanent war" intended to serve American corporate interests.

In offering this indictment, Pauwels's book served as a bridge between the older revisionist literature of the 1990s and the wave that emerged after the turn of the millennium. While his book (which was originally published in Dutch in 2000) was written in the late 1990s in reaction to the US's post-Cold War unilateralism, its publication in English in 2002 allowed him to update it to accommodate the new realities of the post-9/11 world. This new geopolitical context allowed his book's conclusions to resemble Baker's and Buchanan's. This similarity notwithstanding, Pauwels refrained from concluding that the United States would have been better off staying out of the Second World War entirely. Despite challenging the good war consensus, he conceded that the Second World War was "good" in comparison to the many "bad" wars in American history, whether the Indian Wars of the nineteenth century or the War in Vietnam. The fact that the war was fought against "'an enemy of unspeakable evil,'" he declared, "necessarily [made it] a good war."[121] Finally, he affirmed that it was ultimately "a good thing that not the fascists, but rather their opponents, were victorious."[122]

Yet even if Pauwels did not go so far as Baker and Buchanan, his study also reflected a normalized view of the Nazi past. Like Baker, he universalized Nazism's significance by viewing it primarily as an outgrowth of Western capitalism. In the process, he underestimated the singularity of Nazism's ideological radicalism. This explained his strained comparison of Nazi and American racism, a comparison that reached its apogee in his exaggerated claim that "Hitler's attempt to conquer 'living space' in Eastern Europe" was inspired by the United States' Indian Wars in the nineteenth century.[123] Pauwels's blurring of the line between the Nazis and the Americans was meant to critique the latter, not rehabilitate the former. Yet, by focusing on America's shortcomings in fighting Nazi Germany, he effaced the distinction between the two states and diminished the latter's historical specificity.

Echoing many of the conclusions of Pauwels's book was British historian Norman Davies's study, *No Simple Victory: World War II in Europe, 1939–45* (2007).[124] Part historiographical essay, part voluminous encyclopedia, *No Simple Victory* was an angry work that attempted to correct the "myths and legends" that allegedly defined British and American knowledge of the Second World War.[125] Davies enumerated many examples of Anglo-American ignorance about the war, the chief one being the failure to realize that its heaviest fighting took place on the eastern instead of the western front. While average Britons and Americans may have heard of major battles like Stalingrad, most would be surprised to learn that the campaigns of Kiev, Kursk, and Bagration dwarfed major offensives in the west, such as Operation Overlord.[126] Implied within this ignorance, according to Davies, was an Anglo-American reluctance to credit the Soviet Union for making the decisive contribution to Hitler's defeat. This myopia especially defined Winston Churchill's "self-justifying" postwar account of World War II, which credited "the Anglo-American partnership [with] providing the winning combination."[127]

In supporting his claim about the USSR's importance, Davies resembled Baker and Buchanan by employing counterfactual reasoning. Unlike them, however, he did not claim that Allied non-intervention in the war would have made history turn out better by allowing the Nazis to defeat the Soviets. He claimed the opposite, writing that "if the Red Army had been knocked out [of the war], the Germans would not have stood idly by as the USA built up its strength and prepared to drop an atomic bomb on them. The German armed forces would have been immediately turned ... on Great Britain; the outcome of the Battle of the Atlantic could have been reversed; the Western Allies would probably have lost the base for their bombing offensive ... and a European counterpart of Enola Gay would have had nowhere to take off."[128] By imagining how Anglo-American security would have been threatened by a victory of the Nazis over the Soviets, Davies stressed the latter's importance in helping to defeat the former.

Davies was hardly a left-wing apologist for the USSR, however. In his book, he strove to correct yet another aspect of Anglo-American ignorance – the extent of Stalin's wartime crimes. These included the Soviet Union's brutal treatment of Poland, from its invasion of the country in 1939 to the shifting of its borders in 1945; the USSR's inhuman maltreatment of its own soldiers, who were cavalierly sacrificed in risky wartime offensives, routinely shot for minor offenses, and later punished for getting captured; and the Red Army's savage attacks against German civilians, who were raped, expelled, and murdered by the millions at the war's end. Perhaps the biggest misconception that Davies sought to overturn, however, was the Anglo-American notion that "Soviet" suffering in the war was somehow the same thing as "Russian" suffering. He pointed out that 90% of Soviet territory saw no fighting during World War II, adding that the 10% that *did* experience combat was located in the country's western, non-Russian sections.[129] Ukrainians and Belorussians represented the largest groups of Soviet citizens who died in the war, far outnumbering Russians. For Davies, the fact that historians failed to disaggregate the specific victim groups and mistakenly referred to 27 million "Soviet" wartime casualties was a clear example of Western ignorance of the war's reality.

Given the Soviet Union's role in defeating the Nazis, and given the brutal methods used by Stalin in the effort, Davies refused to see the Second World War as a good war. Declaring that "no side in the Second World War possesse[d] ... a monopoly ... of virtue or ... immorality," he asserted that the "good war" was a "dubious" concept that could only be viewed with extreme "skepticism."[130] In attempting to explain why Britons and Americans nevertheless continued to view the war in such positive terms, Davies pointed to what he called the "Allied Scheme of History." For him, this view arose during the Cold War, when Anglo-American scholars "aggrandize[d]" their contribution to victory and ignored that of the East.[131] In willfully using the past for "political purposes," the "Allied Scheme of History" produced "sixty years of historiographical apartheid" and a consciousness of the past marred by blindspots and bias.[132] This "fragmentation of memory" was further reinforced by the end of the Cold War, when the triumph of Western liberalism over Soviet communism led to the emergence of a particularly "Americocentric" view of World War II. It furthermore dovetailed with the Bush administration's "'neoconservative'" approach to world affairs in the years after year 2000.[133]

In leveling these charges, Davies was partly motivated by political views. A British historian of Welsh background born in 1939, Davies is hard to categorize politically. His skewering of English nationalism in his previous scholarship, in addition to his dislike of Churchill and George W. Bush, would seem to place him on the British left.[134] Yet, despite voting for the British Labour party, he has long displayed anti-communist views more typical of conservatives.[135] For the most part, Davies's revisionist position grew out of his work as a historian of modern Poland.[136] Convinced that Poland's historic importance and wartime suffering had long been overlooked in the West, Davies sought to direct critical attention towards the role of the wartime Allies in betraying the country during the years 1939 to 1945.

Davies's empathy for the Poles further explained one of the main consequences of his revisionist position: its subtle relativization of Nazism's criminality. In seeking to overturn the "Allied Scheme of History," Davies challenged the view that "the Nazis were … evil," but the Soviets were not.[137] Davies's shifting of attention to Soviet crimes helped lessen the singularity of the Nazis' own atrocities, most notably the Holocaust. Davies conceded that the Holocaust had "rightly" received attention, but he implied that it had unjustly overshadowed other aspects of the war. While the Holocaust "accounted for the death of nearly 6 million innocents … it was not exceptional …[and] occurred in a context where three or four times that number of other innocents perished. The historian's duty is to remember them all."[138] He attributed the Holocaust's disproportionate impact on Western consciousness to the Cold War, which allowed Western Europeans and Americans to confirm "the irrational evil of Nazism" while ignoring "the wartime sufferings of the people of the Soviet Bloc."[139] He also spoke negatively of Holocaust historians who tried to "enforce a Holocaust orthodoxy" by compelling other scholars to "sign up to the contention that the Holocaust was unique."[140] He furthermore bemoaned laws banning Holocaust denial as blocking "paths to … fuller [historical] understanding."[141] Finally, Davies lessened the singularity of Nazism's evil by arguing that World War II should be historicized as part of a broader Seventy-Five Years War from 1914–1989. In advancing these points, Davies minimized the Holocaust's significance. He was certainly correct that the violence of the twentieth century was linked in important ways. Yet in blurring the substantial differences between the century's separate conflicts, he ensured that the Nazis' distinct contribution would be effaced.

Compared to Davies, American historian Michael Bess offered a more balanced critique of the good war consensus in his book, *Choices Under Fire: Moral Dimensions of World War II* (2006).[142] Bess adopted a broad perspective in his study, surveying the war as it unfolded in both the European and Pacific theaters. He paid special attention to the gap between the righteousness of the Allied cause – defeating Axis aggression – and the morally ambiguous methods used to achieve it. In doing so, he sought to counter the reigning historiographical "stance of celebration" with a new "stance of critical scrutiny."[143]

Bess first challenged conventional views of the war's origins by rehabilitating the controversial Allied policy of appeasement. Rejecting the "facile approach" of previous scholars who "heap[ed] scorn upon British and French policymakers of the 1930s," he viewed appeasement as a reasonable response of the Western powers to Hitler's saber rattling.[144] Bess argued that the Western powers legitimately wanted to avoid another war, honestly believed they could rationally address Germany's outstanding grievances from World War I, and genuinely feared that renewed military conflict would boost the fortunes of the Soviet Union. Driven by a spirit of pacifism, appeasement, he argued, was "intelligent, noble, and proactive diplomacy."[145] The problem, he went on to note, was that Hitler saw appeasement as a sign of "weakness" and exploited it for his own expansionist purposes, a reality that became abundantly clear at the Munich conference in 1938.[146] Bess conceded that appeasement was ultimately a "failure." Yet he argued that there was little alternative to it. Employing counterfactual reasoning, he envisioned several scenarios that might have averted a Second World War, including a British and French military campaign in 1936 to expel the Germans from the Rhineland and a British and French diplomatic offensive to integrate the Soviet Union into a firm alliance. In the end, though, he rejected these scenarios as rooted in "unreality" and concluded that appeasement was the Allies' only viable choice.[147] Yet, instead of siding with previous scholars and moralistically judging the policy as "dishonorable," Bess found a silver lining in it, arguing that it made clear who the war's primary aggressor was. Thanks to appeasement, the Allies acquired a "'moral edge'" that enabled them to frame the war as "a struggle against an unmitigated evil."[148] Indeed, by exposing Hitler as "insatiable," appeasement enabled World War II to be viewed as "the 'Good War.'"[149]

Yet while Bess acknowledged that defeating Nazism was a noble goal, he argued that the means to achieve it were anything but. He focused special criticism on the Allies' aerial bombing campaign against civilians, describing it as "the single greatest moral failure of the Anglo-American war effort."[150] Although he conceded that the bombing campaign "constituted a crucial element in securing Allied victory," it eventually reached a point – in Dresden and Tokyo – where "the military benefit of the operation ... was outweighed by the colossal human cost."[151] Calling the bombing raids on civilian targets "atrocities, pure and simple," Bess condemned them counterfactually, arguing that "the

Anglo-Americans could have won the war without resorting to them."[152] Had they abstained from "area bombing and firebombing" and simply concentrated on military and economic targets, he argued, they would have admittedly prolonged the war, but would still have been able to "severely weaken the enemy's war machine" without indiscriminately killing hundreds of thousands of innocent civilians.[153]

Bess also condemned the US and Britain for relying upon the brutal methods of the Soviet Red Army in fighting the Germans. "The evils of Nazism," he wrote, were only defeated "through an alliance ... with a regime that was in many ways equally as vicious as Hitler's."[154] Citing the fact that nearly 80 percent of Germany's wartime casualties took place on the Eastern front, Bess agreed with Davies that it "was the Russians who broke the back of the German army."[155] Yet, the Red Army used harsh tactics to defeat the Germans, committing atrocities against German civilians and showing "limitless cruelty" towards their own soldiers.[156] Little of this savagery bothered the British and Americans, however. Bess claimed they would have been content to allow the Soviets to defeat the Nazis entirely on their own, were it not for the politically inconvenient result that the Red Army would have ended up conquering all of Western Europe. Only this prospect finally prompted Anglo-American forces to open up a second front in the west with Operation Overlord in June of 1944.[157]

For Bess, these moral shortcomings revealed that there was only a thin line separating Allied virtue from Axis evil. This was further shown by the existence of institutionalized racism in both the Allied and Axis camps. While the German and Japanese regimes were well known for endorsing racist beliefs, the same was true of the United States Army, which consigned most African-American soldiers to menial, non-combat jobs and placed those who were actually sent into combat into segregated units. This shameful fact, together with the eruption of race riots in American cities and the internment of Japanese-Americans in detention camps, led Bess to conclude that, whatever the "distinctions between the various racisms of World War II ... it is ... important to recognize the underlying commonalities among them." While he conceded that the "black G. I. thrown out of a segregated mess hall did not face the same dangers as a Jewish father cradling his child at the ravine of Babi Yar ... for all their differences, they were victims of a fundamentally similar gesture, rooted in hatred."[158]

Given these disquieting realities, Bess concluded that it was difficult to view World War II as a good war. Asserting that "it is time to let go of our nostalgia," he called for a "new mythology" of the war, one that "move[s] beyond the *Star Wars* imagery of pure goodness confronting pure evil in a pure contest with a pure outcome."[159] Even if the Second World War could still be viewed as "a war that needed to be fought . . . this should not prevent us from paying close attention to the conflict's many important gray areas."[160]

In arriving at this conclusion, Bess struck a more balanced position than other revisionists. Unlike Baker and Buchanan, he did not seek to minimize Nazism's evil. Unlike Davies, he did not blame Holocaust consciousness for American and British readers' blind spots about the Second World War.[161] Bess's balanced position reflected his moderate political views. A professor of history born in 1954, he was liberally inclined and sympathetic to pacifism, but did not allow his feelings to lead him to question the war's ultimate necessity.[162] That said, his narrative, especially his comparison of Axis and Allied racism, universalized Nazism's significance and partly obscured its distinctive features. In so doing, his narrative raised the conceptual question of whether it was possible to challenge World War II's reputation as a good war without simultaneously minimizing the Third Reich's criminality.

A possible answer to this question was provided by Niall Ferguson's book, *The War of the World: Twentieth-Century Conflict and the Descent of the West* (2006) (Figure 8).[163] Ferguson's study was a bold work of synthesis that adopted a broader focus than other revisionist texts, covering nearly a century's worth of history in its nearly 650-page narrative. At the book's heart, however, stood an in-depth analysis of the origins and consequences of World War II. Ferguson's discussion of the war was insightful and provocative, but it struggled to question the good war consensus without diminishing Nazism's evil. Because Ferguson was mindful of this pitfall, he did not advance as radical a critique as other revisionists. Throughout the book, he offered many contrarian arguments only to backtrack from them later. By purporting to be more radical than it really was, *The War of the World* resembled a revisionist sheep in wolf's clothing.

From the outset, Ferguson expressed a desire to upend received opinion about World War II. Indeed, he went so far as to question its outright existence, noting that in the process of

A NEW YORK TIMES BESTSELLER

NIALL FERGUSON

THE WAR OF THE WORLD

Twentieth-Century Conflict and the Descent of the West

"A heartbreaking, serious and thoughtful survey of human evil that is utterly fascinating and dramatic, and always has something new to tell us ... superb narrative history."—Simon Sebag Montefiore, *The New York Times Book Review*

Figure 8. The cover of Niall Ferguson's book, *The War of the World* (2006), reflects the historian's revisionist desire to de-romanticize the Second World War.

researching the topic, he came to ask himself whether there was "really such a thing as the Second World War?"[164] The monumental scale, chronological span, and geographical scope of world conflict in the first half of the twentieth century convinced him that World War II should be viewed as part of a larger "Fifty Years War" lasting from 1904–1953.[165] Yet by placing the Allied struggle against Nazism at the center of his narrative, Ferguson implied that the years 1939–45 remained singular in important ways. He thereby highlighted the limits to his revisionism.

These limits were visible in his analysis of the war's origins. Ferguson initially seemed to embrace A. J. P. Taylor's controversial thesis that the conflict "between Germany, France, and Britain was nearly as much the fault of the Western powers [and] … Poland … as of Hitler."[166] Yet he went on to concede that Taylor was only "half-right" in his analysis and quickly reaffirmed the importance of Hitler's expansionist aims for the war's outbreak, writing that the Führer's goal was "to enlarge the German Reich so [as to] … embrace … the entire German *Volk* and in the process to annihilate … the Jews and Soviet Communism."[167] Ferguson also appeared to rehabilitate the disgraced policy of appeasement, arguing that "the arguments for [it] still seem sensible and pragmatic when one reads them today."[168] Yet, he went on to declare that there was "good reason" why the concept had long been "used … as a term of abuse," writing that it should have been abandoned in favor of a policy of "pre-emption."[169] Unlike Bess, who denied that there was any alternative to appeasement at the time, Ferguson argued counterfactually that "an early move to nip in the bud the threat posed by Hitler's Germany … would almost certainly have succeeded" in avoiding the Second World War.[170] Ferguson claimed that because "Germany was simply not ready [militarily] for a European war in 1938," all that "the British had to do was to commit unequivocally to a joint Anglo-French defence of Czechoslovakia" and rebuff calls from Germany for Chamberlain to mediate the dispute.[171] The "chances of a German humiliation would have been high," and even if it had not happened, "almost any outcome, even war itself, would have been preferable to what in fact happened." After all, he insisted, it would "prove much harder to fight Germany in 1939 than it would have proved in 1938."[172] In the end, though, Ferguson refrained from pushing his revisionist argument too far, concluding "we cannot … say for sure what would have happened."[173]

Ferguson was equally indecisive in explaining why the Allies ultimately won the war. Like other revisionists, he questioned the contribution of the "greatest generation" to victory, writing that American soldiers "were far from being the greatest warriors of World War II." He further endorsed Davies's views about the "disproportionate contribution of the Soviets" to the Allies' ultimate triumph.[174] Yet Ferguson also insisted that the role of the US and Britain had been underappreciated, citing statistics related to American industrial production and British imperial troop mobilization.[175] Ferguson also hedged in his use of counterfactual scenarios, presenting multiple ways in which the Nazis could have won the war, only to declare that they "could [never] have triumphed over the overwhelming economic odds against them once they had taken on simultaneously the British Empire, the United States and the Soviet Union."[176] "If anything was inevitable in the history of the twentieth century," he concluded, "it was the [wartime] victory of this overwhelming combination."[177]

The hesitancy of Ferguson's revisionism was further visible in his discussion of the Holocaust. On the one hand, he seemed to follow other revisionists in questioning its uniqueness. This was visible, first of all, in his subsuming of World War II within the larger Fifty Years' War, which diminished the Nazi genocide's particularity by placing it within a half-century of global violence. It was also visible in his frequent comparison of Nazi and Soviet crimes. Ferguson appeared to follow Davies's lead in writing: "We now see just how many of the things that were done in German concentration camps during the Second World War were anticipated in the Gulag: the transportation in cattle trucks, the selection into different categories of prisoner, the shaving of heads, the dehumanizing living conditions . . . the brutal and arbitrary punishments."[178] That said, Ferguson later stepped back from his comparative agenda, noting that while "many aspects of life and death in the Nazi concentration camps . . . had their analogues in the Gulag . . . there was something qualitatively different about the Nazis' war against the Jews and other minorities" – namely, its "modern" character.[179]

Finally, Ferguson was ambivalent about drawing overly revisionist conclusions about the war's morality. On the one hand, he explicitly denied that the Second World War was a "good war," writing that it should not be seen as a war of "evil against good, but of evil against lesser evil."[180] Like Baker, Davies, and Bess, he insisted that the line separating the Nazis from the Allies was often quite thin. "The

Third Reich," Ferguson asserted, "was very far from the world's only racial state in the 1930s"; the United States, he argued, maintained laws against interracial marriage and mandated the sterilization of certain people in accordance with eugenic principles.[181] He also condemned the Anglo-American decision to ally with the Soviet Union, writing that "[in] order to defeat an enemy they routinely denounced as barbaric, the Western powers had made common cause with an ally that was morally little better."[182] The Western powers even began "to adopt [some] of totalitarianism's defining characteristics," such as "dehumanizing the enemy in order more easily to annihilate him," a fact borne out by cases of British and American troops killing German prisoners.[183] At the same time, Ferguson defended the British and American bombing campaign from the "fashionable" claim that it failed to make "any significant contribution to victory," arguing that it "inflicted significant damage on the German war effort" by reducing "potential [economic] output" and thoroughly weakening "civilian morale."[184] He further refused to call the bombing campaign an atrocity comparable to Axis crimes, writing that it was not motivated by hatred.[185] Ferguson ultimately made clear, however, that the war could hardly be viewed as a success from an Anglo-American perspective. Given the fact that its "principal beneficiary was Stalin's Soviet Union," which followed up its military victory over Germany by lowering the Iron Curtain over Eastern Europe, the Allies' ultimate military triumph was a "tainted victory, if indeed it was a victory at all."[186] Rather than solidifying Western supremacy, it represented the "beginning of the end."[187]

This bleak conclusion partly reflected Ferguson's conservative political views. His fear of Western decline, which he shared with Buchanan, was the flip side of his admiration for the British Empire, which he defended in much of his scholarship.[188] Ferguson's conservatism was comparatively moderate, however. He did not go so far as the right-wing British revisionists, John Charmley and Alan Clark, who blamed England's postwar decline on Churchill's decision to take the country to war against Nazi Germany. Ferguson remained an admirer of Churchill and shared the belief that the country's decision to fight the Nazis represented its "finest hour."[189] For this reason, Ferguson's revisionist interpretation of World War II was less radical than that of other scholars. His desire to preserve Churchill's reputation required him to acknowledge Nazism's evil, which served as a foil to Britain's wartime heroism. Unlike the hard revisionists, he refused to imagine British non-intervention allowing history to take a better course.

Beyond the hard and soft revisionist works discussed above, other recent accounts challenged the good war consensus. Some of the more strident contributions came from writers and scholars on the left-liberal wing of the political spectrum. Socialist activist Ashley Smith's article, "World War II: The Good War?" (2000) followed the lead of Pauwels and Baker in claiming that the United States intervened in World War II not to defend democracy, which it hypocritically betrayed, but corporate capitalism.[190] Similarly, leftwing activist and scholar Carl Lesnor's essay, "The 'Good' War" (2005), argued that the Allies' official explanation for intervention set the distressing precedent of "justif[ying] ... all our subsequent wars" by portraying "all our subsequent enemies [as] ... Hitler clones." In making this claim, Lesnor sought to "expose the ideological usefulness" of the "good war" concept by showing how it was "never more apparent than today, when we have taken up arms against the 'Axis' of Evil."[191] The same concern informed liberal American historian David Hoogland Noon's article, "Operation Enduring Analogy: World War II, The War on Terror, and the Uses of Historical Memory" (2004), which criticized President George W. Bush's use of "the rhetoric of the 'good war'" to justify the United States' military campaigns in Afghanistan and Iraq.[192]

Building on these articles, subsequent books by more centrist writers further challenged the idea of the good war. Some questioned World War II's morality by calling attention to Allied misdeeds at the war's end. British journalist Giles MacDonogh's book, *After the Reich: The Brutal History of the Allied Occupation* (2007), graphically chronicled the German people's postwar suffering at the hands of the Allies, describing how German POWs were killed, German women raped, and ethnic Germans expelled by Allied soldiers and Eastern European civilians. The book's accusatory language, which frequently likened the Allies to the Nazis, also made clear that World War II was far from "good."[193] Similarly, American historian William Hitchcock's book, *The Bitter Road to Freedom: A New History of the Liberation of Europe* (2008), explored the "dreadful ugliness" of liberation and showed how the Allied campaign to free occupied Europe from Nazi rule inflicted aerial bombings, hunger, theft, rape, expulsion, and other horrors upon innocent civilians. Hitchcock cited these instances as grounds for challenging "American myopia" about the "good war" and replacing it with an "alternative" narrative that restored the "grim realities . . .[that] have . . . gone missing" from popular consciousness.[194] A comparable agenda underpinned Keith Lowe's *Savage Continent: Europe in the Aftermath of World War II* (2012), which, by chronicling the crime-ridden chaos of the early postwar period, challenged reigning view about the "Greatest Generation" by showing how it was composed not only of "selfless heroes" but "thieves, plunderers, and abusers of the worst kind."[195]

Finally, other studies questioned the Second World War's morality by following Norman Davies's example and focusing on the conflict's long-ignored eastern front. Timothy Snyder's *Bloodlands: Europe Between Hitler and Stalin* (2010) explicitly challenged the tendency of "Americans [to] call the Second World War the 'Good War'" by incorporating certain arguments of Eastern European revisionists and devoting as much attention to the crimes of Stalin as those of Hitler. Whether focusing on Stalin's responsibility for the war's eruption or its many atrocities, Snyder showed how the suffering of Eastern Europeans in the "bloodlands" made it difficult to grant the war any redemptive meaning.[196] The same was true of Max Hastings' *All Hell Let Loose: The World At War, 1939–1945* (2011). Hastings' critique of the Western Allies' betrayal of Poland in 1939, their toleration of Soviet brutality in the east, and the suffering of Eastern European civilians, were part of his larger effort to question "our instinctive assumption that our grandparents fought 'the Good War.'"[197] Finally, Antony Beevor's global history, *The Second World War* (2012), questioned whether it made sense to give "the mantle of a 'good war' . . .[to] the Second World War" by pointing out that "one half of Europe had to be sacrificed to the Stalinist maw to save the other half."[198] These studies, it is important to note, took pains not to relativize Nazism's evil. Indeed, they emphasized Hitler's responsibility for starting the war and perpetrating countless atrocities.[199] Yet by taking specific aim at the concept of the good war, they lent support to the larger revisionist campaign.

Taken together, all of the revisionist studies reflected an important shift in World War II's status in Anglo-American historiography. Driven by a sense of discontent with international political developments, British and American revisionists challenged the idea that World War II was a good war, claiming that its alleged geopolitical lessons – especially the value of military force – were implicated in many of the world's present-day problems. The revisionists' strategies of undermining World War II's "goodness" came in hard and soft versions, but most claimed that the violent methods used by the Allies to defeat the Nazis brought them into a similar immoral orbit and produced endless human suffering. Some revisionists even hypothesized that refraining from intervening in the war might have led history to turn out better. In advancing this line of argumentation, the revisionists both expressed and promoted a normalized view of the Third Reich. Concerned about the shortcomings of the present, they rejected the prevailing view of the Nazi past by relativizing and universalizing its significance.

Responding to revisionism: The good war debate

Yet while the revisionists' representation of the Second World War suggested a shift in British and American memory of the Nazi era, the critical response to it offered a more complicated picture.[200] The revisionist literature reaped considerable attention in the United States and Great Britain, receiving numerous reviews.[201] The responses were sharply polarized, however, with supportive reactions competing with hostile ones. Predictably, the responses tracked along political lines, with the revisionist works receiving support from left-wing pacifists and conservative isolationists, on the one hand, and criticism from liberal and conservative interventionists, on the other.

Baker's and Buchanan's hard revisionist studies were praised by a wide range of critics. *Human Smoke* was predictably admired by left-leaning reviewers. American journalist Mark Kurlansky, writing in the *Los Angeles Times*, commended it for exposing the good war myth as "one ... of the biggest ... lies in modern history," while British journalist Peter Wilby hailed it in *The Guardian* for showing how "romanticising the Second World War has led us into foreign policy traps" like the invasion of Iraq.[202] Other commentators supported *Human Smoke* for its larger ethical lessons. British journalist Sam Leith wrote that Baker's "fascinating and upsetting book" made "a strong case" for pacifism, while Irish novelist Colm Tóibín declared that it represented a "passionate assault on the idea that ... targeting ... civilians can ever be justified."[203] Buchanan's book, meanwhile, also found support, especially among right-leaning critics. A symposium on the book organized by *The American Conservative* in 2008 largely welcomed its claims, with historian Andrew Bacevich hailing it for showing how the good war myth made postwar American foreign policy "excessively militarized, needlessly inflexible, and insufficiently imaginative."[204] Similarly, the libertarian journalist Eric Margolis praised Buchanan's book, agreeing that England was to blame for causing a "general European war" that handed "half of Europe to the Soviet Union."[205] On the extreme right of the political spectrum, finally, neo-Nazi and Holocaust denial websites endorsed Buchanan's book (as well as Baker's) as an important contribution towards dismantling the "Good War Myth of World War II."[206]

By contrast, the two books came in for rougher treatment from other reviewers. More than a few attacked the studies for being based on sloppy and tendentious scholarship. Journalist Anne Applebaum compared *Human Smoke* to an unscholarly "blog post" that failed to "add anything to what we know about World War II," while historian Andrew Roberts cited its many factual errors and dismissed it as "the worst book I have reviewed in eighteen years."[207] Journalist Christopher Hitchens, meanwhile, called Buchanan's study "sinister" and rooted in "ideological bias."[208] Linking these and other responses was the charge that the books implied a "moral equivalence between the Allies and the Axis" and overlooked what historian William Rubinstein called Nazism's "unique evil."[209] Significantly, some critics reversed Baker's and Buchanan's counterfactual assertions by insisting that history would have turned out worse had the Western Allies refrained from fighting the Nazis.[210] Military historian Jeffrey Record argued that if the British and Americans had stayed out of the war, thereby allowing Hitler to defeat the Soviet Union, "all of contintental Europe, rather than just its eastern half, might have been condemned to decades, perhaps even centuries of totalitarian tyranny."[211] Journalist Katha Pollitt agreed, arguing that it was "not so clear . . . that fewer people would have died had Britain and the United States let Germany take over Europe."[212] As scholar Jack Fischel concluded, Anglo-American pacifism "would have only made it easier for Hitler to consolidate his gains and attempt further conquest."[213]

In contrast to the scorching reactions to Baker's and Buchanan's hard revisionism, the softer revisionist studies received a milder response. Pauwels's book was the least widely reviewed, but it earned a favorable reception among left-leaning readers, who praised it for exposing the economic motives behind American interventionism.[214] Bess's study was described as "splendid" by some reviewers, although others called it "muddled" and "murky" for its inconsistent application of moral categories to the war.[215] Ferguson's book received a much wider reading and earned largely positive reviews, most of which underscored the mildness of its revisionist thrust.[216] Historian Simon Sebag Montefiore, for example, wrote that, despite "provocative flashes of revisionism," Ferguson's book was "always sound on the fundamentals, and on the right side," while historian Tristram Hunt described its conclusions as fully within the "liberal mainstream."[217] By contrast, Norman Davies's book received a more polarized response. *No Simple Victory* was hailed for recognizing that the Third Reich's defeat was accompanied by "huge acts of injustice" and for showing that "the Good War was only good in parts."[218] At the same time, the book was faulted for its lack of "proportion" and "moral equivalence" in comparing Soviet and Nazi crimes.[219] As literary scholar Susan Suleiman put it, Davies's encyclopedic book raised "suspicion[s]" by "drown[ing] the ... meaning of the Holocaust in an ocean of mismatched facts."[220] These criticisms revealed that, while there was a willingness to amend the good war consensus, there remained a desire to underscore the singularity of Nazism's evil.

This desire was also demonstrated by the appearance of more orthodox studies of World War II around the same time. In his book, *Moral Combat: Good and Evil in World War II* (2011), historian Michael Burleigh directly attacked the "dubious moral relativism" of Buchanan's and Baker's studies, insisting that the Third Reich's "murderous depredations" made World War II "a necessary war."[221] Similarly, Avishai Margalit, in his book, *On Compromise and Rotten Compromises* (2009), defended the Western Allies' decision to ally with the Soviet Union against Nazi Germany as "morally right," despite Stalin's crimes, because "Hitler's evil was radical evil, undermining morality itself."[222] Still other studies, such as Andrew Roberts's *The Storm of War* (2009), Mark Mazower's *Hitler's Empire* (2008), Richard Evans's *The Third Reich at War* (2008), and Richard Bessel's *Germany, 1945* (2010), stressed the Nazis' ideological extremism and credited the Allies with their defeat. In so doing, they implicitly rejected the revisionist assault on the good war consensus.[223]

Seen in its entirety, the back and forth between the revisionists and their critics revealed several important things about the memory of the Nazi past. First and foremost, it confirmed the dialectic of normalization. From the beginning of the debate, the goal of the revisionists was to overturn the good war consensus by normalizing the legacy of

Nazism. In attempting to do so, however, they engendered efforts to defend its distinctiveness. The resulting controversy impeded the goal of normality: instead of the Allies coming to be viewed like the Axis, their differences were reinforced; instead of the Nazi era becoming viewed as a past like any other, its singularity was solidified. That said, the revisionist literature did not leave the Nazi legacy unaffected. While some of its arguments were rejected, others were accepted. This was particularly true of the soft revisionists' efforts to amend some of the myths about the Anglo-American campaign against the Nazis. These myths included the idea that the Western Allies' role in defeating the Third Reich was as decisive as the Soviets'; that their methods were mostly moral; and that their victory paved the way for a postwar order of freedom and prosperity. The willingness of critics to concede these points revealed that the revisionist campaign registered its share of achievements. While its supporters did not topple the good war consensus, they succeeded in weakening it.

The future of the good war

It is safe to conclude, therefore, that the concept of the good war has probably peaked in influence and will soon begin to decline. This may be for the best. The new revisionism has exposed several problems with the good war as a historiographical concept. For one thing, it is terminologically misleading. Since the adjective "good" glosses over the undeniable horrors that accompany all wars, there is little justification for utilizing it as the defining term for the most destructive of all modern military conflicts. This is especially true given the fact that the idea of the good war is conceptually narrow. While the phrase aptly illuminates the moral dimensions of the Allies' campaign against the Nazis, it obscures the morally questionable means that were ultimately used to defeat them. These flaws, in turn, highlight the good war's third liability, the way in which it serves as a magnet for polemical criticism. Given its misleading and conceptually narrow dimensions, the good war lends itself to being caricatured as a mythic notion surrounded by taboos that allegedly demand immediate correction. This liability explains why individuals and groups representing the extremes of the political spectrum can so easily attack it.

Given these shortcomings, the good war faces several possible fates, none of which bode well for the concept. In theory, the concept could be preserved in amended form by restoring the quotation marks that originally surrounded it in Studs Terkel's pioneering study. Doing this would strip the term of its nostalgic associations, restore its intended ambiguity, and encourage a more critical perspective towards its historical referent. Given the tenor of the recent debate, however, it may be preferable to retire the phrase from circulation altogether. This would help eliminate many of the phrase's current liabilities. Terminologically, it would do away with the misleading implication that any war can be "good." Conceptually, it would allow neglected elements of the war to be included in a wider narrative and foster a fuller understanding of the past. Finally, retiring the phrase would bring an end to polemical attacks by denying critics the ability to make straw-man arguments about the urgency of dismantling reigning "myths."

This latter point is especially important, as much of the revisionist case is based on a weak foundation. It is doubtful, first of all, that ordinary Americans and Britons really subscribe to the caricatured understanding of World War II alleged by revisionists – namely, as a black and white campaign of good against evil. Second, it is doubtful that the good war's historical lessons are responsible for the present-day world's many crises. It was geopolitical, not historical, arguments, after all, that led President George W. Bush to order the invasions of Afghanistan and Iraq. His administration certainly invoked historical analogies drawn from World War II to help justify the war, but they did not inspire it. In claiming otherwise, the revisionists have blamed the concept of the good war for far too much politically. Yet, precisely because its liabilities make it vulnerable to easy attack, it may be best to deny critics the opportunity to make them in the first place by retiring the concept altogether. Some may object that doing so will concede victory to the revisionists. Others may worry that embracing a more self-critical view of World War II will enable the far right to exploit the Allies' historical "dirty laundry" for partisan gain. In the end, though, the free marketplace of ideas will dictate which historical narratives have staying power and which do not. The effective refutation of many of the revisionist' claims in the debate over the good war strongly suggests that their more extreme arguments have little chance of gaining admission into the historical consensus.

This fact should reassure skeptics that, even without the concept of the good war, the fight against Nazism from 1939 to 1945 can still be viewed as a historically necessary campaign. World War II was an undeniably brutal event defined by untold human suffering. But in successfully repelling the Nazis' assault against Western civilization's values – however imperfectly they have been realized in practice – the Allies nevertheless registered a major achievement. While the new revisionism may have succeeded in forcing a rethinking of the war in certain respects, it does not yet appear to have successfully challenged this singular legacy. Whether it will be able to do in the future is unclear. If prior patterns hold true, the present revisionist wave will only run its course following the return of stability in the realm of international relations. That day, however, is probably a long way off, given the current state of world affairs. In the end, our understanding of the Second World War in the near future will probably depend on how today's wars are ultimately resolved.

2 FROM HISTORY TO MEMORY AND BACK AGAIN: DEBATING THE HOLOCAUST'S UNIQUENESS

> As far as historical scholarship is concerned, the uniqueness "debate" has lost most of its steam.[1]
>
> DONALD BLOXHAM

Trendspotting is a risky activity, especially when it comes to history. It is hard enough to identify the causal factors that shape the past, let alone speculate about how it may evolve in the future. During the Cold War, Eastern Europeans living under communism knew better than to try and predict the past, being aware that their governments routinely rewrote it to fit changing needs, airbrushing out those who had become discredited and rehabilitating those who had come back into favor. In the liberal democratic West, by contrast, there have been fewer inhibitions about predicting the past. Especially since the rise of postmodernism, Western academics have prided themselves on their self-reflexive awareness about the forces that shape historical scholarship. Most scholars today consider themselves well informed about how history is subjectively constructed; how the past takes shape in collective memory; and how historiographical trends come and go. All of these skills belong to the repertoire of a scholar like Donald Bloxham and inform his observation that the debate on the Holocaust's uniqueness may have run its course. Whether or not it is accurate, however, is another question.

At first glance, the claim seems persuasive. Many Holocaust historians have made similar assertions in recent years. Alon Confino has written that the idea of the Holocaust's uniqueness "has lost its

intellectual and emotional power ... among scholars."[2] A. Dirk Moses
has agreed, noting that "the genocide studies community has already
conducted the debate about ... uniqueness ... and has moved onto
other research questions."[3] This scholarly shift, according to Dan Stone,
explains why the debate over uniqueness has "died down" and become
largely "irrelevant."[4] It also explains why, according to Jürgen Matthäus,
"perpetuating ...[the] debate over the issue of uniqueness would be
analytically sterile."[5] Convinced that it makes little sense to "flog the
dead horse of uniqueness," Doris Bergen surely speaks for many historians in suggesting that there is little left to say on the topic.[6]

If true, the end of the uniqueness debate would provide further
evidence of the normalization of the Nazi past. Until recently, the question of the Holocaust's uniqueness lacked any semblance of normality.
For over two decades, scholars argued incessantly about whether the
Holocaust was distinct from, or similar to, other genocides. The growing
conviction today that the debate is finally over, by contrast, would seem
to indicate that the idea of uniqueness has shed its divisive character and
become normalized. It would suggest that the Holocaust is no longer
regarded as an exceptional genocide but a "normal" episode of mass
killing. It would furthermore imply that the critics of uniqueness have
successfully universalized the Holocaust's significance. In short, the
alleged end of the uniqueness debate would seem to herald a new era
of consensus in Holocaust historiography.

These suppositions notwithstanding, it is premature to view the
debate as over. Although its intensity may have declined since it erupted a
generation ago, the debate has hardly disappeared. Indeed, since the turn
of the millennium, and especially in the last several years, new scholarly
works have challenged the Holocaust's uniqueness and sparked a new
phase of heated discussion. By examining these works in the context of
the uniqueness debate's larger history, we can better assess whether it is,
in fact, approaching its conclusion or is still very much underway.

The debate about the Holocaust's uniqueness can be divided into
three distinct phases. It began in earnest in the 1990s, when the concept's
supporters and opponents argued vehemently, and often polemically,
about how to interpret the "Final Solution of the Jewish Question."
Much of the discussion focused on matters of history, especially issues
of historical comparison between the Holocaust and other genocides.
By the end of this period, however, scholars began to argue over the
consequences of uniqueness for the issue of memory, specifically whether

the Holocaust's growing presence in Western historical consciousness was overshadowing the popular awareness of other mass killings. This question, in turn, came to stand at the center of the debate's second phase, which began after the turn of the millennium. During this period, scholars dialed down the rhetorical excesses of the previous decade and soberly discussed whether the growing attention to the Holocaust was, in fact, shifting attention away from, or might actually be directing it to, other cases of genocide. By the end of this phase, scholars appeared to have transcended the dialectical clashes of earlier years and reached a new synthesis; while they rejected the idea of the Holocaust's uniqueness, they denied that it had diminished public awareness of other genocides. In fact, most scholars claimed that the perception of the Holocaust's uniqueness actually helped elicit comparisons to other genocides and draw attention towards them. In so doing, they showed that the idea of the Holocaust's uniqueness had actually promoted its universalization. Despite this apparent consensus, however, the recent appearance of books seeking to historicize the Holocaust within the broader history of modern genocide has launched a third phase of the debate. These works of history have been far more balanced than those that appeared in the debate's first phase. But they have still sparked discord, being perceived by certain scholars as promoting apologetic and politically tendentious lines of argumentation. The criticism of these studies, in turn, has led to a vigorous counter-response by their authors and allies, with the result being a new round of intense discussion. Where it will lead is unclear. But it suggests that Donald Bloxham's observation about the end of the uniqueness debate may be wishful thinking. The memory of the Holocaust may not yet be as normalized as many believe.

Phase One: Holocaust history and hyperbole

The idea that the Holocaust is somehow unique has a long history. As a concept, it dates back to the early postwar period, but it only became a topic of interest for scholars in the late 1970s and early 1980s.[7] During these years, historians, philosophers, sociologists, and other academics embraced the concept as part of a defensive response to two larger trends that were perceived as downplaying, if not altogether effacing, the Holocaust's Jewish specificity. One trend involved efforts by scholars to historicize the Nazi genocide with the aid of broader theoretical concepts. Beginning in the 1950s and proceeding into the 1990s, historians and other scholars tried to make sense of the Holocaust by employing such concepts as totalitarianism, fascism, functionalism, modernity, and genocide. These concepts shed light on important aspects of the Final Solution, but they tended to universalize the event and marginalize its Jewish dimensions. A second trend at this same time was the attempt of various groups and individuals outside of the academy to politicize the Holocaust. This phenomenon assumed different forms: it surfaced in the efforts of Eastern European communist governments during the Cold War to "de-judaize" the Holocaust for political purposes; in attempts in the United States to "Americanize" the Holocaust to make it palatable to popular audiences; in campaigns by assorted activist groups to "steal" the Holocaust to draw attention to their own causes; in efforts to deny the Holocaust by right-wing extremists; and in attempts by German conservatives to relativize the Holocaust in order to create a healthy sense of national identity.[8]

Fearing that these trends were obscuring the Holocaust's Jewish dimensions, numerous scholars, mostly from the field of Jewish Studies, such as Emil Fackenheim, Lucy Dawidowicz, Saul Friedlander, Yehuda Bauer, Steven Katz, Deborah Lipstadt, and Daniel Goldhagen, published a series of studies in the 1980s and 1990s that insisted on the Holocaust's singularity. Although their definitions of uniqueness varied, they generally agreed that the Holocaust was historically exceptional – both in the context of the Second World War and the broader sweep of history – by virtue of the intentions that underpinned it.[9] Driven by an irrational and apocalyptic anti-Semitic ideology that branded the Jew a threat of world historical proportions, the Nazis, according to these scholars, planned on exterminating the Jewish people in its entirety.[10] This goal, they argued, stood in contrast to the Nazis' persecution of other groups during the Second World War – the mentally and physically handicapped, Sinti and Roma, Slavs, homosexuals, and others – none of whom were slated for total destruction. The proponents of uniqueness further contended that the totalizing intent behind the Nazis' murder campaign distinguished it from other historical episodes of mass killing that were less sweeping in scope, whether the Turkish CUP's murder of the Armenians, Stalin's starving of Ukrainian Kulaks, or the Khmer Rouge regime's murder of fellow Cambodians. The most emphatic articulation of the uniqueness thesis was presented by Steven Katz's book, *The Holocaust in Historical Context* (1994), which argued that the failure of other mass killings to match the Holocaust's extremity disqualified them from being genuine cases of genocide.[11] To be sure, many scholars were unwilling to go as far as Katz, and some, such as Yehuda Bauer, favored using the terms "holocaust" and "genocide" outside of a Jewish context to describe other historical atrocities. But Katz's call to restrict the term "genocide" solely to the Holocaust, combined with the wave of studies asserting its historical uniqueness, set the stage for a backlash.

Before long, a variety of scholars, mostly from outside the field of Jewish Studies, attacked the idea of uniqueness on multiple fronts. Among the most outspoken were two American specialists in Native-American history, David Stannard and Ward Churchill. In several works published in the 1990s, they rejected the historical claims made by the supporters of uniqueness, asserting that the mistreatment of Native Americans by European settlers over half a millennium qualified it both quantitatively and qualitatively as a case of genocide every bit as severe as the Holocaust.[12] Stannard, for example, argued that the genocide of Native Americans exceeded or matched that of the Holocaust both in the extent of the killing and the intent behind it. The sheer numbers of deaths and the proportion of population killed – between 50–100 million persons in the western hemisphere, comprising 90–95 percent of its indigenous inhabitants – vastly outpaced the Nazis' murder total. Moreover, the "many pre-twentieth century examples of unambiguous official calls by European or white American political leaders for the total annihilation of ... individual Native American peoples" revealed that the Jews were hardly the only people ever to have been slated for total destruction.[13] Churchill, meanwhile, asserted that Jews were not the only group targeted for death by the Nazis, writing that World War II's "invisible victims" – Sinti and Roma, Russian POWs, and Eastern European civilians – should be classified alongside Jews as Holocaust victims. As he argued: "the true human costs of Nazi genocide came to 26 million or more, six million of whom were Jews, a million or more of whom were Gypsies, and the rest mostly Slavs. Only with these facts clearly in mind can we say that we have apprehended the full scope of the Holocaust."[14]

Beyond critiquing the concept of uniqueness for misrepresenting history, Stannard and Churchill attacked it for distorting memory. In one of their most controversial claims, they insisted that the idea of the Holocaust's uniqueness contributed to the "trivialization," if not outright "denial," of other genocides. As Stannard wrote:

> The willful maintenance of public ignorance regarding the genocidal
> and racist horrors against indigenous peoples that have been and
> are being perpetrated by many nations in the Western Hemisphere,
> including the United States ... is consciously aided and abetted and
> legitimized by the actions of Jewish uniqueness advocates, [whose]
> claims of uniqueness for their own people are ... synonymous
> with ...[the] denial of the experience of others.[15]

Churchill went even further, arguing that this form of denial was more
dangerous than the kind promoted by neo-Nazis, for while "the latter
content themselves with denying the authenticity of a single genocidal
process, exclusivists [not only] deny ... the validity of myriad genocides ...
[but] are ... treated as academically credible."[16] Given this claim, it was no
surprise that Stannard and Churchill argued that the idea of uniqueness
was, by its very nature, politically reactionary; canonizing the Holocaust
as the paradigm of genocide provided states with a useful screen behind
which they could hide from, and evade responsibility for, both past and
present misdeeds. Stannard and Churchill highlighted numerous examples of this evasive dynamic, alleging that the US government's decision
to lavish attention on the Holocaust (epitomized by the creation of the
United States Holocaust Memorial Museum in the years 1978–93)
enabled it to ignore the crimes perpetrated against Native Americans
and African slaves; that the Israeli government's constant invocation of
the Holocaust's uniqueness permitted it to distract attention from the
plight of the Palestinians; and that other Western governments' belief in
the Nazi genocide's singularity allowed them to shirk their responsibil-
ities to halt the occurrence of allegedly "lesser" atrocities in such places
as Biafra, Cambodia, Rwanda, and Bosnia.

Many of Stannard's and Churchill's arguments were subsequently
amplified by other American scholars, such as Norman Finkelstein and
Peter Novick. In his polemical study, *The Holocaust Industry* (2000),
Finkelstein criticized the idea of uniqueness at the conceptual level,
arguing that its quasi-metaphysical utilization by scholars like Elie
Wiesel and Steven Katz exposed it as an "intellectually barren" notion
that obfuscated, rather than clarified, the past.[17] He further condemned
the idea for political reasons, claiming that it lent itself to exploitation
by "Zionist" interests. Echoing Stannard and Churchill, Finkelstein
argued that because "unique suffering confers unique entitlement," the
"unique evil of the Holocaust ... not only sets Jews apart from others,

but also gives Jews a 'claim upon those others' ... In effect, Holocaust uniqueness ... serves as Israel's prize alibi."[18] Further still, because anyone who questioned the idea of uniqueness risked being accused of "trivializing the Holocaust," the concept encouraged a kind of "'intellectual terrorism.'"[19] Echoing many of Finkelstein's points, albeit less stridently, was Peter Novick. In his book *The Holocaust in American Life* (1999), Novick agreed that the idea of uniqueness was "fatuous," as it necessitated a kind of intellectual "gerrymandering" that willfully ignored the similarities of the Holocaust to other genocides. He also found the term to be highly political and often "disingenuous," for while its (mostly Jewish) supporters insisted that "'unique' doesn't mean 'worse,'" it was unlikely that anyone "believe[d] that the claim of uniqueness is anything *other* than a claim for preeminence."[20] Finally, Novick decried the idea of uniqueness as a sign of the impoverishment of contemporary Jewish life. The reason it had developed into a "cult," he concluded, was that "many Jews *don't* know who they are except insofar as they have a 'unique' victim identity."[21]

These American critiques of uniqueness were echoed abroad. In Europe, the most vigorous attacks appeared in France.[22] There, intellectuals on both the right and left also attacked the concept for allegedly overshadowing other historical atrocities. Some, such as the conservative French historian, Stéphane Courtois, criticized how it obscured the crimes of communist regimes, writing in his controversial anthology, *The Black Book of Communism* (1999), that the "single-minded focus on the Jewish genocide ... as a unique atrocity has ... prevented an assessment of other episodes of comparable magnitude in the Communist world."[23] Other intellectuals, such as Tzvetan Todorov and Jean-Michel Chaumont, criticized uniqueness for expressing a Jewish preference for a particularistic, as opposed to a universalistic, interpretation of the Holocaust's significance.[24] Still other observers, such as the left-wing philosopher Alain Brossat claimed that the idea of uniqueness served as "an alibi ... for inaction before contemporary catastrophe," especially "Israel's oppression of Palestinians."[25] Outside of France, the most strident critiques of uniqueness appeared in Israel. Left-wing intellectuals, such as Adi Ophir, decried the "religion of uniqueness" and wrote that its supporters "cling tenaciously to an unbridgeable gap between the catastrophe that befell the Jewish people and the disasters that have befallen other peoples," with the result that "their memories prevent ... them from seeing the real victims of their own power in the past and the present."[26] Still other commentators, such as Yehuda Elkana and Amos Elon, pointed to a surfeit of Holocaust memory in Israeli culture and argued that the time had finally come for forgetting.[27]

Whether expressed in the United States, Europe, or Israel, the condemnation of uniqueness reflected deeper cultural and political trends. Throughout the West, the decade of the 1990s witnessed the growing prominence of postmodernism, multiculturalism, and identity politics, all of which contributed to a self-critical and relativistic mood that befit the post-political period following the end of the Cold War. In the United States, the diminished focus on foreign affairs following the victory over the Soviet Union allowed internal social divisions to find greater expression, most notably among Native-American and African-American activists who hoped to call attention to longstanding historical grievances. Stannard's and Churchill's efforts to gain attention for Native-American suffering – and their sense that Holocaust consciousness was impeding their quest – explained their polemical critique of uniqueness. Novick's and Finkelstein's belief that Jewish identity politics lay behind the exploitation of the Holocaust (especially in conjunction with the defense of Israel), meanwhile, explained their own criticism of the concept. Similar debates over identity politics were behind the controversy in France, where the rise of multiculturalism challenged the nation's historic commitment to universal values and predisposed many to criticize the particularistic Jewish forms of Holocaust remembrance that were emerging at the time. This was especially true among intellectuals such as Courtois, who feared that the country's growing attention to the Holocaust was preventing it from acting on the opportunity – provided by the end of the Cold War – to confront its longstanding fascination with communism. Finally, in Israel, the emergence of post-Zionism, which arose following the Palestinian Intifada of 1987–93 and the subsequent Oslo-era thaw in Arab-Israeli relations, prompted left-of-center Israelis to take a more self-critical view of Holocaust consciousness. In short, although it assumed different inflections in different national contexts, the critique of the Holocaust's uniqueness was rooted in the belief that the concept – like Holocaust consciousness in general – was guilty of historical, moral, and political shortcomings.

The diverse attacks against the Holocaust's uniqueness predictably generated angry responses from the concept's supporters. Stannard's and Churchill's works, like those of Finkelstein and Novick, were widely attacked in the United States and abroad.[28] The same was true of the anti-uniqueness literature published in France and Israel.[29] Reviewers cited numerous reasons for their responses, accusing the uniqueness critics of practicing cynically tendentious scholarship, disseminating political propaganda, aping the arguments of Holocaust deniers, and promoting anti-Semitism.[30] This emotional response, however, ultimately ensured that the exchange between the two camps contributed little to a deeper understanding of the larger issues at stake. Few scholars during this phase were able to shed new light on the Holocaust's place in history or its impact on postwar memory.[31]

For this reason, the most important insight to emerge from the debate was the paradoxical recognition that it had provided few insights. As certain scholars noted, most of the debate's central claims – whether about Holocaust history or memory – lacked empirical support. Henry Huttenbach wrote that the argument about "labeling the Holocaust unique ...[has thus far not] elicited a serious academic debate based on expert comparison" of different genocides.[32] Similarly, Berel Lang complained that critics of Holocaust memory, such as Novick, drew "mainly on anecdote" and avoided "a systematic search for evidence" in trying to determine whether "Holocaust-centrism has been responsible for increased rather than decreased moral sensitivity to other atrocities."[33] The opponents of uniqueness were not alone, however, in neglecting to provide support for their claims; the defenders of Holocaust consciousness never proved that it was as salutary as they claimed. These oversights were important, for they motivated subsequent scholars to empirically assess the allegations made in the debate's first phase. In the process, they set the stage for the phase that followed.

Phase Two: Measuring Holocaust memory

After the turn of the millennium, the debate over uniqueness shifted into a new phase as scholars abandoned polemics for analysis. In so doing, they discussed the topic of uniqueness less in the context of history than in memory. To be sure, scholars in the field of genocide studies entered into a highly productive phase, examining multiple historical episodes of mass killings, often with comparative reference to the Holocaust. Yet they refrained from systematically engaging with the topic of uniqueness. As a result, the uniqueness debate shifted to the question of how Holocaust consciousness was shaping the memory of other genocides. Many scholars weighed in on this question after the turn of the new millennium, publishing a variety of important books and articles. By the end of the decade, they seemed to arrive at a new consensus. On the one hand, they largely rejected the concept of uniqueness. On the other, they rejected the claim that Holocaust consciousness had siphoned attention away from other historical atrocities. Indeed, many scholars argued that attention to such atrocities had grown precisely *because* of the spread of Holocaust consciousness. These scholars justified their upbeat assessment by pointing to several factors. One was the humanitarian, interventionist turn that occurred in American and Western foreign policy in the latter stages of the Yugoslav civil war in the late 1990s. A second was the global wave of atoning for historical injustices known as the "memory boom."[34] Given the fact that both trends were partly inspired by the Holocaust's legacy, many scholars began to speak of the "globalization" of Holocaust memory and its emergence as the basis for a universal standard of morality. In so doing, they revealed an interesting paradox: by inviting comparisons to other historical injustices, the idea of the Holocaust's uniqueness had led to its universalization and with it, the expansion, rather than contraction, of historical awareness.

The Holocaust's uniqueness in history

After the turn of the millennium, scholars largely turned away from assessing the Holocaust's uniqueness in history. Most now recognized that the polemical exchanges on the subject had reached a dead end. One of the more eloquent expressions of this sentiment was offered by A. Dirk Moses in his 2002 essay, "Conceptual Blockages and Definitional Dilemmas in the 'Racial Century': Genocides of Indigenous Peoples and the Holocaust."[35] In this article, Moses took issue with both the supporters and opponents of the Holocaust's uniqueness. His main claim was that the two most outspoken groups of scholars in the 1990s – those representing Jewish and Native-American views – each stubbornly clung to subjective authorial positions, rooted in identity politics, that led them to focus on the singularity of their own groups' historical sufferings instead of the broader origins of modern genocide.[36] In order to guide scholars away from partisanship, it was necessary, Moses wrote, for them "to dispense with the vocabulary of uniqueness," for it was ultimately "a religious or metaphysical category" and "not a useful category for historical research."[37] For Moses, analytical clarity could best be gained by integrating the Holocaust into the field of genocide studies.

In making this recommendation, however, Moses argued that the field first needed to surmount some of its own problems. Genocide studies, he pointed out, had long been split into "liberal" and "post-liberal" camps, each of which displayed shortcomings in explaining modern genocide's relationship to Western civilization. The former camp overemphasized the role of the state and ideology; the latter exaggerated the role of deeper structural forces, such as colonialism.[38] For Moses, this competition between agency and structure mirrored the competition between victim groups to prove the singularity of their respective experiences. He also believed it represented an analytical dead end. As a result, Moses called on scholars "to imagine the genocides of modernity as part of a single process rather than merely in comparative (and competitive) terms."[39] By situating the Holocaust within a broader "racial century" from around 1850–1950 and linking it to the forces that later caused genocides elsewhere in the world – "nation-building, imperial competition, and international and intra-national racial struggle" – the similarities of the Nazi murder campaign to other atrocities could be determined.[40] In pursuing this project of historicization, Moses hoped that "mutual recognition of common suffering" could be established among various victim groups, along with the "the solidarity needed to prevent future victims."[41]

In the years that followed, however, most scholars did not follow Moses's recommendation. Instead of historicizing the Holocaust in the context of modern genocide, they did the reverse, examining cases of genocide in relation to the Holocaust. The first decade of the new millennium was notable for the appearance of important studies on genocide by scholars such as Ben Kiernan, Martin Shaw, Adam Jones, William D. Rubinstein, Michael Mann, Eric Weitz, and Moses himself.[42] These studies were distinguished by their efforts to wrestle with the notion of genocide conceptually and examine it comparatively over the broad course of history. In pursuing this ambitious agenda, however, few scholars systematically addressed the Holocaust's uniqueness. If they mentioned it at all, they did so in passing, usually to underscore the concept's theoretical flaws and obsolescence.[43] This trend suggested that most scholars agreed with Martin Shaw's observation that the "sterile 'uniqueness' debate has been transcended" and was unworthy of being continued.[44]

Assessing the Holocaust's implications for memory

As a result, the discussion of uniqueness shifted to the impact of Holocaust memory on the awareness of other genocides. The first contribution to this discussion was Samantha Power's article, "To *Suffer* by Comparison?"[45] Published in 1999, this essay explored the question of whether or not drawing analogies to the Holocaust – or what she called "Holocausticizing" – helped to increase attention to contemporary humanitarian crises.[46] Significantly, Power answered this question by disagreeing with the critics of Holocaust memory. Writing against the background of the Yugoslav Civil War and the Rwandan genocide in the mid-1990s, she affirmed that "the Holocaust analogy may help stir the conscience," noting that "Holocaust-based lobbying may have been one factor behind the large American contributions to UN relief and peacekeeping missions" as well as the UN's creation of "criminal tribunals to punish the perpetrators of genocide ... in Bosnia and Rwanda."[47] At the same time, Power accepted certain arguments advanced by the critics of uniqueness. She conceded that "if we judge the effectiveness of the analogy ...[in terms of whether it succeeded in] getting the United States and its allies to intervene to stop the killings ... the analogy has not 'worked.' The US government has ... never intervened militarily to stop a genocide underway."[48] There were other problems as well. Making Holocaust analogies, she argued, could "cause a backlash by those who believe in the uniqueness of the Holocaust."[49] Such a backlash would entail a campaign of "definitional warfare" devoted to distinguishing the Holocaust from other atrocities, with the final effect being the muting of the need to act. "Once the Holocaust has become the frame through which we view other killings," Power argued, "it can too easily become a ceiling beneath which all else goes ... Once we realize today's crimes are not exactly 'like' those of the Holocaust, we all too quickly soothe ourselves with the further notion that 'the situation is not so bad after all.'"[50] Yet, no matter how much this cautionary conclusion seemed to place Power in the camp of the skeptics, she ultimately exonerated Holocaust memory for American inaction in the face of contemporary genocide. The fact that "American politicians [were] resolutely opposed to intervening to stop these cases of genocide ...[made it] likely that no amount of

Holocaustizing would have generated meaningful action."[51] In the end, she concluded that "invoking the Holocaust in appropriate circumstances probably helps," while "relying upon it [too much] . . . probably hurts."[52]

Several years later, historian Alan Steinweis offered an even more upbeat assessment of Holocaust consciousness in his article, "The Auschwitz Analogy: Holocaust Memory and American Debates over Intervention in Bosnia and Kosovo in the 1990s."[53] Published in 2005, this essay was influenced by the success of the United States-supported NATO campaign against Serbia in the Kosovo crisis of 1998–99. In that year, Steinweis explained, President Bill Clinton took a step he had been unwilling to take earlier in the decade in Bosnia by supporting the NATO bombing of Serbian positions within and outside of Kosovo in order to disrupt the ethnic cleansing of the predominantly Albanian territory. In doing so, Clinton and other major public figures in the United States, such as Elie Wiesel, drew on the Holocaust's legacy to justify their position. In contrast to what the uniqueness critics had alleged, however, they urged intervention while insisting on the Holocaust's singularity. As Steinweis wrote,

> Wiesel distinguished between the situation of 1944 and that of 1999, but claimed that the lesson learned from the Holocaust nonetheless compelled action in the present. President Clinton . . . was pleased to have Wiesel's moral authority behind him [and noted]: "Elie has said that Kosovo is not the Holocaust, but that distinction should not deter us from doing what is right."[54]

This observation, which was echoed by other scholars, suggested that the fears of Novick, Finkelstein, and even Power were unfounded; the idea of the Holocaust's uniqueness – the idea that it represented the apex of evil – did not sap the ability to recognize, or inhibit the will to act against, other injustices.[55] To be sure, some opponents of intervening against the Serbs continued to deny parallels between the Nazi genocide and the Kosovo crisis.[56] But this fact – that people on both sides of the Kosovo crisis could instrumentalize the Holocaust's legacy in support of their positions – weakened the case of the uniqueness critics by showing how Holocaust memory was neither guilty nor innocent, but neutral. In the end, Steinweis concluded on a note of optimism. Although he conceded that the use of Holocaust analogies had become inflated, he praised "the essential idealism of many who have invoked the Holocaust analogy." As he put it, "in the case of Kosovo, the mobilization of popular support for American intervention might well have saved thousands of lives, a result that hardly could be considered an insult to the memory of those who died in the Holocaust."[57] While it was hardly a panacea, Holocaust consciousness had the undeniable capacity to do good.

Other scholars amplified this conclusion by pointing to the Holocaust's importance in fostering the global memory boom. One of the first was sociologist John Torpey in his 2001 article, "Making Whole What Has Been Smashed: Reflections on Reparations."[58] In this essay, Torpey argued that, "contrary to those who regard the Holocaust as a sponge of historical memory that sucks the juices out of alternative commemorative and reparations projects, the very opposite is the case."[59] "Far from obscuring [the] suffering [of other groups]," he declared, "the emblematic status ... of the Jewish Holocaust has helped others who have been subjected to state-sponsored atrocities to gain attention for those calamities."[60] Torpey justified his assertion by pointing to the global wave of reparations claims, all of which shared "the common characteristic that the Holocaust is regarded as the standard for judging the seriousness of past injustices and as a template for claiming compensation."[61] For example, the fact that, in demanding compensation for the crimes of slavery and colonialism, African and aboriginal groups invoked the Nazis' persecution of the Jews proved that "the Holocaust has become the central metaphor for all politics concerned with [historical reparations]."[62] Torpey added that "the Holocaust has emerged as the touchstone of a 'consciousness of catastrophe' that has been perhaps the principal legacy of the twentieth century with respect to the way our contemporaries think about the past."[63] In hailing the virtues of Holocaust memory, Torpey rejected a key allegation of uniqueness critics. Yet he declined to endorse the idea of uniqueness itself. Instead, he suggested that the idea had been rendered irrelevant by the Holocaust's broader universalization.[64] As he put it:

> the victory that went to those who defended the 'uniqueness' of the
> Holocaust in the *Historikerstreit* of the mid-1980s has since been
> overtaken by the efforts of those seeking attention for various historical
> injustices and who, in so doing, find 'holocausts' of many kinds in the
> historical inheritance of our age. The proliferation of holocausts
> inflates the term and undermines the notion of the uniqueness of the

Nazi genocide, but ... given the exemplary role of the Holocaust ... it does encourage attention to other catastrophic pasts.[65]

In short, Torpey showed that while the memory boom had neutralized the idea of uniqueness, it had validated Holocaust consciousness.

Not long after the appearance of Torpey's article, sociologists Daniel Levy and Natan Sznaider advanced similar conclusions in their book, *The Holocaust and Memory in the Global Age* (2006).[66] This work of comparative historical sociology chronicled the formation of Holocaust remembrance in Germany, the United States, and Israel in order to show how the memory of the Nazi genocide had escaped its national confines and assumed a new "cosmopolitan" form. The chief hallmark of this cosmopolitan memory was the shared belief that the Nazi genocide represented the epitome of evil and formed the basis of a new universal morality. Arguing that "the Holocaust has become a moral certainty that stretches across national boundaries and unites Europe and other parts of the world," Levy and Sznaider argued that Holocaust memory had helped "facilitate the formation of transnational memory cultures, which in turn have the potential to become the cultural foundation for global human-rights politics."[67] Unlike Torpey, Levy and Sznaider did not extensively cite examples of groups pressing reparations claims, although, like Power and Steinweis, they noted how the Yugoslav civil war's revival of Holocaust memories prompted Western Europeans and Americans to intervene during the Kosovo crisis of 1998–99.[68] In making these claims, Levy and Sznaider refrained from explicitly commenting on the merits or drawbacks of uniqueness. Fleeting remarks in their book linking uniqueness to conservative political agendas implied that they were unsympathetic to the idea.[69] But they nevertheless affirmed the importance of Holocaust consciousness and explicitly rejected the claims of "those who argue that there is now a surfeit of memory."[70] They thus sided with Torpey in concluding that the Holocaust's universalization had made the issue of uniqueness irrelevant.

Around the same time that Levy and Sznaider published their conclusions, political scientist William F. S. Miles extended them into a non-Western cultural context in his 2004 article, "Third World Views of the Holocaust."[71] Agreeing that the forces of globalization were promoting the Holocaust's universalization, Miles focused on the "extension of Holocaust consciousness to the Third World." This process, he explained, was defined by a pattern of "intellectual nativization," in which "the Third World *indigenizes* the Holocaust and its [multiple] legacies" by tailoring them to its own concerns.[72] An early example of this "progressive expansion of Holocaust consciousness" appeared soon after World War II, when Third World supporters of decolonization cited the Nazis' crimes against the Jews to draw attention to European colonial-era crimes against Africans. More recent examples included groups in Africa and Asia pursuing reparations claims after being inspired by the precedent of German agreements with Israel and other Jewish groups.[73] Miles drew on these instances to conclude that "few instances of historical atrocity have been invoked to draw as many lessons for international morality, politics, and justice as the Holocaust."[74] In endorsing the virtues of Holocaust consciousness, Miles followed the lead of Torpey, Levy and Sznaider in ignoring the event's uniqueness. Although he implied his opposition to the idea in a passing remark about its exploitation by the "apologists for genocide" in Japan and Turkey, he ultimately found it unworthy of extended discussion.[75] In so doing, he confirmed that the Holocaust's uniqueness had been neutralized by its universalization.

Similar to Miles, literary scholar Michael Rothberg also examined the Holocaust's universalization in a non-Western context in his 2009 book, *Multidirectional Memory*: *Remembering the Holocaust in the Age of Decolonization*.[76] In contrast to Miles and other scholars, however, Rothberg positioned his work explicitly against the idea of uniqueness. He declared that the time had come to move "beyond the uniqueness paradigm" because of its role in reducing remembrance to a "competitive," "zero-sum" game, in which one group's quest for recognition occurred at the expense of another's.[77] In making this recommendation, Rothberg criticized scholars like Stannard and Novick for throwing the baby of Holocaust consciousness out with the bathwater of uniqueness. Instead, he agreed with Torpey and Miles that "the emergence of Holocaust memory on a global scale has contributed to the articulation of other ... histories [of victimization]."[78] Rothberg, however, did not focus on recent reparations claims, but on the interrelationship between Jewish and non-Western memories of historic injustice during the early postwar period. In doing so, he arrived at a new and important conclusion; instead of showing how Holocaust memories worked merely in a unilinear direction by drawing attention to the injustices suffered by others (especially in the context of colonialism and decolonization), he demonstrated how both sets of memories worked "multidirectionally" to sustain one another. To demonstrate this, Rothberg pointed to early postwar France, where the violent struggle over Algerian independence – marked by the French government's use of repression, racism, and torture – helped revive long-suppressed memories of the Holocaust, just as those same memories offered a paradigm for subsequent French memory work on the Algerian trauma several decades later.[79] Rothberg thereby offered a more nuanced reading of Holocaust consciousness, concluding that "the Holocaust does not simply become a universal moral standard that can … be applied to other histories; rather, some of those *other histories help produce a sense of the Holocaust's particularity*" (italics in original).[80] In short, Rothberg's idea of memory's multidirectionality represented an effort to split the difference between the Holocaust's uniqueness and its universalization.

The same year as the appearance of Rothberg's book, sociologist Jeffrey Alexander prompted a larger discussion of Holocaust memory with his edited volume, *Remembering the Holocaust: A Debate*.[81] In his main contribution, entitled "The Social Construction of Moral Universals," Alexander was less interested in evaluating whether or not the Holocaust was unique than in emphasizing its positive effects on Western memory. He explicitly rejected Novick's skeptical claim that the Holocaust's extremity prevented it from possessing any larger lessons.[82] Instead, Alexander perceptively argued that the Holocaust's very extremity had led to its "dramatic universalization" into "a generalized symbol of human suffering." This transformation enabled the Holocaust to "deepen … contemporary sensitivity to social evil."[83] By inviting comparisons to other atrocities, the Holocaust functioned as a "bridging metaphor" that contributed to a new moral understanding of minority grievances in the United States and beyond.[84] In making this assertion, Alexander contributed the notable insight that the Holocaust only became a universal symbol of evil *because* of its perceived uniqueness; only thanks to its singular extremity did it become a normative baseline for measuring other historical injustices. He also pointed to another paradoxical feature of Holocaust consciousness: the very comparisons that were inspired by the idea of the Holocaust's uniqueness ultimately served to diminish it. Describing what he called "the dilemma of uniqueness," Alexander concluded that the Holocaust

> could not function as a metaphor of archetypal evil unless it were
> regarded as radically different from any other evil act in modern

times. Yet it was this very status ... that eventually compelled it to become generalized and departicularized ... By providing such a standard for comparative judgment, the Holocaust became a norm ... that deprived it of "uniqueness."[85]

Alexander's claim that the Holocaust's uniqueness had promoted its universalization was the most important conclusion advanced by the scholarship published after the turn of the millennium. Together with the related claim that Holocaust consciousness actually directed attention to, rather than away from, other episodes of mass killing, the conclusion formed the basis of a new scholarly consensus on the question of uniqueness. Unlike the polarized first phase of the debate in the 1990s, scholars in the second phase had less reason to condemn the idea of uniqueness for the simple reason that they believed it had evolved into a progressive concept.

Yet, while scholarly support for Holocaust consciousness was strong, it was not absolute. By the end of the millennium's first decade, expressions of dissent were increasingly voiced. Some were expressed by genocide scholars, who continued to insist that Holocaust consciousness inhibited the awareness of other genocides.[86] Yet dissenting comments also came from observers who had previously supported Holocaust awareness. This shift largely reflected developments in the Middle East in the wake of 9/11. The worsening Arab-Israeli conflict in this period – typified by the second Intifada from 2000 to 2004 and the Israeli invasions of Lebanon and Gaza in 2006 and 2008 – mitigated some of the positive feeling towards Holocaust consciousness that the memory boom had fostered among scholars. This feeling was further weakened by the tendency of right-wing Israeli politicians, such as Benjamin Netanyahu, to invoke Nazi analogies in justifying Israeli policies towards its Arab neighbors. All of these developments led certain scholars to rethink their views and adopt a more critical stance towards Holocaust consciousness.[87]

One of the more notable was historian Tony Judt. During the late 1990s, Judt had supported the idea of the Holocaust's uniqueness, declaring in a critical review of Novick's *The Holocaust in American Life* that, while "the extermination of the Jews of Europe reminds us of similarly obscene undertakings in other times and places ... surely there is no remotely comparable undertaking known to history, whether measured by intention, scale, methods, or outcome."[88] Judt added that "the ubiquity of Holocaust awareness today is not a bad thing," noting that "public interest in the ...[subject] is to be encouraged."[89] After the turn of the millennium, however, the historian changed his position. Events in the Middle East convinced him that Holocaust consciousness was less salutary than he once believed. In 2004, he decried the "exploitation" of the Holocaust, writing that "the claim that the Jewish catastrophe was unique and incomparable" was allowing "Israel to trump any other nation's sufferings (and justify its own excesses)."[90] And in 2008, he worried that the repeated presentation of the "Nazi extermination of the Jews as a singular crime, an evil never matched before or since," would end up "provincializing [the Holocaust's] ... moral significance" and causing it to "lose its universal resonance."[91]

A second scholar to express doubts was Jeffrey Alexander. He admitted to a change of heart in a second essay included in his volume, *Remembering the Holocaust*, entitled "On the Global and Local Representations of the Universal." In it, he responded to critics who claimed that his original article, "The Social Construction of Moral Universals," ignored the political uses of Holocaust memory. By way of explanation, Alexander semi-apologetically declared that his original essay was written in the late 1990s against the hopeful backdrop of the memory boom (the essay was published in article form in 2002 before Alexander expanded it into his 2009 book).[92] He went on to point out, however, that because "we now live in a darker time," shaped by the ongoing crisis in the Middle East, he had become more pessimistic about the virtues of Holocaust memory.[93] Like Judt, he was concerned about the tendency of "conservative Israelis" to use the idea of the Holocaust's uniqueness for nationalistic purposes in their conflict with the Palestinians, a development he condemned for "assault[ing] the universalizing moral principles that the memory of the Holocaust calls upon all of us to sustain."[94] Only by replacing the particularistic usage of memory, which produced "social ... antagonism," with its universalization, which produced "sympathy" for others, could the cause of "ethnic, racial, and religious justice" be advanced.[95]

The fact that scholars who once supported the idea of uniqueness were beginning to criticize it highlighted the shakiness of the consensus supporting Holocaust consciousness. Significantly, this consensus would be further challenged in the third phase of the uniqueness debate, as scholars resumed arguing over the Holocaust's significance not just in memory, but in history.

Phase Three: Historicizing the Holocaust and genocide

The return to history was visible in new studies that focused on the Holocaust's similarities with other genocides. In pursuing this focus, these works once again challenged the idea of uniqueness. They mostly did so indirectly, however. They were part of an effort to avoid the polemical excesses of earlier years and forge a new middle position. Their goal was to historicize the Holocaust within the context of modern genocide without diminishing its particularity.[96] In pursuing this goal, however, these studies met with resistance. Other scholars interpreted the historicization project as an effort at politicization. Fearing that ulterior motives lay behind the new challenges to uniqueness, they responded with sharply worded rebuttals. This response led to heated counter-accusations and soon sparked a new phase of the debate.

New histories of the Holocaust: Bloxham and Snyder

The first major study to historicize the Holocaust was Donald Bloxham's book, *The Final Solution: A Genocide* (2010).[97] This important volume made its interpretive viewpoint clear in its very title. By describing the Holocaust as "a" genocide, Bloxham implied that the event was more similar to, than different from, other historical episodes of mass killing. Bloxham did not challenge the idea of the Holocaust's uniqueness systematically in his study, but did so indirectly by integrating the Holocaust into the larger history of mass atrocities. Echoing A. Dirk Moses's call earlier in the decade to place the Holocaust within a "racial century" from 1850–1950, Bloxham situated his analysis in what he called a "European history of violence" in the years 1875–1945.[98] In this period, he argued, economic and geopolitical forces led to the decline of multi-ethnic empires with calamitous consequences for their minority populations.[99] In Russia, the Ottoman Empire, and Austria-Hungary, the struggle of minorities (whether Jews, Armenians, or Slavs) to achieve emancipation in the decades prior to 1914 threatened the existing social order and led nationalistic elites to view them as subversive revolutionaries. The stigmatization of these minority groups was hastened by the eruption of the Balkan Wars and World War I and ultimately led to horrific episodes of ethnic cleansing. Serbs, Romanians, and Bulgarians expelled Muslims; Turks expelled Greeks, Armenians, and Kurds;

Russians and their Bolshevik successors expelled Jews and other minorities.[100] Mass death – and in the infamous case of the Armenians, outright genocide – was the result.

This wave of killing, according to Bloxham, was the crucial context for understanding the origins of the Holocaust. Europe's ethno-nationalist tradition of intolerance towards minorities, he argued, strongly resembled the Nazis' persecution of the Jews. "Nazi racial policy," he wrote, "was geared not just to Hitler's ... obsession with Jews, but to a host of other biopolitical and geopolitical concerns that would have been entirely recognizable to millions of nationalists ... beyond Germany."[101] Bloxham developed this argument by first describing the nineteenth- and early twentieth-century history of European violence; he then drew comparisons to the Nazis' persecution of Jews in the 1930s, before arriving at the core of his analysis, the conception and implementation of the Final Solution. In discussing this crucial topic, Bloxham explicitly sought to challenge the Holocaust's uniqueness. He made this clear in his book's conclusion, where he took issue with two claims that, in his view, made up the core of the uniqueness thesis. The first claim was that the murder of the Jews was an "ideological" end in itself that was rooted in an "imagined" threat instead of real inter-ethnic conflicts. The second was that the Nazis' murder of the Jews was distinguished by its "totality," "'absolute prioritization,'" and "relentless pursuit of the victims."[102]

Bloxham rejected both of these claims, arguing that they overemphasized the role of ideology. Truly understanding the Holocaust, he insisted, required showing its origins in the interplay between ideological forces and practical considerations.[103] In developing his argument, Bloxham diverged from most scholars by viewing the Holocaust less as an event than as a process. He rejected the idea that the Holocaust had an "'essence'" that was determined by a key event or decision – for example, the Wannsee conference of January, 1942, which most scholars viewed as lending coherence to what was, until then, an uncoordinated series of scattered murder operations.[104] Instead, he argued that "the series of events ... we now call the Holocaust" unfolded organically and changed constantly according to many diverse factors. These included the Nazis' assessment of the military/security situation, their thinking about immediate economic conditions, their prospects of realizing their ambitious colonial plans of Germanization, and their shifting diplomatic relations with Allied and neutral states. Bloxham conceded that there was intent behind the Nazis' murder campaign, writing that "mass death was inherent to Nazi designs from before Barbarossa."[105] But while he admitted that a policy of murder existed, he argued that the extent of its application (how many Jews were to be affected and where) was undecided when the policy was first adopted. Moreover, he showed that the policy was applied inconsistently.[106]

This analytical stance helped Bloxham challenge the twin claims made by the supporters of uniqueness. He rejected their argument that the Nazis' murder of the Jews was irrational and not rooted in any real existing conflict by showing how the latter stood in the way of the Nazis' desire to Germanize Eastern Europe and transform it into a "utopia of blood and soil."[107] This massive colonization project, which was epitomized by the SS's "General Plan for the East" (*Generalplan Ost*), was not only rooted in objective material considerations, he wrote, but mirrored "modern settler colonialism ... in aiming for the systematic removal and mass death of the native population."[108] The murder of the Jews was thus neither irrational nor unprecedented. Bloxham also contested the claim that the Nazis were relentless in pursuing Jews wherever they could find them. Writing that "it is simply not true" that the Nazis "would have gone literally to the ends of the earth to track down each and every living Jew," he argued that the Final Solution was "intertwined with [the Nazis'] war fighting ability" and was often de-emphasized if it conflicted with the prosecution of the war.[109] On the periphery of the Nazi colonial empire and in certain Allied states, for example, the Nazis did not expend as much effort as they might have in tracking down Jews. In France or Bulgaria, they postponed doing so until an unspecified date; in Denmark, they were content with expulsion instead of murder.[110] This apparent laxness reflected the fact that the men responsible for the Final Solution – Himmler, Eichmann, and others – believed that its proper target was the core of Eastern European Jewry, namely the Jews of Poland and the Soviet Union. Eliminating these Jews was thought to be sufficient to cripple Jewry once and for all.[111] By 1943, Himmler believed that the Jewish problem in the German sphere of influence had been essentially "solved" and only mopping up operations remained.[112] This sense of victory may explain why other Jews who should have been mercilessly hunted down were not, such as the thousands of Hungarian Jews who were sent as forced laborers to Germany once it had already been declared *judenrein* in 1944.[113] In the end, Bloxham concluded, the Nazis' murder campaign, while "exceptional ... in the annals of genocide ... was not perpetrated mindless of the economic, political, or logistical cost."[114]

Bloxham did not just challenge the Holocaust's uniqueness on historical grounds, however, but on ethical ones as well. For him, the concept was a myopic expression of Western provincialism. The fact that scholars expressed shock at Western civilization's capacity to perpetrate a horror like the Holocaust was a sign of bad faith, for, as he put it, "Europe had not only witnessed other genocides [before the Holocaust], it had inflicted them on its colonial peripheries."[115] Those who insisted on the Holocaust's uniqueness were thus guilty of blind ignorance rooted in "Western-centrism." Worse still, their desire to grant the Holocaust "universal significance" reflected a long tradition of the West seeking "to universalize its own values."[116] Since it was precisely a penchant for universalism that had shaped "Europe's violent interaction with the rest of the world" in the first place, those who supported uniqueness were implicitly guilty of perpetuating a legacy of persecution.[117] Abandoning the idea of uniqueness was thus especially urgent for moral reasons.

Similar arguments were visible in a second major study to take issue with the concept of uniqueness, Timothy Snyder's celebrated book, *Bloodlands* (2010) (Figure 9).[118] Like Bloxham, Snyder also believed that the concept impeded genuine historical understanding. Truly understanding the Holocaust, he contended, required relocating it from the traditional setting of German and Jewish history during the Second World War to a broader spatial and temporal context that he called the "bloodlands." It was in this vast realm between central Poland and western Russia that, in the years 1933–45, some fourteen million people were murdered by the Soviet and Nazi regimes. By subsuming the Holocaust within this larger wave of killings, Snyder partly followed in the path of Norman Davies and Niall Ferguson, both of whom, as noted in Chapter 1, questioned the Holocaust's uniqueness by showing how Hitler's crimes resembled those of Stalin. Snyder, however, took such comparisons further and historicized the Holocaust more systematically within the context of modern genocide. In the process he, too, ended up courting controversy.

Like Bloxham, Snyder challenged the idea of the Holocaust's uniqueness indirectly. He refrained from invoking the concept as such, preferring instead to show how it produced misconceptions about the genocide's historical significance. One was the mistaken belief that "mass killing is usually associated with the Holocaust."[119] In fact,

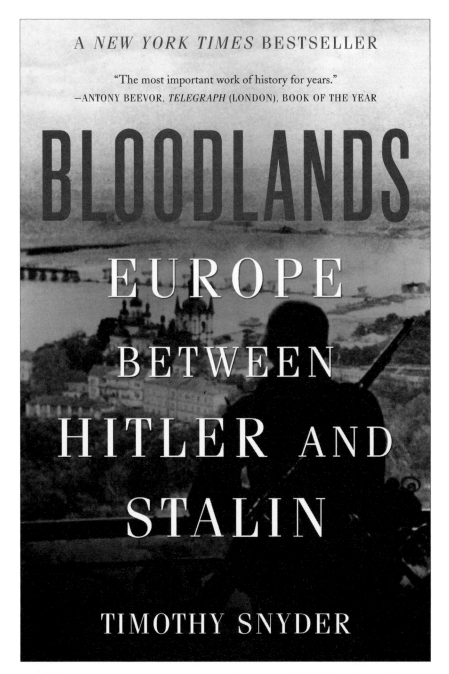

Figure 9. Timothy Snyder's book, *Bloodlands* (2010), subtly challenged the Holocaust's uniqueness by highlighting the similarities between Nazi and Soviet crimes in occupied Eastern Europe.

Snyder noted, it was not the Nazis' murder of six million Jews, but the murder of fourteen million people in the bloodlands that actually represented the "central event" of "European history."[120] A second misconception was that "Auschwitz stands for the Holocaust and the Holocaust for the evil of a century."[121] In truth, Snyder argued, the notorious extermination camp was hardly representative of the Nazi genocide, for while it was "associated . . . with rapid industrial killing,"

> it was not the height of the technology of death: the most efficient shooting squads killed faster, the starvation sites killed faster, and Treblinka killed faster. Auschwitz was also not the main place where the two largest Jewish communities in Europe, the Polish and the Soviet, were exterminated. Most Soviet and Polish Jews under German occupation had already been murdered by the time Auschwitz became the major death factory . . . By the . . . spring of 1943, more than three quarters of the Jews who would be killed in the Holocaust were already dead.[122]

Snyder's conclusion that "Auschwitz is the coda to the death fugue" further underscored his belief that, because much of the killing in the Holocaust was perpetrated with "traditional" instead of "modern" methods, the event was less unique than commonly thought.[123] Finally, while Snyder acknowledged the magnitude of Auschwitz for Jewish Holocaust deaths (pointing out that one sixth of all Jews died there), he showed that it was hardly only a site of *Jewish* suffering. "More non-Jewish Poles died at Auschwitz," Snyder wrote, "than did Jews of any European country, with only two exceptions: Hungary and Poland itself."[124] While not employing the concept of uniqueness, in short, Snyder nevertheless challenged some of the historical corollaries that supported it.

Having questioned the centrality of Auschwitz for understanding the Holocaust, Snyder went on argue that the event could be better understood by comparing how the mass murder of the Jews under Hitler resembled the mass killings perpetrated by Stalin. To begin with, Snyder showed that, prior to the outbreak of World War II, the Soviet dictator was more murderous than Hitler.[125] During the 1930s, the starvation of Ukrainian peasants and the shooting of Soviet "kulaks," ethnic Poles, and other national minorities during the Great Terror claimed the lives of over four million people.[126] By 1938, "the USSR had killed approximately a thousand times more people on ethnic grounds than had Nazi Germany."[127] In probing the reasons behind this murder spree, Snyder argued that Stalin was motivated by the irrational fear that the targeted groups were full of subversive nationalists and spies. At the same time, Snyder demonstrated that Stalin's fears arose from real conditions, especially the failure of his utopian program to collectivize Soviet agriculture and the persistence of geopolitical tensions between the USSR and Poland. In short, the historian employed a "scapegoating" theory to explain the Stalinist regime's vengeful campaign against perceived enemies of the revolution.[128]

Snyder declared that similar forces explained the Nazis' murder of the Jews. When they invaded the Soviet Union in 1941, the Nazis had grand imperial ambitions. The *Generalplan Ost* sought to demographically reorder great swaths of Soviet territory in order to create an agrarian racial utopia. The related *Hungerplan*, conceived by the Nazi Minister of Food, Herbert Backe in 1941, sought to seize the vast agricultural sector of the Ukraine for the benefit of Wehrmacht troops and German civilians on the home front. These Nazi plans, Snyder noted, would have consigned tens of millions of people, mostly non-Jewish Slavs, to deportation and death had they been implemented.[129] Yet due to insufficient manpower, the Nazis were unable to realize their grand plans. Instead, they decided "to extract what was feasible" and reduced the scope of their goals, resolving to murder "only" the Jews as their primary objective.[130] The Holocaust was thus the result of a setback, indeed a failure, in policy. Like Stalin's vengeful reaction against the Soviet Union's internal "enemies" after the failure of collectivization, Hitler's decision to kill the Jews was intended as "a substitute for triumph" over the Soviet Union.[131] As Snyder concluded:

> Hitler and Stalin ... shared a certain politics of tyranny: they
> brought about catastrophes, blamed the enemy of their choice, and
> then used the death of millions to make the case that their policies
> were necessary or desirable. Each of them had a transformative
> utopia, a group to be blamed when its realization proved impossible,
> and then a policy of mass murder that could be proclaimed as a kind
> of ersatz victory.[132]

In showing how Hitler's and Stalin's crimes shared similar origins, in short, Snyder implied that the Holocaust was not unique.

This point was reinforced by Snyder's portrayal of how the Nazi and Soviet murder campaigns unfolded. Once they were underway, Hitler and Stalin's killing policies mutually reinforced one another in a kind of "'belligerent complicity.'"[133] After dividing up Poland in the Nazi-Soviet non-aggression pact, the two regimes collaborated in deporting and murdering millions of Poles, including the mentally and physically handicapped, army officers, and educated elites. The regimes' ensuing occupation of the bloodlands, with their accompanying reigns of terror, sparked waves of collaboration and resistance that ended up victimizing not just Jews but others as well. This important insight showed that the Holocaust did not occur in isolation. Despite often being portrayed in this fashion by Holocaust historians, the killing of Jews consistently took place alongside the killing of other groups. In 1942, for example, the Germans murdered non-Jewish Belarusian "partisans" (nearly always civilians) in the same kinds of mass shootings perpetrated by the Einsatzgruppen against Jews.[134] These and other examples showed that the murder of Jews took place within a larger campaign of mass killing and further challenged the uniqueness of the Jewish experience.

Snyder also subtly challenged the idea of the Holocaust's uniqueness in his book's last chapters dealing with the postwar period. In a chapter on "ethnic cleansings," he chronicled the massive postwar expulsions that took place at the end of World War II, pointing out that 12 million Germans and some 22 million Eastern Europeans (especially Poles, Ukrainians, citizens of the Baltic states, and minorities living in the Crimea and Caucasus) were brutally expelled from their homes. The historian was careful to disaggregate the roughly 1.5 million people killed in these expulsions from the 14 million killed in the bloodlands, conceding that "even at their worst ... the horrors visited upon the Germans ... were not mass killing policies."[135] Nevertheless, the effect of this chapter was to immerse the Holocaust in an even deeper morass of misery.

Finally, Snyder's discussion of memory and its relation to mass killing further challenged the idea of uniqueness. Ever since the end of World War II, he argued, various nations had exaggerated the suffering of their citizens in the conflict, inflating the number of deaths and seeking redemptive significance in them. The result of this nationalistic exploitation of memory was an "international competition for martyrdom."[136] Snyder focused mostly on the efforts of Eastern European states such as

Poland, Ukraine, Russia, and Belarus to foreground their suffering, but the implications for Jews were nevertheless clear. In rhetorically asking, "can the dead really belong to anyone?" Snyder made the case that Jewish victims did not solely "belong to Polish, or Soviet, or Israeli, or Ukrainian history." Because they could easily belong to any of them, it was ultimately preferable "to reckon with each victim as an individual."[137] Instead of enlisting victims "into competing national memories," they should be viewed as part of a common "humanity." With this idealistic recommendation, Snyder concluded his book by rejecting the particularistic reflexes underpinning the idea of uniqueness.

The return of debate

Taken together, Bloxham's and Snyder's provocative books were significant not merely for the arguments they advanced but the controversy they sparked. Although their tone was dispassionate – and although they rarely challenged the Holocaust's uniqueness directly – Bloxham and Snyder were nevertheless faulted for slighting its singularity.

The reception to Bloxham's book was largely favorable, but it received its share of criticism. On the positive side, observers praised *The Final Solution* as a "challenging," "sophisticated," and "thought-provoking" work of synthesis that was "remarkable" for its "breadth and depth."[138] At the same time, however, certain reviewers attacked what they saw as its critique of uniqueness.[139] Two of the most outspoken critics were Doris Bergen and Omer Bartov. Both scholars were concerned by Bloxham's depiction of Holocaust history and its implications for Holocaust memory. Bergen described Bloxham's analytical mission as aiming "to decentre the Holocaust within the study of extreme violence" and declared that it amounted to "an extended criticism of the claim of the Holocaust's uniqueness."[140] She added that his criticism was something of a straw man, given that the concept's most ardent "proponents ... have proven open to comparisons" with other genocides.[141] That Bloxham nevertheless launched his attack against the concept prompted Bergen to wonder about his motives. Asking "Why does it seem so crucial to Bloxham to mount this attack now?", Bergen answered her own rhetorical question by citing Saul Friedländer's injunction for historians to "sidestep political agendas and identity politics" in writing about the Holocaust. Noting that Bloxham had failed "to restrain ...[his own] subjectivity," she implied he was guilty of partisanship.[142]

Bartov, by contrast, was more direct in identifying Bloxham's motives. He began by rejecting Bloxham's claim that the idea of uniqueness privileged the experiences of Jews over others, observing that "other genocides came into public and scholarly view thanks to the emergence of the Holocaust ... and not despite it."[143] Bartov then went on the offensive and asserted that "debates over the uniqueness ... of the Holocaust are ... almost purely political today," noting that the "critics of Holocaust discourse claim it merely serves to cover up or delegitimize criticism of Israeli policies."[144] Bartov argued that Bloxham took a similar position in his book where, in discussing postwar episodes of ethnic cleansing, he laconically observed that the "'nascent Israeli state forced the dispersal of large numbers of Arabs and denied them the right to return.'" For Bartov, the fact that this remark was made "without any contextualization" showed how Bloxham distorted the idea of uniqueness for political purposes. By asserting links between the Holocaust and the "intrinsically genocidal" phenomenon of colonialism, Bloxham, according to Bartov, promoted the delegitimization of Israel as a colonial Zionist enterprise "on the verge of genocide" against the Palestinians.[145]

For his part, Bloxham denied that his book targeted the idea of uniqueness. In a long response to his critics, he declared that Bergen was "wrong ... in thinking that 'uniqueness' is a guiding obsession of mine" and noted that he only devoted "six pages of content" to the subject.[146] He also rejected Bergen's comparison of uniqueness to a "dead horse," insisting that it remained an "influential" idea, having "entered the doxa of ... the public sphere."[147] Moreover, he refused to accept her suggestion that the Holocaust should have a "centred" – that is, privileged – position within the field of genocide studies.[148] In explaining his position, Bloxham argued that historicizing the Holocaust within the history of modern genocide was part of a "moral-cum-political" agenda of "prediction and ... prevention."[149] The "morality of prevention," he argued, required abandoning the idea that the Holocaust was different from other genocides, for it had "allowed ... the international community to legitimate non-intervention" in countries experiencing genocidal violence on the grounds that it was a "manifestation ... not of [a] ... unilateral, utopian desire to exterminate, but the result of bilateral 'tribal atavism' and the like."[150] Bloxham ended his defense by accusing his critics of political mudslinging. Bartov's "outright political allegation" against him, he claimed, served merely to "heighten tensions" between scholars of differing views and carried with it "a nasty whiff of attempted censorship."[151] No scholar, he concluded, had "a monopoly on morally correct approaches to [the Holocaust]."[152]

Soon after Bloxham's response, the debate over his book expanded when A. Dirk Moses published a series of articles defending Bloxham and challenging the supporters of uniqueness. In "Revisiting a Founding Assumption of Genocide Studies" (2011), Moses sought to refute Bartov's criticisms of Bloxham. Moses first argued that Bartov overreacted in insinuating that scholars who viewed the Holocaust as a form of colonialism supported "casting Israel as a settler colonial purveyor of genocide."[153] Such a claim, Moses insisted, read far too much political significance into what was essentially a scholarly approach to historicizing the Holocaust. This point notwithstanding, Moses offered his own political interpretation of Bartov's position, accusing him of pursuing a "regressive" project in "trying to update the uniqueness claims of previous decades."[154] Moses said that Bartov was wrong to claim that the Holocaust had helped other genocides gain visibility. The very fact that the Holocaust had become the "template against which other genocides can be measured" actually helped "occlude ... other genocides," for logic held that if "a genocide must resemble the Holocaust to become visible ...[then a case of] mass violence [that] ... does not resemble the Holocaust ... is screened out as non-genocidal."[155] The belief that a genocide had to involve a state authority pursuing a racist ideology against a helpless victim was unnecessarily limiting and distracted attention from the deeper structural forces related to colonialism that were implicated in genocide. It also had a "distorting" effect on scholarship, making historians think that for an episode of mass killing to qualify as genocide, "the perpetrators must resemble Nazis and the victims must resemble Jews."[156] "Far from providing insight, as Bartov thinks," Moses concluded, the idea of the Holocaust as a paradigm "promoted blindness to genocidal episodes around the world."[157] The only solution was for the Holocaust "to be deprovincialized from its signification within [the] ... exclusively Jewish and Western narrative ... enjoined by Bartov" and placed in a larger world historical context that paid attention to "imperial logics" related to "demography, migration, and state-formation."[158]

Moses amplified his skepticism about the value of Holocaust memory in a second essay, "Paranoia and Partisanship: Genocide Studies, Holocaust Historiography, and the 'Apocalyptic Conjuncture'" (2011).[159] In this article, he pointed out that if "mass violence must resemble the Holocaust to constitute genocide," the implication was that "normal ethnic/national conflict" over "real issues like land, resources, political power, and the like" could not be considered genocidal.[160] This view needlessly narrowed the definition of genocide to a "'hallucinatory' ideology" rooted in "delusional, paranoid, and non-political considerations . . .[like] ethnic purity."[161] Instead, Moses wanted scholars to cease viewing ideology in isolation and link it to geopolitical factors. One method of doing this, he suggested, was to follow Bloxham's lead and recognize how, in all genocides, paranoid elites came to view domestic minority groups as national security threats by virtue of their alleged collusion with rival nations.[162] Moses acknowledged that real geopolitical vulnerabilities were involved in these suspicions, but he stressed that an equally important reason for elites' paranoia was their memory of past suffering. As he wrote, "genocides *generally* are based on traumatic memories of past events in which 'disloyal' peoples are held collectively guilty and then collectively punished or deported or destroyed, *pre-emptively*, to prevent the feared repetition of the previous traumatic experience."[163] This being the case, Moses called for breaking down the "stark dichotomy of ideology and political rationality" and replacing it "with a spectrum that recognizes how paranoid threat assessment leading to pre-emptive strikes against collectives is present in genocide generally."[164] "All genocides," he argued, "could be placed on this spectrum with the Holocaust rather than treated separately." These claims allowed for two important conclusions: first, the dynamics that drove the Holocaust were not unique; second, the specific role of memory could just as easily serve destructive as progressive ends.

Moses added a polemical thrust to these claims in a third essay, "Genocide and the Terror of History" (2011).[165] In this theoretically sophisticated article, Moses drew on the work of Mircea Eliade and the field of trauma studies to argue that traumatic experiences of suffering did not so much promote tolerance and understanding as fantasies of "revenge and retaliation." Rooted in "collective narcissism and paranoia," Holocaust consciousness nurtured "the fear of collective destruction . . . Rather than being the harbinger of a universal human-rights culture . . . transcultural memories . . .of the Holocaust often lead to the 'calamitization' of politics [and]. . . the 'terror of history.'"[166] For Moses, this historical viewpoint sowed the seeds of future violence. Traumatized groups, he argued, were prone to develop "annihilation anxieties" that led them to seek "redemptive solutions," often in the form of "national liberation ... projects," that themselves "can have genocidal implications when they are directed against ... 'foreigners' and 'colonizers.'"[167] Significantly, Moses applied this dynamic to both Jews and Arabs in the context of the modern Middle East, arguing that both groups depicted current events as "reincarnations or perpetuations of the traumatic, often genocidal, experience ... leading to preemptive or anticipatory self-defense."[168] Moses focused particular attention on Jewish historical consciousness and the Holocaust's disproportionate presence within it. Citing Jewish fears of how contemporary anti-Semitism made Israel "existentially threatened" and how it might lead to a "second Holocaust" (from Iran or its allies), he concluded that such reactions were overwrought and did not correspond to reality.[169] Indeed, they reflected a dysfunctional form of "hyper-vigilance" that was "impervious to reality checking."[170] "Rather than promoting awareness, 'Holocaust education' ... promote[s] misperceptions of reality."[171] For this reason, he concluded, "The widespread belief that 'Holocaust education' will make the world a better place was wildly optimistic."[172]

Taken together, Bloxham's book and the responses by Bergen, Bartov, and Moses revealed that some of the core issues of the uniqueness debate remained unresolved. Despite the consensus that scholars had seemingly established earlier in the decade, disagreement remained about whether Holocaust consciousness was a positive or negative force. This disagreement was further underscored by the renewed willingness of scholars to employ polemical arguments in support of their positions. These trends revealed that the topic of uniqueness retained its capacity to divide.

This reality was further confirmed by the scholarly reaction to *Bloodlands*. Snyder's book received a great many positive reviews, but also had its share of detractors. On the one hand, various journalists and scholars hailed *Bloodlands* as a landmark study, calling it "gripping," "magisterial," "shattering," "brave and original," and "a major contribution."[173] The book's receipt of numerous awards and its translation into twenty languages further testified to its critical success.[174] At the same time, however, German historians and Holocaust specialists were more reserved in their praise and some were openly critical. While many acknowledged the book's narrative power and admired it as a work of synthesis, they called attention to certain shortcomings.[175] Some faulted it for not really offering an explanation of the Holocaust. Mark Roseman, for example, wrote that the book does not "tell us something different" or provide "big new answers," while Omer Bartov declared that it "presents no new evidence and makes no new arguments."[176] Others argued that this shortcoming lay in Snyder's core concept of the bloodlands. Speaking for many, James Sheehan explained that the concept was "no more than a geographical expression that describes the physical site of the killing, not a geopolitical category with interpretative power."[177] Jürgen Zarusky, meanwhile, faulted Snyder for using the idea of the bloodlands "inconsistently ... as a spatial concept," often "projecting events upon a realm that was not affected by them in its entirety."[178]

The most critical responses, however, were from scholars who believed *Bloodlands* diminished the Holocaust's uniqueness. Writing that "it was the ... global scale of the Nazis' intentions towards the Jews that marked out the genocide from other mass exterminations of the period," Richard Evans argued that Snyder's comparison of the Holocaust to Stalin's crimes "distracts attention from what was unique about the extermination of the Jews."[179] Dan Diner added that Snyder's "downgrading of Auschwitz ... expose[d] a pivotal weakness in ...[his] argument," namely, its overlooking of the "pan-European topography" of the Holocaust, which aimed for the "total destruction ...[of] all Jews ... *everywhere.*"[180] The Simon Wiesenthal Center's Efraim Zuroff agreed, saying the Nazis' intent to kill "every last Jew in the world regardless of their politics, religious practice or communal affiliation" made the Holocaust "unique among the murder campaigns ... in the Bloodlands."[181] Dovid Katz supported this claim by contrasting the wartime fate of the Jews under Hitler with the milder fate of Eastern Europeans under Stalin. Rejecting the claim that Stalin's crimes amounted to genocide, Katz employed counterfactual reasoning in writing that

> the Estonians, Latvians, Lithuanians, Poles and Ukrainians are still thankfully with us in 2010, as great nations ... precisely because there was no genocide ... East European Jewry is not there anymore ... because there was genocide. Moreover, as Snyder must know, a Nazi victory in the east, with all that was being planned for the various "inferior races" [there] ... would not have left these nations ready for independence in 1991.[182]

Had the Nazis defeated the Soviets, in other words, "the Holocaust would have only been the beginning of the destruction of large segments of the Eastern European population."[183] Indeed, it was precisely the Soviets' eventual victory over the Nazis, reviewers argued, that *prevented* much of Eastern Europe from experiencing genocide. Rather than seeking similarities between Stalin's crimes and the Holocaust, therefore, it was preferable to stress the differences. "Those who liberated Auschwitz are just not the same as those who committed genocide there," Katz concluded. "Genocide is different from the other crimes of the era, and for this reason, the Holocaust was unique."[184]

Beyond identifying *Bloodlands*' shortcomings as a work of history, critics assailed what they regarded as its adverse consequences for memory. Zuroff, for example, feared that *Bloodlands* was destined to become "the bible of ... Holocaust distorters in post-Communist Eastern Europe" by shifting attention away from the collaboration of Eastern Europeans with the Nazis to their victimization by the Soviets.[185] He further feared that the book's implicit support for the double genocide theory "relieve[d] the pressure on ...[Eastern European] societies to confront their past."[186] To be sure, Zuroff and other observers did not accuse Snyder of intentionally supporting this revisionist agenda. Bartov, for example, noted that "by equating partisans and occupiers, Soviet and Nazi occupations ... Snyder ... *inadvertently* [emphasis added] adopts the apologists' argument that where everyone is a criminal no one can be blamed."[187] Yet, for many reviewers, the question of intent mattered less than effect. For Katz, Snyder's comparison of Soviet crimes to the Holocaust was "in concord with Baltic ultranationalists who ... inflate the definition of genocide to include deportation, imprisonment, loss of freedom and much more."[188] For this reason, Zuroff concluded that Snyder's book, despite being written by a scholar of "obvious talent," was destined to "be misused by those intent on distorting the ... worst tragedy in human history."[189]

Evaluating the debate

Just as in the uniqueness debate's first phase during the 1990s, both sides in the most recent phase have largely talked past each other and missed an opportunity to clarify the Holocaust's links to modern genocide. Thanks to the importation of political suspicions from the outside world into the world of academia, scholars misinterpreted and overreacted to one another's work. This was most visible in the responses to Bloxham's and Snyder's studies. Yet, the arguments presented by Bloxham and Snyder, as well those presented by Moses, did not entirely lack agendas of their own. Moreover, they suffered from certain analytical shortcomings that limited their otherwise powerful critiques of the prevailing scholarly literature.

The overreaction to the critique of uniqueness was first visible in the reviews of Bloxham's *The Final Solution*. To a degree, the suspicions raised by Bergen and Bartov rested on a thin foundation. As Bloxham pointed out, his references about Israel amounted to several scattered sentences in a four-hundred-page book.[190] Especially in comparison to the more abundant and overtly polemical remarks made by scholars like Stannard, Churchill, and Finkelstein in the 1990s, Bloxham's references to the Israeli–Palestinian conflict were tame. That Bartov nevertheless seized upon them may have reflected his fear that these earlier polemics – produced by scholars from outside of the field of Holocaust studies – were beginning to influence mainstream Holocaust historiography. As Bartov wrote, while "extreme statements from politically engaged circles may be dismissed as mere propaganda ... the growing chorus of scholarly voices who ... identify links between what they argued is the colonial nature of the Nazi extermination of the Jews and what they believe is the colonial nature of Zionism and the Jewish state is ... more troubling."[191] Bartov's fears were understandable, given their appearance not only in the work of Bloxham and Moses, but in studies published around the same time by prominent scholars, such as Mark Mazower.[192] Yet, since none of these studies were as polemical as earlier texts, Bartov's suspicions about their agendas may have been somewhat exaggerated.

That said, Bloxham's arguments in his own defense were not entirely persuasive. It is hard to believe that he was truly surprised by Bartov's reaction to his laconic reference to Israel's "dispersal" of Palestinians in 1948–49. The remark was, in fact, not well contextualized. Although Bloxham said he "was at a loss to know why the context of the collapse of the Ottoman Empire and the often violent establishment in its wake of a number of smaller states" was "insufficient" for explaining Israel's later actions, he did not mention that Israel's treatment of the Palestinians took place during a war in which the new nation was attacked by hostile Arab states and militias. Given Bloxham's in-depth contextualization of other events in his book, his failure to do so in this instance was notable and may have reflected his own political leanings. Hints to this effect were visible in his response to Bartov's charge that *The Final Solution*'s focus on Nazi perpetrators displayed insufficient empathy with their Jewish victims. Bloxham replied by declaring that if Bartov were "consistent in his prescriptions for the most important sort of historical understanding – i.e. empathy – he would be enjoining me to empathize with the victims of the *Naqba*." The implied message of this pointed declaration – that Bartov did not empathize with Palestinian suffering – taken together with Bloxham's failure to contextualize its complex roots suggested that Bartov's suspicions about Bloxham's motives may not have been entirely unfounded.[193] By implicitly linking Israel's behavior in the military conflict of 1947–49 to deeper forces responsible for modern genocide, Bloxham's study could, at least in theory, be used to criticize Israel in the strident fashion feared by Bartov. To be sure, Bloxham was fully within his rights to make a case for such linkages. Scholars commonly advance political agendas with their analyses. But when political commentary unrelated to the immediate subject is made in passing fashion without being systematically elaborated, it can devolve into rhetoric and, as Bergen warned, "risk ... antagonizing ... audience[s] and undermining the credibility of [one's]... argument."[194] Such commentary, moreover, ran counter to the recommendation by Bloxham's ally, A. Dirk Moses, for genocide scholarship to focus more on analysis than activism.

Yet, Moses himself did not always follow his own advice. In his essay, "Paranoia and Partisanship," he wrote that historians should "practice self-discipline" and "transcend ... partisan identifications" so that they do not perpetuate "paranoid threat assessments that contribute to self-fulfilling prophecies of escalation and destruction."[195] This recommendation, which was made in reaction to Bartov's critique of Bloxham, was commendable on its face; yet it was unduly alarmist.[196] In a sense, Moses's pessimistic perspective represented an inverted version of the whiggish view of Holocaust consciousness embraced by scholars during the second phase of the uniqueness debate. Indeed, Moses came close to suggesting that "paranoid" uses of the Holocaust were inherent to Holocaust consciousness in and of itself. In reality, it is the political dispositions of certain groups (whether on the right or left) that encourage exploitative uses of the Holocaust, "paranoid" ones included. As the uniqueness debate has shown, the Holocaust has served both universalistic and particularistic agendas. Holocaust consciousness is neither left nor right, but neutral.

Moses made other overgeneralizations as well. One was his claim that "Israelis need their terror of history to justify ... their victories of 1948, 1967, and beyond." This may be true of some right-wing Israelis, but hardly of all Israelis, many of whom decry such uses of the past. Moses was on stronger ground when he contextualized the traumatic view of Jewish history in forces beyond Holocaust consciousness, for example, when he linked this view to the "100 year [old] Zionist desire to repudiate ... exile" and prevent "Jews ...[from being] powerless again."[197] Yet, even here, Moses might have gone further, for this traumatic perspective dated back much further in Jewish history, to the typological view of Jewish suffering – diagnosed by Yosef Hayim Yerushalmi in his famous book, *Zakhor* – that perceived new persecutions through older, usually biblical, paradigms.[198] Given these longer traditions, Moses placed too much blame on Holocaust consciousness for the anxiety of contemporary Israelis.

This point is reinforced by several counterfactual observations. If the Holocaust had never happened (and if continued Jewish migration to Palestine had eventually given rise to a state, as most historians believe would have occurred), Israelis would probably still be displaying the same kind of "panicked" perspective identified by Moses, since the country would still be in a precarious existential position, ringed by hostile Arab neighbors. Holocaust consciousness should not be overemphasized, therefore, for Israel's present-day political mood. Moreover, if Holocaust consciousness were so implicated in the Israeli "terror of history," there never would have been any peace agreements between Israel and other Arab states. Israelis, after all, were no less traumatized by the Holocaust – and no less paranoid about external threats – when their treaties with Egypt and Jordan were forged several decades ago than they are now (and one might argue they were collectively *more* traumatized, as more Holocaust survivors were alive at the time than are alive today). Moses's terror of history argument was thus overly deterministic. This was visible, finally, in his explanation of how material circumstances shape memory. Moses was right to advise historians to study the "material conditions of political paranoia" and not just presume "its existence" by employing the concept of ideology.[199] Yet, while it is true that in times of crisis – for example, in eras of "foreign occupation and social decay" – memories can lead to paranoia, in periods of stability memories can become more universal, empathetic, and "other-directed."

Memory in general, and Holocaust consciousness in particular, can just as easily serve progressive as regressive aims.

Similar issues over memory were involved in the debate surrounding *Bloodlands*. Some of the negative responses to Snyder's book were rooted in an overreaction to its perceived political implications. Many of Snyder's critics, such as Zuroff and Katz, were overly alarmist in linking *Bloodlands* to the right-wing agendas of Eastern European nationalists. This was pointed out by a variety of historians who defended Snyder from the charge that his book diminished the Holocaust's singularity. As John Connelly put it, Snyder was a "gentle revisionist" who was driven more by scholarly than political motives.[200] Christopher Browning agreed, writing that "those who suggest that [*Bloodlands*] . . . equates Nazi and communist crimes of mass killing or diminishes the . . . Holocaust have simply not read it carefully . . .[Snyder] firmly establishes that Hitler and the Nazis were more lethal than Stalin . . . and that . . . Jewish victimization was singular."[201] Other critics concurred: James Kirchik declared that "Snyder has not minimized the horror or unique evil of the Holocaust," while Adam Kirsch wrote that he preserved "the singularity of Jewish experience."[202] Snyder, moreover, defended himself admirably, pointing out that he had been widely criticized by, and even received death threats from, right-wing nationalists for highlighting Eastern European collaboration in the Holocaust. He further emphasized that he did not equate the Holocaust with other genocides. Declaring that "questioning the Holocaust's singularity" was "the last thing I want to do," he went on to say that "the mass murder of the Jews was . . . unprecedented in its horror; no other campaign . . . was so tightly bound to the idea that a whole people ought to be exterminated."[203] In short, fears that Snyder sought to relativize the Holocaust were unfounded.

The exaggerated nature of these fears was not their chief liability, however, for they also distracted attention from some of *Bloodlands'* own analytical shortcomings. Of all the arguments used by Snyder to question the Holocaust's uniqueness, one was especially open to challenge: namely, the "scapegoating" theory that he employed to explain both Hitler's and Stalin's crimes. As noted above, Snyder advanced this theory to explain the decision-making process behind the Nazis' turn to mass murder, arguing that it resulted from the failure to realize their colonial plans in the east.[204] This theory stood in tension, however, with Snyder's reluctance to pinpoint the exact timing of the Nazis' decision to pursue the Final Solution – specifically, whether they did so in a climate of euphoria or despair about Germany's prospects in the war.[205] Snyder basically sidestepped the question of timing by asserting that the destruction of European Jewry was implied in Hitler's vision of an eastern colonial empire well before the invasion of the USSR even took place.[206] As he put it, "a Final Solution that would eliminate European Jews after the war" was one of Hitler's four utopian goals prior to launching Operation Barbarossa; indeed, the "Jews were killed because Hitler had defined this as an aim of the war."[207] In other words, Snyder implied that the wholesale elimination of the Jews, whether by slow death or direct killing, was an end in itself. This claim, however, conflicted with the theory that Hitler decided to kill them only as a result of a contingent policy failure.[208]

The conflict between Snyder's two claims is further underscored by several counterfactual considerations. The scapegoating theory implied that if Stalin's and Hitler's original policies had actually succeeded, the two dictators would have had no reason to seek revenge via mass murder. This applied most clearly to Stalin's collectivization program. Had it gone as planned – had Stalin not recklessly pegged the harvest quota for 1931 to the unusually high figures of the bumper crop of 1930 – there would have been no failure and thus no need for scapegoats.[209] This was especially true since Stalin's persecutions, according to Snyder, were a function of paranoia borne of "political vulnerability." The dictator's murder campaign notably ebbed when he felt more secure in the latter part of the 1930s.[210] A more successful Soviet Union, in other words, would have been a less bloody one. By contrast, Hitler's persecution of the Jews obeyed a different dynamic. Unlike Stalin, he did not soften, but instead radicalized, his policies towards the Jews as his grip on power became firmer. This dynamic, which was visible in the years 1933–39 as well as after the eruption of the war, reflected the fact that the elimination of the Jews was one of Hitler's most important ideological priorities. For this reason, if the Wehrmacht had successfully defeated the Red Army in 1941 – if Hitler had not required any scapegoats – it is unlikely that he would have spared the Jews. There still would have been a Final Solution, albeit possibly with different methods. This hypothesis casts doubt on the theory that the Holocaust only resulted from a policy failure in the east. It also suggests that, contrary to Snyder's assertions, the Holocaust's similarities to Stalin's crimes may ultimately be outweighed by its differences.

The scapegoating theory also failed to explain another distinctive feature of the Holocaust – the fact that it was not restricted to the bloodlands but was extended to other parts of Europe. Although Snyder correctly noted that the number of Western European Jews murdered by the Nazis paled in comparison to the number of Eastern European Jews, it was precisely their numerical "insignificance" that was important. For the Nazis gave equal attention to deporting the tiny Jewish communities of the Channel Islands, Norway, and Greece (and also planned to kill the Jews of North Africa).[211] These were Jewish communities where the Nazis had no imperial ambitions related to the *Generalplan Ost*. There was no reason to target them as scapegoats for the Nazis' failure to realize their eastern ambitions. But they were killed all the same. This important fact stood as an important reminder of the global – and ultimately ideological – scope of the Final Solution. It also underscored a final counterfactual point: had the Nazis won World War II, no Jewish community anywhere would have been safe.

These suppositions are especially relevant in light of Snyder's own use of counterfactual reasoning to challenge the idea of the Holocaust's uniqueness. In the introduction to *Bloodlands*, after questioning the centrality of Auschwitz in the Final Solution, he advanced the additional claim that "the Holocaust overshadows other German plans that envisioned even more killing," declaring that

> Hitler wanted not only to eradicate the Jews ...[but] also to ... kill tens of millions of Slavs ... If the German war against the Soviet Union had gone as planned, thirty million civilians would have been starved in the first winter, and tens of millions more expelled, killed, assimilated, or enslaved thereafter.[212]

This claim appears reasonable at first glance. Yet, upon further reflection, it is somewhat puzzling, for it seems to imply that real history has unjustly overshadowed hypothetical history – that the death of nearly six million Jews has overshadowed the tens of millions of Slavs who were never killed. Snyder is correct, of course, in surmising that had the Nazis won the war and tried to implement the *Generalplan Ost* and *Hungerplan*, millions of additional Slavs would have been murdered. Yet even had this scenario come to pass (which is unlikely due to a shortage of German manpower, as is discussed in Chapter 3), it is unclear whether it would have lessened the postwar world's sense of the

Holocaust's singularity. Had the Nazis won the war, they also would have brought the Final Solution of the Jewish Question to completion and killed not just two-thirds, but close to 100 percent, of European Jewry. That nightmare scenario, by virtue of its totality, may still have overshadowed what might have been the numerically larger, but less total, murder of Eastern European Slavs. In other words, it might still have reinforced perceptions of the Holocaust's extremity and, as such, its singularity.

Taken together, the works of Bloxham, Snyder, and Moses exhibited impressive strengths but also certain shortcomings. They represented notable attempts to historicize the Holocaust by situating it within the context of modern genocide. They furthermore pursued this goal in a sober analytical fashion, without the polemical excesses of the earlier scholarship. At the same time, however, their discussion of the Holocaust's uniqueness was marked by certain contradictions. While Bloxham, Snyder, and Moses denied any desire to minimize the Holocaust's distinct features, their studies nevertheless ended up marginalizing them. It was ironic, moreover, that Bloxham and Moses questioned the Holocaust's uniqueness while at the same time insisting that the concept was already passé. If the idea were so discredited as to no longer merit debate, there would have been little reason for them to challenge it. Their effort to do so suggested that their historicization of the Holocaust was part of a push to universalize its significance.

This agenda was further suggested by the three scholars' critique of Holocaust memory. Rejecting the scholarly consensus of the last decade, Bloxham, Snyder, and Moses each questioned the notion that the worldwide spread of Holocaust consciousness represented a progressive development. They implied or stated outright that centering attention on the Nazis' murder of the Jews came at a price: Bloxham identified it as the perpetuation of the Western metanarratives that underpinned modern colonial genocide; Snyder saw it as the reinforcing of national martyrology and myth-making; and Moses linked it to a paranoid "terror of history" mentality. All three scholars preferred, like Judt and Alexander before them, for Holocaust memory to assume a more universal form and avoid particularistic iterations. In advancing these points, Bloxham, Snyder, and Moses were criticized by other scholars, who accused them of diminishing the Holocaust's uniqueness. Their response, in turn, was telling. Although Snyder was conciliatory, Bloxham and Moses did not shy away from employing polemical arguments in their defense, invoking the Israeli–Palestinian conflict in support of their larger historiographical agenda. In so doing, they ironically helped perpetuate the very debate they declared to be over.

The most recent phase of the uniqueness debate thus confirms the dialectic of normalization. The efforts of Bloxham, Snyder, and Moses to historicize the Holocaust and highlight its common features with other genocides succeeded mostly in heightening other scholars' suspicions that they were normalizing the topic for political reasons. These scholars' response, in turn, was to underscore the Holocaust's uniqueness. The result was the renewal of controversy and the blocking of normalization.

Conclusion

It is hard to say what the course of the uniqueness debate means for the evolution of Holocaust memory. The fact that the debate has gone on for two decades suggests that the memory of the Nazi genocide continues to resist normalization. Indeed, the debate's dialectical nature raises the possibility that the idea of uniqueness is destined to be surrounded by conflict. It is important to stress that this conflict has little to do with major academic disagreements. The more scholars have historicized the Holocaust, the more they have abandoned the concept of uniqueness as analytically imprecise and empirically unverifiable. These scholars have maintained the desire to preserve awareness of the Holocaust's distinctive features, but they have largely refrained from referring to them with the term "uniqueness" for fear of raising a red flag. This gesture of conciliation, meanwhile, has been reciprocated by scholars who have rejected the concept of uniqueness, but have conceded that the Jewish experience under the Nazis was marked by special traits missing from other genocides.

Given this pattern of scholarly rapprochement over the last generation, it is clear that the ongoing conflict over the Holocaust's uniqueness is mostly about politics. The debate has shown that the attempt to historicize the Holocaust has consistently been accompanied by the effort to politicize it. For years, scholars and activists have imported various political agendas into the discussion about the Holocaust's uniqueness, whether relating to American identity politics, post-communist Eastern European nationalism, or the Arab–Israeli conflict. The injection of these topics into the debate has largely been determined by the course of political events, intensifying in times of crisis and fading in times of stability. This pattern of politicization has had several important consequences: it has transformed the idea of uniqueness from an analytical construct into a politicized code word. And it has produced a climate of mutual suspicion in which every invocation of uniqueness – whether critical or supportive – is reflexively perceived as an expression of a political position. The positions are familiar: the opponents of uniqueness allege that the idea is an aggressive tool for advancing Jewish and Zionist interests, while its supporters see it as a defense against efforts to minimize Jewish suffering in World War II.[213]

While these mutual suspicions may contain a kernel of truth (some supporters of uniqueness *have* exploited the concept in defense of Israel, while some critics *have* tried to de-judaize the Holocaust), they are ultimately exaggerated. Just as many defenders of uniqueness have not been driven by Zionist goals, many critics have not been driven by anti-Zionist or anti-Semitic agendas. The longstanding politicization of the concept, however, has conditioned both camps to see political agendas where they do not always exist. For this reason, as long as there are political conflicts that touch on competing perceptions of the Holocaust's legacy, the topic of uniqueness will retain the capacity to sow dissension. As long as the Arab–Israeli conflict endures, as long as Eastern European nationalists resist coming to terms with their countries' experiences under Nazi and Soviet occupation, as long as struggles over identity politics continue in the US and Europe – in short, as long as any crisis makes it tempting to employ the Holocaust for partisan ends – there will be no normalization. For better or worse, the Holocaust's status as the contemporary world's secular emblem of evil will continue to make it both a moral measuring stick and a rhetorical weapon for diverse political causes.

The future of the uniqueness debate will thus ultimately depend on how scholars respond to the continuing politicization of the Holocaust's legacy. If recent events are any indication, they will find it difficult to remain unaffected by the dialectic of normalization. Throughout the Western world, ongoing efforts to universalize the Holocaust continue to elicit spirited defenses of it uniqueness. In early 2014, the EU's High Representative for Foreign Affairs, Baroness Catherine Ashton, sparked controversy by failing to mention Jews or anti-Semitism in her official declaration for Holocaust Remembrance

Day – an oversight that critics alleged was meant to appease Europe's Muslims, who are uninterested in hearing about Jewish suffering in a time of ongoing Israeli–Arab tensions.[214] In the United States, meanwhile, conservative critics of President Barack Obama have made headlines by employing Holocaust analogies to attack his policies, whether Tea Party activists' comparison of the Affordable Care Act to the Nazi T4 euthanasia program or the *Wall Street Journal*'s early 2014 endorsement of billionaire venture capitalist Thomas Perkins's comparison of the "progressive war on the American one percent, namely the 'rich,'" with the Nazis' "war [against the] Jews."[215] In Israel, meanwhile, groups on both the left and right continue to employ Holocaust references to condemn everything from the government's treatment of Palestinians to its policies towards Orthodox Jews. Predictably enough, critics have condemned these examples of universalization for effacing the Holocaust's singularity. But they have been unable to bring them to a halt. Indeed, the difficulty of resisting the process of normalization was recently underscored by the firestorm of criticism that was directed at Israeli politicians who, in early 2014, tried to defend the Holocaust's uniqueness by proposing legislation banning "wrong or inappropriate" uses of Nazi terminology and symbols.[216]

Given these ongoing controversies, Holocaust scholars would do well to be aware of the dialectic of normalization as they pursue their future academic research. The better they understand the political forces that hover over their discipline, the more prepared they will be to ensure that future debates about the Holocaust will remain focused on issues of analysis rather than politics. If scholars can remain free of such forces and keep their work dispassionate, the uniqueness debate will likely ebb. If they cannot, there is every reason to suspect that it will continue well into the future.

3 PROBING THE LIMITS OF SPECULATION: COUNTERFACTUALISM AND THE HOLOCAUST

No Hitler, No Holocaust.[1]

— MILTON HIMMELFARB

Without the Holocaust there would be no ... state of Israel.[2]

— HENRY TURNER

Without Hitler, the State of Israel probably would not exist today, so to that extent he was probably the Jews' greatest friend.[3]

— DAVID IRVING

Besides often being false, syllogisms can sometimes be offensive. To suggest, as – collectively – the above counterfactual quotations do, that Adolf Hitler should be hailed as the creator of the State of Israel is clearly both. Highlighting this fact, however, helps to explain why counterfactual speculation has long been viewed with suspicion. For generations, historians have dismissed the use of counterfactual reasoning in the writing of history. From E. H. Carr's and E. P. Thompson's classic put-downs to more recent critiques by Richard Evans, counterfactual thinking has long been viewed as an amusing diversion at best and, at worst, a complete waste of time.[4] It would seem inappropriate, therefore, to apply such reasoning to a subject as serious as the Holocaust.

Nevertheless, in recent decades, counterfactual reasoning has become an important feature of Holocaust historiography. Beginning in the early 1960s and increasing up to the present day, historians and other scholars have discussed many "what if?" scenarios in writing about the origins, course, and legacy of the Nazi genocide. Some have examined the origins of the Final Solution, inquiring whether it would have happened at all, or in the same way, without the figure of Adolf Hitler. Others have explored the conduct of the victims and bystanders, speculating about how greater Jewish efforts at resistance and Gentile attempts at rescue might have helped avert the Holocaust or mitigate its effects. Still others have examined questions pertaining to the Nazi genocide's legacy, most notably: how its uniqueness would have been affected by a Nazi victory in World War II; how the Final Solution might have been averted if the Western Allies had remained neutral in the conflict; and whether the State of Israel would have been created had the Holocaust never occurred.

In exploring these "what if?" scenarios, historians have been driven by various agendas. Some have been purely analytical. Others have been moral. Still others have been political. Regardless of their motives, the ways in which historians have imagined the past have been shaped by their views of the present. For this reason, counterfactual representations of the Holocaust can be seen as significant documents of memory. In speculating about how the past could have been different, historians have revealed their views on how it really was. Predictably enough, historians have arrived at starkly different conclusions in hypothesizing about the Nazi genocide. Some have indulged fantasies and envisioned it turning out better; others have nurtured nightmares and imagined it turning out worse. Whatever their conclusions, the growing willingness of historians to speculate about the Holocaust points to an important mnemonic trend. In focusing on what *might* have happened to the Jews during the Second World War instead of on what actually did, counterfactuals reveal that there are no longer any morally rooted "limits of representation" with respect to the Holocaust. In the process, they highlight the ongoing normalization of the Nazi past.

Why do we ask "what if?" in studying the Holocaust?

The growing scholarly interest in speculating about the Holocaust reflects the heightened prominence of counterfactual reasoning in Western intellectual life. At the most basic level, counterfactual reasoning involves the posing and answering of hypothetical "what if?" questions.[5] This speculative mode of thought has long been employed in the humanities and social sciences, especially in the field of history. Historical counterfactuals imagine how important events in the past might have unfolded differently in light of certain "points of divergence." These points include the deaths of kings and politicians, the occurrence of military victories or defeats, and the rise of grand cultural and religious movements. By imagining history's course being altered as a result of such variables, "what ifs?" emphasize the importance of contingency over determinism in shaping historical events. In so doing, "what if?" scenarios partake in a time-honored tradition. Counterfactual thinking dates back to Antiquity and the famed historians of Greece and Rome. For nearly as long, however, historians have decried speculating about the past, regarding "what if?" history as the fanciful "other" of "real" history.[6] Of late, however, this skepticism has waned. Thanks to various political and cultural trends – the revolutions of 1989, the rise of postmodernism, and the information revolution – an anti-deterministic, relativistic turn has taken hold in Western culture and encouraged scholars to think more speculatively about the past.[7] The result has been a spate of new academic studies employing counterfactual reasoning, many of which have been produced by historians.[8]

In these studies, scholars have come to understand that counterfactual reasoning serves important analytical purposes. To begin with, "what if?" scenarios shed light on the forces of historical causality. When historians claim that "x caused y," they implicitly affirm that "y would not have occurred in the absence of x."[9] To cite a specific example, the assertion that Anglo-American bombing raids on German cities during World War II were crucial for the Allies' ultimate victory is closely related to the counterfactual claim that, had they not employed this controversial tactic, they might not have won the war as quickly. Such a claim underscores the contingent nature of historical events and challenges the tendency to view them deterministically. By imagining how the absence of aerial bombing raids would have affected the war's course, we can better understand the factors that contributed to the Allies' triumph. We can also better appreciate that it was hardly foreordained. Counterfactual reasoning thus shows that choice rather than inevitability stands at the core of all "what ifs?"

Counterfactual reasoning also helps historians make moral judgments in interpreting historical events. The scholarly debate on whether the Allies were morally justified in bombing German cities has long been inseparable from the question of how history might have unfolded had they not done so. Had the Allies abstained from their bombing program, fewer Germans would have been killed from the air during the war. As a result, the morality of the Allies' wartime behavior would be less controversial today. It is far from certain, however, that the absence of aerial bombing would have actually produced fewer total German deaths. Without Allied air raids, the war might have lasted longer, been characterized by extended ground offensives, and claimed *more* civilian victims. Had this outcome transpired, historians today might be debating whether it would have been morally preferable to continue the bombing campaign, end the war sooner, and spare the German civilian population prolonged suffering. These possibilities reveal that moral judgments often depend on whether a counterfactual ends up improving or worsening the course of history.

Finally, in showing how the past might have been different, counterfactuals shed light on how historical events are remembered. Counterfactual scenarios usually alter the past in a positive or negative direction. As a result, they can be categorized either as fantasies or nightmares.[10] Both are highly subjective in the sense that they express the hopes and fears of those who imagine them. All historical counterfactuals are therefore "presentist" in character. They explore the past less for its own sake than to utilize it instrumentally to comment upon the contemporary world. Fantasy scenarios, for example, envision the alternate past as superior to the real past and, in so doing, typically express a sense of dissatisfaction with the way things are today. By contrast, nightmare scenarios, in depicting the alternate past as inferior to the real past, often articulate a sense of contentment with the status quo. Both scenarios also have political implications, serving liberal and conservative purposes in different ways.[11] The larger point, however, is that the inherent subjectivity of counterfactuals makes them ideal documents for studying memory. Historical counterfactuals are informed by many of the same psychological impulses that influence how the past takes shape in remembrance. These impulses are often moralistic and include the twin tendencies of assigning blame for negative historical events and claiming credit for positive ones. These subjective (and often political) desires frequently underpin both fantasy and nightmare scenarios. This fact further explains why counterfactuals often lend themselves to challenging orthodox views of the past. By showing how history might have transpired differently, counterfactuals serve the goals of revisionist history and counter-memory.[12]

Historians have applied counterfactual reasoning to many historical topics, but one of the most important is the Holocaust.[13] The reasons are understandable, for the Holocaust has long confronted historians with the same kinds of analytical, moral, and mnemonic questions that counterfactual reasoning is so well-suited to address. For decades, historians have examined the causal chain of events that led to the Holocaust; they have assessed the moral behavior of the perpetrators, victims, and bystanders; and they have explored how the event has been remembered. In doing so, moreover, scholars have often become embroiled in controversies, with supporters of established paradigms heatedly debating revisionist challengers. Because counterfactuals are prone to fostering historiographical debate, they have played an important, if underappreciated, role in Holocaust scholarship.

Counterfactual reasoning was not initially a major feature of Holocaust historiography. This absence was partly due to the slow development of the field itself. General historical studies on the Nazi genocide were few and far between in the early years after World War II, with the first major syntheses only appearing in the 1960s. In this period, most historians prioritized establishing the basic facts of the Holocaust by plowing through the massive documentary record that survived the war. Given this empiricist imperative, the best-known works of the era – by scholars such as Philip Friedman, Eugen Kogon, Léon Poliakov, Gerald Reitlinger, and Raul Hilberg – featured little counterfactual speculation.[14] Whenever scholars did avail themselves of it, they often added disclaimers. When Poliakov speculated about how other groups besides the Jews might have suffered had the Nazis won the Second World War, he apologetically noted: "Nothing is more useless than to forecast events that have not ... taken place."[15] It was not until the 1970s and 1980s that Holocaust scholars became comfortable making counterfactual claims. By this time, more of the Holocaust's facts had been established and scholars shifted to interpreting their significance. Inevitably, differences of interpretation emerged, competing schools of thought took shape, and public controversies erupted on a variety of issues pertaining to the Holocaust's origins, course, and legacy. In short, as tensions between orthodox and revisionist perspectives increased, the use of counterfactual reasoning became more common.

This trend becomes clear in tracing how counterfactual reasoning has been employed in Holocaust scholarship over the last several decades. Scholars have utilized such reasoning to examine both the Holocaust's history and legacy: they have applied it to assess the behavior of the victims, perpetrators, and bystanders; and they have used it to determine whether the genocide was historically "unique"; whether it could have been prevented through Allied non-intervention in World War II; and whether it helped establish the state of Israel. Scholars initially applied counterfactual reasoning to these topics haltingly. But over time, they began to speculate with growing confidence – so much so that, today, many do so explicitly. Scholars have employed counterfactual reasoning for different purposes. They have utilized it to analyze historical causality, make moral judgments about the past, and revise orthodox interpretations of it. In the process, they have often sparked controversy. By employing counterfactual reasoning just as often as a rhetorical device as an analytical tool, they have often been accused of privileging partisan subjectivity over scholarly objectivity.[16] As a result, many skeptics insist that counterfactual reasoning does not deserve to be taken seriously. In fact, the opposite is true. The growing presence of counterfactual reasoning in Holocaust historiography reflects how the Nazi genocide has evolved in collective memory.

Blaming the victims: Hannah Arendt and the debate over Jewish collaboration

The first topic to feature extended counterfactual argumentation was the behavior of Jewish victims in the Holocaust. A major stimulus was the bitter controversy sparked by the publication of Hannah Arendt's book, *Eichmann in Jerusalem*, in 1963 (Figure 10). Although best known for introducing the concept of the "banality of evil," the book unleashed an especially furious reaction among Jews because of its critical assertions about the responsibility of the Jewish councils (*Judenräte*) for the deportation and murder of the Jewish inhabitants of Nazi-administered ghettos. Significantly, the claim in Arendt's study that elicited the most protest employed counterfactual reasoning. Declaring that "wherever Jews lived ... Jewish leaders ... cooperated ... with the Nazis," Arendt speculated that

Figure 10. Hannah Arendt imagined one of the earliest and most controversial "what if?" scenarios about the Holocaust in her book, *Eichmann in Jerusalem* (1963).

if the Jewish people had ... been unorganized and leaderless, there would have been chaos and plenty of misery but the total number of victims would hardly have been between four and a half and six million people ...[A]bout half of them could have saved themselves if they had not followed the instructions of the Jewish Councils.[17]

In short, Arendt submitted a fantasy scenario: if the Jews had behaved differently, they could have improved the course of Jewish history.

Arendt's motivations in submitting this claim were varied. She partly hoped to revise the heroized portrayal of Jewish victims in the existing scholarly literature on the Holocaust.[18] Yet her speculative vision of a better past also reflected her political disaffection with the present. Arendt was alienated by the postwar development of the Zionist movement, believing it had shifted too far to the right in the wake of the Holocaust. This shift was visible, she believed, in Israeli Prime Minister David Ben-Gurion's politically motivated decision in 1961 to try Eichmann in Israel for crimes against the Jewish people instead of delivering him to an international tribunal, where he could be tried for crimes against humanity. This, however, was not the trial's only flaw, in Arendt's view. She particularly disapproved of its "gravest omission," namely the failure to address the "cooperation between the Nazi rulers and the Jewish authorities."[19] Against this backdrop, Arendt's critique of wartime Jewish leaders in her book functioned as a rhetorical attack via historical analogy against Israel's postwar political establishment.

Arendt's claims sparked heated debate among Jews. Among her numerous critics, some, such as Gershom Scholem, focused on Arendt's alleged lack of empathy for the Jews' plight during the war.[20] Others notably challenged her counterfactual assertions with counterfactual arguments of their own. Lionel Abel, for example, questioned Arendt's causal claim that "Jewish leadership was so necessary to Nazi success in killing Jews" by pointing out that Nazi Einsatzgruppen units killed "over half a million Russian Jews ... in the Ukraine ...[where] there were no *Judenräte*." As Abel noted, "had Miss Arendt dealt with the killing of the Jews in Russia, she would have had to abandon her whole thesis that ... the deaths of so many Jews rests finally with their own leadership."[21] Other critics refuted Arendt's fantasy that Jews could have saved themselves by claiming that her vision would have actually produced a nightmare.[22] According to Jacob Robinson, if Jewish communal organizations had followed Arendt's advice, dissolved themselves after the onset of Nazi occupation, and urged Jews to escape, they would have merely "made conditions worse," for there would have been no Jewish authorities to help refugees looking to immigrate to other countries – something that was still possible in places such as the Protectorate of Slovakia from 1939 to 1941.[23] These and other points made by Arendt's critics revealed that the debate over Jewish behavior was partly a debate about the relationship between contingency and inevitability in the Holocaust. Although Arendt insisted that even "the possibility of *doing nothing*" reflected a "limited freedom of decision" for ghettoized Jews, her critics replied that they had little ability to determine their fate once the Nazis had decreed their destruction. As Norman Podhoretz concluded, the behavior of the Jewish leaders hardly "mattered in the slightest to the final result. Murderers with the power to murder descended upon a defenseless people and murdered a large part of it. What else is there to say?"[24]

As it turned out, there was much to say, at least according to Arendt's supporters, many of whom offered counterfactual claims in her defense. Bruno Bettelheim, for example, wrote: "No doubt the stories of the ghettos would have been different if most Jews and their leadership had not been ... willing ... to cooperate with the Germans ...[and had fought] back. No doubt many Jews ... might have tried to escape."[25] Speculating in more extended fashion, Mary McCarthy added:

> Had the Nazis been obliged to use their own manpower to select Jews for the extermination camps ... they would not only have rounded up fewer Jews but they would have felt the drain in their military effort; had Hitler persisted in the Final Solution, at the cost of diverting troops to carry it out, the war might have ended somewhat sooner. It is clear that the refusal to cooperate would have met with terrible reprisals, but...[they] might have demoralized the army and the civilian population both in Germany and in the occupied countries, and chaos, the nightmare of generals, might have been the result ... To say this is not ... to show a lack of sympathy for ...[the Jews'] plight. To speculate on the past ... is not to blame ... but merely to wish, to regret, to close your eyes and see it done differently.[26]

Finally, Dwight Macdonald defended Arendt against Scholem's accusation that she lacked "a special feeling in favor of her fellow Jews," arguing that "such a prejudice would have made it impossible for her to speculate on how the catastrophe might have been less complete had the Jewish leadership followed different policies."[27] These comments reveal that the debate over Arendt's counterfactual remark was about more than the historiographical question of whether Jews in the Holocaust possessed freedom of choice or were prisoners of fate. It was also rooted in disagreement about the propriety of using counterfactual argumentation for partisan ends.

The flurry of counterfactual debate sparked by Arendt's book was ultimately short-lived. With a few exceptions, scholarship on Jewish behavior in the Holocaust – like Holocaust scholarship in general – ebbed in the period that followed.[28] For the remainder of the 1960s and into the mid-1970s, studies on the Third Reich mostly addressed the political origins of the Nazi dictatorship, its administrative structure, and its ideological relationship to fascism.[29] Little attention was paid to the origins of the Nazi genocide. The same was true of the studies that appeared during the "Hitler Wave," most of which skimmed over the Holocaust in the process of probing the arcane depths of Hitler's biography.[30] None of these works, moreover, was marked by much meaningful counterfactual reflection. The structuralist attention to the social, economic, and bureaucratic forces that marked the Third Reich encouraged a focus on determinism rather than contingency, while the Hitler Wave's interest in sensationalistic biographical detail trumped more speculative claims about history's other possible outcomes. Wondering "what if?" about the Holocaust, in short, seemed to hold little appeal to most scholars.

Analyzing the perpetrators: "No Hitler, No Holocaust"

In the 1980s, however, counterfactual reasoning resurfaced in the context of a new topic – Adolf Hitler's role in conceiving, initiating, and implementing the so-called Final Solution of the Jewish Question. This focus developed alongside the upsurge in Holocaust scholarship that began in the mid-1970s. This scholarship was initially defined by the "intentionalist" belief, best articulated by Lucy Dawidowciz's influential study, *The War Against the Jews* (1975), that the Nazi dictator had played a central role in planning the genocide.[31] By the end of the decade and into the 1980s, however, the rise of the "functionalist" school of thought, associated with Martin Broszat and Hans Mommsen, challenged the intentionalist position by diminishing Hitler's role in the Final Solution and emphasizing forces related to the bureaucratic structure of the Nazi state.[32] It was partly in response to this new line of argumentation that intentionalist scholars moved to defend their position with the help of counterfactual statements. They now began to argue that without Hitler, there would have been no Holocaust.

Ironically, the best-known counterfactual formulation of this "what if?" scenario was neither inspired by the intentionalist–functionalist debate nor produced by an historian. In 1984, essayist Milton Himmelfarb published an article in *Commentary* magazine entitled "No Hitler, No Holocaust." Although the article came to be associated with the intentionalist position, it was not written as a refutation of functionalism, but of several other historiographical trends. Himmelfarb was a conservative supporter of traditional historical methodology and sought to challenge what he believed to be the historical profession's trendy embrace of deep structural forces – "geography, demography, technology, *mentalités*" – over "the biography of great men." The focus on such deterministic forces, he argued, had distorted the history of the Holocaust by leading "Hitler ...[to] disappear ... behind abstractions." Instead, Himmelfarb reasserted the role of contingency in historical events and highlighted Hitler's centrality in the Holocaust, declaring:

> Hitler willed and ordered the Holocaust, and was obeyed.
> Traditions, tendencies, ideas, myths – none of these made Hitler murder the Jews. All that history, all those forces and influences, could have been the same and Hitler could as easily ... not have murdered the Jews ...
> Antisemitism was a necessary condition for the Holocaust, it was not a sufficient condition. Hitler was needed. Hitler murdered the Jews because he wanted to murder them. [33]

For Himmelfarb, the conclusion was inescapable: "No Hitler, No Holocaust."

Himmelfarb's belief in individual agency was not the only historiographical consideration that informed his essay's counterfactual conclusion. His assertion, "No Hitler, No Holocaust," was also meant to refute the deterministic claim that the Holocaust was caused by Christian anti-Semitism. This claim had been advanced several years earlier in two articles published in *Commentary*: one by Polish Jewish writer and Holocaust survivor, Henryk Grynberg, the other by the British Jewish scholar Hyam Maccoby.[34] These articles, according to Himmelfarb, had grossly underestimated the decisive role played by Hitler, whose name was mentioned "only once." In response, Himmelfarb defended Christianity from the deterministic allegation that it paved the way for the Holocaust. To prove his point, he argued that Christian anti-Semitism had neither intended nor permitted the mass murder of the Jews, embracing the principle that "the Jews are to be allowed to live, but not too well." Only with the advent of "anti-Christian anti-Semitism," which he traced back to the Deist thought of "Voltaire the Enlightener," did Jew-hatred become murderous. It was this secular strand of hatred that influenced the "anti-Christian," Adolf Hitler. This causal link allowed Himmelfarb to make the anti-deterministic claim that "Hitler made the Holocaust because he wanted to make it. Anti-Semitism did not make him make it."[35]

In downplaying the role of anti-Semitism in the Holocaust, Himmelfarb, like Arendt before him, was driven by political considerations. At the time he wrote his essay, he was developing his famous neo-conservative political agenda, a key feature of which was the forging of alliances between Jews and Christian conservatives. This goal was impeded, however, by most Jews' belief that anti-Semitism derived from Christian teachings. It was to debunk this association that Himmelfarb exonerated Christian anti-Semitism for the Holocaust and instead blamed it on "anti-Christian anti-Semitism." For good measure, Himmelfarb added that this latter form of Jew-hatred found a comfortable home in the secular thought of the political left, especially in the form of anti-Zionism. This claim revealed the political function of Himmelfarb's counterfactual. In asserting that without Hitler's anti-Christian anti-Semitism there would not have been a Holocaust, he sought to convince Jews that they had "more to fear from anti-Christians than from Christians" and should ally with Christian conservatives.[36]

Himmelfarb's formulation, "No Hitler, No Holocaust," may be the best-known version of this counterfactual premise, but it was hardly alone. Already before its appearance, and increasingly in the years since, many scholars embraced its basic thrust. In the early 1970s, for example, Walter Laqueur flatly declared, "without Hitler . . . no Holocaust," while Joachim Fest famously wrote that "if Hitler had succumbed to an assassination . . . at the end of 1938, few would [have] hesitate[d] to call him one of the greatest of German statesmen . . . [since his] anti-Semitism and . . . design for world dominion . . . would . . . have fallen into oblivion."[37] Similar comments were made in the 1980s by Randolph Braham, Sebastian Haffner, and Philippe Burrin, while in the last two decades they have been echoed by Doris Bergen, Inge Clendinnen, John Connelly, Jonathan Frankel, Daniel Goldhagen, John K. Roth, Richard L. Rubenstein, William D. Rubinstein, and Henry Turner.[38] Significantly, some scholars have explicitly highlighted their embrace of "what if" reasoning. In 2004, for example, Ian Kershaw declared that "a set of counterfactual propositions ... underline how I see Hitler's indispensability [to Nazism] ... No Hitler: no Holocaust, no state policy aimed at wiping out the Jews of Europe."[39] So popular have such formulations become that another supporter, Peter Longerich, has concluded: "Nowadays the vast majority of historians who ...[study] the Third Reich would subscribe to the theory 'no Holocaust without Hitler'. Or, to argue counterfactually, if Hitler had died in 1940, it is extremely questionable whether the Nazi regime would have followed that fateful path under different leadership."[40]

To be sure, other scholars have challenged the premise that without Hitler, the Holocaust would not have happened. Fearing that the premise distracted attention from other factors that contributed to the Nazi genocide, they offered their own counterfactuals to disprove it. One critic of Himmelfarb's original article, for example, asserted that, beyond Hitler's will for extermination, the Holocaust also required modern "devices for mass killing," concluding: "Had the Crusaders had such technology, someone would have willed and ordered a Holocaust back in the Middle Ages." This comment, which implied the genocidal potential of Christian anti-Semitism, was echoed by Lucy Dawidowicz, who declared that while "Christianity cannot be held responsible for Hitler ... the Nazis would not have succeeded in disseminating their brand of racist anti-Semitism had they not been confident of the pervasiveness ... of Christian hatred of Jews."[41] Similarly, John Weiss declared that "it is time to stop believing that 'without Hitler, no Holocaust,' ...[for] anti-Semitism was an explosion waiting to happen; the Nazis would be the beneficiaries, the Holocaust the consequence."[42] These comments revealed how counterfactuals were compatible with a belief in inevitability.

Given such responses, supporters of the "No Hitler, No Holocaust" counterfactual have been careful to resist its monocausal implications. As Longerich put it, "Seen in purely logical terms it denotes a necessary but not a sufficient condition, so the phrase 'no Holocaust without Hitler' cannot be reversed to give the thesis 'the Holocaust took place merely because Hitler willed it.' For the...Holocaust to occur, a whole series of other conditions had to be fulfilled alongside 'Hitler.'"[43] Kershaw has taken a similar position, arguing, on the one hand, that "without Hitler's fanatical will to destroy Jewry ... the Holocaust would almost certainly not have come about," while adding that "it would also not have become reality ... without the active collaboration of the Wehrmacht ... the civil service ... or the leaders of Germany's industries."[44] Relatedly, Robert Paxton has acknowledged the importance of "Hitler's obsessive hatred of Jews" in the Holocaust, while also stressing that without the assistance of "thousands of subordinates," his murderous plans "would have remained ... a fantasy."[45]

There is no simple explanation for why the "No Hitler, No Holocaust" counterfactual has become increasingly popular among historians in the last generation. But the answer may lie in the evolving character of Holocaust scholarship itself. Thanks to the explosive growth of Holocaust historiography, the number of explanations that have been cited by historians – whether anti-Semitism, bureaucratic competition, racial science, modernity, economic rationality, or colonial demographic engineering schemes – has grown so large that it threatens to turn the Nazi genocide into an over-determined event. This being the case, explaining the event counterfactually – in terms of the factors whose absence would have made it impossible (instead of those that made it possible) – enjoys the appeal of analytical simplicity. It further satisfies deeper moral impulses. For while larger theories come and go, the counterfactual premise, "No Hitler, No Holocaust," prevents us from losing sight of the role played by a man whose fanatical desire for a world without Jews has made him an enduring symbol of evil.

Judging the bystanders: What if the world had not remained passive during the Holocaust?

Moral impulses also explain a third major area of counterfactual speculation about the Holocaust – the question of bystander passivity. Beginning in the 1960s and accelerating after the 1980s, scholars began to ask whether various historical bystanders – the United States government, the Papacy, the German people, and even the world Jewish community – could have undertaken more energetic efforts to rescue Jews from the Nazis. These claims challenged the inevitability of the Jews' wartime fate and stressed the role of contingency in fantasizing how history might have turned out better. In so doing, they generated a backlash among critics, who insisted that history was destined to be bad and might even have been worse.

Counterfactual thinking first appeared in studies of the US government's passivity in the face of genocide. The historical examples of American inaction during World War II were numerous and ranged from the restrictive nature of US immigration policy to the US Air Force's refusal to bomb Auschwitz. Some of these failures were criticized counterfactually during the war itself, but historians did not explore them in detail until the 1960s.[46] One of the first was Raul Hilberg who, in *The Destruction of the European Jews*, asserted that "many of those who are dead might have been alive were it not for the refusal and delays by our own State Department ... the War Refugee Board, and other agencies to take immediate measures [on behalf of the Jews]."[47] Subsequent works by scholars such as Arthur Morse, Henry Feingold, Walter Laqueur, Deborah Lipstadt, Yehuda Bauer, and Rafael Medoff, employed similar reasoning.[48]

The best-known and most controversial study, however, was David Wyman's *The Abandonment of the Jews* (1984).[49] This book surveyed many different rescue options for Jews during the Holocaust, but its most powerful counterfactual statements appeared in a chapter on the bombing of Auschwitz. After arguing on behalf of its feasibility in the summer of 1944, Wyman speculated:

> if the killing installations had been destroyed at this stage in the war,
> it would have been practically impossible for the hard-pressed
> Germans to rebuild them ... Without gas chambers and crematoria,
> the Nazis would have been forced to reassess the extermination
> program in light of the need to commit new and virtually non-existent
> manpower ... to mass killing ... If ... the earliest pleas for bombing ...
> had drawn a rapid response, the movement of the 437,000 Jews ...
> from Hungary to Auschwitz would most likely have been broken off
> and ... hundreds of thousands might have been saved.[50]

Indeed, as he added in a rhetorically powerful footnote, had the Allies destroyed Auschwitz, "Anne Frank might possibly have survived," since the train that took her family to the notorious camp in September 1944 "very likely would not have left Holland."[51] Building upon this chapter's claims, Wyman concluded his book with a counterfactual bang in a section entitled, "What Might Have Been Done." In it, Wyman listed a dozen specific policies that the US government could have attempted on behalf of European Jews (but did not), ranging from alerting them to the existence of the Nazi murder plan, pressuring the Germans to release them, and lobbying foreign countries to accept them as refugees. Even if only some of them had been attempted, he argued, "the Nazis ... would have ceased to believe that the West did not care what they were doing to the Jews. That might possibly have slowed the killing ...[and] hastened the decision of the SS ... to end the extermination." Even "if few or no lives had been saved, the moral obligation would have been fulfilled."[52]

Wyman's claims sparked considerable debate. A commercial and critical success, *The Abandonment of the Jews* had many supporters, most of whom agreed with its insistence that the Allies could have done more to shape what, in truth, were contingent events.[53] By contrast, critics highlighted the Allies' limited freedom of action and the inevitability of the Jews' fate under Nazi occupation.[54] This was especially true of the most hard-hitting critique, William D. Rubinstein's book, *The Myth of Rescue* (1997). Like Arendt's critics, Rubinstein pointed out that the odds were strongly stacked against history turning out differently because of the Nazis' unshakeable commitment to murder. In the face of Hitler's "absolute obsession with ridding Europe of the 'biological bases of Jewry,'" he argued, "the rescue of Jews ... was simply beyond the actual power of the Allies." Given the plain fact that "rescue was impossible," to claim otherwise was a naive example of "wishful thinking." Few of the rescue proposals listed by Wyman, according to Rubinstein, were actually considered at the time and most of them were impractical.

Had they been pursued, Rubinstein added, they actually would have made history turn out worse. Bombing Auschwitz, for instance, would have "utterly failed to halt the Nazi death machine" and might have led to bitter postwar claims about the Allies having "killed Jews in a foolish and unnecessary way." Pressuring Nazi Germany's allies not to deport Jews would have backfired and cost, rather than saved, thousands of lives. Pointing to the case of Hungary, Rubinstein argued that precisely when Hungarian dictator Miklós Horthy "halted the deportations ... the Nazis staged a *coup d'état* ... because of his lack of cooperation over the Jewish question. If Horthy had put a stop to the deportations before, Hitler would have staged the *coup* earlier ...[This would have led] to the deportation and extermination of Budapest's Jews, who ...[in actuality, ended up being] spared ... because the Soviet Armies were [by then] closing in on Auschwitz." Because of this counterfactual likelihood, and in view of the equally impractical nature of other hypothetical rescue plans, Rubinstein concluded that Allied behavior should be "viewed much more favourably" than was demanded by critics like Wyman. Instead of casting guilt upon "those who were innocent," it should be assigned where it truly belonged – to "Hitler, the SS, and their accomplices and no one else."[55]

Similar scholarly disputes swirled around the behavior of the Catholic Church and the Papacy during the Holocaust. This literature focused mostly on the sins of omission allegedly committed by Pope Pius XII during the years of the Second World War. These included his failure to publicly denounce the Nazis' murder of the Jews, his refusal to support Catholic clergy who were inclined to speak out against it, and his failure to protest the deportation of Italian Jews, especially those from Rome.[56] In making these points, historians often explored speculative scenarios related to the Church's options for rescue. Already in the early 1960s, for example, Gunter Lewy wrote that "had German Catholicism from the start adhered to a policy of resolute opposition to the Nazi regime, world history might well have taken a different course ... Hitler might not have dared going to war and literally millions of lives would have been saved."[57] More recently, similar points have been made by scholars such as Michael Phayer, John Cornwell, Susan Zuccotti, and Daniel Goldhagen.[58] Representative was Phayer's claim that "had Pope Pius chosen to make a public statement about the ... Jews ... his example would undoubtedly have been emulated by at least some other European bishops, and by many priests and laypersons."[59] Linking all of these studies was the fantasy that Papal action might have improved the course of history.

By contrast, defenders of the Pope's wartime behavior insisted that his pursuit of such actions would have made history turn out even worse. Scholars making this claim included Michael O'Carroll, Pierre Blet, Margherita Marchione, José M. Sanchez, and David G. Dalin, all of whom argued that Papal protests on behalf of the Jews would have led to more severe persecution.[60] As Dalin put it, "one might ask what could have been worse than the mass murder of six million Jews. The answer is the slaughter of hundreds of thousands more."[61] Scholars who shared this perspective argued that the Pope remained silent for fear of endangering *Mischlinge* and Jewish converts to Catholicism, both of whom remained vulnerable throughout the war.[62] One of the main pieces of evidence for this claim, according to Pius's defenders, was that when the Dutch Catholic clergy drafted a protest against the imminent deportation of Dutch Jews in the summer of 1942, the Nazis retaliated by deporting Jews who had converted to Catholicism. This experience apparently convinced Pius – who was then allegedly debating whether to draft his own protest – to keep silent for fear of making matters worse.[63] As Marchione argued: had the Pope actually spoken out, it "would ... not have saved a single victim and instead could have cost thousands ... of additional innocent lives." Worse still, "Pope Pius XII would have borne the blame for the death of additional victims."[64] As a result, it was best that he remained silent.

Similar controversy surrounded the behavior of ordinary Germans during the Holocaust. For some time, scholars have argued that the sporadic occurrence of popular protests against Nazi policies shows that German people could have undertaken more efforts on behalf of the Jews. Discussing the Bishop of Münster Clemens August Graf von Galen's 1941 speech against the T4 program, for example, J. P. Stern argued in *The Führer and the People* (1975) that "if the Churches had opposed the persecution of the Jews as they opposed the killing of the congenitally insane and the sick, there would have been no 'Final Solution.'"[65] More recently, Nathan Stolzfus analyzed the 1943 Rosenstrasse demonstrations of intermarried German women in Berlin on behalf of their arrested Jewish husbands, noting that "it is conceivable ... that under pressure the regime might have made concessions larger than the seventeen hundred persons released following the Rosenstrasse protest."[66] Summing up the position of these scholars, Daniel Goldhagen concluded: "in the face of ... popular opposition ...[the Nazi regime] backed down...Clearly had Germans cared about the welfare of Germany's Jews, then ... the capacity of the regime to pursue its eliminationist program would have been greatly restricted."[67]

Finally, there is the difficult case of Jewish attempts at rescue. This enormous topic deals with the behavior of Jewish leaders both in British-controlled Palestine and the United States. Many studies have addressed this topic, including works by Tom Segev, Shlomo Aronson, Haskell Lookstein, and Rafael Medoff.[68] But one of the most notable for its explicitly counterfactual dimensions was Yehuda Bauer's book, *Jews for Sale?* (1994).[69] In its prologue, Bauer wrote: "this book departs ... from accepted historical writing ...[by dealing] with might-have-beens ... Maybe historians are not supposed to do this, but there is hardly a historian who does not. Here at least I am going to do so consciously."[70] Bauer discussed many "what ifs?" in *Jews for Sale?*, but he mainly sought to determine whether SS chief Heinrich Himmler's willingness to exchange Jews for economic concessions in 1944 should have been further pursued by Jewish groups and the Allies. After studying the evidence, Bauer determined that the SS leader, convinced that the Nazis would probably lose the war, might have been willing to cut deals that would have allowed "tens of thousands, maybe hundreds of thousands [of Jewish lives to be] saved . . . in order for Nazism to survive."[71] But the Allied commitment to winning the war as soon as possible led them to avoid making any deals. "Himmler might have been willing to sell, given certain conditions," Bauer concluded, but "there were no buyers."[72] In making this claim, Bauer drew the causal conclusion that the forces of inevitability triumphed over those of contingency. But his "what if?" perspective also allowed him to make an important moral conclusion – namely, that it was wrong to vilify those Jews, such as Reszoe Kasztner, who tried to negotiate with the Nazis during the Second World War. Instead, they should be viewed as "heroes" for, unlike the Allies, "they did the correct thing at the right time."[73]

The diverse cases of bystander behavior during the Holocaust highlight the advantages and pitfalls of using counterfactual reasoning to draw moral judgments about the past. First, since counterfactuals lend themselves easily to moral judgments – since "could haves" can easily shade into "should haves" – they hold rhetorical appeal for all sides in historical disputes. David Wyman's claim that "Anne Frank might possibly have survived" had the Allies bombed the rail lines to Auschwitz is a clear example of using counterfactuals to appeal to readers' emotions. While this particular claim showing how history could have been improved appeals to our hopes, counterfactual claims depicting how history might have turned out worse exploit our fears. This was the case with David Dalin's assertion that a Papal protest against the Holocaust might have led to "the slaughter of hundreds of thousands" of additional Jewish victims. Both kinds of counterfactuals hold an innate appeal for those who believe that the study of history is not just about explaining, but also judging, the past.

The problem, of course, is that while counterfactuals have often been utilized to judge bystander behavior, they have failed to produce any scholarly consensus. This is partly because, as Michael Marrus has written, "with all . . . historical . . . 'might-have-beens' there is no way of proving or disproving [them]."[74] In the absence of objective facts, subjective agendas – often having to do with politics – play a more prominent role. The debates thus end up being intractable. The responsibility for this state of affairs lies equally with liberal and conservative scholars. Both have been involved in attacking and defending bystander inaction. Liberals have commonly criticized bystander inaction when the institutions responsible for it have been conservative. Many critics of Pius XII's silence during the Holocaust, for example, have been Catholics opposed to the Papacy's recent centralization of power.[75] Conversely, where the holders of institutional power have been on the left, critics predictably have hailed from the right. This was true in early postwar Israel, where right-wing Israelis criticized the Labor government for its alleged shortcomings in rescuing Jews during the Holocaust; it has also been true, more recently, in the United States, where conservative Jews have accused the liberal wartime Jewish establishment of insufficiently fighting for Jewish interests (a charge that is often intended to shore up present-day support for the State of Israel).[76]

Of course, to say that the counterfactual arguments cannot be disproved is not to say they are all equally plausible. For example, scholars have convincingly challenged the claim that Pius XII's silence was justified by the Nazis' retaliatory deportation of converted Dutch Jews in 1942 by showing that converts were due to be deported in any case.[77] It is less easy, however, to disprove the response of the Pope's defenders, who plausibly argue that, since he probably had no way of knowing that the Nazis were committed to killing these converts – or of knowing that the Nazis were committed to killing *all* Jews as they defined them – he was justified in staying silent in order to protect those who remained alive.[78] Here, we arrive at a speculative impasse, where the absence of agreed-upon facts forces us to rely upon personal biases to determine the "odds" of an event actually happening one way or another.

A related and final shortcoming of speculating about bystander behavior is that debating what "might have happened" can distort our understanding of what did. As various scholars have argued, focusing on what bystanders such as the US Government, the Pope, or the German people did *not* do during the Holocaust directs attention away from what the main perpetrators actually did. Representatives of both conservative and liberal positions agree in principle about this peril, although they express it differently. The conservative scholar Ronald Rychlak has tried to deflect guilt from bystanders by insisting that while "many individuals and groups have been blamed for the Nazis' actions ... Hitler and his top advisors ... deserve the vast majority – if not all – of the blame." Conversely, the more liberal historian, Doris Bergen, has directed her critical attention inward, arguing that the debate over Papal silence "can obscure even more terrible acts of commission," such as the fact that "Christians were not merely inactive in the Holocaust: they did the killing."[79] Although the political and moral implications of these comments diverge, they show that the counterfactual focus on secondary, instead of primary, levels of responsibility for the Holocaust can lead to misplaced moralizing.

Assessing the Holocaust's uniqueness: What if the Nazis had won the war?

Moral concerns have also informed counterfactual speculation about the Holocaust's uniqueness. In debating this topic, both the supporters and opponents of uniqueness used the premise of a Nazi victory in World War II to hypothesize how a triumphant Third Reich would have pursued its genocidal policies against Jews and other victims. The former argued that a Nazi victory would have led to the complete eradication of the Jewish people, while the latter claimed that it would have prompted a more destructive genocidal onslaught against non-Jews.

The supporters of uniqueness typically advanced their case with sweeping assertions about the totality of the Nazis' murder plans. Steven Katz, for example, argued in "The 'Unique' Intentionality of the Holocaust" (1981) that because Hitler's goal was "to make the world *judenrein* by the elimination of . . . all Jews as concrete individual human beings," it stood to reason that if "Hitler had had his way . . . there would have been no 'Jews' after the 1940s."[80] Similarly, Yehuda Bauer stressed that the Holocaust was set apart from other genocides by "its intended totality. The Nazis were looking for . . . all Jews. According to Nazi policy, all persons with three or four Jewish grandparents were sentenced to death for the crime of having been born. Such a policy . . . would have undoubtedly been applied universally if Germany had won the war."[81] Finally, William D. Rubinstein speculated that even if World War II had not actually been won by the Nazis, but merely "lasted longer . . . it seems certain that every Jew in Nazi-occupied Europe would have perished."[82]

Other scholars expanded upon these general claims by exploring the scenario of a Nazi wartime victory in specific national contexts. The first such portrayals appeared in the early 1960s and focused on the hypothetical fate of the Jews in Nazi-occupied England and the United States. Comer Clarke's book, *England Under Hitler*, and William Shirer's *Look* Magazine essay, "If Hitler Had Won World War II," both portrayed Anglo-American Jewry being murdered en masse by the Nazis.[83] More recent portrayals, by contrast, have been set in the

Middle East, with studies by Jeffrey Herf, Edwin Black, David Dalin, and John Rothmann, hypothesizing that the region's Jews would have fallen victim to the Nazis in the event of a Nazi military triumph. Of these recent accounts, the most important was Klaus-Michael Mallmann and Martin Cüppers's book, *Nazi Palestine*.[84] Based upon newly discovered Nazi plans to use Einsatzgruppen units to kill the Jews of North Africa, this study reasoned that, if the Nazis had broken through at El Alamein in 1942 and invaded the Jewish Yishuv, they would have found "a vast number of Arabs ... ready to serve as willing accomplices in the central task of ... implement[ing] ... the Holocaust in Palestine."[85] Before long, the authors grimly declared, "the Yishuv would undoubtedly have been completely annihilated."[86] Worse still, Mallmann and Cüppers speculated that if the Wehrmacht had been able to advance into the Caucasus, Einsatzgruppen units would have murdered Persian and Afghani Jews as well.[87] These speculative assertions supported the idea that the Holocaust's uniqueness lay in the relentless Nazi quest to kill all the Jews they could lay their hands on.

By contrast, other scholars have used counterfactual arguments to challenge the Holocaust's uniqueness. They have claimed that the Nazis' plans for other "racially inferior" groups, such as the Slavs, were no different from their plans for the Jews and have speculated that, if the Nazis had actually won the Second World War, they would also have subjected the Slavs to the fate of genocide.[88] The roots of this counterfactual argument date back to the early 1950s when Léon Poliakov hypothesized that "if the fortunes of war had given the Nazis enough time, the ... logic of genocide would have inexorably driven other peoples and races into the gas chambers."[89] Hannah Arendt echoed this point in the early 1960s, speculating that if "the Germans [had] won the war, the Poles would have suffered the same fate as the Jews – genocide."[90] More recently, historians Timothy Snyder, Adam Tooze, Donald Bloxham, Catherine Epstein, and Dan Stone have advanced this argument, citing the role of colonial demographic engineering schemes in the Nazis' decision to kill the Jews.[91] In doing so, they have challenged the Holocaust's uniqueness by drawing attention to what the event shares with, rather than what separates it from, other genocides.

Snyder, Tooze, and Bloxham were particular prone to use counterfactual reasoning in advancing their argument. As noted in Chapter 2, Snyder's book, *Bloodlands*, asserted that "If the German war against the Soviet Union had gone as planned, thirty million civilians would have been starved in the first winter, and tens of millions more expelled, killed, assimilated, or enslaved thereafter."[92] In making this claim, Snyder partly relied on the research of Adam Tooze, which stressed how Nazi plans for occupied Eastern Europe would have claimed additional millions of non-Jewish victims, had the war unfolded differently. Like Snyder, Tooze wanted to direct attention to "the full extent of the Third Reich's genocidal ambition" and argued that the "*Generalplan Ost* set a timetable for the extinction of the entire population of Eastern Europe" in the event that the Nazis were to win the war.[93] He further emphasized the importance of the *Hungerplan*, which envisioned the starvation of 20–30 million Slavs, as evidence of the Nazis' genocidal goals.[94] In reality, the plan exacted a huge toll from Soviet POWs in World War II, claiming 3.3 million victims who died of starvation. This fact prompted Tooze to make the important counterfactual claim that "if the clock had been stopped in early 1942, this programme of mass murder would have stood as the greatest single crime committed by Hitler's regime," exceeding that of the Holocaust.[95] Taking a similar position was Donald Bloxham who, invoking the scenario of the Nazis winning the war, argued that

> had German victory transpired, the death of European Jewry would
> have been only one part of a much larger programme of direct
> and indirect genocide. The swift defeat of the USSR would have
> permitted the enactment of the *Generalplan Ost* with all the horrors
> that that implied for tens of millions of Slavs. To their numbers
> could probably be added increasingly large sections of the ethnic
> German population itself, and many other groups besides, for . . . the
> regime thrived 'upon the supposed threat from the enemies which
> it persecuted so implacably.'[96]

Had a Nazi victory in World War II worsened the course of history, in other words, the genocide of the Jews would paradoxically be viewed as less of a singular atrocity.

   Bloxham employed additional counterfactuals to challenge the Holocaust's uniqueness. In one scenario, he questioned the claim, made by Katz, Bauer, and others, that all Jews would have been killed had "the Nazis won [the war]," arguing: "one might equally posit that, had the USSR been defeated as swiftly as Hitler intended, the policy of immediate killing of the majority of Jews would have not occurred, and the destruction of the Jews would have been a matter of more drawn-out attrition, as some of the unrealized Nazi deportation plans suggested."[97] In another scenario, he wrote:

> An equally plausible counterfactual is to ask what our conception of the Holocaust would be had not the last great episode of the final solution taken place. The murder of Hungarian Jewry in 1944 has done most to entrench the notion of a fully continental genocide. It was also the part of the genocide that hinged most on wartime contingency. In other words, it might well not have happened.[98]

Had the destruction of Hungary's Jews, in fact, been avoided, the Final Solution might not have acquired its unique reputation as an exhaustive hunt for every last Jew.[99] This possibility, moreover, would have had important repercussions for our view of Auschwitz. As Bloxham noted, "our understanding of the Holocaust has greatly been shaped by the murder of Hungarian Jewry. Auschwitz would probably not have achieved its notoriety had it not been the destination for this huge, most public, and arguably most avoidable national killing operation of the final solution."[100] In questioning the centrality of Auschwitz for understanding the Holocaust, Bloxham agreed with Snyder that the camp's infamous reputation had overshadowed the Holocaust's more representative killing centers, not to mention other instances of genocide from the same period.[101] His strategy of counterfactually displacing Auschwitz – and its distinctively modern killing methods – from the center of the Holocaust narrative thus served to emphasize the event's similarities with other genocides and undermine any claims to uniqueness.

The utilization of counterfactual reasoning both to defend and question the Holocaust's uniqueness reveals that it is methodologically neutral. It can be used both to shore up orthodox views and advance revisionist challenges to them. That said, all instances of counterfactual reasoning ultimately stand and fall based on their plausibility. Just as some of the claims made by revisionist critics of bystander passivity during the Holocaust were ahistorical or unlikely to change the course of history, the arguments of uniqueness critics can be questioned on the same grounds. Their claim that a Nazi victory in World War II would have led to a genocide of the Slavs was weakened by the fact that its putative cause – the *Generalplan Ost* – could never have been implemented in the first place. As scholars such as Mark Mazower and John Connelly have shown, there simply were not enough Germans to settle the lands that Hitler envisioned for his eastern empire without depopulating Germany and necessitating the importation of foreign workers.[102] This reality, which would have persisted even had Germany won the war, forced the Nazis to dragoon millions of Slavs to toil as forced laborers in the Reich to make up for its severe labor shortage. Yet since this policy worsened the labor shortage in the east – thereby heightening the value of workers there – the Nazis could not afford to kill the Slavs and instead decided to enslave them.[103] The contradictions of the *Generalplan Ost*, in other words, produced a pragmatic turn in Nazi policy towards the Slavs.

This turn was notable in light of the Nazis' very different treatment of the Jews. While the Nazis' inability to realize their geopolitical goals in the east led them to moderate their policies towards the Slavs, it had no moderating effect on their implementation of the Final Solution, which they continued to pursue relentlessly. An important reason for this divergence was the different status that Jews and Slavs held in Nazi ideology. While the Nazis viewed *all* Jews as posing a racial threat to Germany, they had no consistent ideological view towards the Slavs, whom they classified in hierarchical fashion, with some deserving better treatment than others.[104] This ideological ambivalence – together with the practical considerations involving labor – made it unlikely that a Nazi victory in the war would have led to a genocide of the Slavs. It probably would have worsened the fate of the Jews, however. As Dan Stone has recently argued, a victorious Nazi regime likely would have redoubled its efforts to complete the Final Solution by capturing and killing the Jews that remained in other Axis states.[105] This hypothetical course of events would have further highlighted the difference between the fate of the Jews and the Nazis' other victims in the Second World War. In other words, it would have further underscored the Holocaust's singularity. To be sure, since this scenario is no more empirically verifiable than the one it is meant to refute, neither side in the ongoing uniqueness debate can claim to have made their case decisively. Both sides' use of counterfactual reasoning ultimately served rhetorical purposes.

Averting the Holocaust: What if the Allies had remained neutral in World War II?

The issue of plausibility has also defined counterfactual claims about the Holocaust's non-occurrence. In recent years, scholars and journalists have explored the possibility that the Holocaust could have been prevented had the Allies remained neutral in World War II. As noted in Chapter 1, these claims were a feature of the revisionist effort to challenge World War II's reputation as the "good war." In hypothesizing that the Nazi genocide never would have taken place had the Allies abstained from intervening in the war, the revisionists aimed to diminish the Allies' moral stature by saddling them with a portion of blame for the Holocaust. In the process, however, they enraged critics, who attacked their claim's plausibility with counterfactual arguments of their own.

The claim that Allied neutrality would have prevented the Holocaust came partly from figures on the pacifist left. Nicholson Baker's book, *Human Smoke*, hypothesized that if England had forged a separate peace with Germany in 1940, the Nazis might have deported the Jews to Madagascar instead of killing them. Churchill's decision to fight the Germans, however, prompted them to pursue the Final Solution, with the result being that Britain shared culpability in the Holocaust. Other figures on the left took a similar stance. Peter Wilby, the former editor of the *New Statesman*, endorsed Baker's view in an article in *The Guardian* in 2008 where he asked, "Would the Holocaust have happened if there had been no war or if the Western democracies had acted against Nazi Germany earlier?" His answer was clear: "We can never know – though it is likely that, if Britain had made peace in 1940 after the fall of France, the Jews would have been sent to Madagascar. What is certain is that the war prevented any concerted attempt at rescue."[106]

Similar speculative arguments hailed from the isolationist right. Patrick Buchanan's study, *Churchill, Hitler, and "The Unnecessary War,"* argued that if the Western Allies had refrained from declaring war on Germany in 1939, the Nazis would have focused on invading the Soviet Union and left Western Europe alone. As a result, Western European Jews would have survived. Or as Buchanan laconically put it in a subsequent essay, "no war, no Holocaust."[107] Conservative British journalist Peter Hitchens took a similar position, arguing that if Britain "had stayed out of the war" then "it is certainly hard to argue that the fate of Europe's Jews would ... have been any worse than it was."[108] Indeed, their fate implicitly might have been better. Finally, another conservative scholar, Barry Rubin, drew on Eastern European revisionist arguments to insist that "If the USSR had not backed Hitler during the 1939–1941 period, there would have very possibly not been a Second World War or Holocaust at all."[109]

Whether emanating from the left or the right, these counterfactual claims unleashed a torrent of criticism from reviewers who angrily disputed their plausibility. These reviewers not only rejected the claim that the Holocaust would not have happened had the Allies remained neutral in World War II, they speculated that it would have been even worse. Historian David Engel argued that even if Allied neutrality had allowed the Nazis to realize the Madagascar Plan, its implementation would have produced "conditions for Jews that were supposed to lead to widespread death in any event."[110] Other critics insisted that Hitler eventually would have broken his separate peace with the Western Allies and proceeded, as Winston Groom noted, to "gobble ... up the rest of Europe, North Africa, and the Middle East."[111] This development, Adam Kirsch observed, would have been catastrophic, for "Hitler would have completed the genocide of the Jews, made Poland and Ukraine German slave colonies, depopulated Russia, and committed even more horrors against the 'Christian peoples' for whom Mr. Buchanan professes such solicitude when contemplating their sufferings under communism."[112] The promise of peace in the West, in short, was illusory. Summing up these critics' position, Andrew Roberts concluded: "I find the prospect of a Nazi-dominated Europe – which American and British pacifists would have done precisely nothing to prevent – just as abhorrent as pacifists find 'the obscenity of war.'"[113]

In debating whether or not Allied neutrality would have prevented or worsened the Holocaust, both sides displayed very different views of Nazism. The revisionists, for their part, were motivated by their political views to regard Nazism as comparatively benign: Baker's left-wing beliefs led him to universalize Nazism as a mere variant of traditional Western imperialism, while Buchanan's right-wing convictions led him to relativize Nazism as a lesser evil than communism. As a result of their beliefs, both men believed that Allied neutrality in World War II would have improved the course of history by averting the Holocaust.

By contrast, the defenders of the good war paradigm were convinced of the Nazis' fundamental evil and insisted that if they had triumphed in the war, they would have completed the Holocaust, thereby worsening the course of history. As with many of the other debates about the Holocaust's legacy, this one was also unresolvable. But it was significant for reflecting the ongoing battle to shape the memory of the Nazi past.

No Holocaust, No Israel?

The final counterfactual question related to the Holocaust was whether it was a precondition for the creation of the State of Israel. This premise has long enjoyed support across the political spectrum. Much of it has been expressed by left-wing anti-Zionists. But it has also been visible among conservative scholars and even non-partisan observers. Linking all these groups is their belief that Israel's creation was dependent upon the contingent fact of the Holocaust's occurrence, an event without which the state might not have emerged. Not surprisingly, this counterfactual scenario has sparked fierce opposition among Israel's defenders, many of whom have responded by stressing the inevitability of the Jewish state's creation. In short, competing models of political philosophy and historical causality have underpinned the debate about whether Israel would have been established without the Holocaust.

   Today, the phrase "No Holocaust, No Israel" is associated more with political extremists than academics. This is because in Europe, the United States, and the Middle East, various groups and individuals have made headlines by attributing Israel's birth to Western guilt for the Holocaust, accusing Zionists of manipulating and in some cases fabricating a heritage of victimization to justify the state's existence and its policies towards the Palestinians. This controversial claim has mostly been expressed in declarative rather than counterfactual fashion – that is, in assertions that the Holocaust enabled Israel's creation, rather than in speculative claims that without the Holocaust there would be no Israel. The declarative pattern of argumentation has been visible in recent statements by diverse anti-Zionists, such as former Iranian President Mahmoud Ahmadinejad, American journalist Helen Thomas, and the Ultra-Orthodox Jewish group, Neturei Karta.[114] The counterfactual version of the claim, meanwhile, has been expressed by neo-Nazi groups.[115]

It is not only extremists, however, but also mainstream academics, that have linked the Holocaust to the founding of the State of Israel. Scholars from both the liberal and conservative wings of the political spectrum have expressed support for the concept of "No Holocaust, No Israel." Among the former, Lebanese academic, Gilbert Achcar, has asserted that "without the Holocaust . . . I don't think the Zionist project would have come to fruition," while the post-Zionist Israeli scholar Bernard Avishai has written that "without the Holocaust, Israel might not have arisen in 1948."[116] Among more conservative-leaning historians, Henry Turner has argued that "without the Holocaust there would be no Palestinian problem, because there would be no state of Israel," while comparable statements have been made by Sebastian Haffner and Jeffrey Herf.[117]

Despite these supportive comments, many scholars have rejected the claim that Israel would not have been established without the Holocaust. The best-known refutation was offered by conservative German Jewish historian Michael Wolffsohn in his essay, "Without Hitler, No Israel?"[118] Published in 1988, this essay opposed the claim that the Holocaust helped create the Jewish State by insisting on the inevitability of the Zionist mission's success. As Wolffsohn put it, "Zionism had no need of the Holocaust as testimony to its legitimacy," for it was already "an active force in Palestine long before Hitler's advent" and would have been no less committed to creating a Jewish state in Palestine even "if there had been no Hitler."[119] Israel's creation, in other words, was a foregone conclusion. Viewing "the Second World War . . . and Hitler" as "unwitting catalysts" to "trends already well established," Wolffsohn concluded that "the Jewish State would have been proclaimed sooner or later, with or without the sanction of the United Nations."[120] Other scholars similarly stressed the inevitability of Israel's creation. The left-leaning post-Zionist Israeli historian Tom Segev argued that in light of the fledgling state's firm "social, political, economic, and military foundations," there was "no basis for the frequent assertion that the state was established as a result of the Holocaust."[121] Similarly, the conservative Israeli historian Efraim Karsh insisted that the forces of "global decolonization . . . would have led to the creation of a Jewish State . . . even if the Holocaust had never happened."[122] Still other scholars have shown how, in the absence of the Holocaust, the demographic growth of European Jewry in the mid-twentieth century would have made Israel's creation inevitable and established the state on a much firmer foundation than was the actually the case.[123]

Not all scholars rejected the "No Holocaust, No Israel" premise by insisting on the inevitability of Israel's creation, however. Some argued that the establishment of Israel was nearly *prevented* by the Holocaust. The eminent historians Gerhard Weinberg and Yehuda Bauer each made this claim with the aid of counterfactual arguments. Noting that "the Germans hoped to conquer the Middle East to kill the Jews," Weinberg argued that "if they had succeeded ... there would have been no State of Israel created in the Palestinian mandate ... for no one would have considered seriously the establishment of a Jewish state ...[where] there were no Jews."[124] Relatedly, Bauer speculated that "if the German Reich had held out one more year, it is doubtful whether there would have been any survivors at all. More Holocaust would have equaled less chance for a Jewish state ...Because of the Holocaust ... there were almost not enough Jews to fight for a state."[125] As it was, according to Bauer, "the attempt to establish a state almost failed." In 1946, President Harry S. Truman was aware of the plight of Jews in European DP camps and urged the British to admit 100,000 refugees into Palestine. "If the British had accepted Truman's demand," Bauer mused, "Israel might never have arisen," for "such a development would have taken the fire out of the DPs' demands" and earned Britain the United States' support for its policy of "suppress[ing]... the Jewish armed rebellion." As matters turned out, Great Britain's refusal put Truman at odds with the British government and eventually led him to support a Jewish state.[126] For Bauer, however, "the establishment of the State of Israel was far from being a foregone conclusion."[127]

Related to the claim that the Holocaust nearly prevented the creation of Israel was the hypothesis that the state's creation *before* World War II might have prevented the Holocaust from happening in the first place. Israeli politicians and self-described supporters of the country have long made such claims – most recently, Prime Minister Benjamin Netanyahu, who in 2009 said: "There are those who say that without the Holocaust the State would not have been established, but I say that if the State of Israel had been established in time, the Holocaust would not have taken place."[128] The clearest scholarly articulation of this claim was Lucy Dawidowicz's observation that had a Jewish state existed in 1939 . . . . the terrible story of six million dead might have had another outcome. As a member of the Allied nations . . . a Jewish state . . . might have been able to wield sufficient military and political clout to have inhibited [various Axis states]. . . from collaborating with the Germans in that murder. A Jewish state could have persuaded neutral countries to give Jewish refugees safe passage. A Jewish state would have ensured safe haven. A Jewish state would have made the difference.[129]

Comments such as Dawidowicz's were clearly intended to endorse one of Zionism's main rationales for creating a Jewish State in the first place – the need to protect Jews from persecution. Yet, not all supporters of Israel endorsed Dawidowicz's observation. Yehuda Bauer wrote that it was "sheer nonsense" to imagine that if there "had . . . been a Jewish state in 1939, the Holocaust would not have happened," as there was little chance that "a mini-state with one or two or three divisions would have stopped the German army that overran all Europe."[130] Also rejecting Dawidowicz's claim as "naïve and improbable" was William D. Rubinstein, who pessimistically speculated that "had an independent Jewish state existed in Palestine during the war . . . Hitler might well have made its conquest and destruction a much higher priority than it was actually given."[131] History, in other words, might have turned out even worse.

Such skeptical comments reveal that while counterfactual claims have often served specific political agendas, they have not done so in deterministic fashion. Speculative claims about the Holocaust's relationship to the creation of Israel show that counterfactual reasoning has been used both to attack and defend the Jewish State. In the same way that the scenario, "No Holocaust, No Israel," has been employed to challenge the Jewish state's legitimacy, other "what ifs?" – such as the Holocaust being prevented by Israel's earlier creation – have been used to support it. It is not only that counterfactual reasoning has been used to promote different political agendas, however. Scholars with the same political agendas have often arrived at different conclusions despite their shared use of counterfactual reasoning. The scholars who debated whether Israel's earlier creation might have prevented the Holocaust were all Zionists, yet their shared political affiliation did not produce a counterfactual consensus. These examples confirm that while counterfactual thinking can easily be used in partisan fashion, in the end it is politically neutral.

Conclusion

The considerable energy that historians have exerted exploring "what if?" questions related to the Nazi genocide testifies to the growing importance of counterfactual reasoning in Holocaust historiography. This development partly reflects the increased acceptance of counterfactual thinking within contemporary cultural and academic life. But it also reflects the contentiousness of Holocaust historiography. As the preceding pages have shown, Holocaust historians have employed counterfactual reasoning in the process of debating the origins, course, and legacy of the Nazi genocide. Although the Holocaust is hardly unique in having sparked scholarly debate, it has arguably generated more controversy than other historical topics. Throughout the postwar period, historians and other scholars have worked tirelessly to research the origins and consequences of the Final Solution. Yet despite more than half a century of work, disagreement on key questions persists. Given this reality, counterfactuals have often been a tempting way to resolve scholarly deadlock through rhetorical rather than analytical means. Indeed, "what if?" assertions can be seen as rhetorical trump cards that are used to win over audiences by appealing to their emotions instead of their reason. Social science research has shown that counterfactuals are closely associated with, and are often triggered by, powerful emotions, such as regret, blame, guilt, relief, and hope. People who view past events from these emotional perspectives tend to gravitate to "what if?" scenarios that imagine how the course of history might have been different.[132] Needless to say, these same emotions are closely associated with the Holocaust's legacy. They are emotions felt not only by the event's eyewitnesses and their descendants, but often by the scholars who study it. The growing use of counterfactuals may thus reflect the emotional need among certain scholars to finally resolve some of the Holocaust's lingering historical questions. By rhetorically appealing to people's feelings, counterfactuals may reflect an impatient desire to have the final word on Holocaust history.

If so, what does this trend mean for Holocaust memory? Fittingly enough, it is difficult to answer such a speculative question. But a tentative answer may be found in Saul Friedlander's seminal study, *Probing the Limits of Representation* (1992).[133] This edited volume featured a number of important scholarly interchanges on the implications of postmodern theory for the writing of Holocaust history. One of the most notable for its counterfactual dimensions was the interchange between Friedlander and Hayden White. White's essay, "Historical Emplotment and the Problem of Truth," drew on some of the claims of his famous structuralist study of historical narration, *Metahistory* (1973), to reflect on their consequences for Holocaust historiography. In this book, White argued that, in deciding how to represent the past, historians typically selected from various aesthetic modes of "emplotment" – tragic, romantic, comic, and so on – that shaped how they arranged, and drew conclusions from, historical facts. This claim implied that historians employed similar tools as novelists in representing the past. Indeed, it implied that history differed little from fiction.[134]

These points were provocative in and of themselves, but they became controversial once they were applied to the Holocaust. As various scholars pointed out, White's argument had relativistic implications. The most worrisome was that if history had no greater claim to truth than literature, Holocaust deniers would gain ammunition in their ongoing campaign to undermine belief in the facticity of the Nazi genocide. Uncomfortable with this implication, White used his essay in Friedlander's volume to backtrack somewhat, conceding that "in the case of an emplotment of the events of the Third Reich in a 'comic' or 'pastoral' mode, we would be eminently justified in appealing to 'the facts' in order to dismiss it from the lists of 'competing narratives' of the Third Reich."[135] White's apparent suggestion that historical "truth" inhered in facts independent of subjective narration was intended to be a progressive moral-political gesture, but Friedlander would have none of it. In response, he posited a simple counterfactual scenario to reveal that White's claim was epistemologically flawed. As Friedlander put it, "White's theses...appear untenable...[for] what would have happened if the Nazis had won the war? No doubt there would have been a plethora of pastoral emplotments of life in the Third Reich and of comic emplotments of the disappearance of its victims, mainly the Jews."[136]

Friedlander's use of counterfactual reasoning was significant, for by showing how the Holocaust would have been narrated triumphalistically in a Nazi-ruled world, he implied that there were no longer any limits – aesthetic, moral, or otherwise – to representing the Holocaust. If scholars traditionally saw the limits of representation as lying where historical narratives violated truth, counterfactual modes of representation, by being ungrounded in empirical reality, showed these limits to be unsustainable. Friedlander's conclusion further implied that if there were no limits to representing the Holocaust, there were no limits to speculating about it. There was nothing to keep scholars or anyone else from drawing whatever hypothetical conclusions they wished about the Holocaust.

The absence of limits has been confirmed by the many "what if?" scenarios that scholars have explored in interpreting the Nazi genocide's history and legacy. Over the course of the last generation, scholars have inquired whether Jewish victims during the Holocaust might have used alternate tactics to evade the grasp of their persecutors; they have wondered whether the genocide would have transpired in the absence of the regime's notorious dictator; and they have imagined how the bystanders might have done more to aid the cause of rescue. Scholars have further examined how a Nazi victory in World War II would have shaped views of the Holocaust's uniqueness, how Allied neutrality in the war might have prevented the Holocaust from taking place, and how the Holocaust's non-occurrence would have affected the creation of the State of Israel.

The absence of limits is further reflected in the diverse motives that have inspired scholars to imagine alternate outcomes to the Holocaust. Most scholars have been driven by a combination of analytical, moral, and political objectives. In pursuing them, they have typically displayed a presentist mindset. They have also frequently been revisionist in orientation, being eager to overturn historiographical orthodoxy. Hannah Arendt's speculative observations about Jewish behavior in the ghettos was all of these things: analytical, moralistic, politically motivated, presentist, and revisionist. The same can be said of various scholars' counterfactual critiques of bystander passivity and Allied intervention in World War II. To be sure, defenders of orthodox views have also availed themselves of counterfactual reasoning. Scholarly defenses of the Holocaust's uniqueness and the inevitability of Israel's creation show this to be the case. In light of these facts, speculating about the Holocaust clearly has no inherent analytical, moral, or political limits.

That said, the conclusions that scholars have drawn in answering their "what if?" questions have obeyed certain limits, insofar as they have followed distinct patterns. The first involves the relationship between mode of argumentation and conclusion. Revisionist critics of orthodox views have generally argued that hypothetical history would have turned out better than real history, while defenders of those views have argued that it would have been worse. These lines of argumentation have frequently been correlated – though not always – with the degree of scholarly support for the factors of contingency and determinism in shaping historical events. While revisionists have tried to show how chance circumstances easily could have led history to proceed in a different direction, defenders of orthodox views have argued that history's course was preordained. Thus, while the critics of the Papacy, the US Air Force, and the Jewish leadership of the Yishuv have argued that more could have been done to rescue Jews during the Holocaust, their defenders have replied that nothing would have changed the final outcome.

A second pattern involves the heated debates that have been sparked by such competing conclusions. These debates have been as inevitable as they have been intractable. Every time that scholars have invoked counterfactual scenarios, they have met with resistance because their arguments typically have been phrased in highly rhetorical and moralistic terms. As they evoke powerful emotions – regret, shame, and guilt, among others – these arguments inevitably call forth objections. The problem, however, is that counterfactual arguments, by definition, cannot be disproved. And so the debates between competing scholarly camps have often dragged on without resolution. This feature of counterfactual reasoning could easily be seen as one of its main liabilities. Yet it has thus far not had a detrimental impact upon its reputation.

Indeed, the final pattern that has defined counterfactual representations of the Holocaust has been the absence of a scholarly backlash against them. Rather than condemning counterfactual reasoning as such, scholars in recent debates have instead utilized it for their own purposes. This trend testifies to the pluralistic, inclusive nature of the contemporary historical profession. Having come to accept some of the relativistic implications of postmodern theory for the writing of history, scholars have refrained from objecting to counterfactuals in the manner of earlier, more positivist-minded scholars. Indeed, they have used them openly and will likely continue to do so into the future. With the erosion of the old limits of representation, the stage has been set for unlimited speculation.

The speculative turn in Holocaust historiography has important consequences for Holocaust memory. In important ways, the increasing tendency to ask "what if?" about the Holocaust points to the increasing normalization of the Nazi past. One reason for this is that counterfactual reasoning shares many features with the phenomenon of normalization.

Both involve revising orthodox views of the past, breaking moralistic taboos that surround it, encouraging efforts to universalize and relativize its significance, and – most importantly – employing new aesthetic methods of representing it. Indeed, when all is said and done, this may be counterfactualism's most powerful contribution to normalization. By freeing historical representation from the confines of real history, by emphasizing what might have happened instead of what did, by elevating rhetorical speculation over rational explanation, counterfactualism highlights the absence of limits to representing the Holocaust. In so doing, it shows how the Holocaust has become viewed like other pasts.

At the same time, however, counterfactual representations of the Holocaust have undermined the quest for normality by promoting the dialectic of normalization. Every effort to promote the normalization of the Nazi genocide has generated an attempt to preserve its exceptionality. There has not been a single aspect of the Holocaust that, having been subjected to counterfactual speculation, has been free of controversy. This discord has kept the Holocaust from being viewed in the dispassionate manner enjoyed by other, more "ordinary" pasts. The attempt to produce normality, in other words, has instead created its opposite.

There is little likelihood that this dynamic will change in the future. In all probability, counterfactual representations of the Holocaust will continue to flourish in the years to come. This is because counterfactual reasoning possesses not only a presentist, but also a futurist, orientation. Alternate pasts reflect not only how we view the world of today, but how we imagine possible tomorrows. Their imaginary visions always reflect fears and fantasies, nightmares and dreams, about how the world almost was and still could be. This futurist orientation has long informed thinking about the Holocaust. Historians may disagree about whether the Nazi genocide has – or should have – any "lessons," but fears that ignoring those lessons might lead history to repeat itself have long justified scholarly and popular engagement with the subject. It is no surprise, then, that the tendency of historians to use counterfactuals to derive causal, moral, and political lessons about the Holocaust reflects the larger goal of preventing the recurrence of genocide in the future.[137] However difficult it will be to realize this important goal in practice, one thing is for certain: as long as the Holocaust's legacy continues to inform our fears and fantasies, it will continue to find expression in counterfactual form.

4 NAZIS THAT NEVER WERE: NEW ALTERNATE HISTORIES OF THE THIRD REICH

'There's something wrong.'

They were walking down 25 Mai Strasse. On either side of them was Belgian artillery: captured guns displayed on low plinths.

'You just figured that out?' said Patrick.

'I mean about this place.'

The last time they'd been here was in September 1944, during Operation Sisal, and those final days before the Afrika Korps's assault on the city. With the Belgian administration in chaos and unable to evacuate its citizens, the job fell to mercenaries. The streets thronged with people desperate to escape, but only those with enough 'portable' – gold, jewels – had been saved. Everyone else was left to their fate. Burton felt a stirring of long-suppressed guilt. He could still remember them, the sweat, the panic, wide eyes set in beseeching faces . . .

'There are no blacks.'

'Say what?' said Patrick.

'Look at the faces.'

Apart from the heat, the palms, and baobab trees, they might have been in Hamburg.[1]

British writer Guy Saville's ominous portrayal of Nazi-ruled Stanleystadt, the new capital of the former Belgian Congo, in his recent novel, *The Afrika Reich* (2011), highlights the enduring appeal of imagining how the history of Nazi Germany might have turned out differently. In the half-century after World War II, scores of alternate histories were produced on the subject of Nazism. The appearance of new accounts since the turn of the millennium once more confirms that "what if?"

questions about the Third Reich continue to spark the imagination of writers, scholars, and filmmakers throughout the Western world. Recent alternate histories have appeared in many countries – the United States, Great Britain, and Germany, in particular – and have assumed a variety of forms, including novels, short stories, historical essays, films, television programs, and comic books. They have also tackled a variety of counterfactual questions: what if the Nazis had won World War II? What if Hitler had been assassinated? What if the Führer had survived the war? What if the Holocaust had never happened?

In addressing these and other questions, recent alternate histories resemble earlier accounts in offering divergent portraits of the Third Reich. While some continue to portray the Nazi era in moralistic fashion, most have subjected it to different strategies of normalization. Some alternate histories, produced mostly by figures on the political left, have universalized the Nazi past in order to call critical attention to contemporary problems. Other alternate histories, produced by representatives of the political right, have relativized the Nazi legacy in the pursuit of national self-assertion. In embracing these strategies of normalization, both kinds of narratives have expressed presentist views of the Nazi era influenced by the unsettled political climate of the post-9/11 world. Recent alternate histories have not always been motivated by political concerns, however. Other accounts have aestheticized the Nazi era by employing humor to transform it from a repository of lessons to a source of laughs. These accounts show how the passing of time has dulled the past's moral resonance and promoted unorthodox modes of representing it. Taken together, the depiction of the Nazi era in recent works of alternate history points to the ongoing normalization of memory. That said, countervailing forces remain at work. While many alternate histories have received a positive response, their attraction of criticism shows that memory remains contested.

The Nazis win World War II

The most popular topic in the entire field of alternate history has long been the Nazis winning World War II. Since the turn of the millennium, many new narratives on the subject have appeared in Great Britain, the United States, and Germany. These accounts have varied widely in their conclusions. But by instrumentally using the Nazi past to criticize present-day political trends and by employing humor to diminish Nazism's horror, they have promoted the process of normalization.

Great Britain

In Great Britain, alternate histories of a Nazi victory in World War II have traditionally come in one of two forms: the triumphalistic and the self-critical. The accounts that appeared between 1945 and the year 2000 offered vastly different depictions of a Nazi-ruled world and the British people's behavior in it. Early postwar narratives, such as Noel Coward's 1948 play, *Peace in Our Time*, patriotically endorsed the myth of the finest hour by asserting the exceptionality of British collaboration and the inevitability of the nation's self-liberation from Nazi rule. By contrast, subsequent works, such as Kevin Brownlow and Andrew Mollo's film, *It Happened Here* (1966) and Len Deighton's novel, *SS-GB* (1978), challenged the idea of the finest hour by portraying collaboration as commonplace and Nazi rule as permanent. This divide between triumphalistic and self-critical narratives reflected differing assessments of Britain's development after 1945; while the early patriotic tales expressed the fervent hope for national renewal, the pessimistic narratives that followed reflected the bitter recognition of post-imperial decline. This divided pattern persisted into subsequent decades. During the 1980s and 1990s, upbeat narratives by historians, such as Niall Ferguson and Andrew Roberts, defended the finest hour myth by imagining the British people behaving honorably in the face of a Nazi invasion, while accounts by novelists and journalists, such as Robert Harris and Madeleine Bunting, challenged it by asserting the likelihood of collaboration.[2] Significantly, this latter trend has defined British alternate histories since the turn of the millennium.

An excellent example of the self-critical impulse was provided by the Welsh-born Canadian novelist Jo Walton's "Small Change" trilogy of numismatically-titled books, *Farthing* (2006), *Ha'Penny* (2007), and *Half a Crown* (2008) (Figure 11).[3] Originally published in England, the series features a hard-boiled British detective named Peter Carmichael who becomes progressively enmeshed in his country's descent into fascism after British leaders forge a separate peace with the Nazis. As described in *Farthing*, the counterfactual point of divergence is Rudolf

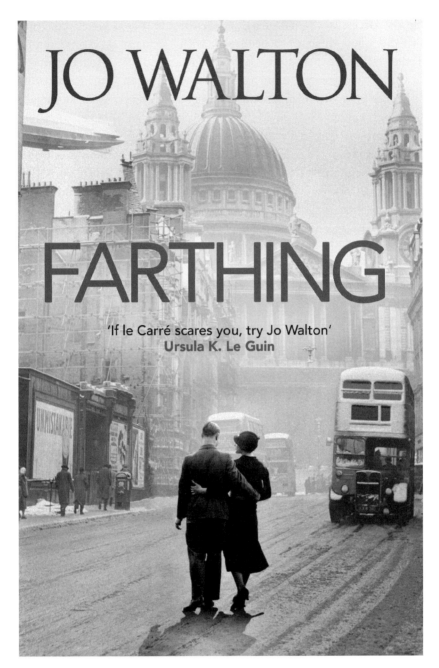

Figure 11. Jo Walton's novel, *Farthing* (2006), portrays England forging an alliance with Nazi Germany. Note the zeppelin on the London skyline.

Hess's successful flight to England in May of 1941, which convinces British leaders to sign a peace treaty with Germany shortly thereafter. The novel is set nearly a decade later in 1949 and focuses on the murder of one of the treaty's main negotiators, Sir James Thirkie, a former MP and prospective candidate for Prime Minister, who belongs to England's ruling aristocratic elite, the "Farthing Set" (named after their headquarters, Castle Farthing, in Hampshire). As the novel opens, Thirkie is discovered stabbed to death in his bedroom with a yellow Star of David pinned to his chest. Suspicion immediately falls upon a Jewish guest staying at the estate, David Kahn, a banker and fierce anti-Nazi, who is married to the daughter of the Farthing Estate's owner and government minister, Lord Eversley. Most of the novel follows Detective Carmichael as he tries to unravel the crime and determine whether Kahn is guilty or being framed for political motives. Carmichael increasingly comes to suspect the latter after Thirkie's brother-in-law, Mark Normanby, is named Prime Minister and tries to seize dictatorial powers using the pretext of a "Bolshevik Jewish menace" facing the country.[4] Eventually the detective discovers that the killers are, in fact, Normanby and his wife Angela, who want to eliminate Thirkie because of his opposition to Normanby's power-grab. Yet when Carmichael informs his boss at Scotland Yard that he has cracked the case, he is told to drop it and charge Kahn with the crime instead. Carmichael protests, but his boss coldly reveals that he knows of the detective's homosexuality and forces him to go along with the frame-up for the sake of political expediency. As the novel concludes, Carmichael reluctantly recognizes that his silence has turned him into a collaborator with his country's fascist government.

The sequel, *Ha'Penny*, picks up the story in 1949 with England sliding deeper into fascism. The novel's main plot focuses on Carmichael's effort to prevent the assassination of Germany's dictator, Adolf Hitler, while on a state visit to England; its primary subplot, however, examines the British people's readiness to collaborate with the Nazis. This readiness is epitomized by the tale's main character, a politically apathetic actress named Viola Larkin, who resists the effort of her politically engaged friends to enlist her in the assassination plot, which is supposed to take place during a theatrical performance attended by Hitler and Prime Minister Normanby. As she tells her Uncle Phil, who is involved with the plot: "You say Normanby had a bloodless coup. What's the difference between that and the bloody coup you're suggesting? ... Nobody cares ... politics is politics. Mr. Churchill ... wouldn't really do anything differently from ... Normanby... As for Hitler, what happens in the Reich isn't any of our business."[5] Larkin goes so far as to declare that ordinary Britons actually "like the idea of our having a proper leader, a fuhrer to sort us out."[6] Finally, Larkin's stance is shown to be representative of other Britons. When she tells one of the plotters, an Irishman named Devlin, that she does not "think Stalin's any better than Hitler," he responds by saying: "England is like a country of sleepwalkers, walking over the edge of a cliff, and has been these last eight years. You're prosperous, you're content and you don't care what's going on the other side of the Channel as long as you can keep on having boat races and horse shows."[7] In the face of such apathy, the efforts of the patriotic plotters predictably fail. At the novel's conclusion, Carmichael warns Normanby and Hitler about the bomb's presence in the theater and the two dictators end up surviving the ensuing blast.

The trilogy's final installment, *Half a Crown*, opens a decade later in 1960 and portrays England as having fully embraced fascist rule. By this time, the Nazis have defeated the Soviets by nuking Moscow, while the Japanese have defeated the United States. In England, domestic anti-Semitism has reached a fever pitch as Normanby's government decides to deport the country's Jews to a new death camp located near the southeastern English town of Gravesend. Most Britons are comfortable in this new dystopian world. As the novel's protagonist, an eighteen-year-old girl under Carmichael's guardianship, Elvira Royston, declares to one of her teenage friends, "fascism ...[is] fun!"[8] By contrast, Detective Carmichael has developed moral qualms about his complicity with the new order. Although he is named director of a British version of the Gestapo called "The Watch," he works behind the scenes to smuggle British Jews to freedom. This activity helps him maintain his dignity. Or as a colleague encouragingly puts it: "You failed a test, yes ... but you have never surrendered your soul. And I believe it's the same for the whole country."[9]

This remark serves as a hopeful beacon that allows the novel to end on a redemptive note. *Half a Crown* goes on to portray the emergence of domestic political upheaval in England after Normanby orders the deportation to Gravesend of a group of British right-wing extremists belonging to the ultra-nationalist Ironsides organization, who are hoping to install the Duke of Windsor on the throne as Edward VIII and establish a more dictatorial fascist government. Most ordinary Britons do not support the radical nationalists, but they believe that Normanby's government has exceeded its authority in indiscriminately deporting British citizens without confirming whether they actually belong to the group. As popular demonstrations erupt, the British people rediscover their democratic values. This trend culminates with the political awakening of the otherwise apolitical Elvira. After she naively betrays Carmichael by exposing his clandestine activity on behalf of British Jews, she makes an about-face after being told the truth about Normanby's role in murdering Thirkie twenty years earlier by Carmichael's confidante, the Foreign Minister, Sir Guy Braithewaite. The novel concludes with Elvira disclosing the explosive news to Queen Elizabeth at a debutantes' ball held at the royal palace and the Queen thereupon appearing on national television to announce Normanby's arrest and new national elections. As the novel ends, the message is clear: "England was taking her first tottering steps towards being free again."[10]

Despite this upbeat ending, Walton's trilogy advanced a self-critical message in asserting Great Britain's potential to embrace fascism. In many ways, the author followed in the tradition of liberal British writers from the 1960s and 1970s in using her novels to subtly express her political views. An award-winning fantasy and science fiction writer born in Wales in 1964 (and currently a Canadian citizen), Walton stands on the liberal wing of the political spectrum and has openly discussed how the events of the post-9/11 world influenced her trilogy. As she put it in a 2009 interview,

> watching the US and the UK defy the UN and invade Iraq on a trumped up excuse was just too much like Hitler's invasion of Czechoslovakia and Poland for me. I'd been furious, and there hadn't been anything I could . . . do about it. Then there . . .[were the violations of] civil liberties . . . I started writing *Farthing* just after the Abu Ghraib revelations. I didn't set out to write something to draw explicit parallels. But it would be disingenuous to say I wasn't thoroughly aware of the implicit ones.[11]

In suggesting that democratic societies were capable of fascist behavior, Walton universalized the significance of the Nazi era in the fashion of earlier liberal writers. That said, her narrative was less self-critical by virtue of its happy ending. Whereas the alternate histories of the 1960s and 1970s saw no escape from fascist rule, Walton's tale ultimately affirmed the British people's ability to liberate themselves and restore their democratic values. Her critique of the finest hour, like her normalization of the Nazi past, was thus comparatively moderate.

Strongly resembling Walton's narrative was bestselling British writer C. J. Sansom's novel, *Dominion* (2012) (Figure 12).[12] Also set in a world in which England made a separate peace with Germany in 1940, the novel takes place over a decade later in the year 1952, in a climate of intensifying collaboration between the two nations. *Dominion* is a fast-paced thriller that focuses on the efforts of a small cell of British resisters to prevent the German Gestapo from capturing a brilliant, but mentally imbalanced, scientist named Frank Muncaster, who possesses confidential information about the United States' atomic bomb project. Much of the novel is composed of cat-and-mouse action scenes set in a variety of locales, ranging from London to the British countryside. *Dominion* is most significant, however, for its bleak portrait of Britain's decline following its peace with Germany. Vividly symbolized by the "shabby and downtrodden" condition of London, which is increasingly swathed in a suffocating fog, the nation's decline prompts the novel's protagonist, a civil servant named David Fitzgerald, to realize that the Anglo-German alliance has failed to preserve Britain's empire. Fearing for his country's future and increasingly concerned about his own fate as a half-Jew, he resolves to join the resistance.[13] His fears soon prove prescient when Britain's Prime Minister Lord Beaverbrook decides to double down on his policy of Realpolitik and deport the country's Jews to Germany in exchange for favorable trade deal with the Reich. Countless ordinary Britons support this collaborationist policy and participate in the ensuing roundup of British Jews. This activity – which is epitomized in the novel by the cooperation between the craven London Special Branch agent, William Syme, and the brutal Gestapo official, Gunther Hoth – underscores Britain's moral collapse. By depicting Britons assisting the evil goals of the Nazis, *Dominion* asserts the British people's capacity to become collaborators. As Fitzgerald's wife, Sarah, bluntly puts it: "We used to think British people could never become Fascists . . . But they can. I suppose anybody can, given the right circumstances."[14]

Like Walton's trilogy, however, *Dominion* also ended on a redemptive note. Although Fitzgerald's cell of resisters fails to accomplish its mission of delivering Muncaster to the Americans (he tragically commits suicide in order to avoid falling into the Gestapo's hands), it ends up benefiting from the capricious course of historical events.

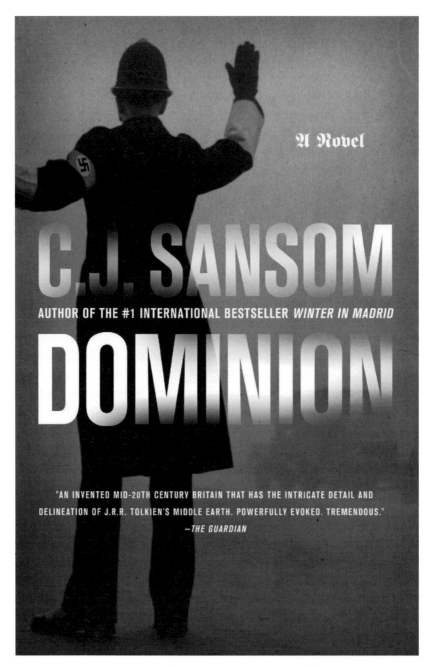

Figure 12. C. J. Sansom's novel, *Dominion* (2012), depicts the British collaborating with the Germans, as is shown by the London bobby with the swastika armband.

Following Hitler's death and the eruption of a civil war in Germany between the SS and the Wehrmacht, British resistance forces led by Winston Churchill exploit the renewed uncertainty in British–German relations to topple the country's fascist government and seize power. In the novel's epilogue, set in October of 1953, resistance forces, supported by the British working class, are well on their way to restoring democracy to the wayward nation. Following tense negotiations with former Fascist officials, who are told they have no future in the country, Churchill makes clear that Britain has turned the corner towards a better future. Signaling his hope for national reconciliation and renaissance, he declares in the novel's concluding lines, "The exiles will be returning soon. To help us rebuild. Rebuild! We need them all now!"[15]

Dominion's hopeful ending, however, did not overshadow its larger cautionary message. Like Walton's trilogy, the novel challenged the myth of the finest hour by asserting the British people's capacity to collaborate with fascism. In submitting this message, Sansom was motivated by some of the same motives as Walton. Born in 1952, the writer stands on the political left (he calls himself a "radical, independent socialist") and has often used his fiction to express his opposition to right-wing politics, nationalism, and war.[16] It was no surprise, therefore, that in writing *Dominion*, he sought to critique present-day trends. Unlike Walton, however, his target was not post-9/11 British foreign policy, but contemporary European nationalism. According to Sansom, Europe's economic crisis (which he attributed to the "free-market ideology that has dominated the world for the past 30 years"), was responsible for making "fiercely nationalist, anti-immigrant, and sometimes openly Fascist nationalist parties ... significant forces in politics again."[17] While pointing to familiar cases, such as Greece and Russia, Sansom was particularly concerned about the efforts of the Scottish National Party to promote the cause of secession from Britain.[18] For the half-English and half-Scottish writer, this "heartbreaking" development prompted him to write *Dominion* as part of a larger effort to expose the dangers of nationalism in the past and present. As he concluded, "if this book can persuade even one person of the dangers of nationalist politics ... in Europe ... it will have made the whole labour worthwhile."[19]

In taking this stance, however, Sansom subtly universalized the significance of the Nazi era. His critique of nationalism was well intended, but his suggestion that all societies had the potential to turn fascist effaced the Third Reich's singularity. Sansom, of course, took pains to emphasize Nazism's evil in his novel. But he did so less for its own sake – that is, to comment about Nazism as a phenomenon – than to criticize the British for abetting it. As with Walton's trilogy, however, his novel's redemptive ending ultimately muted its self-critical thrust and limited its normalizing effect.

By contrast, other recent alternate histories offered less comforting narratives. One of the most notable was prominent Welsh writer Owen Sheers's acclaimed novel, *Resistance* (2007) (Figure 13).[20] Set in the isolated Black Mountains of rural Wales in 1944, *Resistance* takes place in a world in which the failure of the Allied landing at Normandy enables the Germans to launch a successful counter-attack against England. The novel opens dramatically on a September morning when a small group of Welsh women living in the rural Olchon Valley awaken to discover that their husbands, together with the rest of the local men, have vanished. Before long, one of the women discovers a discarded pamphlet in a milking shed that suggests the men have gone underground to join Auxiliary Units belonging to the nascent British resistance movement. *Resistance* goes on to portray the women's struggle to survive the difficult months that follow. They face enormous challenges undertaking the arduous chores that need to be completed on their respective farms. But they face an even greater challenge when a small patrol of German soldiers arrives and announces their assumption of control over the area.

The women initially remain distant from the Germans, but as the novel unfolds, they slowly slide into collaboration. This development is seen most clearly in the relationship between the novel's two main characters, the Welsh farmer, Sarah Lewis, and the Wehrmacht Captain, Albrecht Wolfram. Following the disappearance of her husband, Tom, Sarah has to fend for herself when Wolfram arrives at her cottage to announce his patrol's presence. Her initial instinct is to resist, but she is gradually disarmed by Wolfram's moderate, non-threatening demeanor. Thirty-three years of age, Wolfram is portrayed as "practically geriatric" and "not enough of a Party man to have risen any further" in the Nazi hierarchy.[21] Although he is dedicated to fulfilling his assignment, Wolfram is not ideologically committed to the Nazi worldview. Indeed, he wants nothing more than to drop out of the war, with all of its "fear and fighting," and "give himself and his men a rest."[22] Realizing that the "secretive" valley will provide him cover, Wolfram merely needs to secure provisions to enable his patrol to survive off the grid.[23]

Figure 13. Luftwaffe planes patrol the skies over rural Wales in Owen Sheers's novel, *Resistance* (2007), which imagines Welsh women collaborating with the German invaders.

He therefore turns to Sarah and the other women for help, offering his men's labor in exchange for food.

Their response, in turn, constitutes the novel's dramatic and ethical core. Although the women are initially reluctant to accept Wolfram's offer, the arrival of an unusually harsh winter – and the endangerment of their livestock – leads them change their mind. Before long, the five members of the German patrol are each assigned to work on a different farm. Yet, this "recipe for mutual survival," as Wolfram calls it, gradually evolves into something deeper.[24] As Christmas arrives, the men give the women homemade wreaths and they soon don the work clothes of their vanished husbands in completing their chores. Predictably, one of the men has a fleeting romantic encounter with one of the women's daughters. Even Sarah finds it difficult to resist the Germans' advances, especially when Wolfram gives her a gramophone on her birthday and plays her a beguiling Bach cello suite. Against the backdrop of these developments, the women's resistance begins to break down. As the members of "the patrol were becoming less German in the women's eyes and more just men," the two groups increasingly begin to collaborate.[25]

In the end, however, their ability to work together is shattered by a tragic turn of events. Although Wolfram thinks he has successfully cut off the women from the outside world (he cancels mail service from the local village into the valley, implying that all the inhabitants are deceased), the decision by one of Sarah's friends, Maggie, to enter a young colt in a local agricultural fair (and, more importantly, her decision to bring one of the German soldiers, Alex, to help handle the animal) tips off local resistance forces about the women's collaboration with the Germans. When a sniper's bullet suddenly kills the colt from out of the blue, it becomes clear that the women are marked for death. Wolfram responds by begging Sarah to flee with him, but she ultimately decides to escape by herself into the unknown. As the novel ends, Sarah is shown heading into the hills at night, without food or water (and having just entered the date of her "death" in the family Bible, which she leaves behind on a table). With this conclusion, *Resistance* – true to its name – implies that Sarah successfully resists the temptation to collaborate and preserves her faith in freedom.

This ending notwithstanding, *Resistance* subverted its title's meaning by portraying British opposition to the Nazis as less common than collaboration. In doing so, Sheers was motivated by some of the same considerations as Walton and Sansom. A celebrated poet, novelist, and journalist, Sheers (born in 1974) is known for his anti-war beliefs, which he has often expressed in his poetry and drama.[26] These beliefs clearly colored the plot of *Resistance*. To be sure, Sheers did not write his carefully crafted and highly atmospheric novel purely for presentist purposes. Yet, he made clear that Britain's involvement in the war in Iraq was an important influence. In a 2007 interview, he noted that the novel was "informed by the fact that we are in a very questionable war at the moment" and later observed that "when I'd sat down to write *Resistance*, I wanted to write an anti-war novel that used an alternative Second World War to bring questions of sacrifice, collaboration and occupation close to home. To create a story which tried to use that narrative as a lens through which to ... question all wars."[27] Put differently, Sheers's interest in exploring the "complex territory ... where the lines between resistance and collaboration blur" led him to project the moral ambiguities of the present back into the past.[28]

In the process, however, Sheers exhibited a normalized view of the Nazi era. In explaining the roots of collaboration, he ultimately pointed to such universal human needs as companionship, security, and survival. Sheers's conclusion represented a valuable supplement to earlier alternate histories, many of which explained collaboration as the result of more unseemly motives, such as greed, opportunism, and prejudice. Yet, Sheers overlooked the issue of ideology, especially the appeal that Nazism had for countless collaborators during the Second World War. The downplaying of ideology was reflected in Sheers's humanized portrayal of his German characters, especially Wolfram, whose moderate demeanor made him the prototypical "good German." To be sure, Sheers scattered enough fleeting references to Nazi criminality throughout the novel – to tortured resistance fighters, burned-out villages, and deported Jews – to pre-empt the charge of being soft on Nazism. Yet, such passages in *Resistance* were offset by others depicting the Germans' humanity. Perhaps the most representative appeared midway through the novel, when the sister of a British resistance fighter tells him that the Germans are "no different from you ... If we'd won, our boys ... would be ... doin' the same."[29] This remark, and others like it, had the effect of neutralizing the impression of German criminality and dulling the narrative's moral edge. In the end, by humanizing the Germans; by empathetically explaining, rather than condemning, collaboration; and by rejecting a redemptive ending, Sheers's novel went beyond those of Walton and Sansom in normalizing the Nazi era.

Resembling *Resistance* in its anti-redemptive tone was British writer Guy Saville's novel, *The Afrika Reich* (2011). Saville's account of a Nazi victory in World War II diverged from other alternate histories by being set not in England but Africa. A brisk thriller, *The Afrika Reich* focuses on the struggle of its protagonist, a tough British war veteran named Burton Cole, to complete a secret mission meant to help Great Britain keep pace with Nazi Germany in the two countries' race for colonial supremacy in Africa. The year is 1952 and the Nazis have won the Second World War thanks to Britain's decision to forge a separate peace with Germany following Hitler's capturing of the British Expeditionary Force at Dunkirk in June of 1940. Among the key decisions that follow is Prime Minister Halifax's agreement at the Casablanca Conference of 1943 to divide up Africa with Germany, a move that paves the way for "a decade of peace and prosperity" for both countries.[30] Behind the scenes, however, trouble is brewing, for a power struggle between the SS and the Wehrmacht in Africa threatens to unleash an old-style colonial war between Germany and Britain over the spoils of empire.

The power struggle results from disagreement within the Nazi state over how to run the African continent. For the better part of a decade, the SS has ruled Germany's colonies with an iron fist. Under the administration of the novel's chief villain, the fanatical SS Governor General of the Congo, Walter Hochburg, millions of Black Africans have been put to work as slave laborers for German companies (for example, Volkswagen, which controls the rubber plantations of the Congo) and many are eventually deported to the Sahara desert in conjunction with Heinrich Himmler's decision in 1949 to pursue an ambitious program of "ethnic reallocation and consolidation."[31] Yet, there are problems. The high death rate of African slaves and an insufficient supply of German settlers create a labor shortage that the SS addresses by transporting Russian workers to Africa. The Germans even start transporting Jews to the continent from their reservation on Madagascar (ten million have been deported there by the early 1950s) to solve the problem. These setbacks notwithstanding, Hochburg remains dedicated to his vision of a racial utopia and plots to seize British-controlled Northern Rhodesia to consolidate German control of the region. His plan causes a rift with the Wehrmacht, however, which, desperate to avoid hostilities with Great Britain, resolves to stop Hochburg in his tracks. This background sets the stage for the novel's chief plot line: Burton Cole's commissioning by a cabal of British government officials and Wehrmacht officers to assassinate Hochburg and put an end to his reckless racial engineering agenda.

Much dramatic action ensues, yet the deeds of Cole and the novel's other supporting characters are ultimately less significant than *The Afrika Reich*'s overall portrait of Nazi evil. The novel is full of repellant Nazi sadists and scenes of gruesome torture that straddle the line between the ghoulish and the gothic. Hochburg, for example, paves the Schädelplatz plaza of his SS headquarters with the skulls of murdered Africans; he orders that the corpses of German dead be mixed into the cement used in the German-built freeway system (known as the Pan African Autobahn) for the purpose of "Aryanizing the soil of Africa"; and he devises endless methods of torturing Cole and the members of his assassination team (eye gouging, genital abuse, and auto-da-fés are standard fare).[32] In the end, the SS invasion of Northern Rhodesia is beaten back by the British, Cole escapes with his life, and Hochburg, frothing at the mouth, vows revenge. *The Afrika Reich*, in short, represents a Nazi victory in World War II in dystopian terms.

In its own way, however, the novel also universalized the significance of Nazism. Like Walton, Sansom, and Sheers, Saville underscored the evil of the Third Reich in order to critique the willingness of Great Britain to collaborate with it. The novel makes clear that Britain's decision to pursue "Peace for Empire" entails an unacceptably high moral cost.[33] The British work together with the Germans to build the Pan African Autobahn, for instance, despite the high death toll for African slave laborers. Moreover, British amorality profoundly affects the novel's protagonist, Cole. His assigned task, assassinating Hochburg, is ultimately revealed to be a suicide mission given him by a British official, Jared Cranley, who is bent on revenge after discovering that Cole is having an affair with his wife. Saville, finally, did not merely condemn the amorality of the British, but also the Americans. He portrayed the United States as partly responsible for letting the Nazis win the war by adhering to an isolationist stance of neutrality. He also showed the US helping to sustain the Nazi regime after its wartime triumph by having American companies pursue profitable joint ventures with the SS in Africa.[34] In short, by criticizing the Third Reich's aiders and abettors nearly as much as the Nazis themselves, Saville implied that fascism was hardly restricted to the Germans and could tempt liberal democratic states as well.

Saville wrote from a combination of motives. Having spent time as a journalist living in North Africa, he was well prepared to place his novel in an African setting. He was also inspired by his literary interests, especially his admiration for Joseph Conrad's *Heart of Darkness* and Philip K. Dick's *The Man in the High Castle*.[35] Equally significant in shaping the tone of Saville's narrative, however, were his critical views of Anglo-American foreign policy in the post-9/11 era. In a recent interview, the writer declared his eagerness to challenge British myths about World War II – especially the idea of "the good Allies versus the evil Nazis" – because of how they "set the context for conflicts ever since ... including the invasion of Iraq, which was defined as the morally correct, democratic powers overthrowing the wicked Saddam." Saville also noted his desire to "question the 'finest hour' myth" and challenge "the cherished British notion that fascism 'couldn't happen here,'" stating that "I don't believe there is anything intrinsically anti-fascist in the British character." This explains why he refrained from making his novel's protagonist, Cole, morally admirable and instead portrayed him as a traumatized, opportunistic, and violent figure who fails to achieve his goal of eliminating Hochburg. Symbolizing the "futility of revenge," Cole, Saville observed, "parallel[s] America inasmuch that he 'goes to war' but ultimately achieves little beyond slaughter."[36]

The reception of recent British alternate histories suggested significant support for their universalizing agendas. For one thing, the narratives received considerable attention. Most of them were commercial successes, being published not only in British and American editions, but international ones as well.[37] *Dominion* and *The Afrika Reich* were bestsellers; *Resistance* was turned into a major film (released in 2011), while *Dominion* was serialized for broadcast on BBC Radio in 2013. All of the alternate histories received positive reviews from major journals and newspapers. Walton's trilogy was praised as "terrific," "convincing," and "one of the best speculative works produced in years."[38] Sheers's novel was hailed as "one of the best debuts of recent years ... an original and brilliantly executed work of fiction," while the film version's reviews were equally positive.[39] Saville's *Afrika Reich* was described as "scarily convincing," and "politically sophisticated."[40] And Sansom's *Dominion* was praised as "absorbing," "evocative," and "one of the best books of 2012."[41]

Many reviewers supported the books' normalizing tendencies. One reviewer of Walton's *Farthing*, for instance, noted approvingly that "the analogies of this alternate history to our own world today are there to be drawn," while another agreed that the novel was "as much about Bush and Blair as ... about World War II."[42] Sheers's *Resistance*, meanwhile, received praise for its anti-war subtext. While one observer wrote that the novel was "an eye-opening invitation to imaginatively experience the occupation we [British] inflict so self-confidently on other people," another said that its portrait of German soldiers occupying Britain "provides food for thought on the topic of British military engagement around the world."[43] Similarly, reviewers of *The Afrika Reich* praised its portrait of British–German collaboration as "credible," while reviewers of *Dominion* described it as a convincing "reproof to those who believe that no form of fascism could ever take root here."[44]

At the same time, however, scattered critics expressed discomfort with the ways in which the alternate histories normalized the Nazi era. Some noted the extent to which *Resistance* humanized the Germans, pointing out that in the film version, the German characters "are depicted very differently to most of cinema's Nazis ... they do not wear red armbands decorated by swastikas that might prejudice us against them."[45] This neutral portrait did not bother some reviewers, one of whom praised Sheers for getting readers to "[care] for everyone – Welsh or German or English." Yet another complained that the sympathetic portrait of the Germans ultimately made "*Resistance* ... very strangely, a novel in which Nazism triumphs and yet evil is missing."[46] Other critics expressed reservations about *Dominion*'s portrayal of Britain's willingness to collaborate with Nazi Germany. According to one reviewer, it was doubtful that the British people, a "cross-grained, bloody-minded folk rarely willing to do as they are told," would "have allowed such a dystopia to grow up around them without a fight."[47] On the whole, however, such criticisms were exceptions to the rule.

Taken together, recent British alternate histories about a Nazi victory in World War II suggest that British writers and readers have become more comfortable taking a critical perspective towards their nation's finest hour myth. By emphasizing a British penchant for collaboration, they rejected earlier eras' triumphalistic portraits of heroic British resistance in a Nazi-ruled world. This trend reflected the emergence of a more self-critical streak in the nation's identity in the years since 9/11. At least among left-leaning writers, criticizing British collaboration in alternate history served to critique present day political trends – especially British foreign policy decisions involving US-led wars in the Middle East. It also subtly universalized the Nazi era's significance. Most notable of all was the predominantly positive popular response to these narratives. Unlike the case in the 1960s and 1970s, when like-minded accounts were widely attacked, the relative absence of such critiques in recent years suggests that many Britons have come to embrace a more normalized perspective towards the past.[48]

This trend is confirmed, finally, by the British animated comedy film, *Jackboots on Whitehall* (2010) (Figure 14). Directed by the Scottish filmmaking duo, Edward and Rory McHenry, the film diverged from prior British works of cinema by featuring the use of animatronic puppets to dramatize the premise of the Nazis invading England. The puppets, which are voiced by a distinguished group of A-list British actors, including Ewan McGregor, Alan Cumming, and Richard Griffiths, depict a range of major German and British figures, all of whom are placed in a variety of visually stunning settings that explain the film's six million dollar price-tag. The film's plot, by contrast, was much more down-market. Unlike other British alternate histories, *Jackboots on Whitehall* did not so much dramatize as satirize the premise of a Nazi triumph in World War II.

Jackboots on Whitehall begins its counterfactual narrative with the failure to evacuate British troops from Dunkirk in June of 1940. Buoyed by this failure, the Germans proceed to invade Britain through a tunnel dug beneath the English Channel. Once Wehrmacht troops push to the surface at London's Trafalgar Square, the rest of the film features nonstop combat sequences in which the Nazis pursue British forces all the way to Hadrian's Wall in the north. When all looks lost, however, a stalwart English villager named Christopher volunteers to secure military support from the people of Scotland. At this point, the film lapses into intertextual farce when Christopher succeeds in persuading a hybrid William Wallace/Mel Gibson character to muster a band of ferocious, blue-painted Scottish warriors to attack Nazi forces. After many graphic scenes of Scottish warriors cleaving Nazi skulls with medieval weapons, the Scots emerge victorious. At this juncture, however, the film introduces a clever twist: the Scottish defeat of the Nazis fails to save England. Instead, in a nod to Scottish nationalism, the McHenry brothers send the Scots marching to the south and defeat the English. The nightmare of the thousand year Nazi empire is replaced by the chant "Long Live the Scottish Empire."

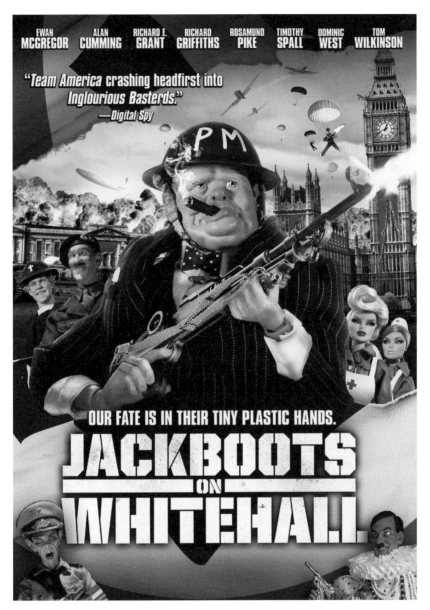

Figure 14. The film *Jackboots on Whitehall* (2010) satirizes the scenario of the Nazi invasion of England, mocking British and Germans alike. The film's stars are all puppets.

  This ironic conclusion is merely one of several ways in which *Jackboots on Whitehall* displayed a normalized view towards the Nazi era. The most important sign of this sensibility was the film's equal opportunity mocking of Nazi perpetrators and their British victims.

The leaders of the Third Reich are all represented in grossly caricatured fashion. Joseph Goebbels is a screaming ape, Hermann Goering serves as his gay lover, and Hitler prances about in a ball gown. Viewers are presumably expected to chortle, but there is little that is genuinely funny about the film's mocking of the Nazi leadership. Ordinary German soldiers, meanwhile, are portrayed as mindless automatons (the only exception being a squad of buxom, leather-clad, female Nazi dominatrixes). Nothing the Nazis do is shown to be particularly evil; they simply fire their weapons and pursue their British enemies across the country in the pursuit of victory. The film thus subtly de-demonizes the Nazis. At the same time, it de-heroizes the English. Churchill is portrayed as pompous and indolent, being fast asleep in his bunker during the invasion (he wakes up in time to utter the double-entendre that the Nazis have come "right into our back entrance"). The civilian Home Guard is represented as smug and dim-witted. Finally, in showing the English being conquered by the Scots, the film discards the triumphalistic idea of the finest hour.

To be sure, *Jackboots in Whitehall*'s primary goal was to entertain, not teach history. The film's directors (both of whom were born in the 1980s) belonged to a younger generation far removed from the war and they predictably exhibited a more lighthearted view towards it. In interviews, they genially described having created an "epic comedy action adventure [that's] got something for everybody . . . romance . . . action, Nazis, Romans, lots of explosions . . . and fireballs."[49] In lending their blithe perspective to the topic, the directors radically transfigured it, subverting both the finest hour myth of British resistance and the revisionist counter-myth of British collaboration. Prior to *Jackboots in Whitehall*, all British alternate histories either defended one premise or the other. By dispensing with both – by abandoning any pretense of seriousness in representing a hypothetical Nazi invasion of England – the film nihilistically subverted the entire scenario. It thereby suggested that the scenario may be nearing the end of its lifespan.

This possibility was partly supported by responses to the film. Reviews of *Jackboots in Whitehall* in the British media were strongly divided. On the one hand, critics attacked it as a "boorish," "puerile," and "pointless" film that "sadly plumps for lowest-common-denominator idiocy."[50] Other observers, however, contrasted the film favorably to previous British alternate histories. Several commentators praised the filmmakers for trying to update a familiar topic for a younger generation – or as *The Observer* put it: "for people for whom the last war belongs in the distant past."[51] This agenda explained why, according to one reviewer, the film "adopt[ed] a tone a thousand times less solemn than Kevin Brownlow and Andrew Mollo's 'It Happened Here'."[52] This reviewer praised the film's satirical approach and argued that it should have gone even further in offering an original perspective on "a subject that is 70 years old and done to death."[53] Another reviewer agreed, declaring

> It's about time someone took the piss out of all this again, because most of the work in this field has had a very grim tone over the years . . .
>
> It's vaguely disturbing how often we, the uninvaded descendants of the allied victors, try imagining how we might have behaved had we gone through the ordeal of . . .Poland . . . Do we secretly wish . . . to blow trains off their tracks and tar-and-feather prominent collaborators? I wonder. But I fear that soon enough we'll see an American rightwing variant in which Muslims – or liberals – are the favoured enemy.[54]

In celebrating the film's subversive tone, these comments signaled a growing exhaustion among certain Britons with the scenario of a Nazi invasion of England. One likely reason for this exhaustion, if the last comment is any indication, was the growing skepticism towards smug displays of patriotism in the post-9/11 period. Rooted in a critical view towards British involvement in the wars in Afghanistan and Iraq, this skepticism perceived the finest hour myth as implicated in the country's foreign policy mistakes and therefore supported any effort to undermine it. It is hard to gauge how much support this perspective enjoys. But the more that Britons willingly satirize the scenario of a Nazi victory, the more they will advance the process of normalization.

The United States

Compared to the relative uniformity of recent British alternate histories, American depictions of a Nazi triumph in the Second World War have followed a less consistent pattern. For much of the postwar period, American alternate histories tended to be less self-critical than British accounts. Most emphasized Nazism's evil in order to justify the United States' intervention in the "good war."[55] This general consensus reflected the relative stability of postwar American history, which was largely marked by prosperity and self-confidence. To be sure, in times of crisis, as in the 1960s and 1970s, self-critical alternate histories appeared; but they represented an exception. For the most part, American narratives triumphalistically validated the past. Over the last decade, this trend has largely continued. But, in a reflection of the internal divisions that have emerged in American political and social life since 9/11, self-critical narratives also appeared. As in England, they too universalized the Nazi era's significance.

A clear example of the first trend was provided by Harry Turtledove's novel, *The Man With the Iron Heart* (2008) (Figure 15).[56] It offered a new spin on the theme of the Nazis winning World War II by imagining them losing the military struggle against the Allies but launching a successful guerilla insurgency against them after 1945. The novel's point of divergence is May 29, 1942, the day on which Reich Main Security Office (RSHA) chief, Reinhard Heydrich, survives what in real history was a successful assassination attempt against him by Czech resistance fighters outside of Prague. Because he ends up living long enough to see the war go badly after 1943, he decides that Germany's only possible hope lies in a guerilla war after the end of hostilities, and he informs SS chief Heinrich Himmler of his desire to lead it.[57]

Against this backstory, *The Man With the Iron Heart* opens after V-E day in 1945 with Germany defeated and Allied troops patrolling the country in an effort to secure the peace. A variety of characters populate the novel, most of which conform to familiar stereotypes. The Americans, who get top billing, are a mix of Midwestern hayseeds, northeastern ethnics, and southern rednecks – all of whom pepper their remarks with abundant profanity. French, British, and Russian characters also adhere to predictable character types. Character development in the novel, however, largely takes a back seat to action scenes and plot twists. Much of the narrative portrays German "Werewolf" attacks against Allied forces. At first, the insurgents, who call themselves the "German Freedom Front," use bazookas to attack Allied troop convoys, in one episode killing General George Patton.[58] But they soon embrace more daring tactics, employing "kamikaze Nazis" to launch suicide attacks against higher-profile targets.[59] They twice succeed in disrupting scheduled war crimes trials against imprisoned Nazis (first by using a truck bomb to destroy the Palace of Justice in Nuremberg, second by flying a hijacked C-47 transport plane into the Berlin municipal courthouse); they assassinate moderate German politicians, such as Konrad

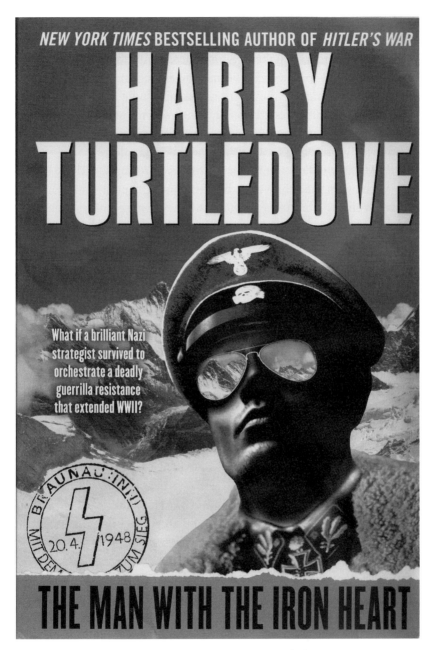

Figure 15. In Harry Turtledove's novel, *The Man With the Iron Heart* (2008), a Nazi insurgency against Allied occupying forces in postwar Germany serves as an allegory about the challenges faced by the United States in Iraq.

Adenauer, to prevent centrist political parties from gathering popular support; and they kidnap German atomic scientists held in the British zone and force them to make a radium-laced "dirty bomb," which they detonate in the US compound in Frankfurt, leaving the city contaminated with radiation. Finally, the Werewolves also take their fight to the French and British. A truck bomber brings down the Eiffel Tower into the Seine in Paris, while other insurgents detonate payloads in front of Westminster Abbey and St. Paul's Cathedral in London.

The Man With the Iron Heart does not simply wallow in violence for its own sake, however, but examines the political fallout that emerges from it. The many military and civilian casualties caused by Werewolf attacks predictably contribute to the growth of anti-war sentiment on the American home front. Turtledove's portrayal of this development features a variety of characters who lead this pacifist agenda: Diana McGraw, whose loss of her son, Pat, in Germany prompts her to form a movement to "bring the boys home"; Tom Schmidt, a journalist from the anti-interventionist Chicago Tribune, who harasses President Truman about his commitment to stay the course; and Jerry Duncan, a Republican congressman from Indiana, who exploits the anti-war feeling for political gain. Before long, throngs of anti-war activists march in front of the White House and debate erupts in Congress about the wisdom of leaving Germany altogether. Some representatives urge staying there, arguing, as one New York Democrat does, that "If we leave, Heydrich wins ...[Our country will] pay a much higher price if we cut and run. We might pay the price of World War III." Yet, the failure to quash the insurgency and the fear – articulated by Congressman Duncan – that "if we stay, we throw away ... billions of dollars," ultimately prevail.[60] The midterm elections of 1946 bring defeat for the Democrats and a big victory for the GOP, which proceeds to cancel funding for American troops. President Truman thus has no choice but to bring US forces home.[61]

The results of this decision are ambiguous but shade towards the negative. On the one hand, just as American troops are withdrawing from Germany, they get a lucky break from a Jewish DP and Auschwitz survivor, Shmuel Birnbaum, whose wartime experience as a slave laborer digging tunnels for Heydrich's hideout near Bad Tölz enables him to remember the site's location and lead American forces to it. Once there, an ordinary soldier, Bernie Cobb, spots the Werewolf leader making a night-time escape and kills him with a hand grenade and grease gun.[62] This outcome partly validates the continued American presence in Germany. As a buoyant President Truman subsequently tells journalists, "a few months from now, we wouldn't have had the manpower to do anything about ... Heydrich [and he] would still be down there thumbing his nose at us."[63] At the same time, however, the novel ends on ominous note. After Heydrich's death, his designated successor, Waffen-SS officer Jochen Peiper, takes control of the insurgency and launches a series of spectacular attacks culminating in the hijacking of a TWA airliner to Spain and a Soviet airliner to Prague. Convinced that "whoever has the most patience ... wins," Peiper is confident that, while the Soviets will be difficult to dislodge from the East, the Americans and British will eventually pull out of Western Germany and the result will be "a free and independent and National Socialist Deutsches Reich."[64] In the novel's last scene, a German civilian is shown watching the last convoy of American troops leave the country; gazing into the distance, he removes a hidden NSDAP membership badge from under his collar and prepares to "wear it openly again." "The white inner circle" of the badge, the tale concludes, "held a black swastika. Every Party member had one just like it. Pretty soon, they'd all be showing it, too."[65]

In implying that the Nazis eventually would have returned to power in alternate history, Turtledove vindicated the United States' real historical decision to fight against Germany in World War II and pursue a reconstructionist policy towards the defeated country afterwards. He thus confirmed that the conflict was a good war. Turtledove reinforced this message in the novel by emphasizing the importance of remembrance. A key element in the plot is the fact that American troops only kill Heydrich thanks to the novel's silent hero, the Jewish survivor, Birnbaum, whose razor-sharp memory enables them to locate the RSHA chief's underground hideout. President Truman's remark that Heydrich's "own past came back to bite him" endorsed the notion that memory equals justice.[66] The novel's sympathetic portrayal of other Jewish characters – such as Lieutenant Lou Weissberg, who vocally insists on the need for the US to stay in Germany and prevent a Nazi revival – further suggested the need for remembrance. This point was supported, finally, by the novel's negative portrayal of ordinary Americans making anti-Semitic remarks about Jews being unable to forget the past and thirsting for revenge against the Germans. "You can't expect those people to be reasonable," one anti-war activist says of a disembarking Jewish soldier upset about leaving Germany, "Most regular Americans appreciate what we're doing."[67]

In suggesting that the United States made the right decision by staying in Germany after World War II, Turtledove was not only making a comment about the past but also the present. As was obvious from countless references, *The Man With the Iron Heart* was a thinly veiled allegory about the American War in Iraq. Many of the novel's plot elements and characters were taken right from recent years' headlines, whether the Iraqi insurgency's use of suicide bombs, the anti-war activity of American mothers like Cindy Sheehan, or references to Colin Powell's "Pottery Barn rule" (at one juncture, Lou Weissberg sees a sign in a German shop window reading, "YOU BREAK IT, YOU PAY FOR IT").[68] Whether or not Turtledove wanted his novel to be read as a policy brief for what the United States should do in Iraq, it is hard not to view his text as offering a conservative set of conclusions, namely to stay the course and remain in the country at whatever price. Although Turtledove recognized the moral costs of occupying another country (he showed the US using brutal counterinsurgency tactics, such as shooting hostages and torture, to stem the Werewolf campaign), he seemed to conclude that it was justified in order to avoid a worse evil.[69] This is suggested near the novel's end when President Truman ominously declares, "'If we run from Germany, the first thing the Nazis will do if they get back into power is start working on an atom bomb ... And the second thing ...[they] will do ... is start working on a rocket that can reach the United States from Germany ...[Then] nobody is safe any more.'"[70] This remark, which tapped into American fears about Iran's pursuit of nuclear weapons, further seemed to place Turtledove in a conservative camp.

That said, Turtledove's primary motive in writing the novel was probably more analytical than political. Born in 1949, he is a professionally trained historian with a Ph.D. in Byzantine History from UCLA and has long described his interest in alternate history as rooted in his curiosity about the deeper causal forces – for instance, structure versus agency – that drive historical change.[71] He has scrupulously avoided discussing his personal political views in public forums, moreover, leading to confusion among his many readers about whether he stands on the socialist left or libertarian right.[72] Although *The Man With the Iron Heart* (like many of his other stories) could be interpreted as having a political message, Turtledove's real goal in writing it was probably to explore the historical parallels between the American occupations of Germany and Iraq and to hypothesize about the outcome of the former had the US been confronted with the same challenges that plagued the latter.[73] In a recent interview, Turtledove implied that his narrative was mostly a thought experiment and resisted the suggestion that it had a specific political slant, noting: "I don't think that it holds any particular lessons. Anyone is going to bring to it whatever his or her own preconceptions already are."[74] Be that as it may, Turtledove clearly wrote from a different political perspective than Walton and Saville. His novel drew on the Nazi past not to critique, but to endorse, America's present-day interventionist foreign policy.

In the process, however, *The Man With the Iron Heart* universalized the Nazi era's significance. Turtledove was hardly the first writer to draw parallels between the American occupations of Germany and Iraq.[75] In doing so, however, he elided the substantial differences between them. These included the different level of threat posed to the US by the two countries (and the accompanying rationales for invasion); the extent of the crimes perpetrated by the respective regimes (and the degree of moral imperative for postwar occupation); and the importance of the two countries for a peaceful postwar order. In the process of being employed to understand Iraq, in short, the Nazi legacy lost its distinctiveness.

Strongly resembling Turtledove's tale was Alan Glenn's novel, *Amerikan Eagle* (2011) (Figure 16).[76] Set in Portsmouth, New Hampshire in 1943, the novel is a detective thriller featuring a hardscrabble police inspector, Sam Miller, whose life begins to unravel after being entrusted with a mysterious case involving the appearance of a man's corpse in a railroad yard. In examining the body, Sam is puzzled by a strange series of numbers tattooed on the man's wrists and he begins the painstaking work of discovering their meaning. Before he can begin, however, his superiors order him to drop the case. Suspecting murder, Sam is reluctant to obey, but he does not want to risk his job. After all, times are tough in America. The nation remains mired in an economic depression, with unemployment hovering around 40 percent. It also has a president, Huey Long, who has yet to make good on his assurances that good times are around the corner.

The reason for this dire situation, *Amerikan Eagle* explains, lies a decade in the past, on the fateful day of February 15, 1933, with the murder of President Franklin D. Roosevelt by an assassin in Miami.

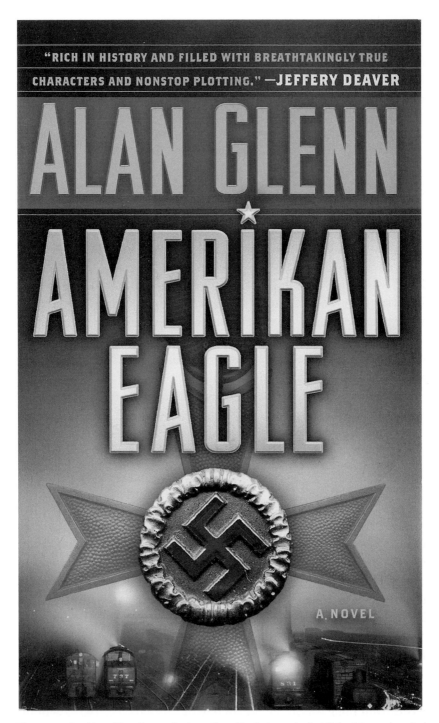

Figure 16. In Alan Glenn's novel, *Amerikan Eagle* (2011), the United States is ruled by the authoritarian President, Huey Long, and collaborates with Hitler's Germany.

In the wake of this tragedy, FDR's successor, John Nance Garner, refrains from passing New Deal legislation, the nation's economic woes continue, and Louisiana Governor Huey Long is elected president in 1936. Long proceeds to crush labor unions, restrict the free press, and create a one-party state defended by southern thugs known as "Long's Legionnaires." More ominously, Long creates labor camps for leftists and dissidents, one of whom is Sam's brother, Tony, who has run afoul of the authorities while trying to stoke labor activism in the Portsmouth shipyards. Sam disapproves of his country's right-wing political tilt, yet career pressures give him no choice but to collaborate with Long's dictatorship.

His collaboration becomes harder to sustain, however, once America's drift towards fascism gradually brings it into the orbit of Nazi Germany. Thanks to Long's isolationism, the United States refrains from getting involved in the Second World War. This decision greatly benefits Germany, which defeats Great Britain in 1940 and takes over its imperial possessions. Although the Nazis remain engaged in hostilities with the Soviet Union, they appear to have the resources to win a war of attrition. Their fortunes are further strengthened when President Long decides to undertake a bold foreign policy initiative and establish closer relations with the Third Reich through a new trade and peace treaty. According to the treaty's terms, the US agrees to supply the Germans with weapons, thereby stimulating the American armaments industry and boosting employment; the US also agrees to extradite "criminal" elements back to the Reich.[77] In a gesture of rapprochement, Hitler decides to come to Portsmouth to sign the treaty, thereby setting the stage for later drama.

These events quickly drag Sam into the maw of the era's political intrigue. After some covert sleuthing, Sam discovers that the corpse at the center of his murder case is that of a German national of Jewish background who has escaped from one of a series of secret concentration camps housing Jewish prisoners working as slaves for the American government. Sam learns this information the hard way, getting nabbed by Long's thugs while investigating one of the camps, a marble quarry in Vermont, where he is briefly interned as an inmate. While there, he learns from one of the other prisoners that Long and Hitler have agreed to secretly transport European Jews to the United States on seized British ships in contravention of the US ban on foreign immigration. The idea stems from Long's Secretary of the Treasury, Henry Morgenthau, who has devised it as a way of saving Europe's Jews from the Holocaust. After being released from the camp, Sam has time to reflect on his experiences, which profoundly shape the events that stand at the novel's denouement. Once back in Portsmouth, Sam learns of a conspiracy of leftist dissidents led by his brother, Tony, to assassinate Hitler during the treaty signing ceremony. Yet thanks to a series of lucky breaks, Sam succeeds in thwarting the assassination plot and disrupting a related effort to kill President Long.

As the novel concludes, the question remains whether Sam has done the ethically correct thing. His main motivation for acting as he does is to free his wife and son, who have been arrested and kept as hostages in a labor camp to ensure that he cooperates with the FBI's hunt for his brother. But Sam has other reasons as well. When his wife – who belongs to a resistance group funneling refugees to Canada via an underground railroad – questions his decision to prevent the assassination of the two dictators, Sam hints that his actions have served a greater good. Although he cannot divulge the existence of Jewish refugees working in secret American concentration camps, Sam recognizes that their continued existence – and by extension, the cooperative relationship between Hitler and Long – is the only thing preventing the Holocaust from resuming in Europe. Thus, while Sam is aghast that Jewish inmates are being economically exploited in America, he cannot help but side with his boss, Hanson, who tells him "it's better to be here overworked and underfed, than to be back in Europe, slaughtered."[78] This is why Sam ultimately shoots Long's would-be assassin before he can kill the president. Seconds before acting, in a moment of indecision, Sam thinks to himself: "Let the goddam kingfish get killed. Why not? The bastard deserved it as much as Hitler did ... And yet ... there were thousands of ... Jewish refugees alive in the United States because of Long ... And thousands more were on their way ... But with Long dead, thousands more ... would die."[79] In the end, Sam defends his collaborationist relationship with the two fascist regimes in order to prevent greater evil.

In depicting the nightmare scenario of the United States turning into an ally of Nazi Germany, Glenn was driven by several motives. One was to vindicate the United States' real historical decision to fight against the Third Reich in World War II. Like Turtledove, Glenn showed the disastrous effects of the United States pursuing a path of isolationism. His reasons for doing so, however, were rooted in different political considerations. Whereas Turtledove seemed to condemn isolationism and justify the foreign policy of the Bush administration, Glenn took a more critical stance towards it. This was suggested by scattered references in *Amerikan Eagle* to President Long's approval of "enhanced interrogation techniques" and waterboarding against labor unionists and other dissidents. These references to some of the Bush administration's most controversial policies in Iraq suggested that Glenn intended *Amerikan Eagle* to be read as a cautionary parable about the US's rightward turn after 9/11.[80] Glenn partly confirmed this supposition about the book's political message in a 2012 interview. A self-described "crusty New Hampshire Independent," Glenn (the pseudonym of the successful crime fiction writer Brendan Dubois) noted that while he did not write his novel with a specific political agenda in mind, some of his reservations about the Bush administration's policies – for example the Patriot Act – "seeped into some of my plotting."[81] Glenn pointed out, however, that his fears about the abuse of government power were "not limited to just one party," adding that he was equally concerned that "the Obama Administration still has Guantanamo Bay open." This comment revealed that *Amerikan Eagle* was less of a left-liberal critique of the Bush administration than a libertarian parable about the abuse of government power.[82]

Yet while Glenn may have had different political motives than Turtledove in crafting his nightmare scenario, his book also universalized the Nazi legacy. To be sure, the writer left little doubt about his distaste for Nazism. At one point in the novel, Sam's sympathetic wife, Sarah, makes this clear in declaring, "the whole bunch of them – Nazis, SS, Gestapo – they're pure evil."[83] Still, while Glenn depicted the Third Reich negatively throughout the novel, he did so less for its own sake than to condemn America for collaborating with it. *Amerikan Eagle* includes numerous examples of the two regimes' affinities for one another, the most dramatic being the American government's creation of a "Waffen-SS George Washington" brigade to fight with the Nazis against the Soviets in Europe. Yet Glenn went beyond merely portraying collaboration and suggested an equivalence between the United States and Nazi Germany. No passage indicated this better than Sam's exchange with a German Gestapo agent, Hans Groebke, who comes to Portsmouth to oversee security for Hitler's visit. When Sam accuses the German agent of serving a brutal regime, Groebke relativizes Nazism's evil, declaring:

'So let us speak of death, then, Sam. Who slaughtered the red Indian last century, who stole their lands and put them on reservations?

Who is shooting auto workers in Detroit, fruit pickers in Oregon, strikers in Manhattan, yes? Your own hands, how clean are they Herr Miller? Did you not participate a few days ago in a . . . *cleansing* [of] refugees and undesirables . . .?'

'I do not judge you for what you do . . . You are similar, you and I. Our nations. We have both made empires on the back of other peoples . . . Even our symbols are the same. The eagle, yes? . . . [B]oth of our nations, so similar.'[84]

Significantly, Sam has no response to Groebke's observation. Although he is an outspoken character up until this point of the novel, his sudden inability to refute the German agent's comment tacitly assents to its underlying truth. It is unclear whether or not Groebke's claim echoed Glenn's personal views, but *Amerikan Eagle*'s equation of Nazi and American imperialism – foregrounded in its title – effaced the considerable differences between them.

Reviews of Turtledove's and Glenn's novels were comparatively scarce and generally mixed. Tellingly, *The Man With the Iron Heart* was praised by conservative reviewers. *The Washington Times* called the novel "extraordinary," "chilling," and "thought-provoking" and declared that it confronted readers with the "exceptionally relevant" question of "how far [the] . . . occupation of a belligerent nation by a Western democratic power . . . ought to go."[85] *The National Review* praised Turtledove's work in an online interview and tried to draw out the conservative implications of his novel (Turtledove largely demurred). By contrast, ordinary readers complained that Turtledove's parable was politically transparent, heavy-handed, and implausible.[86] For its part, *Amerikan Eagle* received less print media attention, but Internet reviews tended to be critical. Some readers were skeptical that the United States would so easily have abandoned its democratic traditions.[87] Others said the novel went overboard in creating an "oppressive atmosphere" in 1940s America.[88] These comments suggested that most readers rejected Glenn's claims about America's susceptibility to Nazism and preferred to see the Third Reich as singular in its historical significance.

By contrast, other alternate histories expressed a more normalized perspective towards the Third Reich by satirizing the premise of a Nazi victory in World War II. On May 15, 2010, the popular television show, *Saturday Night Live*, broadcast the skit, "The Timecrowave," in which a fictional inventor, Gram Lamton

Figure 17. In the *Saturday Night Live* skit, "Timecrowave" (2010), Alec Baldwin and Kristin Wiig send food back through time, thereby inadvertently allowing the Nazis to conquer America. Note the swastika flags in the background.

(played by Alec Baldwin), stars in a mock infomercial promoting a device that enables prospective buyers to prepare meals more quickly by sending them back in time to the moment when they are desired.[89] In making his pitch, Lamton cautions his studio audience that consumer negligence might occasionally "create a paradox, where small differences may start to occur in the space-time continuum." He reassures viewers, however, that "I'm sure ... something like that will never happen!" At this point, the skit's running gag kicks in, and Lamton is shown, first, sporting a moustache (earlier in the skit, he is clean-shaven) and secondly, being turned into an African American. Soon thereafter, Lamton's sidekick, Penny Schmeer (played by Kristen Wiig), is depicted praising the machine's wonders, while through the window behind her, houses can be seen draped with American flags sporting swastikas (Figure 17). Thanks to the time-crowave, the Nazis have somehow won World War II and conquered America. The premise is meant to be funny, and the live audience obliges by laughing heartily.

There have been other comic portrayals of a Nazi triumph in World War II. The American film, *Hot Tub Time Machine* (2010), featured a character who, concerned about the consequences of traveling back in time, voices the fear that "We're gonna do something to make Hitler president!"[90] The manic way in which the character

articulates this potential outcome, however, makes it clear that it is
meant to elicit guffaws rather than goose bumps. The same is true of a
recent YouTube video parody of the film, *Downfall* (2004), featuring
Hitler in his Berlin bunker declaring to his generals that he has built a
time machine and is about to use it to "escape this shit hole we're in and
make us victors in this war." Predictably, the plan fails and Hitler's
bunker is portrayed collapsing in on him, with the dictator repeatedly
screaming out "Fegelein!" in anger.[91] Here again, the premise of a
Nazi victory provides an opportunity for laughter, as Hitler's angry
invocation of Hermann Fegelein (an SS officer and Eva Braun's
brother-in-law) has become a wildly popular Internet meme denoting
intense frustration.[92] Finally, various Internet websites have taken a
humorous approach to portraying a Nazi wartime triumph, with one
site, TV Tropes, glibly citing the premise as the basis of a new universal
law: "As the amount of time-traveling you do increases, the probability of Hitler winning World War II approaches one." The site explains
the law as follows:

> You return home from your jolly time travel adventure . . . having
> saved the world and being careful not to upset history and . . . hold on
> a moment? Are those *swastikas*?! Hanging from the *White House*?!
> Looks like you've been hit by Godwin's Law of Time Travel.
>   Talked to the wrong person? Nazi Victory! Left technology back
> before the dinosaurs were wiped out? Nazi Victory! Stepped on a
> bug? Nazi victory! Left a tap running? Nazi Victory! Prevented a
> Nazi victory? Nazi Victory!

This passage, like the others noted above, points to the further normalization of memory. When the TV Tropes site declares that "the strangest
thing about Time Travel is probably that . . . the Nazis winning WWII is
the most common accidental timeline shift," it implies that the premise
has become hackneyed. When it declares that "in reality, a Nazi victory
[was] . . . improbable [since the]. . .Allies were in reality *much* more
powerful," the passage shows how the premise has become viewed as
implausible.[93] If these comments are at all representative of wider views,
they may explain why a scenario originally meant to frighten is being
transformed into one meant to amuse. As in Britain, the satirical portrayal of a Nazi wartime victory in America may reflect a growing sense
of fatigue with the topic.

Germany

In contrast to Britain and the United States, Germany has traditionally produced fewer alternate histories on the subject of a Nazi victory in World War II. For obvious reasons, the scenario has inherent appeal to neo-Nazis and has thus been treated from a strictly moralistic perspective by most mainstream writers. That this continues to be the case was demonstrated by the most significant work of fiction to appear in recent years, Siegfried Langer's novel, *Alles bleibt anders* (*Everything Remains Different*) (Figure 18).[94] Published (and also set) in the year 2008, the novel opens dramatically with its protagonist, a young German named Frank Miller, wandering the streets of Berlin in a daze, having lost his memory. Frank barely recognizes any of the city's landmarks and only through a stroke of luck runs into a neighbor who tells him how to find his mother's apartment. Once he arrives there, his mother is overjoyed for, as she explains, it has been three years since she has last seen him – or to be precise, seen his body, which she tells him was found mangled on the tracks of Berlin's Görlitz train station in 2005. As the story unfolds, Frank tries to unravel the mystery of his death by learning about his previous life in Berlin – his family, his studies at the university, his fiancée. Soon the reader discovers that the world he inhabits is a strange one in which the German monarchy reigns, horse-drawn carriages rule the streets, and Jews exist in abundance. Before long, however, strange events begin to happen: Frank's fiancée refuses to see him, her new husband is shocked to learn of his reappearance, and a strange assailant tries to attack him in a park near the Müggelsee.

The reason for these events, *Alles bleibt anders* gradually reveals, is that Frank is stuck in the middle of a parallel world story. To explain Frank's memory loss, the novel rewinds to the year 2004, when – in an alternate world – he had just begun a course of study at the University of Oxford, in German-occupied England, following a four-year stint serving in the Wehrmacht near the *Stadt des Endsiegs* (City of the Final Victory), formerly known as Stalingrad. In this world, Nazi Germany has won the Second World War and imposed a system of draconian rule across Europe. Poland has been Germanized and erased from the map; the United States has retreated into isolation ever since a German nuclear attack against its troops in North Africa in 1945; and the Soviet Union, while remaining restive, has ceased to be a serious threat. As a soldier, Frank has witnessed many of the latter-day atrocities necessary to

Figure 18. Siegfried Langer's 2008 novel, *Alles bleibt anders* (*Everything Remains Different*), is set in a world in which the Nazis win World War II. Albert Speer's massive *Volkshalle* in Berlin is featured on the cover.

uphold this order and is only too glad to return to civilian life to pursue a degree in physics.

Once in England, however, his life takes a dramatic turn when he becomes involved in a conspiracy of fellow graduate students aiming to overthrow the Nazi regime. Frank's involvement begins after being invited one evening to a gathering of students at the home of his physics teacher, Professor Gothaer, and hears them tell horrific tales of "stolen human organs, Gestapo [crimes], experiments on children, violence, mangled women, arbitrary rule, forced abortions, terror, state violence, militarism, occupied territories, expulsion, torture, executions, [and] genocide."[95] Increasingly convinced of the Nazi system's inherent evil, Frank and his friends plan to overthrow the regime by reversing the course of history. They plan on using a device invented by Professor Gothaer to transport them to certain parallel worlds where "alter-egos" of themselves already exist (they are able to travel there and displace their alternate selves once the latter fall asleep). They hope that once the professor locates a world where Nazism never achieved success, they can identify the point of divergence that enabled its creation and bring the information back to their own world. Through a series of intricate calculations, Professor Gothaer soon locates such a world, one in which the death of the infant Johannes Gutenberg in 1399 prevents the success of Martin Luther's Reformation, the eruption of the Thirty Years War, centuries of German division and, ultimately, the rise of Nazism. Before long, Frank and another student named Dieter are sent back to this world in its present-day form, essentially the *Kaiserreich* of 2005. But before Frank can unlock its secrets, he is betrayed. Dieter turns out to be a Gestapo spy who kills Frank once they are transported to this parallel world, throwing him into the path of an oncoming train at the Görlitz train station. In a clever twist, however, the Frank whom Dieter kills is not his time-traveling companion, but Frank's alter ego (it turns out that the other Frank has just gotten engaged to his fiancée and is too excited to go to sleep, thereby preventing the time-traveling Frank from displacing him, and leading Dieter, who has arrived earlier, to mistake him for his intended murder target). This mind-bending set of circumstances, which also explains Frank's memory loss at the novel's outset, sets the stage for a dramatic climax, an old-fashioned shoot-out, in which Dieter is killed and his plan to establish the NSDAP in the *Kaiserreich* is thwarted.

This positive turn of events notwithstanding, *Alles bleibt anders* is anything but a feel-good novel with a happy ending. Because Frank's best friend and love interest, Karen, is mortally wounded in the shootout with Dieter, Frank resolves with Professor Gothaer to save her by seeking out a second parallel world in which Nazism fails to achieve success. They soon determine that such a world exists thanks to Dwight D. Eisenhower's decision to launch the D-Day invasion of Normandy on June 6 rather than June 5, 1944 (the day on which, in Frank's own world, stormy weather leads to the failure of the Allied landing and the Nazis' eventual victory). Frank and another student, Tristan, briefly explore this alternate world – our world – in its present-day form, visiting Berlin and experiencing its chaotic mix of ethnic groups, religions, and rebellious teenagers. The two students are bewildered by Berlin's multi-cultural reality, but they decide that it is vastly preferable to their own criminal world and resolve to go back in time and convince Eisenhower's staff to wait an extra day before launching the Anglo-American invasion of Normandy. In a deflating turn of events, however, Frank discovers after returning to his own world that his alteration of this key point of divergence has not, in fact, removed the Nazis from power. Instead, changing one event has simply created an infinite number of new parallel worlds, the existence of which is rapidly registered on Professor Gothaer's overtaxed machine. As Frank concludes, "the past has proved to be unalterable."[96]

In arriving at this sober conclusion, *Alles bleibt anders* strove to communicate clear moral lessons about the Nazi era. Like earlier German alternate histories by writers such as Otto Basil and Ralph Giordano, Langer's novel was unsparing in its portrait of Nazi evil.[97] Beyond narrating brutal details about the ways in which the Nazis hang on to power, it imagined the Gestapo agent, Dieter, vowing to spread Nazism throughout the whole universe, declaring that once the Nazi regime gets control of Professor Gothaer's machine, there will be "endless numbers of worlds … for the securing of our power, for the spreading of our goals … Our own world will not suffice."[98] The novel was equally clear in refusing to relativize Germany's responsibility for Nazism. When Karen, midway in the narrative, argues in favor of eliminating Nazism from history by killing Hitler as an infant, Professor Gothaer professes skepticism that "Hitler's premature end would not have hindered the emergence of National Socialism … Its ideas emerged and grew in part independently of Hitler … He was hardly responsible for them alone."[99] This remark highlighted the German people's share of responsibility for the Nazi disaster. Since this claim has usually been avoided in German alternate histories (it is far more common in Anglo-American accounts), its presence in Langer's novel was significant.[100]

Beyond describing the horror of a Nazi ruled world, however, *Alles bleibt anders* was notable in how it portrayed the attempt to change it. The novel powerfully depicted the emotional pull for ordinary

Germans of changing the past. So desperate are Frank and his friends to eliminate Nazism and redeem their country that they are willing to make extreme sacrifices. Even when Frank's friend, Tristan, points out that allowing the Allies to win the war will result in suffering for the German people (he notes that the "eastern territories will be stripped away and millions of Germans will be expelled"), Frank decisively replies: "We want no master race ... to raise itself above another ... The dictatorship must be eliminated. Oppressed people throughout Europe associate ... death with the Germans: this must come to an end forever. No Nazism on German soil in the year 2008."[101] Yet while the novel flirted with the fantasy of undoing the past, it ultimately rejected it. By portraying Frank failing to change German history for the better, *Alles bleibt anders* offered a didactic point about Germany's obligation to remember the Nazi legacy. Marianne, a fellow resister with Frank, makes this point clear at the novel's end when she declares: "even if we bear no personal guilt, we cannot sneak away from our responsibility ... we have to live with the past, whether or not we like it; it is not our job to change it. It is impossible to fight Nazism in 1944 or 1933; only in the present, that is the only era that matters."[102]

In offering this conclusion, Langer was motivated by a simple moral agenda. Born in 1966, he was too young to have experienced the events of the Nazi years personally. But he had a deep interest in the ethical questions raised by this period of German history. For the writer, the most important was "how would you yourself have behaved if you had been born fifty years earlier?"[103] Significantly, this question resonated with German critics. *Alles bleibt anders* was nominated for several prizes and was positively reviewed both on German science fiction websites and in the print media.[104] *Der Standard* of Vienna, for example, praised the "exciting debut novel" for finding "a unique approach" to exploring the topic of a Nazi victory in World War II.[105] Other reviewers praised the book for its "thought-provoking" way of dealing with the difficult subject of "Germany's struggle to come to terms with its Nazi past."[106] Indeed, more than a few commentators admired the novel for "soberly" exploring the everyday brutality of the "terror state" without "lifting an index finger" in a crudely didactic way.[107] Still others, finally, praised the novel for offering German readers a method of deriving moral lessons from "a distant episode of history that is not much more real than the Roman Empire."[108] These positive comments pointed to a German desire to resist normalization.

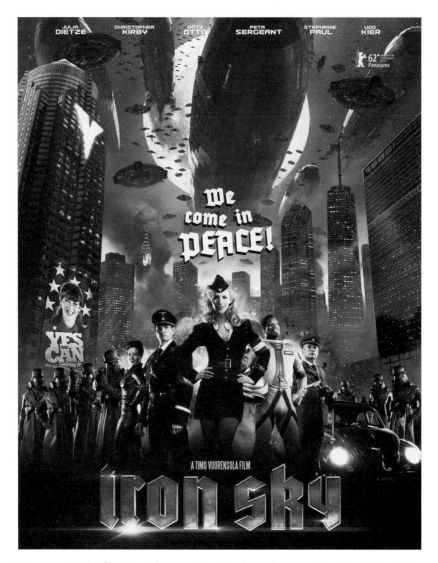

Figure 19. In the film *Iron Sky* (2012), Nazis from the moon invade Earth with the goal of establishing a Fourth Reich.

By contrast, the German response to another work of alternate history, the film *Iron Sky* (2012), revealed a more complicated picture (Figure 19). A multinational production with a major German contribution in terms of cast, funding, shooting location, and dialogue (much of the film is in German with English subtitles), *Iron Sky* is, strictly speaking, less of an alternate history than a future history.[109] It does not so much portray the Nazis winning World War II as parlaying their wartime defeat into an opportunity for future triumph.[110] That said, the film drew on many of the same fears that traditionally informed the scenario of a Nazi victory in the war. It did so in a radically new way, however. Like *Jackboots on Whitehall*, *Iron Sky* used satire to subvert the scenario's gravitas, playing it for laughs instead of chills.

Set in 2018, the film is based on the outlandish premise – widely believed by conspiracy theorists – that, unbeknownst to the world, a group of Nazi scientists at the end of World War II secretly escaped Earth in flying saucers and established a colony on the dark side of the moon. In the film, the lunar Nazis' existence accidentally comes to light when a pair of American astronauts on a mission to the moon accidentally stumble upon the colony, which is housed in a giant stone fortress built in the shape of a swastika. The Nazis capture one of the astronauts, an African American named James Washington (Christopher Kirby), who quickly meets the "Fourth Reich's" leaders and learns of their diabolical plans for world conquest. The lunar Nazis, at first glance, seem to be unambiguously evil. Hitler's successor as Führer, Wolfgang Kortzfleisch (Udo Kier), is coolly menacing. His rival, the aspiring Führer-to-be, Klaus Adler (Götz Otto), is gratuitously violent (he shoots and kills the other American astronaut at the film's beginning). A mad scientist, Doktor Richter, is a latter-day Josef Mengele who conducts medical experiments on his helpless American prisoner. And his daughter, Renate (Julia Dietze), a Nazi elementary school teacher, indoctrinates her students with lessons about Aryan racial superiority. Factor in an arsenal of fearsome weapons, epitomized by an enormous death ship called the *Götterdämmerung*, and *Iron Sky*'s Nazis appear well-suited to fulfill their assigned roles as formidable villains.

The film's plot initially reinforces this impression by showing the Nazis wreaking havoc on the course of history. Events kick into motion when Adler and Washington (together with the stow-away, Renate) travel back to Earth in the effort to locate an energy source to power the *Götterdämmerung*. With Washington's help, Adler and Renate arrange a meeting with the President of the United States, a Sarah Palin-like Republican conservative (Stephanie Paul), who takes a liking to them and, on the advice of her marketing adviser, Vivian Wagner (Peta Sergeant) hires them to revive her moribund re-election campaign. Having gained access to the levers of power, Adler proceeds with his plot to overthrow Kortzfleisch (whom he eventually kills) and launch the invasion of Earth with an armada of Nazi space zeppelins. Before long,

Earth is taking missile fire and the planet's great powers are forced to rally together to defeat the alien invasion. Thanks to nuclear proliferation, however (all the major powers have built nuclear-equipped space vessels, in contravention of UN agreements), the Allies repel the Nazi threat and the *Götterdämmerung* crash lands on the moon before it can arrive on Earth. This apparent triumph, however, is short-lived. After news emerges that the Nazis have stockpiled an enormous supply of the valuable element, Helium-3 (which is used in nuclear fusion), the Allies start fighting with one another to control it and become embroiled in a world war. As the film ends, the camera pans away from planet Earth as nuclear explosions flare on its surface. The Nazis may not have succeeded in taking control of the planet, but they succeed in laying waste to it.

In its broader contours, *Iron Sky* offered a moralistic portrait of Nazism, yet its narrative was strikingly normalized in many ways. First of all, the film aestheticized its subject through its embrace of satire. Compared to the melodramatic way in which the scenario of the Nazis returning to power was alluded to in early postwar films, such as Alfred Hitchcock's *Notorious* (1946) and Orson Welles's *The Stranger* (1946), *Iron Sky* drained the premise of any real suspense. The film was much less concerned with plot than gags. Much of *Iron Sky* was devoted to spoofing other films. One scene, for example, pokes fun at the blockbuster movie, *Downfall*, when Vivian Wagner, speaking with her marketing staff, launches into profanity-laced tirade in the style of Bruno Ganz's Hitler lambasting his generals in the Berlin bunker. *Iron Sky* also sought laughs via crude racial humor. The film introduces one of its running sight gags early on when Doktor Richter injects Washington with an "albinizing" serum to turn his skin white (and his hair blonde) for his return trip to Earth. This premise is then repeatedly milked for comic effect – as when Washington, dressed in a Nazi uniform, asks a group of black street kids in New York City for directions, with predictable consequences. The film also featured sexual innuendo and comic violence. In one scene, Adler is about to have sex with Wagner when Kortzfleisch walks into the room, thereby forcing him to stand up and give the Führer greeting with his drawers dropped; near the film's conclusion, meanwhile, Renate heroically kills Adler by stabbing him in the forehead with her high-heeled shoe. Finally, there are numerous scenes mocking Nazi symbolism, as when helmeted Nazi stormtroopers looking through a pornographic magazine liken the similarity of the centerfold's shaved pubic region to the Führer's moustache. All of these scenes diminish the frightfulness of a Nazi return to power.

Iron Sky also normalized the Nazi past by universalizing its significance. Although the film was mostly an exercise in slapstick, it also contained political elements. Most notably, it suggested the existence of parallels between the Third Reich and the government of the United States. A good example of this comparison is when the American President hires Adler and Renate as her campaign spokespersons after hearing Renate speak glowingly of the Nazis' way of life – especially their desire "to make the world healthy once again. With hard work and honesty. With clarity. With decency." The fact that the President swiftly embraces this values-oriented rhetoric – despite its Nazi pedigree – implies a similarity between fascist ideas and the conservative domestic policies advocated by recent GOP politicians. Still other scenes in *Iron Sky* criticized American foreign policy. When the President learns of the Nazi invasion of Earth, she welcomes it as improving her re-election prospects. She is also portrayed as sparking Earth's civil war by trying to claim all the moon's Helium-3 for the United States. The film even depicts the American government committing war crimes. When the commander of the American spaceship, the *USS George W. Bush*, orders a nuclear attack on the Nazis' lunar fortress, a lower-ranking officer objects by noting the presence of "women and children," to which the commander replies, "we don't negotiate with terrorists." By showing the Nazis precipitating such bellicose American behavior, the film implied an affinity between the Third Reich and the US.

Significantly, the creative team behind *Iron Sky* confirmed that it possessed a normalizing agenda. The film's Finnish director, Timo Vuorensola, explained that its comic treatment of Nazism was meant as an alternative to prevailing moralistic modes of representation. Although he described Nazism as "ultimate evil," the director declared "it's about time for the more comedic approach. The sinister side has become maybe a little bit like aesthetic noise. With the comedic approach, I think you maybe unearth something that makes you realize what this was all about."[111] This statement showed that while the film had its lighthearted features, it was meant to be a "political satire."[112] The film's main political point was that Nazism, far from expiring in 1945, had survived into the present. *Iron Sky*, Vuorensola observed in an interview, was about "the rhetoric, the language of fascism, and how we can hear it in today's worldwide politics as well." When asked whether the film was meant to suggest "that modern American politics has fascistic elements?" he replied, "Yes, but what I want to say is that it's not just modern-day America … It's happening all over Europe, because financial crisis has always been a great breeding ground for fascist ideologies. They use the same language every time. Nobody learns."[113] The only solution to fascism's ubiquity, the director suggested, was tolerance. This was visible in the film's last scene, which advanced what Vuorensola called a "hippie" message of "peace and love."[114] In it, Renate and Washington share a kiss against the backdrop of Earth's conflagration, thereby suggesting the possibility of human understanding in the midst of hatred.

Despite concluding with this unobjectionable message, the reception of *Iron Sky* was mixed. Although the film received scattered reviews in Great Britain and the United States, it found its widest reception in Germany.[115] *Iron Sky* premiered at the Berlin Film Festival in April, 2012 and received considerable media attention. A good number of reviewers praised the film's B-movie sense of humor and hailed it as a successful satire of fascist aesthetics and loony conspiracy theories.[116] These and other critics were inclined to view it as a guilty pleasure. As the reviewer for *Stern* noted, it was a "trash spectacle that one should … not take seriously."[117] This response suggested a desire to view the film in a normalized fashion despite its controversial theme. Other reviews indicated support for *Iron Sky*'s rejection of moralistic forms of representing Nazism. Wolfgang Höbel, writing in *Der Spiegel*, praised the film for "succeeding in making even the most sober moral preacher laugh." To be sure, Höbel hastened to add that laughing at *Iron Sky* was made easier by the fact that a non-German directed it. "If a German filmmaker had been involved," he noted, "one would have serious concerns about … the mischief that was being made with the … German past."[118] As it was, however, the movie's international authorship provided Germans with cover to indulge their craving for normalcy. Or as another *Spiegel* reviewer put it following *Iron Sky*'s Berlin premiere: "laughing about the Nazis has an especially liberating effect in the [German] capital."[119]

By contrast, other German commentators criticized the film for a host of failures. Some focused on its cinematic shortcomings. Summing up many of them was Daniel Erk, who, writing in *Die Zeit*, called *Iron Sky* "boring, flat, and timid" and declared "there is practically nothing good about this film, not the plot, the gags, the casting, the digs, and certainly not the desire to break taboos."[120] Others faulted the film for universalizing the Nazi era's significance. These critics insisted that *Iron Sky* was not really about Nazism at all. One said the film was mostly about the "mendacity of the mass media, which serves as the henchmen of the powerful and their PR strategists."[121] Others said it was less interested in condemning Nazism than making "sharp digs against the present-day United States."[122] These digs diluted Nazism's meaning, however, for, as Henryk Broder argued, if the American President's cynical exploitation of fascist ideas to win votes "is the criterion for embracing a fascist ideology, then this applies ... to all political parties everywhere. Everyone is [thus] fascist."[123] Further still, film critic Michael Meyns astutely observed that in critiquing "[America's] crude behaviour ... under the Bush administration," the film made "the Nazis ... appear ... harmless ... Although [they seek] world domination, their foolish costumes and kooky plans make them come across as no more threatening than typical James Bond villains." "It appears," he concluded, "that the Nazis have become stereotypical components of a popular cultural inventory that are as easy to parody as Crusaders, Huns, and Vikings."[124] Meyns's comments, by criticizing the depiction of the Nazis as no different from other historical villains, showed a commitment to resisting the process of normalization. Yet it was offset by the desire of other critics to laugh at the Nazi era. This fact, in addition to the sharp split in Internet responses to *Iron Sky* among ordinary Germans – between those who found it hilarious and those who found it puerile – revealed that Germans had become increasingly divided on the merits of normalizing the Nazi past.[125]

Killing Hitler

After the subject of the Nazis winning World War II, one of the most popular themes in alternate history has been Hitler's removal from history.[126] Many writers and scholars have imagined how history's course would have changed had Hitler's life taken a different direction. What if he had never been born? What if he had been accepted into art school? What if he had been assassinated? This last scenario, in particular, has been actively explored in recent years, especially in Germany. German accounts have often disagreed, however, on how Hitler's elimination would have changed the course of history. While some have portrayed it as turning out better, others have viewed it turning out worse. In the process, they have offered diverging views of the Nazi past. Fantasy scenarios, by imagining the German people acting responsibly after Hitler's elimination and putting their country back on a path of political moderation, have relativized German guilt for Nazism by blaming it mostly on the Nazi dictator. By contrast, nightmare scenarios, by showing Germany going down the path of political extremism even without Hitler, have underscored the German people's broader responsibility for Nazism. Predictably, these accounts respectively reflect diverging conservative and liberal views of the Nazi experience.

Representing the first group was eminent German historian Alexander Demandt's recent anthology of counterfactual essays, *Es hätte auch anders kommen können* (*It Could Have Happened Differently*). Published in 2010, this volume explored a wide range of counterfactual topics, but it included a brief discussion of several assassination attempts against Hitler that might have substantially changed the course of history had they succeeded.[127] Interestingly, Demandt dismissed the most famous attempt of all – the July 20, 1944 assassination plot against Hitler known as Operation Valkyrie – as having taken place much too late to have substantially changed the course of historical events (aside from sparing Germany much needless destruction). Instead, Demandt focused his attention on the possible consequences of an earlier, lesser-known assassination plot – that of British military attaché, Noel Mason-Macfarlane, to kill the Führer in the spring of 1939. Had Mason-Macfarlane successfully carried out his plan to shoot Hitler with a high-velocity rifle in Berlin, the course of history, according to Demandt, would have been changed substantially. Echoing the views of previous German historians, such as Joachim Fest and Sebastian Haffner, Demandt argued that Hitler would have been celebrated as ranking among "the greatest Germans" of all time and honored with the placement of his bust in the famed Valhalla monument near Regensburg. He would have been credited with the economic recovery of the 1930s, and Austria would have been permitted to remain part of Germany. The Nazi regime's early misdeeds would have been dismissed, and World War II and the Holocaust would never have happened.

More importantly, the Nazi system eventually would have given way to a more moderate regime. Initially, Demandt asserted, there would have been a "power struggle between Hitler's paladins." Yet regardless of whether a "moderate like Hermann Goering or a radical like Goebbels or Himmler emerged in charge," the regime "would have quickly stabilized."[128] The reason was larger geopolitical imperatives. Without Hitler in charge, the Nazis would have refrained from launching an aggressive war in the east and Stalin's Soviet Union would have emerged as the greatest threat to the Western powers. They, in turn, would have sensed Stalin's desire to attack them and therefore forged an alliance with Germany to defend the capitalist system. Facing this united front, Stalin would have had to remain content merely with conquering Poland.[129] Without the massive territorial gains acquired by Stalin in the "Great Fatherland War," the USSR's "lifespan would have been shortened in the ensuing cold war" and the important cities of "Breslau, Danzig, and Königsberg would have remained undamaged and German."[130] Perhaps most importantly, the Nazi regime itself would not have lasted. Without the "state of emergency produced by a foreign war" reinforcing the power of the police state, "splinter groups would have formed, followed by a [real political] opposition, a multiparty system and eventually a democracy, albeit maybe only in the 1950s or 1960s." Just as other European military dictatorships, such as Spain and Greece, democratized after World War II, "Germany would not have been an exception," as the country's bourgeoisie would have demanded a "say in government" and the creation of "a free democratic political system."[131]

In outlining this fantasy, Demandt echoed the conclusions of previous German writers that removing Hitler from history would have improved its course. Like the short stories of Hans Pleschinski and Sabine Wedemeyer-Schwiersch, Demandt's essay embraced the argument, associated with the "intentionalist" school of German historians, that Hitler was the chief authority within the Nazi system. This standpoint preserved a sense of Hitler's evil. Yet by saddling the Nazi dictator with the blame for Germany's crimes, it implicitly absolved the German people of their share of responsibility.[132] By contrast, British and American alternate histories have traditionally cast doubt on the idea that Hitler's elimination would have improved history's course, arguing that the German people's nationalistic tendencies would have remained a structural source of instability. Demandt's essay followed the traditional German pattern, for it expressed a deep faith in the German people's ability to transcend the misdeeds of the Nazis and return the country to the path of normal historical development. This upbeat vision of German history has been typical of conservatives, who have long strived to establish a positive sense of national identity; it further corresponded to Demandt's own political leanings.[133] At the same time, however, this vision displayed a comparatively benign view of Nazism that de-emphasized the significance of its crimes. The clearest evidence of this tendency in Demandt's essay was its lack of attention to the Nazis' persecution of the Jews. Demandt did not address how the Kristallnacht pogrom might have sullied Hitler's reputation after his assassination; nor did he comment on how the institutions entrusted with the "Jewish Problem," especially the SS, would have gone about solving it in the Führer's absence. Demandt's one laconic reference to the Jews' fate – "the majority would have been expelled from Germany" – was not followed by any description of its consequences. This absence of attention was glaring, but it was predictable. Only by ignoring the fate of the Jews could Demandt's upbeat portrait of the German people after Hitler be sustained.[134]

A similar set of considerations informed the prominent German writer Dieter Kühn's book of short stories, *Ich war Hitlers Schutzengel* (*I Was Hitler's Guardian Angel*) (Figure 20).[135] Published in 2010, the volume contained four short stories, three of which focused on the consequences of Hitler's assassination for German history. In the first, "Elser jagt Hitler in die Luft" ("Elser Blows Hitler into the Sky"), Kühn imagined Georg Elser succeeding in his famous assassination attempt against the Nazi dictator in Munich's Bürgerbräukeller on the night of November 8, 1939. In the tale, Hitler haughtily ignores a note passed to him by his personal adjutant Julius Schwab urging him to finish his speech in order to catch a waiting train to Berlin (his airplane is grounded due to foggy weather). As a result, the Führer keeps speaking and is killed when Elser's time bomb – hidden in a column behind his podium – explodes, destroying much of the building. Since Kühn portrayed the bomb also killing Nazi leaders Joseph Goebbels, Heinrich Himmler, Alfred Rosenberg, Martin Bormann, and Wilhelm Frick, the question of who will succeed Hitler is quickly resolved in favor of the most prominent Nazi still on the scene, Hermann Goering. Like Demandt, Kühn speculated that Hitler would have gone on to be celebrated as an illustrious figure in German history. This is largely thanks to Goering, who organizes an elaborate funeral ceremony at Munich's Feldherrnhalle and thereafter announces plans to inter Hitler's body in a massive mausoleum on his estate at Carinhall outside of Berlin.

Kühn's tale differed from Demandt's, however, in offering a more detailed exploration of Germany's ensuing political development after Hitler's death. In a symbolic sign of things to come, Goering takes up residence as the new Reich Chancellor in Berlin's Hohenzollern Palace and fills important government positions in the army, bureaucracy,

Figure 20. Dieter Kühn's volume of short stories, *Ich war Hitlers Schutzengel* (*I Was Hitler's Guardian Angel*) (2010), features several tales that explore the consequences of Hitler's assassination.

and foreign office with old elites, such as Ludwig Beck, Carl Goerdeler, and Ulrich von Hassel. Under the influence of these moderate figures, Goering pursues a more peaceful foreign policy, shelving plans to attack France and England and pursuing a path of diplomatic rapprochement. Domestically, Goering relaxes anti-Semitic restrictions against Jews and places the moderate *Schutzpolizei* instead of the fanatical SS in charge of running the concentration camps. In the realm of culture, finally, Goering fashions himself into Germany's leading aesthete, expanding his collection of Old Masters paintings and pursuing Hitler's dream for a monumental art museum in Linz. As the story ends, Kühn writes:

> the popularity of Reich Chancellor Goering grows. He allows himself to be celebrated as a "man of peace" and displays his brilliance as a "renaissance count." [He organizes] elaborate press balls ... pompous New Years' receptions ... opulently decorated premieres in "his" State Opera ...[and] grand parades ... in front of numerous State guests ...
> Headline in *The Times*: "Has the German Reich Reverted to the Era of the Kaisers?"[136]

Hitler's removal from history, in short, leads Germany to abandon the fanaticism of Nazism and return to its older monarchical traditions.

A second story by Kühn, "Auf Hitler folgt Rommel" ("After Hitler Comes Rommel"), featured a similar turn of events. In this tale, Hitler is killed in a plane crash in March of 1943, when a bomb placed on his flight from Smolensk to Berlin by Wehrmacht officer, Henning von Tresckow, actually explodes (in real history, the bomb's plastic explosives froze at high altitude and failed to detonate). With Hitler removed from the scene, a power struggle ensues between the SS and the Wehrmacht. Himmler initially seizes the upper hand by blaming the Führer's death on Wehrmacht negligence (he alleges Soviet planes carried out the attack). But at precisely the time that Himmler undertakes provisional talks with the Western Allies about the possibility of a separate peace, Abwehr chief Wilhelm Canaris notifies General Erwin Rommel, who sends soldiers to arrest the SS leader and forcibly subordinate his feared organization to the Wehrmacht.

As in Demandt's account, Kühn's tale showed German history taking a more moderate course. Following negotiations between Rommel and General Montgomery on the island of Guernsey, Winston

Churchill agrees to give the Wehrmacht a free hand against the Soviet Union and, before long, the British and Americans join in an anti-communist crusade against the USSR. To be sure, the Western Allies first insist that Germany makes certain concessions: the country has to submit to a token "occupation" by Allied forces, who march through German territory on the way into the Soviet Union; the NSDAP is banned; Himmler is hanged; and Cologne replaces Berlin as the nation's capital. Overall, however, Germany is spared war in the West and escapes much of the destruction it suffered in real history. Guiding Germany into this fantasy is Erwin Rommel. In his capacity as Reich President, he appoints old elites to positions of power and inaugurates a return to the "rule of law." He also presides over the reinstitution of conservative values in culture; literature is suffused with militaristic themes and music remains committed to "simple melodies, healthy harmony, and solid rhythm."[137] In short, Rommel is "the man of the hour," a hero who facilitates "the restoration of a conservative Europe."[138]

In offering this upbeat portrayal of German history following Hitler's assassination, Kühn's stories resembled Demandt's in displaying conservative tendencies. Their portrayal of Germany going down a restorationist path under the post-Hitler governments of Goering and Rommel affirmed the inherent moderation of the German people, who are able to successfully turn away from National Socialism. As with Demandt's narrative, however, Kühn's upbeat portrayal of Germany returning to a path of political moderation rang false because of its marginalization of the Jewish question. Neither of the tales said much about how the Jews' fate would have been affected by Hitler's death. Given the fact that the Jews already suffer intense persecution before Hitler's assassination, readers are left to assume that they will continue to experience it after his demise; this is especially true in Kühn's second story, which takes place in 1943, a point at which most Jews killed in the Holocaust had already been murdered. Needless to say, Kühn could not tackle the Jews' fate directly and still maintain the integrity of his tale's premise. Addressing the Holocaust would have cast the German people in an unflattering light and weakened the plausibility of their self-rehabilitation by exposing their complicity in genocide. Because dealing with the fate of the Jews would have undermined his allohistorical fantasy, Kühn, in short, ignored it. In so doing, he avoided dealing with Germany's guilt for the Holocaust.

This avoidance was also visible in the ending to "After Hitler Comes Rommel." In the tale's last paragraph, Winston Churchill is sitting outdoors painting a landscape scene overlooking the Rhine River, "his back to the events on the eastern front." The British Prime Minister is busy thinking about the "need to establish a bulwark against the red flood," but he reminds himself "not to care about the war in the east any longer" and to "finally leave everything behind him." The act of painting allows Churchill "to forget present-day plagues" and "purify the spirit!" Oil paints, in particular, possess the advantage of "painting over" what has been painted before and "enabling it to disappear." The story then closes with the line, "There is currently an enormous need for oil paint!"

The meaning of this concluding paragraph is murky, but it arguably contained a conservative message. By depicting Churchill turning his back to the east, Kühn symbolically portrayed the British Prime Minister ignoring the human suffering caused by the joint Allied–German assault against the Soviet Union. Kühn may have intended this passage to be a blanket indictment of Realpolitik. Yet, it was telling that he made this point by using a British instead of a German leader. By portraying Churchill (instead of, say, Rommel) ignoring the carnage in the east, Kühn diminished German responsibility for it. Indeed, he implied the existence of a moral equivalence between Allied and German behavior. In so doing. he employed the familiar conservative strategy of blurring the line between the Allies and Germans in the effort to relativize the guilt of the latter.

That said, it is possible to pursue an alternate reading of Kühn's tales and view them as offering a more self-critical commentary on German history. Although the writer ostensibly showed the German people redeeming themselves by rejecting Nazism, they end up exchanging it for monarchical, instead of parliamentary, rule. They thereby reveal that their political instincts are far from democratic. Kühn seemed to suggest such a reading in the conclusion of his book's third story, eponymously titled, "I Was Hitler's Guardian Angel." Located between – and thus intertextually linked to – the book's two other counterfactual tales, this lengthy story was not a traditional work of alternate history, in which history's course is altered, but an inverted one that depicted the *prevention* of history's alteration. In this sense, it was more akin to a "secret history" that disclosed to readers the unknown events that determine the course of real history.

The story is narrated from the perspective of an angel – Hitler's guardian angel – who recounts his pivotal role in protecting the dictator from multiple attempts on his life. In describing the many occasions when he prevented assassination attempts against the Führer (whether by Elser, Tresckow, or Stauffenberg), the angel defends his actions by claiming he was simply doing the job that all guardian angels are entrusted with. At the same time, he recognizes that "as long as I kept Hitler alive, the murder and destruction [he unleashed] would continue."[139] The angel looks to the Archangel Michael and to God himself for a sign that his actions are part of a larger plan, but to no avail. In the end, he takes solace in the fact that while he prevents Hitler's opponents from killing him, they probably would not have had much success realizing their ultimate goals. As the story concludes, the angel exclaims that his role in history's disastrous course has been

> over-estimated, indeed radically! for the subsequent actions that followed the assassination attempts, the attempts to topple the state, would have failed in any case! In every instance, there were too few people whom the conspirators could trust: too few helpers with authority and power. In short, with the few people of the resistance, there was little chance to create a new state.[140]

It is impossible to know whether the angel's self-justifying remarks reflect Kühn's own views, but they can plausibly be interpreted as expressing the author's belief that the German people were never capable of freeing themselves from Nazism and establishing a true democracy through their own actions. If true, this reading would show Kühn to be holding the German people accountable for the crimes of the Nazi era rather than exonerating them of any responsibility for them.

The ambiguous implications of Kühn's stories partly reflected the author's idiosyncratic literary style. A prolific, prize-winning writer, Kühn is well known for his best-selling biographies of famous Germans throughout the ages, such as Wolfram von Eschenbach, Neidhart, Oswald von Wolkenstein, and Ludwig van Beethoven.[141] These works (and others on non-German historical figures such as Napoleon and Josephine Baker) have long attracted readers with their postmodern mixing of fact and fiction. Reviewers, however, have often described them as "making every historian's hair stand on end" for their loose allegiance to historical fact.[142] Indeed, while critics admire his "falsified histories," they confess to being bewildered about their "underlying intentions."[143] Given Kühn's literary playfulness, it is hard to say what message, if any, he wanted the stories in *I Was Hitler's Guardian Angel* to communicate. Yet while they were clearly critical of Nazism, they were reluctant to probe the depths of its evil.

This reluctance probably reflected Kühn's personal background. Born in 1935, the writer belonged to the same generation as Demandt – one that personally witnessed the war and its destructive effects. Given the fact that he experienced Allied bombing raids on his home city of Cologne as a young boy, he was understandably inclined to participate in the renewed German tendency after the turn of the millennium to focus on their wartime victimization. Like Demandt, Kühn has wistfully fantasized about how Germany's cities might have avoided wartime destruction. In a recent interview, he noted that under a Goering-led Germany, "we would have been spared a world war" and the appearance of German cities "would look entirely different."[144] Whether or not Kühn was willing to accept the political price for this fantasy scenario is unclear. In the interview, Kühn speculated that under a Goering regime, the German people would have accepted "a kind of "National Socialism lite" as their political system, especially if they could have foreseen that, under Hitler's more radical brand of Nazism, "everything would ultimately end in destruction."[145] When asked in another interview whether or not it was "embittering" to realize that Hitler's assassination would not have led to democracy – that Germany's political rehabilitation was "only enabled by the total collapse of 1945" – Kühn sidestepped the question's political implications and replied that the assassination would have been worth it, "since it would have spared us the worst. How many cities, after all, were destroyed by bombs after the July 20th assassination plot?"[146] These remarks suggested that Kühn's alternate histories were geared more towards fictionally helping the German people avert their own victimization than ameliorating the suffering of the Nazis' millions of non-German victims. So powerful was the fantasy of Germany avoiding destruction that embracing a kinder and gentler form of Nazism was worth it. It is unclear whether Kühn had any political reasons for implying this message (the writer has rarely discussed his political views in public). But given his longtime affiliation with the conservative Free Democratic Party (FDP), his interest in Germany's wartime victimization can be seen as echoing the goals of the center-right rather than the left.[147] In the end, by offering an upbeat portrait of Germany's development under Goering and Rommel – and by marginalizing the Holocaust in order to achieve it – Kühn subtly relativized the singularity of the Third Reich's crimes.

This conclusion is supported by contrasting Kühn's and Demandt's tales with a more critical account of Hitler's assassination, Wolfgang Brenner's novel, *Führerlos* (*Führerless*) (Figure 21). Published in 2008, the novel, at first glance, resembled Kühn's short story, "Elser Blows Hitler into the Sky," insofar as it also portrayed Elser's bomb killing Hitler in 1939. Brenner did not imagine the blast killing any of the other major Nazis, however, and so his novel's ensuing narrative mostly chronicled the complex power struggle that erupts following the Führer's death. This struggle is mostly between Joseph Goebbels and Hermann Goering. Through his position as Reich Propaganda Minister, Goebbels initially tries to cover up Hitler's death by fabricating a story about him dying in a plane crash following the expected victory. In so doing, the Propaganda Minister hopes to prevent the German people from becoming demoralized and losing their appetite for invading France. Goering, meanwhile, is Hitler's designated successor and recognizes Goebbels' maneuvers as part of a joint attempt with Himmler's SS to seize power. In response, Goering quickly dispatches a team of Luftwaffe officers to arrest Himmler and, in short order, convinces Reinhard Heydrich to eliminate him and take over his job (Himmler's death is attributed to suicide).

Through these measures, Goering appears to get the upper hand over Goebbels and begins to consolidate power. His first step is to earn the German people's trust by pursuing a moderate kind of foreign policy. After offering Germany's old elites a conciliatory gesture by inviting Kaiser Wilhelm II back to Germany from Dutch exile, Goering instructs Germany's armed forces to refrain from pushing ahead with attacks against France and England. For good measure, he pursues a path of rapprochement with the Soviet Union, refusing to take sides after the Soviets invade Finland. These steps reassure the German people – who, in the meantime, have begun to organize sporadic anti-war protests – and enhance Goering's popularity.

This development, however, does not keep Goebbels from pursuing his own power grab. The Propaganda Minister soon hatches an elaborate plan involving the woman whom he now stylizes into Hitler's "widow," Eva Braun. While Goering amasses power for himself, Goebbels concocts the news that Eva is pregnant with Hitler's child. His long-term goal is to act as Germany's secret regent until the child – who presumably will be "produced" at the proper time – is old enough to take the reins of power. In the short term, Goebbels hopes that the story of Hitler's offspring will keep the Führer-myth alive among the German

Figure 21. Wolfgang Brenner's 2008 novel, *Führerlos* (*Führerless*), depicts how Hitler's assassination in 1939 sparks a fierce power struggle between Hermann Goering and Joseph Goebbels.

masses. (They confirm his expectations by rushing to buy magazines trumpeting the latest updates on Eva's comings and goings.) At the same time, Goebbels undertakes a major film project, a bio-pic on the Führer's life, which he hopes will further help to keep Hitler in the public eye and counteract Goering's efforts to wean the German people away from their previous Führer-worship.

Goering is largely able to outflank Goebbels, however, through further foreign and domestic policy initiatives. His master-stroke is his forging of contacts with the Swiss-based American OSS chief, Allen Dulles, whom he convinces to consider a German plan to guarantee England's and France's borders in the West in exchange for Allied recognition of Germany's gains in Poland and a joint campaign to contain any Soviet advances into Eastern Europe. At the ensuing Paris Conference of January 1940, Goering succeeds in getting FDR and Churchill to agree to these terms, thereby ending the prospect of a dangerous two-front war. Goering now starts to envision himself as the "peace chancellor" who restored stability to Europe.[148] Domestically, meanwhile, Goering permits something of a cultural thaw, allowing the German media to ask critical questions about the "Hitler era," especially the dictator's brinkmanship of the late 1930s. He also assembles a team of pragmatic advisers to help him construct a "reformed kind of National Socialism" based on more "rational and modern policies," in particular, "vigorous economic activity and full peace along the Reich's borders."[149] To achieve this goal, Goering's advisers, including Ludwig Erhard, seize upon the idea of mass-producing Volkswagen Beetles to satisfy pent-up consumer demand among the German people. This plan generates headlines nationwide and seems to promise great success.

Yet, despite Goering's best intentions, his plans are thwarted by the inherent contradictions of the Nazi system. Goering's efforts to chart a new course are undermined by his inheritance of policies begun under Hitler. The most important is the SS's Germanization program in occupied Poland. Begun during the Wehrmacht's Blitzkrieg invasion of the nation in the fall of 1939, the violent expulsion of Polish civilians from their homes continues even after Hitler's death, as the SS officials in charge of them retain their authority to fulfill the Führer's original orders. Goering, listening to his pragmatic advisers, initially tries to curtail the SS's abuses and orders Heydrich to treat Polish civilians humanely. But the problems prove insurmountable. Not only does Goering have no answer for the unrest in Poland, he does not know how to tackle the ongoing T4 Euthanasia campaign, the revelation of which shocks his advisers. Most serious of all, Goering has no humane solution for the "Jewish question." While his advisers recommend suspending anti-Semitic laws against German Jews and reintegrating them into the *Volksgemeinschaft* as economic catalysts, Goering dismisses this as politically impossible, especially as radicals like Julius Streicher increasingly accuse him of being a sell-out. At the same time, Goering recognizes that the growing chaos in occupied Poland (caused by the ongoing deportations of Jews to the Polish interior) may sabotage Germany's good relations with the West. At this juncture, Goering faces a dilemma: shelve the regime's anti-Semitism and preserve peace with the West? Or remain committed to anti-Semitism and war? Significantly, Goering ultimately accepts Heydrich's recommendation that the only way to pacify Poland and solve the intensifying Jewish problem is to invade the Soviet Union, which will provide the necessary cover for a more radical "Final Solution" through murder.

In the end, *Führerlos* revealed the impossibility of creating a "reformed" kind of National Socialism. Brenner partly attributed this to the chaotic system of rule created by Hitler – one that persists even after his death. Near the end of the novel, Goering, frustrated by his inability to satisfy the demands raining down upon him from various officials, thinks angrily to himself:

> they lurked everywhere: the Führer's creations. Brazen bigmouths, breezy opportunists, eel-like functionaries. They had no ideological commitments except to get whatever they could for themselves.
> Now they sat in important positions in the new Nazi state and threw sand into the machinery unless they were ... fawned over. Although Hitler had been dead for some time, they behaved the same way as when he was alive.[150]

This passage testified to Brenner's belief that the Nazi system – supported by countless Germans – possessed its own deterministic logic that would have survived even after Hitler's removal from power. Like a giant mechanical clock, it followed its own evil dynamic once it had been wound up and switched on by the Führer. Hitler's success in committing the Nazi economic, military, and police establishments to a policy of war meant that, even after his death, there were too many groups – especially the Wehrmacht and the SS – with a vested interest in continuing down the path of aggression to behave any differently. Even reform-minded Nazi leaders, such as Goering, could not have stuffed the evil genie back into its bottle.

Brenner underscored this point at the novel's end by depicting the tragic fate of Eva Braun. After Goebbels' jealous wife, Magda, discovers that Eva is not really pregnant, she throws a fit that prompts the young woman to flee to Munich. Since the Propaganda Minister cannot risk Eva revealing details of his plan, he has her detained and placed in a sanatorium, where she is kept under sedation. Before long, however, Goering's decision to go to war allows him to reconcile with Goebbels and the latter now comes to view Eva as expendable. As the novel ends, she is consigned to the T4 program and ultimately murdered in a gas van. Just as the Nazi system is able to survive the death of its creator, so too can it do without its first lady.

In offering this bleak view of German history without Hitler, Brenner contradicted the fantasy visions of Demandt and Kühn. His novel implied that Hitler's assassination would have made history worse, not better. Although *Führerlos* ends without showing the outcome of the planned German invasion of the Soviet Union, it implies that the Wehrmacht would have been successful. Thanks to Goering's separate peace with the Allies, Germany only has to fight a one-front war against the Soviets, who no longer enjoy American economic and military aid. In hinting at the Allies' role in enabling a German victory, Brenner could theoretically be seen as trying – like Kühn – to deflect attention away from Germany's sole responsibility for the coming war in the east. Yet Brenner ultimately held the German people primarily responsible. By showing them upholding the Nazi system even after Hitler's death, he rejected Demandt's and Kühn's optimistic belief that they would have pursued a path of political moderation. Brenner thereby expressed his allegiance to a different philosophy of history – one that emphasized the importance of deep structural forces instead of great individuals in shaping historical events. Removing Hitler, in his view, would have done little to improve history, because the evils of the Nazi system and the investment of the German people in its perpetuation would have persisted.

Brenner's judgment partly reflected his personal background. Born in 1954, he belonged to a younger generation than Demandt and Kühn and did not experience the war first hand. He thus did not have the same wistful feelings of a lost childhood that stimulated the fantasies of older Germans. Moreover, while Brenner was not a member of the 1968 generation, he grew up in a more self-critical left-wing political environment that strove to wrestle more directly with the Nazi regime's crimes. This outlook was visible in his other creative work. A professional journalist, Brenner has long identified with the victims of German right-wing extremism, a fact exemplified by his sympathetic biography of Walter Rathenau (murdered by right-wing fanatics in 1922) and his documentary film about Kreisau Circle member and resistance figure Adolf Reichwein (executed by the Nazis in 1944).[151] Given the subject matter of these works, it is clear why Brenner devoted more attention in *Führerlos* to the Nazis' victims, whether the Poles, the Jews, or the mentally and physically handicapped. Unlike the stories of Demandt and Kühn, which ignored these groups in focusing on the German people's return to the values of the *Kaiserreich*, Brenner made sure they stayed at the center of the narrative. Only by doing so could Nazism's inherent evil be recognized.

The popular reaction to the tales of Demandt, Kühn, and Brenner was mixed. Most reviewers of Demandt's anthology of essays offered generic words of praise for his "entertaining historical diversions."[152] But specific remarks about his account of Hitler's assassination were more dismissive. One reviewer called Demandt's account "unusually imprecise," compared with his counterfactual musings about earlier periods of history.[153] Another criticized its conservative political implications, describing Demandt's claim that Hitler's death would have tempted Stalin to attack the West as amounting to a "rewarming of the long dismissed legends of a Nazi preventive war against the Soviets in 1941."[154] Ironically, the conservative political implications of Demandt's essay were confirmed by its endorsement by extreme right-wing groups, which hailed the historian for saying "exactly the same thing" that the "national camp had said in back rooms for years" – namely, that if Hitler had been assassinated in 1939, he would have been hailed as a great statesman.[155] Reviewers of Kühn's book, by contrast, disagreed about its political implications. Some saw it as a critique of the German people, writing that it exposed "how many in Germany would have accommodated themselves with a dictatorship under Goering or Rommel."[156] Others sensed that the book had a more conservative agenda. One commentator declared that Kühn's tale "comes alarmingly close to right-wing dreams of a continued battle against Bolshevism," while another noted that its idealized portrait of Goering left her with a "stale aftertaste."[157] Brenner's book also met with a mixed response. Some praised it for its "authenticity" and "radical shift in perspective," with one reviewer hailing it for "making clear to readers that 'evil' has not disappeared with Hitler's death and that there is no possibility of a 'good' ... form of National Socialism coming into existence."[158] Others questioned the plausibility of the Allies actually forging a separate peace with the Germans.[159] In short, readers were divided on the texts' stance on normalization. While left-liberal Germans were quick to criticize passages that seemed to relativize German responsibility for Nazi crimes, conservative readers praised them for doing so. In the end, the divided reception of these German narratives mirrored ongoing German debates about responsibility for the Third Reich.

Hitler's survival

Similar German divisions over memory were brought to light with the appearance of Timur Vermes's bestselling novel, *Er ist wieder da* (*He's Back*) (Figure 22).[160] Published in 2013, the novel dealt with another familiar counterfactual theme related to the Third Reich – Hitler's survival of World War II. Since 1945, numerous accounts have portrayed Hitler escaping death and going into hiding, whether in the jungles of Latin America or the sewers of Berlin.[161] Most accounts published before the turn of the millennium directly addressed the moral question of the Führer's evasion of justice and the postwar world's effort to hold him accountable for his crimes. Vermes's novel, by contrast, took a very different approach by playing the scenario for laughs. Although it displayed something of a moralistic streak in places, its overwhelmingly satirical tenor – and its popularity among German readers – provided further evidence of a growing German desire to normalize the Nazi era.

Unlike previous alternate histories on the topic, *Er ist wieder da* was unique for being narrated by Hitler himself. Speaking in a long-winded, histrionic style familiar to readers of *Mein Kampf*, Hitler, at the novel's outset, explains his befuddlement at having just awakened in an empty lot in the middle of Berlin still dressed in his gasoline-soaked uniform. The novel never explains the origins of this *deus ex machina*, but it deftly explores its comic consequences. As Hitler shakes off the initial shock of being alive, he tentatively sets out to explore his new surroundings. Like a Japanese soldier emerging from decades of

Figure 22. Timur Vermes's bestselling 2012 novel, *Er ist wieder da* (*He's Back*) depicts Hitler coming back to life in contemporary Berlin. The cover reflects the current aesthetic trend of reducing Hitler's visage to his parted hair and signature toothbrush moustache. See also Figures 30 and 46.

self-imposed jungle isolation, the former Führer is utterly confused by present-day German life and comically misinterprets its significance. Having missed out on nearly seventy years of the country's postwar history, he perceives everything from an obsolete Nazi perspective. He believes, for example, that the presence of Turks on Berlin's streets is a legacy of his successor, Karl Doenitz's effort to bring Turkey into the war on Germany's side. He thinks Berlin's modern appearance is the result of the implementation of his scorched earth policy at the end of the war. And after learning about the Internet, he erroneously thinks that the linguistic resemblance of Wikipedia to the German word for Vikings (*Wikinger*) means that the website has Aryan roots.[162] In these and other ways, *Er ist wieder da* allows readers to laugh directly at Hitler. They can laugh at his ignorance, his destitution (he has no money, no job, no home), and at the incongruous image of him wearing a pair of blue jeans and sneakers donated to him by an empathetic Berlin kiosk operator.

Above all, readers can laugh at Hitler's struggle to cope with his loss of power. One of the novel's funniest features is the ex-dictator's attempt to preserve his delusions of grandeur despite his lowly circumstances. Throughout the novel, Hitler insists that "destiny" has enabled him to survive in order to rescue Germany from its present-day plight. As he pompously thinks to himself:

> I slapped myself on my forehead. It was so obvious that I scolded myself for not having recognized it sooner. It was not the first time that destiny had seized control. Was it not the same in 1919, at the depth of Germany's misery? Was it not then that an unknown corporal emerged out of the trenches . . . and led the Fatherland to the highest heights of its glory?
> If destiny has . . . seen the need to play such a conjuring trick [today], then the situation must be even more desperate than it was back then.
> The Volk must be in even greater danger! . . .
> I now understood fully. I alone was meant to save the Volk.[163]

Unfortunately for Hitler, however, no one else is aware of his new historical mission. Wherever he goes, the ex-dictator remains unrecognized by those whom he meets. The kiosk owner mistakes him for a comedian committed to a life of method acting, while a group of teenagers at a laundromat think he is the actor and frequent Hitler impersonator, Christoph Maria Herbst, from the hit German television comedy, *Stromberg*.

Er ist wieder da did not satirize Hitler for its own sake, however. It also showed the potential dangers of laughing at him. Early in the novel, the kiosk owner's admiration of Hitler's "impersonation" of the Führer prompts him to introduce the ex-dictator to a friend who works for a television station. Before long, the novel (in an homage to the film *Network*) portrays how the station, seeking to boost its ratings, invites Hitler to appear as a guest on the talk show of a Turkish comedian. In his brief appearance, Hitler launches into an epic rant about foreigners (among other things, he complains that "Germans today today separate their trash more carefully than they separate their races") and becomes an immediate hit, a veritable YouTube sensation.[164] The joke is that while Hitler is being deadly serious, his fans think he is being ironic. No amount of evidence convinces the German public otherwise. Journalists try to get Hitler to divulge his "real" name and explain why he never breaks character. No one wants to consider the possibility that his racist rants are genuine. The public is only capable of seeing him as an avant-garde comedian. Ironically, by sustaining the public's desire to laugh at Hitler, the German media boosts his popularity and turns him into a celebrity. Before long, he gets his own TV show and is contracted to write a book. His colleagues congratulate him by ironically referring to him as the "Führer" and giving him mock Hitler salutes. As the novel concludes, however, ominous signs begin to mount. Posters prepared for Hitler's upcoming show display the slogan, "Not Everything was Bad," and German political parties compete to recruit him into their ranks. Laughing at Hitler, *Er ist wieder da* suggests, may help to rehabilitate him and facilitate his return to power.

In arriving at this cautionary conclusion, Vermes tempered his novel's slapstick style with a moral message. Although the journalist and first-time novelist denied wanting to hold up an "admonishing index finger" to readers, he explained that his comic depiction of Hitler was meant to humanize him and thereby challenge the traditional German portrait of him as a monster.[165] Vermes's background may have inclined him to challenge this prevailing view. Born in 1967 of a German mother and Hungarian father, he belonged to the generation that came of age in the 1980s and 1990s, at a time when Germans were embracing a more self-critical view of the Nazi era. He thus rejected the tendency to demonize Hitler because it "obscured the obvious attraction that [he] exerted as a human being ... on countless people who adored him." It further provided Germans with an easy postwar alibi with which to avert blame for their country's descent into evil. "A monstrous Hitler,"

Vermes noted, "makes it easy for us [Germans], because the more irresistible evil is, the less guilty those are who eagerly helped him [to power]." By portraying Hitler as a human being with his "positive sides," by contrast, Vermes intended to show readers "why so many people cooperated with him" once upon a time and remind them that "even today . . .[he] might be successful" again.[166]

Despite being informed by a moral agenda, however, Vermes's humanization of Hitler normalized the Nazi past by encouraging Germans to laugh at it. In contrast to British and American audiences, which have long enjoyed lampooning Hitler and the Nazis, Germans have traditionally been more inhibited about doing so. For much of the postwar period, they followed an implicit taboo – rooted in lingering sensitivities about the nation's wartime suffering and concerns about its international image – against making Nazism's horrors into the stuff of humor. Since the 1990s, however, comic representations of the Nazi era have become more common in German popular culture. This trend, which has been visible in films, television shows, and comic books, reveals that Germans have begun to abandon their previous moralistic attitudes in favor of a more normalized perspective typical of their Anglo-American neighbors.[167] *Er ist wieder da*, by prompting German readers to laugh at Hitler, both reflected and promoted this desire for normality.

In so doing, however, the novel ran the risk of trivializing the Nazi era's criminality. Like certain controversial comedy skits by Howard Stern and cartoon strips by Robert Crumb, *Er ist wieder d*a gave a platform to racist ideas in the process of spoofing them.[168] When the novel portrays Hitler attributing Germany's postwar "economic miracle" to "the disappearance of the Jewish parasites" and the Turks' limited German language skills to the Nazi policy of denying a full education to "subjugated peoples," it assumes that readers will understand the inanity of the dictator's beliefs without having to have them explicitly repudiated. Yet in loosening the moralistic reigns on his narrative, Vermes opened himself up to the charge of being soft on Nazism.[169] To be sure, the writer insulated himself from this charge by making sure that Hitler receives his come-uppance at the novel's end, when he ironically gets beaten up by neo-Nazis who think that he is a Jew trying to discredit Nazism with his "comedy act." But even here, by depicting Hitler ultimately receiving the support of the German public (which thinks that any victim of neo-Nazism, even Hitler, must be "good"), the novel ends up making Hitler sympathetic. Indeed, it is notable that while readers begin the novel by laughing *at* Hitler, they gradually end up laughing *with* him. Throughout *Er ist wieder da*, Hitler launches into rants against things that many of us despise: vapid television shows, soulless chain stores, noisy leaf blowers, and opportunistic politicians. Like the ubiquitous *Downfall* parodies on YouTube (discussed in Chapter 6), *Er ist wieder da* turned Hitler into a mouthpiece for numerous contemporary grievances. In the process, the novel not only led readers to identify with Hitler (something reinforced by the text's first person perspective); it also universalized his significance. By inserting Hitler into the present instead of the past, the novel shifted attention away from his real historical importance.

In the end, *Er ist wieder da* highlighted fading fears of Nazism. Until recently, the counterfactual premise of Hitler surviving World War II and trying to return to power was portrayed as a nightmare. As seen in a wide range of novels, television shows, and films from the 1950s through the 1990s, the prospect of a Hitler-led Fourth Reich originally reflected real historical anxieties that Nazism had not entirely been banished from history.[170] In the last generation, however, Germany's post-unification stability and the quickening pace of organic normalization have diminished these fears. This explains why the impulse to bring Hitler to justice for his crimes, once so prominent in alternate histories of Hitler's survival, was entirely absent from Vermes's novel. As Germans have become more self-confident about the present, they have displayed a growing desire to normalize the past by tempering its tragedy with comedy.

This trend was confirmed, to an important degree, by the novel's popular reception. *Er ist wieder da* was an enormous commercial success. By late 2013, it had sold over one million copies in Germany and had reached the top spot on *Der Spiegel*'s bestseller list. The novel is also being translated into more than thirty languages and made into a film.[171] This overwhelmingly positive response was echoed in countless reader comments on German websites, the majority of which praised the book as "hilarious."[172] The novel was also praised in published reviews, which enthusiastically described it as an "insanely comical," "roaringly funny," and overwhelmingly "successful . . . satire."[173] At the same time, however, dissenting voices were heard.[174] Some reviewers faulted *Er ist wieder da* for being overly long and repetitive, but others levied the more serious charge that the novel's popularity signaled a worrisome shift in German memory. One observer feared that the novel's ironic tone was being overlooked by its many fans, declaring that it was "politically naïve" to expect that "the [German] public stands on the correct side and is in the position to reflect on what it reads."[175] Other commentators agreed, with one noting that it was "highly dangerous" for Vermes to place readers in the position of "identify[ing] with Hitler" – especially since, as another argued, it made them "ruminate over countless Nazi ideas."[176] The fact that many ordinary readers confessed to agreeing with Hitler at various junctures in the novel lent confirmation to this fear.[177] Indeed, even Vermes expressed concern about the desire of many readers "to see the world through Hitler's eyes" – a desire that made him wonder about the motives behind many readers' requests for a sequel.[178] It is impossible to know the extent to which such views were behind *Er ist wieder da*'s popularity. But certain reviewers' fears that the book was promoting questionable attitudes towards the Nazi past revealed that not all Germans were comfortable with normalizing it.

Alternate Holocausts

Similar debates were also sparked by alternate histories about the Holocaust. In the decades after 1945, most "what if?" narratives relating to the Nazi genocide have been fantasies. Some have focused on the attempt to undo the Holocaust; others have dealt with the effort to punish the Germans more severely for having perpetrated it.[179] Since the turn of the millennium, a new version of the fantasy has appeared dealing with a previously unasked question: how would history have been different if the Holocaust had never occurred in the first place?

The most prominent exploration of this scenario was American writer Michael Chabon's 2007 novel, *The Yiddish Policemen's Union* (Figure 23).[180] Like *Amerikan Eagle*, *The Yiddish Policemen's Union* took the form of a traditional detective novel, albeit one whose counterfactual elements lay more on the margins than at the center of its narrative. The novel's plot, at first glance, appears to be a straightforward story of two detectives trying to solve a murder. Yet, the tale's setting and the identity of the characters add an unusual twist. Set in the present, the novel takes place in the remote town of Sitka, Alaska and features a pair of Jewish detectives, Meyer Landsman and Berko Shemets, who are trying to solve the murder of a Hasidic Jewish chess prodigy. The incongruousness of the characters and setting is not immediately explained. But readers gradually come to learn that *The Yiddish*

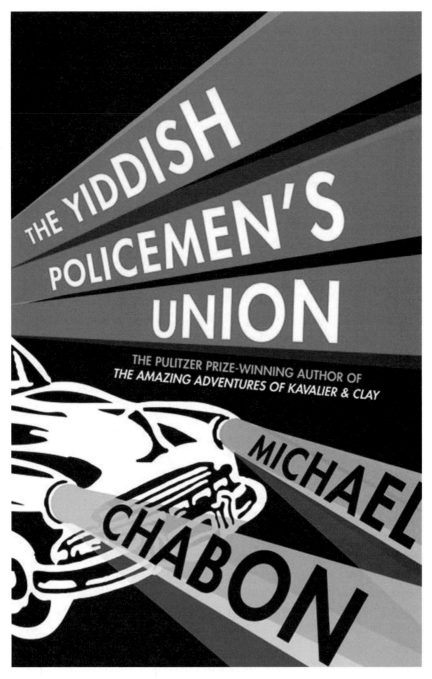

Figure 23. Michael Chabon's novel, *The Yiddish Policemen's Union* (2007), imagines European Jews partly escaping the Holocaust by fleeing to a new homeland in Alaska.

Policemen's Union is set in an alternate world in which the United States government decided in 1940 to establish a territorial home for European Jewish refugees in Alaska.

Based on a real document, known as the Slattery Report (which was produced by the Department of the Interior in 1939), this fateful political decision changes history in numerous ways. Thanks to President Roosevelt's passing of the Alaska Resettlement Act in 1940, two million Jews are able to escape from war-torn Europe to the American territory (Alaska is not yet a state) and establish a vibrant community full of social, cultural, and religious diversity. Most of the novel is devoted to describing the varied Jewish characters who inhabit this alternate world, whether secular proletarians or devout Hasidim. But lurking in the background is the fact that the Holocaust (at least as we know it in real history) never occurs. Although two million Jews fall victim to what becomes known as the Nazi "Destruction," the lives of four million others in Europe are spared. (Chabon never really explains the reason for this Nazi decision, but it seemingly results from Germany's early defeat of the Soviet Union in 1942.) Regardless of the reason for this turn of events, *The Yiddish Policemen's Union* initially appears to endorse the fantasy that averting the Holocaust – or at least dramatically mitigating its magnitude – would have made history turn out for the better.

In reality, however, the novel cast doubt on whether the course of alternate history would have been superior to that of real history. On the one hand, far more European Jews survive the Nazi onslaught and many are privileged to partake in the creation of a Yiddish-speaking homeland in Alaska. Moreover, Germany's defeat of the Soviet Union means there is no Cold War, a conclusion implied by the novel's references to a "Third Russian Republic" and a "Polish Free State."[181] On the other hand, the state of Israel is never created, as the Jews lose the 1948 War of Independence and are "driven into the sea" by the Arabs.[182] Moreover, the Jews of Alaska are themselves in a precarious situation. The Roosevelt administration's original granting of independence to the Alaskan Jewish settlement is only intended to last for sixty years, at which point it is supposed to be reconsidered. At the time the action of the novel takes place – our present – the President of the United States is inclined to have the territory revert to the United States, thereby ending the Jews' dreams of political autonomy. Moreover, friction is growing between the Jews of Sitka and the native Alaskan population, further underscoring their vulnerability.

This political setting provides the backdrop for the novel's main plot, a complicated conspiracy of Jewish religious fundamentalists and Christian Zionists – including the President himself – to destroy the Dome of the Rock in Jerusalem and prepare the groundwork for a messianic-inspired Jewish return to Palestine. At the novel's conclusion, detectives Landsman and Shemets discover the reason for the murder of the Hasidic chess prodigy – he is killed because he is unwilling to play the role of the messiah in the conspiracy. They also learn the distressing news that the Dome of the Rock has, in fact, just been bombed. Even without the occurrence of the Holocaust, in short, the future looks bleak, with potentially apocalyptic strife on the horizon between Jews and Arabs. As Shemets's wife, Ester Malke, laments to Landsman near the book's conclusion,

> let me tell you something . . . All these people rioting on the television
> in Syria, Baghdad, Egypt? In London? Burning cars. Setting fire to
> embassies. Up in Yakovy . . . they were dancing, those fucking
> maniacs, they were so happy about all this craziness, the whole floor
> collapsed right onto the apartment underneath. A couple of little
> girls. . . got crushed to death. That's the kind of shit we have to look
> forward to now. Burning cars and homicidal dancing.[183]

In arriving at this ominous conclusion, *The Yiddish Policemen's Union* subtly normalized the Nazi past by universalizing its significance. This effect reflected Chabon's political motives in writing the novel, which was partly meant to critique the conservative political turn in Israel and the United States after the turn of the millennium. A self-identifying member of the political left, Chabon (who was born in 1963) vocally opposed the hardline policies of Prime Minister Ariel Sharon (especially the expansion of Jewish settlements in the West Bank) and questioned the unstinting support given the Israeli leader by President George W. Bush.[184] These concerns were reflected in the novel's plot, especially its unflattering portrayal of the unseemly and ultimately disastrous alliance between extremist Zionism and fundamentalist Christianity.[185] *The Yiddish Policemen's Union* further appeared to critique contemporary Zionism by seemingly endorsing the counterfactual claim, popular among leftists, that without the Holocaust, the State of Israel would never have been created.[186] Chabon, however, was no anti-Zionist. Indeed, he recognized and defended the need for a Jewish homeland. Explaining his goals in writing the novel, he observed:

> This story ... is about the status quo of the Jews, who are always on
> the verge of being thrown out, of being shown the door ...
>
> [B]ecause of the absence of Israel in ... my book, the Jews are
> in ...[the] position of being guests ... I felt I ... had to confront ...
> the very real ... possibility of expulsion ... I realized ... it's still the
> status quo for us today. We may feel secure, with Israel having the
> fifth-largest military force in the world. But I guess that sense of
> fragility, of always being on the verge of being expelled ... is
> something ... we're still living with even if we prefer not to think
> about it.[187]

In short, Chabon wrote his novel from a deep awareness of the dilemmas of modern Zionism. While he shared the age-old Jewish sense of vulnerability and believed in the need for a Jewish state, he recognized the tragic consequences of the Zionist effort to overcome it. In showing how Jewish life in Alaska remained precarious even in the absence of the Holocaust, he made clear that the establishment of a Jewish national home was destined to cause problems wherever it was ultimately located. This assertion was clearly informed by moral considerations. Yet, in advancing it, Chabon ended up treating the Holocaust as a means to a larger political end, thereby universalizing its significance and contributing to its further normalization.

The same was true of historian Walter Laqueur's 2008 essay, "Disraelia: A Counterfactual History, 1848–2008."[188] Like Chabon's novel, this article also focused on the Holocaust's non-occurrence in order to comment on contemporary problems facing the State of Israel. In Laqueur's essay, the Nazi genocide never transpires thanks to the creation of a Jewish homeland in the Ottoman Empire in the year 1848. Motivated by the desire to stem the rising tide of anti-Semitism and prop up the declining Turkish regime, a coalition of interested parties led by Benjamin Disraeli and the Rothschild family convinces the Turkish Grand Vizier that it is in his empire's financial interest to accept a massive wave of Jewish immigration to Palestine. Jewish doubts about the scheme disappear because of the flare-up of anti-Jewish violence in parts of Central and Eastern Europe during the revolutions of 1848. And so, between the years 1849–1855, some two million European Jews migrate to the Ottoman Empire, settling in "eight cantons ... from Jaffa to Kirkuk."[189] The influx of immigrants has far-reaching historical consequences. The region of Jewish settlement, which comes to be known as "Disraelia," industrializes intensively after the 1860s and becomes "the richest and most powerful region" of the Ottoman Empire.[190] It gains outright independence following the empire's collapse in World War I and proceeds to increase its strength in the years that follow. The country's key achievement is its development of nuclear technology in the 1930s, which allows the Disraelian government to force Adolf Hitler to cease his anti-Semitic agitation against Germany's 200,000 Jews. As a result, there is no Second World War and no Holocaust. To cap the fantasy, Laqueur concluded by noting that Disraelia

> would have some sixty million inhabitants at the beginning of the 21st century. It would have advanced industries ... It would be the fifth-largest oil producer in the world, economically ... competitive with Europe, America and even Asia. It would have powerful armed forces, living in peace with its neighbors ... No one would dare to question its right to exist.[191]

This conclusion revealed that Laqueur's narrative was influenced by present-day Middle Eastern politics. Unlike Chabon, Laqueur has long stood on the center-right of the political spectrum.[192] That said, his essay bore certain signs of a left-wing sensibility. Its suggestion that history would have turned out better if the quest for a Jewish homeland had proceeded in a less particularistic direction resembled the position long held by the (mostly left-wing) supporters of binationalism. In the essay, Disraelia is established not as a Jewish, but rather a multi-ethnic state, one in which Jews, Arabs, Kurds, and others all have "absolute equality in the administration of the region."[193] The country has two capitals, Tel Aviv and Mosul, and there is a "principle of alternation" in the presidency "by which a Jew is invariably followed by a Kurd or an Arab." Jerusalem is turned into an "internationalized city" out of respect for the "world's leading religions."[194] Moreover, "Hebrew, Turkish, and Arabic are official languages." Most importantly, separatist efforts by "Jewish fanatics" to divide the country and expel all non-Jews are mercilessly crushed following the assassination of the country's Jewish president in 1929.[195] In short, Laqueur implied that the development of Jewish nationalism within a multi-ethnic framework would have improved history's course.

Compared to Chabon's bleak narrative, Laqueur's portrayal of the Holocaust's non-occurrence was more of a utopian fantasy. His references to Disraelia becoming "a model of friendly coexistence between the Muslim world and the people of the book" – not to mention a haven for "distinguished political refugees," such as Ayatollah Khomeini and "the Saudi entrepreneur Osama bin Laden" – made clear that his counterfactual narrative was inspired by the desire to avoid many of Israel's real historical problems.[196] Laqueur suggested as much in the conclusion, where he argued that Israel's tragedy was to have been born eighty years too late, after the tragedy of the Holocaust and the awakening of Arab nationalism. This gap in time made all the difference between the Jewish homeland being "a strong and rich state, universally respected, and a small and relatively weak country, isolated, without important natural resources." Laqueur added that the contemporary moral condemnation of Israel was largely due to its small size, writing, "What is considered normal behavior in . . . a state counting sixty million is a moral outrage when done by a small country."[197] By exposing the criticism of Israel as contingent upon its size, Laqueur essentially defended the Jewish state. His essay thus took a more conservative stance than Chabon's novel. At the same time, it also universalized the Holocaust's significance by employing it to comment on contemporary political realities.

The response to both texts recognized their underlying agendas. For the most part, *The Yiddish Policemen's Union* was praised by reviewers, many of whom hailed it as a "blockbuster" and a "beautiful work of literature."[198] Yet certain conservative critics attacked it for displaying a liberal political slant. Deriding Chabon as a "leftwing atheistic Yiddishist . . .[from] Berkeley," James Lewis sharply criticized his novel as an expression of "Jewish self-hatred" sure to appeal to "paranoid anti-Semite[s]."[199] This was largely due, the *New York Post* opined, to the novel's unsympathetic portrait of Hasidic Jews, who were shown as "willing to do anything, including massacring other Jews, in the cause of Zionism."[200] John Podhoretz declared that this portrait amounted to the "reverse-image [of] fanatic Muslims" and cast doubt on Chabon's self-proclaimed Zionist allegiances.[201] Indeed, as Samuel Freedman claimed, Chabon was an outright anti-Zionist, a man so "apparently imbued with the belief that Israel is a colonial, imperialistic oppressor" that he "has found joy in, at least on paper, making it cease to exist."[202] Interestingly, Laqueur's essay came in for similar criticism. Although less widely reviewed, it was also attacked for allegedly having a left-wing political agenda, with historian Martin Kramer accusing the historian of having "de-Israelized" the Jewish state with a fantasy that was patently unrealistic given the realities of the Middle East.[203] These comments were all notable for their sharpness, but their relevance for the issue of normalization is hard to measure, given the fact that they focused mostly on the two alternate histories' representation of Israel and ignored their universalization of the Holocaust. In all likelihood, however, their disapproval of the former implied a rejection of the latter. Yet again, the effort to advance the cause of normalization met with resistance.

Conclusion

Taken together, recent alternate histories have normalized the memory of Nazism in different ways. Most have universalized the significance of the Third Reich in the process of commenting on the crises of the post-9/11 world. These works have largely been produced by left-leaning writers eager to criticize the conservative policies of President George W. Bush and his European allies. This was especially true of British and American portrayals of a Nazi victory in World War II. The nightmare narratives of Walton, Sansom, Sheers, Saville, and Glenn, by imagining Britain and the US collaborating with Hitler's Reich, advanced a strong critique of contemporary Anglo-American foreign policy. Also universalizing the Nazi past were Chabon's novel and Laqueur's essay, both of which utilized the premise of the Holocaust's non-occurrence to direct attention to the deepening crisis of Zionism. Laqueur, however, wrote from a more conservative perspective defending the State of Israel, and his essay, like Turtledove's novel, showed that efforts at universalization did not always serve liberal agendas. Yet they, too, instrumentalized the Nazi past for present-day purposes.

Other alternate histories relativized the Nazi past. This trend was most pronounced in Germany and was visible in Alexander Demandt's and Dieter Kühn's tales about Hitler's assassination, all of which expressed the conservative fantasy that, following the Führer's death, the German people redeem themselves by putting their country on a more moderate political path. In doing so, these narratives lessened the German people's responsibility for the Third Reich and offered a normalized perspective on the Nazi era. They reflected the ongoing effort of conservative Germans to put their country's shameful Nazi past behind it and promote a more assertive national agenda, a trend that also accelerated in the post-9/11 world. Of course, not all German accounts accepted such a vision. The novels of Siegfried Langer and Wolfgang Brenner, by underscoring the Third Reich's criminality, resisted the normalizing trend by representing the Nazi era from a strongly moralistic perspective.

Still other narratives aestheticized the Nazi past by satirizing it. This trend was visible in the films, *Jackboots on Whitehall* and *Iron Sky*, the American television program, *Saturday Night Live*, the German novel, *Er ist wieder da*, and various Internet websites. These works' humorous representation of the Nazi past revealed a readiness to spoof certain counterfactual premises (the Nazis winning World War II and Hitler's survival) that once inspired fear. This satirical impulse reflected the fading of older nightmares and a growing sense of exhaustion – perhaps even boredom – with topics that have been portrayed many times before. In the process, it reflected the natural process of organic normalization.

Finally, recent British, American, and German alternate histories confirm the persistence of national variations in the memory of Nazism. British and American narratives have displayed the greatest willingness to universalize the Nazi past, mostly to promote liberal political agendas. German narratives, by contrast, have revolved around the question of relativizing the Nazi era, with conservative and liberal writers respectively promoting and resisting it. Only one thing links all three countries, and that is the growing willingness to laugh at the Nazi legacy by producing works that aestheticize it through humor. These diverging patterns are confirmed by the reception of recent alternate histories. British reviewers have praised most of the tales that have universalized the Nazi era; American reviewers have been more split; while German reviewers have generally criticized the counterfactual effort to relativize Nazi criminality. These patterns suggest that the British remain most inclined to normalize the Nazi past, while Americans and Germans remain divided. Recent alternate histories thus confirm that normalization and moralism continue to coexist in a dialectical relationship.

5 HUMANIZING HITLER: THE FÜHRER IN CONTEMPORARY FILM

> 'You're an awfully hard man to like,
> Hitler, but I'm going to try.'

German Jewish art dealer Max Rothman's exasperated remark to the struggling artist, Adolf Hitler, in the 2002 film, *Max*, highlights an important new trend in recent cinematic representations of the Nazi dictator. Since the turn of the millennium, there has been a notable surge of films featuring Hitler. Directed by an array of American and European filmmakers, these films have focused on several aspects of the Führer's life. Some, such as *Hitler – The Rise of Evil* (2003) and *Mein Kampf* (2009), have followed the lead of *Max* and concentrated on Hitler's early years. Others, such as *Downfall* (2004), *Mein Führer* (2007), and *Inglourious Basterds* (2009), have portrayed Hitler's last days, examining the circumstances that precede his death. These films have differed substantially in style. Some have aimed for documentary authenticity, while others have embraced historical fiction. Some have adopted the narrative trope of tragedy, while others have pursued the path of comedy. No matter how much they have varied in their subject or method of representation, however, most of the films have been linked, to one degree or another, by their attempt to humanize Hitler. Like Max Rothman, the directors of these films have tried to overcome their distaste for the Nazi dictator in order to understand him.

In so doing, these films have departed significantly from prior cinematic representations of Hitler. Prior to the turn of the millennium, most films about the Führer portrayed him from a strongly moralistic perspective. Whether depicting his meteoric rise or catastrophic fall, they tended to demonize him as the epitome of evil. Recent films, by contrast, have adopted a less judgmental stance and depicted Hitler as a human being who can be understood in conventional historical terms. In the process, these motion pictures have both reflected and contributed to the increasing normalization of the Nazi past. Recent films have promoted this trend in several ways. They have done so, first of all, by aestheticizing the Nazi era. By using documentary-style realism, satire, or a combination of the two to portray the Führer's human side, they have de-emphasized his evil. These films have also universalized the Third Reich's significance. In trying to understand Hitler, they have identified his deviant development as the result of general modern forces, thereby effacing the specificity of his misdeeds. Finally, recent films have also relativized the Nazi era's criminality. By imagining Hitler being involved in close relationships with fictional Jewish characters at the beginning and end of his political career, they have blurred the line between German perpetrators and Jewish victims, lessening the guilt of the former and increasing that of the latter. In representing the Nazi past in these ways, these films have met with sharp criticism, sparking vigorous debate in Western Europe and the United States. The ensuing controversy, in turn, has paradoxically undermined the very process of normalization that the films have promoted.

Hitler in twentieth-century film

Hitler has long played a leading role in the movies.[1] He made his cinematic debut in Germany in the late 1920s, appearing in a variety of UFA newsreels and NSDAP-sponsored documentaries.[2] These motion pictures were predictably propagandistic, a trend that continued after 1933 when the Nazi Ministry of Propaganda controlled the dictator's image in the weekly *Deutsche Wochenschau*. Hitler's appearance in feature films was equally stage-managed, a trend epitomized by Leni Riefenstahl's motion pictures, *Victory of Faith* (1933), *Triumph of the Will* (1935), and *Olympia* (1938). These films were extremely effective in stylizing the Führer into a figure of omnipotence, so much so, that no other films of him were ever commissioned.[3] Although footage of Hitler was included in scattered documentaries, he did not appear in any other major German films during the war years.[4] His absence from cinematic representation was part of a deliberate policy to sustain the "Führer myth" and accent his aura of authority.[5] As part of this policy, Hitler only "appeared" in subsequent films via historical analogy, in features on such political ancestors as Frederick the Great and Otto von Bismarck.[6] By the war's end, Hitler's absence from German films mirrored his withdrawal from German public life. His last appearance in a March, 1945 newsreel left no visual indication that his final weeks would be spent underground in his Berlin bunker, away from the camera eye.

Outside of Germany, Hitler was the subject of more critical cinematic attention. He first appeared in Allied propaganda films, being portrayed in such early works as the British motion picture, *The Lion Has Wings* (1939), as a bloodthirsty warmonger, an image that persisted in subsequent Allied wartime newsreels. By contrast, feature-length commercial films mostly depicted Hitler from a satirical perspective. Charlie Chaplin's *The Great Dictator* (1940) and Ernst Lubitsch's *To Be or Not to Be* (1942) famously mocked the Nazi dictator. Chaplin's classic depiction of Adenoid Hynkel dreamily balancing the globe on his fingers poked fun at the Führer's monomaniacal ambitions, while Lubitsch's famous scene featuring a Polish Hitler impersonator uttering the immortal line, "Heil Myself," lampooned the dictator's cult of personality (Figure 24). Both films were undeniably funny, but they situated their humor within a clear moral context. *The Great Dictator* concluded with the Jewish barber's plea for humanity to embrace tolerance, while *To Be or Not to Be* featured a Polish Jewish actor reciting Shylock's famous speech for tolerance from Shakespeare's *Merchant of Venice*. On the whole, these and other wartime films – whether Three Stooges comedies or Disney animated shorts – used humor as a weapon to puncture Hitler's mythic aura of omnipotence.[7] To a degree, they were successful. They were a predictable hit among Allied audiences, and they may have even affected Hitler himself. The Nazi dictator hated being mocked and vowed vengeance against those responsible for it.[8] If nothing else, Hitler's reaction made clear that the Allies' wartime use of cinematic humor was hardly innocuous. Indeed, it was a form of war by other means.

After the defeat of the Nazis in 1945, however, comic portrayals of Hitler became taboo. Following the revelation of the Nazis' crimes during the Holocaust, it became next to impossible to portray the Nazi dictator in any manner that could be interpreted as light-hearted. Any attempt to exploit the Nazi past for humor or entertainment was

Figure 24. In this famous scene from Ernst Lubitsch's 1942 film, *To Be or Not to Be*, Polish actor and Hitler impersonator Frederick Bronski utters the immortal line, "Heil Myself!"

frowned upon as aestheticizing its criminal legacy. Charlie Chaplin made this clear after the war when he famously noted that he "could not have made fun of the homicidal insanity of the Nazis" in *The Great Dictator* had he "known the about the horrors of the German concentration camps."[9] Because of this sentiment, new cinematic methods of representation had to be devised.

Before long, directors settled on a realistic, documentary style of filmmaking as the most suitable for representing the Nazi dictator.[10] This sober approach dated back to the war years, in works such as John Farrow's *The Hitler Gang* (1944), and it continued well into the 1960s. German filmmaker G. W. Pabst's 1955 production, *Der letzte Akt* (*The Last Ten Days*) unambiguously underscored Hitler's evil, portraying him in his Berlin bunker as a deranged figure unconcerned with Germany's imminent destruction, while the 1962 low-budget American film, *The Private Life of Adolf Hitler*, focused on his dysfunctional romantic life before depicting his mental breakdown in the bunker

Figure 25. In this scene from G. W. Pabst's 1955 film, *Der letzte Akt* (English version, *The Last Ten Days*), the Führer defiantly dictates his last will and political testament.

(Figure 25).[11] Other documentary-style films about the Nazi dictator appeared during the "Hitler Wave" of the 1970s. Some, such as Ennio De Concini's *Hitler: The Last Ten Days* (1973), George Schaefer's *The Bunker* (1980), and Marvin J. Chomsky's *Inside the Third Reich* (1982), focused on Hitler's demise, with veteran actors Alec Guinness and Anthony Hopkins portraying Hitler as a madman descending into hysteria. Others, such as Joachim Fest's *Hitler: A Career* (1977), adopted a broader view and surveyed the full scope of the Führer's rise and fall. The culmination of this documentary approach appeared in the 1990s with German television impresario Guido Knopp's series of documentaries on Hitler and the Third Reich, all of which portrayed the Führer as the evil genius of the Nazi state.[12]

More imaginative, fictionalized portrayals of Hitler also appeared in the years after 1945. The films were fewer in number, but they were notable for rejecting realism in favor of fantasy. A well-known sub-genre of such films exploited the counterfactual scenario of the "survival myth" and depicted Hitler escaping to a foreign hideout after World War II and eluding justice for his crimes. This premise was explored directly in the pulp classics, *They Saved Hitler's Brain* (1963) and *Flesh Feast* (1967), as well as in modified form, in the Hollywood blockbuster, *The Boys From Brazil* (1978).[13] These films posited Hitler's survival in order to indulge in the fantasy of killing him, thereby holding him accountable for his misdeeds.[14] Subsequent examples of this genre, such as Armin Mueller-Stahl's *Conversation With the Beast* (1996) and Barry Hershey's *The Empty Mirror* (1996), also posited Hitler's survival and subjected him to some form of rough or symbolic justice. In so doing, they generally maintained the cinematic tradition of moralistically portraying him as a symbol of evil.

This adherence to moralism notwithstanding, some of these films exhibited normalizing tendencies. Signs of a new willingness to humanize Hitler were visible in *Hitler: The Last Ten Days* and *The Bunker*, whose stars, Alec Guinness and Anthony Hopkins, depicted him less as a demonic madman than a demoralized has-been.[15] Similarly, *Conversation With the Beast* and *The Empty Mirror* humanized Hitler by respectively portraying him as a comic and introspective figure prone to seek forgiveness for his crimes.[16] Still other motion pictures normalized the Nazi past by aestheticizing it. The best example was German filmmaker Hans Jürgen Syberberg's postmodern extravaganza, *Hitler, A Film From Germany* (1977), whose quasi-theatrical collage of competing Führer images refrained from offering a morally grounded view of the Nazi dictator and reproduced much of his regime's mythic, irrationalist imagery.[17] The same was true of Fest's film, *Hitler: A Career*, and Knopp's series of Hitler documentaries, whose use of seductive Nazi-era film footage, dramatic scores, and skilled re-enactments, replicated the allure of fascist aesthetics and transformed the Third Reich into a ratings-grabbing form of "docutainment."[18]

Despite these signs of normalization, however, most Hitler films prior to the turn of the millennium displayed a preference for moralism, a fact that was further confirmed by their reception. Ever since the war years, films featuring Hitler have garnered tremendous attention. Much of it has been positive, with critics hailing the majority of motion pictures for tackling the historically fraught topic of the Third Reich from an ethically grounded perspective. Yet even when negative reviews of Hitler films appeared, they too confirmed the moralistic consensus about representing him. The most common complaint among reviewers was that certain films gave insufficient attention to the Nazi dictator's criminality. Satirical portrayals of Hitler during the war years were widely criticized for this shortcoming, with Lubitsch's *To Be or Not to Be* being faulted by British and American reviewers for making light of Polish suffering at the hands of the Nazis.[19] Later motion pictures, such as those by Fest and Syberberg were also criticized, especially in Germany, for paying more attention to the reasons for Hitler's popularity among the German people than to the severity of his crimes, an omission that reviewers feared could distort younger Germans' understanding of the Nazi period.[20] Even the Hitler biopics of the 1970s were occasionally criticized for going too far in humanizing the Nazi dictator.[21] These responses pointed to the ongoing desire to view the Nazi past from a moralistic perspective.

That said, there were occasional signs of dissent. Some reviewers, especially in the US and England, criticized the moralistic tone of certain Hitler films for being predictable and boring. Pabst's film, *The Last Ten Days*, was described by one critic as "tiresome"; De Concini's *Hitler: The Last Ten Days* was called "as exciting as a parent-approved comic book"; and *The Bunker* was described as proving that "even evil can be dull."[22] These reviewers felt obliged to give these films what one called "a certain somber respect," but they admitted that it was ultimately "a begrudging one."[23] In Germany, meanwhile, reviewers faulted the moralistic tone of certain Hitler films for a very different reason. Critics of Fest's film and Knopp's television documentaries argued that their demonization of Hitler and their focus on his centrality in the Nazi state shifted attention away from the German people's culpability for the regime's crimes and thus served a self-exculpatory function.[24] Taken together, these responses pointed to a growing exhaustion with, and suspicion of, moralistic modes of portraying Hitler. This sentiment remained exceptional prior to the turn of the millennium. But it soon became more common.

Hitler films since the turn of the millennium

Since the year 2000, the cinematic depiction of Hitler has undergone a notable transformation. While certain motion pictures have adhered to moralistic modes of representation, most have embraced a more normalized approach. Recent films about Hitler have focused on different aspects of his career. Some have chronicled his early life. Others have addressed the events immediately preceding his death. These films have assumed different narrative forms, with realistic, documentary works coexisting with satires and counterfactual fantasies. All of them, however, have normalized the

Nazi past by aestheticizing, universalizing, and relativizing it. In the process, they have sparked controversy about the future of memory.[25]

The fledgling Führer: Hitler's early life

Not all the motion pictures that have appeared since the year 2000 have aimed to normalize Hitler. The exception that proved the rule was the made-for-television film, *Hitler – The Rise of Evil* (Figure 26). As was made abundantly clear by its subtitle, the film embraced a moralistic approach in portraying the dictator. Directed by the French Canadian filmmaker, Christian Duguay, and aired in two parts on CBS television in May of 2003, the miniseries was a conventional biopic in the realistic tradition of the Hitler films of the 1970s and 1980s. Rather than focusing on the Führer's last days in the bunker, however, *Hitler – The Rise of Evil* surveyed his transformation from down-and-out Austrian bohemian to monomaniacal dictator. The film's moral agenda was clear from the very outset. Before it displayed any images on the screen, the film showed viewers a quotation by Edmund Burke that read: "The only thing necessary for the triumph of evil is for good men to do nothing." From this point on, over a span of three hours, the film imparted a simple message about Hitler: he was evil from the beginning. As a child, Hitler is shown to be sullen and mischievous (in one early scene, he destroys his father's beehives by setting them on fire); as a result, the young Hitler suffers regular beatings. His father is exasperated about his son's deviant ways and exclaims in frustration, "He's God's curse on me for marrying my niece," implying that Hitler's evil is genetically determined. As the film chronicles Hitler's path to adulthood, it follows the narrative outlined in his self-serving autobiography, *Mein Kampf*. In short order, the by-now grown-up Hitler (played by Robert Carlyle) tries to cope with his mother's death, his failure to gain admission to art school, his growing destitution, and his resentment against ethnic and religious minorities in Vienna. He absorbs anti-Semitic ideas in the Habsburg capital, develops them during his military service in World War I, and refines them after his return to Munich in 1918. Once back in his adopted city, he becomes even more fanatical, telling his military superior, Captain Karl Mayr, that the country's "nationalist agenda must include elimination of the Jews." When Mayr replies "it's just not feasible," Hitler replies ominously, "We just drive them out. Deport them if necessary. Can you imagine a world without them? How pure? How holy?"

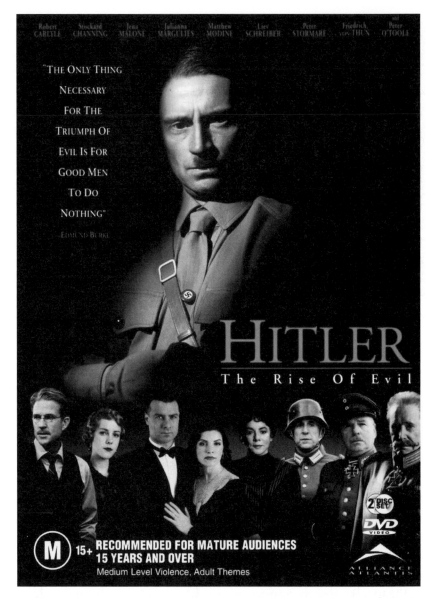

Figure 26. The CBS television movie, *Hitler – The Rise of Evil* (2003), offered a traditional moralistic depiction of Hitler's rise to power in the years 1918–33.

The film then shows Hitler's entry into politics and his gradual rise to power. After joining the DAP, the aspiring Führer gains support from lower middle-class and bourgeois Germans in beer hall speeches and fancy dinner parties, before attempting to topple the Berlin

Figure 27. In this scene from *Hitler – The Rise of Evil* (2003) the aspiring Führer (Robert Carlyle) uses his demagogical gifts to attract a political following in the early 1920s.

government in his ill-fated putsch of 1923 (Figure 27). Following his conviction for treason and his confinement in Landsberg prison, Hitler pursues a romantic dalliance with his niece, Geli Raubal, who further confirms his evil, telling his chauffeur, Emil Maurice, at one juncture, "He's a monster. You can't imagine what he asks of me." Alongside this chronicle of Hitler's political career, the film intersperses scenes of Munich journalist Fritz Gerlich (Matthew Modine) trying to serve as a "voice of sanity" by urging his fellow citizens to stand against Hitler's "party of intolerance and hatred." Gerlich also confirms Hitler's evil, demonizing him at one point with the remark, "He's not human; he's studied people in order to appear human." None of Gerlich's efforts are of any use, however. Germany's political crisis soon leads the NSDAP to gain further electoral support from the German people and prompts President Hindenburg to appoint Hitler chancellor. Following the eruption of the Reichstag fire, the passing of the Enabling Act, and the party's violent reckoning with its political opponents (Gerlich is shown getting beaten to death at Dachau), Hitler quickly consolidates power and solemnly proclaims: "the thousand year Reich has begun." With this climax, the film confirmed Hitler's evil. Before it concluded, however, it offered one final moral lesson. In the penultimate scene, the film cuts away once final time to Burke's quotation about good men doing "nothing." *Hitler – The Rise of Evil* thereby implied that Hitler was not alone; other people were complicit in his rise to power and his regime's ensuing crimes. To drive home this point, the film closes with documentary photographs of the Nuremberg Laws, Kristallnacht, World War II, and the Holocaust, complete with captions detailing the horrific death toll that Hitler's evil brought to Europe.

In crafting this narrative, the producers of *Hitler – The Rise of Evil* were motivated by a variety of considerations, the most important being their desire to pre-empt criticism that they had humanized the Nazi dictator. When the film was originally conceived in 2001, it was entitled *Hitler: The Early Years* and was intended to focus on the dictator's entry into politics. In 2002, CBS's President, Leslie Moonves, explained the approach by alluding to the large number of films on Hitler's demise, declaring: "We know how the story ends, but we don't know how the story begins."[26] The film's producers emphasized that they would strive for historical accuracy, noting that the film would be based on historian Ian Kershaw's bestselling study, *Hitler, 1889–1936: Hubris* (1998). The film's director, Christian Duguay, meanwhile, underscored its critical perspective on the dictator, noting "You watch this movie and you never forget here's a man who is demonic."[27] Yet despite these assurances, various groups and individuals feared that the film would humanize Hitler. The Anti-Defamation League's director, Abraham Foxman, expressed his frustration that "people would spend talent, time and money to make this man human."[28] Historian Michael Berenbaum warned that "if [the film]... shows us Hitler's humanity and makes him a sympathetic character it's a total outrage."[29] Finally, the Simon Wiesenthal Center complained that, because the movie only covered the Third Reich's history to 1935, it would "tell ... only half of a terrible story" and ignore the regime's later crimes.[30] In response to these and other criticisms, CBS revised the script and planned a donation to a Jewish or Holocaust-related group.[31] The network further produced a "Guide for Educators," complete with discussion questions for teachers and students.[32] More importantly, it gave the film a new subtitle, adding the "The Rise of Evil" to clarify its moral intentions.

These efforts had an ambiguous impact on the film's reception. On the one hand, *Hitler – The Rise of Evil* was a modest critical success, winning two Emmy awards and extensive praise for Carlyle's performance as the Nazi leader.[33] Calling it "brilliant" and "compelling," many reviewers were relieved that the film did not make Hitler sympathetic and praised it as "tasteful and responsible."[34] Many endorsed the film's moralistic portrait of the dictator. One observer wrote that the motion picture showed that "Hitler was born insane and got worse," while another affirmed that it portrayed him "more as a satanic force than a human being."[35] On the other hand, certain commentators critiqued the film's predictability, noting that it lacked "suspense, drama, and passion" and ultimately did not make for "great television."[36] Part of the problem, one reviewer pointed out, was that *Hitler – The Rise of Evil* was a "politically correct depiction" that went "out of its way to be inoffensive."[37] As another commentator noted, the producers' fear of being "accused of making Hitler 'sympathetic'" prevented the film from exploring "Hitler's humanity" and confronting "the undeniable allure he exerted to coerce people to follow him."[38] The result, another observer concluded, was that "in its refusal to view Hitler as anything but a monster," the film ended up being "nothing more than a political puppet show with swastikas."[39]

By contrast, other critics insisted that *Hitler – The Rise of Evil* raised important moral questions. More than a few commentators praised the motion picture for counterfactually speculating about how the rise of the Nazis might have been averted. In truth, *Hitler – The Rise of Evil* did not ask any explicit "what if?" questions. But reviewers perceived an implicit counterfactual lesson in the film's central claim – epitomized by the Burke quotation – that too many people had neglected to stop Hitler before he became too powerful. Abraham Foxman said the film depicted "how many times [Hitler] ... could have been challenged and wasn't."[40] The film's producer Peter Sussman agreed, noting that "Hitler's career could have ended a dozen times ... [but] he always managed to slip by."[41] Actor Robert Carlyle echoed this point, declaring, "He was lucky he didn't get blown up in the First World War a couple of times ... If he had, the world might have been a very different place."[42]

Yet while these responses signaled a desire to view the Nazi past from a moralistic perspective, other comments highlighted a tendency to normalize it. This was visible in the ways in which the film and its reception universalized the Nazi era's significance. Given the fact that *Hitler – The Rise of Evil* was planned and ultimately broadcast in the turbulent period between 9/11 and the start of the Iraq War, many observers interpreted it as a parable about the danger of appeasing Al Qaeda and Saddam Hussein. CBS's Moonves implied as much in 2002, when he said that the film was tackling "a very timely subject – how bad guys get into power."[43] Various journalists made similar points, with one writing that the film's portrayal of evil was particularly relevant in light of "each new discovery of some monstrousness that occurred under Saddam Hussein in Iraq."[44] Other observers, by contrast, objected to this line of reasoning. Historian Charles Maier objected to how the film "hypostasized" the concept of evil and supported the tendency "in contemporary America, to [make]... evil (as in axis of ...) ... into a major historical agent."[45] Historian Nathan Stolzfus agreed, noting "there is little in this series to challenge ... our notion that Saddam Hussein of 2003 should be compared with Hitler."[46]

Liberal critics did not just reject comparisons between Hitler and Saddam Hussein, however, but offered their own comparisons between the Nazi leader and President George W. Bush. No less than the film's executive producer, Ed Gernon, saw a parallel between Hitler's rise to power and Bush's drive to go to war in Iraq, noting "it basically boils down to an entire nation gripped by fear, who ultimately chose to give up their civil rights and plunged the whole world into war ... I can't think of a better time to examine this history than now."[47] More conservative observers, meanwhile, angrily rejected this comparison, calling it "an act of slander against the president of the United States."[48] Such conservative allegations were exaggerated. But as Ron Rosenbaum perceptively noted, *Hitler – The Rise of Evil* did contain one tendentious reference to contemporary events. By pointedly showing Hitler using the word "terrorists" to describe the arsonists responsible for the Reichstag fire and by depicting the Nazi dictator proceeding to suspend civil liberties, the film made a thinly veiled allusion to President Bush's citation of 9/11 to justify the Patriot Act.[49] In the end, Gernon was fired and conservatives were appeased. But the debate showed how even a moralistic portrait of Hitler could be vulnerable to the charge of universalizing the Nazi past.

In stark contrast to *Hitler – The Rise of Evil*, another major film released around the same time, *Max* (2002), adopted a more normalized perspective in portraying the Nazi leader (Figure 28). Written and directed by the Oscar-nominated Dutch-American filmmaker, Menno Meyjes, the film focused on the vexing historical question of why Hitler abandoned his dream of becoming an artist and instead went into politics. In so doing, *Max* flirted with the genre of counterfactual history, raising questions about how historical events might have been different if Hitler had succeeded in becoming a painter. In prompting viewers to reflect on this "what if?" question, the film encouraged them

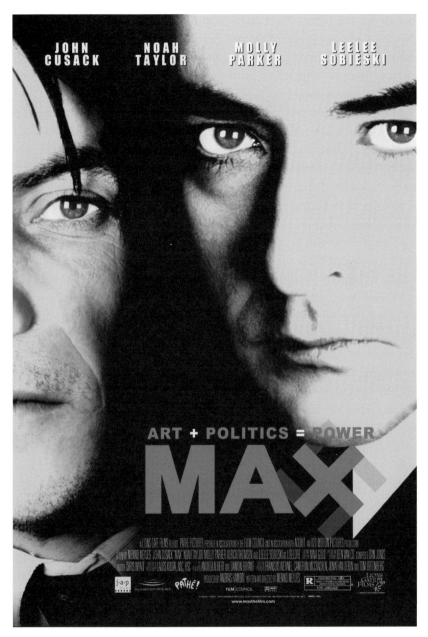

Figure 28. The film, *Max* (2002), chronicles Hitler's failure to become an artist and his ensuing turn to political extremism in early postwar Munich.

to root for the future Nazi dictator and hope that, by making different choices, he might somehow avoid the disastrous path he pursued in real history. *Max* ultimately ended up dashing viewers' hopes. But in challenging them to empathize with Hitler, the film took a notable step towards humanizing him.

Max begins its humanization of Hitler by portraying him returning to Munich after World War I in a state of profound financial and psychological distress. As the film opens, Hitler (played by Noah Taylor) walks dejectedly through the city towards a soup line, where he glumly waits with other drifters for a hot meal. Having just returned from the war, he still hopes to become an artist, but his prospects initially appear bleak. Before long, however, he meets a man who renews his career ambitions, the (fictional) Jewish art dealer Max Rothman. Rothman (played by John Cusack) is himself a wounded war veteran, and he declares his willingness to look at Hitler's portfolio to see if he has the necessary talent to succeed. In looking through Hitler's realistic charcoal sketches, Rothman – who favors modern art – sees some promise, but senses certain shortcomings. "I think you can go even deeper," Rothman tells him, noting, "what I'm missing is an authentic voice … One gets the feeling that you're holding something back." Hitler's reply is calm, but it displays obvious hurt: "When I came back from this war," he tells Rothman, "I came back to nothing. Really nothing. No homeland. No home. No parents. No family. No fiancée. No profession. No job. No food. Not even an address. All I have in this world is the conviction that I am a great artist … And you just stole from that, from the one thing that's mine." With this remark, Hitler earns the viewer's sympathy by defending himself – the mediocre everyman – against the elitist judgment of the privileged Jewish critic, Rothman.

More importantly, Hitler's reaction stirs a sense of guilt and pity in Rothman that guides the rest of the film. As *Max* unfolds, it becomes a story about Rothman's attempt to steer Hitler towards a life of art instead of politics. Rothman learns early on about Hitler's dabbling in right-wing politics when he sees him deliver a clumsy anti-Semitic speech to soldiers at his military base. When Hitler approaches Rothman after the speech and shyly asks him what he thinks of it, the latter patiently advises him, "if you were to put the same amount of energy into your art as you do your speaking you may have something going." This remark shows that Rothman regards Hitler less as a serious menace than a redeemable lost soul. He proceeds to challenge Hitler on his anti-Semitism, telling him that it is a refuge for people who

Figure 29. In this scene from *Max* (2002) the Jewish art dealer Max Rothman (John Cusack, right) urges the struggling artist Adolf Hitler (Noah Taylor, left) to express himself more honestly on the canvas.

feel "cheated." When Hitler denies having such feelings, Rothman tries to lure him "out of politics" by taking some of his work on consignment and giving him an advance. Hitler gratefully replies, "you've saved my life. You know, maybe you're right. Maybe I've yet to find my authentic voice. Maybe I should get more modern." Rothman then advises Hitler to overcome his inhibitions, telling him to "take all this pent-up stuff that you're quivering with and ... hurl it on the canvas ... It doesn't have to be good and beautiful, it just has to be true" (Figure 29). In watching these exchanges, viewers cannot help but hope that Rothman's tough love will succeed and Hitler will go on to pursue a career in genuine artistic creativity.

Hitler squanders his opportunity, however. Confronted with the challenge of introspectively expressing himself in his art, Hitler suffers from painter's block and ends up smashing his canvas in a fit of rage. Driven by self-pity and resentment, he decides to throw himself into political activism. When he next sees Rothman, Hitler rationalizes his failure to produce any modern art by loudly proclaiming: "Politics is the new art! 'Go deeper,' you said. Well I went ... deeper than any artist has gone before ... I am the new avant-garde!" By all rights, Rothman at this point should give up any hope of Hitler becoming an artist. Yet when he visits Hitler one last time and sees his new sketches of grandiose architectural ensembles, leather-clad stormtroopers, and buxom Nordic vixens, he realizes that Hitler indeed has a "coherent vision" rooted in a paradoxical form of "future kitsch" and he resolves to organize a show of his work. Hitler is thrilled at this prospect and he agrees to meet Rothman at a café later in the evening to settle the details. Beforehand, however, he reluctantly agrees to his military superior's request to make one last anti-Semitic speech on behalf of the fledgling NSDAP. This decision proves fateful. Hitler's invective wins over the crowd and causes such a surge in anti-Semitic feeling that several sailors in attendance decide after the gathering to go out and beat up Jews, one of whom turns out to be Rothman, who is viciously attacked while on his way to meet Hitler. At this same point, Hitler is waiting in vain for Rothman to appear at the café and by closing time is convinced he has been stood up. The film ends with Rothman bleeding to death in the snow and the audience keenly aware that his efforts on Hitler's behalf have been for naught. Hitler's career as an artist is over and his career as a politician is just beginning.

Despite its tragic ending, *Max* nevertheless displayed a strikingly normalized perspective towards the Nazi past. This was visible, first of all, in the intentions behind the film's humanization of Hitler. Many of the figures associated with *Max* explained that the film rejected prevailing moralistic portraits of the dictator by seeking to understand, rather than merely condemn, him. Director Meyjes and producer András Hámori explained this agenda in personal terms, citing their parents' reluctance to speak openly about the Nazi experience as grounds for challenging the taboos against portraying the dictator as a human being. Meyjes (born in Amsterdam in 1954) asserted that his father's wartime suffering in a Nazi slave labor camp and the death of his grandparents in the "hunger winter" of 1945 explained why his family had long viewed Hitler "as a one-dimensional beast."[50] Similarly, the Hungarian-born Hámori said that the death of many relatives in the Holocaust made "the very word Hitler ... taboo in my family."[51] Both men, however, rejected the taboos that surrounded the Nazi dictator. By humanizing Hitler in their film, they sought to demythologize him. As Meyjes put it, "What Hitler did was so awful that we all desire an extreme grandeur to surround him. We want to believe he was a force born in a cloud of sulfur that disappeared in a puff of gasoline and now, thank God, we're rid of that forever. But ... Hitler was a human being, and it is the fact that he made a choice to become a monster that is essential to understanding him."[52] Noah Taylor agreed, noting, "I think it's way too convenient to view Hitler as a satanic figure who just appeared for no reason ... What makes him truly frightening ...[is] that he's entirely human …[Ultimately]…people make their own choices about whether to behave well or badly."[53] Finally, John Cusack asserted that "the fact that [Hitler]… is human doesn't make the man less culpable, it makes him more culpable. If he's not human, then he's beyond human reckoning."[54]

Max also aestheticized the Nazi past. In the effort to humanize Hitler, the film employed black humor to produce a light-hearted portrait of the future dictator. Certain scenes in the film were comical by virtue of their incongruousness. When Rothman, early in the film, invites the future dictator out for a drink by saying "come on Hitler, I'll buy you a glass of lemonade," the effect is jarring because of the inherent absurdity of the twentieth century's most notorious criminal being offered a refreshing beverage. Other scenes displayed a darker form of humor by exploiting viewers' awareness of Hitler's political future to ironic effect.[55] One example is when Rothman fleetingly introduces Hitler to the painter, George Grosz, in his gallery. After being told Hitler's name, Grosz says he's "never heard of him," to which Rothman replies confidently, "you will." In another instance, Hitler is sitting in a bar with Rothman and several female companions and begins to pontificate about blood purity. Rothman reassures the women that "Hitler's very concerned with blood. We think – we hope – it is a metaphor." Finally, after Rothman floats the idea of a show for the struggling artist, Hitler says, "I'd kill for you if you gave me a show!" to which Rothman anxiously responds: "Don't kill for me – please." All of these examples derive their bite from viewers' awareness of what the future holds. Yet they inspire laughter nonetheless.

Max also drew universal lessons from the Nazi experience. Rather than portraying Hitler's turn to Nazism as the result of factors rooted in Germany's unique circumstances after World War I, Meyjes explained it in more general terms. As he put it, "in the end, the roots of Fascism are always the same: fear, rage, envy, and frustration."[56] Conceptualizing Nazism's origins in such universal terms was intimately connected to the director's intention to create "a historical fable," that is, a tale offering lessons of general, as opposed to specific, applicability.[57] Moreover, it enabled him to highlight his film's present-day relevance. Meyjes noted that he "thought about [Serbian dictator Slobodan] Milosevic a lot" in preparing the film, declaring that "the time is especially ripe to ask how figures like Hitler can come to be."[58] He added that "there are Hitlers of the future lurking, and if you want to comprehend what makes evil tick, you have to begin with ordinary human emotions."[59] Cusack made a similar point in noting that *Max*'s message "resonates today," observing, "It would be much easier for me if Osama bin Laden didn't have a mother or father . . . But he's a human being like you and me."[60] Cusack added that Hitler's merging of aesthetics and politics had implications for the administration of George W. Bush, whose policies after 9/11 amounted to a "successful con job" and whose "propaganda machine is gearing us up toward war."[61]

Finally, *Max* came close to relativizing the Nazi era's criminality. To a degree, the film blurred the line between German perpetrators and Jewish victims by raising the question of whether Rothman himself is partly to blame for Hitler's turn to politics. Rothman, after all, is a source of constant disappointment to the future dictator and arguably hastens his decision to abandon art. After humiliating Hitler by exposing his artistic backwardness, Rothman tries to encourage him to seek new opportunities for creative expression. Yet, every time Rothman raises Hitler's expectations, he ends up dashing them: he is responsible for Hitler's failed attempt to try his hand at modernism; and his failure to show up to his meeting with Hitler about his promised exhibition convinces the artist to abandon art for good. All of Rothman's actions contribute to the film's muting of Hitler's criminality. They put Hitler in the position of being a victim and diminish his responsibility for his turn to politics. They also place Rothman in the role of collaborating with evil. His collaboration may be unwitting, but his underestimation of Hitler's political potential and his naive belief that he can redeem him gives him a share of historical guilt. In the process, *Max* came close to blaming the victim.

To be sure, the film ultimately exonerated its title character of the charge of collaboration. Indeed, *Max* clearly shows that Rothman never had much of a chance to shape Hitler's fate. Throughout the film, Hitler's actions are portrayed as guided by the competing forces of contingency and inevitability. *Max* certainly contemplates the counterfactual possibility that, if Rothman had kept his scheduled meeting with Hitler, he could have steered him away from politics to art. At the same time, though, the film suggests that Hitler's political turn may have been inevitable. By depicting how Rothman's missed meeting is the result of Hitler's anti-Semitic speech, the film showed how the young artist's growing political engagement closes off any alternate path of development. By eliminating Hitler's last lifeline to a better future in the form of Rothman, *Max* showed how the future dictator's anti-Semitism inevitably leads him to abandon art for politics. Hitler, in short, may never have been redeemable in the first place. That said, *Max* never-theless emphasized that Hitler's decision to embrace politics over art was ultimately a matter of choice. In so doing, the film underscored Hitler's humanity. Unlike *Hitler – The Rise of Evil*, *Max* rejected the idea that the future Nazi dictator was born demonic. Cast into circumstances not of his choosing, he made conscious decisions that sealed his fate and that of the world.

Given *Max*'s humanized depiction of Hitler, reactions to the film were predictably divided. As a commercial endeavor, the film was a failure. Costing approximately 11 million dollars, *Max* grossed just over $500,000.[62] Even before it was completed, the film's goal of humanizing Hitler was widely viewed with suspicion. Producer Hámori had difficulty securing financing for *Max*, recalling that "everyone turned us down ... especially the Europeans ... Nobody wanted to touch the subject."[63] Major filmmakers who were approached to direct the film, such as Steven Spielberg, begged off, saying they could not afford to be associated with it. These suspicions intensified just before *Max*'s North American release. The right-wing Jewish Defense League called the movie "a psychic assault on Holocaust survivors" and pressured distributor, Lions Gate Films, to keep it from public view, saying "there is nothing human ... about the most vicious ... murderer in world history."[64] The Anti-Defamation League also initially expressed concerns – later withdrawn – that the film would trivialize the Nazi period.[65] In a gesture of unintentional irony, the Museum of Tolerance in Los Angeles betrayed its name by declining to host a screening of the film.[66] *Max*, moreover, never found a distributor in Germany, where it remained unreleased.

These reactions reflected deep opposition to normalizing Hitler and were further visible in the film's critical reception. Some reviewers were confused by *Max*'s narrative style, saying it could not decide whether it wanted to be a farce or a drama.[67] Others took issue with its humorous elements, describing the film as "inappropriately comic" and complaining that it came "uncomfortably close to a Mel Brooks satire."[68] Still others faulted the film's "what if?" narrative for failing to hold Hitler accountable for his crimes; one critic faulted *Max* for glibly suggesting that Hitler's career path "was a matter of sheerest chance," while another said that "the movie winds up reducing the tragic history of the 20th century to a paradox of bad timing."[69] As one observer concluded, the movie seems "to absolve Hitler by saying "he wasn't evil, he was just undiscovered.""[70]

By contrast, other reviewers hailed *Max* as a cinematic triumph. Various critics described it as "intelligent," "engrossing," and "provocative," with some singling it out for "break[ing]... a lot of taboos."[71] Chief among these taboos was the prohibition of portraying Hitler as a human being. Reviewers called the film "brave," "brashly inventive," and "revolutionary" for "its humanized portrayal of Hitler. As one put it, "what we are given here is as close to a human portrait of Hitler ... as we have yet seen in any art form."[72] Some observers saw this humanization as a healthy corrective to his traditional demonization. Roger Ebert said that to "dehumanize him is to fall under the spell which elevated him into the Führer, a mythical being who transfixed Germans."[73] Critics denied that humanizing Hitler exonerated him for his crimes. While one conceded that the film made Hitler "pitiable," another asserted that, "no one who sees this film is ... likely to ... feel ... twinges of sympathy for Hitler. Indeed, in making Hitler more human, *Max* accomplishes the considerable feat of making him more culpable as well."[74] In short, the positive responses to *Max*'s humanization of Hitler reflected a weakening of the moral consensus about how best to cinematically represent him.

Following *Max*, the next major motion picture to focus on Hitler's early years was *Mein Kampf* (2009) (Figure 30). Directed by the Swiss filmmaker Urs Odermatt and officially released in 2011, the German-language production was based on the 1987 play by the famous Hungarian Jewish playwright, George Tabori. *Mein Kampf* differed from *Max* and *Hitler – The Rise of Evil* by focusing exclusively on Hitler's time in Vienna prior to the outbreak of World War I. But it addressed a similar set of themes and questions: when and why did Hitler become a political fanatic? How inevitable or contingent was his path towards extremism? To what extent should he be portrayed as a demon or human being? In approaching these questions, *Mein Kampf* resembled *Max* in displaying a speculative and fantastical narrative style combining drama with black humor. For this reason, it, too, sparked controversy about the proper way to represent the Nazi dictator.

Like *Max*, *Mein Kampf* offered an empathetic and humanized portrait of the future Führer. As the film opens, the year is 1910 and Hitler (played by Tom Schilling) is traveling by train from Linz to Vienna. Nervous and poor, he suffers several strokes of bad luck, being ejected from his compartment by a conductor for errantly taking a seat in

Figure 30. The film *Mein Kampf* (2009) portrays Hitler's early years of destitution in Vienna prior to 1914 and his intensifying hatred of Jews. Compare the stylized portrayal of Hitler's face with Figure 22.

first class and then, while switching cars, losing his portfolio of drawings, which fly out of the train as it races towards the Habsburg metropolis. Forced to jump from the train to retrieve his work, Hitler ends up walking to his destination. When he finally arrives in Vienna, he is

awestruck by the city's monumental architecture, but is quickly brought
back to earth after he arrives at his new place of residence, a derelict
boarding house inhabited by a ragtag group of elderly homeless men.
These introductory scenes effectively generate sympathy for the young
twenty-one-year old as he struggles to become an artist.

Before long, however, *Mein Kampf* shows less flattering glimpses
of Hitler's darker side. These emerge after he encounters two elderly Jews
living in the shelter, an itinerant Hungarian-Jewish Bible salesman named
Shlomo Herzl (Götz George) and his clarinet-playing companion,
Lobkowitz (Bernd Birkhahn) (Figure 31). In one of many exchanges that
are meant to ironically foreshadow later historical events, Hitler arrives in
the shelter when Shlomo is telling Lobkowitz about his ongoing efforts to
write his memoirs. Shlomo explains that he is struggling with a title, wryly
noting that he has already eliminated "My Memoirs," "Shlomo and Juliet,"
and "Lady Chatterley's Shlomo." When he asks Lobkowitz what he thinks
about "Mein Kampf" as a possible title, Hitler, who has just walked into
the room, exclaims "that's it!" Instead of being grateful for the suggestion,

Figure 31. In *Mein Kampf* (2009), the young artist Adolf Hitler (Tom Schilling) is
befriended by two itinerant Jews, Shlomo Herzl (Götz George, right) and his clarinet-
playing companion, Lobkowitz (Bernd Birkhahn, left).

however, Shlomo upbraids Hitler for his interruption, saying "who asked you?" From this point, Hitler develops a fraught relationship with Shlomo that reveals his less appealing character traits. Hitler presents himself as both rebellious and egocentric, telling Shlomo that he possesses an "ingrained reluctance to obey authority" and an "unshakeable resolve ... to seek my fortune in the city of the waltz, a vocation predestined by my considerable artistic talent." Yet, he also earns Shlomo's sympathy by alluding to his "generational conflict" with his father, who is shown in a flashback angrily telling his son, "I'll beat you to death" for a bad report card. Even though Hitler squanders some of this sympathy by showing signs of prejudice (in one initial exchange, he dismisses Shlomo as a "foreigner"), he has not yet proven himself to be irredeemable.

This point is driven home in the film by Shlomo's determination to steer Hitler in a positive direction. As with the character of Max Rothman in *Max*, Shlomo functions as the Jewish symbol of counterfactual possibilities, a character who – however naively – tries to redeem Hitler and guide him toward a path of moderation and respectability. The first evening in the shelter, Shlomo gives Hitler his coat to use as a blanket. He goes on to treat the future dictator in a fatherly manner, warmly waking him up each morning with the chirpy (and to viewers' ears, highly incongruous) line, "Good Morning Hitler! Rise and shine my little artist." Shlomo further encourages him as he prepares for his entry exam to the Vienna Academy for Fine Arts. Because viewers naturally identify with Shlomo's benevolence, they cannot help but hope that he will succeed in preventing Hitler from heading down a path of fanaticism. By placing viewers in this empathetic position of hoping Hitler achieves his goal *Mein Kampf* succeeds in humanizing him.

Mein Kampf also accomplishes this by making Hitler the butt of numerous jokes. As in wartime films, the presence of satirical scenes in *Mein Kampf* is meant to demythologize him. In one instance, Shlomo is shown benevolently escorting Hitler to the Academy when the young artist suddenly darts into a store to ask about the price of a book displayed in the window. It turns out that the storefront houses the office of the local Jewish mohel (ritual circumciser), who mistakes Hitler for a Jew. Hitler leaves the store humiliated and screams to Shlomo that "my blood is as pure as driven snow." Later on, Shlomo and Lobkowitz tease him about having Jewish origins, saying "there are twenty-three Hitlers in Vienna, all from Odessa and Munkacevo." In a subsequent scene, Hitler is suspected of being Jewish by some of the neighborhood's nationalist thugs after he tells them of his artistic interests (they reply doubtfully that "painters, musicians, and vegetarians are often . . . Jews"). These scenes poke fun at Hitler and allow viewers to laugh at his expense. At the same time, they normalize him by making him pitiable.

Soon enough, however, Hitler reverts to type and becomes less sympathetic. He soon falls in with the neighborhood nationalists who expose him to their anti-Semitic views, giving him propagandistic literature and validating his resentments. As a result, he quickly becomes more outspoken in his hate-filled opinions. Hitler liberally quotes social Darwinistic theories, telling Gretchen, a young blond employee at the boarding house, about animals needing to mate only with their own species; and he blames Shlomo "for the murder of Jesus Christ." Later, when Hitler receives the crushing news that he has been rejected from art school, he blames his bad luck on "a worldwide conspiracy by the Elders of Zion!" Increasingly destitute, he starts to commit petty acts of criminality, stealing bread from a little girl and panhandling in the guise of a wounded war veteran.

Hitler's increasing turn towards evil sets the stage for *Mein Kampf*'s final method of normalization, blurring the line between German perpetrators and Jewish victims. As Hitler increasingly displays unflattering character traits, Shlomo is portrayed as abetting, if not facilitating, his negative transformation. He does this by continuing in his effort to redeem the future Führer, despite the mounting evidence of its futility. Shlomo consistently tries to motivate Hitler to get a legitimate job and he even sells some of his painted postcards to earn him some money. Most pivotally, he saves him from death. Shlomo rescues Hitler after a failed suicide attempt (he jumps off of a bridge tied to a rope, but escapes with only bruises); then, in a highly metaphorical scene, Shlomo convinces an elderly neighborhood postal worker named Frau Death to take Hitler's name off her list of imminent victims. Yet despite his efforts on Hitler's behalf, Shlomo fails to redeem his young acquaintance.

Indeed, in an ironic turn of events, Shlomo inadvertently paves the way for Hitler's future political activity. After having to listen to another one of Hitler's tirades, Shlomo tells him in frustration, "you're a miserable actor. You should go into politics." Before long, Hitler is practicing his public speaking style using arm gestures borrowed from Shlomo's histrionic method of selling Bibles to Viennese pedestrians. Shlomo also indirectly gives Hitler the title of his not-yet-written autobiography, *Mein Kampf*. He even gives Hitler his distinctive physical appearance, trimming his moustache and slicking his hair to the side in preparation for his art exam. In response, Hitler thanks him with the portentous remark, "Jew, I appreciate your assistance. When my time has come I shall reward you suitably. When you are old, I will find a neat solution for you." This allusion to the coming Final Solution, following on the heels of the other scenes, reveals that Shlomo is deluding himself in trying to reform the future dictator. As Lobkowitz tells him, "The way you're mothering that painter borders on masochism." Shlomo never-theless insists that "the holy scriptures say love thy enemy as you love yourself." And he adds, "Hitler is not even my enemy. He is just young and ... foolish. Do I know what will become of him? Maybe he'll be just a man? It might be my assignment to help him become it." In a telling response, however, Lobkowitz tells Sholomo that "if [Hitler]... becomes a criminal ... then you're his accomplice." Shlomo's Jewish humanitari-anism ends up paving the way for Nazi totalitarianism.

Despite these normalized features, *Mein Kampf* ended on a moral-istic note by acknowledging Hitler's evil. When Shlomo finally loses patience with Hitler and complains "you're abusing my humanism," the failed artist engineers the elderly Jew's downfall. He first convinces Shlomo's longtime friend, Gretchen, to abandon him, and he subsequently fabricates a fraudulent child abuse charge against him that ends up landing him in jail together with Lobkowitz. As the two men fall asleep in their cell, the film concludes with a surreal dream sequence that foreshadows coming historical events. In it, Hitler accosts Shlomo and demands he give up his memoir, "Mein Kampf," which he fears contains incriminating observa-tions about his youthful struggles. Shlomo refuses, and Hitler and his gang of nationalist thugs ransack the boarding house in the effort to find it. Unable to do so, they spring Shlomo out of prison in order to force the book from him. At this point, Hitler threatens the elderly Jew by saying "what shall I do with you? If you had a nice tattoo we could at least make a lampshade out of you." A penultimate scene, in which Hitler forces Frau Death to bend to his will makes the film's main point clear: as Hitler puts it, "We'll teach death its job. The beginning of a wonderful friendship." This lesson is driven home in the film's final scene when Shlomo and Lobkowitz, dressed in striped prisoner uniforms, march out of their cell toward a mysterious white light, symbolizing the Holocaust. Hitler, in short, has become the master of death.

By adding this ending to its humanized portrait of Hitler, *Mein Kampf* emerged as an unusual example of normalization. Because it was based on an older play, it is unclear whether the film's narrative reflected the priorities of its director, Odermatt, or those of its original author, Tabori. Significantly, Tabori originally wrote *Mein Kampf* as a farce that used humor to cope with the horrors of the Holocaust. This idiosyncratic approach reflected the playwright's own personal experiences. Born in Budapest in 1914, Tabori moved to Germany in 1932, but eventually fled to England in 1936. His parents were less fortunate. His father was killed at Auschwitz, while his mother survived after barely escaping deportation. In much of his dramatic work after 1945, Tabori embraced a "laughter of despair" informed by the belief that "humor is how one copes with personal and historical catastrophes."[75] This being the case, he intended *Mein Kampf* to be a satire that demythologized Hitler by exposing the absurdity of his anti-Semitism.[76] Tabori's masterstroke was the ironic, fictional premise of a Jew giving Hitler his start in politics and his signature physiognomy. Yet *Mein Kampf*'s satirical tone ultimately served a moral purpose. In portraying the failure of Shlomo's altruism to triumph over Hitler's anti-Semitism, the play functioned as a bleak parable about the inability of good to triumph over evil.[77] That said, the play's use of pastiche, combining the defamiliarizing strategies of Beckett and Brecht, brought a comparatively light-hearted approach to the subject of Nazism.[78] Indeed, Tabori's description of the play as a work of "theological slapstick" – and his stated opposition to "taboos and clichés" – made clear that his approach to the subject was highly unconventional.[79]

By all appearances, Odermatt strove to follow Tabori's lead. He, too, exhibited a more normalized approach to the topic because of his personal background. Where Tabori's Jewish identity led him to embrace black humor as an alternative to simplistic moralism, Odermatt did so as a result of his Swiss heritage. "Being from Switzerland," he told an interviewer, "I do not have the same historical background as a German or Austrian. Maybe I am a little less historically burdened and more curious, maybe I have a bit more distance and can more easily venture beyond a stance of demonstrative moral concern [*Betroffenheit*]."[80] Odermatt endeavored to keep much of Tabori's original dialogue in the film and preserve its function as a "parable of good that serves evil." At the same time, he shifted the narrative focus from Shlomo to Hitler, saying that the film aimed to create a "psychological profile" of the Nazi dictator.[81]

Odermatt's film, however, did not receive the same response as Tabori's play. When *Mein Kampf* was originally performed in Germany in the late 1980s and 1990s, it was a smash hit and earned rave reviews. By contrast, the response to Odermatt's film was mixed and tended to be critical. The most positive reviews appeared in Britain and the US, where observers hailed the film as "remarkably brave" for its "sympathetic ... humaniz[ation]... of Hitler."[82] In Germany and Austria, however, the reviews were uniformly negative. Most commentators offered an aesthetic critique of the film, complaining that Odermatt had dulled the comedic edge of Tabori's play by transforming it from a satirical farce into a realistic drama. As with certain reviews of *Max*, critics attacked the film for being unable to decide whether it wanted to be a satire or a work of realism.[83] One observer griped that the film was "not funny enough to be a comedy," a shortcoming that others attributed to its overly dramatic tone.[84] The film's "seriousness drove out every joke," one reviewer wrote, while another said that it "did not trust itself to embrace the absurd, surreal, or anarchic."[85] According to *Der Spiegel*, the fault lay in Odermatt's misguided attempt to present Tabori's "cock and bull story" as a "historical drama."[86] Certain commentators criticized the film's rigorous pursuit of authenticity, mocking the actors' efforts to learn local Austrian dialect and the director's attempt to find period-appropriate costumes and shooting locations.[87] The end result, other observers complained, was that the film "shrunk Tabori's [satire] into a work of Guido Knopp historicism."[88]

In addition to these aesthetic critiques, reviewers attacked what they took to be the film's moralistic tone. As with certain reactions to *Hitler – The Rise of Evil*, reviewers faulted *Mein Kampf* for being too heavy-handed in its message. In the words of one reviewer, the film's portrayal of Hitler employed "didactic methods ... worthy of a school lecture."[89] Another criticized the film for simplistically portraying Hitler as "genetically evil from the outset" instead of undergoing "a process of development as in Tabori['s original play]."[90] These criticisms were puzzling, given *Mein Kampf*'s satirical, humanized portrait of Hitler. Yet they may have represented a logical reaction to the film's divergence from the play. One reason for the original popularity of Tabori's work was that it offered German audiences one of their first opportunities after 1945 to laugh about the Nazi past. Because of Tabori's Jewish background, German audiences felt permitted to mock Hitler in ways that would have been impossible had the play been written by a non-Jewish playwright. They were thereby able to distance themselves from a sense of responsibility for Hitler's crimes.[91] Odermatt's film, however, offered fewer opportunities for laughter. Indeed, its more realistic approach may have discomfited audiences by reminding them of the deeper social roots of Hitler's hatred. This discomfort may explain one disappointed reviewer's remark that Odermatt's film was a "dejudaized version of Tabori's play," as it lacked the original's specifically "Jewish" sense of humor.[92] Without its presence, the film lost its transgressive, cathartic potential. It is unclear whether other criticisms of Odermattt for abandoning the humor of Tabori's play were informed by this belief.[93] But if so, they too highlighted a German yearning for normalcy.

Farewell to the Führer: Hitler's death

If *Hitler – The Rise of Evil*, *Max*, and *Mein Kampf* focused on Hitler's early years, other films concentrated on his last days. One of the most prominent was the blockbuster German film from 2004, *Downfall* (*Der Untergang*) (Figure 32). Directed by Oliver Hirschbiegel and produced by Bernd Eichinger, who also wrote the script, the film resembled the biopics of the 1970s in depicting the well-known events of Hitler's last days in Berlin. Yet while *Downfall* did not break any new ground in its focus, it portrayed Hitler in a much more humanized light. In so doing, the film courted considerable controversy.

From the beginning of *Downfall*, Hitler (played by Bruno Ganz) displays a human side. The film opens in November of 1942 with a group of young women arriving in the middle of the night at Hitler's *Wolfsschanze* Headquarters in East Prussia, hoping to land a job as the Führer's secretary. They are told to wait in an antechamber because Hitler "is feeding his dog," Blondi, whom he later kisses on the head and praises for having a "very sharp mind." When Hitler finally greets the applicants, he senses their nervousness and conscientiously tries to put them at ease, asking them about their hometowns and telling them to dispense with formal salutations. The viewer's first impression of Hitler, in short, is that of an animal lover and charmer of women. This benevolent image continues when the eventual recipient of the position, Traudl Junge (Alexandra Maria-Lara), takes dictation immediately after getting hired and botches the job, making numerous errors in her typing. Hitler, however, does not lose his temper and reassures her, gently saying, "I suggest that we try it again."

This humanized portrayal continues as the film shifts two-and-a-half years into the future, to the fateful month of April 1945. By now, the Soviets are closing in on Berlin and Hitler has begun to melt under the pressure of staving off the impending defeat. As he walks through

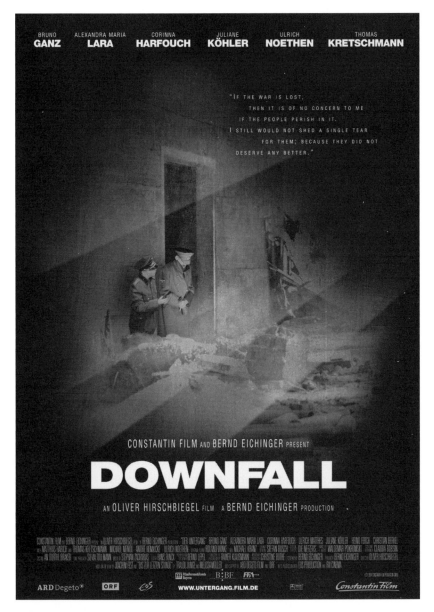

Figure 32. The 2004 film *Downfall* (*Der Untergang*) portrays Hitler's last days in the bunker of the Reich Chancellery.

the bunker, his left hand shakes with tremors, thereby symbolizing human frailty. He also has to contend with what he takes to be military and political treason on all fronts. His generals fail to hold their positions; his longtime supporters, Goering and Himmler, undertake

Figure 33. In this scene from *Downfall*, Hitler (Bruno Ganz) shows affection to his future wife, Eva Braun (Juliane Köhler).

unilateral diplomatic initiatives without his permission; and he is convinced that he has been betrayed by "cowards, traitors, and failures." When asked by his remaining supporters what they should do, he fatalistically replies, "The war is lost ... Do whatever you like." *Downfall* does not attempt to generate sympathy for Hitler through these scenes, as it assumes viewers know that the Führer's failures stem from his own hubris. But the film nevertheless portrays his reaction to failure in human terms. After Eva Braun (Juliane Köhler) tells Hitler, "You know I'll stay with you. I won't let you send me away," he appears genuinely moved and shows his appreciation by giving her an extended kiss on the lips (Figure 33). Even as Hitler nears his decision to commit suicide, he benevolently watches the Goebbels children sing German folk songs and politely compliments his cook for his last meal.

To be sure, while *Downfall* humanized Hitler, it also called attention to his evil side. As Traudl tells Eva in a revealing remark near the film's conclusion: "In private, [Hitler]... can be such a caring person, but then he says such brutal things." Hitler's brutality is partly explained by Germany's looming defeat. His famous rants from the film (now immortalized in countless YouTube parodies) are understandable as a human response to failure. Yet *Downfall* also showed that Hitler's evil is grounded in his Nazi ideology. This was made clear at various junctures when he expresses callous social Darwinistic views about the wartime suffering of the German people. Late in the film, when Albert Speer objects to Hitler's scorched earth policy, saying it will "hurl Germany back to the Middle Ages," the Nazi dictator declares, "If the war is lost, it's immaterial if the people perish too . . . They have proved themselves too weak, and it is a law of nature that they will be exterminated." This mercilessness is further displayed when the Führer orders the execution of Eva Braun's brother-in-law, Hermann Fegelein, for collaborating with Himmler, saying to his horrified bride-to-be, "there is no compassion for traitors." Still other scenes of German civilians dying needlessly in the effort to defend Berlin and being executed by fanatical SS vigilantes confirmed the cruelty of Hitler's ideology. These scenes round out the film's depiction of the Nazi dictator and counterbalance its otherwise humanized portrait of him.

Downfall's narrative reflected Hirschbiegel's and Eichinger's effort to create a documentary-style film that depicted Hitler's last days as authentically as possible. Their striving for authenticity was visible in the film's reliance on historical texts, most notably journalist Joachim Fest's book, *Der Untergang* (2002), and Traudl Junge's autobiography, *Bis zur letzten Stunde* (2002).[94] In drawing on these sources, Hirschbiegel and Eichinger sought to depict historical events on the screen as they had happened in real life. Eichinger, for example, claimed his film was "more authentic than all previous ones" as it avoided melodrama and showed Hitler in all of his human complexity.[95] It was wrong, Eichinger believed, to portray Hitler as a demon. "Hitler was a human being," he said; "he wasn't humane . . .[but] he could be friendly, even courteous."[96] The example of Hitler, indeed, proved that that "the most inhuman things can emerge from a human being."[97]

Eichinger's humanization of Hitler did not just reflect his desire for verisimilitude but his rejection of taboos in representing the Nazi era. Arguing that "moralizing never did anyone any good," he rejected the reluctance of postwar filmmakers to feature Nazis as cinematic protagonists, arguing that they should be depicted as "people with three dimensional character, people who one could even find sympathetic."[98] He dismissed the charge that this stance could be likened to "relativizing evil," explaining that "I am just not demonizing." Similarly, while Eichinger denied having any sympathy for Hitler, he acknowledged that "at certain places in the film one can sense empathy."[99] These remarks revealed that, in making the film, Eichinger was more interested in "relating . . . than commenting."[100] Rather than seeking to offer a political lesson in the film, he declared that "[it is] a very important message for me that whoever wants to remain resistant to the appeal of ideologies must form his own opinion, even it turns out to be wrong."[101] In effect, Eichinger embraced a non-judgmental form of cinematic historicism that strove for a wholly objective focus on the facts of the historical record.[102]

Eichinger's rejection of moralism reflected a conservative desire to create a normalized view of German history. Like Hirschbiegel and Fest, he stood on the conservative wing of the German political spectrum and "despised" what he saw as the German left's moralistic view of the country's history.[103] He also resented the fact that the representation of Hitler had been "usurped by non-German, and in particular Hollywood or Anglo-American, television productions."[104] In making *Downfall*, Eichinger asserted what he took to be a more authentically German perspective on the Nazi period. Arguing that "the sensibility of Germans is very different from that of Americans, who feel like their liberators," he insisted that

> we have to be able once more to reenter our own history instead of merely trying to 'take care of it.' This is not possible by debating whether we are a perpetrator nation (*Tätervolkdebatte*). As a people, we have imposed a level of guilt upon ourselves that we will never be able to erase . . . We need a new attitude and a national identity. Otherwise we will stagnate culturally. With this film, it is easier for me to say that I am German and that I am not embarrassed about it.[105]

In making *Downfall*, in short, Eichinger humanized Hitler as part of a larger attempt to normalize German history, memory, and identity.

Downfall's agenda predictably sparked vigorous debate. On the one hand, many reviewers approved of the film's mission. In Britain and the US, *Downfall* was praised for lacking "the habitual moralizing, preaching and self-flagellation connected with this sorry chapter [of German history]."[106] It was hailed for advancing the "inexorable process of seeing the Hitler era as history"; and it was admired for showing "how far the Germans have come in laying to rest their ghosts."[107] Such sentiments were commonly expressed in Germany, especially by conservative reviewers. Journalist Eckhart Fuhr, for instance, approvingly noted that the film inaugurated a "more relaxed" view of the Nazi era, one defined by a greater sense of "understanding" for the "generation of the perpetrators." As he put it, "today, Germans have their history, but they are no longer burdened by it. This allows them to look Hitler directly in the eyes."[108] An even more enthusiastic review was penned by Frank Schirrmacher in the *Frankfurter Allgemeine Zeitung*. Calling the film a "masterpiece," he emphasized that Eichinger portrayed Hitler in such a way as to make him "controllable." By this, Schirrmacher meant that the director had succeeded in using his own artistic methods to portray Hitler, instead of permitting the dictator's self-created documentary traces – visible in weekly newsreels, speeches, or writings – to posthumously shape his image. For Schirrmacher, this represented a breakthrough. Rhetorically asking, "is this what normality is?", he declared that Eichinger's status as "the first artist not to let himself be dictated to by Hitler is an act of normalization." This achievement made *Downfall* "an important milestone in our history of coming to terms with the past."[109]

By contrast, other critics faulted the film for abandoning a moral perspective and failing to pass judgment on the Nazi era.[110] Sociologist Harald Welzer said *Downfall*'s pretence to neutrality and authenticity was problematic, for it implied that the subject of Nazism could be narrated without contextualization and judgment, as if the facts could merely speak for themselves.[111] Other critics faulted the film for failing to provide a clear narrative stance. Historian Götz Aly declared that "analytically, the film points nowhere," while filmmaker Wim Wenders noted that it "has no opinion ... about fascism or Hitler" and "leaves the question of perspective for viewers" to decide.[112] This anti-editorializing stance left other observers wondering about the nature of the film's ultimate agenda.[113]

Critics also complained that *Downfall*'s humanization of Hitler perpetuated rather than dismantled his mythic aura. Journalist and media critic Georg Seesslen noted the ironic fact that while "the film's pursuit of exactitude ... strove for the opposite of mythologization," its neutral pursuit of authenticity succeeded merely in creating "the paradox of an 'authentic myth.'"[114] Put differently, *Downfall*'s rigid pursuit of objectivity failed to explain Hitler and left him a mythical cipher. This re-mythologization, according to various critics, was epitomized by the film's refusal to depict Hitler's actual death. This reluctance, combined with *Downfall*'s readiness to portray the death of countless ordinary Germans, prompted Wenders to exclaim: "What explains this failure of representation, this sudden prudery? . . . Why not show that the pig is finally dead? Why grant the man this honor that it denies the others who die en masse?"[115] The film's "non-display" of Hitler's death, Wenders feared, turned him into a "mythical figure." Indeed, as historian Michael Wildt noted, it fulfilled Hitler's own wish to die on his own terms by killing himself in private.[116]

Finally, critics attacked *Downfall* for blurring the line between the war's perpetrators and victims. Historian Jost Dülffer said the motion picture "broke a taboo" by placing the German people's victimization at its narrative center and shifting attention away from their culpability for Hitler's crimes.[117] For historian Hannes Heer, this exonerating effect of the film reflected a growing tendency within German society to "blame Hitler" alone for the Nazi catastrophe.[118] The inclination to absolve ordinary Germans of historical responsibility was also cited by Welzer, who observed that "when the only thing depicted [in the film] is the Third Reich's end, and when . . . the prehistory of the downfall . . . is no longer of any interest, then the 'human aspects' of the actors suddenly push to the foreground instead of what they perpetrated."[119] The film's eagerness to absolve the German people was further visible, American film critic David Denby noted, in its focus on the "noble behavior" of the "stoical defenders of Berlin who persist in the face of certain defeat," even honoring the "the good S.S. doctor who takes care of the wounded."[120] The problem with this portrayal, various historians pointed out, was that the "good Germans" who were trying to mitigate the destructiveness of Hitler's orders were less innocent of wrongdoing than the film implied, with many of them being ardent Nazis with considerable blood on their hands.[121] The film's tragic tone was thus fraudulent. Not only did it identify with the perpetrators, it ignored the victims. As critics noted, *Downfall* had only one line of dialogue related to the Holocaust.[122] The film showed Hitler in all kinds of human situations, but it did not show him to be a mass murderer.[123] In short, *Downfall* assumed the mantle of tragedy by marginalizing the Third Reich's criminality under the pretext of objectivity.

Following *Downfall*, the next major film to portray Hitler at the end of his life was *Mein Führer* (Figure 34). Directed by the Swiss Jewish filmmaker Dani Levy and released in 2007, the film was pioneering in several ways. First, it embraced a blatantly comic approach in portraying

Figure 34. The film *Mein Führer* (2007) features a buffoonish Hitler attempting to maintain his sanity as the Nazi Reich struggles to hold out against the approaching Allies.

the Nazi dictator. Unlike *Max*, whose humorous references were scattered and subtle, *Mein Führer*'s were overt. The film thus marked something of a throwback to the satirical motion pictures of the 1940s. Its goal was different, however. While wartime films spoofed the Führer for political reasons, namely to undermine his power, *Mein Führer* did so for moral and aesthetic reasons. Indeed, Levy embraced comedy in order to refute *Downfall*'s transformation of Hitler into a figure of tragedy. To be sure, *Mein Führer*'s humor was distinctly black. It was tempered, moreover, by the inclusion of elements of a counterfactual revenge fantasy. The film was novel, however, in being the first-ever German language comedy about Hitler. If *Downfall* controversially raised the question of whether the Germans should be allowed to humanize Hitler, *Mein Führer* sparked debate by asking whether they should be allowed to laugh at him.[124]

At first glance, *Mein Führer* resembled *Downfall* by portraying the Führer in a state of psychological distress. As the film opens, the date is December, 1944, and Hitler (played by Helge Schneider) has become so demoralized by Germany's declining fortunes that Propaganda Minister, Joseph Goebbels (Sylvester Groth), fears that he will be unable to help the German people maintain their morale for much longer. In order to forestall defeatism, Goebbels decides to call on Hitler's old acting coach from the 1920s, Adolf Grünbaum (Ulrich Mühe), to help the Führer recover his oratorical skills. The complicating factor is that Grünbaum is a Jew who is imprisoned, along with his family, in the concentration camp of Sachsenhausen. Not one to let obstacles stand in his way, Goebbels soon secures Grünbaum's release in the hope that he can help Hitler "rekindle in his heart that fire of 1939" in time to deliver a high-profile speech five days later in Berlin that will rally the German people to fight on to victory. What Goebbels does not tell Grünbaum is that he secretly expects him to revive Hitler's oratory by reanimating the "hatred" that the dictator will presumably feel through his encounter with the Jewish acting coach. (Goebbels also keeps a second, more ominous plan secret: namely, his conspiracy, hatched together with Heinrich Himmler, to seize power by killing Hitler with a bomb hidden in the podium where his speech is to be given and blaming the attack on the Jews.)

Against this backdrop of intrigue, the film brings Grünbaum and Hitler together for an extended series of interchanges that portray the Führer in a distinctly humanized light. When Grünbaum first meets

Hitler, the latter is standing in the Reich Chancellery staring out the window. As Grünbaum approaches, Hitler orders him to "heil me" – but then quickly adds, "heal me . . . I'm not doing well." Calling himself "a hopeless case," Hitler has entirely lost his self-confidence. He has not yet lost his pride, however, and at first refuses to let Grünbaum help him with his upcoming speech, ejecting him from his office. Grünbaum thereupon tells Goebbels that he cannot accept his order, as Hitler is "a broken man" beyond help. Yet he quickly changes his mind after getting the Propaganda Minister to release his family from Sachsenhausen. From this point on, Grünbaum endeavors to return Hitler to his old vigorous self.

Following this turn of events, the film abandons realism and shifts to a satirical mode of representing Hitler. It begins when the Führer agrees to follow Grünbaum's first piece of advice, which is to shed his stiff army uniform and don a bright green tracksuit for doing stretching and breathing exercises (Figure 35). The incongruous image of

Figure 35. In this scene from *Mein Führer* (2007) Hitler (Helge Schneider), incongruously clad in a bright green tracksuit, receives a lesson in breathing exercises from his Jewish acting coach, Adolf Grünbaum (Ulrich Mühe).

the leisurely attired dictator doing pushups and shadowboxing makes him look ridiculous. So does the ensuing scene when the Führer, having just asked Grünbaum a series of provocative questions – "Why doesn't the Jew fight back? Why do you let us deport you?" – ends up being punched in the nose and knocked unconscious by the insulted Jewish acting coach. Other scenes similarly mock the Nazi dictator: for example, when he gets down on his hands and knees to imitate a barking dog and ends up being mounted by his German shepherd, Blondi; when he suffers from erectile dysfunction while attempting to have sex with Eva Braun; and when half of his signature moustache is accidentally shaved off by a clumsy hairdresser prior to his big speech. All of these scenes are meant to shatter Hitler's mythic aura. Yet, by depicting him as a hard luck schlemiel, they also humanize him and make him the potential object of sympathy.

Other scenes are more overt in making Hitler a sympathetic figure. These occur after Grünbaum begins to employ psychoanalytical methods to help Hitler recover his old fighting spirit. In one scene, Grünbaum sits on a chair and says to Hitler, who is lying on a couch: "I'd like you to relive a moment that enraged you. Feel that rage again. Feel it crawl into your body." Hitler responds without words by clenching his fists, at which point Grünbaum shifts gears and asks him to recall a moment that made him happy. When Grünbaum inquires about the memory, Hitler replies, "My beloved father gave me a slingshot." Hitler is later shown having a nightmare in bed, stammering in his sleep, "Thank you Father, Thank you, Father." Still later, after Grünbaum partly hypnotizes Hitler, the dictator acts out older childhood memories – this time of abuse – shouting, "Don't touch me, Father! . . . Tell him to stop it. Tell him! Please, don't touch your son." Hitler then exclaims: "Do you know how often my father beat me? Every day." At this point, the dictator begins sobbing, thereby earning Grünbaum's sympathy and perhaps that of viewers as well.

The film's sympathy for Hitler was most clearly demonstrated by its refusal to kill him. One of *Mein Führer*'s running themes is that Grünbaum has numerous opportunities to assassinate the Führer but does not take advantage of them. Unlike the characters of Max Rothman and Shlomo Herzl, who have no foreknowledge of Hitler's political destiny and never contemplate killing him, Grünbaum knows that he can change the course of history by doing so. In the scene where Grünbaum knocks the Führer unconscious, he spies a sharp letter opener on the dictator's desk and briefly considers stabbing him. But Hitler revives before he can do so. When Grünbaum's wife later asks him whether he is planning on killing Hitler, he replies hesitantly: "I have to. Don't I?" Grünbaum also prevents his wife from killing Hitler. In an absurd scene near the film's conclusion, Hitler, suffering from insomnia, climbs into bed with the Jewish couple and promptly falls asleep. Grünbaum's wife immediately starts to smother the dictator with a pillow, but the acting coach stops her while she is sitting on Hitler's head, saying "you are … killing a defenseless human." These scenes further highlight *Mein Führer*'s normalized perspective towards Hitler. If the postwar pop culture fantasy of killing the Führer (and thereby improving the course of history) traditionally rested on his reputation as the epitome of evil, the fact that *Mein Führer* refrained from consummating the fantasy suggested its fading appeal. Hitler the human has begun to compete with Hitler the demon.

This shift explains why Grünbaum – following the example of Rothman and Shlomo – ultimately decides to redeem Hitler. When Grünbaum initially accepts Goebbels's request to tutor the Nazi dictator, he does so purely to save his family. But the acting coach gradually comes to sympathize with his student. Through their conversations, Grünbaum comes to realize that Hitler is a damaged human being who needs therapy. By using the (Jewish) science of psychoanalysis to help Hitler gain a new level of introspection about his childhood, Grünbaum helps him recover his voice. In effect, *Mein Führer* anticipated the central narrative conceit of the Oscar-winning film, *The King's Speech* (2011), where an acting coach helps King George VI overcome his stutter by coming to terms with his own strict father. More importantly, by portraying Hitler's capacity for redemption, the film shows Hitler to be a human being rather than a demon, a man whose evil had prosaic, as opposed to otherworldly, origins. So fully does Grünbaum appear to rehabilitate Hitler that the dictator later refers to him jovially as "my Jewish friend" and even "my Führer." In a play on the film's title, the Jew, Grünbaum, ironically becomes the "leader" who guides the Nazi to a new stance of tolerance. Unlike Rothman and Shlomo, Grünbaum seems poised to realize the counterfactual possibilities involved in the Jewish project of redeeming the Führer.

Yet *Mein Führer* ultimately ends on a tragic note. Although the Nazi dictator is well prepared for his speech, he loses his voice just before he is to take the podium after loudly berating his clumsy hairdresser for errantly shaving off his moustache. Hitler thereupon asks Grünbaum to fill in and mimic his voice from beneath the stage with a hidden microphone, while the dictator lip syncs for the crowd. Grünbaum does not stay on script, however, and instead delivers a more subversive message to the throngs of German listeners. "I thank you for your blind trust in me," he declares. "As loyal Germans you have followed me and made the world into Sauerkraut. Today our fatherland lies in ruins. And all of you are Aryans, blond and blue-eyed, except for me. And yet you cheer me. Heil myself!" At this point, the crowd roars out "heil!" and Grünbaum continues: "Why do you do it? I am a bed-wetter, a drug addict. I can't get an erection! I was beaten by my father so often that I ... torture defenseless people as I was once tortured myself. I take revenge all over Europe on Jews, homosexuals, and the sick for the agony I suffered when I was a child." Grünbaum is about to go on, but several Nazis, led by Albert Speer, burst into his hiding place and shoot him several times with pistols. His last words to the German people, stammered in agony, are "heal your...selves!" As the film nears its end, Grünbaum is shown with blood running down his head while Hitler looks down towards him in confusion before starting to flee the stage. The very last scene shows the Führer's podium being destroyed by the explosion of Goebbels' hidden bomb. Whether or not the dictator escapes the explosion is never disclosed.

The significance of this ambiguous ending is unclear. The main problem is that *Mein Führer* never clarifies the counterfactual consequences of Grünbaum's actions. On the one hand, the film appears to endorse Grünbaum's strategy of appeasing Hitler. Instead of choosing violence and assassinating Hitler, Grünbaum pursues a verbal strategy of intercession – the time-honored Jewish tradition of *shtadlanut* – by using words to tame the Nazi beast. He also verbally appeals to the German masses to recognize the foolishness of their Führer-worship. This strategy of non-violence enables Grünbaum to preserve his morals and sense of dignity. It allows to him to win Hitler's allegiance. And it offers the Jews a modest form of revenge for their suffering. At the same time, however, *Mein Führer* ultimately portrays Grünbaum's appeasement of Hitler as failing. Not only does he end up getting shot, his family presumably will be deported back to Sachsenhausen. Grünbaum's decision to spare Hitler's life, moreover, will have no positive consequences for the course of history. The film's ambiguous ending allows different readings, but the result appears to be the same: if Hitler is killed in the bomb blast, Goebbels and Himmler will take his place and the Nazis will remain in power. If Hitler survives, Goebbels will exploit the attempted assassination to stoke German anti-Semitism and reanimate the moribund war effort. In either case, the outcome is negative. This being so, *Mein Führer* raises the possibility – also suggested in *Max* and *Mein Kampf* – that the Jewish effort to redeem Hitler amounts to collaboration. The film thus comes close to relativizing Nazi criminality by blurring the line between Nazi perpetrators and Jewish victims.

However one interprets it, *Mein Führer*'s ambiguous ending reflected Levy's opposition to moralistic methods of portraying the Third Reich. Like the creative team behind *Max*, Hámori and Meyjes, the director grew up in a family that was directly affected by the Nazi experience (his mother fled from Berlin to Switzerland in the 1930s and chose not "to speak about it"). Levy rejected the "rigid taboo" that surrounded the topic, however, insisting that it was "important to be open to things that are forbidden ... Only by taking this approach can one arrive at a true confrontation [with the past]."[125] Levy also opposed "the moralistic confrontation with the Nazi past" for aesthetic reasons. Movies about the Third Reich had arrived "at a dead end" because of their tendency to depict it from a realistic, documentary-style perspective. Levy pointed to *Schindler's List* and Guido Knopp's series of Third Reich documentaries as examples of a tradition of "authoritarian historiography" in film, one that was defined by a "dogmatic"confidence in the medium's representational possibilities.[126] Levy, however, argued that "film is a lie" and denied that the Holocaust was at all representable, accusing movies like *Schindler's List* of "selling viewers simulated reality as truth."[127] The worst offender, though, was *Downfall*. Levy rejected the film's pretensions to objectivity, saying that "the solemn manner in which it slavishly tries to reproduce reality is simply grotesque."[128] He also complained about its crude didacticism, noting that its use of "dramatic music" and "authoritative ... voice-over[s]" to show "who the bad guys are" failed to challenge viewers to adopt a perceptual stance that was anything but "morally secure."[129] In short, Levy's aversion to taboos, moralism, and realism in films about the Nazi era led him to seek an alternative approach.

Indeed, it prompted him to narrate the Third Reich from a comic perspective. "Annoyed" and "bored" by documentary-style films, Levy recalled that "when I first heard [that *Downfall* was being developed], I began itching to do a counter-film that would stand as a subversive response to it."[130] He hoped a comedic approach would be able to shake things up, "turn morality on its head, make people insecure, and prompt questions."[131] He specifically wanted to parody *Downfall*'s humanization of Hitler, which he believed accepted the dictator's self-representation at face value. "I don't want to give this cynical, psychological wreck of a person the honour of a realistic portrayal," Levy argued. "I had [to be]... able to exaggerate through comedy."[132] The director also wanted to parody *Downfall*'s claim to be more truthful than previous cinematic portraits of the dictator. This explained why he chose a sarcastic subtitle for *Mein Führer* – "The Truly Truest Truth about Adolf Hitler" (*Die wirklich wahrste Wahrheit über Adolf Hitler*). In expressing Levy's belief in the impossibility of realistically depicting Hitler, the subtitle displayed what he called the film's palpable tone of "scurrilous irony."[133]

This skepticism was further reflected in the film's subversion of its own authenticity. At the end of the movie, Levy has Grünbaum speak as an off-screen narrator who frames the film's story from an undetermined vantage point some time after the Third Reich's collapse. This voice-over comes as a jarring surprise for viewers convinced that they have just witnessed Grünbaum's death. They are left to assume either that he has somehow survived to tell his tale, or that he is a German version of *Sunset Boulevard*'s Joe Gillis, posthumously narrating the story of his own death. The reality is never fully clarified in the film. But the ambiguity was probably intended to expose Grünbaum as an unreliable narrator who may be spinning his story – like the true actor he is – out of whole cloth. This possibility was further suggested by Grünbaum's last lines in the film: "That was my story. It's absolutely true. I promise. Okay, perhaps I exaggerated a few things. You don't believe me?" Grünbaum recites these lines at the same time he tells viewers that, in reality, Adolf Hitler died "by taking cyanide and shooting himself" in April of 1945. This statement served as the film's admission of its own fraudulence. Why *Mein Führer* subverts its own veracity is unclear. But Levy probably intended Grünbaum's unreliability to illustrate the director's skepticism about cinema's ability to arrive at historical truth. As Grünbaum says at the film's conclusion: "one hundred years from now, authors will still write about [Hitler]... Why? Because we want to understand what we will never understand." The film thus ends on a note of irony by declaring that the goal of all Hitler films – historical understanding – is itself unattainable.

A greater irony, however, was the fact that *Mein Führer* submitted its own explanation of the Nazi dictator – one that was strongly moralistic to boot. Levy, to be sure, embraced moralism in his film to challenge rather than reaffirm accepted truths. Admitting that he was a "humanistic moralist," he explained that "the great thing about a comedy is that it is allowed to raise moral questions and provoke."[134] Levy's specific goal was to use comedy to challenge the reigning demonic portrait of the Führer with a more humanized version that viewers could identify with. As he put it, *Mein Führer* was meant to bring viewers to an "unexpected closeness to Hitler" that involved "empathy [or even]... pity."[135] Levy advanced this goal in the film by showing the Nazi dictator to be the innocent victim of child abuse. In writing the film's screenplay, Levy embraced Swiss psychoanalyst Alice Miller's claim that the nineteenth-century Central European child-rearing tradition known as "black pedagogy" (*Schwarze Pädagogik*) was partly responsible for causing Nazism. (This tradition's emphasis on corporal punishment, according to Miller, had a traumatic impact on children, leading them to blindly obey authority and fantasize about avenging their pain and suffering.)[136] Levy was convinced that this tradition had strongly affected Hitler. Arguing that it made the future dictator "a divided personality, manic depressive, sexually incapable, and emotionally ... crippled," Levy concluded that "the 'black pedagogy' of this era had a direct influence on National Socialism. Of this I am certain."[137]

Levy did not advance this claim simply to put viewers in the unconventional position of empathizing with Hitler, however. He also sought to indict German culture for the Third Reich. Aware of the tendency of many Germans to blame the Nazi experience solely on Hitler, Levy showed that the Nazi dictator's behavior lay in the nation's abusive child-rearing traditions. This explanation allowed him to refute the central narrative of *Downfall*, whose focus on Hitler's responsibility for the German people's wartime suffering enabled them to evade their own guilt for the Nazi regime. At the same time, however, Levy's explanation subtly universalized the Nazi past. By pointing to child abuse as an explanation for Nazism, *Mein Führer* focused on a factor that was universal in nature, thereby downplaying the relevance of Germany's specific political situation after World War I.[138] This decision somewhat diluted the film's focus on the Third Reich's German origins.

In the end, however, *Mein Führer*'s conclusion reflected Levy's conviction that Nazism should ultimately be seen as a German phenomenon. By refusing to make clear whether Hitler actually dies in the film, Levy pointed to its basic irrelevance. Regardless of the Führer's fate, Nazism will survive. Grünbaum's apparent "choice" about whether to collaborate with, or kill, Hitler is no choice at all. This is because the deeper, more intractable problem is the German people. Their blind obedience to the Nazis, the film revealed, is what allows the regime to pursue its destructive policies. *Mein Führer* made this point clear at its conclusion, when Grünbaum, having just been shot, utters two final words to the throngs of onlookers listening to his fake Hitler speech: "heal yourselves." In offering this admonition, Levy showed that he shared the historiographical view that Nazism was not the result of a historical accident but was deeply rooted in German history. *Mein Führer*'s humanization of Hitler – like his refusal to kill him – helped reaffirm this larger point. By implying that Hitler's hypothetical redemption and death would have had no positive effect on history, the film exposed the deeper sources of Nazism. Levy's humanization of Hitler was thus the opposite of what it appeared to be. Despite departing from prior moralistic modes of portraying the dictator, it ironically served a larger moral agenda.

In yet another irony, however, critics largely overlooked *Mein Führer*'s moral agenda and perceived it to be normalizing the Nazi past. This was especially true of observers in Germany, who attacked the film for its light-hearted portrayal of Hitler. The general secretary of the Central Council of Jews in Germany, Stephan Kramer, called *Mein Führer* "superficial ... and even dangerous," saying that Hitler "does not deserve the sympathy of the public."[139] Other critics agreed that the film humanized the Nazi dictator far too much, with journalist Ralph Giordano declaring that it "could be damaging if it gets the public to treat Hitler as a comedic figure."[140] Representatives of the German Catholic Church saw *Mein Führer* as a "trivialization" of Hitler, while playwright Rolf Hochhuth saw it as a "distortion."[141] Summing up the view of many, one critic said that by putting "Adolf on the couch," the film had arrived at an overly sympathetic view of dictator, concluding, "Hitler is not exactly the ideal star witness for the thesis that crimes have their causes in screwed-up childhoods ... At a certain point, one reaches a limit of understanding."[142] Such elite reactions also found an echo at the mass level. According to polls, 56 percent of Germans spoke out against the film, while only 35 percent approved of a comedy about Hitler.[143] These reactions were most likely reinforced by survey results reporting that viewers who had actually seen the film came away from it with a more sympathetic view of the Nazi dictator.[144]

To be sure, *Mein Führer* had defenders who recognized its moral agenda. Yet even they saw it as weakened by its satirical streak, noting that it could not decide whether it wanted to be a comedy or a drama.[145] As journalist Henryk Broder wrote, the film had "two parts…one absurd and the other moral," but it had difficulty harmonizing them. "The absurd part," he observed, "isn't absurd enough [and the]…moral part … is too moral. No matter how skilled the cook, a pork chop can never be turned into a kosher delicacy."[146] Outside of Germany, reactions echoed similar points. In the United States, most reviewers panned the film because it was "not laugh-out-loud funny" and failed to be provocative. As one critic put it, the only taboo it violated was "thou shalt not bore the audience."[147] Others agreed that Levy's humanized portrait was overly normalized. As film critic Stephen Holden put it in the *New York Times*, "blaming Hitler's monstrosity on a miserable childhood is an egregiously sentimental explanation for the Nazi horror."[148]

These criticisms notwithstanding, other reviewers described the film as a milestone in the Germans' normalization of the Nazi past. Some welcomed the idea of a German comedy about Hitler, believing that laughing at the dictator was a sign of Germany's democratic credentials.[149] Others, arguing that "jokes help expel demons," suggested that the film would have a cathartic effect for the German people.[150] Journalist Horst von Butlar made this clear when he predicted that "Germany will give [Levy] a hug" for "showing Germany something funny about [the Nazis]," since "it was time that Germans, too, could laugh at Adolf Hitler."[151] *Mein Führer*, in short, was praised for doing what Odermatt's widely-panned film, *Mein Kampf*, could not – deliver a cathartic release. Other commentators, however, were more skeptical. One German critic asserted that "laughing about Hitler was no sign of German normalcy," adding that the subject of Nazism was "too serious" for "teaching history through tomfoolery."[152] Others saw ulterior motives in the readiness of Germans to laugh at Hitler in Levy's film. One was discomfited by allusions to the director's Jewish background as proof of the permissibility of laughing at Hitler, suspecting that it smacked of subtle anti-Semitism and reflected a sign of the ongoing attempt of Germans to "draw a line under the Nazi past" (*Schlussstrichpolitik*).[153] Another said that the tendency to view Levy as a "moral authority" reflected a German tradition of "finding a model Jew ...[to sanction] every non-kosher opinion."[154] These diverging responses confirmed the claim of still other observers that the Federal Republic was anything but "relaxed" about the topic of Hitler and the Nazis.[155] For these critics, normality remained a distant goal.

The final film to explore the subject of Hitler's death was Quentin Tarantino's *Inglourious Basterds* (2009) (Figure 36). Like *Mein Führer*, the film rejected the realistic style of *Downfall* and displayed a more hybrid approach in representing the Nazi era. Loosely based on Italian director Enzo G. Castellari's film, *The Inglorious Bastards* (1978), Tarantino's motion picture blended the genres of realistic drama, comic farce, and counterfactual history. The film even displayed the influence of non-cinematic elements borrowed from literature by being divided into five chapters. Only one of the chapters involved Hitler, but it was important, for it explicitly portrayed the Führer's death. In contrast to *Downfall*, which declined to depict Hitler's demise, and *Mein Führer*, which portrayed it ambiguously, *Inglourious Basterds* showed it in graphic fashion. In so doing, the film rejected *Downfall's* mythologization and *Mein Führer's* humanization of Hitler in favor of an approach that moralistically demonized him as a crucial element of a larger revenge fantasy. The film thus seemed to reject any normalization of the Nazi past. Yet by aestheticizing violence and dissolving the line between Jewish victims and German perpetrators, *Inglourious Basterds* undercut its moral claims and advanced the normalizing process in its own unique way.

Inglourious Basterds features several major story lines that parallel one another until colliding in an explosive conclusion. The first involves the efforts of a brutal SS major, Hans Landa (played by Christoph Waltz), to hunt down Jews hiding in Nazi-occupied France. Shortly after the film opens in the year 1941, Landa is depicted interrogating a nervous French peasant about his knowledge of Jews in the region; Landa gradually realizes the peasant is hiding a Jewish family in his basement and abruptly orders his SS men to shoot through the floorboards of his house, killing most of them. Only one of the Jews, a young woman named Shoshanna (Mélanie Laurent) survives. She provides the film with its second plot line, namely her effort to get revenge for her family's murder. After escaping from Landa, Shoshanna flees to Paris

Figure 36. Quentin Tarantino's film, *Inglourious Basterds* (2009), shows Hitler falling victim to an assassination plot carried out by a band of American Jewish hit men.

where, by 1944, she has taken on an assumed name and opens up a movie theater. She soon meets a young Wehrmacht soldier named Fredrick Zoller, whose wartime exploits as a sniper have landed him a starring role in a new propaganda film, *Nation's Pride*, produced by

Joseph Goebbels. Realizing that Zoller is smitten with her, Shoshanna has him persuade the Propaganda Minister to premier the film in her theater with top Nazi officials in attendance. This gives her the chance for vengeance, and she begins planning a scheme to set the theater on fire during the performance, killing all in attendance. The movie's third plot line profiles a group of young American Jewish soldiers who have been dropped behind enemy lines in France just before D-Day in order to terrorize Nazi soldiers with sadistic revenge attacks. The group, which is known as the "basterds," is led by a Tennessee hillbilly named Aldo Raine (Brad Pitt), and features various Jewish characters who scalp their victims after killing them (for variety's sake, one member, Donnie Donowitz – the "Bear Jew" – beats them to death with a baseball bat).

These characters converge in Paris for the climactic scene featuring Hitler's death. As part of an Allied-sponsored plot called "Operation Kino," the basterds are sent in to provide support for Shoshanna's arson plan. Hitler attends the premiere and the basterds, dressed in tuxedos, are there to meet him. Here, the film abruptly changes its narrative style in order to aestheticize the grand finale. Up until this juncture, most of *Inglourious Basterds* is narrated from a realistic perspective taut with dramatic tension. The scenes at the Paris movie theater, however, adopt a blatantly comic tone. This section of the film begins when Shoshanna is standing on a balcony surveying the premiere's guests milling about below. Suddenly, super-imposed upon the screen next to a Nazi official, appear the words "Hermann" and "Goering," written in white block letters with a white arrow pointing towards the corpulent Nazi *Luftwaffe* minister. A similar graphic, reading "Martin Bormann," subsequently identifies Hitler's secretary and party chancellery chief. These defamiliarizing gestures, which combine text with image, pull the film away from realism and into comic book territory. The satirical tone of this chapter is further shown when Raine and his two basterd colleagues incompetently pose as Italian cameramen, stumbling through insufficient vocabulary, atrocious accents, and absurdly stereotypical hand gestures.

The film reverts somewhat to realism for the scene portraying Hitler's death, but it, too, is highly aestheticized. As the cinema audience watches Goebbels' film, a new section of footage spliced into the reel by Shoshanna depicts her divulging her revenge plan. The scene features a close-up of her supersized face telling the audience that they

Figure 37. Hitler (Martin Wuttke) dies in a hail of bullets near the climax of *Inglourious Basterds* (2009).

"are all going to die" and giving the signal to her African assistant in the theater, Marcel, to "burn it down." At this point, Marcel flicks a lit cigarette in slow motion towards an enormous pile of highly flammable film canisters, which burst into flame to the audience's horror. Two of the basterds then force their way into Hitler's private theater box and riddle him and Goebbels with bullets (Figure 37). As Shoshanna's face diabolically laughs that "this is the face of Jewish vengeance," the film offers further slow motion scenes of the basterds shooting into the panicked crowd. The conflagration culminates when sticks of dynamite left by the basterds detonate and the theater explodes into flames.

The scene's purpose is to make viewers cheer Hitler's death, a reaction that is further encouraged by the film's portrayal of the Führer – and the Nazis in general – as the essence of evil. Although Hitler (played by Martin Wuttke) only has a few scenes in the movie, he is shown to be a fanatical anti-Semite. When told, for example, about a recent attack by the basterds, he becomes irate – screaming "how much more of these Jew swine must I endure?" – and demands that they be captured so that he can "hang them naked by their heels, from the Eiffel Tower." Unlike *Downfall* and *Mein Führer*, *Inglourious Basterds* displays little of Hitler's human side. Moreover, the film clearly shows Nazism to be evil. This is made clear when Raine tells his men, "I sure as hell didn't come down from the goddamn Smoky mountain ... to teach the Nazis lessons in humanity. Nazis ain't got no humanity. They're the foot soldiers of a Jew-hating, mass murdering maniac, and they need to be destroyed."

In underscoring Nazism's evil, the film sought not only to boost viewers' enjoyment of Hitler's death, but satisfy their expectations of its counterfactual consequences. In contrast to *Mein Führer*, which denied viewers the pleasure of knowing how Hitler's possible death affects the course of history, *Inglourious Basterds* implied that the Führer's death would help improve it. The film portrays Hitler's assassination as bringing about an earlier end to World War II. Thanks to the assassination of the Nazi top brass, Germany ends up surrendering to the Allies months before it does in real history. (This event ironically transpires thanks to Hans Landa, who, despite easily uncovering the basterds' assassination plot, opportunistically allows it to go forward in exchange for a boatload of rewards from the US government, including American citizenship.) *Inglourious Basterds* further sought to satisfy viewers' desires by preventing Landa from avoiding accountability for his earlier crimes. At the film's end, Raine ensures that the SS man will not be able to blend anonymously into postwar American society by carving a swastika into his forehead, thus branding him for life. In so doing, the film delivered a modicum of justice for Landa's victims and ended on a note of moral closure.

Yet while *Inglourious Basterds* portrayed the Nazi past mostly in moralistic fashion, it normalized it in one important respect. Like *Downfall*, *Max*, *Mein Kampf*, and *Mein Führer*, it, too, blurred the line between Nazi perpetrators and Jewish victims. *Inglourious Basterds* did so in a new way, however. While *Downfall* portrayed the Germans as victims, and while *Max*, *Mein Kampf*, and *Mein Führer* depicted Jews as collaborators, *Inglourious Basterds* brought them into the realm of perpetrators. In pursuing vengeance, the film's Jewish characters employ violence worthy of the Nazis. Shoshanna's desire to avenge her family's murder, for example, leads her to threaten an innocent French film developer with death unless he assists her revenge plan, an act that in the film's original script she defends by declaring: "In a wolf fight, you either eat the wolf, or the wolf eats you. If we're going to obliterate the Nazis, we have to use their tactics."[156] Similarly, the basterds' sadistic murder of their Nazi opponents inverts the treatment that the Jews suffered at their hands. To be sure, the film did not exhibit an entirely amoral view of Jewish violence and depicted its adverse consequences. Shoshanna ends up being killed by Zoller before she can enjoy her revenge. And two of the Jewish basterds involved in Operation Kino, Hirschberg and Donowitz, presumably meet their demise in the theater fire after detonating their sticks of dynamite. Yet, because their actions ultimately help history turn out for the better, the film endorsed the Jewish quest for vengeance.

In placing the behavior of Jews in the same orbit as that of the Nazis, Tarantino did not intentionally set out to normalize the Nazi past. Unlike most of the filmmakers who directed or produced recent Hitler films, he was uninterested in politics and history.[157] Where other filmmakers were personally invested in the Nazi era's historical legacy, he displayed a more neutral attitude that reflected his interest in aesthetics over ethics. *Inglourious Basterds*' aestheticization of violence, particularly through its use of comedy, reflected the director's trademark practice of "getting you to laugh at things that really aren't funny."[158] The film's setting in the Second World War, meanwhile, mostly reflected his longtime fascination with genre films and not any particular interest in the event's history. Finally, the film's focus on vengeance addressed a topic that dominated many of his films, such as *Reservoir Dogs*, *Pulp Fiction*, and *Kill Bill*. In exploring these themes in *Inglourious Basterds*, Tarantino explained that he wanted to do "something different" and not just portray Jews as victims; instead, he wanted to depict "Germans that are scared of Jews."[159] His motives in doing so, however, were less moralistic than cinematic. At its root, *Inglourious Basterds* was a film about film.[160] To the extent that Tarantino was at all interested in German history, he was interested in the history of German cinema. The director observed that his movie made film itself responsible for killing the Nazi elite in the form of the reels that Shoshanna sets on fire in her theater. Saying he got "a kick" out of the fact that "the power of cinema is going to bring down the Third Reich," Tarantino gleefully speculated that among the films set on fire would have been works "banned by the Nazis, Lubitsch, Chaplin, Pabst … that blow the Third Reich into the sky."[161]

Yet while Tarantino's normalization of the Nazi past had little to do with politics, the critical response to *Inglourious Basterds* was highly politicized. Many of the reviews addressed the film's aestheticization of the Nazi era. On the one hand, certain observers hailed the film for its artistic merits, praising its visual style and self-conscious borrowing from film history.[162] Others approvingly noted how it "abolished the clichés of war films and liberated the Jew from his cinematic role as victim."[163] German critics, in particular, said that, especially after such historically grounded films as *Downfall*, the motion picture had a "liberating" effect.[164] The belief that the film was a "masterpiece" was confirmed by its nomination for eight Oscars and its impressive commercial success.[165] Yet *Inglourious Basterds* was also critiqued for exploiting the Nazi era without delving into its deeper issues. Journalist Jens Jessen compared the motion picture to a pornographic movie in the sense that its plot and setting were incidental to the main agenda of "getting down to business" and wallowing in gratuitous violence.[166] Other reviewers, however, concluded that it was too much to expect Tarantino to "grapple with history in any meaningful sense," since he had proven himself in his previous work to be "the most talented filmmaker in America who prides himself on having absolutely nothing to say."[167]

Still other commentators said that *Inglourious Basterds* did not just aestheticize Nazi violence but relativized it by blurring the line between Nazis and Jews. Many critics objected to the film's fictional depiction of Jews doing to the Nazis what they had actually suffered at their hands in real history.[168] Whether showing Jews burning Nazis in buildings or carving swastikas in their foreheads, Tarantino, according to writer Daniel Mendelsohn, asked audiences to "applaud [the]... inversion . . .[and] take a deep emotional satisfaction in turning the tables on the bad guys." In the process, however, the director encouraged "audiences [to] cheer . . . for a revenge that turns Jews into carbon copies of Nazis."[169] Film critic J. Hoberman went further, arguing that the film's portrait of "Jews ... acting like Nazis" implied that they were pursuing a "just Holocaust" against the Germans.[170] These reviewers sensed that the film advanced a normalizing dynamic. Film critic Neil Gabler wrote that the film "conventionalizes Jews" by having them succumb to the revenge impulse like "everybody else."[171] German observers cited this fact in explaining the film's popularity in the Federal Republic, noting that German audiences' "jubilation" at the basterds' vengeance "is an expression of . . . relief towards the film for sparing viewers a bad conscience. The Nazis were brutal and so are the Jews, thus there is no need for shame or atonement."[172] Conversely, other reviewers worried that the film normalized the Nazis. One commentator feared that the film's portrayal of Jews sadistically torturing Nazis risked creating "sympathy" for them as victims.[173] Another worried that Tarantino had made SS man Landa the film's most appealing character, depicting him as "a most delightful Nazi," who had no equivalent on the Allied side.[174]

Still others argued that *Inglourious Basterds'* portrayal of Jewish violence universalized the significance of the Nazi period. Some Jewish critics found the film to have worrisome implications about Jews' capacity for violence in the contemporary Middle East. This was the claim of journalist Jeffrey Goldberg, who fretted that several people associated with the film took pleasure at the prospect of producing a "Jewish revenge fantasy," in particular, actor Eli Roth, who made headlines for referring to the film as "kosher porn."[175] Goldberg worried that the film's depiction of Jews as vengeance-seekers could justify aggressive Israeli policies towards the Palestinians.[176] In fact, Tarantino acknowledged that "conception[s] of ... post-Israel Jew[s]" subtly informed his portrayal of his film's Jewish vigilantes. In a 2010 interview, he described a trip to Israel in which he learned about the country's "kick ass army," which left him impressed with the "awesome" concept that "every young person ... is gonna know what it means to be a warrior." For critics like Goldberg, however, Tarantino's take-away lesson about Israeli self-defense – "We will never be caught sleeping again" – could legitimize the kind of violence that encouraged comparisons of Israelis to Nazis.[177]

Still other observers worried that Tarantino's portrayal of violent Jews would not so much associate them with Nazi sadists but Arab terrorists. One particular scene in the film implied such a connection. At the grand finale in the Paris movie theater, two of the basterds are seated in the audience with sticks of dynamite strapped to their legs. This image – and Tarantino's subsequent description of them as "suicide bombers" – drew an implicit equivalence between Jews and present-day Islamic radicals, thereby casting the former in an unflattering moral light. Indeed, it threatened to diminish the Jews' status as historical victims. As journalist Danielle Berrin explained, "if Jews get their revenge, then they have less claim to victimhood. Which means less sympathy for the many existential threats facing Israel."[178] The fact that certain German critics interpreted *Inglourious Basterds'* narrative as a sign that "Israeli hawks ... had arrived in Hollywood" revealed a readiness to see Jews as aggressive perpetrators instead of innocent victims.[179] Similarly, the anxious attempt of other Jewish reviewers to dismiss Tarantino's vision as "un-Jewish" reflected the fear that the film's portrayal of Jewish violence could negatively affect views of Israel.[180] In short, despite not being inspired by political considerations, *Inglourious Basterds* sparked its share of politicized debate.

Conclusion

Over the last decade, films about Hitler have represented the Nazi dictator in increasingly normalized fashion. Whether focusing on his early years in Vienna or his last days in Berlin, whether chronicling his path into politics or its catastrophic effects, recent films have broken with reigning cinematic practice and have sought to understand rather than condemn him. Rejecting the moralistic tradition of demonization, they have pursued a normalizing strategy of humanization. These films have promoted this strategy by employing the methods of aestheticization, universalization, and relativization. In so doing, they have met with resistance, sparking debate about their impact on the memory of the Nazi past. In generating this reaction, recent Hitler films have confirmed, yet again, the dialectic of normalization. They have also revealed that *all* methods of representing Hitler and the Third Reich – whether normalized or moralistic – possess merits and drawbacks for remembrance.

Since the turn of the millennium, many films have attempted to humanize Hitler via the method of aestheticization. They have done so by focusing attention on the two phases of his life when he was at the nadir of his power: his early years, when he struggled to find a place in the world, and his last days, when he decided to depart from it. By concentrating on these two periods, recent films have humanized the Nazi dictator by cutting him down to size; instead of portraying him as an omnipotent figure to be feared, they have shown him as a decrepit figure to be pitied. *Max* and *Mein Kampf*, for example, depicted the young Hitler struggling to cope with the indignities of poverty and the humiliation of thwarted dreams. *Downfall* and *Mein Führer* portrayed the dictator as weakened by the frailties of old age, ill health, and imagined betrayal. These films pursued their humanizing agenda via different modes of representation. *Downfall* embraced realism and portrayed Hitler as an everyman performing everyday tasks, such as eating dinner and kissing his wife. *Max*, *Mein Kampf*, and *Mein Führer* embraced satire and made him the pitiable butt of jokes. These modes of humanizing Hitler undeniably normalized him by rejecting moralistic methods of representation. In most cases, they did so with respectable intentions. The cinematic effort to humanize Hitler was largely driven by the desire to demythologize him, to reduce his stature from larger-than-life to run-of-the-mill. This effort was underpinned by the moral goal of preventing

Hitler from ever again serving as an object of fascination or attraction. But it came with a price. Realistic methods run the risk of reproducing the aesthetic effects that underpinned Hitler's original appeal. Humorous methods, meanwhile, risk trivializing his crimes and distracting from his evil. These trade-offs involving the aestheticization of the Nazi past highlight some of the inescapable ambiguities of normalization.

The same can be said of the cinematic effort to humanize Hitler via the strategy of universalization. Many recent films about Hitler have sought universal lessons in the Nazi past. Some have highlighted the role of general, as opposed to particular, forces in explaining Hitler's embrace of political extremism. In directing *Max*, for example, Menno Meyjes explained Hitler's turn to Nazism as a result of basic human emotions, such as rage and frustration. Dani Levy's *Mein Führer* explained Hitler's political turn as the result of abusive nineteenth-century Central European child-rearing traditions. Other films universalized the Nazi legacy by drawing parallels between the Third Reich and present-day political events. The directors and producers behind the films, *Hitler – The Rise of Evil* and *Max*, cited the political dangers represented by Saddam Hussein, Slobodan Milosevic, and even George W. Bush in underscoring the relevance of Hitler's rise to power. Reviews of *Inglourious Basterds* and statements by its director, Quentin Tarantino, meanwhile, linked the film to Israel's precarious status in the Middle East. As with the strategy of aestheticization, these instances of universalization were driven by respectable motives. There is nothing inherently problematic with seeking universal lessons in the Nazi era. Showing how a particular historical period provides larger insights about the human condition broadens its historical relevance and enables it to speak to a wide audience. At the same time, universalizing the past runs the risk of ignoring its specificity and distorting its reality. By overlooking the role of German cultural and political traditions in Hitler's rise to power, recent films missed an opportunity to deepen the cause of historical understanding.

Similar ambiguities defined the phenomenon of relativization. Recent films about Hitler relativized the Nazi past by blurring the line between Nazi perpetrators and Jewish victims. *Downfall* did so by casting the Germans as victims and marginalizing Jewish suffering. *Inglourious Basterds* did so by portraying Jews behaving like their Nazi tormentors. Most films, however, blurred the line by suggesting the capacity of Jews to collaborate with the Nazis. *Max, Mein Kampf,* and *Mein Führer* each featured Jewish protagonists who work with, and try to redeem, Hitler. Max Rothman, Shlomo Herzl, and Adolf Grünbaum all extend themselves towards Hitler out of a sense of sympathy with his plight. But they all fail to achieve their objectives and pay for it with their lives. The films clearly depicted these characters' fates as tragic. But by stressing their naiveté in trying to redeem Hitler, the films came close to blaming the Jewish characters for their own demise. By depicting Jews in such a critical light – and by portraying Hitler in a more humanized light to begin with – recent films have subtly relativized Nazi criminality. To be sure, this normalizing effect was largely unintentional. Rather, it was the collateral effect of these films' decision to subvert the counterfactual fantasy that Hitler might have been redeemable with the proper assistance. By exposing the fantasy's folly, these films inevitably cast a negative light on the Jews who try to steer Hitler away from his historical destiny. At the same time, the films unintentionally pointed to a positive feature of relativization. They showed that the strategy can function as a corrective to moral absolutism and promote a greater appreciation for history's complexity. They showed that while the Nazis were evil, they had their helpers – even Jewish ones, as we know from the notorious example of the *Judenräte* – a fact that enables a more nuanced understanding of the Nazi era. To be sure, relativization can lead to minimization, but it need not do so and should therefore not be judged in blanket fashion. This fact, too, highlighted the ambiguities of normalization.

In the end, there are no simple answers to the question of how Hitler and the Nazi past should be cinematically represented. The divided reception of recent Hitler films makes this difficulty all the more clear. While many of the films have been hailed by critics and been a hit with audiences, they have been faulted for breaking with moralistic forms of representation. This divided reception highlights the elusiveness of normality. At the same time, it underscores the crisis of moralism. Not only are fewer films adhering to ethically grounded traditions of representation, those that have done so – such as *Hitler – The Rise of Evil* – have been widely criticized. The exhaustion of moralism is partly due to its long postwar run as the orthodox mode of representing Hitler. But it is also due to its core liability, the inability to foster historical understanding. As long as films portray Hitler as an evil demon instead of a human being, they will have difficulty advancing the task of understanding him. Their goal of judgment will impede the goal of explanation. At the same time, however, rejecting moralism in favor of normalization brings its own problems. The more that films insist on humanizing Hitler – through whatever aesthetic means – the more they risk trivializing him.

It is hard to know whether rigid moralism or creeping normalization represents the greater threat to the memory of the Nazi era. Views diverge in different parts of the world. In Germany today, many observers are troubled by moralistic representations of Hitler as an evil demon. Pointing to the film *Downfall* and to Guido Knopp's Hitler documentaries, critics argue that focusing on Hitler's evil shifts attention away from the role of the German people in abetting his crimes. These commentators therefore support the cinematic effort to humanize Hitler. This effort, they maintain, helps draw attention to the reasons why Germans originally supported him and underscores their historical responsibility for his rise to power. Believing in the necessity of this larger goal, these critics are not concerned that Hitler's humanization will promote his trivialization. In the United States and England, by contrast, the opposite is true. In both countries, the inflated invocation of Hitler in political discourse and his increasingly satirical portrayal in popular culture have stoked concerns that his criminal reputation is becoming diminished. Believing in the importance of preserving Hitler's status as Western culture's yardstick of evil, they have urged portraying him through moralistic modes of representation. Implicit in their position is the recognition that while such modes can become repetitive, predictable, and stale – while they may shift attention away from the culpability of the German people – they alone can preserve Hitler's demonic aura of menace, without which the Third Reich as a historical epoch is incomprehensible. Needless to say, it is extremely difficult to simultaneously demonize and humanize Hitler. The increasing tendency of recent films to pursue the latter strategy, however, suggests that as long as the dialectic of normalization continues to function, a return to moralism may eventually be on the horizon.

6 BETWEEN TRAGEDY AND FARCE: NAZISM ON THE INTERNET

Adolf Hitler ... was an Austrian-born German politician and the leader of the National Socialist German Workers Party ... Hitler's supremacist and racially motivated policies resulted in the systematic murder of eleven million people, including nearly six million Jews.[1]

WIKIPEDIA

Hitler did his best for his people. He was only a man and a man can only do his best. It was the traitors who led white nations against Hitler that messed it up for white people, not Hitler. Hitler was for whites and his enemies were agianst [sic] whites. Hitler deserves our respect.[2]

STORMFRONT

All cats want to rule the world, that's part of the nature of the species, but to be a genuine Kitler there has to be some other similarity ... to that ever popular German/Austrian dictator. We're looking for that toothbrush 'tache ...Or the flock-of-seagulls hairdo. Perhaps an evil glint in its eye ...Of course, the best Kitlers will have all of the above.[3]

CATS THAT LOOK LIKE HITLER.COM

Anyone using the Internet to learn about the history of the Third Reich had better beware. Typing key words associated with the history of Nazi Germany, such as "Hitler," "Nazism," or "Holocaust," into search engines like Google or Yahoo instantly yields a cacophony of results. The first hits appear on largely reputable websites, such as Wikipedia, Encyclopedia Britannica, and Answers, as well as sites connected to major research institutions, such as the United States Holocaust Memorial Museum and Yad Vashem. A few more clicks, however, bring the unsuspecting web user to extreme right-wing sites, such as Stormfront, Committee for Open Debate on the Holocaust, and Institute for Historical Review. Still further clicks lead in a more humorous direction: to Uncyclopedia, which offers mock entries about Hitler and Nazism; to Hipster Hitler, which features comic strips of the bespectacled Führer wearing ironic, Nazi-themed T-shirts; and to YouTube, with its innumerable video parodies of the Führer. Finally, the intrepid web surfer will arrive at sites that can only be described as bizarre, such as Cats That Look Like Hitler, which displays adoring photographs of fascist-looking felines, and – taking things a step further – Things That Look Like Hitler, which purports to detect the Führer's face in photographs of random objects, ranging from smoke detectors to fried zucchini. In short, surfing the web reveals a basic truth about Nazism's place on the Internet: what one initially encounters – the plain facts about the Third Reich, as well as extremist distortions of those facts – communicates a sense of the Nazi era's tragedy; what one eventually becomes mired in – cheeky satire, puerile parody, and freakish kitsch – is pure farce.

The representation of the Nazi legacy on the Internet provides further evidence of the normalization of memory. Like the many novels, short stories, essays, and films that have portrayed the events of the Third Reich in recent years, Internet content (whether texts or images) has played an important role in shaping our views of the Nazi past. In contrast to other cultural artifacts, however, Internet texts and images are distinct in crucial ways. The ways in which they represent Nazism have been profoundly affected by the unique features of the Internet as a medium. By providing a venue for the expression of all ideas, no matter what their quality, and by fostering new habits of reading, thinking, and remembering, the Internet has granted unprecedented attention to the sensational and the trivial. Websites committed to spreading awareness of the history of the Third Reich have thus faced increasing competition from sites devoted to distorting and spoofing it. As the online representation of Nazism has expanded to encompass history, hatred, and humor, it has fostered a shift away from moralism to normality. This new pattern of representation has predictably met with a stormy reception and sparked considerable debate. But its massive scale and limitless reach seem to be overwhelming any efforts to oppose it.

The Internet and memory

The rise of the Internet has profoundly shaped how we remember. Ever since it gained mainstream status in the 1990s, the Internet – together with other innovations, such as personal computers, mobile phones, digital cameras, wireless networking, broadband, email, text messages, and the like – has revolutionized the ability of human beings to produce, transfer, and access information.[4] This development, by enabling access to information that otherwise might have remained obscure (or entirely forgotten), has turned the Internet into an insurance policy of sorts for memory. Nothing ever dies on the Internet. Facebook profiles survive for years after their creators have passed away. Old blogs and online comments can be accessed long after their initial posting. Thanks to the wonders of digitization, information has become nearly immune to destruction. Its ability to be infinitely reproduced, stored, and distributed online has provided unprecedented protection against the kinds of catastrophes – such as the destruction of the ancient library of Alexandria – that have historically robbed humanity of irreplaceable texts.

The Internet's role in preserving and safeguarding information has been indispensable in fostering knowledge about history. For obvious reasons, the Internet has been a godsend for anyone interested in learning about the past. All kinds of historical sources are readily available online. Primary sources can be found in abundance on websites like the Internet History Sourcebooks Project at Fordham University (created in 1996), which offers materials on all historical eras spanning the ancient to the modern world. Secondary sources, meanwhile, can easily be accessed on the websites of libraries, archives, and museums, as well as large compilation sites, such as Best of History Websites.[5] Most of these sites enable users to do keyword searches, which dramatically ease access to information. The same is true of websites, such as Google Books, which have digitized and expanded access to hard-to-find historical books and articles. Beyond fostering research, the Internet has enabled historians and interested lay people to engage with one another's ideas in discussion forums, such as those sponsored by the H-Net (Humanities and Social Sciences Online) discussion network, established in 1995.[6] All of these developments have led professional historians to enthusiastically welcome web-based opportunities for historical research, teaching, and learning.[7] By allowing researchers and readers alike to gain unprecedented access to historical knowledge, in short, the Internet has been a boon to historical memory.

At the same time, however, the Internet has had unintended consequences that have adversely affected remembrance. Various observers have recently pointed to the Internet's deleterious effects on human cognition. Nicholas Carr has argued in his book, *The Shallows: What the Internet is Doing to Our Brains*, for example, that the Internet conveys information in such a way as to promote "cursory reading ... distracted thinking, and superficial learning."[8] These liabilities ironically derive from some of the Internet's chief assets. Although it allows untrammeled access to infinite amounts of information, the Internet leads many web users to feel a sense of information overload. In attempting to cope with the deluge of data, Carr notes, they embrace new modes of reading, such as skimming and scanning, that sacrifice depth for speed.[9] Similar trade-offs come with the Internet's enabling of multitasking. Thanks to interactivity, hyperlinks, searchability, and multimedia, we can simultaneously navigate multiple websites while receiving email alerts, watching video clips, listening to music, and skyping with friends.[10] This intensive multitasking can be liberating, but it can also have the effect of making the Internet into a de facto "interruption system" that distracts us from what we are doing.[11] As it weakens our powers of concentration, the Internet can diminish our attention spans. The average Internet user in the United States, Carr reports, spends between twenty and thirty seconds on a website before moving on to another one.[12] No wonder that the Internet inclines us to privilege small, digestible, and attention-grabbing items of information – blurbs, headlines, and summaries – over longer and more nuanced texts. Increasingly, the visual and the aural – whether in the form of photos, videos, audio tracks, or multimedia combinations of all three – seem to be supplanting the textual. The result is that we have begun to abandon deeper forms of reading, thinking, and reflecting in our pursuit of the immediate and the trivial.[13]

All of these trends have potentially worrisome consequences for memory. As our capacity to concentrate declines, we may not be able to retain information as effectively as before.[14] Our ability to remember may thus be threatened. Studies have shown that the flow of information on the web is so large and rapid that we cannot easily transfer what we read from our working memories to our long-term memories.[15] One result is that we have begun to outsource remembrance to the Internet itself, thereby turning it into "an external storage system."[16] Recent scientific research on the "Google effect" shows that ordinary people cease to actively remember information if they believe they can easily look it up on the web. To be sure, other observers have noted that people in earlier eras have had to contend with similar outsourcing challenges – most famously with the transition from oral to written culture during Antiquity – and have made the adjustment successfully.[17] Yet in the same way that previous technological changes have posed challenges to human memory, the Internet is undeniably doing so as well.

Responsibility and remembrance: Representing the history of Nazism online

These trends have important consequences for the memory of Nazism. To begin with, the Internet has undeniably helped foster awareness of the history of Nazi Germany. There is abundant web-based historical source material on the subject of the Third Reich, whether the history of the Nazi dictatorship, the Second World War, or the Holocaust. There are countless websites devoted to chronicling all of these topics, based in the United States, Europe, and elsewhere. The largest and most general is Wikipedia, which has thousands of entries on Nazism, from the familiar to the obscure. One can choose to read the lengthy entry about "World War II" or just as easily skim any of the nearly 6,000 individual entries on minor Nazi party members, such as Max Erwin von Scheubner-Richter or Jakob Grimminger.[18] Beyond Wikipedia, many other websites are exclusively devoted to the topic of Nazism. Some are associated with universities, such as the massive compilation site, A Teacher's Guide to the Holocaust, which was created at the University of South Florida in 1997.[19] Others are associated with Holocaust museums, whether the United States Holocaust Memorial Museum in Washington DC, or regional museums in New York, Chicago, Houston, and Los Angeles.[20] Private research and advocacy institutions have also created sites, the most noted being Facing History and Ourselves, the Simon Wiesenthal Center, and the Anti-Defamation League.[21] Still other sites have been established outside of the United States, most notably in Europe, and are associated with various cultural and political institutions. In Germany, concentration camp memorial sites and documentation centers in Berlin, Munich, Nuremberg, and Cologne, offer extensive websites, as do national museums and research institutions, such as the German

Historical Museum, the German Historical Institute, and the Goethe Institute.[22] Regional and city museums also provide similar, if more limited, services.[23] Eastern European sites also exist, whether in Poland, Hungary, or the states of the former Yugoslavia.[24] Finally, important websites are based in Israel, most notably the site of the country's Holocaust remembrance authority, Yad Vashem.[25]

Websites on the subject of Nazism have also been created by private individuals. Some are run by scholars, a good example being the German Propaganda Archive, created by Calvin College communications professor, Randall Bytwerk, which features an extensive array of Nazi propaganda posters.[26] Others have been created by lay people who are personally interested in the Nazi era. Some sites, such as World War II Remembered and Lost Images of World War II, have been established by the grandchildren of American World War II veterans and are devoted to displaying photos of their time in combat.[27] Others, such as Third Reich Locations, Third Reich in Ruins, and The Hitler Pages, feature countless archival and contemporary photographs of architectural sites associated with the years of the Nazi dictatorship.[28]

All of these sites allow casual web users to learn a tremendous amount about Nazism, World War II, and the Holocaust. Unlike traditional printed sources, they employ diverse methods of representing the past and enjoy the advantages of multimedia and interactivity. Links to documentary film clips, visual images, audio soundtracks, and other supplementary materials give these sites unparalleled depth in what they can teach about the past. Anyone who goes onto the German Historical Museum's web page, LeMO (Lebendiges Museum Online), and clicks on "Adolf Hitler," for example, does not merely gain access to facts about the Nazi dictator, but audio links to his speech to the German people prior to the Reichstag elections of July, 1932 and video footage of the Day of Potsdam, March 21, 1933.[29] Web users who visit the site, Third Reich in Ruins, meanwhile, acquire an entirely different perspective on the Nazi past by being able to compare the appearance of the Third Reich's many physical sites at the time of their creation (as documented in photographs, postcards, and maps) with their appearance after the passage of more than half a century. In these and many other ways, the Internet has encouraged historical awareness of the Nazi era and anchored it more firmly in cultural memory.

That said, it is unclear whether the abundance of information available about the Nazi past actually translates into more active remembrance. Indeed, if skeptics are right, web users may be less likely to internalize knowledge about the Nazi era than to rely on the Internet as an external storage system of information that can readily be accessed. While the Internet may broaden access to knowledge, it also may be making it shallower. It is an open question whether this represents a step backwards or forwards from the pre-Internet era. In the old world of hard copy texts, knowledge was limited to those with access to libraries and book budgets. There were probably fewer people with a basic knowledge of the Nazi era, but they may have been better informed on the subject. Today, more people than ever have probably been exposed to the history of the Third Reich, but their exposure may be more fleeting and superficial. In short, there are clear trade-offs with the rise of Internet-based historical knowledge. While we can now educate the many instead of the few, we may be sacrificing depth for breadth.

There are other potential problems to consider. The websites discussed above have undeniable merits, but they are not without short-comings. By their very nature, websites are always adapting, but they are not always up to date. Entries on Wikipedia may appear to be thorough at first glance, but they often have not incorporated the most recent scholarly research. Entries can contain information that is unsourced (therefore making it unreliable) and links to sites that have vanished.

Many of these shortcomings are visible in the short Wikipedia entry on the "uniqueness" of the Holocaust. The entry (a subheading within the larger entry on "The Holocaust") is just under 300 words long and neglects to mention most of the important contributions to the discussion on the topic. The entry cites a very small and unrepresentative selection of scholars (one of whom is an outlier, Norman Finkelstein) and their blurbs are listed in no particular chronological or thematic order. The larger Holocaust entry, to which the uniqueness subheading belongs, also features certain questionable assertions about the subject. In a subheading entitled "extermination camps," one reads that "the use of camps equipped with gas chambers for the purpose of systematic mass extermination of peoples was a unique feature of the Holocaust and unprecedented in history."[30] This assertion is not only unsourced, it never defines the meaning of the term "uniqueness." Moreover, it is followed by the misleading claim, also unsourced, that gas chambers "were established at Auschwitz, Belzec, Chełmno, Jasenovac, Majdanek, Maly Trostenets, Sobibór, and Treblinka."[31] Holocaust scholars might be inclined to question the inclusion of Jasenovac and Maly Trostenets in this list, as gassings there took place to a far lesser degree than at the Aktion Reinhard camps and Auschwitz.[32] (Moreover, the list omits other small-scale instances of gassing that were conducted at camps such as Sachsenhausen and Mogilev, not to mention the major gassings that transpired in Germany during the T4 program, whose relevance for the question of uniqueness is not even broached.) Yet despite these misleading claims, they persist in the entry. Similar shortcomings surely define other Wikipedia entries. It would be easy enough for scholars to flag and correct such errors. Yet, most have little incentive to do so, as such editorial work is time consuming and does not count towards their publication record. The consequences of this reality are several: it produces a division of labor, in which lay contributors, rather than scholars, preside over web-based information; it contributes to the decline of peer review, which in the pre-Internet world held information to higher professional standards; it leads to the diminished authority of Internet-based information; and it places web users in a default position of cognitive suspicion when accessing it.

This sense of suspicion is reinforced by uncertainty about the motives behind certain websites devoted to Nazism. While institutionally sponsored sites raise few suspicions, the same cannot be said about those created by private individuals. These sites are often ambiguous about their intentions. To be sure, nearly all go out of their way to offer disclaimers that they are "not political" and are "for pure historical use only."[33] But it is not always easy for ordinary web users to know whether such claims are genuine or disingenuous. In some cases, it is easy to tell when a website is underpinned by a moral agenda. Anyone who accesses the extensive collection of photographs on The Hitler Pages, for instance, is immediately told at the bottom of the first page that the site has "nothing to do with dubious political ideas or right wing movements." The site thereafter refers web users to view its photographs of Auschwitz, which are described as "the best warning there is" for understanding "what Hitler brought Europe."[34]

By contrast, other sites lack such moral admonitions. Third Reich Locations, for example, offers few commentaries about its contemporary photographs of Nazi-related sites. Many of its captions are strictly neutral. Its description of Munich's Hofbräuhaus, for example, merely notes that it is the place where "Adolf Hitler often spoke." Other buildings, such the Haus Elephant Hotel in Weimar and the Deutscher Hof Hotel in Nuremberg, are described as places where "Hitler stayed." Such captions are factually accurate, but for web users accustomed to seeing

Ottens Hof, close to Wewelsburg, use to be an old SS hang out, as can be seen on the old wood carvings.

Figure 38. The website Third Reich Locations displays contemporary photographs of sites associated with the history of Nazi Germany. Note the morally neutral description of the Ottens Hof country inn.

Nazi material embedded within a strict moral framework, they may appear insufficiently critical. This is especially true of images whose captions might be interpreted as endorsing Nazi sites. The description of the Ottens Hof guest house near Heinrich Himmler's Wewelsburg Castle as "an old SS hang out" is so casual as to make the site potentially seem inviting (Figure 38); its description of Albert Speer's studio for Nazi sculptor Josef Thorak outside of Munich as an "amazing building" flirts with admiration; and its display of Rudolf Hess's grave site in the Franconian town of Wunsiedel (despite the grave's removal by authorities in 2011) raises fears that the image might inadvertently appeal to neo-Nazis eager to make Internet "pilgrimages" to the Third Reich's important physical remnants.[35] The fact that the site is anonymously run, finally, raises suspicions about whether it has an unspoken agenda. In the case of Third Reich Locations, such suspicions turn out to be unfounded. The creator, Jon Reffs, has noted that his interest in Nazi sites reflects no "hidden agenda" and is "purely documentary in nature," being mainly devoted to showing how the passage of time has shaped key sites associated with the regime.[36] That said, the case of Third Reich

Locations reveals how the absence of moralistic signposting on sites dealing with the Nazi era can foster suspicions.

Hatred and history: Neo-Nazism on the Internet

It is especially hard to avoid suspicions, given the fact that the Internet has become a fertile medium for neo-Nazi and extreme right-wing political organizations. The presence of neo-Nazism on the Internet represents the negative counterpoint to the numerous websites that have tried to promote awareness about the Third Reich. Indeed, it represents something of a tragic development, as it has corrupted the Internet's power to educate by using it to spread misinformation. Ironically, the Internet itself is partly to blame for this development. For decades, neo-Nazi, anti-Semitic, and Holocaust denial literature existed, but was kept largely underground. The Internet's democratic character, however, has allowed this previously marginal material to gain mainstream status.[37] Whereas extremist tracts once had difficulty getting published by reputable presses, today they can be published with online presses or simply be uploaded to individual websites. Moreover, readers who once might have been reluctant to publicly purchase such literature can now access it privately via their home computers. Finally, the Internet has lent extremist texts greater legitimacy. The openness of the World Wide Web – especially its commitment to free speech and its resistance to censorship – means that blatant lies can commingle with objective information. The generic format of search results, moreover, often makes it difficult to distinguish between the two. In short, as the Internet has enabled toxic misinformation to flow into the existing stream of historical knowledge, it has polluted its moral orientation.

The exact number of extremist websites is unclear, but it has grown considerably since the web's arrival in the 1990s. Neo-Nazi and other right-wing groups were among the earliest adopters of web technology to spread their views.[38] Today, they probably number in the hundreds.[39] The first major extremist sites were established in the mid to late 1990s, such as Stormfront (1995), the Committee for Open Debate on the Holocaust (1996), and Jew Watch (1998). Well-known Holocaust deniers, such as David Irving and Ernst Zündel, established their own personal sites around the same time.[40] These prominent sites are often linked to smaller sites. Most of them are marginal, but the online encyclopedia, Metapedia, established in 2007, has pretensions of being an all-encompassing storehouse of right-wing "knowledge."[41] Whether large or small, all of these sites have disseminated predictable claims: that Nazi Germany was not responsible for World War II; that the Holocaust is a postwar myth; that Jews run the world, and so forth – none of which requires further elaboration. More "moderate" neo-Nazi sites, such as that of Germany's Nationaldemokratische Partei Deutschlands (NPD), are more careful about making such extreme claims, but its party platform makes its allegiance to National Socialist ideas clear.[42]

It is difficult to gauge these sites' impact on popular views of Nazism. Some sites have considerable traffic. Stormfront, for instance, ranks in the top one percent of Internet sites in terms of use, allegedly attracting more than 40,000 users each day.[43] Others rank far below. Indeed, the presence of neo-Nazism on the web may be less than what one might initially think. The website, Directory of Nazi Websites, lists nearly three hundred sites; many, however, are inactive.[44] That said, neo-Nazi sites retain the capacity to cause serious harm. The fact that the perpetrators of recent hate crimes – most notoriously, Anders Breivik in Norway – have been active visitors to neo-Nazi Internet forums shows that such sites may be implicated in inspiring violent acts.[45]

Right-wing extremists have also sought to smuggle their claims onto mainstream websites. Exploiting the Internet's openness to user contributions, they have particularly tried to influence entries on Wikipedia. The site's editors are on the lookout for such efforts, of course, and often delete extremists' claims. In 2008, for example, a user who tried to submit biased content for the Wikipedia entry on the extreme right-wing Liberty Lobby, founded by Holocaust denier Willis Carto, was rebuffed by a Wikipedia editor who noted, "This article is the biggest train wreck of unsourced claims of racism I have ever seen."[46] As a result, the Wikipedia entry on the Liberty Lobby, and many others on the site, presently include warnings about their trustworthiness, the most common being the message, "the neutrality of this article is disputed." This message has been affixed to numerous entries related to Nazism, usually about controversial topics, such as "Comparison of Nazism and Stalinism," "Bombing of Dresden," and "Flight and Expulsion of Germans (1944–1950)."[47] In the most charitable view, these cautionary messages confirm the reality of historiographical disagreement. Yet, they may also cast suspicion on all Internet-based information and lead web users to view it as potentially compromised. Indeed, in recent years, suspicions have thrived that neo-Nazis are actively manipulating the Internet. In 2004, for example, web users were shocked to see that typing the word "Jew" into Google's search engine listed, as its first hit, the anti-Semitic website, Jew Watch. Despite Google's claim that such results were the unintended result of computer algorithms (which were influenced by the frequent usage of the word "Jew" in anti-Semitic contexts), skeptical observers feared right-wing attempts to doctor online information.[48]

The most successful effort to disseminate neo-Nazi views on the Internet came to light in late 2013 when world attention was directed towards the sudden proliferation of the anti-Semitic gesture, known as the "quenelle," on sites such as YouTube, Twitter, and Facebook. Popular among European right-wingers, especially in France, the gesture is an inverted Nazi salute in which the person displaying it holds one arm stiffly down while the other arm, elbow bent, grabs the opposite shoulder in exaggerated fashion. The quenelle was popularized by the avowed anti-Zionist French comedian, Dieudonné M'Bala M'Bala, who first used it when running for European Parliamentary elections in 2009 (Figure 39). In recent years, the gesture has spread virally across the Internet, where many individuals – employing the narcissistic digital-age practice of taking "selfies" – have defiantly posted images of themselves making the gesture in front of synagogues, Holocaust memorials, and even concentration camps. For those who employ the gesture with hateful intent, the goal is to mock Jews by exhibiting support for Nazi ideas at sites of Jewish religious significance or historic suffering. It has even become something of an Internet game, with participants trying to outdo one another in the brazenness of their choice of locations for their gestures. Some people have even taken to displaying the quenelle (whose right-wing meaning was unknown until very recently) in the presence of unsuspecting Jews, whether orthodox Hasidim or Israeli soldiers.[49] While confusion has surrounded the quenelle because of its use by European celebrities (especially athletes), who have defended it as an "anti-establishment" sign, the gesture has undeniably anti-Semitic and pro-Nazi features. A generation ago, it would have remained a cult sign with a limited following. But thanks to the Internet, it has become a widespread signifier for intolerance and hatred.

There have been efforts to combat neo-Nazism on the Internet. As early as the late 1990s, the Anti-Defamation League publicly raised concerns about the proliferation of web-based hate speech and tried to spread awareness of the problem through educational initiatives and

Figure 39. This poster featuring the avowed anti-Zionist French comedian, Dieudonné M'Bala M'Bala, displays the controversial inverted Nazi salute known as the "quenelle."

lobbying efforts. Grassroots attempts to halt neo-Nazism online have also emerged, whether in the form of general anti-fascist websites or specific Twitter pages opposed to the quenelle.[50] These populist efforts have faced major obstacles, however. One is the Internet's democratic character. In 2005, opponents of Jew Watch organized an Internet petition drive to remove the site from Google, gathering 125,000 signatures. Google refused to comply, however, citing the principle of free speech. Jew Watch thus continues to rank high in searches of the word 'Jew.'[51] Other efforts have foundered on the Internet's global character. Because it transcends the boundaries of the nation-state, the Internet resists national laws that attempt to restrict the flow of information. Neo-Nazi sites can be shut down by the government of a given country, but their content can reappear on foreign sites. This problem has also affected Internet commerce involving Nazi-related literature, artifacts, and memorabilia. The sale of such items has been big business on the Internet in recent years, but not in countries like Germany, where it has been restricted.[52] Yet while it is impossible to purchase a copy of *Mein Kampf* from a German website, one can easily be purchased from foreign vendors.[53] There have been some successes in opposing these trends. In 2001, Yahoo Auctions and eBay banned the sale of Nazi memorabilia after fielding complaints from the Simon Wiesenthal Center that the sites were selling items that "symbolize hate" and "glorify Nazism."[54] In 2012, moreover, the rogue hacker group, Anonymous, launched a series of attacks against neo-Nazi websites, successfully closing down some fifteen sites associated with Germany's NPD.[55] These efforts notwithstanding, neo-Nazism on the Internet persists as a problem.

The consequences of extremist sites for the memory of Nazism remain unclear. But they may further increase webs users' skepticism about the reliability of the Internet as a repository of information. While scholars and other specialists may have little difficulty distinguishing between legitimate and fraudulent information about Nazism online, lay users may have more trouble. Some may respond by recoiling from the topic as hopelessly mired in bias. The diminished faith in objectivity may lead to a growing belief in the relativity of truth and, with it, the acceleration of normalization. That said, the efforts of watchdog groups to protest neo-Nazi sites will keep the history of the Third Reich in the public eye and may prevent it from fading into irrelevance.

Irony and the Internet: The unbearable light-heartedness of Nazism

The process of normalization is not just being promoted by websites peddling hatred, however, but also by sites promoting humor. In recent years, the representation of Nazism on the Internet has taken a comic turn. This development has been visible in many forms, ranging from the creation of video parodies, comic strips, and images involving Hitler to the proliferation of Nazi-related puns in online discourse. This humorous turn is yet another by-product of the Internet's democratic character. Most of the humorous sites have emerged as the result of individual initiative. People have always sought to express their idiosyncratic ideas in public, but only since the rise of the Internet have they had a platform to present them to a larger audience. Their ideas may be odd or offensive, but they are destined to secure attention. Since the Internet encourages short attention spans and superficial forms of reading, unusual representations of the Nazi past are destined to get a second look from web surfers seeking their next diversionary fix. This explains why the most common of these representations are those that subvert Nazism's traditional meaning to ironic effect. What better way is there to gain attention, after all, than by taking the Western world's classic symbol of evil and employing it for the sake of humor?

The rise of the "Hitler meme"

The clearest proof of this trend is provided by the transformation of Adolf Hitler into an Internet "meme." In recent years, scholars and journalists have increasingly employed this neologism to make sense of contemporary cultural trends. At the most basic level, a meme refers to an idea that, like a gene, uses the methods of self-replication, mutation, and mimicry to seep into the minds of individual human beings and eventually society at large. Memes are usually described as developing through an evolutionary process that enables them to claim a dominant cultural presence. They can take the form of videos, catch phrases, or images. They can spread through any medium. But they have especially proliferated on the Internet. The Internet's ability to rapidly spread information has led to the creation of "Internet memes" through email, blogs, social networking sites, and other methods of transmission. Internet memes have included viral videos, such as KONY 2012 (about the brutal Ugandan guerilla leader, Joseph Kony); phrases, such as LOL ("laughing out loud" and its variants, ROFL and lulz); rage comics (short comic strips with primitively-drawn "rage faces" expressing displeasure); image macros (photographs with ironic, superimposed texts); and the typed expressions known as emoticons.[56]

Among the many memes that have risen to prominence in recent years, one of the most surprising has been that of Adolf Hitler. Since the year 2008, when its appearance was first reported, the existence of a "Hitler meme" has become widely acknowledged, although never clearly defined.[57] At the most basic level, the Hitler meme is a concept that refers to the Nazi dictator's transformation into a convenient symbol for any number of purposes. Whether employed in online videos or photographic images, whether inspiring bad puns or mindless games, Hitler has become an infinitely malleable icon. Numerous websites have featured him, but what links them all is the use of humor. These sites have employed different forms of humor, including irony, parody, and satire; they have also employed it for different purposes, with some aiming to critique, others to endorse.[58] The images of Hitler that have appeared on these sites have circulated widely on the Internet thanks to social networking sites, such as Facebook, Twitter, and Tumblr, as well as mainstream news sites, such as CNN and the Huffington Post.[59] In the process, they have reaped immense attention, both positive and negative.

The rise of the Hitler meme reflects the ongoing process of normalization. To be sure, humorous portrayals of Hitler are hardly unique to the Internet. Indeed, they have become increasingly prevalent throughout Western popular culture. In the United States, Germany, Great Britain and elsewhere, Hitler has been used to generate laughs in numerous films, television shows, and comic books.[60] The Internet has simply democratized this trend and opened it up to the masses, allowing anyone who is sufficiently inspired to mock, spoof, or satirize Hitler online.

The underlying motivations, however, remain the same: to subvert and ultimately reverse the symbolism that has traditionally surrounded the Nazi dictator. As an Internet icon, Hitler has acquired dual semiotic significance. He has become both a symbol of evil *and* a symbol of humor. Indeed, he has become a symbol of humor precisely *because* he has long been a symbol of evil. Theories of humor stress that incongruity – the "simultaneous activation of two contradictory perceptions" – is a key element of laughter. So too is disparagement, which involves bringing "something exalted ... into contact with something trivial or disreputable" in order to produce a feeling of superiority.[61] Both of these theories explain the appeal of the Hitler meme. What better way to elicit laughs than to take a symbol of evil and undermine it through incongruous disparagement? Moreover, humor can also serve a positive political function. As is well known from Hans Christian Andersen's famous tale, "The Emperor's New Clothes," mocking power weakens it. Humor can also serve an important emotional function. Because it evokes pleasurable feelings and relieves tension, humor is a necessary component of good mental health.[62] All of these claims help explain why humor has been applied to the Nazi period. For both the descendants of the perpetrators and the descendants of the victims – for Germans, Jews, and others – laughing at Hitler holds out the promise of gaining relief from an emotionally burdensome past.[63] That said, laughing at Hitler is not without its problems. It runs the risk of aestheticizing the Nazi past; of universalizing its significance by using it as a means for other ends; and of relativizing its criminality. In short, Hitler's transformation into a meme promotes the process of normalization.

The best-known incarnation of the Hitler meme is arguably the *Downfall* parody. Ever since the first example was uploaded onto YouTube in August of 2006, thousands of videos have combined clips of Bruno Ganz's famous German-language meltdown scenes from the film with humorous subtitles expressing complaints about unrelated topics.[64] The first documented example, entitled "Sim Heil," was a Spanish language critique of the Microsoft video game, *Flight Simulator X*, portraying Hitler ranting about the product's deficiencies ("there are bugs even in the installer," the Nazi dictator angrily exclaims to his generals at one juncture).[65] This parody addressed a relatively narrow topic, but subsequent ones applied its underlying impulse to a broader range of themes.

So many video parodies have appeared, in fact, that they can be placed in separate categories. Some have focused on political topics, for example, the videos, "Hitler Rants about Former President George W. Bush," "Hitler Rants about Obama Health Care," and "Hitler Finds out that Osama bin Laden Is Dead." Others have focused on popular culture, including: "Hitler Doesn't Like How *Harry Potter* Ends," "Hitler Reacts to Kim Kardashian's Divorce," and "Hitler Finds Out Kanye West Disses Taylor Swift at the VMAs." Many videos have addressed current events, as with "Hitler Reacts to Joe Paterno and Penn State" and "Hitler Rants about Casey Anthony Verdict." Still others have articulated the frustrations of daily life: "Hitler is Informed His Pizza Will Arrive Late" and "Hitler Phones an Indian Call Center."[66] All of these examples are American, but similar parodies have been produced in other nations, ranging from Israel (where Hitler rants about the lack of parking spaces in Tel Aviv) to the Philippines (where he complains about the 2010 elections).[67]

As the number of such videos mounted in 2008, they began to attract the attention of the mainstream media, which further boosted their visibility.[68] They also attracted the attention of lawyers representing Constantin Film AG, which produced the original film, who sued to have them removed from YouTube for copyright infringement.[69] Despite this legal intervention, the parodies did not disappear. In fact, they proliferated further, and most can be found on YouTube. Others have been posted on specially designated websites that rank them according to different criteria.[70] By now, the *Downfall* parodies have attained such canonical status on the Internet that they have reached a meta level of self-referentiality. There are now parodies of Hitler ranting about the removal of Hitler parodies from YouTube.[71] There are also intertextual parodies of different cinematic Hitlers complaining about the existence of each other (in one mashup video, the Hitler of *Inglourious Basterds* rants about being upstaged by Bruno Ganz's "dumbass bunker Hitler").[72]

Despite their diversity, the parodies uniformly derive their humor from the incongruity between the desperate emotionalism of Ganz's original cinematic rant and the flippancy of the topic being commented upon. Among countless examples, two are representative. One is the video, "Hitler Rants about Rebecca Black – Friday." In it, Hitler is sitting in the bunker with Joseph Goebbels when a Nazi officer enters the room and announces, "My Führer, we have some music for you." The officer proceeds to play a recording of teen sensation Rebecca Black's much-maligned pop song from 2011, "Friday." For the next thirty seconds, Black's peppy music and inane lyrics intone in the background – "seven a.m. waking up in the morning . . . gotta have my bowl, gotta have cereal" – as Hitler's impassive face turns sour. His left hand starting to tremble, the Führer eventually explodes, "This has got to be the worst music I have ever heard!" The camera quickly shifts to Albert Speer greeting Hitler's secretary, Traudl Junge, outside the dictator's office, while Hitler is heard shouting, "You're all idiots. Turn off that crap now." At this point, Junge tells Speer, "He really hates that . . . song," to which the armaments minister replies, "I warned them not to play that music to the Führer."[73] Another video is "Hitler Rants About Carmageddon." In this parody, Hitler is told by his generals that construction work on Los Angeles's 405 freeway is continuing through the month of June "and many commuters will be affected." Hitler replies calmly, "as long as they are finished with this nonsense by the 17th. I have to pick up my cousin at the airport." At this remark, his generals look nervously at each other and give him the bad news that "the city is closing the 405 . . . for two full days. People are calling it Carmaggedon." Hitler takes a second to process the news and explodes in a long rant in which he exclaims: "This is a fucking outrage! How am I supposed to get to LAX?" After venting further about the inadequacy of public transportation, Hitler finally collapses into a state of resignation and dejectedly concludes: "Maybe I will ask my cousin to reschedule his trip. It would be so much easier if he could fly into Burbank."[74]

As shown by these and many other examples, parodies of the film *Downfall* dramatically transfigured the Nazi past. It is impossible to determine the motives of the many individuals who have made such videos. The creators of *Downfall* parodies are a unique group of individuals who operate within a tight-knit community of "Untergangers," some of whom are incredibly prolific (one has posted upwards of 600 separate videos that have received over 31 million views). They closely guard their privacy, however, and typically do not divulge their names or their views of the Nazi legacy.[75] That said, several traits have defined their work. First, by using Western society's reigning symbol of evil for comic purposes, the parodies have diverted attention away from Hitler's criminality and dramatically humanized him. They have done so most notably by transforming the Nazi dictator into a champion of the aggrieved. All of the *Downfall* parodies have been motivated by the desire to express frustration with a specific topic. As expressions of "the human id," they have epitomized the Internet's culture of complaint, with its penchant for "flaming" and "trolling."[76] In turning Hitler into a mouthpiece for diverse grievances, however, the parodies have universalized his significance. By utilizing him to address contemporary issues, they have placed his significance into the present instead of the past, thereby distracting attention away from his real historical importance. To be sure, anyone yearning to vent about a specific topic cannot be blamed for turning to one of history's most charismatic demagogues to articulate their grievance. Yet doing so – as Timur Vermes's novel, *Er ist wieder da* also showed – makes the Nazi dictator into a figure of sympathy. Because many of the issues that Hitler complains about are legitimate, he becomes someone that viewers cheer for. Anyone who hates Rebecca Black's song "Friday," or traffic jams, or late pizzas, or anything else, will be inclined to root for Hitler as the designated ranter who can provide emotional relief from any number of perceived frustrations. The danger, of course, is that the more we assume this perspective towards the Führer, the more we may end up normalizing him.

That said, some *Downfall* parodies resisted this pitfall and promoted a morally informed stance of remembrance. In the video, "Hitler Finds Out Americans are Calling Each Other Nazis," the Führer's generals enter the bunker war room and tell him that, throughout much of the world, "your name is synonymous with pure evil." "I don't care about that shit," Hitler replies, "I want to know what the Americans think about me." His generals hesitate and then relay the bad news that "the people in America call everybody they disagree with 'Hitler' to the point that it is completely trite and meaningless." Hitler takes several seconds to process the news and then rants: "do you have any idea how hard I have worked to become the most singularly evil person ever to have lived? Tell me what the Americans are saying! I am the Prince of Darkness! I was belched from the fiery depths of hell!" One of his officers thereupon responds: "The Democrats call conservative activists 'brownshirts' and claim they wear swastikas. And everybody draws your little moustache on their political opponents." Hitler thereupon exclaims,

> You cannot be fucking serious. I have been wearing this ridiculous
> thing for years so that it might be the very symbol of evil, not
> some convenient talisman for unthinking Americans ... To think
> I could have had a normal moustache all along like Stalin! I have had
> it with these Americans. If they cannot tell the difference between
> a genocidal maniac and those fucking teabaggers, they can all go
> to hell![77]

With this clever monologue, the video condemned the instrumentalization of Hitler for political gain and endorsed preserving the distinctiveness of his evil.

The same is true of the video, "Hitler Gets a Report on His Death." In it, Hitler is speaking with one of his officers who tells him matter-of-factly: "My Führer, it seems you're dead. You shot yourself and then you were barbecued. The world celebrated your death ... Since 2006, you've been mocked in thousands of *Downfall* parodies. My apologies ... I didn't realize you were still alive." Hitler processes the information and then complains, "How many times do I have to prove that I'm not bloody dead?" The scene then shifts to Albert Speer greeting Traudl Junge outside

Hitler's office, while we hear the Führer shouting off camera, "Can't people see I'm alive? This is madness." Junge then asks Speer, "Did you know Hitler was alive?" to which he replies, "No I didn't. I've always thought the Führer was the undead." At this juncture, another officer helpfully chimes in, "he does look like a zombie sometimes."[78] This dialogue also showed how, in certain instances, satire could underscore Hitler's evil.

On balance, most *Downfall* videos promoted the universalization of the Nazi past, a fact that was confirmed by their reception. The media coverage of the parody wave was predominantly positive, with most observers diagnosing it as a harmless phenomenon. If they saw any importance in the videos, it was their significance for copyright law, not their relevance for the memory of Nazism.[79] Internet responses, meanwhile, were even more positive. Although it is hard to generalize about the massive number of comments received by individual videos, most were enthusiastic.[80] Although certain videos occasionally sparked profanity-laced flame wars between web users, most expressed appreciation for the videos' humor and creativity.[81] Some posts even implicitly supported normalizing the Nazi legacy. Certain responses to the "Friday" parody, for example, showed that ordinary web users identified with Hitler as a representative of justified grievances. One critic of the song wrote: "I never thought I would say this, but I agree with the Fuhrer!", while another noted "How right Hitler truly is about Friday astonishes me."[82] Similar comments were posted about the "Hitler Rants About Casey Anthony Verdict," with one exclaiming, "U GO HITLER!!! I AGREE WITH YOU!!!"[83] Other comments displayed sympathy for Hitler as a person. When the Nazi dictator dejectedly reschedules his cousin's visit in the video, "Hitler Rants About Carmageddon," one commentator wrote, "I feel bad for Hitler."[84] To be sure, there were dissenting views. Reacting to Hitler's rant about Casey Anthony's acquittal for murder, one user wrote, "so this video says that Hitler, after all he did to millions of people, has the right to make such a verdict? Is Hitler now considered a good person? The person who made this video is sick."[85] Such comments, however, were exceptional.

Downfall parodies were not the only videos to make use of Hitler for comic purposes. Countless music videos have combined images of Hitler with familiar songs.[86] One of the better known was "Hitler Disco." Uploaded onto YouTube in 2009, "Hitler Disco" synced documentary photographs and film footage of the dictator to the 1999 techno song, "Heut' Ist Mein Tag" ("Today is My Day") by the German pop singer, Blümchen. In certain segments of the video, color footage of Hitler (from Eva Braun's 1938 home movies at Berchtesgaden) is repeatedly played forward and backward making the dictator appear to be dancing a jig. In another segment, Hitler's head, wearing a pair of digitally super-imposed headphones (Figure 40), is set in motion to the music's rapidly thumping beat (for good measure, the heads of Rudolf Hess and Heinrich Himmler are also included). Later in the song, the dictator's arms are rapidly animated to give the "Sieg Heil" salute to the music's rhythm.[87] Similar uses of documentary footage are found in other YouTube videos, such as "Hitler is the Scatman" (which also employs the Berchtesgaden

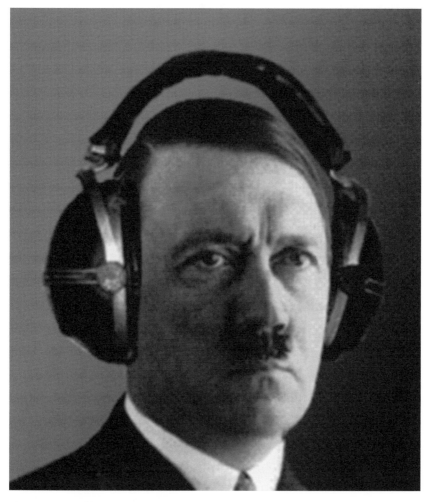

Figure 40. "Hitler Disco" is one of countless music video parodies on the Internet featuring the Nazi dictator.

footage); "Hitler – Born to Be Alive" (which coordinates the lyrics of the 1979 Patrick Hernandez song to footage of various Hitler speeches); and "Hitler is Walking on Sunshine!" (which matches the drums and horns from Katrina and the Waves' 1983 hit song with footage of Hitler Youth members manically drumming in the film, *Triumph of the Will*).[88]

Probably the best-known Hitler music video, however, was the German-language video, "Ich hock' in meinem Bonker" (I'm Sitting in My Bunker). Created by the German comic book author Walter Moers and included as a bonus DVD in his 2006 comic book, *Der Bonker* (*The Bunker*), the animated music video quickly made it onto the Internet where it became a web sensation, receiving millions of views.[89] The video shows Moers's comically rendered Adolf and his dog Blondi ensconced in the Berlin Führerbunker, trying to persevere in the face of ongoing Allied aerial attacks. As the video begins, Hitler is sitting naked on the toilet (Figure 41). A reggae soundtrack kicks in and

Figure 41. In this still from Walter Moers's animated 2006 music video, "Ich hock' in meinem Bonker" (I'm Sitting in My Bunker), the bulbous-nosed dictator takes a bathroom break.

the dictator begins to rap a ludicrous song commenting on the state of the war. "I'm sitting in my bunker in the middle of Berlin," he intones. "I have cynanide capsules and enough gasoline. The Luftwaffe is bust, the marines and army, too. I'm having no more fun with World War II." A female chorus then chimes in, singing, "Adolf, you old Nazi pig, just surrender!" to which Hitler repeatedly responds, "I will never surrender!" After all, he explains, "I have Blondi and a bottle of Chantré." Another set of verses follows, describing the Allied carpet-bombing of Germany and Hitler's continued refusal to surrender, before the song ends with the dictator telling Blondi not to be afraid as "we still might win the war." The visual images that accompany the music are uniformly satirical. Hitler is shown standing naked in front of his medicine cabinet, his posterior visible, and sitting in a bubble bath with Blondi and rubber ducks bearing Hitler moustaches. All of these images are meant to mock. In contrast to most of the *Downfall* parodies, however, Moers lampooned Hitler from a clear moral perspective. In the video, the camera occasionally pans away from the bunker's interior to show the ruined city of Berlin at night, searchlights thrusting skyward in the attempt to spot Allied aircraft. The exterior of the bunker is spraypainted with graffiti slogans: "Nazis Out!", "Peace," and "Make Love Not War." These touches absolved the video of minimizing Hitler's impact on history by showing its destructive consequences.

Indeed, they helped ensure the video's generally positive reception. Most reviews of "Ich hock' in meinem Bonker" in the German media praised its humorous tone and said that it confirmed the permissibility of "making fun of Hitler."[90] Comments by ordinary Germans on chat forums were equally positive, with countless respondents calling the video "super" (*geil*) and "awesome" (*der Hammer*).[91] To be sure, some responses were more negative; one commentator wrote that the video was "funny but macabre," while another dismissed it as "tasteless."[92] In response to such criticisms, however, many web users actively defended the video. As one observer put it, "why [call the video] tasteless? Adolf H. is lampooned in the song. Sixty-one years after [the end of] National Socialism, [this] is the right method of coming to terms with the past …[for it employs]… the language of young people and protects against the brown swindlers."[93] Another commentator argued that the video "makes Hitler so laughable that no one can [possibly]… regard him as a model."[94] Still other observers underscored the video's effectiveness in mocking the dictator by contributing their own insults, calling him a "bedwetter," a "son of a bitch" (*Hurensohn*), and a "monstrosity" (*Missgeburt*).[95] In short, most comments showed that Germans were eager to employ strategies of humor – especially disparagement – to deal with the Nazi legacy. As one commentator concluded, "Hitler will never be forgotten . . .[But] a little humor in view of this dark chapter does Germany good."[96] This belief – which was echoed by the popularity of other satirical German-language videos at the same time – revealed that Germans were increasingly eager to laugh at Hitler.[97]

In addition to being expressed in videos, the impulse to mock the Nazi dictator was visible on diverse Internet websites. One of the best known was Hipster Hitler. Established in 2010, the site features a regular comic strip, whose main character is a hipster version of the Nazi dictator (Figure 42). Sporting dark, thick-rimmed eyeglasses, skinny jeans, and white t-shirts sporting Nazi-themed puns, Hitler interacts with a variety of other Nazi figures – Goebbels, Goering, and Himmler, among others – in small, eight- to ten-panel story lines. The plots are slight in nature, but they generally deride hipster culture. One of the earliest, entitled "Juice," satirizes hipster irony. In it, Hitler walks into a room wearing a t-shirt featuring the words, "I ♥ Juice." Irritated, Goering responds: "Mein Führer, do you realize that it seems like your shirt is saying you love Jews?" Hitler replies, "Gah, yeah I know. It's called being ironic, Goering."[98] Another comic, entitled "Typewriter," pokes fun at hipster couture. It portrays Goebbels bringing Hitler a typewriter, which he uses to type out the title page of his latest text: "*Mein Kampf II, or How I managed to get my wallet out without ripping my skinny jeans.*"[99] Other installments of the strip poke fun at vintage clothing stores (Hitler visits one looking for inspiration for a new SS uniform), art school (Hitler loses his slot to Winston Churchill), and manscaping (Hitler relocates his signature moustache to his crotch, noting "razor burn is so avant garde!").[100] Each installment also features different Nazi-related puns on Hitler's t-shirts, covering such themes as music ("Under Prussia" and "You Make Me Feel Like Danzig") and film ("Back to the Führer" and "Reign Man").

The rationale of the comic strip is difficult to determine at first glance, but a link on the site explains its origins. It says that Hipster Hitler was established with the goal of mocking

> both hipster culture and the exploits of the Third Reich using a
> combination of puns, parody, dark humor, anachronisms, and

Figure 42. The Internet comic strip and website, Hipster Hitler, portrays the Führer as a bespectacled, skinny-jeans-wearing bohemian.

visual gags . . . In constructing Hitler as a Hipster we're offering a new way of disliking Hitler and laughing at the "lazy dictator" he was . . . In the process of satirizing Hitler's thoughts, actions and logic, we're taking a few digs at a contemporary subculture of urban, middle-class youth that fetishize the "authentic" and conform to non-conformism.[101]

This elaborate explanation notwithstanding, the site originated as a lark. It was created in 2010 by two recent college graduates from Australia, James Carr and Archana Kumar. At the time, Carr was living in Williamsburg, Brooklyn, and had become annoyed by the area's hipster scene. He complained about it in a series of Skype conversations with Kumar, who at the time was based in Berlin. In one conversation, the two friends tried their hand at coining new insults for hipsters, one of which was "Hipster Hitler." Inspired by this fortuitous pun, Carr and Kumar began producing short comic strips (the former doing the writing, the latter producing the art) and soon developed an entire website devoted to lampooning hipster culture. Indeed, they came to believe that there were many similarities between hipster culture and Hitler's own bohemian past. As Carr explained in an interview, these similarities included Hitler's identity as "a failed artist, his vegetarianism, his laziness, and support for animal rights." Carr assumed, moreover, that others shared his annoyance with hipster culture. "Everyone ... hates hipsters," he asserted, because they are "against the mainstream and ... disparage the lesser tastes of the general populous [sic]."[102] Before long, what began as a private grievance expanded into a popular website. By late 2010 the site had 65,000 Facebook fans and began attracting increasing attention.[103] This attention increased especially after the founders began to sell merchandise – most notably, t-shirts – based on the site's comic strips.

The popularity of Hipster Hitler illustrated the dynamics of normalization. On the one hand, the site clearly aestheticized the Nazi past, stripping it of horror and replacing it with humor. The strip also universalized Hitler's significance by following in the tradition of *Downfall* parodies and utilizing the Nazi dictator to express grievances on an array of topics. In the process of comparing Hitler to hipster culture, moreover, the site relativized his criminality. While hipster culture may be annoying, it hardly compares to the culture of death and destruction that Hitler established in Nazi Germany. To be sure, the site took pains to defend itself against accusations that it was defending Hitler, insisting, "We are clearly not glorifying or celebrating Hitler but, instead, mocking him."[104] The site's creators added: "We see ... laughing at a cruel and horrible man like Hitler as more of a cathartic process."[105] It is doubtful, however, that any of the teenage and twenty-something users who visit the site have any need for catharsis. With the Nazi era lying seventy years in the past – too far back in time for them to have personally experienced it – the only emotion likely to have driven interest in the site was the desire to laugh. Other disclaimers similarly lacked credibility. The site noted that "this comic is not written with the intent of offending people and refrains from making the holocaust or any other similar horrific event ... the subject matter of a strip." This hands-off policy was honored in the breach, however, as was shown by the strip's inclusion of t-shirt slogans that included the puns, "East Side, West Side, Genocide" and "Death Camp for Cutie."[106]

Predictably, the response to Hipster Hitler was divided. User comments on the strip's Facebook page described the site as "hilarious" and "absolutely genius."[107] Individual strips received hundreds of likes and dozens of comments, mostly supportive. Many among them praised the site for demythologizing the Nazi dictator. One German reviewer wrote: "to poke fun at Hitler ... takes away power from those who wish to lure the young into their glorification of ...[him]."[108] Another said that the comic transformed Hitler "into a non-threatening cat, or a non-threatening nancy boy."[109] Still other comments insightfully explained the site as an understandable reaction of young people to being "inundated with Holocaust education."[110] By contrast, other voices expressed concerns about the site, especially its sale of Nazi-themed merchandise. Some German bloggers argued that the site was "disrespectful towards the many victims [of Nazism]."[111] Others feared that it was attracting neo-Nazis, who were attracted by its provocative t-shirts.[112] As one observer explained, an "objective viewer ... on the street who sees the t-shirts out of the context of the ... comic, would fail to see the satire/parody in the merchandise" – indeed, he or she would believe that its slogans were "pandering to Neo-Nazi ideology."[113] Another worried that commercializing Hitler in t-shirts would make the Nazi dictator not merely "lulzy" – that is, a source of laughter – but "cool."[114] Such fears culminated in 2011, when the Australian B'nai B'rith Anti-Defamation Commission launched a protest against an Australian website, Red Bubble, which was selling the shirts, for promoting "pro-Hitler merchandise." Shortly thereafter, the site withdrew the products from the market (though they are once again available today).[115]

Another humorous site that caused controversy was Cats That Look Like Hitler. True to its name, the site is a repository of amateur, user-contributed photographs of felines that allegedly resemble the Nazi dictator (Figure 43). There are thousands of photographs archived on the site – a bonanza for cat lovers everywhere (although non-cat-owners may find them repetitive).[116] The rationale for the site's existence is explained

Figure 43. This image from the Cats That Look Like Hitler website offers a representative image of the many fascist felines that populate the site.

on its opening page, where web visitors are asked: "Does your cat look like Adolf Hitler? Do you wake up in a cold sweat every night wondering if he's going to up and invade Poland? Does he keep putting his right paw in the air while making a noise that sounds suspiciously like 'Sieg Miaow'? If so, this is the website for you."[117] After reading this tongue-in cheek introduction, most visitors to the site will probably be charmed by the first cats they view. They may even agree with the site's claim that the cats resemble the Nazi dictator by virtue of "unfashionable moustache-like marking[s] under . . .[their] nose[s]." How they will respond to the site's description of such cats as "Kitlers," however, is anybody's guess. Fortunately, Cats That Look Like Hitler offers other distractions for web users who eventually tire of gazing at endless photographs of mustachioed felines. It also sells backpacks, t-shirts, coffee mugs, and calendars emblazoned with the site's iconic Kitler logo as well as posters featuring cat-related puns (to wit: "The Furred Reich").[118]

Like Hipster Hitler, Cats That Look Like Hitler was originally created as a lark. It was started in 2006 by a Dutchman named Koos Plegt, who posted photos of several Kitlers, which received modest attention from other Internet users. One of them, a British man named Paul Neve, was particularly enthusiastic and received permission to develop the site's full potential.[119] From that point on, it was merely a matter of time before the Internet's tendency to bestow attention on the bizarre kicked in and made the site a web sensation.

Not surprisingly, the response to the site was divided. It received considerable coverage in the mainstream media, both in Europe and the United States. The British press, which gravitates to all things Nazi, featured the site in *The Sun*, the *Daily Mail*, and on several television shows.[120] In the US, the site was featured in 2010 on *The Colbert Report* and was also covered by CNN.[121] Much of this coverage was non-judgmental and sought mostly to elicit chuckles from readers and viewers. User responses to the Cats That Look Like Hitler website were also positive, with many appreciating the site's sense of humor as "just screwed up enough to be brilliant."[122] Other comments, by contrast, were more critical. Some respondents saw the site as offensive to Hitler's victims. As one put it, "I don't think anything about Hitler is funny and I think I am speaking on behalf of the MILLIONS of Jews that he tortured and killed (some of which were my family)." Others found the site disrespectful to animals, writing "no cat deserves any connection with Hitler."[123] Predictably, the site's creator, Paul Neve, sought to reassure viewers that the site was uninterested in "glorifying Hitler." As the site reads: "Let's get this straight. Hitler was an arsehole. Hitler was a disgusting, pus-ridden lump of excrement from the devil's own anus . . . As such, I think it's entirely appropriate to reduce him to an object of ridicule by comparing his physical appearance and styling to a bunch of fluffy, cute moggies."[124] There is no reason to doubt this statement's sincerity. But there is also no doubt that the site's comic tone made light of the Nazi legacy.

Websites did not merely perceive Hitler in the faces of cats, however, but in myriad other objects as well. In recent years, European and American media outlets have featured many stories of the Nazi dictator's visage being located in unexpected places. In 2011, the press reported the discovery of a "Fish that looks like Hitler."[125] It was soon followed by a stinkbug with markings on its shell that resembled Hitler.[126] There was also a "House that looks like Hitler," whose slanted roof and front door evoked the dictator's haircut and moustache (Figure 44).[127] And in 2013, a JC Penney teapot, designed by Michael Graves, was perceived as bearing a resemblance to Hitler.[128] The impetus for these stories is uncertain. They may have been spin-offs of earlier reports about the discovery of "hidden" swastikas in unexpected locations. In 2000, for example, the German press reported the existence of a grove of trees forming a swastika pattern in a remote East German forest.[129] Somewhat later, in 2006, the American press reported the revelation (courtesy of Google Earth) that a complex of buildings belonging to the US Navy in San Diego had been built in the shape of a swastika.[130] What prompted the publication of these stories – apart from the enduring popularity of "news of the weird" – is unclear. What is undeniable, however, is that the impulse to see signs of Nazism in the built or natural environment has become something of a fad.

Indeed, it has reached the point that a new website, Things That Look Like Hitler, has been established to document and promote the practice.[131] Anyone who goes onto this user-generated compilation site will find an enormous number of photographs of people, animals, and random objects allegedly displaying signs of the Führer's physiognomy, especially his moustache, parted hairstyle, and upright arm. They include animals (dogs, cats, horses, sheep, fish, even ferrets) with dark markings under their noses; toddlers with baby food smeared on their philtrums; Japanese anime cartoons; light switches; smoke alarms; belly buttons; lotion bottles; car grilles; flowers; random vegetables; and assorted bric-a-brac. The obvious question is why people would take so many photographs of ordinary objects supposedly bearing a resemblance to Hitler in the first place. The website gives few clues. Unlike Hipster Hitler or Cats That Look Like Hitler, both of which offer programmatic agendas on their home pages, Things That Look Like Hitler does not explain its

Figure 44. The British media's claim that this ordinary townhouse in Swansea, Wales, "looks like Hitler" is an example of a larger fad – seeking Hitler's face in random objects.

raison d'etre. Established in March, 2012, the site offers only a single explanatory text: "Hitler is back. And we need to warn the world. Tell everyone you know. Link to the site on Facebook. Tweet about it. Blog its existence. Print out posters and stick them up everywhere you go. Tattoo the URL on stray dogs. Write it on the back of dirty motor vehicles. Thanks, and Heil (Things That Look Like) Hitler."[132] The questionable taste of this text's salutation notwithstanding, the site is clearly meant to be humorous. This is visible in some of the captions that accompany the photographs. Most are purely descriptive: "This dog looks like Hitler," "This baby looks like Hitler," "This house looks like Hitler," and so on. Yet, signs of sardonic humor creep in every so often. Describing the appearance of a certain house facade, one caption reads: "This house looks like Hitler. Although not as much as the other house that looks like Hitler looks like Hitler."[133] In another example, the caption describing a handwoven doll reads: "This knitted figure looks like Hitler. Well, Knitler."

Besides channeling a desire to laugh at the incongruous, the reason why people are seeking signs of Hitler in random objects remains puzzling. It can partly be explained, however, by seeing it as part of a larger Internet phenomenon. Many present-day websites are devoted to cataloging "things that look like other things."[134] These include people who look like other people (for example, Men Who Look Like Kenny Rogers or Lesbians Who Look Like Justin Bieber); objects that look like people (Things That Look Like Brits); and the ever-popular category, things that look like genitals (Things That Look Like Penises, Things That Look Like Buttholes, Vegetables That Look Like Genitals). The tendency to see things in other things further taps into an age-old human impulse towards anthropomorphism, which has long been visible in everything from Giuseppe Arcimboldo's Renaissance-era vegetable portraiture to Jesus sightings in grilled cheese sandwiches.[135] And it probably also reflects the workings of obscure perceptual phenomena like pareidolia, which refers to the human tendency to spot figurative images in abstract forms, such as clouds.[136]

The tendency to see Hitler in random objects can also function as a game. In the same way that Scrabble challenges players to assemble words out of random letters, some web users clearly find it challenging to gaze at assorted objects and figure out how they might resemble the Führer. Moreover, in the same way that a scavenger hunt pits people against one another in the effort to locate hidden objects, posting photos of things that look like Hitler online can easily become a competitive enterprise with bragging rights going to those who come up with the most creative examples. Some of the photographs on Things That Look Like Hitler are, in fact, quite creative. Take, for instance, the example of a simple lotion bottle. Whoever recognized that the slant of its black cap resembles the slant of Hitler's hairline; that the vertical bar code on its rear resembles his moustache; and that the horizontal text describing its active ingredients approximates his eyes, deserves credit for his or her ability to "see" Hitler's face in such an abstract form. Like discovering the answer to a difficult crossword puzzle question, seeing Hitler's presence in random objects provides a sense of intellectual satisfaction. Because his presence in them is highly incongruous, moreover, discovering it is inherently funny and satisfies the perennial desire to demythologize the Nazi dictator. Finally, as was shown by the wave of publicity that surrounded the Hitler Teapot "controversy" in 2013, invoking Hitler online provides an instant way for Internet bloggers and others to get attention.[137] That said, turning Hitler into a game transforms him from a symbol of evil into one of amusement.

The playfulness of the website, Things That Look Like Hitler, has been echoed in actual Internet games involving the Nazi dictator.[138] The best known is Six Degrees of Hitler. This game employs the Wikipedia website to try and land on Hitler's entry in the fewest possible clicks from an initial random entry. To start the game, players go to the left hand menu bar of the Wikipedia site and click "random article." If the word "portmanteau" appears, for instance, the challenge is to locate another linked word on the entry that will quickly bring the player to Hitler. Soon enough, one finds on the portmanteau entry a category, "other languages," that contains a listing for "German." Clicking on the link presents a menu of options, including one for "Heinrich Heine" (who coined some sixty portmanteau words). Clicking on that link brings one to Heine's biography, which contains a reference to "Hitler" (who is listed in the context of the Nazi party's burning of Heine's books in 1933). In short, three clicks bring one from "portmanteau" to "Hitler" – a relatively efficient performance. Other randomly selected articles appear, at first glance, to be more challenging to navigate. What, after all, should one do with "Fillaeopsis"? In fact, it takes merely four clicks to get from this "genus of flowering plants in the legume family" to Hitler. One first clicks on "French" (the language from which the word legume derives), then "Europe" (listed as part of the French language's "geographic distribution"), then the island of "Guernsey" (where it is spoken), which contains "Hitler" (who is listed as obsessed with defending the German-occupied island from Allied attack during World War II).

The origins of Six Degrees of Hitler trace back to an article with the same title that was written by journalist Timothy Noah in *Slate Magazine* in 2008.[139] Penned during the US presidential campaign, when conservatives were criticizing then-candidate Barack Obama for his alleged association with radical figures like William Ayers, Noah made the point that such guilt by association was absurd because all people were linked to everyone else eventually. To prove this, he cited John Guare's well-known play from 1990, *Six Degrees of Separation*, and the pop culture spin-off game, Six Degrees of Kevin Bacon (in which players try to connect a randomly selected actor to the ubiquitous movie star, Kevin Bacon, through as few movies as possible). Mocking the practice of assigning guilt by association, Noah facetiously invited readers "to connect ... *Der Führer* with any one of the three remaining major presidential candidates. Whoever is able to connect a candidate to Hitler with the fewest number of 'degrees,' or steps, will be named the winner." Following the appearance of Noah's article, comedians Lewis Black and Stephen Colbert subsequently mocked the practice of linking people to Hitler, and the concept soon became an Internet game.[140] By 2009, searches for Hitler and Kevin Bacon spiked on Google, talk of Wikipedia searches for Hitler appeared on chat forums, and talk about the game began to appear in the mainstream media.[141] In 2012, an actual app for the game became available on Google Play.[142] (Spoiling all the fun, there is now a website called "Hitler Hops," which automatically tells web users how many entries will be necessary to go from any randomly inserted word to Hitler.)[143]

In all of its variations, Six Degrees of Hitler reflected no larger agenda and served mainly as a diversion. One hardly needs to ask what accounts for the game's appeal. It is merely one of the countless ways to procrastinate on the Internet. Like updating one's Facebook status or playing Words With Friends, seeing how many clicks are required to arrive at Hitler's Wikipedia entry represents an easy method of fending off boredom and getting immediate gratification. Needless to say, in serving this function, the game divorced Hitler from his historical context and transformed him into a symbol of triviality.

That said, Six Degrees of Hitler is in better taste than another new Internet pastime, creating humorous image macros related to the Nazi dictator. In recent years, image macros have become a ubiquitous Internet phenomenon. Classic examples include LOLcats (photos of cats with grammatically stilted slogans, such as "I Can Has Cheezburger?"); Scumbag Steve (featuring photos of a stoned-looking young male wearing a sideways baseball cap accompanied by rude captions such as "Hey, Can I Borrow – Everything?"); and Musically Oblivious 8th Grader (showing a young teenage girl uttering ignorant statements about popular music, such as "John Lemon is my favorite Beetle").[144] Since then, many image macros featuring Hitler have also appeared. Many are parodies of existing memes: for example, an image that pokes fun at LOLcats by portraying a Kitler with the accompanying caption, "I Can Has Poland?"[145] Others are based on groan-inducing puns, for example, the image of a leaping dolphin with a photoshopped Hitler head stuck on its body and the caption, "Hey Look Adolfin!"[146] These traits can all be found in abundance on websites like Meme Generator, which features tens of thousands of image macros of the Nazi dictator. The most popular are found in the category of "Advice Hitler," which features more than 35,000 images of the Führer spouting phrases, such as "I Can Haz Europe?" and "Wall Street Boring. Occupy France."[147] Meme Generator also features thousands of images of "Disco Hitler," "Bedtime Hitler," "Successful Hitler," and "Hitler Says Nyan," all of which are accompanied by a variety of humorous and nonsensical captions.

These and countless other similar images suggest that we may be witnessing the emergence of a new Internet law: the more popular the meme, the more likely it will be Hitlerized.[148] This Law of Ironic Hitlerization, as it might be called, fulfills a function similar to that of adding spices to food. Adding a Hitler moustache, hairstyle, or Nazi uniform to a meme automatically lends it a powerful kick of irony, sensationalism, and tastelessness. Inspired, most likely, by the *Downfall* parodies, the practice has become an automatic reflex that has been applied to all kinds of themes. As seen with the Advice Dog and LOLcat parodies, image macros have been among the most likely Internet memes to be Hitlerized.[149] Memes in other formats, however, have been subjected to similar treatment. Animated videos represent one notable category. The ubiquitous Nyan Cat video (featuring an animated cat with a Pop-Tart body flying through space to a repetitive computer generated soundtrack) was spoofed with a "Hitler edition." In one version, the cat's body was replaced with a swastika flag; in another, it was replaced with a Hitler head (in both, its tinny "nyan nyan nyan" soundtrack was replaced with an angry male voice screaming, "Nein Nein Nein").[150] Emoticons have also been Hitlerized. Merely a few keystrokes on a computer keyboard – two backslashes, a colon, an equals sign, and a vertical bar – enable one to produce a "typical Hitler," as seen here: //:=l. (Variations include a "stoned Hitler," which looks like, //8=), and a "bombastic Hitler," which looks like //:=O).[151] Finally, besides Internet memes, other well-known visual images have been Hitlerized on the Internet. Children's cartoon characters have frequently been targeted, with Hitler moustaches and Nazi uniforms being digitally applied to such otherwise blameless characters as My Little Pony, Hello Kitty, Pikachu (from the Pokémon series), and all four of the Teletubbies.[152] Corporate logos and products have also been Hitlerized in the spirit of Wacky Packages: Burger King has been adjusted to read "Führer King"; "I Can't Believe It's Not Butter!" has been transformed into "I Can't Believe It's Not Hitler!"; and Listerine has been turned into "Hitlerine."[153] Finally, there are cases of accidental Hitlerization, in which glitches in photographs of public figures have made them appear to sport Hitler moustaches. In one instance, a blacked-out pixel in front of right-wing British politician Nigel Farage's face on BBC television made him resemble the Nazi dictator; in another, a shadow cast by the finger of Israeli Prime Minister Benjamin Netanyahu upon the upper lip of German Chancellor Angela Merkel made her resemble her notorious predecessor.[154] The fact that these examples swiftly attained viral status on the web, prompting endless laughter, confirms a simple truth: adding Hitler to a visual image dramatically enhances its comic effect.

This is further confirmed by the persistence of more traditional, textual forms of poking fun at Hitler on the Internet. In the same way that venerable satirical journals, such as *National Lampoon* and *Mad Magazine*, exploited the Nazi dictator for comic effect before the rise of the Internet, web-based satirical journals have done so as well.[155] The online version of *The Onion*, for example, has often invoked Hitler in its fake news stories, publishing pieces about his survival and postwar life ("My precious Deutschland will rise again," the spunky nursing home resident exclaimed in one article) and imagining him winning World War II with the help of a "vortex gun."[156] Other online periodicals have posted similar articles, with the British *Daily Mash* running headlines such as, "France is Basically Hitler, Agrees Everyone," "Are You More German Than Hitler?" and "Germans Use [Gordon] Brown Video for Hitler Spoof."[157] Even college newspapers have used Hitler for humorous purposes, with the Rutgers University newspaper, *The Medium*, causing controversy in 2012 by publishing a mock op-ed entitled, "What About the Good Things Hitler Did?" and falsely attributing it to a Jewish student activist.[158]

Among the many textual parodies of Hitler, one of the most elaborate can be found on the website, Uncyclopedia. Known as the "content free encyclopedia," Uncyclopedia is something of a cross between Wikipedia and *The Onion*. It offers thousands of entries on all kinds of topics, including the history of the Third Reich. In the website's American edition (there are foreign editions as well), there is an extensive entry on Hitler, coming in at around 7,500 words.[159] Like much of the site's content, the entry on Hitler is dominated by irreverent and often crude humor, little of which is especially funny. The biographical entry surveys the life of "Adolf 'Chuckles' Hitler" from his birth to his twelve years in power as the "Chancellor of Germany (and Fücker) from 1933–1945." Some of the content is mildly amusing. Spoofing the obsession with Hitler's family tree, the entry explains that his father, "Alois Hitler ... was a customs official in Australia-Hungary ... and his mother, Gretta Pölzl, Alois' second cousin, was his father's third wife who was also her own grandmother." By contrast, other biographical details fall flat, mostly due to their obsession with puns. The entry describing Hitler's adolescence, for example, notes that after high school, the young Hitler started a "small garage band" and wrote songs such as "Dachau Side of the Moon," "Kampftown Races," and "Hitler Baby One More Time." Other details come across as arbitrary. The entry reports that, during World War I, Hitler learns to play the banjo and sings in a male chorus, which motivates him to go into show business. Following the war, he returns to Munich and has an acid-fueled religious experience that prompts him to go into politics. He then begins his slow rise to power, which he accomplishes by besting a political rival, Adolf Schmittler von Knorring, whose memoir, *My Cough*, is unable to compete with Hitler's own autobiography. Within this narrative, the entry provides numerous details about Hitler's personal life. Some are meant to be ironic. Hitler serves for a stretch as "vice president of the Anti-Defamation League," for example, but is "removed from this office after it was discovered that he didn't pay his membership fees." Other details are simply incongruous; for example, the fact that Hitler is a "watermelon aficionado" who nurtures an "irrational fear of applesauce." Against this silly backdrop, the entry winds down with a perfunctory survey of World War II, which Hitler unleashes after being taunted by Polish generals who show him "pictures of Brad Pitt without a shirt." Few details are provided about the war, and the entry wraps up by explaining that Germany is defeated when "the Soviet Onion began closing in on Berlin from the east and other Allies from the west, while Middle Earth invaded from the South." In the end, Hitler goes to "his local McDonald's" where he dies of "food poisoning."[160]

The Uncyclopedia entry on Hitler can generally can be dismissed as a jejune example of Internet humor, but it is significant in one respect. Near its conclusion, the entry contains a small section on the Holocaust that highlights the thin line between normalization and moralism. At first glance, the 500-word section comes across as a tasteless example of the former. The first few sentences read:

> The supposed slaughter of 12 million Jews and countless other minority groups in Europe by Hitler and the Nazi regime was used as justification for the creation of Israel. However, it's a little known fact that Hitler supported the formation of a Jewish homeland, and was the first to come up with the idea. He wanted to move the 12 million Jews by train to a site in Palestine. However he soon found out that a train ticket that far was approximately over $500 . . . and cyanide gas tablets were $3 . . . Hitler did the math, and what we were left with was a few ~~dead~~ unconscious, but totally fine Jews.

Although this section initially reads like an endorsement of Holocaust denial, it actually critiques it. "The absence of bodies," the entry continues, is "proof that such events did not take place. While some may suggest that the bodies were incinerated in the large body incinerators found at Auschwitz . . . [they] were in fact large ovens used to bake many delicious baked goods for the Jewish population." The entry then goes on to state: "given the size of the incinerators, the SS could incinerate roughly 400 Jew bodies a day taking into consideration size and weight ratio and the average length to completely burn a body given the incinerators' heat settings. In summation, it would've been impossible to burn even 1/4 of the Jews in the given time that the supposed Holocaust took place. Therefore, it never happened." This statement mocking the crude vocabulary ("Jew bodies") and pseudo-scientific logic of Holocaust deniers makes clear that the entry is, at least partly, underpinned by a moralistic agenda. That said, its flippant tone and glib sidebars – one shows jubilant concentration camp prisoners at liberation with a caption reading, "concentration camps were actually nice places to live" – puts the entry quite close to the line of bad taste.[161]

Indeed, the entry highlights how humor can coincide with hatred on the Internet. While the Hitler meme offers many opportunities to poke fun at the Nazi dictator, it has also been used to express support for his ideas. Many online images of Hitler have been laced with anti-Semitism and racism. It is hard to determine exactly when a phrase crosses the line from being satirical to hateful, from being offensive to malicious. But countless examples of the Hitler meme emerge as likely candidates for the latter. The most egregious examples involve the Holocaust. One of the best-known early Nazi-related image macros was of a present-day toddler dressed in a Nazi uniform and holding an empty cup with the caption, "I have eliminated all the juice."[162] Similar versions have proliferated in other formats, for example, an Advice Hitler macro with the phrase, "I Say Its Time for the Jews to Forgive and Forget. And Let Zyklon B Bygones."[163] Other offensive phrases have been added to other Hitler macros, such as "Gas Bill? I Wondered When It Was Jew," "What Happens at Auschwitz Stays at Auschwitz," and "Let's Party Til' the Last Jew."[164] Few people outside of right-wing circles would find any of these phrases remotely funny. Unfortunately, they are hardly exceptional. There are also countless examples of images spouting pure invective (ie. "Fuck Jews," and worse) without a pretense of satire. Besides image macros, equally offensive send-ups of popular products in the spirit of Wacky Packages have been produced. They include a Hitlerized version of Kentucky Fried Chicken's Colonel Sanders, who has been transformed into a bow-tie wearing Hitler and framed with the phrase, "Kentucky Fried Jews," and a mock advertisement for Microsoft Windows, which has been recast as "Nazi Soft Vindows: Final Solution Edition."[165] Still other image macros of Hitler attack various minority groups, with captions such as "Fucking Mexicans Go Back to Mexico," "Fuck! Forgot the Koreans," and "Fucking Niggers."[166]

Such images obviously express hatred. Indeed, they mimic the intolerant sentiments expressed in the comments section of

YouTube and other video sites, many of which routinely spit out vitriol about Jews and others. Such comments reveal how blurred the line can be between humor and hatred. Indeed, with the Hitler meme, it appears that the Internet has created a space where they actually merge. Ordinary web users, of course, can easily ignore such memes while online. However, there may be a subtle cumulative effect to such exposure. Seeing neo-Nazi style image macros alongside more harmless ones on the website, Meme Generator, for example, effaces the differences between their underlying agendas and subtly legitimizes the illegitimate. This leveling effect is merely another worrisome by-product of the Internet's populist character, which makes it impossible to consign to the margins what arguably belongs there. As humor commingles with hatred, intolerance seeps further into the mainstream.

All of these trends are visible, finally, in the way that language itself is increasingly being used to discuss Nazism on the Internet. As scholars such as Victor Klemperer and George Steiner noted decades ago, the Nazis created a new vernacular during the Third Reich – a *Lingua Tertii Imperii* – that employed superlatives and euphemisms to mask the brutal realities of the regime's policies.[167] Today, a different phenomenon is underway, but with similar consequences. The Internet has given rise to a digital age patois – "Internet-speak" – that has created neologisms, slang, and abbreviations that govern much of web discourse.[168] As part of this trend, words related to the Third Reich have been appropriated, inflated, and universalized. Unlike in the Nazi era, they have not been mobilized for a single political purpose, but rather in the service of a wide range of agendas, ranging from the critical to comic. The effect, however, has been to mute Nazism's historic evil.

The first example of this trend is the inflation of the word "Nazi" into an all-purpose term of opprobrium. This has been seen most clearly with the creation of neologisms (either blended nouns or two word phrases) that incorporate "Nazi" into them. Common examples include: "feminazi," "grammar Nazi," "gym Nazi," "stroller Nazi," "breast-feeding Nazi," and so forth (Figure 45). Many of these terms preceded the creation of the Internet, having first appeared on television and radio.[169] Their appearance has also been promoted by the polarized political environment in the United States, which also predates the Internet. All of this said, the Internet has accelerated the inflationary use of the term "Nazi." The medium's encouragement of flaming makes

Figure 45. The concept of the grammar Nazi, here immortalized with its own Swastika-like flag, reflects how the process of normalization has manifested itself in language.

Nazi-related terms preferred weapons of choice in online disputes. The Internet's unparalleled ability to spread new words once they emerge has been crucial as well. According to Urban Dictionary, the word "Nazi" has become "a slang term used to describe people who are overly concerned about details (in an unhealthy way), and like to correct others on every occasion they get. Especially evident on Internet forums, blogs, and YouTube."[170] This definition not only identifies the web's role in inflating the term "Nazi," it shows how present-day usage has diluted the term's meaning. If most people have come to view the term "Nazi" as merely "denoting people seen as controlling" (as another online reference tool, Wikpedia's Wiktionary defines it), then this, too, is a sign of normalization.[171] While the groups that have been called "Nazi" may be overbearing at times, it hardly needs stating that feminists, exercise addicts, and stroller moms bear no resemblance to the leaders of the Third Reich.

The normalizing trend has been further promoted on the Internet through the creation of Nazi-related puns. Many have cropped up in image macros. One of the more prominent is the phrase, "I did Nazi that coming," often used as a statement of surprise – as in the response of a cartoon Hitler who, when told, "Mein Fuhr! [sic] The Allies have invaded Normandy!" replies "Wow, I did nazi that coming!"[172] Another phrase uses Anne Frank's name to express annoyance, as in, "I hate it when people joke about the holocaust, Anne Frankly, I won't stand for it."[173] (Merging both phrases is a Facebook page entitled, "Anne Frankly I did Nazi That Coming.")[174] Some of these puns seem to have first appeared in Facebook messages and were subsequently posted on its comedic counterpart, Lamebook.[175] From there, they have been endlessly reproduced and circulated on social media sites, such as Twitter, Tumblr, 4chan, and Reddit.[176]

A similar development is the creation of Nazi-related neologisms based on puns. One new word is "lolocaust," merging the term "LOL" and the suffix, "caust," to create a word that the Urban Dictionary defines as "Funny on a scale that kills 6 million people," to wit: "man that joke cause da lolocaust."[177] Other web users have used the suffix "caust" to create humorous terms of disparagement; one critic of Rebecca Black's music video, "Friday," commented: "Time for the Final Solution: Rebeccacaust!"[178] Relatedly, the phrase, "How much does the challah cost?" has circulated widely after having been popularized by the (half-Jewish) comedian, Chelsea Handler.[179] Still other puns have made use of Auschwitz. The term "Cowschwitz" has been invoked to critique cattle ranches.[180] And an image macro of a smiling Hitler features the phrase, "They told me caffeine causes anxiety, so then I said Auschwitz [ie. I switch] to Decaf."[181]

The transformation of Nazi-related words into puns reflects trends within the larger culture. It partly stems from the presence of similar puns in works of literature, such as Art Spiegelman's use of the term "Mauschwitz" in his graphic novel, *Maus*, and John Boyne's usage of the term "Out With" to refer to Auschwitz, in *The Boy in the Striped Pajamas*. These examples, in addition to older ones, such as the term, "Shoah business," to refer disparagingly to the academic discipline of Holocaust studies, may have helped to legitimize Nazi-related puns and paved the way for them to develop into an Internet phenomenon. In the process of being embraced by the masses, however, punning has lost its original moral purpose and become an end in itself. Indeed, it has become something of a game. Theories of humor hold that puns originated in "ancient 'duels of wits,' in which people attempted to display their intellectual superiority over others by means of their facility with words."[182] This appears to be confirmed by the desire of web users to outdo one another in their ability to use the Nazi period as an arsenal of verbal weapons.[183] The recent Hitler teapot controversy, for example, witnessed Reddit users dueling with one another to come up with the best tea-related Nazi puns, including: "Schindler's Mint," "Ceylon B," and "Night of the Oolong Knives."[184] In employing historically fraught words and phrases in such a blithe fashion, however, present-day pun-meisters further show the waning of a moralistic perspective on the Nazi past.

There have been some attempts to resist this linguistic form of normalization. One of the most important has been the creation of a code of Internet etiquette known as "Godwin's Law of Nazi Analogies."[185] Conceived by the lawyer and Internet blogger Mike Godwin, the law states that "as an online discussion grows longer, the probability of a comparison involving Nazis or Hitler approaches one." Godwin arrived at this insight in 1990, in the early days of the Internet, after noticing that many online discussions were plagued by commentators dismissing each other's ideas as "Hitler-like." Although the law did not say so outright, it implied that reckless comparisons to Hitler automatically invalidated them (subsequent corollaries to the law made this point explicit).[186] Godwin adopted this position for moral reasons. After reading the work of Primo Levi, he developed what he called a "greater psychological understanding of why the Holocaust happened" and became unable "to tolerate the glib comparisons I encountered on the Internet." He thus developed the law out of a position of "moral outrage" in order to get "folks who glibly compared someone else to Hitler or to Nazis to think a bit harder about the Holocaust."[187] Significantly, the law had something of an effect. As Godwin began to invoke his law as a "counter-meme" in Usenet and chat room discussions, he found that it prompted web users to argue more responsibly without rhetorical excesses.[188] Since then, it has achieved canonical status as the Internet's "most famous law."[189]

Indeed, it has inspired others to counteract the Nazification of online language. Many journalists, bloggers, and other pundits have invoked Godwin's Law in criticizing the proliferation of Nazi analogies. Media Matters did so in 2010 in reporting on Fox News commentator Glenn Beck's more than five hundred references to Nazism, Hitler, or fascism in the eighteen months following the inauguration of President Obama in 2009. The online journal, as a result, concluded that "Godwin's Law should be renamed Beck's Law."[190] The concept became so widespread that Godwin's name became a verb (as when an online commentator, having been rebuked for a Nazi comparison, complained about having been "Godwinned").[191] To be sure, many critics protested such analogies without invoking Godwin's Law.[192] The Anti Defamation League and the American Jewish Committee, among others, have long opposed the Nazification of public discourse. Moreover, representatives of the entertainment industry, especially the satirical news shows, *The Daily Show With Jon Stewart* and *The Colbert Report*, ridiculed the inflated use of Nazi terminology in American cultural life.[193] These groups' efforts (all of which have an online presence through their websites) show that the Internet has also been used to resist the trivialization of Nazism.

It is questionable, however, whether these efforts have had much effect. Neither Godwin's Law nor the admonitions of watchdog groups have succeeded in ridding the Internet of Nazi comparisons, which continue to flourish. Perhaps for this reason, growing numbers of commentators have expressed a sense of impatience with the topic of Nazism altogether. Reacting to the ubiquity of Hitler references, one observer sarcastically declared that "even Hitler must be sick of himself."[194] Another complained that the Nazi dictator had become a "shortcut" reference to "evil personified" and had limited people's awareness of earlier historical villains.[195] Still other observers sensed that invoking Hitler had come to function like crying wolf and had lost believability. "In a culture where Hitler is the plaything of advertisers, filmmakers, and pundits," one journalist wrote, "the Nazis are not ... effective as a warning."[196] Agreeing, a German commentator complained that his

country's "highly sensitive alarm system" for tracking the revival of Nazi
ideas had begun to malfunction by focusing on trivial, instead of major,
threats, concluding: "this is the result of an exaggerated historical didacticism. Where parallels to the Nazi era are everywhere, eventually there
will be none that are visible. We need less instead of more speeches about
Hitler."[197] For these and other observers, memory had become a liability
that was best de-emphasized, if not abandoned. Leon Wieseltier
expressed this view in chastising Jews for recklessly drawing analogies
between events in the Middle East and the Third Reich, demanding they
recognize, once and for all, that "Hitler is dead."[198] Another blogger
went further and bluntly declared, "It's time to stop letting Hitler live
rent-free in our heads ... Hitler has outlived his usefulness. It's time to
put him back in his bunker and bulldoze the rubble over him."[199] To be
sure, other observers continued to insist that certain comparisons
to Hitler and the Nazis were perfectly legitimate and should not be
prohibited out of hand.[200] For increasing numbers of commentators,
however, the time had arrived to throw the baby of memory out with its
dirty bathwater.

In the final analysis, the rise of the Hitler meme and its related
offshoots confirms the Internet's importance in fostering the normalization of memory. Some skeptics may question the value of rigorously
examining the meme's origins, dissemination, and function, given its
frequently crass character. Seen in isolation, of course, each individual
expression of the meme amounts to little more than a trivial piece of
ephemera. Taken together, however, their effect may be more substan-
tive. Thanks to the exponential powers of digital reproduction, the
Hitler meme has reached countless millions of people worldwide with
unknown cumulative effects. Most gainfully employed adults probably
do not spend enough time on the Internet to be familiar with the countless memes that have been ironically Hitlerized. Lacking the necessary
cultural "literacy," they will probably dismiss them as inane and unworthy of serious consideration. Those who are immersed in web culture,
however, intuitively understand that the Hitler meme is as an ironic,
self-referential example of intertextuality. They may not verbalize it as
such, but many young web users have probably begun to see Hitler as a
familiar, amusing, and reassuring Internet presence. The enthusiastic
embrace of ironic Hitlerization by ordinary web users points to the
rejection of moralistic methods of representing the Nazi past. There is
little hard data to buttress this supposition, but one item of information is

sobering. When one goes onto the website, What Does the Internet Think? and types in the words, "Nazis" and "Adolf Hitler," one receives dramatically more favorable ratings for the latter than the former.[201] Whether or not these ratings are accurate or representative is unclear, but they suggest that the signifiers "Nazi" and "Hitler" may be in the process of acquiring different connotations. While the former has become solidified in our culture as an insult, the latter is turning into something more benign.

Conclusion

The representation of Nazism on the Internet presents a contradictory picture. While much of the online information about the Third Reich communicates a clear sense of its tragic dimensions, a considerable amount is farcical. This coexistence of opposites testifies to the democratic character of the Internet and the inevitable trade-offs that have come with it. On the one hand, by making information accessible to all, new possibilities have emerged for promoting education and awareness about the Nazi past. On the other hand, by allowing ordinary people to shape that information without the benefit of elite gate-keeping, much of it ends up being of questionable quality. Put differently, access has fostered crassness.[202] To be sure, this is nothing new. Ever since Plato, democracy has been suspected of promoting mediocrity. For all the high-level opportunities to learn about the Nazi legacy from websites linked to universities, museums, and research institutions, there are just as many ways to become distracted by dreck. Whether it is the hate sites of neo-Nazi groups or the humorous sites of self-proclaimed satirists, the Internet offers countless ways to be diverted and dumbed-down. This is especially true as the weirder representations of Nazism have been widely circulated by mainstream social networking and news sites. These sites have not only legitimized otherwise fringe information, they have taught us to crave it. Because the Internet weakens our attention span and powers of concentration, it makes us susceptible to information that is simplistic, superficial, and sensational. These dynamics have given rise to previously unseen phenomena like the Hitler meme, which is arguably the clearest sign of the Internet's acceleration of normalization.

The question remains what effect this new pattern of representations will have on the effort to portray Nazism from a serious moral perspective. Does normality threaten to undermine morality? Or can the two coexist? On the one hand, there is no reason why the latter cannot be the case. After all, if both modes of representing Nazism on the Internet have coexisted up until now, they should be able to do so in the future. The Internet, if it is anything, is inclusive. At the same time, however, normalized representations of Nazism may undermine those that are more morally rooted. The more that people become accustomed to laughing at the subject of Nazism, the more its aura of gravitas may be weakened to the point where no one takes it seriously anymore. In the same way that a disruptive student can ruin a classroom learning environment, the juxtaposition of ironic and serious material related to Nazism on the Internet may compromise the entire topic. If every web search on the Third Reich turns up textual and visual material that is humorous instead of serious – and if people succumb to this material's diversionary pull – then easy entertainment may triumph over labor-intensive learning. The more that people develop a taste for the former, the more they may neglect the latter. Some may contend that web users are intelligent enough to be able to compartmentalize their approach to the topic and partake of both modes of representation. Indeed, even the intellectually minded can enjoy being connoisseurs of bad taste. It is hard to imagine, however, that people can regularly consume information in both serious and comic modes and not be affected at a deeper level. It seems doubtful that the same people who post flippant messages about the Nazi past on chat forums, create irreverent image macros, and laugh at *Downfall* parodies at one moment will visit websites that impart its more sober historical lessons the next. In the end, there may simply be two different audiences for these two opposing modes of representing the Nazi past. Although they exist in a single digital medium, they may as well exist in parallel universes. One thing is certain: no amount of criticism can halt the normalizing wave, which obeys its own populist principles. At least on the Internet, the new discourse on Nazism is decidedly democratic.

CONCLUSION

[It is] the undeniable and terrible truth of the universe. Look within yourself ... you know it to be true.

There is no use pleading, no use denying. The sooner you accept the truth the sooner the real work can begin.

Everyone is Hitler.[1]

UNCYCLOPEDIA

Well, maybe not everyone. But it sometimes seems like it given how frequently people these days are compared to the Nazi dictator. Since the turn of the millennium, Hitler comparisons have multiplied all over the world. In the United States, Presidents George W. Bush and Barack Obama have been repeatedly likened to Hitler, as have countless other politicians, ranging from prominent national figures like Sarah Palin, John McCain, and Hillary Clinton to more minor local officials.[2] Various world leaders have come in for similar treatment, whether European heads of state, Angela Merkel, Silvio Berlusconi, and Vladimir Putin; Middle Eastern leaders, Ariel Sharon, Mahmoud Ahmadinejad, and Bashar al-Assad; and non-Western political figures, such as Hugo Chavez, Hu Jintao, and the Dalai Lama.[3] Beyond politicians, many other prominent people have been likened to Hitler, including religious leaders, comedians, sports figures, and Hollywood directors.[4] So common have such comparisons become that the Internet now boasts multiple lists of "People ... Who Have Been Compared to Hitler."[5] To be sure, these lists do not include "everyone," as asserted in Uncyclopedia's satirical claim. But they are extensive enough to suggest that it is only slightly off the mark.

At the same time that everyone seems to have become Hitler, Hitler seems to be everywhere. His name and image, his ideas and legacy, have repeatedly been invoked, reproduced, and exploited for myriad purposes. In the United States and Europe, celebrities and other public figures, such as Hank Williams Jr., Joan Rivers, Megan Fox, Kanye West, Tom Coughlin, G. Gordon Liddy, Oliver Stone, Boris Johnson, Lars von Trier, and John Galliano have recently made headlines for ill-considered remarks involving the Führer.[6] Advertisers around the world have sparked controversy by employing the Nazi dictator's image to sell wine in Italy, condoms in the Netherlands, televisions in India, eggs in South Africa, pizza in New Zealand, and tea in Turkey (Figure 46).[7] In the United States, journalists, pundits, and activists from the liberal and conservative wings of the political spectrum have raised hackles by invoking Hitler's legacy in discussing such disparate topics as stem cell research, environmentalism, the IRS, health insurance, evolution, gun control, abortion, smoking bans, the separation of church and state, the use of the filibuster, the Patriot Act, and the existence of Guantanamo Bay military prison.[8] Elsewhere in the world, Hitler's legacy has been utilized to condemn politicians and their policies in such diverse countries as North Korea, India, Venezuela, Ukraine, and South Africa.[9] On top of all of this, the Third Reich continues to have a major presence in contemporary cultural and intellectual life, whether in literature, film, television, music, drama, art, and academic scholarship. In short, wherever one looks, Hitler and the Nazis are everywhere.

And yet, not all is as it seems. While Hitler and the Nazis superficially appear to be everywhere, in a deeper sense, they are nowhere. The inflated use of the Nazi legacy for tendentious purposes threatens to drain it of much of its historical distinctiveness and turn it into an empty signifier.[10] This development marks a notable change in Western consciousness of the Third Reich. Once upon a time, Hitler and the Nazis were viewed as admonishing symbols of extremity. Today, their ubiquity has lent them an aura of normality. For increasing numbers of people, the Nazi era has lost its sense of historical specificity. It has come to mean almost anything. If Hitler and the Nazis once inspired fear, today they are just as likely to elicit laughs. Indeed, if present-day trends continue, they may soon induce yawns.

This transformation of the Nazi legacy is the result of a powerful wave of normalization that has swept much of the world since the turn of the millennium. Prior to this point – that is, for much of the postwar

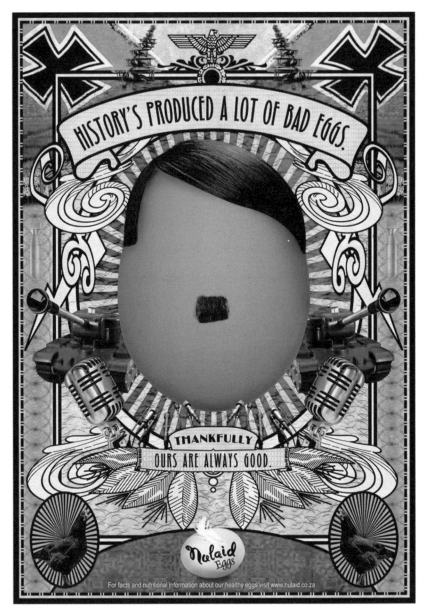

Figure 46. The commercialization of the Nazi past is an increasingly common feature of our present-day world. In this South African advertisement, Hitler's face is employed to sell eggs. Compare with Figures 30 and 22.

era – the events of the Third Reich and Second World War were predominantly viewed from a moralistic perspective. Although there were periodic efforts to normalize the Nazi legacy, they were too weak to threaten the era's moral consensus. Since the year 2000, however, these efforts have intensified. They have assumed different forms wherever they have appeared, but they have generally been defined by the attempt to relativize, universalize, and aestheticize the Nazi past. The supporters of these strategies have relativized Nazism's criminality by blurring the line between the Third Reich's perpetrators and victims; they have universalized Nazism's significance by highlighting its similarity to, and relevance for, contemporary problems; and they have aestheticized the Nazi era by diminishing its horror through unconventional narrative methods, such as humor. These trends have manifested themselves differently in different parts of the world. But wherever they have appeared, they have challenged moralistic patterns of remembrance and eroded the Nazi era's aura of exceptionality.

The new wave of normalization traces its origins to recent social, political, and cultural trends. To begin with, it reflects the quickening pace of organic normalization. With the passing of time and the passing away of the eyewitnesses to the actual events of the Third Reich, the communicative memory of the period has begun to yield to cultural memory. Although representatives of the older generation are still around to tell of their personal experiences during the Nazi era, they no longer exist in sufficient numbers to reinforce older moralistic views of the past. As a result, younger people born in the decades since 1945 have increasingly shaped present-day cultural memory. Representatives of this generation have played a leading role, for example, in promoting historiographical forms of normalization. Many of the scholars who have challenged the idea of the Holocaust's uniqueness and the concept of the "good war" were born in the 1960s or after.[11] Having grown up in an increasingly globalized world that has been shaped by the end of the Cold War, the onset of the memory boom, and the eruption of the "war on terror," these scholars have been inclined to universalize the Nazi past by stressing its relevance for present-day problems.[12] Young people have also led the push to aestheticize the past. Younger scholars have shown a greater willingness to use counterfactual reasoning in academic scholarship; younger writers have predominated in the literary genre of alternate history; and young directors have been responsible for many recent Hitler films.[13] Finally, young people – especially teenagers and twenty-somethings – have radically transfigured the Nazi past on the Internet. The rise of the Hitler meme and countless other comic representations of Nazism would be unimaginable without the contributions of the Facebook generation. In all of these cases, young people have directly challenged traditional moralistic modes of representing the Nazi era. Their motives in doing so cannot be known with any certainty, but they seem to be rejecting their elders' canonization of remembrance. Since the 1980s, the growth of state support in Europe and the United States for Holocaust education, the spread of highly ritualized commemorative ceremonies marking key dates in the history of the Third Reich, and the explosion of the memory boom have given young people in the West unprecedented exposure to the Nazi past. It is possible, however, that some of them have begun to feel suffocated by this exposure and have rebelled against it by pursuing unconventional ways of representing the subject.[14] Their use of humor, in particular, testifies to their skeptical and irreverent attitude towards the Nazi era. Indeed, it further confirms the importance of organic normalization. Humorists have often observed that "tragedy plus time equals comedy."[15] If true, the comic turn in the representation of the Nazi era makes perfect sense. As the new millennium marches forward and as the events of the past recede further in time, we can expect that gravitas will increasingly be replaced by guffaws.

The new normalization has also been promoted by the political circumstances of the post-9/11 world. During the relatively peaceful years of the 1990s, the Nazi legacy was optimistically viewed as yielding moral lessons and promoting international understanding. The return of crisis since the turn of the millennium, however, has produced a far more pessimistic attitude towards memory's efficacy. The attacks of September 11th in the United States, the wars in Iraq and Afghanistan, ongoing tensions between Israel and its Arab neighbors in the Middle East, the rise to prominence of China and India, and the global economic crisis of 2008, have all shaped Western views of the Third Reich by promoting the tendency to universalize and relativize its significance. The first strategy has generally been promoted by people on the political left, who have sought to draw critical attention to present-day events by highlighting their alleged parallels to the Nazi era. This universalizing strategy has been visible in revisionist histories of World War II, scholarly challenges to the Holocaust's uniqueness, alternate histories about the Nazi era, and films about Hitler. Revisionist attacks against the idea that World War II was a "good war," for example, have sought to criticize present-day American foreign policy by blurring the differences between the wartime behavior of the Allies and that of the Nazis, describing both as the result of capitalist and imperialist forces. A similar critical agenda has influenced alternate histories portraying the US and Great Britain collaborating with the Third Reich in a world where the Nazis won the Second World War. The desire to criticize present-day Israeli policies, meanwhile, has shaped certain scholars' attempts to question the uniqueness of the Holocaust by locating its origins in universal modern forces, such as nationalism and imperialism. And various films about Hitler have identified universal factors as responsible for his entry into politics. The effort to relativize the Nazi past, by contrast, has generally been promoted by representatives of the political right, who have sought to minimize the Third Reich's significance altogether. This effort has also been influenced by recent political developments. Conservative attacks against the "good war" in the United States and Great Britain have minimized the threat posed by the Third Reich to the Western Allies in World War II as a means of submitting a neo-isolationist critique of present-day Anglo-American foreign policy. Conservative alternate histories in Germany, meanwhile, have portrayed Hitler's assassination as improving the course of German history in order to minimize the German people's responsibility for Nazism and boost their sense of national pride in the post-9/11 world.

The new normalization has also been promoted by the information revolution. The rise of new digital technologies and, above all, the Internet has accelerated the aestheticization of the Nazi past. It has done so, to begin with, by encouraging the spread of counterfactual thinking. The rise of the virtual world of cyberspace has promoted a willingness to entertain virtual visions of history that are untethered to reality. Since the turn of the millennium, speculative "what if?" thinking has increasingly influenced the representation of the Nazi era. It has been visible in revisionist critiques of the "good war," with historians claiming that history would have turned out better had the Allies abstained from fighting the Nazis. It has been employed in countless academic studies on the Holocaust, especially the subject of uniqueness, with scholars disagreeing about whether the Nazi genocide's singularity would have been underscored or effaced by a Nazi victory in World War II. Counterfactual thinking has predictably been visible in the steady stream of alternate histories about the Nazi era. And it has surfaced in recent

Hitler films, many of which have teased viewers with speculative scenarios involving the beginning and end of the Führer's political career. The information revolution has also aestheticized the Nazi past by encouraging humorous representations of it. The use of parody and satire to portray the Third Reich has been visible in alternate histories, Hitler films, and countless websites. These comically oriented works have not been directly inspired by the information revolution, but they have been widely disseminated by its chief product – the Internet. The viral spread of the Hitler meme and other satirical representations of the Nazi past would be unimaginable without the Internet and other digital technologies.

The new wave of normalization has assumed different forms in different countries. It has been most apparent in the United States. Much of the scholarship on the "good war," the Holocaust's uniqueness, and counterfactual topics related to the Third Reich has been produced by Americans, as have Hitler films and Nazi-themed websites. All of these works have sought to normalize the Nazi past for different reasons. Some have done so in the pursuit of political goals. This is true of works that have sought to overturn triumphalistic views of America's wartime role in defeating the Nazis and works that have challenged the Holocaust's centrality in American historical consciousness. Other accounts have normalized the Nazi past simply to get attention, elicit laughs, and spark controversy, the best example being the multiple iterations of the Hitler meme. In Great Britain, the story has been similar. There, normalization has taken aim at the redemptive myth of the "finest hour." British historians have questioned this myth in their revisionist accounts of the Second World War; writers and filmmakers have respectively challenged and spoofed it in their alternate histories; and ordinary people (and the mass media) have exploited it for laughs in their websites about various things that "look like Hitler." In Germany, by contrast, normalization has focused less on overturning a triumphalistic view of the past than a guilt-ridden one. It has mostly appeared in the form of efforts to relativize and aestheticize the Nazi era. Revisionist films about World War II and conservative alternate histories about Hitler's assassination have sought to minimize the German people's responsibility for Nazism. Meanwhile, German-language films, novels, satirical music videos, and comic books about Hitler have expressed a yearning to laugh at the Nazi era.[16] The fact that Germans now feel bold enough to follow the lead of their Anglo-American neighbors and poke fun at the Third Reich means that they, too, are starting to resemble everyone else. In a word, they are becoming normal.

All of these trends notwithstanding, the normalization of the Nazi past has not gone unchallenged. The effort of some to normalize the past has reinforced the determination of others to preserve its exceptionality. The defenders of moralism have launched fierce attacks against revisionist critiques of the "good war," against efforts to overturn the Holocaust's uniqueness, against counterfactual interpretations and alternate histories of the Nazi period, against Hitler films, and against humorous websites. They have attacked them for relativizing, universalizing, and aestheticizing the Nazi past; for trivializing its significance; for muting its aura of evil; and for stripping it of its historical singularity. The defenders of moralism have not merely criticized the new wave of normalization, they have produced their own works to counteract it. They have written scholarly studies defending the "good war" and the Holocaust's distinctiveness; they have crafted alternate histories describing the evils of a Nazi-ruled world; and they have created websites that document the Third Reich's criminal reality. All of these works testify to the ongoing desire to view the Nazi past from a moralistic perspective, keep it in the public eye, and heed its lessons.

As the new millennium progresses, then, what can we conclude about the future of the Nazi past? In light of recent trends, it is tempting to speculate that we have arrived at a new stage of the normalization process. Indeed, in view of some of the extreme representations of Nazism on the Internet, it is tempting to surmise that we may be approaching certain limits of normalization, beyond which the Nazi past cannot be normalized any further. Considering all the evidence, however, it seems likely that the dialectic of normalization will be with us for some time to come. If current patterns hold, every effort to normalize the Nazi past will elicit defenses of its exceptionality. Debates will continue to erupt between the proponents of normality and morality. Nothing will be resolved. Dynamic deadlock may become the normal condition of memory.

It will be highly ironic if the dialectic of normalization comes to be viewed as normal, for up until now, it has meant the opposite. Throughout the postwar period, the debates sparked by the Nazi legacy have shown it to be a past unlike most others. Yet, there is a certain logic to the abnormal becoming normal. Normality, after all, is a slippery, relativistic concept whose meaning rests upon its "other," the abnormal.

The meaning of both terms can easily become inverted; the abnormal can become viewed as normal and the normal abnormal. Appropriately enough, this dynamic has been visible in recent German history. Germany's abnormal postwar division into two separate countries eventually became viewed as normal by most of its citizens. The country's reversion to a "normal" state of unity after 1990, meanwhile, was initially perceived by most Germans as anything but.[17] Similarly, Germany's postwar struggle with memory, once viewed as abnormal, has become seen as normative since the memory boom, with the inhabitants of other countries following the Germans' lead and intensely debating their own painful pasts.[18] Given this reality, the dialectic of normalization may actually be a sign of normality instead of its absence. Whatever one calls it, there is no guarantee that the current balance of power between the proponents of normalization and the defenders of moralism will last. Indeed, it may be disrupted at any point in the future. Patterns of remembrance always change in the face of new events. Today's definition of normality may not be tomorrow's.

There is a final irony about the quest to predict the future of the Nazi past. The very process of determining whether we have reached a point of normality may prevent such a point from ever being reached. Isaiah Berlin once noted that "to be normal means to not feel under observation."[19] It means not feeling scrutinized by others. It can also mean not subjecting one's self to endless scrutiny. In both cases, normality means not living in a constant state of self-consciousness about whether one is normal to begin with. For this reason, merely to ask the question whether the Nazi past will ever truly be normalized is to prevent it from ever occurring. In some respects, historians may be guilty of the "observer effect," insofar as they influence their object of study in the process of studying it. In tracing the normalization of Nazism, in charting its trajectory, in wondering about its final destination, they are contributing to its endless deferral. It is unclear to what degree this effect is intentional. All historians want to stimulate interest in the past and enhance its resonance in the present. This is especially true of historians of memory and particularly of scholars who specialize in the memory of the Nazi era. All of them study it, comment upon it, and strive to keep it in the public eye in order to prevent it from fading into oblivion. (Some have even alleged that they do so to keep themselves in business as skilled observers of the phenomenon they themselves are perpetuating.)[20] Yet historians are hardly alone in delaying the arrival of normality. So, too, are the proponents of normalization. Every time German observers have declared that the Nazi past has been mastered, every time they have asserted that Germany has become a normal nation, they have underscored its ongoing abnormality. People who are truly normal, after all, do not go around proclaiming how normal they are. Only once we no longer care about the subject of normalization, only once we lose interest in the memory of the Nazi era, only then will it truly become normalized.[21]

Whether or not readers of this book will accept this prediction depends on whether they trust an analysis that itself is entangled in such interpretive conundrums. Without question, this book is guilty of the observer effect. Its analysis keeps its subject alive instead of allowing it to fade. Its conclusion – that struggles over memory will likely persist into the future – carries with it the whiff of a self-fulfilling prophecy. In short, this book is implicated in impeding the very normality whose future it seeks to forecast. Yet, it can hardly do otherwise. As a work of history, it is incapable of fulfilling the one precondition that normality requires – leaving the past alone. It cannot help but subject the past to the same critical scrutiny identified by Isaiah Berlin as negating the possibility of normality. All it can offer, by way of compensation, is to admit as much and openly concede that studying the phenomenon of normalization deeply affects it.

With this in mind, it is appropriate to end on a metaphorical note of self-reflexivity. The subject of this book – the Nazi past – has been likened over the years to many things: a workplace accident, a diverging road, a clogged toilet. But here at the book's conclusion, as its argument circles back on itself, another image comes to mind: the Moebius strip. Fittingly conceived by a German scientist in the mid nineteenth century, this confounding invention has always symbolized endless futility. One can only empathize with the ants portrayed in M. C. Escher's famous drawing, fated to walk indefinitely along the strip's path, never being able to stop, and never arriving at any destination. While hardly perfect, the image comes close to describing the never-ending debate over the Nazi past. It reminds us that the paths of remembrance are not linear, and that the goal of normality, while visible, lies perpetually out of reach beyond a curving horizon.

NOTES

Introduction

1. Many of the photographs can be found in the Fotoarchiv Hoffmann at the Bavarian State Library in Munich: www.fotoerbe.de/bestandanzeige.php?bestnr=1948.

2. Hoffmann recalled that Hitler sought to "vet gestures and expressions" from the series of photographs. Hoffmann added that Hitler forbade the publication of still other images, including ones of the Nazi party leader wearing Lederhosen and eyeglasses. See Heinrich Hoffmann, *Hitler Was My Friend: The Memoirs of Hitler's Photographer* (Barnsley, 2012), pp. 50–51, 250. The volume was originally published in London in 1955. See also Frederick Spotts, *Hitler and the Power of Aesthetics* (New York, 2004), pp. 45–47.

3. A Google search reveals that the first Disco Hitler image was uploaded onto Meme Generator between 2011 and 2012. It originally premiered in animated form (with Hitler being made to look as if he is "dancing" back and forth as the mirror ball pulsates) in the parody video, "Hitler Disco," which was created and uploaded onto YouTube by a web user using the screen name, Lizard2176, in 2009. Email from Lizard2176 to author, Summer 2013. See www.youtube.com/watch?v=-ghmoPn_b6I&skipcontrinter=1.

4. http://knowyourmeme.com/memes/image-macros.

5. http://memegenerator.net/Disco-Hitler.

6. For these and other captions, see http://memegenerator.net/DiscoHitler/images/new/alltime/page/8 (see also page/5, page/57).

7. Total figures can be tabulated at http://memegenerator.net/memes/search?q=hitler and http://memegenerator.net/Advice-Hitler/images/popular/alltime/page/5; Among other sites, see: www.memes.com; www.cheezburger.com; www.memecenter.com; www.quickmeme.com/

8. See http://memegenerator.net/Bed-Time-Hitler and www.quickmeme.com/ Chilling-Hitler.

9. Hitler's head has been photoshopped onto a supermodel's body for a Christian Dior ad, "Hitler j'adore." https://lh6.googleusercontent.com/-Nhsn6HzHaDs/TW5aOFYjvtI/AAAAAAAAC4M/jc5jLKnJc-U/gal1.jpg'; Hitler's face has been superimposed onto the head of pop singer, Adele. http://www.funnyjunk.com/channel/4chan/Adelef+Hitler/TXrBGGK/ and onto the body of rapper/actor Will Smith, http://nonciclopedia.wikia.com/wiki/File: Hitler_rapper.jpg.

10. http://memegenerator.net/instance/34200265; www.memes.com/advice-hitler/6 http://desmotivaciones.es/438818/Hi-Hitler; www.keepcalmandposters.com/ poster/keep-calm-and-hi-hitler; http://cheezburger.com/1007243008; http:// cheezburger.com/1223610624; https://i.chzbgr.com/maxW500/2089963776/ h93B88308/; https://i.chzbgr.com/maxW500/2512920320/hC629780D/.

11. See Ian Kershaw, *The "Hitler Myth": Image and Reality in the Third Reich* (Oxford, 1987).

12. See, for example, the query by one web user in 2010 what the phrase "Hi Hittler" (sic) means: www.godlikeproductions.com/forum1/message1034211/ pg1. In 2012, Lithuanian police arrested a youth for spraying the words "Hi Hitler" on a Holocaust memorial: *Baltic News Service*, August 23, 2012.

13. Virginia Heffernan, "The Hitler Meme," *New York Times*, October 24, 2008: www.nytimes.com/2008/10/26/magazine/26wwln-medium-t.html? pagewanted=all. For a general discussion of Hitler's current place in Western popular culture, see Daniel Erk, *So viel Hitler war selten: Die Banalisierung des Bösen, oder Warum der Mann mit dem kleinen Bart nicht totzukriegen ist* (Munich, 2012).

14. Many of the studies on normalization come from the German context. See, for example, Stefan Berger, *The Search for Normalcy: National Identity and Historical Consciousness in Germany Since 1800* (Providence, 1997); Jeffrey K. Olick, "What Does It Mean to Normalize the Past?" *Social Science History*, Winter 1998, pp. 547–71; Aleida Assmann and Ute Frevert, *Geschichtsvergessenheit, Geschichtsversessenheit: Vom Umgang mit deutschen Vergangenheiten nach 1945* (Stuttgart, 1999), pp. 59–63; Stuart Taberner and Paul Cooke, eds., *German Culture, Politics, and Literature into the Twenty-First Century: Beyond Normalization* (Rochester, NY, 2006).

15. See Emile Durkheim's chapter, "Rules for the Distinction of the Normal from the Pathological," in *The Rules of Sociological Method* (New York, 1982), pp. 85–107.

16. All of these perils were highlighted by the famed German historian Leopold von Ranke, who recommended an objective, empathetic view of the past that

evaluated it on its own terms rather than the subjective moral standards of the historian.

17. The notion of "official" memory is implied in Maurice Halbwachs's undifferentiated notion of "collective" memory and finds elaboration in Pierre Nora's discussion of the nation-state's role in shaping memory to suit the needs of national identity: Maurice Halbwachs, *The Collective Memory* (New York, 1980); Pierre Nora, "Between Memory and History: *Les Lieux de Mémoire,*" *Representations,* 26, Spring 1989, pp. 7–25. The notion of counter-memory can be traced back to Michel Foucault in *Language, Counter-memory, Practice: Selected Essays and Interviews* (Ithaca, 1977).

18. Jan Assmann, "Kollektives Gedächtnis und kulturelle Identität," in Jan Assmann and Tonio Holscher, eds., *Kultur und Gedächtnis* (Frankfurt am Main, 1988), pp. 10–13.

19. Relativization and universalization represent different forms of tendentious historical comparison. At the risk of oversimplifying, relativization seeks to diminish the significance of the object of comparison, while universalization seeks to inflate it.

20. In traditional Western historiography, the scholarly pursuit of realism has entailed determining the objective truth about the past. In literature, realism and its offshoot, naturalism, have played an important role in historical fiction ever since the nineteenth century. See Donald Drew Egbert, *Social Radicalism and the Arts* (New York, 1970). For the importance of realism in historical films, see Robert Rosenstone, *History on Film, Film on History* (Harlow, UK, 2012), pp. 17–22, 53.

21. In employing this concept, I differ from Jürgen Habermas's use of the phrase, which referred to the Federal Republic of Germany's paradoxical achievement of postwar normalcy via the embrace of an abnormal national identity. Jürgen Habermas, *The Past as Future* (Lincoln, NE, 1994), p. 28. I also differ from Caroline Pearce's narrower notion of a "dialectic of normalcy." Caroline Pearce, *Contemporary Germany and the Nazi Legacy: Remembrance, Politics and the Dialectic of Normality* (London, 2008). Pearce's notion describes the "conflict between the perceived need for remembrance and the desire for 'normality'" (p. 2).

22. Aleida Assmann has argued that "every call for … a *Schlussstrich* [drawing a line under the Nazi past] has brought about the exact opposite and caused the resurrection of memory," in Assmann and Frevert, *Geschichtsvergessenheit, Geschichtsversessenheit,* p. 53.

23. As Salomon Korn has put it, "it is just as impossible to talk normalcy into existence as it is to decree spontaneity." Salomon Korn, *Geteilte Erinnerung* (Berlin, 1999).

24. Among the more important works on the subject of *Vergangenheitsbewältigung* are: Charles Maier, *The Unmasterable Past: History, Holocaust, and German*

National Identity (Cambridge, MA, 1988); Jeffrey Herf, *Divided Memory: The Nazi Past in the Two Germanys* (Cambridge, MA, 1997); Ulrich Brochhagen, *Nach Nürnberg: Vergangenheitsbewältigung und Westintegration in der Ära Adenauer* (Hamburg, 1994); Manfred Kittel, *Die Legende von der zweiten Schuld: Vergangenheitsbewältigung in der Ära Adenauer* (Berlin, 1993); Helmut Dubiel, *Niemand ist frei von der Geschichte* (Munich, 1999); Bill Niven, *Facing the Nazi Past: United Germany and the Legacy of the Third Reich* (London, 2002).

25. For comparative studies of the phenomenon, see: Ian Buruma, *The Wages of Guilt: Memories of War in Germany and Japan* (New York, 1994); Elazar Barkan, *The Guilt of Nations: Restitution and Negotiating Historical Injustices* (Baltimore, 2000); John Torpey, ed., *Politics and the Past: On Repairing Historical Injustices* (Lanham, MD, 2003); Richard Ned Lebow, Wulf Kansteiner, and Claudio Fogu, eds., *The Politics of Memory in Postwar Europe* (Durham, NC, 2006); Małgorzata Pakier and Bo Stråth, eds., *A European Memory? Contested Histories and Politics of Remembrance* (New York, 2010).

26. These four strategies are outlined in Martha Minow's book, *Between Vengeance and Forgiveness: Facing History after Genocide and Mass Violence* (Boston, 1999).

27. In 1966, Theodor Adorno described the emergence of "a new categorical imperative," namely, "that Auschwitz will not repeat itself." Theodor W. Adorno, *Negative Dialectics* (London, 2004), p. 365.

28. For a survey, see Gavriel D. Rosenfeld, "A Looming Crash or a Soft Landing? Forecasting the Future of the Memory 'Industry,'" *Journal of Modern History*, March 2009, pp. 122–58.

29. Eric Langenbacher alludes to this dynamic in his article, "Changing Memory Regimes in Contemporary Germany?" *German Politics and Society*, Summer 2003, p. 52.

30. In pursuing this strategy, Adenauer defeated the call of his SPD rival, Kurt Schumacher, for Germans to take responsibility for the Nazis' crimes. For important studies, see Herf, *Divided Memory*; Robert Moeller, *War Stories: The Search for a Usable Past in the Federal Republic of Germany* (Berkeley, 2003); Norbert Frei, *Adenauer's Germany and the Nazi Past* (New York, 2002); Y. Michal Bodemann, *In den Wogen der Erinnerung: Jüdische Existenz in Deutschland* (Berlin, 2002).

31. Hermann Lübbe, "Der Nationalsozialismus im politischen Bewusstsein der Gegenwart," in Martin Broszat, ed., *Deutschlands Weg in die Diktatur* (Berlin, 1983), pp. 333–34.

32. For an excellent survey, see Hans Kundnani, *Utopia or Auschwitz?: Germany's 1968 Generation and the Holocaust* (New York, 2009).

33. Niven, *Facing the Nazi Past*, p. 186.

34. This push by the conservative CDU to normalize the past was preceded by the tentative effort to do so by the pragmatic SPD Chancellor, Helmut Schmidt. Schmidt made headlines when he said that "German sovereignty should no longer be held hostage to Auschwitz." See Olick, "What Does It Mean to Normalize the Past?" p. 550.

35. For the impact of national division on German memory, see Herf, *Divided Memory* and Niven, *Facing the Nazi Past*.

36. The Neue Wache memorial blurred the differences between the victims of the First and Second World Wars and of the Nazi and Communist dictatorships. See Andrew Beattie, "The Victims of Totalitarianism and the Centrality of Nazi Genocide: Continuity and Change in German Commemorative Politics," in Bill Niven, ed., *Germans as Victims: Remembering the Past in Contemporary Germany* (Houndmills, UK, 2006), pp. 147–63. The Day of Commemoration for the Victims of National Socialism was established in 1996 and is celebrated on January 27th, the day of Auschwitz's liberation.

37. Dubiel, *Niemand ist frei von der Geschichte*, pp. 290, 292. See also Barkan, *The Guilt of Nations*, p. xi.

38. Karl Wilds, "Identity Creation and the Culture of Contrition: Recasting 'Normality' in the Berlin Republic," *German Politics*, April 2000, pp. 95, 94–98. Ruth Wittlinger and Martin Larose, "No Future for Germany's Past: Collective Memory and German Foreign Policy," *German Politics*, 4, 2007, pp. 481–95. Ruth Wittlinger and Steffi Boothroyd, "A 'Usable' Past at Last? The Politics of the Past in United Germany," *German Studies Review*, 3, 2010, p. 492.

39. Alvin H. Rosenfeld has written that "German 'normalization' is only achievable with the consent of the Jews." Alvin Rosenfeld "Feeling Alone, Again: The Growing Unease of Germany's Jews," *American Jewish Committee Global Jewish Advocacy*, 2002. www.ajc.org/site/apps/nlnet/content3.aspx?c=ijITI2PHKoG&b=846637&ct=875099.

40. On the concept of the "double past" involving the Third Reich and the communist East German dictatorship, see Niven, *Facing the Nazi Past*, chapter 2. Other scholars warned against relativizing Nazi crimes in this way. See Bernd Faulenbach, Markus Meckel, and Hermann Weber, eds., *Die Partei hatte immer Recht: Aufarbeitung von Geschichte und Folgen der SED-Diktatur* (Essen, 1994). On the use of the idea of modernity, see Uwe Backes, Eckhard Jesse, and Rainer Zitelmann, eds., *Die Schatten der Vergangenheit: Impulse zur Historisierung des Nationalsozialismus* (Berlin, 1990); Michael Prinz and Rainer Zitelmann, eds., *Nationalsozialismus und Modernisierung* (Darmstadt, 1991).

41. Niven, *Facing the Nazi Past*, chapter 7.

42. Henryk M. Broder, "Ende der Schonzeit," *Der Spiegel*, 23, 2002, pp. 26–27.

43. For general studies, see Mark Connelly, *We Can Take It! Britain and the Memory of the Second World War* (Harlow, UK, 2005); Malcolm Smith, *Britain*

and 1940: History, Myth and Popular Memory (London, 2001). See also Geoff Eley, "Finding the People's War: Film, British Collective Memory, and World War II," *AHR*, June, 2001, pp. 818–38.

44. See Churchill's postwar memoir, *The Second World War:Vol. II, Their Finest Hour* (Boston, 1949), pp. 225–26. Connelly notes that British memory of the war has focused on its early phase, especially the year 1940, when Britain was under assault by the Nazis, as opposed to its middle and latter phases, when Britain went on the attack against Germany, bombing its cities: Connelly, *We Can Take It!* p. 14. This reflects a preference to remember the past from the perspective of a victim rather than of a perpetrator.

45. British historiography on appeasement offers an excellent example of the orthodox view of the finest hour. See Chapter 1, footnote 4, of the present study. Cinematic endorsements of the war experience can be found in films, such as *The Dam Busters* (1955), *Dunkirk* (1958), and *Sink the Bismarck* (1960). See Connelly, *We Can Take It!, passim.* Roger Manvell, *Films and the Second World War* (New York, 1974). See also Noel Coward's play, *Peace in Our Time* (1947). The television program *Dad's Army* (which began in 1968 and ran for nine years) focused on the British Home Guard. Connelly, *We Can Take It!*, p. 76. Commemorative reenactments of the Dunkirk evacuations have been held every five years since the 1960s: ibid., p. 89. More recent gestures confirming World War II in as Britain's finest hour include the erection of a monument to Arthur "Bomber" Harris in front of St Clement Dane's RAF church in London in 1992, the official declaration of January 27th as Holocaust Memorial Day in 2001 and the erection of the Bomber Command Memorial in Green Park/Hyde Park Corner in 2012.

46. Various works of alternate history portrayed the Nazis as the epitome of evil. See, for example, Sarban, *The Sound of His Horn* (1949) and Comer Clarke, *England Under Hitler* (1961). The Nazi era has regularly been played for laughs in British film and television comedies. The phenomenon has been examined in Jacques Perretti's documentary film, *Hitler: The Comedy Years* (2007). Notable examples include the Monty Python sketch, "Hitler in England" (1970) and "The Germans," an episode in the BBC sitcom, *Fawlty Towers* (1975). www.youtube.com/watch?v=VdJpDxlI8Ho *Heil* and www.imdb.com/title/tt0578590/quotes.

47. Certain literary and cinematic alternate histories portrayed the British collaborating with the Germans following a Nazi invasion of England. See, for example, Kevin Brownlow and Andrew Mollo's film, *It Happened Here* (1966), Ewan Butler's novel, *Without Apology* (1968), the BBC2 television miniseries, *An Englishman's Castle* (1978). See Rosenfeld, *The World Hitler Never Made* (Cambridge, UK, 2005), chapter 1. A similar trend was visible in mainstream historical films, such as *The Battle of Britain* (1969) and *The Eagle Has Landed* (1976), both of which distinguished between "good" Germans and evil Nazis.

48. Connelly, *We Can Take It!*, pp. 275–77. Thatcher also employed World War II analogies to combat British labor unions, especially Arthur Scargill's National Union of Mineworkers. Smith, *Britain and 1940*, p. 126. This conservative form of universalization dated back to the 1950s, when politicians such as Hugh Gaitskell and Anthony Eden likened Gamel Abdel Nasser to Hitler.

49. The nationalism of the Thatcher years encouraged the tendency to demonize Germany, especially at the time of German unification. Thereafter, revisionist histories questioning the "finest hour" proliferated. See Ruth Wittlinger, "British-German Relations and Collective Memory," *German Politics and Society*, Autumn 2007, pp. 46–48.

50. For a discussion of revisionists texts, see Chapter 1 of the present study.

51. Hugo Young, "Germano-phobia Grips Us as the British Refuse to Forget the War," *The Guardian*, February 16, 1999, p. 16; Jason Cowley, "Forgotten Victims," *The Guardian*, March 26, 2002.

52. Hasia Diner, *We Remember With Love and Reverence: American Jews and the Myth of Silence after the Holocaust, 1945–62* (New York, 2009); Jeffrey Shandler, *While America Watches: Televising the Holocaust* (New York, 1999); James E. Young, *The Texture of Memory: Holocaust Memorials and Meaning* (New Haven, 1993); Edward Linenthal, *Preserving Memory: The Struggle to Create America's Holocaust Museum* (New York, 1995).

53. Rosenfeld, *The World Hitler Never Made*, chapter 2.

54. In the 1960s, James Baldwin referred to America as the "Fourth Reich," while Paul Goodman argued that "the family is the American fascism." Cited in Benjamin DeMott, "The Age of Overkill," *New York Times*, May 19, 1968. Betty Friedan's 1963 book, *The Feminine Mystique* likened the suburban homes of American housewives to "comfortable concentration camps." Cited in Kirsten Fermaglich, *American Dreams and Nazi Nightmares: Early Holocaust Consciousness and Liberal America, 1957–1965* (Waltham, MA, 2007), p. 58 (and generally chapter 2). For a critique of this practice, see Edward Alexander, "Stealing the Holocaust," *Midstream*, November 1980, pp. 46–50.

55. The Catholic Church invoked the Nazi era in opposing abortion, while the NRA did so in opposition to gun control. See "Bishop Rebuts Criticism of a Holocaust Analogy," *New York Times*, March 14, 1984, p. B3; "An Angry Bush Ends His Ties to Rifle Group," *New York Times*, May 11, 1995, p. 1.

56. Tony Judt, "The Past Is Another Country: Myth and Memory in Postwar Europe," *Daedalus*, Fall 1992, pp. 83–118.

57. This dilemma is a major theme of the recent survey by John-Paul Himka and Joanna Beata Michlic, eds., *Bringing the Dark Past to Light: The Reception of the Holocaust in Postcommunist Europe* (Lincoln, NE, 2013).

58. On the Poles' killing of Jews at Jedwabne in 1941, see Jan Gross, *Neighbors: The Destruction of the Jewish Community in Jedwabne, Poland* (New York, 2002); Antony Polonsky, *The Neighbors Respond: The Controversy over the*

Jedwabne Massacre in Poland (Princeton, NJ, 2003). On Croatia's struggle to balance the collaborationist Ustasha regime's killings of Serbs and Jews at the Jasenovac concentration camp with the subsequent killing of Ustasha soldiers by communist partisans in the Austrian town of Bleiburg in 1945, see Ljiljana Radonic, "Transformation of Memory in Croatia," in Eric Langenbacher, Bill Niven, and Ruth Wittlinger, eds., *Dynamics of Memory and Identity in Contemporary Europe* (New York, 2012), pp. 166–79. Other Eastern European examples are discussed in Chapter 1 of the present volume.

59. Tom Segev, *The Seventh Million: The Israelis and the Holocaust* (New York, 1993), pp. 464–65; Idith Zertal, *Israel's Holocaust and the Politics of Nationhood* (Cambridge, UK, 2005).

60. For decades there was tremendous opposition in Israel to translating the controversial scholarship of Hannah Arendt and Raul Hilberg, as well as Adolf Hitler's manifesto, *Mein Kampf*; Segev, *Seventh Million*, pp. 464–65; Zertal, *Israel's Holocaust*, p. 132; Amos Goldberg, "Filling the Gaps in Israel's Holocaust Reading List," *Haaretz*, December 13, 2012. See also Amos Elon, "The Politics of Memory," *New York Review of Books*, October 7, 1993.

61. "'Hitler' Heater Ads Draw Fire From All Quarters," *Taipei Times*, Nov. 23, 1999. http://www.taipeitimes.com/News/local/archives/1999/11/23/11877; David Cohen, "The Rise and Fall of the Third Reich Café," *The Jerusalem Report*, May 22, 2000, p. 42; "Manga Version of Hitler's 'Mein Kampf' a Hit in Japan," *The Telegraph*, September 30, 2009, http://www.telegraph.co.uk/news/worldnews/asia/japan/6247568/Manga-version-of-Hitlers-Mein-Kampf-a-hit-in-Japan.html; "Bangkok's 'Hitler Chic' Trend Riles Tourists, Israeli Envoy," CNNGo, http://www.cnngo.com/bangkok/life/hitler-chic-trend-138530.

Chapter 1 A "good war" no more: The new World War II revisionism

1. Norman Davies, *No Simple Victory: World War II in Europe, 1939–45* (New York, 2007), p. 71. The book first appeared in the UK in 2006.

2. On the finest hour, see Connelly, *We Can Take It!* and Smith, *Britain and 1940*. On the Soviet case, see Nina Tumarkin, *The Living and the Dead: The Rise and Fall of the Cult of World War II in Russia* (New York, 1995); on France, see Henry Rousso, *The Vichy Syndrome: History and Memory in France since 1944* (Cambridge, MA, 1991), p. 10.

3. In Great Britain, both the Tory and Labour parties employed the idea of the "finest hour" to rally public support for their respective administrations; in the Soviet Union, hard-line rulers like Joseph Stalin as well as reformers like Nikita Khrushchev utilized the idea of the "Great Patriotic War" to bolster their regimes; and in France, both Gaullist and Socialist-led governments stylized the war into a national triumph enabled by heroic deeds of resistance. Smith, *Britain and 1940*,

pp. 111–13; Tumarkin, *The Living and the Dead*, chapters 4–5; Rousso, *The Vichy Syndrome*, chapters 1–2.

4. To be sure, British, French, and Soviet histories of the war disagreed about how much the Western Allies and the USSR respectively abetted Hitler's plans for war, the former highlighting the Nazi–Soviet pact of 1939, the latter highlighting Western appeasement of Hitler. Despite this disagreement, these histories still foregrounded German culpability. On the whole, postwar histories of the war justified their respective governments' prewar and wartime behavior. British studies defended interventionism and criticized appeasement. See Winston Churchill, *The Second World War: Vol. I, The Gathering Storm* and *Vol. II, Their Finest Hour* (1948); John Wheeler-Bennett, *Munich: Prologue to Tragedy* (New York, 1948); Alan Bullock, *Hitler: A Study in Tyranny* (London, 1952); Lewis Namier, *In the Nazi Era* (New York, 1952). In France, historians sought to preserve national self-esteem and initially avoided politicized debates over the Vichy period. See Charles De Gaulle, *Mémoires de guerre: L'Appel 1940–1942* (Paris, 1954); Robert Aron and Georgette Elgey, *Histoire de Vichy* (Paris, 1956); Henri Amouroux, *La Grande Histoire des Français sous l'Occupation (The Full History of the French under the Occupation)*, in eight volumes (Paris, 1976–1993). Soviet studies, epitomized by Stalin's *Falsifiers of History* (1948), explained the war as a by-product of capitalist-inspired imperialism and the Western Allies' failure to stand up to Germany. See Patrick Finney, *Remembering the Road to World War Two: International History, National Identity, and Collective Memory* (London, 2011), chapter 1; Teddy J. Uldricks, "War, Politics and Memory: Russian Historians Reevaluate the Origins of World War II," *History & Memory*, 2, Fall/Winter 2009, pp. 62–65; Sergei Kudryashov, "Remembering and Researching the War: The Soviet and Russian Experience," in Jörg Echternkamp and Stefan Martens, *Experience and Memory: The Second World War in Europe* (New York, 2010), pp. 86–115.

5. The first major studies were written by military figures, such as Dwight D. Eisenhower in *Crusade in Europe* (Garden City, NY, 1948) and Lucius Clay in *Decision in Germany* (Garden City, NY, 1950). Later studies included William Shirer, *The Rise and Fall of the Third Reich* (New York, 1960), Gerhard L. Weinberg, *The Foreign Policy of Hitler's Germany* (2 vols., 1971, 1980), and Norman Rich, *Hitler's War Aims* (New York, 1973).

6. Studs Terkel, *"The Good War": An Oral History of World War II* (New York, 1984). Terkel clarified that he was made aware of the phrase by the journalist, Herbert Mitgang, and pointed out that it had long been in usage among "men of his and my generation." Terkel, p. xi. The phrase itself only came into widespread usage in the 1990s. A Lexis-Nexis search reveals that between 1984 (the date of the book's publication) and 1989, there were only 175 references to the "good war" in relation to World War II. Between 1990 and 1999, by contrast, the phrase appeared some 764 times.

7. Michael C. C. Adams notes in his study, *The Best War Ever: America and World War II* (Baltimore, 1994), that "as American ... power ...[has] waned ... the Good War ... has become hallowed, almost above criticism"(p. 6).

8. For a discussion of mainstream revisionism in the American historical profession, see Peter Novick, *That Noble Dream: The "Objectivity Question" and the American Historical Profession* (Cambridge, UK, 1988).

9. Many Holocaust deniers, for example, have tried to legitimize their work by describing it as "revisionist." This appropriation of the term has led it to fall into disrepute in certain circles. This fact notwithstanding, there is no reason to view revisionism in and of itself as inherently suspicious.

10. I exclude from the category of "revisionism" studies that reassessed the war's origins and consequences but accepted its basic legitimacy and morality. For example, American historians have disagreed about when and why President Roosevelt ultimately had the US intervene in the European conflict; British historians have debated the origins and efficacy of appeasement; and German historians have argued over the driving forces behind Hitler's foreign policy. See Justus Doenecke, "U. S. Policy and the European War, 1939–1941," *Diplomatic History*, 4, Fall 1995, pp. 669–98; Keith Robbins, *Appeasement* (Oxford, 2001); Andrew David Stedman, *Alternatives to Appeasement: Neville Chamberlain and Hitler's Germany* (New York, 2011); Ian Kershaw, *The Nazi Dictatorship: Problems and Perspectives of Interpretation* (London, 2000), chapter 6.

11. Charles A. Beard, *President Roosevelt and the Coming of the War, 1941* (New Haven, 1948); Harry Elmer Barnes, ed., *Perpetual War for Perpetual Peace: A Critical Examination of the Foreign Policy of Franklin D. Roosevelt and Its Aftermath* (Caldwell, 1953); William Henry Chamberlin, *America's Second Crusade* (Chicago, 1950). David Hoggan's *Der erzwungene Krieg: Die Ursachen und Urheber des 2. Weltkrieges* (Tübingen, 1977) was originally completed as a dissertation in 1955 and published in book form in Germany in 1961. For a larger discussion, see Warren I. Cohen, *The American Revisionists: The Lessons of Intervention in World War I* (Chicago, 1967).
Deborah Lipstadt's, *Denying the Holocaust: The Growing Assault on Truth and Memory* (New York, 1993), shows how some revisionists later gravitated to Holocaust denial.

12. Robert Gale Woolbert criticized Beard's book for its "distortion of fact" in his review of *President Roosevelt and the Coming of the War, 1941, in Foreign Affairs*, October 1948, p. 157. Julius Pratt attacked Barnes's edited volume as marred by "prejudice" in his review of *Perpetual War for Perpetual Peace*, in *Political Science Quarterly*, March 1955, pp. 135–37. William McNeill called Chamberlin's book "a travesty of history" in his review of *America's Second Crusade*, in *International Affairs*, October 1951, pp. 537–38. According to Doenecke in "U. S. Policy and the European War, 1939–1941," the dawn of the

1960s witnessed the "demise of anti-interventionist right . . . and . . . the revisionism that went with it" (p. 671).

13. A. J. P. Taylor, *The Origins of the Second World War* (London, 1961).

14. Bruce M. Russett, *No Clear and Present Danger: A Skeptical View of the U.S. Entry into World War II* (New York, 1972). Melvin Small, *Was War Necessary? National Security and U. S. Entry into War* (Beverly Hills, CA, 1980).

15. Taylor, who was a leftist involved in the postwar nuclear disarmament movement, may have intended his book to be an indictment of postwar western anticommunism. His portrayal of Hitler as a rational, non-ideological leader was meant to convince Western politicians to see Nikita Khrushchev similarly and take a less confrontational diplomatic attitude towards him. William Roger Louis, ed., *The Origins of the Second World War: A. J. P. Taylor and His Critics* (New York, 1972), pp. 103–04. Taylor claimed that the West's reluctance to take a conciliatory policy towards the USSR after 1945 was due to "the recollection of the appeasement towards Germany that failed a decade ago." Gordon Martel, "Introduction," in *The Origins of the Second World War Reconsidered* (London, 1986), p. 14. Russett opposed America's involvement in Vietnam, which he blamed on the interventionist tradition that was established in World War II. Not all the revisionist studies of this period emanated from the left, as was shown by conservative British scholar Maurice Cowling's *The Impact of Hitler: British Politics and British Policy, 1933–1940* (Cambridge, UK, 1975), which claimed that Britain's intervention against the Nazis caused the country's postwar decline.

16. The most fiercely attacked study was Taylor's, which was perceived as whitewashing Hitler, an impression solidified by the praise it received from right-wing and neo-Nazi organizations in Germany. In truth, Taylor's comparatively mild portrayal of Hitler (he described him as "no more wicked than . . . other contemporary statesmen") was meant to underscore the role of ordinary Germans in taking the country to war (Taylor wrote that "Hitler's foreign policy was that of his predecessors and . . . of virtually all Germans"). These statements reflected Taylor's longstanding anti-German attitudes and embrace of the *Sonderweg* paradigm for explaining the Third Reich's origins. See Louis, *A. J. Taylor and His Critics*, pp. 8–9. For the critical responses to Russett's book, see Rosenfeld, *The World Hitler Never Made*, p. 138. Reviews of Small's book were more respectful. See Lawrence S. Kaplan, *American Historical Review*, June 1981, pp. 673–74; David S. Patterson, *The Journal of American History*, December 1981, pp. 642–43.

17. Paul Fussell, *Wartime: Understanding and Behavior in the Second World War* (New York, 1989); Adams, *The Best War Ever*.

18. James Bacque, *Other Losses: An Investigation into the Mass Deaths of German Prisoners at the Hands of the French and Americans After World War II* (Toronto, 1989). Alfred-Maurice De Zayas, *A Terrible Revenge: The Ethnic*

Cleansing of the East European Germans, 1944–1950 (New York, 1994). This book was based on De Zayas's earlier study, *Nemesis at Potsdam: The Anglo-Americans and the Expulsion of the Germans. Background, Execution, Consequences* (Boston, 1977). *A Terrible Revenge* first appeared in hardback under the title, *The German Expellees: Victims in War and Peace* (New York, 1993).

19. Adams cited the US-led invasion of Iraq in 1991 as an example of the lessons of World War II – specifically the dangers of appeasement – being misapplied in a new setting: Adams, *The Best War Ever*, p. 4. Bacque seems to have been driven by his moral empathy with ex-German POWs to take up their cause. See S. P. Mackenzie, "Essay and Reflection: On the 'Other Losses' Debate," *The International History Review*, November, 1992, p. 727. De Zayas, a longtime human rights activist, was motivated by the ethnic cleansing of the Yugoslav civil war to focus on the suffering of ethnic Germans.

20. Bacque's book was condemned as empirically flawed, while De Zayas's was largely ignored. Mackenzie, "Essay and Reflection: On the 'Other Losses' Debate," pp. 717–31. Bacque's book was extensively refuted in Stephen Ambrose and Günter Bischof, eds., *Eisenhower and the German POWs: Facts against Falsehood* (Baton Rouge, LA, 1992). Notably, both Bacque's and De Zayas's books were warmly greeted by right-wing audiences, who cited German suffering as a method of relativizing German guilt for the war.

21. Correlli Barnett, *The Audit of War* (London, 1986); John Charmley, *Churchill: The End of Glory: A Political Biography* (New York, 1993). Both books were also attacked for concluding that the country would have been better off staying neutral in the conflict. These texts reflected British disaffection with the nation's decline from great power status, a fact underscored by the United States's enhanced superpower status after 1989.

22. Clive Ponting, *1940: Myth and Reality* (London, 1990); Madeline Bunting, *The Model Occupation: The Channel Islands under German Rule* (New York, 1995). For the critical response, see Rosenfeld, *The World Hitler Never Made*, pp. 71, 88. Other books that challenged wartime myths included Angus Calder's *The Myth of the Blitz* (London, 1995) and Stuart Hylton's *Their Darkest Hour: The Hidden History of the Home Front 1939–1945* (London, 2001) which exposed the existence of social tensions on the home front during the war.

23. John Bodnar, *The "Good War" in American Memory* (Baltimore, 2010), chapter 2.

24. Denise Youngblood, *Russian War Films: On the Cinema Front, 1914–2005* (Lawrence, KS, 2006), pp. 117–18.

25. Bodnar argues in *The "Good War" in American Memory* that, despite critiquing the violence and brutality of the war, most works did "not question the crusade against Fascism" and "supported the goal of destroying Hitler's regime" (pp. 131, 135).

26. In the case of the United States, Bodnar points to films, such as *White Christmas* (1954), *The Longest Day* (1962), and *Patton* (1970), which supported the orthodox view of the war, in addition to memorials, such as the US Marine Corps Memorial (1954) and the USS-Arizona Memorial (1962), which hailed soldierly sacrifice (ibid., pp. 142–45, 87–90). In the case of Great Britain, the enormous number of war films during the 1950s and 1960s testified to the hold of the finest hour on British national memory. In the Soviet Union, finally, the "cult" of World War II remained unchallenged. See Tumarkin, *The Living and the Dead*.

27. German historians agreed with their European and American colleagues that Hitler was responsible for the war's eruption. See, among other studies, Friedrich Meinecke, *The German Catastrophe* (Cambridge, MA, 1950) (first published in German in 1946); Karl Dietrich Bracher, *The German Dictatorship* (New York, 1970); Eberhard Jäckel, *Hitler's Weltanschauung* (Middletown, CT, 1972); Klaus Hildebrand, *The Foreign Policy of the Third Reich* (Oakland, CA, 1973); Andreas Hillgruber, *Hitlers Strategie: Politik und Kriegführung, 1940–1941* (Bonn, 1975). An exception to this trend was right-wing historian Dirk Bavendamm's studies, *Roosevelts Weg zum Krieg: amerikanischer Politik, 1914–1939* (Frankfurt, 1983) and *Roosevelts Krieg, 1937–45* (Munich, 1993), both of which blamed Roosevelt instead of Hitler for World War II.

28. Hans-Ulrich Wehler referred to the "emotional inhibitions" of German historians. "Die Debatte wirkt befreiend," *Der Spiegel*, March 25, 2002, p. 62.

29. This was seen in the critical reaction to Andreas Hillgruber's *Zweierlei Untergang* (Berlin, 1986), which focused on the suffering of German civilians on the Eastern Front in the last phase of the war. See Perry Anderson, "On Emplotment: Two Kinds of Ruin," in Saul Friedlander, ed., *Probing the Limits of Representation: Nazism and the 'Final Solution'* (Cambridge, MA, 1992), pp. 54–65.

30. Bill Niven, "Introduction: German Victimhood at the Turn of the Millennium," in Bill Niven, ed., *Germans as Victims*, p. 7.

31. See Niven, *Facing the Nazi Past*, chapter 4.

32. In 1984, Helmut Kohl took offense at being excluded from the Allies' 40th anniversary celebrations of D-Day. On May 8, 1985, President Richard von Weizsäcker spoke of VE Day as a day of liberation for Germany. Memorials marking liberation from Nazism were built in cities such as Munich. See Gavriel Rosenfeld, *Munich and Memory: Architecture, Monuments, and the Legacy of the Third Reich in Postwar Munich* (Berkeley, 2000), pp. 284, 390, n. 17.

33. Foreign Minister Joschka Fischer invoked Auschwitz to justify German intervention in Kosovo. Chancellor Gerhard Schroeder justified German participation in the NATO campaign in Afghanistan as part of the struggle against "totalitarian challenge" represented by Al Qaeda. Kundnani, *Utopia or*

Auschwitz? p. 270; Wittlinger and Larose, "No Future for Germany's Past?" pp. 481–95.

34. Niven, *Facing the Nazi Past*, pp. 114–15.

35. Hans Erick Nossack's *Der Untergang* (Frankfurt, 1996) was originally published in 1948 (the English-language version, *The End: Hamburg, 1943*, was published 2004); W. G. Sebald, *Luftkrieg und Literatur* (Munich, 1999), the English-language version, *On the Natural History of Destruction*, appeared in 2002; Jörg Friedrich, *Der Brand: Deutschland im Bombenkrieg, 1940–1945* (Berlin, 2002), the English-language version, *The Fire: The Bombing of Germany, 1940–1945*, was published in 2008.

36. Günter Grass, *Im Krebsgang* (Göttingen, 2002).

37. Anonymous, *Eine Frau in Berlin, Tagebuch-Aufzeichnungen vom 20. April bis 22. Juni 1945* (Munich, 2005).

38. On the museum project, see Samuel Salzborn, "The German Myth of a Victim Nation: (Re-)presenting Germans as Victims in the New Debate on their Flight and Expulsion from Eastern Europe," in Helmut Schmitz, ed., *A Nation of Victims? Representations of German Wartime Suffering from 1945 to the Present* (Amsterdam, 2007), pp. 91–92. An additional proposal to establish a new "National Holiday for the Victims of Expulsion" commemorating their wartime experiences was proposed in 2011: "Ein Fatal falsches Signal," *Süddeutsche Zeitung*, February 2, 2011.

39. See A. O. Scott, "A History Lesson, Airbrushed," *New York Times*, January 14, 2014.

40. Friedrich, *Der Brand*, p. 110. Sebald's original German phrase, *Vernichtungsaktion*, was translated into the milder English phrase "destruction." See Annette Seidel Arpaci, "Lost in Translation? The Discourse of 'German Suffering' and W. G. Sebald's *Luftkrieg und Literatur*," in Schmitz, ed., *A Nation of Victims*, pp. 164–65.

41. "So muss die Hölle aussehen," *Der Spiegel*, 2, 2003, p. 50, see also p. 5. *Der Spiegel* also referred to Allied bombers as "flying terrorists," p. 46. Luke Harding, "German Tabloid Demands Apology from Queen for Wartime Air Raids," *The Guardian*, November 2, 2004.

42. Friedrich's 600-page book had sold 200,000 copies by the end of 2003. www.spiegel.de/spiegel/print/d-29410542.html. Grass's novel had sold 400,000 copies by 2006. www.rp-online.de/kultur/buch/grass-buch-ist-schon-ein-bestseller-aid-1.2039388. At its highest levels, the television film, *Dresden*, had over 12 million viewers and a 32% market share of the overall viewing audience. "Dresden"-Quote: Feuersturm mit Millionenpublikum," *Spiegel Online*, March 7, 2006. *Die Flucht* registered 11 million viewers and a 29% market share: www.presseportal.de/pm/29876/966297/das-erste-bleibt-die-nr-1-14-0-marktanteil-im-ersten-quartal-2007-platzierung-vor-zdf-und-den. *Unsere Mütter, unsere Väter* attained over 7.5 million viewers and a 24% market share:

Primetime-Check: Mittwoch, 20. März 2013, www.quotenmeter.de/n/62772/
primetime-check-mittwoch-20-maerz-2013.

43. "Die Debatte wirkt befreiend," *Der Spiegel*, March 25, 2002, p. 62.

44. Peter Schneider, "The Germans Are Breaking an Old Taboo," *New York Times*,
January 18, 2003.

45. Nikolaus von Festenberg, "Von der Couch in die Hölle," *Der Spiegel*, February
25, 2006.

46. Frank Schirrmacher, "Die Geschichte deutscher Albträume," *FAZ*, March 15,
2013. Historian Götz Aly agreed that the film had the potential to generate
intergenerational conversation: "Vereiste Vergangenheit," *Die Zeit*, March 14,
2013. See also Eckhard Fuhr, "Wie der Zweite Weltkrieg wirklich war," *Die
Welt*, January 24, 2014.

47. Hofmann (born in 1959) discussed his left-liberal political leanings, as well as his
personal motivations for making his series of World War II films, in "Töten oder
getötet werden," *Der Spiegel*, March 11, 2013. Kolditz (born in 1956) grew up
in East Germany. See "Mit den Kategorien Gut und Böse kommst du nicht
weit," *FAZ*, March 19, 2013.

48. See Pearce, *Contemporary Germany and the Nazi Legacy*; Wilds, "Identity
Creation and the Culture of Contrition"; Wittlinger and Larose, "No Future for
Germany's Past?"; Niven, *Germans as Victims*, p. 8; Leftists felt no need to dwell
on the Nazis' crimes because they viewed them "as a given." Ian Buruma,
"Many German Civilians Died in the Second World War," *The Guardian*,
November 26, 2002, p. 6. See also Wolfgang Sofsky, "Die halbierte
Erinnerung," *SZ*, December 5, 2002, p. 13.

49. Christopher Rhoads, "Behind Iraq Stance in Germany: Flood of War
Memories," *Wall Street Journal*, February 25, 2003; Mariam Lau,
"Bücherverbrennung nie da gewesenen Ausmaßes," *Die Welt*, January
9, 2003.

50. This was the assertion of Corelli Barnett, quoted in "Schillerndes Ungeheuer,"
Der Spiegel, 49, 2002, p. 156. Critical reviews of Sebald included:
Daphne Merkin, "Cordoning off the Past," *New York Times*, April 6, 2003,
p. 14 and Ruth Franklin, "Rings of Smoke," *New Republic*, September 22,
2002, especially pp. 37–38. See also, Bartosz Jalowiecki, "Lies the Germans Tell
Themselves," *Commentary*, January, 2004, pp. 43–46. In Britain, Tony Blair
worried that Germany was developing a culture of victimhood. Niven,
Germans as Victims, p. 8.

51. Pawel Lutomski, "The Debate about a Center against Expulsions: An
Unexpected Crisis in German-Polish Relations?" *German Studies Review*, 3,
October, 2004, pp. 449–68. Israel's reaction to the Center for Expulsions is
discussed in Margalit, "Increased German 'Suffering.'"

52. Evelyn Finger, "Der englische Pilot," *Die Zeit*, March 2, 2006. See also
David Crossland, "World War II: German Film Recalls Dresden Bombing,"

Spiegel International, February 13, 2006. On *Die Flucht*, see Christian Buß, "Go West, Gräfin!" *Der Spiegel*, March 2, 2007.

53. In his essay, "Nazis sind immer die anderen," *TAZ*, March 21, 2013, Ulrich Herbert argued that the film failed to show how the very generation to which the film's (unrealistically apolitical) protagonists belonged was itself strongly influenced by Nazi ideological indoctrination. See also Stefan Schmitz and Matthias Weber, "Das gespaltene Urteil der Historiker," *Stern*, March 23, 2013. Poland's ambassador to Germany officially protested the film's distorted portrayal of the Polish resistance, whose anti-Semitism was not offset by any depiction of Polish efforts on behalf of Jews. "Vollkommen falsches Bild," *SZ*, March 27, 2013.

54. German critics were especially vocal about this possibility. Norbert Frei expressed this view in *1945 und Wir: Das Dritte Reich im Bewußtsein der Deutschen* (Munich, 2005), esp. pp. 7–22, while Aleida Assmann did the same in her recent book, *Das neue Unbehagen an der Erinnerungskultur: Eine Intervention* (Munich, 2013).

55. See "NPD-Mann spricht von Dresdner 'Bomben-Holocaust,'" *Der Spiegel*, January 21, 2005. This right-wing trend was also promoted by the publication of books, such as Klaus-Rainer Röhl's *Verbotene Trauer* (*Forbidden Mourning*) in 2002. Niven, *Germans as Victims*, pp. 11–12.

56. See Salzborn, "The German Myth of a Victim Nation," pp. 91–92. The right-wing party the NPD was a vocal supporter of the Center Against Expulsions. In 2011, Steinbach sought to relativize Germany's guilt for the war by claiming that Poland was eager to fight with Germany in 1939. "How Far to the Right Can Germany's Conservatives Go?" *Der Spiegel*, October 9, 2010. "Charges of Historical Revisionism Stir Up Berlin," *Der Spiegel*, April 8, 2010.

57. "Warum ich nach sechzig Jahren mein Schweigen breche," *FAZ*, August 11, 2006, www.faz.net/aktuell/feuilleton/debatten/guenter-grass-im-interview-warum-ich-nach-sechzig-jahren-mein-schweigen-breche-1357691.html.

58. Ruth Wittlinger, "The Merkel Government's Politics of the Past," *German Politics and Society*, 4, Winter, 2008, pp. 9–27. In 2008, Merkel's governing coalition called into existence the "Stiftung Flucht, Vertreibung, Versöhnung," (Foundation Flight, Expulsion, and Reconciliation), under the aegis of the German Historical Museum, which proceeded to plan the new documentation center, which will be housed in the Deutschlandhaus in Kreuzberg. Dagmar Kift, "Neither Here nor There? The Memorialization of the Expulsion of Ethnic Germans," in Bill Niven and Chloe Paver, eds., *Memorialization in Germany since 1945* (New York, 2010), pp. 78–90.

59. Mikhail Gorbachev's glasnost policy encouraged a new mood of historical revisionism. In 1988, Baltic protesters demanded the publication of the Hitler–Stalin pact's secret protocol allowing Soviet annexation of Eastern Poland and the Baltic states. Russian historian Dmitiri Volkogonov was the first scholar

in the USSR to take a critical view of the pact. Finney, *Remembering the Road to World War Two*, pp. 48–52.

60. The three Baltic countries established their commissions in 1998.

61. The Latvian commission used the term "genocide," while the Estonian one refrained from doing so. Eva-Clarita Onken, "The Politics of Finding Historical Truth: Reviewing Baltic History Commissions and Their Work," *Journal of Baltic Studies*, March 2001, p. 113.

62. For the text of the declaration see www.victimsofcommunism.org/media/article. php?article=3849.

63. www.victimsofcommunism.org/media/article.php?article=3849.

64. "Estonia to Remove Soviet Era Memorial," *BBC News*, January 12, 2007, http://news.bbc.co.uk/2/hi/europe/6255051.stm; "Georgia Smashes History for New Parliament Site," *RT*, December 17, 2009, http://rt.com/politics/georgia-parliament-monument-outrage; "Russia Outraged by Desecration of Monument to Soviet Soldiers in Bulgaria," *RT*, June 22, 2011, http://rt.com/politics/russia-bulgaria-monument-ministry/. In the Estonian town of Parnu in 2002, a controversy erupted over the erection and later removal of a memorial honoring Estonian soldiers who fought with the Waffen SS against the USSR. "Estonia Revmoves SS Monument," *BBC News*, July 24, 2002, http://news.bbc.co.uk/2/hi/europe/6255051.stm.

65. Efraim Zuroff, "Eastern Europe: Anti-Semitism in the Wake of Holocaust-Related Issues," *Jerusalem Center for Public Affairs*, Spring 2005.

66. "Estonia's PM Denies Waffen-SS Parade Tied to Nazi Ideology," *Ria Novosty*, July 21, 2011, http://en.rian.ru/world/20110722/165327473. html; Neo-Nazi groups were allowed to march in Estonia and Latvia in support of local SS veterans groups. "David Cameron's Rightwing 'Allies' March in Riga to Commemorate the SS," *The Guardian*, March 13, 2010, www.guardian.co.uk/world/2010/mar/14/latvia-divided-communists-nazis. Ceremonies were held in 2010 and 2011 honoring the fascist Ustashe leader, Ante Pavelic, in Croatia, and nationalist Stepan Bandera in Ukraine. Efraim Zuroff, "Don't Rehabilitate the Guilty," *Haaretz*, January 13, 2012. www.haaretz.com/print-edition/opinion/don-t-rehabilitate-the-guilty-1.407063.

67. Finney, *Remembering the Road to World War Two*, p. 2.

68. "Russia Rebukes Estonia for Moving Soviet Statue," *New York Times*, April 27, 2007.

69. "Vladimir Putin Condemns Appeasement of Hitler on 70th Anniversary of WW2 Outbreak," *The Telegraph*, September 1, 2009, www.telegraph.co.uk/news/newstopics/world-war-2/6122748/Vladimir-Putin-condemns-appeasement-of-Hitler-on-70th-anniversary-of-WW2-outbreak.html. The three Baltic states also boycotted the 60th anniversary ceremonies in Moscow marking the end of World War II in 2005.

70. "Putin Blames Britain for Russia's Invasion of Poland on the 70th Anniversary of WWII," *Daily Mail*, September 2, 2009, www.dailymail.co.uk/news/article-1210264/Putin-condemns-Moscow-signing-1939-treaty-Berlin–blames-Britain-wartime-pacts-Nazi-Germany.html.

71. "The War? Nothing To Do With Stalin, Says Russia's President, Dmitry Medvedev," *The Guardian*, August 30, 2009, www.guardian.co.uk/world/2009/aug/30/war-stalin-russia-medvedev.

72. Elizabeth Wood, "Performing Memory: Vladimir Putin and the Celebration of WWII in Russia," *The Soviet and Post-Soviet Review* 38, 2011, p. 1785.

73. "Russia: OSCE Distorts History," *Pravda*, July 10, 2009, http://english.pravda.ru/russia/politics/10-07-2009/108043-russiaoscetruth-0/; "OSCE Resolution: The case against Estonia," *Pravda*, July 14, 2009, http://english.pravda.ru/russia/politics/14-07-2009/108127-esceestonia-0/

74. Oleg Kozlovsky, "Medvedev Imposes Control Over Russian History," *Huffington Post*, May 19, 2009, www.huffingtonpost.com/oleg-kozlovsky/medvedev-imposes-control_b_205349.html.

75. Efraim Zuroff, "Right of Reply: A Threat to Holocaust Memory," August 27, 2010, www.jpost.com/LandedPages/PrintArticle.aspx?id=186060. See also Dovid Katz's writings on defendinghistory.com.

76. See Timothy Snyder, "Fascism, Russia, and Ukraine," *New York Review of Books*, March 20, 2014.

77. Nicholson Baker, *Human Smoke: The Beginnings of World War II, the End of Civilization* (New York, 2008); Patrick Buchanan, *Churchill, Hitler, and "The Unnecessary War": How Britain Lost Its Empire and the West Lost the World* (New York, 2008).

78. Baker, *Human Smoke*, pp. 473–74.

79. Ibid., p. 106.

80. Ibid., p. 206.

81. Ibid., p. 204.

82. Ibid., p. 233.

83. Ibid., pp. 328, 362, 397.

84. Ibid., pp. 114, 283, 456.

85. Ibid., pp. 206, 407.

86. www.radioopensource.org/nicholson-bakers-human-smoke/.

87. Baker also overlooked the fact that the Nazis would not have had sufficient ships to transport Europe's Jews to Madagascar even with British neutrality; and that Hitler continued to seriously consider the Madagascar Plan's viability even after it became clear that England would not agree to a separate peace. See Peter Longerich, *Holocaust: The Nazi Persecution and Murder of the Jews* (Oxford, 2010), pp. 161–64.

88. "I've never really understood the Second World War II," Baker observed, "but I always chalked it up to my own ignorance of history."www. radioopensource.org/nicholson-bakers-human-smoke/.

89. These include the works of Maurice Cowling, A. J. P. Taylor, Correlli Barnett, William Henry Chamberlin, John Charmley, Alan Clark, and Niall Ferguson.

90. Buchanan, *Churchill, Hitler, and "The Unnecessary War,"* p. 260.

91. Ibid., p. 282.

92. Ibid., p. 262.

93. Ibid., pp. 328, 362.

94. Ibid., p. 367.

95. Ibid., p. 324.

96. Ibid., p. 383.

97. Ibid., p. xvii.

98. Ibid., p. 293.

99. Ibid., p. 301.

100. Ibid., p. 312.

101. For a discussion, see Rosenfeld, *The World Hitler Never Made*, pp. 149–51, 157–58.

102. Buchanan, *Churchill, Hitler, and "The Unnecessary War,"* p. 417.

103. Ibid., pp. xix, 423.

104. Ibid., pp. xx, 420.

105. Ibid., p. xx.

106. Ibid.

107. Ironically, A. J. P. Taylor, upon whom Buchanan relied so much, believed the opposite, arguing that "I was convinced . . . that Soviet predominance in eastern Europe was the only alternative to Germany's and I preferred the Soviet one." Quoted in Norman Rich, "Hitler's Foreign Policy," in Martel, *The Origins of the Second World War Reconsidered*, p. 127.

108. Buchanan, *Churchill, Hitler, and "The Unnecessary War,"* p. 320. Buchanan took this argument from A. J. P. Taylor.

109. Ibid., p. 363.

110. Alexander B. Rossino, *Hitler Strikes Poland: Blitzkrieg, Ideology, and Atrocity* (Lawrence, KS, 2005); Phillip T. Rutherford, *Prelude to the Final Solution: The Nazi Program for Deporting Ethnic Poles, 1939–1941* (Lawrence, KS, 2007). Adam Tooze's important book, *The Wages of Destruction: The Making and Breaking of the Nazi Economy* (New York, 2008), argues that Hitler's entire foreign policy was shaped by the belief that the United States was Germany's most dangerous long-term rival and eventually would need to be confronted.

111. Jacques Pauwels, *The Myth of the Good War: America in the Second World War* (Toronto, 2002).

112. Ibid., p. 14.

113. Ibid., pp. 54–58.

114. Ibid., pp. 34–35.

115. Ibid., pp. 37, 66.

116. Ibid., p. 128.

117. Ibid., p. 238.

118. Ibid., p. 61.

119. Ibid., p. 37.

120. Ibid., p. 88.

121. Ibid., p. 238.

122. Ibid., p. 238.

123. Ibid., p. 237. In making this claim, Pauwels ignored an enormous body of German geopolitical thinking rooted in *völkisch* thought.

124. Norman Davies, *No Simple Victory*.

125. Davies, p. 11.

126. Ibid, pp. 24–25.

127. Ibid., p. 463.

128. Ibid., p. 485.

129. Ibid., pp. 19–20.

130. Ibid., p. 487

131. Ibid., p. 430.

132. Ibid., p. 6.

133. Ibid., pp. 6, 479.

134. Davies's mammoth book, *The Isles: A History* (Oxford, 2000), took an iconoclastic approach to the prevailing Anglocentric view of British history.

135. Davies recalled with distaste a dinner party in the mid-1980s where A. J. P. Taylor and his Hungarian communist wife denied Soviet involvement in the Katyn massacre. Davies, *No Simple Victory*, p. 14. See also Anne Applebaum's review of Davies's controversial book, *Europe*, in the *New Criterion*, May, 1997: www.newcriterion.com/articles.cfm/oldcliches-applebaum-3340.

136. See for example the interview www.bbc.co.uk/radio3/johntusainterview/davies_transcript.shtml.

137. Davies, *No Simple Victory*, p. 14.

138. Ibid., p. 296. Note that Davies referred to six million "innocents" instead of "Jews."

139. Ibid., p. 466.

140. Ibid., p. 466.

141. Ibid., p. 489.

142. Michael Bess, *Choices Under Fire: Moral Dimensions of World War II* (New York, 2008). The book originally appeared in hardback in 2006.

143. Ibid., p. 17.

144. Ibid., p. 69.

145. Ibid., p. 71.

146. Ibid., p. 71.
147. Ibid., pp. 72–74.
148. Ibid., p. 74.
149. Ibid., p. 75.
150. Ibid., p. 110.
151. Ibid pp. 108–09.
152. Ibid.,. p. 110.
153. Ibid., p. 106–08.
154. Ibid., p. 166.
155. Ibid., pp.168, 170.
156. Ibid., p. 177.
157. Ibid., p. 172.
158. Ibid., p. 40–41.
159. Ibid., p. 340.
160. Ibid., p. 340.
161. Indeed, Bess devoted an entire chapter of his book to the moral question of bystander passivity in the face of the Nazi genocide
162. Bess's previous scholarship displayed an interest in pacifism and ecology, but not from any dogmatic perspective. See, for example, *Realism, Utopia, and the Mushroom Cloud: Four Activist Intellectuals and their Strategies for Peace, 1945–1989* (Chicago, 1993) and *The Light-Green Society: Ecology and Technological Modernity in France, 1960–2000* (Chicago, 2003).
163. Niall Ferguson, *The War of the World: Twentieth Century Conflict and the Descent of the West* (New York, 2006).
164. Ibid, p. lxx.
165. Ibid., p. lxxi
166. Ibid., p. 313.
167. Ibid., p. 315.
168. Ibid., p. 319.
169. Ibid., p. 382.
170. Ibid., p. 319.
171. Ibid., p. 362.
172. Ibid., p. 368.
173. Ibid., p. 366.
174. Ibid., pp. 521, 511.
175. Ibid., pp. 511–30.
176. Ibid., p. 514.
177. Ibid., pp. 515, 522.
178. Ibid., p. 220.
179. Ibid., pp. 508–09.
180. Ibid., p. 510.
181. Ibid., p. 274.

182. Ibid., p. 532.
183. Ibid., p. 547.
184. Ibid., p. 568.
185. Ibid., p. 571.
186. Ibid., pp. 511, 587.
187. Ibid., p. lxvii.
188. These views emerged clearly in his books, *Empire: The Rise and Demise of the British World Order and the Lessons for Global Power* (New York, 2004) and *The Pity of War* (New York, 1999).
189. Rosenfeld, *The World Hitler Never Made*, pp. 90–91.
190. Ashley Smith, "World War II: The Good War?" *International Socialist Review*, 10, Winter, 2000.
191. Carl Lesnor, "The 'Good' War," *The Philosophical Forum*, Spring, 2005, pp. 84–85, 77. Lesnor (1933–2011) was an independent scholar and associate editor of the *Philosophical Forum*, who was affiliated with the left-wing Radical Philosophy Association.
192. David Hoogland Noon, "Operation Enduring Analogy: World War II, the War on Terror, and the Uses of Historical Memory," *Rhetoric & Public Affairs*, 3, Fall 2004, p. 340.
193. Giles MacDonogh, *After the Reich: The Brutal History of the Allied Occupation* (New York, 2007). MacDonogh's book presented disturbing facts about German civilian suffering, but employed language that made the Allies seem no better than the Nazis. MacDonogh judgmentally (but erroneously) referred to an Allied "policy" of "collective guilt" towards the Germans (p. xiv); said the Allies "came in hate" to Germany (p. 3); believed Germans were "subhuman" (p. 235); employed "weapons of mass destruction" against them (p. 46); and used "SS methods" in interrogating Nazi war criminals (p. 406).
194. William Hitchcock, *The Bitter Road to Freedom: A New History of the Liberation of Europe* (New York, 2008), pp. 367–69. In a nod to the post-Iraq political climate, Hitchcock argued that wars of liberation against dictators always entail immense human suffering. He ultimately concluded, however, that the Allied campaign "was an honorable struggle . . . [against] a vile and barbaric regime" (p. 373).
195. Keith Lowe, *Savage Continent: Europe in the Aftermath of World War II* (New York, 2012), p. 57. Lowe also at times equated Nazi and Allied behavior, see p. 59.
196. Timothy Snyder, *Bloodlands: Europe Between Hitler and Stalin* (New York, 2010). The promotional blurb for the book read: "Americans call the Second World War 'The Good War.' But before it even began, America's wartime ally Joseph Stalin had killed millions of his own citizens – and kept killing them during and after the war. Before Hitler was finally defeated, he had murdered

six million Jews and nearly as many other Europeans." Snyder wrote that
"Stalin allowed Hitler to begin a war" (p. xi).

197. Max Hastings, *All Hell Let Loose: The World At War, 1939–1945* (London,
2011), p. 675.

198. Antony Beevor, *The Second World War* (New York, 2012), p. 781.

199. In *All Hell Let Loose*, Hastings called Hitler's crimes against the Jews
"satanic," and concluded that "the Allied cause deserved to triumph"
(pp. 674, xix). In *The Second World War*, Beevor wrote "there can be no doubt
that Adolf Hitler was the chief architect of this new ... conflagration" (p. 10).

200. Understanding memory requires examining both the representations of the
past and the reactions to them. See Alon Confino, "Collective Memory and
Cultural History: Problems of Method," *American Historical Review*,
December 1997, pp. 1386–403.

201. German reviews also echoed the criticisms of Anglo-American reviewers. For a
representative response to Baker's *Human Smoke*, see Gustav Seibt,
"Menschen mögen Krieg," *Die Süddeutsche Zeitung*, March 3, 2009.
Buchanan's book was translated into German but was less widely reviewed.
One of the few to appear was Franziska Augstein, "Hitler? Harmlos!" *SZ*,
September 5, 2008.

202. Mark Kurlansky, Review of *Human Smoke, Los Angeles Times*, March 9,
2008. Peter Wilby, "The Last Excuse For The Iraq War Is Founded On A
Myth," *The Guardian*, April 25, 2008.

203. Sam Leith, "Were We any Better than the Nazis?" *Spectator*, April 26, 2008,
pp. 32–33. Colm Tóibín, "Their Vilest Hour," *New York Times*, March 23,
2008.

204. "How Good Was the Good War," *American Conservative*, July 14, 2008.

205. Eric Margolis, "Churchill's Great Mistake," *Toronto Sun*, November 16,
2008. www.torontosun.com/comment/columnists/eric_margolis/2008/11/16/
7427861-sun.html. Margolis's praise of Buchanan's book is partly explained
by the fact that he was a founding editor of Buchanan's *American Conservative*
magazine. See also Eric Margolis, "Don't Blame Hitler Alone for World War
II," September 7, 2009, www.ericmargolis.com/political_commentaries/dont-
blame-hitler-alone-for-world-war-ii.aspx.

206. See, for example, Mark Weber's essay by the same title on the website of the
Institute for Historical Review, www.ihr.org/news/weber_ww2_may08.html.
This essay also listed the studies of Baker, Davies, and MacDonogh as books
for "further reading." For reviews of Baker and MacDonogh, see the websites
of Stormfront, Codoh and Inconvenienthistory.com.

207. Anne Applebaum, "The Blog of War," *New Republic*, May 28, 2008,
pp. 41–44. Andrew Roberts, "Historical Method," *History Today*,
September 2008, p. 1. See Roberts's review, "Up in Smoke," *New Criterion*,
June, 2008. For similar claims about Baker's sloppy scholarship, see

Jeffrey Herf, "Nicholson Baker's Human Smoke," *Chicago Tribune*, March 29, 2008; David Cesarani, "Human Smoke, by Nicholson Baker," *The Independent*, April 25, 2008.

208. Christopher Hitchens, "A War Worth Fighting," *Newsweek*, June 23, 2008.

209. David Pryce-Jones, "Human Smoke by Nicholson Baker," *Commentary*, March, 2008; William Rubinstein, Review of *Human Smoke*, *History Today*, July 2008, p. 65.

210. Christopher Hitchens, "Just Give Peace a Chance?" *New Statesman*, May 19, 2008, pp. 54–55.

211. Jeffrey Record, Review of *Churchill, Hitler, and 'The Unnecessary War,'" Parameters*, Autumn, 2008, pp. 150–52.

212. Katha Pollitt, "Blowing Smoke," *The Nation*, April 3, 2008.

213. Jack Fischel, "Questioning the Good War," *Virginia Quarterly*, Summer 2008. www.vqronline.org/articles/2008/summer/fischel-human-smoke/.

214. Review of *The Myth of the Good War*, at www.historycooperative.org/ journals/llt/55/br_23.html. See also left-wing German historian Kurt Pätzold's review in *Junge Welt*, December 14, 2001.

215. Frederic Smoler called it splendid but "exasperating." Fredric Smoler, "How Good Was the Good War, Really?" *American Heritage*, November 27, 2006 www.americanheritage.com/events/articles/web/20061127-world-war-ii-howard-zinn-kamikaze-battle-midway-atomic-bomb-hiroshima-crimes.shtml. The book's complexity was praised by Antoine Capet: Review of Michael Bess's Choices Under Fire, http://hnn.us/roundup/entries/33697.html. R. Werner called it "murky" in *"Review of Choices Under Fire," Choice*, April, 2007. Left-leaning historian Robert Westbrook said it was "too timid" in its critique of the Good War. "Not So Good War," *Christian Century*, May 29, 2007, pp. 36–38.

216. There were a few exceptions, however, as certain reviewers faulted Ferguson for errors of fact and excesses of interpretation. Gerhard Weinberg said Ferguson's book was filled with "blatant errors" and "distort[ed]... the evidence to ... fit with his preconceptions." Gerhard L. Weinberg, "The War of the World," *The Historian*, Spring, 2008, pp. 188–90. See also Paul Johnson, "Niall's Saga," *National Review*, September 25, 2006, pp. 48–50 and Edward Luttwak, "The Variability of Violence," *Commentary*, March, 2007, pp. 74–76.

217. Simon Sebag Montefiore, "Century of Rubble," *New York Times*, November 12, 2006; Tristram Hunt, "Massy Ferguson," *The Guardian*, June 3, 2006, agreeing that the book "lacked a sustained polemical thrust." See also Rana Mitter, "A Post-Modern History?" *Times Higher Education Supplement*, June 30, 2006. Still others argued that while "Ferguson's arguments may be revisionist in some elusive sense ... they're hardly new." Peter Paterson, "The History of Celebrity," *Daily Mail*, July 22, 2006, p. 55.

218. Noel Malcolm, "Review of No Simple Victory," *Sunday Telegraph*, November 12, 2006, p. 44; Jan Morris, "All Trite on the Western Front," *The Observer*, December 3, 2006, p. 24.

219. "The Madness of Myths; Rewriting History," *The Economist*, November 11, 2006; Hew Strachan, "War by Numbers," *The Times*, November 19, 2006, p. 48. Strachan added that the book was "written in haste" and full of errors, a claim also made by Jan Morris, "All Trite on the Western Front," p. 24. Other critics likened Davies's thesis about Anglo-American ignorance of Stalin's evil to a "straw man." Philip H. Gordon, Review of "No Simple Victory," *Foreign Affairs*, March–April, 2007, p. 173. Piers Brendon, "Eyes on the East," *The Guardian*, November 11, 2006, p. 8. Brendon wrote that Davies "for the most part . . . labours the obvious."

220. Susan Rubin Suleiman, "Eastern Front," *New York Times*, September 9, 2007, p. 16.

221. Michael Burleigh, *Moral Combat: Good and Evil in World War II* (New York, 2011), pp. viii–xi. Burleigh concluded that "some patriotic myths are not only useful but true."

222. Avishai Margalit, *On Compromise and Rotten Compromises* (Princeton, NJ, 2009), p. 179.

223. Andrew Roberts, *The Storm of War: A New History of the Second World War* (New York, 2010); Mark Mazower, *Hitler's Empire: How the Nazis Ruled Europe* (New York, 2008); Richard Evans, *The Third Reich at War* (New York, 2008); Richard Bessel, *Germany, 1945: From War to Peace* (New York, 2010).

Chapter 2 From history to memory and back again: Debating the Holocaust's uniqueness

1. Donald Bloxham, *The Final Solution: A Genocide* (Oxford, 2010), p. 319.

2. Alon Confino, *Foundational Pasts: The Holocaust as Historical Understanding* (Cambridge, UK, 2012), p. 155, n. 25.

3. A. Dirk Moses, "The Fate of Blacks and Jews: A Response to Jeffrey Herf," *Journal of Genocide Research*, June, 2008, p. 271.

4. Dan Stone, *Histories of the Holocaust* (Oxford, 2010), p. 212.

5. Jürgen Matthäus, "The Precision of the Indefinite," *Journal of Genocide Research*, March–June 2011, p. 107.

6. Doris Bergen, "Challenging Uniqueness: Decentring and Recentring the Holocaust," *Journal of Genocide Research*, March–June, 2011, p. 107.

7. Already in the 1960s, David Ben-Gurion described the Holocaust as "a unique episode that has no equal." Quoted in Segev, *The Seventh Million*, p. 329.

8. For a more detailed discussion, see Gavriel D. Rosenfeld, "The Politics of Uniqueness: Reflections on the Recent Polemical Turn in Holocaust and Genocide Scholarship," *Holocaust and Genocide Studies*, 1, Spring 1999, pp. 28–61.

9. Definitions of uniqueness have been numerous since the concept's emergence. David B. MacDonald has identified fifteen different variations of the uniqueness claim in his book, *Identity Politics in the Age of Genocide: The Holocaust and Historical Representation* (London, 2008), chapter 2.

10. Yehuda Bauer claimed that "the uniqueness of the Holocaust" lay in "planned total annihilation . . . and the . . . apocalyptic ideology that motivated the murder." Yehuda Bauer, "Whose Holocaust?" *Midstream*, November 1980, p. 45.

11. Rosenfeld, "The Politics of Uniqueness," pp. 35–37.

12. Ibid., pp. 38–42.

13. Ibid., pp. 181, 184.

14. Ibid., p. 49.

15. David Stannard, "Uniqueness as Denial: The Politics of Genocide Scholarship," in Alan Rosenbaum, *Is the Holocaust Unique? Perspectives in Comparative Genocide* (Boulder, 1996), p. 198.

16. Ward Churchill, *A Little Matter of Genocide: Holocaust and Denial in the Americas, 1492 to the Present* (San Francisco, 1997), p. 64.

17. Norman Finkelstein, *The Holocaust Industry: Reflections on the Exploitation of Jewish Suffering* (London, 2000), p. 47. Finkelstein first attacked uniqueness in his book, co-written with Ruth Bettina Birn, *A Nation on Trial: The Goldhagen Thesis and Historical Truth* (New York, 1998).

18. Finkelstein, *The Holocaust Industry*, pp. 47–48.

19. Ibid., p. 47

20. Peter Novick, *The Holocaust in American Life* (Boston, 1999), pp. 9, 196–97.

21. Ibid., p. 198.

22. There was no similar critique of the Holocaust's uniqueness in Germany. As a result of the Historians' Debate of 1986, questioning the Holocaust's singularity was thoroughly discredited among German intellectual and political elites. See Maier, *The Unmasterable Past*.

23. Stéphane Courtois, et al., eds., *The Black Book of Communism: Crimes, Terror, Repression* (Cambridge, MA, 1999), p. 23.

24. Carolyn J. Dean, *Aversion and Erasure: The Fate of the Victim After the Holocaust* (Ithaca, 2010), p. 76.

25. Ibid., pp. 93–96.

26. Cited in Elhanan Yakira, *Post-Zionism, Post-Holocaust: Three Essays on Denial, Forgetting, and the Delegitimation of Israel* (Cambridge, UK, 2010), pp. 63, 64. These quotations appeared in Ophir's book, *The Worship of the*

Present: Essays on an Israeli Culture for our Time, which was originally published in Hebrew in 2001.

27. Alvin H. Rosenfeld, "The Assault on Holocaust Memory," *American Jewish Year Book*, 2001, pp. 5–6.

28. On the responses to Stannard and Churchill, see Rosenfeld, "The Politics of Uniqueness," p. 42. See also Omer Bartov, "A Tale of Two Holocausts," *New York Times*, August 6, 2000; Michael Berenbaum, "Is the Memory of the Holocaust Being Exploited?" *Midstream*, April, 2004, pp. 2–8. Michiko Kakutani accused Novick of "deliberate cynicism" in its treatment of Holocaust memory in "Vexing New Book," *New York Times*, August 17, 1999. Paul Bogdanor said Finkelstein's book "systematically falsifies quotes and references," in "The Finkelstein Phenomenon," *Judaism*, Fall, 2002, p. 505; David Roskies, "Group Memory," *Commentary*, September, 1999, pp. 62–65. Notably, Novick himself criticized Finkelstein's book, calling it the "hateful tirade of a fanatic," in "Finkelstein hat meine Arbeit ausgebeutet," *Die Welt*, February 8, 2001, p. 30. Finkelstein's reception in Germany is discussed in Ernst Piper, ed., *Gibt es wirklich eine Holocaust-Industrie? Zur Auseinandersetzung um Norman Finkelstein* (Zurich, 2001). For an Israeli perspective, see "The Finkelstein Polemic," *Ha'aretz Magazine*, March 30, 2001. Positive reviews appeared as well. See Jon Wiener, "Holocaust Creationism," *The Nation*, July 12, 1999 and Lilian Friedberg, "Dare to Compare: Americanizing the Holocaust," *American Indian Quarterly*, 24:3, Summer 2000, p. 356.

29. For the most sustained critique of the French responses, see Dean, *Aversion and Erasure*, chapter 2. Martin Malia discusses the background to the French debate in the preface to the *Black Book of Communism*. Omer Bartov points out some of the main contributions to the debate in his essay, "Extreme Opinions," *Kritika: Explorations in Russian and Eurasian History*, 3:2, Spring 2002, pp. 296–97.

30. Kurt Jonassohn cited Churchill's "biased ... use of sources" in his review in *The American Historical Review*, June, 1999, pp. 867–68. Paul Bogdanor compared Churchill and Stannard to Holocaust deniers in 2004, www.paulbogdanor.com/antisemitism/wardchurchill.html. Oren Baruch Stier called Finkelstein's argument "cynical" in "Holocaust, American Style," *Prooftexts*, 22:3, Fall 2002, p. 387. Tobias Abse said Finkelstein's book resembled a "neo-Nazi tract" and indulged in "anti-Semitic stereotyping" in "Finkelstein's Follies: The Dangers of Vulgar Anti-Zionism," *New Interventions*, 2, 2000. See also Yair Sheleg, "The Finkelstein Polemic," *Ha'aretz Magazine*, March 30, 2001. Neo-Nazi websites praised the Holocaust Industry. See www.codoh.com/revisionist/review/tro5holoind.html.

31. One important exception was John Connelly's essay, "Nazis and Slavs: From Racial Theory to Racist Practice," *Central European History*, 1, 1999, pp. 1–33.

See also Guenter Lewy, "Were American Indians the Victims of Genocide?" *Commentary*, September, 2004, pp. 55–63.

32. "From the Editor: A Reply to Fackenheim," *Journal of Genocide Research*, 2000, 2, p. 9.

33. Berel Lang, "On Peter Novick's *The Holocaust in American Life*," *Jewish Social Studies*, Spring/Summer 2001, pp. 151–52. Similarly, Tony Judt observed that Novick provided no measure of "how much Holocaust awareness . . . is appropriate and in what form?" "The Morbid Truth," *New Republic*, July 19–26, 1999, pp. 36–40. Hillel Levine said that Novick had argued his case "without presenting much evidence" in "The Decline of the Incredible," *New Leader*, June 14, 1999, pp. 23–25. See also Bogdanor, "The Finkelstein Phenomenon," p. 506.

34. Gavriel D. Rosenfeld, "A Looming Crash or a Soft Landing?"

35. A. Dirk Moses, "Conceptual Blockages and Definitional Dilemmas in the 'Racial Century': Genocides of Indigenous Peoples and the Holocaust," *Patterns of Prejudice*, 4, 2002, pp. 7–36.

36. Ibid., pp. 10, 18.

37. Ibid., p. 18.

38. Ibid., pp. 22–27.

39. Ibid., p. 28.

40. Ibid., p. 33.

41. Ibid., p. 36.

42. Ben Kiernan, *Blood and Soil: A World History of Genocide and Extermination from Sparta to Darfur* (New Haven, 2007); Michael Mann, *The Dark Side of Democracy: Explaining Ethnic Cleansing* (Cambridge, UK, 2004); Adam Jones, *Genocide: A Comprehensive Introduction* (New York, 2007); Eric Weitz, *A Century of Genocide: Utopias of Race and Nation* (Princeton, NJ, 2005); Martin Shaw, *What is Genocide?* (Cambridge, UK, 2007); William D. Rubinstein, *Genocide: A History* (Harlow, UK, 2004); A. Dirk Moses, ed., *Genocide and Settler Society: Frontier Violence and Stolen Indigenous Children in Australian History* (New York, 2004); A. Dirk Moses and Dan Stone, eds., *Colonialism and Genocide* (London, 2006).

43. In his book, *Genocide*, Jones rejected the idea that the Holocaust was "uniquely unique" (pp. 162–63). In *A Century of Genocide*, Weitz said that the Holocaust was unprecedented but not unique (p. 12). In *What is Genocide*, Shaw spent a few pages critiquing uniqueness but devoted the majority of his analysis to establishing a "general framework" for discussing genocide instead of doing "case-to-case comparisons" (p. 39). In *Genocide*, Rubinstein avoided taking a stand on the question of the Holocaust's uniqueness, noting merely that the event highlighted the difficulty of defining genocide (pp. 1–2). Other scholars showed greater support for uniqueness, but mostly in passing. In *The Dark Side of Democracy*, Mann wrote that "The Final Solution was the most single-

minded attempt at genocide the world has ever seen" (p. 188). Kiernan in *Blood and Soil* said the Holocaust "has no parallel before or since" (p. 454).

44. Shaw, p. 46.
45. Samantha Power, "To *Suffer* by Comparison?" *Daedalus*, 2, Spring 1999, pp. 31–66.
46. Ibid., p. 32.
47. Ibid., pp. 50–51.
48. Ibid., p. 52.
49. Ibid., p. 32.
50. Ibid., pp. 57–58.
51. Ibid., p. 61.
52. Ibid., p. 61.
53. Alan Steinweis, "The Auschwitz Analogy: Holocaust Memory and American Debates over Intervention in Bosnia and Kosovo in the 1990s," *Holocaust and Genocide Studies*, Fall, 2005, pp. 276–89.
54. Ibid., pp. 282–83.
55. Michael Berenbaum argued that "'just because Kosovo is neither Warsaw nor Auschwitz does not free us from an obligation to respond.'" Ibid., p. 284.
56. Ibid., pp. 284–85
57. Ibid., p. 286.
58. John Torpey, "Making Whole What Has Been Smashed: Reflections on Reparations," *The Journal of Modern History*, June 2001, pp. 333–58.
59. Ibid., p. 337.
60. Ibid., p. 341.
61. Ibid., pp. 337–38.
62. Ibid., pp. 337–38.
63. Ibid., p. 338.
64. Ibid., p. 341.
65. Ibid., p. 341.
66. Daniel Levy and Natan Sznaider, *The Holocaust and Memory in the Global Age* (Philadelphia, 2006). For an earlier articulation of their ideas, see Daniel Levy and Natan Sznaider, "Memory Unbound: The Holocaust and the Formation of Cosmopolitan Memory," *European Journal of Social Theory* 5:1, 2002, pp. 87–106.
67. Levy and Sznaider, *The Holocaust and Memory in the Global Age*, pp. 18, 4.
68. Ibid., pp. 165–79.
69. For example, they pointed out how American Jews' embrace of uniqueness during the Vietnam War led them to reject claims that the US government's policies were genocidal. Ibid., p. 115.
70. Ibid., p. 18.

71. William F. S. Miles, "Third World Views of the Holocaust," *Journal of Genocide Research*, September 2004, pp. 371–93.

72. Ibid., pp. 371, 379.

73. Ibid., pp. 380, 381.

74. Ibid., p. 389.

75. Ibid., p. 386.

76. Michael Rothberg, *Multidirectional Memory: Remembering the Holocaust in the Age of Decolonization* (Palo Alto, CA, 2009).

77. Ibid., pp. 179. 11. Rothberg opposed uniqueness because it created a "hierarchy of suffering" (p. 9).

78. Ibid., p. 6.

79. Rothberg cited Jean Rouch and Edgar Morin's film, *Chronicle of a Summer* (1961), Marguerite Duras' essay, "Two Ghettos" (1961), and media coverage of the October 17, 1961 massacre of Algerian demonstrators in Paris as advancing comparisons between the Algerian crisis and the Holocaust.

80. Ibid., p. 244.

81. Jeffrey Alexander, *Remembering the Holocaust: A Debate* (Oxford, 2009).

82. Ibid., n. 57, pp. 85–88.

83. Ibid., pp. 3, 35.

84. Ibid., pp. 49, 52.

85. Ibid., pp. 58–59.

86. Mark Levene stressed that while the idea of uniqueness had become a "yardstick for . . . evil," it was used in such a way to discourage comparisons to other episodes of genocide: *Genocide in the Age of the Nation State: The Meaning of Genocide* (London, 2005), p. 2. Martin Shaw in *What is Genocide?* complained about the "debilitating effect of the Holocaust paradigm," which "narrow[ed] genocide to killing" (p. 46).

87. For examples, see Avraham Burg, *The Holocaust Is Over; We Must Rise From its Ashes* (New York, 2008), pp. 56–57. Israeli politicians have dwelled on the threat that Iran poses to Israel in terms of the Holocaust: Jones, *Genocide*, p. 253. For a recent example, see "By Conjuring the Holocaust, Netanyahu Brought Israel Closer to War with Iran," *Haaretz*, March 6, 2012.

88. Tony Judt, "The Morbid Truth," *New Republic*, July 19–26, 1999, p. 39.

89. Ibid., p. 40.

90. Tony Judt, "Goodby to All That," *The Nation*, January 3, 2005.

91. Tony Judt, "The 'Problem of Evil' in Postwar Europe," *New York Review of Books*, February 14, 2009.

92. Alexander, *Remembering the Holocaust*, p. 177. He was partly responding to criticisms by Robert Manne and Bernard Giesen in the same volume.

93. Ibid..

94. Ibid., p. 185.

95. Ibid., pp. 177–78.

96. Dan Stone, "Beyond the Auschwitz Syndrome: Holocaust Historiography after the Cold War," *Patterns of Prejudice*, 44:5, 2010, p. 466. A subset of this larger effort was the debate among German historians about the extent to which the Holocaust's roots should be seen as an example of colonial genocide – specifically Imperial Germany's colonial crimes in German Southwest Africa in the early 1900s. The debate between supporters of this claim, such as Jürgen Zimmerer, and critics is recounted in Dan Stone, *Histories of the Holocaust*, pp. 222–24. I do not discuss this debate in the current chapter as it does not explicitly engage the question of the Holocaust's uniqueness.

97. Donald Bloxham, *The Final Solution*. Bloxham made an earlier attempt to historicize the Holocaust in his co-written volume with Tony Kushner, *The Holocaust: Critical Historical Approaches* (Manchester, 2005). Interestingly, like Judt and Alexander, Bloxham and Kushner were originally more sympathetic to the idea of uniqueness, writing that "the early scholarship of exceptionalism did have clear merit," for "in a world which ... tended to subsume the Jewish fate within the larger tragedy of war," it "performed the valuable historical ... service of differentiating Nazi racial policies." "Had that not been done, it would be the duty of present-day historians of the period to do it. The Jews had a paramount ... place in Nazi ideology and the relentlessness of the 'final solution' when it was under way was unquestionably greater than in other Nazi programmes" (p. 83).

98. Bloxham, *The Final Solution*, p. 33.

99. Bloxham described these forces as "borderless high finance, international minority 'protection,' and the great powers' arbitration of borders" following military conflicts. Ibid., p. 332.

100. Ibid., pp. 78–91.

101. Ibid., p. 130.

102. Ibid., pp. 316–17.

103. Ibid., p. 218. He said that the expansion of genocide was determined just as much by "contingent" factors as anti-Semitic ideological intent. Ibid., p. 317.

104. Ibid., pp. 330–31.

105. Ibid., p. 221.

106. Ibid., pp. 221–22.

107. Ibid., p. 180.

108. Ibid., p. 181.

109. Ibid., p. 187.

110. Ibid., pp. 241, 237.

111. Ibid., p. 188.

112. Ibid., pp. 244–45.

113. Ibid., pp. 252–53.

114. Ibid., p. 316.

115. Ibid., p. 318.
116. Ibid., p. 318.
117. Ibid., p. 318.
118. Timothy Snyder, *Bloodlands*.
119. Ibid., p. xiv.
120. Ibid., p. 380.
121. Ibid., p. viii.
122. Ibid., pp. xiv, 383. Snyder noted that only 1% of Soviet Jewish deaths and 7% of Polish Jewish deaths were at Auschwitz.
123. Ibid., p. 383. Snyder further claimed that the use of poison gas was hardly modern and dated back to antiquity. Snyder, p. xv.
124. Ibid., p. 406.
125. Ibid., pp. 86–87, 111.
126. Ibid., p. 411.
127. Ibid., p. 111.
128. Snyder referred to the "scapegoating of Poles for Soviet policy failures." Ibid., p. 91.
129. Ibid., p. ix.
130. Ibid., pp. 187, 214–16.
131. Ibid., p. 215.
132. Ibid., p. 388.
133. Ibid., p. 392.
134. Ibid., p. 240.
135. Ibid., pp. 331–32, 405.
136. Ibid., p. 402.
137. Ibid., p. 407.
138. Among the more favorable reviews were the contributions of Matthäus and Shaw in the *Journal of Genocide Research*, March–June 2011, pp. 107–20. See also Larry Eugene Jones, Review of *The Final Solution*, in *English Historical Review*, June 2010, p. 776; David Cesarani, Review of *The Final Solution*, in *History Today*, April 2010, p. 56; Eric Ehrenreich, Review of *The Final Solution*, in *The American Historical Review*, October 2010, p. 1244. Mark Mazower called Bloxham's book "thought-provoking," in "God's Grief," *TLS*, September 17, 2010; Jutta Helm, Review of *The Final Solution*, in *German Politics and Society*, Winter 2010, p. 109.
139. While Cesarani affirmed that Bloxham "successfully undermines the ground for claiming the Holocaust as 'unique' ... he re-fights an old battle and many of his targets are hardly representative of historical scholarship today." Eric Ehrenreich wrote that, while Bloxham was "successful at demonstrating similarities" between the Holocaust and other genocides, "he does not adequately explain differences," such as the reason why the Nazis decided to kill the Jews,

despite the fact that "no actual ethnic conflict [existed] between the primary perpetrators and the victims."

140. Bergen, "Challenging Uniqueness: Decentring and Recentring the Holocaust," p. 129.

141. Ibid., p. 134.

142. Ibid., p. 134.

143. Omer Bartov, "Locating the Holocaust," *Journal of Genocide Research*, March–June, 2011, pp. 123, 127.

144. Ibid., p. 127.

145. Omer Bartov, "Genocide and the Holocaust: What Are We Arguing About?" reprinted in Uffa Jenesen et al., eds., *Gewalt und Gesellschaft: Klassiker modernen Denkens neu gelesen* (Göttingen, 2011), pp. 382, 392. Bartov's line of reasoning also took issue with the work of Dirk Moses and Mark Mazower.

146. Donald Bloxham, "Response – Discussing Genocide: Two Moralities and Some Obstacles," *Journal of Genocide Research*, March–June, 2011, p. 138.

147. Ibid., pp. 138, 143.

148. Ibid., p. 137.

149. Ibid., p. 140.

150. Ibid., p. 143.

151. Ibid., pp. 147–48.

152. Ibid., p. 148. Dirk Moses agreed that Bartov overreacted in insinuating that those who viewed the Holocaust within the context of colonialism necessarily supported "casting Israel as a settler colonial purveyor of genocide" in "Revisiting a Founding Assumption of Genocide Studies," *Genocide Studies and Prevention*, December, 2011, p. 293.

153. Ibid., p. 293.

154. Ibid., p. 290.

155. Ibid., pp. 291–92.

156. Ibid., p. 297.

157. Ibid., p. 298.

158. Ibid., p. 299.

159. A. Dirk Moses, "Paranoia and Partisanship: Genocide Studies, Holocaust Historiography, and the 'Apocalyptic Conjuncture,'" *The Historical Journal*, 2, 2011, pp. 553–83.

160. Ibid., p. 554.

161. Ibid., p. 555.

162. Ibid., p. 572.

163. Ibid., pp. 573–74.

164. Ibid., p. 574.

165. A. Dirk Moses, "Genocide and the Terror of History," *Parallax*, 4, 2011.

166. Ibid., p. 91.

167. Ibid., p. 93.

168. Ibid., pp. 95–96
169. Ibid., p. 96.
170. Ibid., p. 102.
171. Ibid., p. 103.
172. Ibid., p. 104.
173. *The Economist* called Snyder's book "gripping," "History and its Woes," *The Economist*, October 14, 2010. Andrew Moravcsik called it "magisterial" in *Foreign Affairs*, January/February 2011. "Shattering" was the description of Istvan Deak, in "The Charnel Continent," *New Republic*, December 2, 2010. Anne Applebaum called it "brave and original," in "The Worst of the Madness," *New York Review of Books*, November 11, 2010, p. 8. Christopher Browning called it a "major contribution" in the H-Diplo Roundtable Discussion of *Bloodlands*, 1, 2011. For a full listing of reviews see www.yale.edu/history/faculty/snyder-book-reviews.html.
174. See www.yale.edu/history/faculty/snyder-book-reviews.html.
175. A good example of this balanced approach was Samuel Moyn, "Between Hitler and Stalin," *The Nation*, November 17, 2010. Moyn wrote that the book "may not add up to a comprehensive explanation [of the Holocaust]," but was "a remarkable accomplishment" all the same.
176. Mark Roseman, "Bloodlines," *Journal of Genocide Research*, September 2011, p. 326; Omer Bartov, Review of *Bloodlands* in *Slavic Review*, Summer 2011, p. 425. Anne Applebaum wrote "scholars will find nothing in *Bloodlands* that is startlingly new," in "The Worst of the Madness," p. 10. See also Mark Mazower, "Timothy Snyder's *Bloodlands*," *Contemporary European History*, 21.2, 2012, p. 121.
177. James Sheehan, "Europe's Darkest Hours," *Commonweal*, February 25, 2011 and Richard Evans, "Who Remembers the Poles?" *London Review of Books*, November 4, 2010, p. 22. Zuroff called the bloodlands "an artificial geographical entity," in "The Equivalency Canard," p. 1. Bartov wrote that the bloodlands "lack any historical existence" in his review of *Bloodlands*, p. 425. Connelly agreed that the location of the killing mattered little for explaining it ideologically, in "Gentle Revisionism," *Journal of Genocide Research*, September 2011, p. 316. Roseman added in his review that Snyder's focus was too regional and omitted continental ambitions of policy (p. 325).
178. Jürgen Zarusky, "Timothy Snyders 'Bloodlands,'" *Vierteljahreshefte für Zeitgeschichte*, 1, 2012, pp. 27–28. For example, Snyder ignored the links between the Ukrainian famine of 1932–33 and famines that occurred elsewhere in the Soviet Union outside the bloodlands (28); the impact of World War II combat on the Russian population living outside of the bloodlands (23–25); and the reach of Stalinist terror "into the tiniest corner of the Soviet Union" (11).
179. Evans, "Who Remembers the Poles?" p. 22.

180. Dan Diner, "Topography of Interpretation: Reviewing Timothy Snyder's *Bloodlands*," *Contemporary European History*, 21.2, 2012, pp. 129–30.

181. Efraim Zuroff, "The Equivalency Canard," *Haaretz Books*, May 2011, p. 4.

182. Dovid Katz, "Why Red Is Not Brown in the Baltics," *The Guardian*, September 30, 2010, http://www.guardian.co.uk/commentisfree/cifamerica/2010/sep/30/baltic-nazi-soviet-snyder.

183. Felix Wemheuer, "Nolte Mortale," *Jungle World*, December 1, 2011. http://jungle-world.com/artikel/2011/48/44446.html. As Omer Bartov noted in his review of *Bloodlands* in *Slavic Review*, "Nazi rule would have been even more destructive of nations and cultures and would have likely made impossible the revival of Eastern Europe … after the fall of communism." Yehuda Bauer made a similar point even before the appearance of Snyder's book in "Remembering Accurately on International Holocaust Remembrance Day," *Jerusalem Post*, January 25, 2010.

184. Katz, "Why Red Is Not Brown in the Baltics."

185. Zuroff, "The Equivalency Canard," p. 4.

186. See also Jonathan Freedland, "I See Why 'Double Genocide' Is a Term Lithuanians Want. But it Appalls Me," *The Guardian*, September 14, 2010.

187. Bartov, Review of *Bloodlands*, p. 428.

188. Katz, "Why Red Is Not Brown in the Baltics."

189. Zuroff, "The Equivalency Canard," p. 4.

190. Bloxham, "Response," p. 146.

191. Bartov, "Genocide and the Holocaust," p. 128.

192. Near the conclusion of his book, *Hitler's Empire: How the Nazis Ruled Europe*, Mazower saw the legacy of Nazi ethnic cleansing and demographic engineering policies manifesting itself in "ethnic expulsion in Palestine and the establishment of a Jewish national state there" (p. 597). He also linked postwar Israeli settlement strategies to the planning ideas of SS theorists, who had helped draft Himmler's *Generalplan Ost* colonization plan (p. 599).

193. Bloxham, "Response," p. 147.

194. Bergen, "Challenging Uniqueness: Decentring and Recentring the Holocaust," p. 131.

195. Moses, "Paranoia and Partisanship," p. 583.

196. It was also made in response to Jeffrey Herf. See A. Dirk Moses, "The Fate of Blacks and Jews: A Response to Jeffrey Herf," *Journal of Genocide Research*, June, 2008, pp. 269–87.

197. Moses, "Genocide and the Terror of History," p. 24.

198. Yosef Yerushalmi, *Zakhor: Jewish History and Jewish Memory* (Seattle, 1982).

199. Moses, "Paranoia and Partisanship," p. 576. The "material conditions of political paranoia" include "foreign occupation and social decay."

200. Connelly, "Gentle Revisionism."
201. Browning, H-Diplo Roundtable Discussion of *Bloodlands*, 1, 2011, p.11.
202. James Kirchick, "The Butchery of Hitler and Stalin," *Policy Review*, June 1, 2011, www.hoover.org/publications/policy-review/article/80201; Adam Kirsch, "Devastated," *Tablet*, November 30, 2010, www.tabletmag.com/arts-and-culture/books/51671/devastated/
203. He told this to *Der Spiegel*. Klaus Wiegrefe, "Ein Apparat effizienten Tötens," *Der Spiegel*, July 11, 2011. Timothy Snyder, "The Fatal Fact of the Nazi-Soviet Pact," *The Guardian*, October 5, 2010, www.guardian.co.uk/commentisfree/cifamerica/2010/oct/05/holocaust-secondworldwar/print
204. Some scholars addressed this point, but without addressing its relevance for uniqueness. Evans, for example, in "Who Remembers the Poles?" said Snyder's claim that the Holocaust arose out of "Hitler's rage and frustration at not being able to win the war against the Soviet Union does not stand up to scrutiny." Evans, "Who Remembers the Poles?" pp. 21–22. In "Europe's Darkest Hours," Sheehan also rejected the "argument that the murder of Europe's Jews was a substitute for military victory, a proposition for which there seems little evidence."
205. See Snyder, *Bloodlands*, pp. 207–09.
206. Peter Longerich also made this point in his major study, *Holocaust: The Nazi Persecution and Murder of the Jews*. Longerich's key idea of Nazi *Judenpolitik* posited that the Nazis always envisioned realizing their goal of a racial utopia via "the . . . elimination of the Jews" (p. 4). He added that the so-called "territorial solution" for the Jewish question, involving expulsion, "was . . . always conceived as a 'final solution,' because . . . its goal was the annihilation of the vast majority of the Jews." Before World War II even started, therefore, "those involved in *Judenpolitik* began to gear themselves up for the extermination of the European Jews" (p. 424). See also Dan Stone, *Histories of the Holocaust*, p. 67 and, generally, Alon Confino, *Foundational Pasts*.
207. Snyder, *Bloodlands*, pp. 187, 263.
208. Connelly is one of the few scholars to note the contradiction between viewing the Holocaust as a substitute victory and an end in itself. Connelly, "Gentle Revisionism," p. 317.
209. Snyder, *Bloodlands*, p. 33.
210. Ibid., pp. 84–85.
211. The Jews of Hungary represent an exception to this pattern, as they were numerically large, but also did not occupy space claimed by the Nazis for their colonization scheme.
212. Snyder, *Bloodlands*, p. ix.

213. Jewish scholars have long feared that challenges to the Holocaust's uniqueness may reflect anti-Semitic motives. In "Whose Holocaust?" Yehuda Bauer surmised that, because the Holocaust "created a pro-Jewish reaction among large numbers of non-Jews . . .[a] reversion back to 'normalcy' regarding Jews requires the destruction of the Holocaust-caused attitude of sympathy . . . This is achieved by claiming that the Holocaust was not really something unique, but rather something that happened to many millions of others . . . the Holocaust then becomes . . . flattened out, a meaningless term, and a 'normal' attitude of anti-Jewishness becomes possible again" (p. 45).

214. Her statement referred blandly to "the victims of the Holocaust [who were] . . . brutally murdered in the darkest period of European history," and it generically attributed their fate to "prejudice and racism" instead of anti-Semitism: "Ashton's Lapse," *Jerusalem Post*, January 29, 2014, www. jpost.com/Opinion/Editorials/Ashtons-lapse-339781.In response, the *Post* accused Ashton of "robbing the Holocaust of its uniqueness" and universalizing its significance in order to appease Europe's Muslims, who "chafe . . . against Holocaust commemoration lest it even theoretically imply sympathy for Jews."

215. "Progressive Kristallnacht Coming?" *Wall Street Journal*, January 24, 2014, http://online.wsj.com/news/articles/ SB10001424052702304549504579316913982034286.

216. Jodi Rudoren, "Israel's Efforts to Limit Use of Holocaust Terms Raise Free-Speech Questions," *New York Times*, January 15, 2014.

Chapter 3 Probing the limits of speculation: Counterfactualism and the Holocaust

1. Milton Himmelfarb, "No Hitler, No Holocaust," *Commentary*, March 1984, pp. 37–43.

2. Henry Turner, "Hitler's Impact on History," in David Wetzel, ed., *From the Berlin Museum to the Berlin Wall: Essays on the Cultural and Political History of Modern Germany* (Westport, CT, 1996), p. 118.

3. Quoted in Michael Shermer and Alex Grobman, *Denying History: Who Says the Holocaust Never Happened and Why Do They Say It?* (Berkeley, 2009), p. 49.

4. E. H. Carr dismissed "what ifs" as little more than a "parlour game"; E. P. Thompson referred to them as "'*Geschichtswissenschlopf*, unhistorical shit." Quoted in Niall Ferguson, ed., *Virtual History: Alternatives and Counterfactuals* (New York, 1999). For Evans's critiques, see Richard Evans, "Telling It Like It Wasn't," in Donald A. Yerxa, ed., *Recent Themes in Historical Thinking: Historians in Conversation* (Columbia, SC, 2008), pp. 77–84. See also Richard Evans, *Altered Pasts: Counterfactuals in History* (Waltham, MA, 2014).

5. For an extended definition of counterfactuals, see Richard Ned Lebow, *Forbidden Fruit: Counterfactuals and International Relations* (Princeton, NJ, 2010), chapter 2.

6. To be sure, historians have never entirely rejected "what if" premises in their work. As Johan Huizinga put it, "the historian ... must always maintain ... an indeterminist point of view ...[and consider] different outcomes. If he writes of Salamis, then it must be as if the Persians still might win." Quoted in John Lukacs, *The Legacy of the Second World War* (New Haven, 2010), p. 14.

7. For a full discussion of these and other factors, see Rosenfeld, *The World Hitler Never Made*, pp. 6–10.

8. In addition to Lebow's *Forbidden Fruit* and Ferguson's *Virtual History*, see Robert Cowley's edited volumes, *What If? The World's Foremost Military Historians Imagine What Might Have Been* (New York, 1999), *What If? 2: Eminent Historians Imagine What Might Have Been* (New York, 2001), and *What Ifs? of American History* (New York, 2003). See also, Alexander Demandt, *History That Never Happened: A Treatise on the Question, What Would Have Happened If ...?* (Jefferson, NC, 1993); Karen Hellekson, *The Alternate History: Refiguring Historical Time* (Kent, OH, 2001); Philip E. Tetlock, Richard Ned Lebow, and Geoffrey Parker, eds., *Unmaking the West: 'What-If?' Scenarios That Rewrite World History* (Ann Arbor, MI, 2006); Johannes Bulhof, "What If? Modality and History," *History and Theory*, 2, 1999, pp. 145–68.

9. Richard Ned Lebow, "Counterfactuals, History and Fiction," in *Historical Social Research*, 2, 2009, p. 57.

10. Occasionally, counterfactual histories portray the historical record turning out more or less the same. Tetlock and Parker refer these instances as "reversionary counterfactuals" in *Unmaking the West*, p. 19.

11. Fantasies tend to be liberal, for by imagining a better past, they offer an indictment of the present and express the desire to change it. Nightmares, by contrast, tend to be conservative, for by portraying the alternate past in negative terms, they ratify the present as the best of all possible worlds and discourage the need for change. These political implications are not ironclad, however, and should not be viewed deterministically. Nightmare scenarios can be also used for the liberal purpose of critique, while fantasy scenarios can express conservative dissatisfaction with the present.

12. As is discussed below, however, counterfactual premises can just as easily be used to defend orthodox perspectives.

13. In the United States, the most popular include the American Revolution and the Civil War. On the American Revolution, see the classic works by Robert Sobel, *For Want of a Nail: If Burgoyne Had Won at Saratoga* (Greenhill Books, 1997) and Richard Dreyfuss and Harry Turtledove, *The Two Georges* (New York, 1996). On the Civil War, see Ward Moore, *Bring the Jubilee*

(New York, 1953) and MacKinlay Kantor, "If the South Had Won the Civil War," *Look Magazine*, November 22, 1960, pp. 30–62.

14. In *Roads to Extinction: Essays on the Holocaust* (New York, 1980), Philip Friedman preferred historical description over judgment, which he said had to be postponed until the completion of further research (pp. 379, 564–65). In his famous study, *Theory and Practice of Hell* (New York, 1964), Eugen Kogon made one short counterfactual remark, speculating that "there can be little doubt that had Germany won the war Himmler would have succeeded in ... creating a durable ... network ... that would have held Germany and Europe in its firm grip" (p. 28). In his book, *The Final Solution* (London, 1953), Gerald Reitlinger cited the Nazis' difficulty in deporting Dutch Jews living in mixed marriages to hypothesize that "had Germany won the war, the climate would have been ... unfavourable for extending the Final Solution" (p. 179).
    Leon Poliakov's *Harvest of Hate: The Nazi Program for the Destruction of the Jews of Europe* (New York, 1951) and Raul Hilberg's *The Destruction of the European Jews* (New York, 1961) include a few scattered counterfactual assertions. But none of them stimulated any larger historiographical debates, in contrast to the use of counterfactuals in later works.

15. Poliakov, *Harvest of Hate*, p. 264.

16. Richard Ned Lebow, "Counterfactual Thought Experiments: A Necessary Teaching Tool," *The History Teacher*, February, 2007, www.historycooperative.org/journals/ht/40.2/lebow.html

17. Hannah Arendt, *Eichmann in Jerusalem: A Report on the Banality of Evil* (New York, 1963), p. 125.

18. In pursuing this goal, Arendt drew heavily on Raul Hilberg's critical portrayal of the *Judenräte* in *The Destruction of the European Jews*, which had been published two years earlier in 1961.

19. Arendt, *Eichmann in Jerusalem*, p. 124.

20. For a discussion, see Michael Marrus, "Eichmann in Jerusalem: Justice and History," in Steven Aschheim, ed., *Hannah Arendt in Jerusalem* (Berkeley, 2001), p. 205.

21. Lionel Abel, "The Aesthetics of Evil," *The Partisan Review*, Summer, 1963, pp. 212–13. Supporting this claim was Harold Weisberg, in "Arguments," *The Partisan Review*, Spring, 1964, p. 259.

22. Jacob Robinson viewed the position of Jewish leaders as "unutterably tragic" in *And the Crooked Shall Be Made Straight: The Eichmann Trial, the Jewish Catastrophe, and Hannah Arendt's Narrative* (New York, 1965), p. 226.

23. Ibid., p. 211.

24. Quoted in Michael Ezra, "The Eichmann Polemics: Hannah Arendt and Her Critics," *Democratiya* 9, Summer 2007, pp. 148, 153.

25. Ibid., p. 146.

26. Mary McCarthy, "The Hue and Cry," *The Partisan Review*, Winter, 1964, p. 86.

27. Dwight Macdonald, "Arguments," *The Partisan Review*, Spring, 1964, p. 269.

28. An important exception was Isaiah Trunk's 1972 study, *Judenrat: The Jewish Councils in Eastern Europe under Nazi Occupation*, which emphasized the Jews' minimal freedom of action with Nazi authorities. In this study, Trunk counterfactually defended the *Judenräte*'s stance of trying to keep Jews alive as long as possible, writing: "Had the war ended earlier, a sizable number of the labor elements [in the ghettos] might have survived . . . In August, 1944, when the Soviet armies had already reached . . .Warsaw, approximately 70,000 Jews still lived in Lodz . . . Had the Soviet army not stopped its advance till January 1945, a large number of these 70,000 people would certainly have escaped the gas chambers of Auschwitz" (p. 413). Similarly, Gerhard Weinberg has speculated that "had the German central front collapsed in January–February 1942, as it did in June–July 1944, a substantial portion of the ghetto inhabitants would have been liberated by the advancing Red Army": Gerhard Weinberg, "Two Separate Issues? Historiography of World War II and the Holocaust," in David Bankier and Dan Michman, eds., *Holocaust Historiography in Context: Emergence, Challenges, Polemics, and Achievements* (Jerusalem, 2008), p. 385. In *The War against Jews* (New York, 1976), Dawidowicz agreed that "even if the ghetto bureaucracies had been more efficient, they could not have halted the course of events that the Germans actuated" (p. 473).

29. Some of the more important studies were Karl-Dietrich Bracher, *The German Dictatorship* (New York, 1970); Martin Broszat, *The Hitler State* (London, 1981); Ralf Dahrendorf, *Society and Democracy in Germany* (New York, 1967); David Schoenbaum, *Hitler's Social Revolution: Class and Status in Nazi Germany, 1933–1939* (New York, 1967); Ernst Nolte, *Three Faces of Fascism* (New York, 1966).

30. Albert Speer, *Inside the Third Reich* (New York, 1970); Werner Maser, *Hitler* (New York, 1973); Joachim Fest, *Hitler* (New York, 1973). See also Peter Wyden, *The Hitler Virus: The Insidious Legacy of Adolf Hitler* (New York, 2001).

31. This belief was already accepted in earlier Holocaust studies, for example, in Poliakov's *Harvest of Hate*, which claimed "undoubtedly it was the master himself, Adolf Hitler, who signed the Jews' death warrant" (p. 108).

32. The functionalist claim that the Final Solution arose out of an unexpected situation in Nazi-occupied Soviet Union in late 1941 was rooted in a belief in the importance of contingency in historical events.

33. Himmelfarb, "No Hitler, No Holocaust," p. 37.

34. Henryk Grynberg, "Appropriating the Holocaust," *Commentary*, November, 1982; Hyam Maccoby, "Theologian of the Holocaust," *Commentary*, December, 1982, pp. 33–37.

35. Himmelfarb, "No Hitler, No Holocaust," pp. 37, 40, 43.

36. Ibid., pp. 40, 43.

37. Walter Laqueur, *A History of Zionism* (New York, 1972), p. 381; Fest, *Hitler*, p. 9. Lucy Dawidowicz in *A Holocaust Reader* (New York, 1976) agreed, noting that "without Adolf Hitler . . . the Final Solution would not have been planned . . . and carried to its irrevocable end" (p. 26).

38. Randolph L. Braham wrote, "In all probability, a Jewish Holocaust would not have happened in Germany at that time without Hitler": Randolph L. Braham, ed., *Perspectives on the Holocaust* (Houten, 1983), p. 20. Sebastian Haffner wrote, "After 1933, something like a Führer state would probably have come into being without Hitler. . .But not the murder of millions of Jews": *The Ailing Empire: Germany from Bismarck to Hitler* (New York, 1989), p. 216. Philippe Burrin argued, "If Hitler had died in the summer of 1941,. . .the final solution['s]. . .decisive thrust would probably have been absent": *Hitler and the Jews: The Genesis of the Holocaust* (New York, 1994), p. 150. Doris Bergen declared, "Without Hitler . . . World War II and the Holocaust would have taken very different forms, if they had occurred at all": *War and Genocide: A Concise History of the Holocaust* (Lanham, MD, 2009), p. 30. Inga Clendinnen observed, "had there been no Hitler, there would have been no Holocaust": *Reading the Holocaust* (Cambridge, UK, 2002), pp. 95, 111. Jonathan Frankel wrote, "had Hitler been killed, and not wounded, on October 7, 1916 . . . the Holocaust would almost certainly not have taken place": *The Fate of the European Jews, 1939–1945: Continuity or Contingency?* (New York, 1997), p. 27. Daniel Goldhagen insisted, "Without Hitler . . . there would have been no Holocaust": *Worse Than War: Genocide, Eliminationism, and the Ongoing Assault on Humanity* (New York, 2009), pp. 268–69. Richard L. Rubenstein and John K. Roth wrote, "Without Hitler, there would have been no Final Solution": *Approaches to Auschwitz: The Holocaust and its Legacy* (Atlanta, 1987), p. 194. William D. Rubinstein declared, "If Hitler had been assassinated . . . in 1933 . . . his successor . . . would soon have moderated the . . . murderously anti-semitic aspects of [Nazism]": *The Myth of Rescue: Why the Democracies Could Not Have Saved More Jews From the Nazis* (New York, 1997), p. 70. Henry Turner noted that "if Hitler had died in 1930 . . . the world would have been spared the Holocaust": "Hitler's Impact on History," in David Wetzel, ed., *From the Berlin Museum to the Berlin Wall*, pp. 115, 111–12. John Connelly wrote, "without Hitler there would have been no Holocaust": "Gentle Revisionism," *Journal of Genocide Research*, 13:3, 2011, p. 320.

39. Ian Kershaw, "Hitler and the Uniqueness of Nazism," *Journal of Contemporary History*, 2, 2004, p. 245.

40. Peter Longerich, *The Unwritten Order: Hitler's Role in the Final Solution* (Charleston, SC, 2001), p. 9.

41. Lucy Dawidowicz, "How They Teach the Holocaust," in Lucy Dawidowicz, ed., *What is the Use of Jewish History?* (New York, 1992), p. 71.

42. John Weiss, *Ideology of Death: Why the Holocaust Happened in Germany* (Chicago, 1997), pp. 389, 155.

43. Longerich, *The Unwritten Order*, p. 9.

44. Kershaw, *The Nazi Dictatorship*, p. 132.

45. Robert Paxton, *The Anatomy of Fascism* (New York, 2004), p. 158. Other scholars have counterfactually described the Holocaust being prevented by the absence of other factors. Zygmunt Bauman declared that "without modern civilization ... there would be no Holocaust," in *Modernity and the Holocaust* (New York, 1989), p. 87. John Roth wrote, "no Christianity ... equals no Holocaust," in *Holocaust Politics* (Atlanta, 2001), p. 191.

46. In 1943, the Bergson group ran an advertisement in various newspapers that read: "Is There Something You Could Have Done to Save Millions of Innocent People?" Cited in Deborah Lipstadt, *Beyond Belief: The American Press and the Coming of the Holocaust, 1933–1945* (New York, 1986), p. 224. Scholars have shown that many observers at the time recognized that the War Refugee Board could have saved more Jews if it had been created earlier: Arthur Morse, *While Six Million Died: A Chronicle of American Apathy* (New York, 1968), p. 383; Henry Feingold, *The Politics of Rescue: The Roosevelt Administration and the Holocaust, 1938–1945* (New York, 1970), p. 292.

47. Hilberg, *Destruction of the European Jews*, p. 671 (1961). Already in 1951, Poliakov argued that "the bombardment of the death factories ... would have thrown the entire extermination machine into confusion": *Harvest of Hate*, p. 261.

48. Morse wrote that "Allied indignation over ... Nazi brutality might have stimulated greater resistance ... within the Axis satellites ...[and] strengthened ... opposition ... in Germany": *While Six Million Died*, p. 338. Feingold speculated that the threat of Allied "retaliatory bombing" against Germany and its Allies "might have led more rational-minded leaders in the Nazi hierarchy to a re-evaluation of the Final Solution": *The Politics of Rescue*, pp. 320–21. In *The Terrible Secret: Suppression of the Truth about Hitler's "Final Solution"* (Boston, 1980), Laqueur argued that "some [Jews] could have been saved if Hitler's satellites had been threatened ... and many ... could ... have been saved in 1944 by bombing the railway lines leading to the extermination centres" (p. 208). In *Beyond Belief*, Lipstadt declared, "It is possible that Washington's behavior would have been different if the American public had demanded that this country not stand 'idly by' while innocent human beings were destroyed" (p. 2). In *American Jewry and the Holocaust: the American Jewish Joint Distribution Committee* (Detroit, 1981), Yehuda Bauer

criticized US immigration policies, noting that the filling of the quota for Jews in Germany, Austria, and Czechoslovakia "might have saved a considerable portion of [them]... between 1939 and 1941" (p. 50). More recently, Rafael Medoff's *FDR and the Holocaust: A Breach of Faith* (Washington, DC, 2013) repeated many of the same arguments originally advanced by Wyman.

49. David Wyman, *The Abandonment of the Jews: America and the Holocaust* (New York, 1984). See also David Wyman, *Paper Walls: America and the Refugee Crisis, 1938–1941* (New York, 1985).

50. Wyman, *The Abandonment of the Jews*, p. 304.

51. Ibid., p. 305.

52. Ibid., pp. 334–35.

53. The book appeared on the *New York Times* bestseller list and sold over 100,000 copies, www.jewishbookcenter.com/
abandonmentofthejewsamericaandtheholocaust1941-
1945paperbackbydavidswyman.aspx. Among the positive reviews: John Gross, Review of *The Abandonment of the Jews*, *New York Times*, November 23, 1984, p. C25, stated that "a great deal could have been done to save lives"; similarly, Leonard Dinnerstein praised the fact that "'if' predominates throughout ... the book" in *The Journal of American History*, 72:1, June 1985; see also Henry L. Feingold, *Annals of the American Academy of Political and Social Science*, July, 1980, p. 120 and Paul B. Miller, "David S. Wyman and the Controversy over the Bombing of Auschwitz," *Journal of Ecumenical Studies*, Fall 2003, pp. 370–80.

54. See, for example, John S. Conway, who said Wyman's steps for rescue were "wishful thinking": Review in *German Studies Review*, 8:2, May 1985, p. 356.

55. Rubinstein, *The Myth of Rescue*, pp. xxiv, xxvi, 180–81, 206, 210, 216. See also Robert Joseph White, "Target Auschwitz. Historical and Hypothetical German Responses to Allied Attack," *Holocaust and Genocide Studies*, 16:1, 2002, pp. 54–76.

56. This literature also deals with some of the decisions of Pius XII's predecessor, Pius XI, involving the 1937 encyclical, *Mit brennender Sorge*, and the "hidden" encyclical, *Humani Generis Unitas*, "the Unity of the Human Race."

57. Gunter Lewy, *The Catholic Church and Nazi Germany* (1964), p. 320. Similarly, in *The Silence of Pius XII* (Boston, 1970) Carlo Falconi argued that Pius XII could have released German Catholics from "national obedience" and donned the yellow star as a powerful gesture. Falconi, pp. 99–100. Unlike these two works, Saul Friedlander's *Pius XII and the Third Reich* (1966), adopted an empirical approach and avoided counterfactual musings. Rolf Hochhuth's famous play, *The Deputy* (1964) declared in its afterword: "who can ... claim that the Nazis would not have drawn back if during the war Pius had threatened them with the interdict?" (p. 298).

58. John Cornwell, *Hitler's Pope* (New York, 1999); Garry Wills, *Papal Sin: Structures of Deceit* (New York, 2001); Michael Phayer, *The Catholic Church and the Holocaust, 1930–1965* (Bloomington, IN, 2001); Susan Zuccotti, *Under His Very Windows: The Vatican and the Holocaust in Italy* (New Haven, 2002); Daniel J. Goldhagen, *A Moral Reckoning: The Role of the Catholic Church in the Holocaust and Its Unfulfilled Duty of Repair* (New York, 2002). Cornwell critiqued Pius's tentative Christmas 1942 speech against racism by saying "plain speaking might have made a difference" for Jews: *Hitler's Pope*, p. 268. Phayer speculated that "[if] Pius XI [had] lived five more years" or "if Angelo Roncalli [the later John XXIII] had been elected pope in 1939 instead of 1959," then "historians would have more words of praise and fewer words of regret for the history of the church during the Holocaust": *The Catholic Church and the Holocaust*, pp. xv, 224. Zuccotti wrote that "a public papal condemnation would have warned . . . Jews to hide and convinced more Christians to open their doors to them": Zuccotti, *Under His Very Windows*, pp. 97, 310. Goldhagen asked, "[if] Pius XII had instructed every bishop and priest across Europe. . .to declare in 1941 that. . .killing Jews is an unsurpassable transgression and mortal sin. . .[does] anyone really believe that many more Jews would not have been saved?": *A Moral Reckoning*, p. 55.

59. Phayer, *The Catholic Church and the Holocaust*, p. 110.

60. Michael O'Carroll, *Pius XII, Greatness Dishonored* (Chicago, 1980); Pierre Blet, *Pius XII and the Second World War* (Mahwah, NJ, 1999); Margherita Marchione, *Pope Pius XII: Architect for Peace* (New York, 2000); José M. Sanchez, *Pius XII and the Holocaust: Understanding the Controversy* (Washington, DC, 2002); David G. Dalin, *The Myth of Hitler's Pope: How Pope Pius XII Rescued Jews from the Nazis* (Washington, DC, 2005).

61. Dalin, *The Myth of Hitler's Pope*, p. 80.

62. Sanchez, *Pius XII and the Holocaust*, p. 177.

63. Pius himself was quoted as saying, "no doubt a protest would have gained me the praise and respect of the civilized world, but it would have submitted the poor Jews to an even worse fate." Quoted in Rychlak, *Hitler, the War, and the Pope* (Columbus, MS, 2000), p. 270.

64. Marchione, *Pope Pius XII*, pp. 21, 71.

65. J. P. Stern, *Hitler: The Führer and the People* (Berkeley, 1975), p. 104.

66. Nathan Stolzfus, *Resistance of the Heart: Intermarriage and the Rosenstrasse Protest in Nazi Germany* (New York, 1996), p. 248.

67. Goldhagen, *A Moral Reckoning*, p. 119.

68. Among other works, see: Tom Segev, *The Seventh Million*; Shlomo Aronson, *Hitler, the Allies, and the Jews* (Cambridge, UK, 2004); Saul S. Friedman, *No Haven for the Oppressed: United States Policy Toward Jewish Refugees, 1938–1945* (Detroit, 1973); Haskell Lookstein, *Were We Our Brothers' Keepers? The Public Response of American Jews to the Holocaust, 1938–1944*

(New York, 1985); Rafael Medoff, *The Deafening Silence: American Jewish Leaders and the Holocaust* (New York, 1986).

69. Yehuda Bauer, *Jews for Sale? Nazi-Jewish Negotiations, 1933–1945* (New Haven, 1994).

70. Ibid., p. 4.

71. Ibid., p. 255.

72. Ibid., p. 119.

73. Ibid., p. 260.

74. Michael Marrus, Carol Rittner and John K. Roth, eds., *Pope Pius XII and the Holocaust* (Leicester, 2002), p. 53

75. Studies such as Cornwell, *Hitler's Pope*, Garry Wills's *Papal Sin, Structures of Deceit* and James Carroll's *Constantine's Sword, The Church and the Jews* (New York, 2001) have all seen the present-day Papacy's postwar centralization of power as inspired by Pius XII's strong papal rule. For a response, see Philip Jenkins, *The New Anti-Catholicism: The Last Acceptable Prejudice* (Oxford, UK, 2003).

76. Rubinstein, *Myth of Rescue*, p. 5; Deborah Lipstadt, "The Failure to Rescue and Contemporary American Jewish Historiography of the Holocaust: Judging from a Distance," in Michael J. Neufeld and Michael Berenbaum, eds., *The Bombing of Auschwitz: Should the Allies Have Attempted It?* (Lawrence, KS, 2003), pp. 227–37; Laurence Zuckerman, "FDR's Jewish Problem," *The Nation*, July 17, 2003.

77. Phayer, *The Catholic Church and the Holocaust*, pp. 55, 94; Cornwell, *Hitler's Pope*, p. 287; Wills, *Papal Sin*, pp. 67–68; Goldhagen, *A Moral Reckoning*, p. 50. They have also shown that the Pope's defenders have vastly exaggerated the number of lives the Pope believed had been lost by the protest (40,000 is usually cited instead of "only" 92, including Edith Stein). Marchione, *Pope Pius XII*, claims this figure on p. 23.

78. Sanchez, *Pius XII and the Holocaust*, pp. 119, 177.

79. Ronald J. Rychlak, *Hitler, the War, and the Pope* (Columbus, MS, 2000), p. 272; Doris Bergen, "An Easy Target?" in Marrus, Rittner and Roth, eds., *Pope Pius XII and the Holocaust*, p. 109.

80. Steven T. Katz, "The 'Unique' Intentionality of the Holocaust," *Modern Judaism*, 1:2, 1981, p. 162.

81. Yehuda Bauer, *Rethinking the Holocaust* (New Haven, 2001), p. 49.

82. Rubinstein, *Genocide: A History*, p. 168.

83. On the case of England and the United States, see the works of Comer Clarke, Adrian Gilbert, Madeleine Bunting, and William Shirer, as discussed in Rosenfeld, *The World Hitler Never Made*, chapters 1 and 2.

84. Jeffrey Herf, *Nazi Propaganda for the Arab World* (New Haven, 2009), p. 138. David G. Dalin and John Rothmann, *Icon of Evil: Hitler's Mufti and the Rise of Radical Islam* (New York, 2008), features an entire chapter, "The Mufti's

Reflection: What If Germany Had Conquered Palestine and Britain?," that explores the scenario of the Holocaust transpiring in Palestine. See also Edwin Black, *Farhud: Roots of the Arab-Nazi Alliance in the Holocaust* (New York, 2010).

85. Klaus-Michael Mallmann and Martin Cüppers, *Nazi Palestine: The Plans for the Extermination of the Jews in Palestine* (New York, 2010), p. 125.

86. Ibid., p. 153.

87. Ibid., p. 163.

88. Significantly, not all scholars have used the topic for this purpose. Ben Kiernan's book, *Blood and Soil*, discussed the *Generalplan Ost* without stressing how a Nazi wartime victory might have affected the Slavs. Kiernan, chapter 11.

89. Poliakov, *Harvest of Hate*, p. 264.

90. Arendt, *Eichmann in Jerusalem*, p. 217. In 1958, the Polish scholar, Karol Marian Pospieszalski argued that "had the Nazis remained in power ... they might also have undertaken to annihilate the Poles." Quoted in Lucy S. Dawidowicz, *The Holocaust and the Historians* (Boston, 1981), p. 103. Not all scholars argued counterfactually, as was shown by Czesław Madajczyk's pioneering essay, "General Plan Ost," *Polish Western Affairs*, 2, 1962, pp. 391–442.

91. Snyder, Tooze, and Bloxham are discussed below. Catherine Epstein, in her book, *Model Nazi: Arthur Greiser and the Occupation of Western Poland* (Oxford, 2010), argued that "had the Nazis triumphed in World War II, the Third Reich would have seen a wholesale slaughter of many non-German peoples" (p. 12). Dan Stone wrote: "the evidence suggests that the Slav nations of Europe were also destined, had Germany won the war, to become victims of systematic mass murder": *Histories of the Holocaust* (Oxford, 2010), p. 2.

92. Snyder, *Bloodlands*, p. ix.

93. Tooze, *The Wages of Destruction*, p. 468.

94. Ibid., pp. 476–77.

95. Ibid., p. 483. Tooze's claim echoed a similar one made by Christopher Browning in his book, *The Path to Genocide* (Cambridge, UK, 1992), p. ix. Browning wrote at the beginning of his preface: "If the Nazi regime had suddenly ceased to exist ... in the spring of 1942, its historical infamy would have rested on the 'war of destruction' against the Soviet Union. The mass death of some two million prisoners of war in the first nine months of that conflict would have stood out even more prominently than the killing of approximately one-half million Jews in that same period." Of course, given the implausibility of the Nazis simply disappearing, Browning's counterfactual, like Tooze's, served mostly rhetorical purposes.

96. Bloxham, *The Final Solution*, p. 246.

97. According to Bloxham, the idea that the Nazis would have ceaselessly pursued killing Jews is based on the erroneous idea of a "constant trajectory [of killing] rather than the changing trajectory that actually existed": ibid., p. 245.

98. Ibid., p. 250.

99. Similarly, Michael Marrus asserted that "Had the war ended a year earlier . . . Hungarian Jewry might have survived; had it continued for another year or so, there would have been too few Jews left alive anywhere in Europe to constitute significant 'national differences'": *The Holocaust in History* (New York, 1987), pp. 57–58. Dan Stone speculated that "Had Hungary not sought to switch sides in early 1944, it is likely that the occupation of March 1944 would not have occurred and . . . the Jews . . . would have been spared": *Histories of the Holocaust*, p. 47.

100. Bloxham, *The Final Solution*, p. 250.

101. Snyder wrote that the gassing of Jews at Auschwitz "is misleading as a guide to the Holocaust." Snyder, *Bloodlands*, p. 383. "By the time [the camp's] . . . gas chambers . . . began their deadly work [in the spring of 1943]," the vast "majority of all of the people . . . killed by the Soviet and Nazi regimes, well over ninety percent, had already been killed." He added that "whether or not there was a camp at Auschwitz, the Holocaust would have happened": Timothy Snyder, "The Causes of the Holocaust," *Contemporary European History*, 21:2, 2012, p. 155. Other scholars have continued to defend Auschwitz's centrality, with Richard Evans recently describing it as "the largest mass killing centre in the history of the world": *The Third Reich at War* (New York, 2008), p. 297.

102. Mazower, *Hitler's Empire*, chapter 7, especially pp. 217–20; John Connelly, "Nazis and Slavs," pp. 27–32.

103. Insufficient manpower also sidelined the *Hungerplan*, as the Wehrmacht lacked the troop strength to enforce the blockade of Soviet cities. Tooze, *The Wages of Destruction*, p. 483.

104. Connelly, "Nazis and Slavs," pp. 20–24, 27.

105. Dan Stone wrote: "one suspects that a victorious Third Reich would sooner or later have successfully pressed for the deportation of Jews in all . . .[of the states with which it was allied], as it did the Jews of Rhodes or Salonica, and as it tried (but failed) to do in Albania." Stone, *Histories of the Holocaust*, p. 50. Gerhard Weinberg agreed, writing "After victory over the Allies, Germany could easily bludgeon any recalcitrant government into surrendering its Jews." Weinberg,"Two Separate Issues?" p. 392.

106. www.guardian.co.uk/commentisfree/2008/apr/25/foreignpolicy.iraq.

107. Patrick Buchanan, "Was the Holocaust Inevitable?" *Human Events*, June 20, 2008. http://www.humanevents.com/article.php?id=27107

108. Peter Hitchens, "If We Hadn't Fought World War 2, Would We Still Have a British Empire?" *Daily Mail*, August 31, 2009, www.dailymail.co.uk/debate/

article-1209890/PETER-HITCHENS-If-hadnt-fought-World-War-2-British-Empire.html

109. Barry Rubin, "Those Who Neglect Their Past Have No Future," *Jerusalem Post*, August 13, 2010.

110. Eric Herschth, "The Limits of Pacifism," *The Jewish Week*, June 21, 2011. www.thejewishweek.com/arts/books/limits_pacifism

111. Winston Groom, "Apparently, the Good War was a Bad Idea," *Weekly Standard*, August 11–18, 2008.

112. See also Adam Kirsch, "Patrick J. Buchanan's Know-Nothing History," *New York Sun*, June 11, 2008.

113. See Roberts's review, "Up in Smoke," in *New Criterion*, June, 2008.

114. In 2009, Ahmadinejad insisted that the Western powers "launched the myth of the Holocaust . . .[as a] pretext for establishing the Zionist regime": www. adl.org/main_International_Affairs/ahmadinejad_words.htm? Multi_page_sections=sHeading_4. On Helen Thomas's controversial 2010 remarks, see www.ynetnews.com/articles/0,7340,L-3899361,00.html. See Neturei Kara Rabbi Yisroel Dovid Weiss's speech at the Tehran Holocaust Denial conference in 2006: www.nkusa.org/activities/Speeches/2006Iran-WeissSpeech.cfm.

115. For neo-Nazi support, see http://forum.codoh.com/viewtopic.php? f=2&t=3720.

116. Gilbert Achcar noted, "Without the Holocaust and without the rise of the Nazis I don't think the Zionist project would have come to fruition": www. israeli-occupation.org/2010-05-13/gilbert-achcar-interview-the-league-against-denial/ Other scholars sympathetic to Arab interests have argued similarly. Lance Selfa has declared, "Without the Holocaust, the state of Israel probably wouldn't have been founded": Lance Selfa, *The Struggle for Palestine* (Chicago, 2002), p. 15. One Arab respondent in Samar Dahmash-Jarrah's and Kirt M. Dressler's volume, *Arab Voices Speak to American Hearts* (Charles City, VA, 2005), wrote, "Without the Holocaust, Israel would not have been established" (p. 83). Bernard Avishai argued, "without the Holocaust, Israel might not have arisen in 1948," in *The Tragedy of Zionism: How Its Revolutionary Past Haunts Israeli Democracy* (New York, 2002), p. 168.

117. Sebastian Haffner wrote, "without Hitler there would be no Israel," in *The Meaning of Hitler* (Cambridge, MA, 1983), p. 100. Henry Turner speculated that, "Without the Holocaust there would be no Palestinian problem, because there would be no state of Israel," in "Hitler's Impact on History," p. 118. Jeffrey Herf argued that "if the Nazis had not carried out a genocide of Europe's Jews, there would have been far less political support in the United States and elsewhere for realization of Zionist hopes in Palestine," in *Nazi Propaganda for the Arab World*, p. 212.

118. The essay appears in: Michael Wolffsohn, *Eternal Guilt: Forty Years of German-Jewish-Israeli Relations* (New York, 1993).

119. Ibid., p. 4.

120. Ibid., pp. 6–7.

121. Tom Segev, *One Palestine, Complete: Jews and Arabs Under the British Mandate* (New York, 2001), p. 491.

122. Efraim Karsh, *Israel: The First Hundred Years, Volume 1* (New York, 2001), p. 2.

123. "If Not For The Holocaust, There Could Have Been 32 Million Jews In The World Today, Expert Says," *Science Daily*, April 24, 2009, www.sciencedaily. com/releases/2009/04/090422121852.htm. Israeli journalist Sever Plocker argued that "If the Holocaust had never occurred, the mass immigration of European Jews to Palestine-Israel would have commenced in the 1950s . . . and no Arab protest could have prevented this from happening." He added: "The Holocaust did not beget Israel; rather, the Holocaust almost foiled the country's establishment . . . Without the Holocaust, today Israel would have been more heavily populated and stronger": Sever Plocker, "It wasn't the Holocaust," *YNetNews*, March 27, 2005, www.ynetnews.com/articles/ 0,7340,L-3063943,00.html. Evyatar Friesel has agreed, noting, "Israel came forth smaller and poorer, in the physical and spiritual sense, than she would have had the huge reservoir of manpower and talent within European Jewry attended her birth and kept watch over her cradle": Evyatar Friesel, "The Holocaust: Factor in the Birth of Israel?" *Shoah Resource Center, The International School for Holocaust Studies*, p. 25, www1.yadvashem.org/ odot_pdf/Microsoft%20Word%20-%203575.pdf.

124. Weinberg, "Two Separate Issues?" p. 384.

125. Bauer, *Rethinking the Holocaust*, p. 258.

126. Ibid., pp. 249–51.

127. Ibid., p. 257. Bauer added that "if the United States had opened its gates to Jewish immigration . . . it is highly probable . . . that a much larger proportion of Jewish D. P.s would have gone to the United States than . . .[went to Palestine]" (ibid., p. 258).

128. Prime Minister Benjamin Netanyahu made this remark in his June 14, 2009 foreign policy speech at Bar Ilan University. Moshe Philips, "The Land of Israel: Is There an Alternative?" www.renewamerica.com/columns/phillips/ 090626.

129. Lucy Dawidowicz, *What is the Use of Jewish History*, pp. 177–78. In *The Future of the Holocaust* (Ithaca, 1999), Berel Lang agreed: "the existence of a Jewish state would have made a difference" in helping to "avert . . . the 'Final Solution'" (pp. 187–88).

130. Bauer, *Rethinking the Holocaust*, p. 259.

131. Rubinstein wrote that "Rommel had only ten divisions in North Africa; with the destruction of Israel and the extermination of perhaps 1 million Jews there as his goal, Hitler might have agreed to give him twenty, thirty or whatever number of Axis divisions was necessary for a successful drive . . . to Palestine." Rubinstein, *The Myth of Rescue*, p. 216.

132. Janet Landman, *Regret: The Persistence of the Possible* (New York, 1993), pp. 37–38; Igor Gavanski, Paula M. Niedenthal, and June Price Tangney, "'If Only I Weren't' Versus 'If Only I Hadn't': Distinguishing Shame and Guilt in Counterfactual Thinking," *Journal of Personality and Social Psychology*, October 1994.

133. Saul Friedlander, *Probing the Limits of Representation: Nazism and the 'Final Solution'* (Cambridge, MA, 1992).

134. White's essay, "The Politics of Historical Interpretation: Discipline and De-Sublimation," which appeared in *The Content of the Form: Narrative Discourse and Historical Representation* (Baltimore, 1987), earned additional criticism for claiming that "when it comes to apprehending the historical record, there are no grounds to be found in the historical record itself for preferring one way of construing its meaning over another" (p. 75).

135. Hayden White, "Historical Emplotment and the Problem of Truth," in Saul Friedlander, ed., *Probing the Limits of Representation*, pp. 50–52.

136. Quoted in Friedlander, *Probing the Limits of Representation*, pp. 40, 10.

137. Scholars who have explored what might have happened to the Jews of the Middle East had the Nazis won the Battle of El Alamein in 1942 are clearly concerned about the possibility of a "second Holocaust," resulting from a future conflict between Israel and its Arab and Muslim neighbors.

Chapter 4 Nazis that never were: New alternate histories of the Third Reich

1. Guy Saville, *The Afrika Reich* (London, 2011), p. 127.

2. Rosenfeld, *The World Hitler Never Made*, chapter 1.

3. Jo Walton, *Farthing* (New York, 2006); Jo Walton, *Ha'Penny* (New York, 2007); Jo Walton, *Half a Crown* (New York, 2008).

4. Walton, *Ha'Penny*, pp. 228, 244.

5. Ibid., pp. 84–85.

6. Ibid., p. 209.

7. Ibid., pp. 174–75.

8. Walton, *Half a Crown*, p. 19.

9. Ibid., p. 92.

10. Ibid., p. 316.

11. Lyda Morehouse, "Subversive Pixel-Stained Technopeasant: An Interview with Jo Walton," *The Internet Review of Science Fiction*, March 2008. http://www.irosf.com/q/zine/article/10407.

12. C. J. Sansom, *Dominion* (London, 2012). Sansom is well known for his series of bestselling novels featuring the sixteenth-century lawyer, Matthew Shardlake. See www.cjsansom.com/Homepage.

13. Ibid., pp. 54, 44.

14. Ibid, p. 138.

15. Ibid., p. 569.

16. Quoted in "A Life in Books: C. J. Sansom," *The Guardian*, November 12, 2010, www.guardian.co.uk/culture/2010/nov/15/cj-sansom-interview Before becoming a writer, Sansom worked as a lawyer representing the underprivileged. His views are visible in his novel, *Winter in Madrid* (2006), about the Spanish Civil War. In discussing the novel's plot, he noted, "I have a personal slant on what is going on . . .[and it] will not take the reader long to realize that I do not like Franco or his regime":www.bookbrowse.com/author_interviews/full/index.cfm/author_number/1517/cj-sansom; www.cjsansom.com/Homepage.

17. Sansom, *Dominion*, p. 590.

18. C. J. Sansom, "My Nightmare of a Nazi Britain," *The Guardian*, October 19, 2012, www.guardian.co.uk/books/2012/oct/19/sansom-dominion-nightmare-nazi-britain.

19. Ibid., p. 593.

20. Owen Sheers, *Resistance* (New York, 2007). See also Welsh writer Murray Davies's novel, *Collaborator* (London, 2003), which also portrayed ordinary British people working with their German occupiers until finally liberating themselves. Davies's novel won the 2003 Sidewise Award for Alternate History, www.uchronia.net/sidewise/complete.html#2003.

21. Sheers, *Resistance*, p. 33.

22. Ibid., p. 111.

23. Ibid., p. 56.

24. Ibid., p. 159.

25. Ibid., p. 236.

26. A longtime contributor to the left-leaning *Guardian* newspaper, Sheers has expressed his anti-war views in his plays, *If I Should Go Away* (2007), *The Two Worlds of Charlie F.* (2011) and his narrative poem, *Pink Mist* (2013). See www.owensheers.co.uk/index.html. For some of these works, Sheers interviewed British veterans from the wars in Afghanistan and Iraq. Owen Sheers, "Rescued From Hell: The War Veterans Who Took to the Stage," *The Guardian*, January 18, 2012.

27. Susan Mansfield, "The Valley of the Lost Men," *The Scotsman*, August 14, 2007. Owen Sheers, "Hay Festival: When the Nazis came to Hay," *The*

Telegraph, May 23, 2011, www.telegraph.co.uk/culture/hay-festival/8523902/Hay-Festival-When-the-Nazis-came-to-Hay.html. Sheers explained that while he was researching how local Welshman might have resisted the Nazis, "I was intrigued by the moral questions and dilemmas this situation ... would have thrown up. At the time, things were already happening in Iraq": Karen Price, "Old Memories of How Country People Were Armed to Resist a Nazi Invasion Sow the Seeds," *The Western Mail*, June 2, 2007.

28. Alice Jones, "A Writer Who's Hard to Resist," *The Independent*, November 24, 2011, www.independent.co.uk/news/people/profiles/a-writer-whos-hard-to-resist-6267092.html.

29. Sheers, *Resistance*, p. 270. It is true that such remarks in the novel are typically voiced by characters eager to justify their collaborationist activity.

30. Saville, p. 34.

31. Ibid., p. 52.

32. Ibid., p. 234.

33. Ibid., p. 265.

34. Ibid., pp. 55, 129.

35. http://networkedblogs.com/ltha8

36. Author interview with Guy Saville, August 31, 2011.

37. *Dominion* was on *The Sunday Times* bestseller list, January 20, 2013. *The Afrika Reich* was also a respectable commercial success, selling more than 10,000 copies in the first six months. Author interview with Guy Saville, August 31, 2011.

38. Douglas Barbour, "Government by Fear," *The Gazette* (Montreal), October 28, 2008, p. I13. Frida Murray, Review of *Farthing* in *Booklist*, October 1, 2007, 104:3, 40; Kelly McManus, "Ghosts of SF Past," March 31, 2007, *The Globe and Mail*, D27. See also Brian Bethue, "A Very Unpleasant Kind of 'Cozy,'" *Maclean's*, September 29, 2008, 64; Saul Austerlitz, "Reshuffling History's Deck," *The Forward*, March 9, 2007, B6.

39. www.economist.com/blogs/prospero/2011/09/how-911-changed-fiction.

40. Graeme Blundell, Review of *The Afrika Reich*, in the *Daily Australian*, June 11, 2011, p. 20; "A Clever What-If," *The Economist*, February 17, 2011; see also Peter Millar, Review of *The Afrika Reich*, in *The Times*, January 29, 2011, hailing the book for its "horrific reimagining of the Dark Continent."

41. Marcel Berlins, Review of *Dominion*, *The Times*, October 20, 2012; Matthew Denison, "Nightmare of a Nazi Britain," *The Express*, November 2, 2012, p. 55; Pam Norfolk, Review of *Dominion*, *The Visitor*, November 12, 2012.

42. Barbour, "Government by Fear"; Adrienne Martini, "Heil Britannia," *Baltimore City Paper*, December 12, 2007, www.citypaper.com/arts/story.asp?id=14955. Similarly, one reviewer commented that Walton wrote *Farthing* "to say something about our own times": Ronni Philips, "Crimes Past, Present,"

Canberra Times, September 13, 2009. Another reviewer opined that the book "reads as if it was written just this morning." Lisa Goldstein, Review of *Farthing*, in *Locus*, May, 2006, www.brazenhussies.net/Goldstein/Review-Farthing.html

43. Laura Miller, "Guerrillas Rise up in Nazi-occupied Britain," Salon.com, March 18, 2008, www.salon.com/2008/03/18/owen_sheers/; Andrew Connelly, "Resistance – and the Irresistible Owen Sheers," *Hackney Citizen*, January 9, 2012, hackneycitizen.co.uk/2012/01/09/resistance-film-owen-sheers/

44. The review of *The Afrika Reich* in *Kirkus Review* said that the book's "realpolitik seems credible": www.kirkusreviews.com/book-reviews/guy-saville/afrika-reich/; Allan Massie, Review of *Dominion*, *The Scotsman*, November 3, 2012.

45. www.theartsdesk.com/film/resistance.

46. "The Germans are Coming," *Washington Post*, April 27, 2008; Craig Seligman, "Nazism Triumphs Yet Evil Is Missing," *Windsor Star* (Ontario), March 8, 2008.

47. Paul Muir, "A Difficult-to-imagine Dystopian Europe," *The National* (Abu Dhabi), November 10, 2012.

48. See Rosenfeld, *The World Hitler Never Made*, chapter 1.

49. See "Interview With the Crew," *Jackboots on Whitehall* DVD.

50. Tim Robey, Review of *Jackboots on Whitehall*, in *The Telegraph*, October 7, 2010; Allan Hunter, Review, www.screendaily.com/reviews/latest-reviews/jackboots-on-whitehall/5015200.article, June 18, 2010; Philip French, Review in *The Observer*, October 10, 2010.

51. French, Review of *Jackboots on Whitehall*.

52. www.timeout.com/film/reviews/89299/jackboots-on-whitehall.html

53. Ibid.

54. John Patterson, "Jackboots On Whitehall is a Reich Royal Riot of a What-If War Movie," *The Guardian*, October 2, 2010.

55. See Rosenfeld, *The World Hitler Never Made*, chapter 2.

56. Harry Turtledove, *The Man With the Iron Heart* (New York, 2009).

57. Ibid., p. 10.

58. Ibid., pp. 20–23, 59.

59. Ibid., p. 33.

60. Ibid., p. 258.

61. Ibid., pp. 316, 438.

62. Ibid., p. 480.

63. Ibid., p. 489.

64. Ibid., p. 520.

65. Ibid., p. 528.

66. Ibid., p. 488.

67. Ibid., pp. 440–41.

68. Ibid., p. 325.

69. Ibid., p. 79.

70. Ibid., p. 419.

71. See Turtledove's interview with Darrell Schweitzer, *Speaking of the Fantastic III: Interviews with Science Fiction Writers* (Rockville, MD, 2011), pp. 128–38. Methodologically, Turtledove wrote that he appreciated the role of both the "Great Man" and "vast socioeconomic forces" in historical events (ibid., p. 135).

72. See, for example, the discussion threads: http://rec.arts.sf.written.narkive.com/ELPzWOGV/turtledove-s-politics and www.alternatehistory.com/newtest/threads/the-man-with-the-iron-heart.163465/

73. Turtledove cautioned readers of his 2007 story "News From the Front" (which criticized FDR) that its plot should not be seen as reflective of his political views, http://turtledove.wikia.com/wiki/News_From_the_Front

74. "Between the Covers," Interview with Harry Turtledove, *National Review Online*. No date (probably 2008). http://radio.nationalreview.com/betweenthecovers/post/?q=ZjdjNjFlZGRjYjhjOGQyMDY2NmM2NmViYWQyODMxMDE= As Turtledove observed, "Any resemblance between what happens here and … what's happening in Iraq is not altogether coincidental. I was wondering how we would cope with asymmetrical warfare if we ran into it in at the end of the 1940s."

75. Jeffrey Herf, "Liberalism, Germany and the War in Iraq," *FrontPageMagazine. com*, May 26, 2003, http://archive.frontpagemag.com/readArticle.aspx?ARTID=18055

76. Alan Glenn, *Amerikan Eagle* (New York, 2011).

77. Ibid., pp. 176–77, 211.

78. Ibid., p. 362.

79. Ibid., pp. 473–74.

80. Ibid., pp. 274, 504

81. Dubois's popular alternate history novel about the Cuban Missile Crisis, *Resurrection Day* (1999) was a vigorous defense of the administration of John F. Kennedy and revealed the author's sympathies for the Democratic President.

82. Emails from Brendan Dubois (Alan Glenn) to author, February 22 and February 24, 2012.

83. Glenn, p. 174.

84. Ibid., pp. 384–85.

85. Martin Sieff, "If Reinhard Heydrich Had Lived," *Washington Times*, October 19, 2008.

86. See www.amazon.com/The-Iron-Heart-Harry-Turtledove/dp/0345504348.

87. As one reader put it, "I just do not believe that Americans would be willing to ignore the more than century long history of democractic government." http://

alternatehistoryweeklyupdate.blogspot.com/2011/08/review-amerikan-eagle. html.

88. http://davebuttoned.blogspot.com/.

89. http://screen.yahoo.com/timecrowave-19860785.html.

90. http://www.tgrantphoto.com/blog/archives/107.

91. The video is entitled, "Hitler Plans to Time Travel," www.youtube.com/ watch?v=QtcSNEN0Xl0/.

92. http://hitlerparody.wikia.com/wiki/Hermann_Fegelein

93. http://tvtropes.org/pmwiki/pmwiki.php/Main/GodwinsLawOfTimeTravel

94. Siegfried Langer, *Alles bleibt anders* (Stolberg, 2008).

95. Ibid., p. 104.

96. Ibid., p. 239.

97. See Rosenfeld, *The World Hitler Never Made*, chapter 3.

98. Langer, *Alles bleibt anders*, p. 189.

99. Ibid., p. 122.

100. See Rosenfeld, *The World Hitler Never Made*, chapter 6.

101. Langer, *Alles bleibt anders*, p. 224.

102. Ibid., p. 239.

103. www.buechertitel.de/Von_70_Absagen_zum_Spitzentitel.html.

104. The novel was nominated for the Kurd Laßwitz prize in German science fiction in 2009. It was nominated for the Deutscher Phantastik Preis in the year 2009. www.pirandot.de/dpp/?Jahr=2009.

105. "Unschöne Dinge," *Der Standard* (Austria), February 28, 2009, http:// derstandard.at/1231151768805/Rundschau-Unschoene-Dinge? sap=2&_slideNumber=3&_seite=1.

106. Marco Behringer, Review of *Alles bleibt anders*, July 1, 2010, http://suite101. de/article/buch-rezension-alles-bleibt-anders-siegfried-langer-a79996. See also the review from geisterspiegel, cited at http://siegfriedlanger.blogspot.com/ 2010/09/alles-bleibt-anders-neue-rezension_29.html.

107. www.siegfriedlanger.de/fileadmin/user_upload/Alles_bleibt_anders/ AllesbleibtandersRezensionphantastisch.jpg. One reviewer praised the novel's portrayal of horror as "restrained": www.siegfriedlanger.de/fileadmin/ user_upload/Alles_bleibt_anders/Kritik-0003.jpg. Another noted that the novel proved that "one does not always need loud cannon fire to warn readers about ... the dangers of intolerance, indoctrination, and radicalism." www. phantastik-news.de/modules.php?name=Reviews&rop=showcontent&id =2696.

108. www.siegfriedlanger.de/fileadmin/user_upload/Alles_bleibt_anders/ abaRezensionDeutschunterrichtOriginal.jpg.

109. *Iron Sky* received a lot of attention for being partly "crowd funded" by individual Internet users, who contributed some 10 percent of the film's

budget. Other funding sources included HessenInvestFilm. Much of the film was shot in Frankfurt.

110. A comic book prequel to the film, entitled "Bad Moon Rising," functions as a "secret history" that explains how Nazi scientists, based in Antarctica, engineer the departure from Earth, via spacecraft, to the moon, www.ironsky. net/sneakpeek/issueone/

111. "Back To The Führer: *Iron Sky* Director Interviewed," *The Quietus*, March 7, 2012. http://thequietus.com/articles/08177-iron-sky-interview-timo-vuorensola.

112. http://mancave.cbslocal.com/2012/03/26/interview-iron-sky-director-timo-vuorensola/.

113. http://thequietus.com/articles/08177-iron-sky-interview-timo-vuorensola.

114. "Interview: *Iron Sky* Director Timo Vuorensola," *Man Cave Daily*, March 26, 2012, www.fffyeah.com/2012/02/interview-with-timo-vuorensola-from-iron-sky/.

115. British and American reviewers restricted their criticism to the film's aesthetic shortcomings, noting that while the film boasted lavish CGI special effects, it was an "ineptly plotted" piece of "chaotic nonsense" whose "dismal script fail[ed]... to understand the potential of its own brilliant premise": Alex von Tunzelmann, "Iron Sky Loses the Nazi Plot on a Cheap Moon Set," *The Guardian*, May 24, 2012, www.guardian.co.uk/film/2012/may/24/iron-sky-nazi-plot-moon; Jeff Shannon, "'Iron Sky': Out-of-This-World Nazi plot Lands in Chaos," *Seattle Times*, August 23, 2012, http://seattletimes.com/html/movies/2018978802_mr24iron.html; Matthew Turner, Review of *Iron Sky*, *The ViewLondon Review*, May 25, 2012, http://www.viewlondon.co.uk/films/iron-sky-film-review-45691.html. Others criticized the film for failing to deliver any laughs. As *Variety* put it, the film was "neither good enough to rep a proper breakout hit nor bad enough that it might attain cult status. It's just kind of lame, the worst of all possible worlds": Leslie Felperin, Review of *Iron Sky*, *Variety*, February 12, 2012.

116. See the review in the online journal *Das Manifest*: www.dasmanifest.com/01/ironsky.php. Many other reviewers acknowledged it as "trashy" cinema, but in a good way. See Peter Zander, Review of *Iron Sky*, *Berliner Morgenpost*, April 5, 2012; "Nazis kommen vom Mond," *Berliner Kurier*, April 5, 2012; Joachim Mischke, "Kommt ein Nazi geflogen," *Hamburger Abendblatt*, April 5, 2012.

117. "Nazis im Weltall," *Stern*, April 2, 2012, www.stern.de/kultur/film/iron-sky-neu-im-kino-nazis-im-weltall-1808472.html.

118. Wolfgang Höbel, "Nazis im Weltall," *Der Spiegel*, February 12, 2012.

119. Andreas Borcholte, "Fahr zur Hölle, Mönch!" *Der Spiegel*, February 13, 2012.

120. Daniel Erk, "Kryptofaschistischer Weltraumschrott," *Die Zeit*, February 14, 2012. Others criticized its "uninspired direction" and likened the film to a

"slap in the face": Markus Keuschnigg, "Trashfilm 'Iron Sky' Mond! Nazis! Udo Kier!" *Die Presse*, April 3, 2012. Most complained that the film was simply not funny. "Die Nazis vom Arsch der Welt," *Der Tagesspiegel*, April 5, 2012.

121. Ulrich Gutmair, "Nazis leben hinterm Mond," *TAZ*, April 5, 2012.

122. Rüdiger Suchsland, "Hart wie Kruppstahl und dumm wie Hitler," www.artechock.de/film/text/kritik/i/irsky.htm. See also Ciprian David, Review of *Iron Sky*, in *Negativ*, February 12, 2012, www.negativ-film.de/2012/02/iron-sky-berlinale-2012-panorama-special.

123. Henryk Broder, "Nazis herrschen auf dem Mond," *Berliner Morgenpost*, April 2, 2012.

124. Michael Meyns, Review of Iron Sky. www.programmkino.de/cms/links.php?link=1778&PHPSESSID=524b4a8789853990ccc74afa60174a54. Another critic agreed, noting that in comparison to the Americans, the "Nazis appear ... sympathetic" to the point that one almost wants to "grant [them] a victory in the space battle": Markus Hesselmann, "Iron Sky: Nazi-Trash, Crowdfunding und mehr," *Der Tagesspiegel*, February 11, 2012, www.tagesspiegel.de/kultur/kino/berlinale/premiere-bei-der-berlinale-iron-sky-nazi-trash-crowdfunding-und-mehr/6199700.html.

125. See the comments at www.amazon.de/product-reviews/B007YPTTME/ref=dp_db_cm_cr_acr_txt?ie=UTF8&showViewpoints=1 and www.imdb.de/title/tt1034314/reviews.

126. See Rosenfeld, *The World Hitler Never Made*, chapter 6.

127. Alexander Demandt, *Es hätte auch anders kommen können* (Berlin, 2010).

128. Ibid., p. 217.

129. Demandt said this in an opinion piece adapted from his book and published in *Die Welt*. "Was, wenn 1939 ein Hitler-Attentat geglückt wäre," *Die Welt*, January, 31, 2011, www.welt.de/kultur/history/article12371067/Was-wenn-1939-ein-Hitler-Attentat-geglueckt-waere.html

130. Demandt, *Es hätte auch anders kommen können*, p. 222.

131. Ibid., p. 220.

132. Pleschinski and Wedemeyer-Schwiersch's works are discussed in Rosenfeld, *The World Hitler Never Made*, pp. 278–85.

133. Demandt does not openly broadcast his political views, but his contribution to a 2003 volume in honor of Ernst Nolte's 80th birthday and his recent keynote address on Oswald Spengler at the newly opened Library of Conservatism in Berlin clearly show his orientation. The volume was Helmut Fleischer and Pierluca Azzaro, eds., *Das 20. Jahrhundert: Zeitalter der tragischen Verkehrungen. Forum zum 80. Geburtstag von Ernst Nolte* (Munich, 2003). "Bibliothek des Konservatismus in Berlin eröffnet," *Junge Freiheit*, November 26, 2012, http://jungefreiheit.de/kultur/2012/bibliothek-des-konservatismus-in-berlin-eroeffnet/

134. Demandt also ignored the fact that countless Germans besides Hitler were involved in the regime's crimes. This was shown at the chapter's end, when the German people learn of the Holocaust and express a "scream of shock" and display "horror, shame, and regret," as if they had known nothing: Demandt, *Es hätte auch anders kommen können*, pp. 230–31.

135. Dieter Kühn, *Ich war Hitlers Schutzengel* (Frankfurt, 2010).

136. Ibid., p. 54.

137. Ibid., pp. 159–66.

138. Ibid., p. 156.

139. Ibid., p. 93.

140. Ibid., p. 124.

141. Kühn has been awarded the Carl-Zuckmayer-Medaille, the Hermann Hesse Prize, and the Großer Literaturpreis der Bayerischen Akademie der Schönen Künste, www.fischerverlage.de/autor/dieter_kuehn/3069.

142. Christoph Driessen, "Ich war Hitlers Schutzengel," *Kölnische Rundschau*, January 26, 2010.

143. See, for example, Gregor Keuschnig, "Dieter Kühn: Den Musil spreng ich in die Luft," *Begleitschreiben* (blog), July 11, 2012, www.begleitschreiben.net/dieter-kuehn-den-musil-spreng-ich-in-die-luft/.

144. See the interview with Jürgen König on Deutschlandradio, www.dradio.de/dkultur/sendungen/thema/1135034/.

145. Ibid.

146. Bücherwelt: *Hitlers Schutzengel*. http://podster.de/episode/1290249.

147. Kühn served as an FDP city councilman in the town of Düren. Walter van Rossum, "In die Labyrinthe der eigenen Erinnerung," *Deutschlandfunk*, December 22, 2013, www.deutschlandfunk.de/buch-der-woche-in-die-labyrinthe-der-eigenen-erinnerung.700.de.html?dram:article_id=272648.

148. Kühn, *Ich war Hitlers Schutzengel*, p. 203.

149. Ibid., pp. 178–79.

150. Ibid., p. 273.

151. Wolfgang Brenner, *Walther Rathenau: Deutscher und Jude* (Munich, 2008) and *Der Mut des Fliegers – Adolf Reichwein, Pädagoge im Widerstand* (1998).

152. Johannes Willms, *SZ*, December 7, 2010, cited at www.ullsteinbuchverlage.de/propylaen/buch.php?id=15829&page=buchaz&sort=&auswahl=a&pagenum=3.

153. See Martin Muno's review of the book for the *Deutsche Welle* July 24, 2011. http://www.dw-world.de/dw/article/o,,6366747,00.html.

154. See Herbert Gebert's review of the book at www.wiesentbote.de/2011/01/10/herbert-geberts-buchkritik-alexander-demandt-es-hatte-anders-kommen-konnen/.

155. This was the opinion of the extreme right-wing National Journal and Globalfire Information and News service, http://globalfire.tv/nj/11de/zeitgeschichte/ah_groesster_staatsmann.htm.

156. Rudolf von Bitter, "Dieter Kühn, Ich war Hitlers Schutzengel," July 12, 2010, www.br-online.de/bayerisches-fernsehen/lesezeichen/dieter-kuehn-ich-war-hitlers-schutzengel-lesezeichen-2010-07-12-ID1278598569949.xml.

157. Maria Renhardt, "Haben die Schutzengel der Opfer versagt?" *Die Furche*, June 2, 2010, www.furche.at/system/downloads.php?do=file&id=1751.

158. Review in *Die Welt*, September 27, 2008; Thomas Neumann, "Hitler starb in Bürgerbräukeller," Literaturkritik.de, December, 2008, www.literaturkritik. de/public/rezension.php?rez_id=12511

159. Stefan Sase, Review of *Führerlos* in *Roter Dorn*, August 1, 2010, www. roterdorn.de/inhalt.php?xz=rezi&id=16447.

160. Timur Vermes, *Er ist wieder da* (Cologne, 2012).

161. See Rosenfeld, *The World Hitler Never Made*, chapter 5.

162. Vermes, *Er ist wieder da*, pp. 19, 87, 133.

163. Ibid., pp. 46–47, 54.

164. Ibid., pp. 162, 192.

165. Fabian Röger, "10 Fragen an Timur Vermes," August 12, 2013, http://koeselsche.de/index.php?option=com_content&view=article&id=236.

166. "Wir haben zu viel vom gleichen Hitler," *SZ*, December 13, 2012. Tony Patterson, "Hitler's Return: Timely Satire or a Joke Too Far?" *The Independent*, February 24, 2013.

167. These works included the films, *Schtonk!* (1992) and *Goebbels und Geduldig* (2001), the popular television show hosted by comedian Harald Schmidt, and comic books, such as Walter Moers's two-volume *Adolf, die Nazi-Sau* (1998–99) and Achim Greser's *Der Führer Privat* (2000).

168. Stern's show often ran a segment called "Guess Who's the Jew?" presided over by a fictional Kurt Waldheim, www.youtube.com/watch?v=fboXaOSY9LY. Crumb's satirical cartoon, "When the Niggers Take Over America!" (1993) has been embraced by white supremacists, www.newyorker.com/archive/1994/11/14/1994_11_14_048_TNY_CARDS_000370902

169. Vermes, *Er ist wieder da*, pp. 148, 122–23

170. These works included, among many others, the films *Notorious* (1949), *Verboten* (1959), and *Zentropa*, (1990) and the novels *The Odessa File* (1972) and *The Holcroft Covenant* (1978).

171. "Er ist wieder da – bald auch im Film," *Börsenblatt*, June 28, 2013, www. boersenblatt.net/628021.

172. See, for example, the review, "Mein Freund, der Führer" (October 22, 2012), on amazon.de, which received over 800 positive responses. There were over 1,300 reviews listed on the website.

173. See "Stimmen zum Buch," www.luebbe.de/Eichborn/Details/Id/978-3-8479-0517-2; Stefan Reckziegel, Review of *Er ist wieder da*, *Hamburger Abendblatt*, November 22, 2012.

174. Some reviews described the book as overly long, with some going so far as to call it "mind-numbingly boring": Marc Reichwein, "*Er ist wieder da* – Eine Hitler-Satire mit Überlänge," *Die Welt*, July 20, 2013; Volker Surman, "Lustig-blöder Hitlerkrampf," *TAZ*, March 27, 2013.

175. Cornelia Fiedler, "Ha ha Hitler," *SZ*, January 9, 2013.

176. Stefan Schmitz, "Heiße Ware unter dem Weihnachtsbaum," *Stern*, December 13, 2012; Surman, "Lustig-blöder Hitlerkrampf."

177. See "Mein Freund, der Führer" (October 22, 2012); "Unheimlich gut" (September 12, 2012); "Fiktion und Wahrheit" (August 25, 2013), among many others, on amazon.de.

178. Hermann Weiss, "Ein unheimlicher Erfolg," *Welt am Sonntag*, January 27, 2013.

179. See Rosenfeld, *The World Hitler Never Made*, chapter 7.

180. Michael Chabon, *The Yiddish Policemen's Union* (New York, 2007).

181. Ibid., pp. 88, 109.

182. Ibid., p. 29.

183. Ibid., p. 406.

184. In 2003 Chabon signed a petition to bring back Israeli settlers from the West Bank to Israel's pre-1967 borders. www.btvshalom.org/pressrelease/041404.shtml.

185. In a 2007 interview, Chabon expressed a liberal fear of ultra-orthodox yearnings to build a Third Temple in Jerusalem and American evangelical support for breeding a red heifer, a precondition for the messiah's return. "Arctic Jews: An Interview with Michael Chabon," April 14, 2007, www.dissentmagazine.org/online.php?id=10.

186. See Chapter 3 of the present study.

187. Quoted in Sarah Goldstein, "Jews on Ice," Salon.com, May 4, 2007, www.salon.com/books/int/2007/05/04/chabon/index.html.

188. Walter Laqueur, "Disraelia: A Counterfactual History, 1848–2008," *Middle East Papers: Middle East Strategy at Harvard*, April 1, 2008, pp. 1–21. The essay was later published in the volume, *Harvest of a Decade: Disraelia and Other Essays* (New York, 2011).

189. Ibid., p. 14.

190. Ibid., p. 16.

191. Ibid., p. 20.

192. See, for example, his recent book, *The Last Days of Europe: Epitaph for an Old Continent* (New York, 2007). See also www.laqueur.net.

193. Laqueur, *The Last Days of Europe*, p. 16.

194. Ibid., p. 9.

195. Ibid., p. 16.

196. Ibid., p. 17.

197. Ibid., p. 20.

198. Sam Anderson, "The Frozen People," *New York Magazine*, May 7, 2007; Mark Oppenheimer, "Jewish Noir," *The Forward*, April 20, 2007; see also Benjamin Lytal, "The Zany Integrity of Chabon," *New York Sun*, April 18, 2007; Michiko Kakutani, "Looking for a Home in the Limbo of Alaska," *New York Times*, May 1, 2007.

199. James Lewis, Review of *The Yiddish Policemen's Union*, *The American Thinker*, July 5, 2008, www.americanthinker.com/2008/07/the_ultimate_pc_novel.html.

200. "Novelist's Ugly View of Jews," *New York Post*, April 22, 2007, www.nypost.com/p/pagesix/item_eRYqGj48hB4cCsvJDEaV2M; jsessionid=31BF7D93ED4E6611FC86A1C9C89544D7.

201. John Podhoretz, "Zion on Ice," *Weekly Standard*, June 25, 2007: "Like all those who express a great sentimental love for their 'heritage,' Chabon loves his just so long as it's in the rearview mirror."

202. Samuel Freedman, "In the Diaspora: Chabon's Choice," *Jerusalem Post*, July 12, 2007. Further confirming the liberal slant of Chabon's novel was the praise given it by liberal reviewers. See, for example, Joshua Furst, "A Long Way from Zion," *Zeek Magazine*, July 2007, www.zeek.net/707zion/.

203. http://sandbox.blog-city.com/disraelia.htm.

Chapter 5 Humanizing Hitler: The Führer in contemporary film

1. Charles Mitchell's book, *The Hitler Filmography: Worldwide Feature Film and Television Miniseries Portrayals, 1940 through 2000* (Jefferson, NC, 2002), discusses one hundred films featuring Hitler, while noting the existence of many more.

2. David Welch, *Propaganda and the German Cinema, 1933–1945* (Oxford, 1983), pp. 6–7.

3. Erwin Leiser, *Nazi Cinema* (London, 1974), p. 29.

4. One documentary was *Feuertaufe* (1940), which portrayed him as a man of peace defending Germany against Polish attack.

5. See Jo Fox, *Film Propaganda in Britain and Nazi Germany* (Oxford, 2007), pp. 200–06. David Welch in *Propaganda and the German Cinema* writes that "any dramatization of such a God-like figure on the cinema screens would be considered blasphemy" (p. 147).

6. These films included *Der große König* (1942) and *Bismarck* (1940).

7. The Three Stooges films included such shorts as *You Nazty Spy* (1939) and *I'll Never Heil Again* (1941). The most famous Walt Disney animated film was *The Führer's Face* (1943). Other wartime comedies included Gordon Douglas's

film, *The Devil With Hitler* (1942), which showed Hitler cavorting with Lucifer in hell (Mitchell, *The Hitler Filmography*, p. 8). These films' moral agenda was made clear by Charlie Chaplin who famously said that in making *The Great Dictator*, he was "determined to ridicule [Hitler's]. . . mystical bilge about a pure-blooded race": *My Autobiography* (New York, 1992), p. 392–93. See also the British film, *Let George Do It!* (later titled *To Hell With Hitler*, 1940), which showed the Nazi dictator getting punched in the face by a British ukelele player, played by comedian, George Formby. For a recent discussion of wartime anti-Nazi films, see Sabine Hake, *Screen Nazis: Cinema, History, and Democracy* (Madison, 2012), chapter 1.

8. Just before unleashing World War II, and then again during the conflict, Hitler claimed to have been laughed at by Jews and venomously gloated that "those who laughed then [will] perhaps no longer laugh a short time from now." Quoted in Claudia Schmölders, "Der Führer privat – aber für wen?" *Frankfurter Rundschau*, January 16, 2007. See also Andreas Platthaus, "Der Diktator als Prügelknabe," *FAZ*, January 6, 2007.

9. Chaplin, *My Autobiography*, pp. 392–93.

10. There were hardly any satirical portrayals of Hitler during the early postwar period, with the notable exception of Mel Brooks's film, *The Producers* (1968) and his 1983 remake of Lubitsch's *To Be Or Not To Be*. Neither film focused much on Hitler himself, however.

11. *The Last Ten Days*' portrayal of Hitler at the nadir of his devilish power was meant to impart the lesson that all dictatorships ultimately meet with an unceremonious demise. See Michael Töteberg, "'Hitler's Shadow Still Looms over Us,': G. W. Pabst's The Last Ten Days as Film and Event," in Karolin Machtans and Martin A. Ruehl, eds., *Hitler Films from Germany: History, Cinema and Politics since 1945* (New York, 2012), pp. 63–64. The film's moral agenda was made clear in its opening credits, which included the words "This film describes the history of an era as it transpired and should never be allowed to transpire again": www.youtube.com/watch?v=6vdBxwmDpAU

12. Knopp's films included, among many others, *Hitler: Eine Bilanz*, *Hitlers Helfer*, and *Hitlers Krieger*. See Wulf Kansteiner, *In Pursuit of German Memory: History, Television, and Politics after Auschwitz* (Athens, OH, 2006), pp. 160–80.

13. *The Boys From Brazil* did not portray the survival of Hitler himself, but rather his genetic material in the form of cloned children.

14. Donald McKale, *Hitler: The Survival Myth* (New York, 1981).

15. Guinness said that in playing the role of Hitler, he consciously tried to "make him human": "Alec Guinness: 'I Cannot Possibly Make Hitler Sympathetic," *New York Times*, September 10, 1972, p. D19.

16. Rosenfeld, *The World Hitler Never Made*, pp. 256–59.

17. Syberberg's experimental film was meant to illustrate his belief that "Hitler served the Germans as a screen onto which they could project all their wishes, anxieties, and hopes": Anton Kaes, *From Hitler to Heimat: The Return of History as Film* (Cambridge, MA, 1989), p. 51; See also Annette Insdorf, *Indelible Shadows: Film and the Holocaust* (Cambridge, UK, 2003), pp. 187–92.

18. Kaes, *From Hitler to Heimat*, pp. 6–7; Kansteiner, *In Pursuit of German Memory*, p. 382.

19. Insdorf, *Indelible Shadows*, pp. 67–68.

20. Michael Getler, "Germans Confront the Führer Again," *Washington Post*, August 1, 1977, p. A12.

21. One reviewer of *The Bunker* wrote that Anthony Hopkins's portrayal of Hitler made him "a little too understandable" and "just that more 'acceptable' as a … historical character": John O'Connor, "'Bunker': On Hitler's Last Days," *New York Times*, January 27, 1981, p. C19. Another reviewer said that *The Bunker* made Hitler into "a figure of pathos, quivery and muttering in his underground headquarters": Tom Shales, "Back in the Bunker," *Washington Post*, January 27, 1981, p. B1.

22. Bosley Crowther, "Screen: 'Last Ten Days': German Film Tells of Hitler's Downfall," *New York Times*, April 12, 1956, p. 26; Vincent Canby, "Screen: 'Last Ten Days,'" *New York Times*, May 10, 1973, p 57; Rick Groen, "Hitler Saga Proves Even Evil Can Be Dull," *Globe and Mail*, January 27, 1981; Roger Ebert noted that he left the film "bored" with Alec Guinness's performance, http://rogerebert.suntimes.com/apps/pbcs.dll/article?AID=/19730522/REVIEWS/305220301/1023.

23. Tom Shales, "Back in the Bunker."

24. These criticisms were already visible in the response to *Hitler – Eine Bilanz*, see Kansteiner, *In Pursuit of German Memory*, pp. 169, 380, n. 73. Notably, Knopp was disinclined to indict the German people for any responsibility for Hitler's crimes, a fact that explains why the projected series, *Hitlers Volk*, was never produced (ibid., p. 172).

25. I have omitted from this chapter recent films in which Hitler is a comparatively marginal presence, such as the Hollywood production, *Valkyrie* (2008) and the German television film, *Speer und Er* (2005).

26. Gayle MacDonald, "The Furor over Hitler," *Globe and Mail* (Canada), May 14, 2003, p. R1.

27. Ibid.

28. Gayle MacDonald, "The Fuhrer on Screen," *Globe and Mail* (Canada), July 27, 2002.

29. Sally Ogle Davis and Ivor Davis, "Making Hitler human," *Ottawa Citizen*, August 14, 2002. Canadian historian Irving Abella argued that the film "gives

[Hitler]... a degree of normalcy that might detract from the enormity of his crimes." Quoted in MacDonald, "The Fuhrer on Screen."

30. "Furore over the Fuehrer," *Ottawa Citizen*, August 28, 2002, p. A14.

31. "CBS Revises Script for Hitler Miniseries," *AP Online*, January 13, 2003. Maureen Dowd accused CBS of exploiting the Nazi past for ratings in "Swastikas For Sweeps," *New York Times*, July 17, 2002, p. A19.

32. www.cbs.com/specials/rise_of_evil/

33. David Wiegand, "An Attempt to Fathom Hitler," *San Francisco Chronicle*, May 16, 2003; Linda Stasi, "Fuhrer – Don't Be Afraid of the Hitler You Never Knew – He's Still a Monster," *New York Post*, May 15, 2003, p. 83; Tom Shales, "CBS's 'Hitler,' Digging at the Roots of Evil," *Washington Post*, May 18, 2003.

34. Charlie McCollum, "Drama About Early Years of Hitler Wins Over Skeptics," *San Jose Mercury News*, May 18, 2003, p. 6 E; Alessandra Stanley, "Architect of Atrocity: The Formative Years," *New York Times*, May 16, 2003, p. E1; "ADL endorses 'Hitler' miniseries," *United Press International*, May 2, 2003.

35. Robert Bianco, "Ultimate Lessons Redeem 'Hitler,'" *USA Today*, May 16, 2003, p. 9E; Andy Smith, "Nothing New in This TV Movie Look at Hitler," *Providence Journal-Bulletin*, May 18, 2003.

36. Stanley, "Architect of Atrocity: The Formative Years."

37. David Kronke, "'Hitler' Rarely Takes Risks," *Daily News of Los Angeles*, May 18, 2003, p. U11.

38. Ken Tucker, "Review of Hitler – The Rise of Evil," *Entertainment Weekly*, May 16, 2003.

39. Steve Murray, "Caricature of a Monster," *Atlanta Journal-Constitution*, May 17, 2003, p. 4C.

40. www.adl.org/PresRele/HolNa_52/4258_52.htm.

41. Mike Hughes, "Producers Found Fascinating Facts in Making 'Hitler' Miniseries," *Gannett News Service*, May 2, 2003.

42. MacDonald, "The Furor over Hitler."

43. MacDonald, "The Fuhrer on Screen."

44. Shales, "CBS's 'Hitler,' Digging at the Roots of Evil."

45. Charles Maier, Comments on "Hitler: The Rise of Evil," *H-German*, May 23, 2003. http://h-net.msu.edu/cgi-bin/logbrowse.pl?trx=vx&list=h-german&month=0305&week=d&msg=FwwJsiTcjpOy5f/6K1SXMA&user=&pw=.

46. Nathan Stolzfus, Comments on "Hitler: The Rise of Evil," *H-German*, May 23, 2003. http://h-net.msu.edu/cgi-bin/logbrowse.pl?trx=vx&list=h-german&month=0305&week=d&msg=1TY007gH/9%2bLuZqfMzGqFg&user=&pw=.

47. Quoted in Howard Rosenberg, "He Fought Our Fear, and the Fear Won," *Los Angeles Times*, April 14, 2003.

48. John Podhoretz, "A Hitler Miniseries Meant to Bash Bush," *New York Post*, April 9, 2003.

49. Ron Rosenbaum, "It's Sweepstime For Hitler, but Winter for Truth," *New York Observer*, May 12, 2003.

50. Naomi Pfefferman, "'Max' Paints Hitler as Human," *Jewish News of Greater Phoenix*, January 10, 2003; Jamie Malanowski, "Human, Yes, But No Less a Monster," *New York Times*, December 22, 2002, Section 2, p. 1.

51. www.culture.com/articles/1866/max-production-notes.phtml

52. "Interviews: Max: What if Hitler was a Successful Artist," www.emanuellevy. com/interview/max-what-if-hitler-was-a-successful-artist-4/.

53. www.culture.com/articles/1866/max-production-notes.phtml.

54. http://movies.about.com/library/weekly/aamaxinta.htm.

55. This point is made by Ed Gonzalez at: http://celebritywonder.ugo.com/movie/2002_Max_ed_gonzalez.html.

56. "Interviews: Max: What if Hitler was a Successful Artist," www.emanuellevy. com/interview/max-what-if-hitler-was-a-successful-artist-4/.

57. Anita Schwarz, Review of *Max*, *Detroit Metro Times*, February 12, 2003. www2.metrotimes.com/screens/review.asp?rid=19715.

58. Max Gross, "Portrait of Der Führer as a Young Man," *Forward*, December 20, 2002, p. 13.

59. "Interviews: Max: What if Hitler was a Successful Artist," www.emanuellevy. com/interview/max-what-if-hitler-was-a-successful-artist-4/.

60. Pfefferman, "'Max' Paints Hitler as Human."

61. www.beliefnet.com/Entertainment/Movies/2003/01/Is-Art-Mightier-Than-War.aspx?p=3.

62. www.imdb.com/title/tt0290210/business?ref_=tt_dt_bus.

63. David Talbot, "Was Hitler Human?" www.salon.com/2002/09/09/cusack_3/.

64. Malanowski, "Human, Yes, But No Less a Monster."

65. Andrew Gumbel, "Portrait of the Fascist as a Young Man," *The Independent*, September 24, 2002, pp. 4–5. See also "Cusack's Hitler Film Finds Jewish Ally," *New York Daily News*, December 22, 2002.

66. Pfefferman, "'Max' Paints Hitler as Human."

67. Terry Teachout, "Sympathy for the Devil," *Sight & Sound*, 6, June 2003.

68. Gumbel, "Portrait of the Fascist as a Young Man"; Dan Gire, "Naive Premise Fails to Take Hitler Drama to the 'Max,'" *Chicago Daily Herald*, January 24, 2003.

69. Todd McCarthy, Review of *Max*, *Variety*. September 11, 2002. www.variety. com/review/VE1117918685?refcatid=31; J. Hoberman, "Portraits of the Artist," *Village Voice*, December 24, 2002, www.villagevoice.com/2002-12-24/film/portraits-of-the-artist/2/

70. Stephen Hunter, "'Max': Tenderizing Adolf," *Washington Post*, February 7, 2003, p. C5.

71. Mick LaSalle, "A Bemusing What-If About Adolf Hitler," *San Francisco Chronicle*, January 24, 2003, p. D5; Rex Reed, "Adolf Hitler, Wannabe Artist," *New York Observer*, January 13, 2003; Martin Knelman, "Max Takes History Down a Treacherous Road," *Toronto Star*, September 14, 2002.

72. Lou Lumenick, "Think Time For Hitler In Max'," *New York Post*, December 27, 2002, p. 46; Stephen Holden, "Hitler Before the Führer," *New York Times*, December 27, 2002, http://movies.nytimes.com/movie/review? res=9904E1DA113CF934A15751C1A9649C8B63 Teachout, "Sympathy for the Devil."

73. Roger Ebert, Review of *Max*, *Chicago Sun-Times*, January 24, 200, http://rogerebert.suntimes.com/apps/pbcs.dll/article?AID=/20030124/REVIEWS/301240303/1023.

74. Peter Bradshaw, Review of *Max*, *The Guardian*, June 19, 2003, www.guardian.co.uk/culture/2003/jun/20/artsfeatures3; Malanowski, "Human, Yes, But No Less A Monster."

75. Klaus L. Berghahn writes that for Tabori, "making fun of Hitler is a kind of self-therapy in the service of survival": "'Hitler and His Jew': Notes on George Tabori's *Mein Kampf*," in Klaus L. Berghahn and Jost Hermand, eds., *Unmasking Hitler: Cultural Representations of Hitler from the Weimar Republic to the Present* (Bern, 2005), p. 199; Claire Horst, "Die Katastrophe als Witz," www.kino-zeit.de/filme/mein-kampf

76. Berghahn, "'Hitler and His Jew,'" pp. 198, 202; Michael Ranze, "Mein Kampf," *Hamburger Abendblatt*, March 3, 2011.

77. Berghahn, "'Hitler and His Jew,'" p. 197.

78. Ibid., pp. 197–201.

79. Tabori was opposed to lazy moralism, saying, "if we don't look past taboos and clichés and start treating each other as people and not abstractions, we may as well light up the ovens": Jörn Siedel, "Trittbrettfahrer der Hitlerei," *Die Zeit*, March 2, 2011.

80. "Interview with Regisseur Urs Odermatt," *Mein Kampf*, Presseheft.

81. www.nordwestfilm.ch/mein_kampf_inhalt.html.

82. Liam Trim, "Review of Dawn of Evil: Rise of the Reich," http://flickeringmyth.blogspot. This reviewer concluded, however, that *Mein Kampf* ended up being "a mediocre tale" with a "baffling … ending." Another reviewer approved of the fact that Odermatt was "attempting to offer a more 'humanized' Hitler," but concluded that the film ended up being "messy and unintentionally tongue-in-cheek": Jodie Sims, ""Review of Dawn of Evil: Rise of the Reich," www.thefilmpilgrim.com. *The Economist* described the film as "a very serious

attempt to once again understand the pathology of a profoundly sick and commanding man": "Imagining a Young Hitler," *The Economist*, March 24, 2011. *The Hollywood Reporter* called it "uninspired" and compared it to a "play [that] someone filmed": Karstein Kastelan, Review of *Mein Kampf, Hollywood Reporter*, July 20, 2010

83. Siedel, "Trittbrettfahrer der Hitlerei."

84. Claire Horst, "Die Katastrophe als Witz," www.kino-zeit.de/filme/mein-kampf.

85. "Wahnwitz im Männerheim," *Stuttgarter Nachrichten*, March 3, 2011; Sonja M. Schulz, "Mein Kampf," www.critic.de/film-main-kampf-2492.

86. Wolfgang Höbel, "Als Hitler noch Klein-Adolf war," *Der Spiegel*, March 3, 2011.

87. Jörn Siedel, "Trittbrettfahrer der Hitlerei."

88. Jan Schulz-Ojala, "Sein Krampf," *Der Tagesspiegel*, March 3, 2011.

89. Anke Westphal, "Ein Gnatze, mehr nicht," *Berliner Zeitung*, March 3, 2011.

90. Dietrich Kuhlbrodt, "Mein Kampf," *Filmgazette*, www.filmgazette.de/index.php?s=filmkritiken&id=283. This essay was originally published in *Konkret* in March, 2011.

91. Berghahn, "'Hitler and His Jew,'" p. 211.

92. Kuhlbrodt, "Mein Kampf."

93. Other reviews did in fact note that viewers expecting to see "Jewish humor" in the film would be disappointed, www.news.de/medien/855135667/verfilmung-von-taboris-mein-kampf/1/.

94. Joachim Fest, *Hitler und das Ende des Dritten Reiches* (Berlin 2002), in translation, *Inside Hitler's Bunker: The Last Days of the Third Reich* (New York, 2004) ; Traudl Junge, *Bis zur letzten Stunde* (Berlin 2002), in translation *Until the Final Hour* (London, 2003).

95. Michael Wildt "*Der Untergang*: Ein Film inszeniert sich als Quelle," *Zeithistorische Forschungen*, 1, 2005, www.zeithistorische-forschungen.de/site/40208312/default.aspx.

96. John Bendix, "Facing Hitler: German Responses to *Downfall*," *German Politics and Society*, 1, 2007, p. 76.

97. Hellmuth Karasek, "Der jämmerliche Dictator," *Der Tagesspiegel*, September 11, 2004.

98. Frank Schirmacher, "Hitler Spielen," *FAZ*, August 22, 2004.

99. "Hitler ist greifbarer geworden," *Frankfurter Rundschau*, September 11, 2004, www.filmportal.de/node/69095/material/544449.

100. Bendix, "Facing Hitler," p. 74.

101. "Hitler ist greifbarer geworden."

102. David Bathrick, "Whose Hi/story Is It? The U. S. Reception of *Downfall*," *New German Critique*, Fall 2007, p. 9.

103. Ibid., p. 9.

104. Ibid., p. 73.

105. "Hitler ist greifbarer geworden": Wildt "*Der Untergang*."

106. Gina Thomas, "Bunker Mentality," *The Guardian*, August 26, 2004.

107. Ian Kershaw, "The Human Hitler," *The Guardian*, September 16, 2004; Mark Landler, "The All-Too-Human Hitler, on Your Big Screen," *New York Times*, September 15, 2004, p. A4.

108. Quoted in Wildt, "*Der Untergang*."

109. Frank Schirrmacher. "Die zweite Erfindung des Adolf Hitler," *FAZ*, September 14, 2004.

110. Wildt "*Der Untergang*"; Hans-Georg Rodek, "Das Ende des Schwarzweiss Phantoms," *Die Welt*, September 15, 2004.

111. Harald Welzer, "Der erratische Führer," *Frankfurter Rundschau*, September 18, 2004, p. 15.

112. Goetz Aly, "Ich bin das Volk," *SZ*, September 1, 2004; Wim Wenders. "Tja, dann wollen wir mal. Warum darf man Hitler in "Der Untergang" nicht sterben sehen? Kritische Anmerkungen zu einem Film ohne Haltung," *Die Zeit*, 44, October 21, 2004.

113. Jens Jessen, "Stilles Ende eines Irren unter Tage," *Die Zeit*, August 26, 2004, p. 33.

114. Georg Seesslen, "Das faschistische Subjekt," *Die Zeit*, September 16, 2004.

115. Wenders, "Tja, dann wollen wir mal."

116. Wildt, "*Der Untergang*."

117. Quoted in Sven Felix Kellerhoff, "Die deutschen Historiker sahen 'Der Untergang,'" *Die Welt*, September 17, 2004; Joachim Frank, "Täter die am Ende zu Opfer werden," *Kölner Stadt-Anzeiger*, September 18, 2004.

118. See Hannes Heer, *Hitler war's: Die Befreiung der Deutschen von ihrer Vergangenheit* (Berlin, 2005). He added that this trend was also visible in Guido Knopp's Hitler-focused television documentaries.

119. Welzer, "Der erratische Führer."

120. David Denby, "Back in the Bunker," *New Yorker*, February 14, 2005.

121. See Heer, *Hitler war's*, pp. 14–17; David Cesarani and Peter Longerich, "The Massaging of History," *The Guardian*, April 7, 2005.

122. Julia Anspach, "Der Untergang – ein Tauerspiel," *Kritische Ausgabe*, 2, 2004.

123. Ibid.

124. Jutta Brückner, "Das späte Kind," *Freitag*, January 12, 2006.

125. Anke Westphal, "Jedes Volk sucht sich seinen Diktator," *Berliner Zeitung*, January 6, 2007; Bert Rebhandl, "Adolf Hitler? Hast du das denn nötig?" *Der Standard* (Austria), January 10, 2007; Johanna Adorján, "Dürfen wir über Hitler lachen?" *FAZ*, December 17, 2006.

126. Ibid. Moritz Holfelder, "Das Dritte Reich ist Kabarettstoff," *Frankfurter Rundschau*, January 8, 2007.

127. Bert Rebhandl, "Adolf Hitler? Hast du das denn nötig?"
128. Ibid.
129. Adorján, "Dürfen wir über Hitler lachen?"
130. Peter Zander, "Levy: Der Kontext von Sex und Macht ist sehr interessant," *Die Welt*, January 5, 2007.
131. Holfelder, "Das Dritte Reich ist Kabarettstoff."
132. Thomas Stephens, "Swiss Directs Controversial Führer Farce," January 12, 2007. www.swissinfo.ch/eng/Home/Archive/ Swiss_directs_controversial_Fuehrer_farce.html?cid=5661024.
133. Rebhandl, "Adolf Hitler? Hast du das denn nötig?"
134. "Levy schreibt an die Kino-Besucher: 'Lachen ist ein Politikum," *Die Welt*, January 20, 2007. Also www.faz.net/-oond78.
135. Adorján, "Dürfen wir über Hitler lachen?"
136. See www.meinfuehrer-derfilm.de/downloads/MEINFUEHRER_Schulheft.pdf.
137. www.meinfuehrer-derfilm.de/downloads/MEINFUEHRER_Schulheft.pdf.
138. Levy said that the "environment [in which the] leaders and followers of National Socialism [grew]... up [in]" constituted "the moral tragedy of that time." Statement by Director Dani Levy.
139. Stephan J. Kramer, "'Mein Führer'" – oberflächlich, überflüssig, gefährlich," *Der Tagesspiegel*, January 11, 2007, p. 8; "Weitere Kritik an 'Mein Führer,'" *Die Welt*, January 10, 2007.
140. Jan Schulz-Ojala, "Alles auf Adolf," *Der Tagesspiegel*, January 6, 2007; "Giordano: Neuer Hitler-Film kann Schaden anrichten," *Die Welt*, January 3, 2007.
141. "Weitere Kritik an 'Mein Führer,'" *Die Welt*, January 10, 2007; "Massive Kritik an Levys Hitler-Satire," *Der Spiegel*, January 9, 2007.
142. Harald Martenstein, "Adolf auf der Couch," *Die Zeit*, January 4, 2007.
143. Lothar Müller, "Lachnummer Adolf," *Der Tagesspiegel*, January 11, 2007, p. 26.
144. Wilhelm Hofmann and Anna Baumert, "Hitler als Figur der psychologischen Medienforschung," in Rainer Rother and Karin Herbst-Meßlinger, eds., *Hitler Darstellen: Zur Entwicklung und Bedeutung einer filmischen Figur* (Munich, 2008), pp. 140–42.
145. Christian Ihle and Horst Motor, "Review, Mein Führer," *TAZ*, January 12, 2007. See also Holden, "Hitler Before the Führer."
146. Henryk Broder, "Dani Levy's Failed Hitler Comedy," *Der Spiegel*, January 9, 2007.
147. Derek Elley, Review of *Mein Führer*, *Variety*, January 22, 2007, p. 25. See also Eric Hansen, Review of *Mein Führer*, *Hollywood Reporter*, January 9, 2007, www.ethansen.de/Pro/THRReviews.html; Nick Pinkerton, "My Führer Lacks Gall," *Village Voice*, August, 11, 2009, www.villagevoice.com/2009-08-11/film/my-f-uuml-hrer-lacks-gall/.

148. Stephen Holden, "Some Unexpected Behavior Therapy for the Not-So-Great Dictator," *New York Times*, August 13, 2009.

149. Schmölders, "Der Führer privat – aber für wen?" p. 15.

150. Elmar Krekeler, "Adolf Hitler einfach wegzaubern," *Die Welt*, January 13, 2007.

151. Horst von Butlar, "Hi- Hi- Hitler," *Financial Times Deutschland*, January 5, 2007, pp. 1–2.

152. This was the opinion of Manfred Funke. Quoted in Regina Krieger, "Lizenz zum Lachen über Peinlichkeiten," *Handelsblatt*, January 10, 2007.

153. Jutta Brückner, "Das späte Kind," *Freitag*, January 12, 2006.

154. Alan Posener, "Der Jud tut gut," *Jüdische Allgemeine*, January 11, 2007. Levy himself recognized that he was a "welcome taboo breaker for non-Jewish Germans": "Wie soll man Hitler verharmlosen?" *Jüdische Allgemeine*, January 11, 2007.

155. Christiane Peitz, "Kennen sie den?" *Der Tagesspiegel*, January 12, 2007.

156. www.imsdb.com/scripts/Inglourious-Basterds.html.

157. "Der Fingerabdruck des Joseph Goebbels," *FAZ*, August 20, 2009.

158. "Glorious Bastard," *Forward*, December 4, 2009.

159. Jeffrey Goldberg, "Hollywood's Jewish Avenger," *The Atlantic*, September, 2009.

160. Daniel Mendelsohn, "'Inglourious Basterds': When Jews Attack," *Newsweek*, August 13, 2009; Manohla Dargis, "Tarantino Avengers in Nazi Movieland," *New York Times*, August 20, 2009.

161. J. Hoberman, "Quentin Tarantino's *Inglourious Basterds* Makes Holocaust Revisionism Fun," *Village Voice*, August 18, 2009; "Ich bin ja kein Nazi," *SZ*, August 17, 2009; Andreas Hartmann, "Die Rache an Guido Knopp," *Jungle World*, August 20, 2009, http://jungle-world.com/artikel/2009/34/37577.html.

162. Roger Ebert, Review of *Inglourious Basterds*, August 19, 2009. http://rogerebert.suntimes.com/apps/pbcs.dll/article?AID=/20090819/REVIEWS/908199995/1023; Peter Travers, Review of *Inglourious Basterds*, in *Rolling Stone*, August 20, 2009; Stephanie Zacharek, Review of *Inglourious Basterds*, in Salon.com August 21, 2009, www.salon.com/2009/08/21/inglourious_basterds/.

163. Sophie Albers, "Mehr als eine jüdische Rachefantasie," *Stern*, August 20, 2009.

164. Hartmann, "Die Rache an Guido Knopp"; see also Denise Peikert, "Retter der Geschichte," August 20, 2009, www.news.de/medien/5334/retter-der-geschichte/1/.

165. Jan Schulz-Ojala, "Das schönste Attentat der Welt," *Der Tagesspiegel*, May 20, 2009. In its first four months, it took in a worldwide gross of more than $300 million, www.imdb.com/title/tt0361748/.

166. Jens Jessen, "Skalpiert die Deutschen!" *Die Zeit*, August 20, 2009.

167. http://articles.boston.com/2009–08–21/ae/29264139_1_christoph-waltz-m-lanie-laurent-tarantino-film/3.

168. Mendelsohn, "Inglourious Basterds"; Jessen, "Skalpiert die Deutschen!"

169. Mendelsohn, "Inglourious Basterds."

170. Hoberman, "Quentin Tarantino's *Inglourious Basterds* Makes Holocaust Revisionism Fun."

171. Goldberg, "Hollywood's Jewish Avenger."

172. Martin Engelberg, "Märchen aus vergangenen Zeiten," *Die Presse*, August 22, 2009, http://diepresse.com/home/meinung/debatte/503491/Maerchen-aus-vergangenen-Zeiten.

173. Goldberg, "Hollywood's Jewish Avenger."

174. Dargis, "Tarantino Avengers in Nazi Movieland,"

175. Karine Cohen-Dicker, "Jewish Revenge Porn," *Forward*, June 12, 2009.

176. Goldberg, "Hollywood's Jewish Avenger."

177. Danielle Berrin, "Quentin Tarantino Calls Israeli Army Service 'Awesome'" *Jewish Journal of Los Angeles*, February 9, 2010.

178. Danielle Berrin, "Oscar Buzz: The impact of 'Inglourious Basterds' on the Jews," *Jewish Journal*, February 24, 2010. www.jewishjournal.com/hollywoodjew/item/oscar_worthy_the_impact_of_inglourious_basterds_on_the_jews_20100224/.

179. Albers, "Mehr als eine jüdische Rachefantasie."

180. For Liel Liebowitz, the film illustrated a non-Jewish sensibility: "Inglorious Indeed," *Tablet*, August 21, 2009. Daniel Mendelsohn agreed, arguing that "an alternate and morally superior form of revenge for Jews would be to do precisely what Jews have been doing since World War II ended: that is to preserve and perpetuate the memory of the destruction that was visited upon them": Mendelsohn, 'Inglourious Basterds.'

Chapter 6 Between tragedy and farce: Nazism on the Internet

1. http://en.wikipedia.org/wiki/Hitler.

2. www.stormfront.org/forum/t830473/.

3. www.catsthatlooklikehitler.com/cgi-bin/seigany.pl?faq.html.

4. For a useful discussion of the Internet and the information revolution, see Johnny Ryan, *A History of the Internet and the Digital Future* (London, 2010).

5. www.fordham.edu/Halsall/index.asp; http://www.besthistorysites.net/.

6. www.h-net.org/.

7. Carl Smith, "Can You Do Serious History on the Web?" *Perspectives*, February, 1998, www.historians.org/perspectives/issues/1998/9802/9802COM.CFM; Andrew McMichael, "The Historian, the Internet, and the Web: A Reassessment," *Perspectives*, February, 1998.

8. Nicholas Carr, *The Shallows: What the Internet is Doing to Our Brains* (New York, 2011), p. 116.
9. Ibid., pp. 138, 170.
10. Ibid., p. 91.
11. Ibid., p. 131
12. Ibid., p. 136.
13. Nicholas Carr, "The Web Shatters Focus, Rewires Brains," *Wired Magazine*, May 24, 2010, www.wired.com/magazine/2010/05/ff_nicholas_carr/all/1
14. Carr, *The Shallows*, p. 193.
15. Ibid., pp. 124–25.
16. Patricia Cohen, "Internet Use Affects Memory," *New York Times*, July 14, 2011.
17. Gez Hebburn, "The 'Google Effect' Debunked: Human Memory Changes Did Not Start with Search Engines," *Search Engine Journal*, July 25, 2011, www.searchenginejournal.com/the-google-effect-debunked-human-memory-changes/31264/.
18. http://de.wikipedia.org/wiki/Kategorie:NSDAP-Mitglied.
19. http://fcit.usf.edu/holocaust/.
20. www.ushmm.org/; http://www.mjhnyc.org/findex.html; www.holocaustcenter.org/; www.hmh.org/; www.museumoftolerance.com; www.lamoth.org/; www.ilholocaustmuseum.org/.
21. www.facing.org/; www.adl.org/main_Holocaust/default.htm; www.wiesenthal.com.
22. www.topographie.de/de/topographie-des-terrors/nc/1/; www.museen.nuernberg.de/dokuzentrum/; www.ns-dokumentationszentrum-muenchen.de/ centre www.museenkoeln.de/ns-dok/; www.dhm.de/; www.ghi-dc.org/; www.goethe.de/ges/pok/enindex.htm.
23. See, for example, Munich's City Museum site: www.stadtmuseum-online.de/dauerausstellungen/nationalsozialismus.html.
24. See, for instance, the website for Auschwitz, http://en.auschwitz.org/m/, Hungary's Holocaust Museum in Budapest, http://old.hdke.hu/index.php?changelang=eng; and the Croatian concentration camp Jasenovac at www.jusp-jasenovac.hr/Default.aspx?sid=5020.
25. www.yadvashem.org/; other Israeli Holocaust museums also have sites, such as the Ghetto Fighters' House Museum, www.gfh.org.il/Eng/.
26. www.calvin.edu/academic/cas/gpa/.
27. www.ww2remembered.com/; http://www.lostimagesofww2.com/.
28. http://www.thirdreichlocations.com/; www.thirdreichruins.com/; http://hitlerpages.com/.
29. For the audio: www.dhm.de/medien/lemo/audios/hitler; for the video: www.dhm.de/medien/lemo/videos/potsdam.
30. http://en.wikipedia.org/wiki/The_Holocaust.

31. http://en.wikipedia.org/wiki/The_Holocaust.

32. Writing of Jasenovac, Wolfgang Benz cites survivor testimonies that camp officials may have experimented with gassing children, but stresses that they never introduced this killing method in systematic fashion. Overall, he concludes, "the murder of prisoners did not take place in gas chambers … but through torture, beatings … sickness and hunger": Wolfgang Benz, *Der Ort des Terrors: Geschichte der nationalsozialistischen Konzentrationslager* (Munich, 2009), vol. 9, pp. 328–29. At Maly Trostinets, near Minsk, gas vans were used to kill Jews for three days in late July, 1942, but otherwise, Jews were killed there in mass shootings, www.holocaustresearchproject.org/nazioccupation/malytrost.html.

33. See, for example: http://www.thirdreichlocations.com/.

34. www.hitlerpages.com/index.html; www.hitlerpages.com/pagina56.html; www.hitlerpages.com/pagina11.html.

35. www.thirdreichlocations.com/WEWELSBURG/OTTENSHOF/Ottenshof.html; www.thirdreichlocations.com/MUNCHEN/STUDIOTHORAK/Studiothorak.html; www.thirdreichlocations.com/WUNSIEDEL/Graverudolfhess.html.

36. Email from Jon Reffs to author, October 14, 2013. In a follow-up message, Reffs related that he had not previously considered the possibility of neo-Nazis misinterpreting his site and resolved to alter the site's captions.

37. John Sutherland, "Mainstreaming Neo-Nazism," *Dimensions: A Journal of Holocaust Studies*, 13:1, 1999, www.adl.org/braun/dim_13_1_neonazism.asp.

38. A 1996 article cites 70 neo-Nazi websites, www.independent.co.uk/news/eu-racism-watchdog-demands-Internet-neonazi-censorship-1326493.html.

39. Estimated at 500 in 1999. http://news.bbc.co.uk/2/hi/americas/600876.stm.

40. Irving's website is www.fpp.co.uk/; Zundel's is www.zundelsite.org/.

41. http://www.metapedia.org/.

42. See "Das Parteiprogramm der NPD" at www.npd.de/html/1939/artikel/detail/1830/.

43. This claim is found on Wikipedia: http://en.wikipedia.org/wiki/Stormfront_(website).

44. http://www.mathaba.net/www/nazi/index.shtml.

45. Breivik belonged to the Swedish neo-Nazi forum, Nordisk, www.bbc.co.uk/news/world-europe-14259989. For other cases see, Christopher Wolf, "Hate on the Internet Leads to Hate Crime: What Is Society's Best Response?" in Barbara Perry et al., eds., *Hate Crimes: Volume 5, Responding to Hate Crimes* (Westport, CT, 2009), pp. 213–24.

46. http://en.wikipedia.org/wiki/Talk:Liberty_Lobby

47. This remark can often be found on the "talk page" sections of Wikipedia entries. See for example: http://en.wikipedia.org/wiki/Talk%3ABombing_of_Dresden_in_World_War_II/Archive_6#Neutrality_dispute.

48. John Brandon, "Dropping the Bomb on Google," *Wired Magazine*, May 11, 2004, www.wired.com/culture/lifestyle/news/2004/05/63380.

49. Scott Sayre, "Concern over an Increasingly Seen Gesture Grows in France," *New York Times*, January 2, 2014; See the French postings on Twitter: https://twitter.com/search?q=%23laquenellenestpasunsignenaziouantisemite&src=hash as reported in Robert Mackey's important article, "French Comic's 'Anti-System' Salute Is Frequently Used to Mock Jewish Suffering" http://thelede.blogs.nytimes.com/2013/12/31/french-comics-anti-system-salute-is-frequently-used-to-mock-jewish-suffering/?_php=true&_type=blogs&_r=0. See also Noah Gur-Arieh, "The Anti-Semite Quenelle Salute is Sweeping Europe, and the World Stands Still," *Jewish Journal*, December 30, 2013.

50. See the website Anti-fascists Online at www.anti-fascists-online.com/ See also the Twitter feed, "antiquenelle" at https://twitter.com/antiquenelles.

51. www.google.com/explanation.html; The ADL responded favorably to Google's explanation, www.adl.org/PresRele/Internet_75/4482_75.htm.

52. In 2002, eBay reported that an estimated 1,125 Hitler related items were for sale, ranging from postage stamps to cuff links: Marc Fisher, "The Art of Evil," *Washington Post*, April 21, 2002.

53. A German annotated edition is forthcoming, however. See "Bavaria Plans New Edition of 'Mein Kampf'," *Der Spiegel*, April 24, 2012, www.spiegel.de/international/germany/bavaria-plans-to-publish-new-edition-of-adolf-hitler-s-mein-kampf-a-829513.html.

54. "Ebay Is Told that It Sells Nazi Items," *New York Times*, November 25, 1999, www.nytimes.com/1999/11/25/business/ebay-is-told-that-it-sells-nazi-items.html

55. "'Anonymous' Declares 'Blitzkrieg' on Neo-Nazis," The Local: Germany's News in English, January 2, 2012, www.thelocal.de/society/20120102-39867.html.

56. For a representative selection see the website Know Your Meme, http://knowyourmeme.com/.

57. Virginia Heffernan, "The Hitler Meme," *New York Times*, October 24, 2008. www.nytimes.com/2008/10/26/magazine/26wwln-medium-t.html?pagewanted=all. A search of Know Your Meme lists 64 results for "Hitler," http://knowyourmeme.com/search?utf8=✓&q=hitler.

58. See Rod A. Martin, *The Psychology of Humor: An Integrative Approach* (Burlington, MA, 2007), p. 13. These and other forms of humor have different functions; irony ("a figure of speech that communicates the opposite of what is said") is mostly observational and points out states of contradiction (ibid., p. 98). Parody is mostly devoted to mimicry, while satire pursues active critique. On satire, see Avner Ziv, "Humor as a Social Corrective," in Laurence Behrens and Leonard J. Rosen, eds., *Writing and Reading Across the Curriculum*, 3rd edn (Glenview, IL, 1988), pp. 356–60.

59. Many, as a result, have had to offer disclaimers reassuring web users about their intentions.

60. Beyond the films mentioned in Chapters 4 and 5, Hitler has been featured on such American television shows as *Saturday Night Live, The Daily Show with Jon Stewart, The Colbert Report, The Simpsons,* and *Family Guy*; he has also repeatedly appeared on the hit German show, the Harald Schmidt Show; and the short-lived British sitcom, *Heil Honey I'm Home!* Hitler has also been spoofed in comic books, such as Walter Moers's two volume, *Adolf, die Nazi-Sau* (1998–99) and Achim Greser's, *Der Führer Privat* (2000).

61. In *The Psychology of Humor*, Martin defines incongruity on p. 63 and discusses it more broadly on pp. 62–75. See also pp. 6, 22. He discusses disparagement at pp. 44–56. Disparagement is often referrred to as the "superiority theory": see the discussion by D. H. Monro, "Theories of Humor," in Behrens and Rosen, eds., *Writing and Reading Across the Curriculum*, p. 351.

62. Martin, *The Psychology of Humor*, pp. 7–20.

63. Of course, the forms and functions of humor vary for victims and perpetrators. For the former, humor often takes a "gallows" form, in which laughter is meant to help "maintain … one's sanity in seemingly hopeless … situations." For perpetrators and their descendants, laughter is meant to serve as a defense mechanism that enables one to evade a sense of guilt (ibid., p. 49).

64. http://knowyourmeme.com/memes/downfall-hitler-reacts. Typing the words "Downfall Parody" into YouTube's search engine yields approximately 47,000 hits.

65. The creator of the meme is DReaperF4. The original video (now translated into broken English) can be found at www.youtube.com/watch?v=Gz1_pUMwnEo. See also http://knowyourmeme.com/memes/downfall-hitler-reacts; http://hitlerparody.wikia.com/wiki/Sim_Heil.

66. All of these videos can be found on YouTube.

67. Robert Mackey, "Israeli Hitler Parody Upsets Holocaust Survivors," *New York Times*, February 18, 2009, http://thelede.blogs.nytimes.com/2009/02/18/israeli-hitler-parody-outrages-holocaust-survivors/. "Hitler on 2010 Philippine Elections: Manny Villar" can be found at www.youtube.com/watch?v=oOdoJVQ-s_c&feature=relmfu.

68. David Smith and Rowan Walker, "Meet the New Face of Satire as Hitler Web Craze Goes Viral," *The Guardian*, September 27, 2008, www.guardian.co.uk/media/2008/sep/28/youtube.Internet; "Hitler Downfall Parodies: 25 Worth Watching," *The Telegraph*, October 6, 2009, www.telegraph.co.uk/technology/news/6262709/Hitler-Downfall-parodies-25-worth-watching.html.

69. Benny Evangelista, "Parody, Copyright Law Clash in Online Clips," *San Francisco Chronicle*, July 23, 2010.

70. www.ranker.com/list/top-10-hitler-downfall-parodies-of-all-time/the-master.

71. www.youtube.com/watch?v=cqqxRPZdfvs.
72. Hitler rants about Hitler http://www.youtube.com/watch?v=8B3H_tHH8jw.
73. www.youtube.com/watch?v=AFbHr-nKkTc.
74. www.youtube.com/watch?v=xlLZ4RWyyAw
75. hitlerparody.wikia.com/wiki/Hitler_Rants_Parodies; http://hitlerparody.wikia. com/wiki/Unterganger.
76. Know your meme. "Flaming" involves expressing one's immediate emotions instantaneously via email or blogging without stopping to self-censor; "trolling" involves expressing cynical comments to other users' posts with the intention of starting an argument.
77. www.youtube.com/watch?v=a4lJ9vsZjMU.
78. www.youtube.com/watch?v=Q9X5jV2LxoQ% 26list=UUSEu_9uWST6nOtHbjYLvG5A%26index=8%26feature=plcp.
79. Finlo Rohrer, "The Rise, Rise and Rise of the Downfall Hitler Parody," *BBC Magazine*, April 13, 2010, http://news.bbc.co.uk/2/hi/uk_news/magazine/ 8617454.stm; Mercedes Bunz, "Just how many Hitler videos does the world need?" *The Guardian*, February 2, 2010; www.guardian.co.uk/media/pda/ 2010/feb/01/digital-media-youtube-hitler-parody; T. Kniebe, "Schaum vorm Mund," *SZ*, April 20, 2010, www.sueddeutsche.de/kultur/untergang-parodien-schaum-vorm-mund-1.937357
80. There have literally been tens of thousands of comments, as shown by the numbers for videos, such as "Hitler Finds Out Americans are Calling Each Other Nazis," (1,462), "Hitler is Informed His Pizza Will Arrive Late (975), and "Hitler rants about Rebecca Black – Friday," (741). All figures are from YouTube.
81. A good example was provided by the nearly 1,000 comments on the Obama Health Care parody.
82. The first comment was by, oortiz915, www.youtube.com/watch?v=AFbHr-nKkTc (posted April, 2012), the second by SuperColodude.
83. www.youtube.com/watch?v=UTgPLVANbD8, PhantomOperaluver75.
84. CosmicCrater1 (no date listed).
85. www.youtube.com/watch?v=UTgPLVANbD8, 29Essan (no date listed).
86. The first music video satirizing Hitler may well be Mel Brooks's promotional "Hitler Rap" video for the film, *To Be Or Not To Be* (1983), http://blog. starwreck.com/2007/09/25/hitler-rap/.
87. www.youtube.com/watch?v=-ghmoPn_b6I&skipcontrinter=1.
88. www.youtube.com/watch?v=m5TbJ7ODi2Y.
89. One of the several versions of the video on YouTube has nearly four million views, www.youtube.com/watch?v=Pq4gQPReH2E. Another has over 700,000. Thomas Meister, "Viel Lärm um den 'Bonker' – aber eigentlich lohnt es nicht," *Tages-Anzeiger*, 22. September 2006.

90. See, for example, Thomas Meister, "Viel Lärm um den 'Bonker'"; Wiebke Brauer, "Moers-Parodie: Schrumpfkur für Hitler," *Der Spiegel*, July 4, 2006, www.spiegel.de/kultur/gesellschaft/moers-parodie-schrumpfkur-fuer-hitler-a-424980.html; See also Andreas Platthaus, "Die Wanne ist voll Führer," *FAZ*, September 5, 2006, www.faz.net/aktuell/feuilleton/buecher/moers-hitler-clip-die-wanne-ist-voll-fuehrer-1357830.html.

91. www.cartoonland.de/archiv/adolf-ich-hock-in-meinem-bonker/.

92. Headstrong5472 (no date listed). www.youtube.com/all_comments?v=Tv47iWKUv5A, www.cartoonland.de/archiv/adolf-ich-hock-in-meinem-bonker/.

93. Posting by www.reviersheriff.de, July 14, 2006, www.cartoonland.de/archiv/adolf-ich-hock-in-meinem-bonker/

94. The comment was by psychedelicSwing, www.youtube.com/watch?v=Tv47iWKUv5A.

95. The comment was by 7Hip7Hop7; Drea1960.

96. The comment was by xxxmvtxxx (no date listed). www.youtube.com/all_comments?v=Pq4gQPReH2E.

97. One of the most popular videos was "Hitler Leasing", which combined footage of a Hitler speech with audio from a comedy sketch about a customer being ripped off by a car leasing company. See "Das Florians-Prinzip," *Focus Magazin*, October 5, 2006, pp. 184–85.

98. http://hipsterhitler.com/hhcomic/wp-content/uploads/2011/10/02_juice.jpg.

99. http://hipsterhitler.com/comics/typewriter/.

100. http://hipsterhitler.com/comics/new-uniforms/; http://hipsterhitler.com/comics/art-school/; http://hipsterhitler.com/comics/halloween/.

101. http://hipsterhitler.com/about-us-2/.

102. "HH Finds His Heimat," *Exberliner*, February 10, 2011. www.exberliner.com/articles/hipster-hitler-finds-his-heimat; See also www.sunday-guardian.com/technologic/hitler-goes-hip-webcomic-satirises-the-fuehrer.

103. The figure of 65,000 is cited at http://silencingprotestsonredbubble.wordpress.com/2011/05/18/a-rb-members-reply-to-the-hipster-hitler-interview/. The figure rose above 100,000 by the fall of 2012. www.socialbakers.com/facebook-pages/141986212505362-hipster-hitler-www-hipsterhitler-com.

104. "HH Finds His Heimat."

105. Ibid.

106. http://hipsterhitler.com/category/store/shirts/.

107. See posts on September 8, 2010. As one put it, "Absolutely genius. If there was a button, I would totally Reich this."

108. See the comment by A_German on May 8, 2011, www.jewlicious.com/2010/10/hipster-hitler/.

109. See the comment by icarus from November 11, 2010 on www.jewlicious.com/2010/10/hipster-hitler/.
110. http://liamgetreu.com/2011/05/18/trying-to-censor-hipster-hitler/.
111. http://tookalook.de/wissenswertes/hipster-hitler-die-generation-die-sich-daruber-lustig-macht-2/.
112. "Update: Reflections on the "Hipster Hitler" Saga: Lawyers, Censorship and Professional Ethics," Firmspy, June 1, 2011, http://firmspy.com/big-firms/allens-arthur-robinson/5752/reflections-on-the-hipster-hitler-saga-lawyers-censorship-and-professional-ethics. Reports of offensive posts on the site can be found on www.nerve.com/news/web/hipster-hitler-t-shirts-get-sued-are-taken-offline. See offensive posts at www.facebook.com/pages/Hipster-Hitler/131291990251318?ref=ts.
113. http://webcache.googleusercontent.com/search?q=cache:z5EXoSL7H4AJ:firmspy.com/big-firms/allens-arthur-robinson/5752/reflections-on-the-hipster-hitler-saga-lawyers-censorship-and-professional-ethics+hipster+hitler+interview+jc+apk+neo+nazis&hl=en&client=safari&gl=us&prmd=imvns&strip=1.
114. See comment by sh'muel October 23, 2010 at www.jewlicious.com/2010/10/hipster-hitler/.
115. http://blogs.jpost.com/content/holocaust-free-speech-v-hate-speech; www.crikey.com.au/2011/05/30/hipster-hitler-sends-redbubbles-law-firm-fleeing/?wpmp_switcher=mobile.
116. The site reports the existence of more than 7,000 photos, www.catsthatlooklikehitler.com/cgi-bin/seigmiaow.pl?7326.
117. www.catsthatlooklikehitler.com/cgi-bin/seigmiaow.pl?7326.
118. www.cafepress.com/kitlerware.
119. www.catsthatlooklikehitler.com/cgi-bin/seigany.pl?faq.html.
120. "Heil Kitler!" *Daily Mail*, March 31, 2011, www.dailymail.co.uk/news/article-1371854/Cats-look-like-Hitler.html; "Mein Furrer," *The Sun*, March 31, 2011. www.thesun.co.uk/sol/homepage/news/3500747/Cats-that-look-like-Adolf-Hitler.html; the site was profiled on BBC2's *Graham Norton Show* in 2009. http://fliiby.com/file/626384/048ziir39p.html.
121. For the Colbert report, www.colbertnation.com/the-colbert-report-videos/341469/july-26-2010/racial-pro-firing; for the CNN report, www.chicagotribune.com/news/nationworld/sns-viral-video-cats-hitler,0,5369851.htmlstory.
122. Comment by "Amber," www.catsthatlooklikehitler.com/cgi-bin/seigany.pl?love.html.
123. www.catsthatlooklikehitler.com/cgi-bin/seigany.pl?hate.html.
124. www.catsthatlooklikehitler.com/cgi-bin/seigany.pl?faq.html.
125. www.telegraph.co.uk/news/newstopics/howaboutthat/9206989/Fish-that-looks-like-Hitler.html.

126. www.dailymail.co.uk/news/article-2012804/He-looks-like-Nazi-piece-work-Meet-bug-resembles-Hitler.html.

127. www.dailymail.co.uk/news/article-1371091/Swansea-house-looks-like-Hitler-complete-naff-parting.html.

128. Derek Thompson, "JC Penney's 'Hitler Tea Kettle' Sold Out in Hours Because This Is the Internet," *The Atlantic*, May 29, 2013, www.theatlantic.com/business/archive/2013/05/jc-penneys-hitler-tea-kettle-sold-out-in-hours-because-this-is-the-Internet/276334/

129. "Hakenkreuz aus Lärchen," *Der Spiegel*, November 23, 2000, www.spiegel.de/politik/deutschland/0,1518,104321,00.html.

130. "Navy Considers Modifying Swastika Barracks following Inquiries from Congresswoman, ADL," *San Diego Jewish Times*, December 13, 2006, www.jewishsightseeing.com/dhh_weblog/2006-blog/2006-12/2006-12-13-coronado-swastika.htm;http://www.theregister.co.uk/2005/07/18/hitler_san_diego/.

131. http://thingsthatlooklikehitler.com/.

132. http://thingsthatlooklikehitler.com/page/3.

133. http://thingsthatlooklikehitler.com/page/4.

134. www.thedailybuggle.com/4-websites/.

135. www.guardian.co.uk/world/gallery/2011/jul/21/jesus-food-sightings#/?picture=377121666&index=4.

136. See Thompson, "JC Penney's 'Hitler Tea Kettle' Sold Out in Hours."

137. Cori Faklaris, "This 'Hitler' Teapot From JC Penney is the Talk of the *Internet!*" *Indianapolis Star*, May 29, 2013. The controversy began after a Reddit user posted the photo. www.indystar.com/article/20130529/NEWS09/305290034/This-Hitler-teapot-from-JC-Penney-talk-Internet-

138. One can place wigs and eyeglasses on Hitler on "Hitler Styler." http://mostplays.com/play/hitler_styler_30781. One can also make Hitler act as a disc jockey at www.newgrounds.com/portal/view/502713. One can kill Hitler at www.pictogame.com/en/play/game/AncSVifb6bPN_kill-hitler.

139. Timothy Noah, "Six Degrees of Adolf Hitler," *Slate*, April 17, 2008, www.slate.com/articles/news_and_politics/chatterbox/2008/04/six_degrees_of_adolf_hitler.html.

140. Black attacked Glen Beck for linking President Obama's choice of a Supreme Court justice to Hitler's T4 program via the sentiment of empathy, www.thedailyshow.com/watch/wed-may-12-2010/back-in-black—glenn-beck-s-nazi-tourette-s. For Colbert's remarks, see www.jewcy.com/post/obama_endorsed_hamas_only_six_degrees_hitler.

141. www.google.com/insights/search/#q=hitler%20kevin%20bacon&cmpt=q. Searches also spiked for the terms, "Hitler" and "Wikipedia Game." For an example of one chat forum in the summer of 2009, see www.quartertothree.com/game-talk/archive/index.php/t-54105.html. See also knowyourmeme.

com/memes/six-degrees-of-hitler. See also "Sandi Toksvig Goes Clicking for Hitler," *The Telegraph*, February 19, 2012.

142. https://play.google.com/store/apps/details?id=com.anthonythomas. sixDegrees&hl=en.

143. www.hitlerhops.com.

144. http://knowyourmeme.com/memes/image-macros; http://knowyourmeme. com/memes/happy-cat; http://memegenerator.net/Scumbag-Steve; http:// memegenerator.net/Musically-Oblivious-8th-Grader.

145. http://www.roflcat.com/i-can-has-poland-.

146. http://iwastesomuchtime.com/on/?i=3251.

147. Total figures can be tabulated at http://memegenerator.net/memes/search? q=hitler; http://memegenerator.net/Advice-Hitler/images/popular/alltime/ page/5.

148. For a list of Internet laws, see www.telegraph.co.uk/technology/news/ 6408927/Internet-rules-and-laws-the-top-10-from-Godwin-to-Poe.html. The Ironic Hitlerization Law can be seen as a corollary of Godwin's Law (see below) and is a variant of Rule 34, "If it exists, there is porn of it": www. telegraph.co.uk/technology/news/6408927/Internet-rules-and-laws-the-top-10-from-Godwin-to-Poe.html.

149. Other examples include adding Hitler moustaches to the angry faces on Rage Comics – with one image playing off of the familiar phrase, "Y U No," to read "Mein Führer – Y U No Love Your Neighbors?", http://files. sharenator.com/hitler_Y_U_No_Meme-s1024x768-170779-580.jpg.

150. www.youtube.com/watch?v=QH2-TGUlwu4&feature=related; www. youtube.com/watch?v=oKNtaM_J_Cg.

151. www.cobracountry.com/articles-cobra/humordept-cobra/hitler.html.

152. http://dailyhitler.blogspot.com/2010/09/my-little-nazi-pony.html; http:// uncyclopedia.wikia.com/wiki/File:Kitty.gif; http://uncyclopedia.wikia.com/ wiki/File:Pikachu_Hitler.jpg; http://www.yummymummyclub.ca/blogs/ mummy-buzz/why-hitler-is-hip-in-thailand.

153. http://spoof-or-not-spoof.deviantart.com/art/Fuhrer-King-182523076?q=sort %3Atime+gallery%3Aspoof-or-not-spoof&qo=1; http://uncyclopedia.wikia. com/wiki/I_Can't_Believe_It's_Not_Hitler; http://uncyclopedia.wikia.com/ wiki/File:Hitlerine2_copy.jpg

154. "UK Politician Accidentally Gets Hitler Moustache on TV," www.dailyedge. ie/nigel-farage-hitler-moustache-1092954-Sep2013/; Joshua Keating, "Unfortunate Photo-Op Hall of Fame," Slate.com, February 25, 2014, www. slate.com/blogs/the_world_/2014/02/25/ unfortunate_photo_op_hall_of_fame.html?wpisrc=burger_bar.

155. See Michel Choquette's photo essay, "Stranger in Paradise," from the March, 1972 issue of *National Lampoon*; see also the examples from Mad *Magazine* from 1969 and 1975, respectively: http://www.flickr.com/photos/

mytravelphotos/2027133743/; http://yesterdaysmagazines.com/images/pic_17272a.jpg.

156. www.theonion.com/articles/crazy-oldtimer-wants-to-create-master-race,20429/; www.theonion.com/articles/alternateuniverse-scifi-channel-show-asks-what-wou,2846/.

157. www.thedailymash.co.uk/news/international/france-is-basically-hitler-agrees-everyone-201204235151; www.thedailymash.co.uk/news/society/are-you-more-german-than-hitler-201106213972; www.thedailymash.co.uk/news/international/germans-use-brown-video-for-hitler-spoof-200906041803.

158. http://issuu.com/rutgersmedium/docs/dailymedium2012print/1; www.huffingtonpost.com/2012/04/09/rutgers-university-hitler-spoof-the-medium-criticized_n_1412988.html.

159. Wikipedia's entry is over 17,000 words. Significantly, the German version of the website, Stupidedia, is a tiny a fraction of the entry's size on the American site. It lists Hitler as having been born in Kotzen (to vomit) Austria in 1898 (not 1889) and committing suicide in 1962. This meager profile may show an ongoing German reluctance to spoof Hitler. www.stupidedia.org/stupi/Adolf_Hitler.

160. http://uncyclopedia.wikia.com/wiki/Adolf_Hitler.

161. Other entries related to the Third Reich cross the line entirely. An entry on "Auschwitz Theme Park" contains material that is highly offensive without being the least bit funny. See for example, the reference to the Auschwitz II Extermination Waterpark, which is described as "by far the most popular attraction . . . created to honor the original extermination camps. The Water Park actually uses the old Jewish blood of the millions who died in the said area." http://uncyclopedia.wikia.com/wiki/Auschwitz_Theme_Park

162. This was related to another well-known photo of an anti-Israel protester holding up a misspelled sign with the phrase "Death to all Juice." http://knowyourmeme.com/memes/death-to-all-juice.

163. http://memegenerator.net/Advice-Hitler/images/popular/alltime/page/10.

164. http://memegenerator.net/Disco-Hitler.

165. http://www.meh.ro/2009/12/01/kfj/; http://uncyclopedia.wikia.com/wiki/File:NazisoftVindowsSupreme.jpg.

166. http://memegenerator.net/instance/20240043; memegenerator.net/instance/12230548; http://memegenerator.net/Disco-Hitler/images/new/alltime/page/31; http://memegenerator.net/instance/21487610.

167. Victor Klemperer, *Language of the Third Reich: LTI: Lingua Tertii Imperii* (New York, 2006); George Steiner, *Language and Silence: Essays on Language, Literature, and the Inhuman* (New York, 1967).

168. Kate Knibbs, "Kthxbai! How Internet-speak is Changing the Way we Talk IRL (in Real Life)," *Digital Trends*, May 22, 2013, www.digitaltrends.com/social-media/how-the-Internet-is-changing-the-way-we-talk/.

169. Indeed, they were probably boosted by the sitcom, *Seinfeld*, whose famous character, the "soup Nazi," became a pop cultural meme.
170. www.urbandictionary.com/define.php?term=nazi.
171. http://en.wiktionary.org/wiki/-nazi.
172. www.tumblr.com/tagged/holocaust-puns.
173. http://chan4chan.com/archive/154738/ I_hate_it_when_people_joke_about_the_holocaust,_Anne_Frankly, _I_won't_stand_for_it.
174. www.facebook.com/pages/Anne-Frankly-I-did-nazi-that-coming/ 210374795676820.
175. http://www.lamebook.com/jacked-up/.
176. http://twitter.com/#!/damnitstrue/statuses/15870200742164o705; www. tumblr.com/tagged/i-did-nazi-that-coming; dis.4chan.org/read/lounge/ 1157831259; www.reddit.com/r/circlejerk/comments/toglj/ i_call_dibs_on_i_did_nazi_that_coming_next_time_a/.
177. www.urbandictionary.com/define.php?term=lolocaust.
178. Comment by Kingofeurope (no date listed), www.youtube.com/all_comments? v=AFbHr-nKkTc.
179. www.youtube.com/watch?v=AFulztJFv3Q.
180. http://www.urbandictionary.com/define.php?term=cowschwitz; http://en. wikipedia.org/wiki/Harris_Ranch.
181. http://puns.icanhascheezburger.com/tag/auschwitz/.
182. Martin, *The Psychology of Humor*, p. 45.
183. See the punning duel between several Facebook users at: www.nerdnirvana. org/2010/06/30/nazi-puns/; http://uberhumor.com/hitler-puns.
184. www.reddit.com/r/LosAngeles/comments/1f2g9f/ the_jc_penney_hitler_tea_kettle_spotted_just_east/?sort=controversial.
185. http://en.wikipedia.org/wiki/Godwin's_law.
186. Dodd's Corollary is probably the best known. Drawing on the "Reductio ad Hitlerum" argument first mentioned by Leo Strauss in 1952, it argues, "When debating a particular subject, if a comparison or implied connection is drawn between the opponent's argument and Hitler and the Nazi Party, the maker of that statement is automatically discredited and the debate is automatically lost by the person or group who referenced the connection to Hitler or the Nazis."
187. www.jewcy.com/arts-and-culture/i_seem_be_verb_18_years_godwins_law.
188. www.wired.com/wired/archive/2.10/godwin.if_pr.html.
189. www.telegraph.co.uk/technology/news/6408927/Internet-rules-and-laws-the-top-10-from-Godwin-to-Poe.html.
190. http://mediamatters.org/blog/200910140053.
191. www.huffingtonpost.com/lori-day/godwins-law_b_1028785.html; www. jewcy.com/arts-and-culture/i_seem_be_verb_18_years_godwins_law.

192. www.huffingtonpost.com/2010/11/11/adl-beck-soros_n_782420.html.

193. To be sure, these comedic attacks against the spread of Nazi analogies unfortunately has had the effect of reinforcing the tendency to use Hitler as a punchline. Satire, even if used for critical ends, can reproduce the normalizing tendencies it seeks to oppose.

194. Kathleen Parker, "Summertime for Hitler," *Washington Post*, August 23, 2009.

195. http://ask.metafilter.com/47155/Who-was-Hitler-before-Hitler#718451.

196. Eric Lidji, "Tarantino Crafts a Powerful, but Uneasy, Tale of Jewish Vengeance," *Jewish Chronicle*, August 25, 2009, pp. 14–15.

197. Jens Jessen, "Was macht Hitler so unwiderstehlich," *Die Zeit*, 40, 2004.

198. Leon Wieseltier, "Against the Ethnic Panic of American Jews: Hitler Is Dead," *New Republic*, May 27, 2002.

199. gatesofvienna.blogspot.com/2008/02/imagine-theres-no-hitler.html.

200. http://reason.com/archives/2005/07/14/hands-off-hitler; www.salon.com/2010/07/01/godwin/. A similar point was made in more satirical fashion by the website, Uncyclopedia, which reacted to Godwin's Law by proposing a self-referential counter-law, known as "Godwin's Law's Law," which decrees that "as an online discussion grows, if the probability of invoking Hitler approaches one, then the probability of invoking Godwin's Law approaches one as well. By citing Godwin's Law's Law, however, the user is usually implying that Godwin's Law does not make a Hitler comparison invalid, as Hitler comparisons can sometimes be very justifiable": http://uncyclopedia.wikia.com/wiki/Godwin's_Law's_Law.

201. The results of the search (on July 23, 2013), for "Nazis" were: 95.6% "negative," 4.1% "positive, "and 0.3% "indifferent." For "Adolf Hitler," they were: 25.8% "negative," 70.6% "positive," and 3.5% "indifferent": www.whatdoestheInternetthink.net/.

202. Carr, *The Shallows*, p. 2.

Conclusion

1. http://uncyclopedia.wikia.com/wiki/Everyone_is_Hitler.

2. On Bush and Obama as Hitler, see Wayne Madsen, "Bush and Hitler, the Unappetizing Similarities," *Counterpunch*, January 31, 2003, www.counterpunch.org/2003/01/31/bush-and-hitler-the-unappetizing-similarities/; Liz Brown, "Howard Stern compares Sarah Palin to Hitler and Spiro Agnew," Examiner.com, July 27 2009, www.examiner.com/article/howard-stern-compares-sarah-palin-to-hitler-and-spiro-agnew-video. For comparisons of other politicians to Hitler, see: Danielle Berrin, "Madonna, McCain & Hitler," *Jewish Journal*, August 25, 2008; "Savage Called Clinton's Rutgers Speech 'Hitler Dialogue,'" April 25, 2007, http://mediamatters.org/video/2007/04/25/savage-

called-clintons-rutgers-speech-hitler-di/138698; in early 2014, the mayor of New London, Connecticut, Mayor Daryl Justin Finizio, was compared to Hitler, http://connecticut.cbslocal.com/2014/01/22/mayor-wants-facebook-page-shut-down-after-being-compared-to-hitler/; Michigan Republican State Speaker of the House, Jase Bolger, suffered the same fate in the spring of 2013, www.freep.com/article/20130503/NEWS05/305030054/Brooks-Patterson-Jase-Bolger-Hitler.

3. "Is Angela Merkel 'Europe's Most Dangerous Leader'?" *Maclean's*, June 21, 2012, www2.macleans.ca/2012/06/21/is-angela-merkel-europes-most-dangerous-leader/; "Umberto Eco compares Berlusconi with Hitler," *The Telegraph*, February 25, 2011; "Obama adviser compares Putin to Hitler," www.guardian.co.uk/world/2008/aug/12/georgia. For comparisons of Israeli leaders to Hitler, see "Anti-Semitism in the Egyptian Media," www.adl.org/egyptian_media/media_2002/comparison.asp; on Ahmadinejad, see "Ahmadinejad – Hitler – Comparison," *Free Republic*, April 22, 2009, www.freerepublic.com/focus/news/2234981/posts; Patrick Brennan, "Assad Joins Hitler, Saddam," *National Review*, September 1, 2013, www.nationalreview.com/corner/357354/kerry-assad-joins-hitler-saddam-patrick-brennan; "Rumsfeld Likens Venezuela's Chavez to Hitler," msnbc.com, February 3, 2006, www.msnbc.msn.com/id/11159503/ns/world_news-americas/t/rumsfeld-likens-venezuelas-chavez-hitler/#.UD4SzI5TNiE; "Beijing's Olympics vs. Hitler's Olympics," *United Daily News* editorial (Taipei, Taiwan, ROC), August 21, 2008, http://lifeinmotion.wordpress.com/2008/08/25/beijings-olympics-vs-hitlers-olympics/; "PRC claims Dalai Lama has 'Nazi' tendencies," *Taipei Times*, March 30, 2012.

4. Jesus was compared to Hitler by Glenn Beck, http://crooksandliars.com/2007/09/24/glenn-beck-jesus-and-hitler-had-a-lot-in-common; Henry Stewart, "Jay Leno is Hitler," *The L Magazine*, January 27, 2010, www.thelmagazine.com/TheMeasure/archives/2010/01/27/jay-leno-is-hitler; NBA coach Rick Adelman was compared to Hitler by coach Phil Jackson, http://en.wikipedia.org/wiki/Rick_Adelman; Director Michael Bay was compared to Hitler by actress Megan Fox: "Megan Fox Compares Michael Bay to Hitler," September 3, 2009, http://blog.moviefone.com/2009/09/03/megan-fox-compares-michael-bay-to-hitler/.

5. See, for example, "43 People (and 1 Cat) Who Have Been Compared to Hitler," www.ideagrove.com/blog/2009/10/44-people-and-1-cat-who-have-been-compared-to-hitler.html; see also, "11 People Who Have Unfairly Been Compared To Hitler," www.huffingtonpost.com/2010/06/10/wtf-people-who-have-unfai_n_606810.html#s98556&title=Jesus_Christ; and List of Entities Compared to Hitler, www.dagorret.net/list-of-entities-compared-to-hitler/.

6. "Hank Williams Jr. Compares Obama To Hitler," *Huffington Post*, October 3, 2011, http://www.huffingtonpost.com/2011/10/03/hank-williams-compares-obama-to-hitler_n_992513.html; Joan Rivers compared Tommy Lee Jones to Hitler: "Joan Rivers on Tommy Lee Jones: 'He Makes Hitler Look Warm and

Fuzzy,'" January 21, 2011, www.popeater.com/2011/01/21/joan-rivers-tommy-lee-jones-naughty-but-nice-with-rob/; "How Hated? Kanye West Likens Himself to Hitler," *New York Times*, August 8, 2011; on Coughlin, see "'Hitler and Then Me,' Giants' Coughlin Says," March 29, 2007, http://nbcsports.msnbc.com/id/17858558/; on Liddy, see http://mediamatters.org/research/2004/11/23/g-gordon-liddy-listening-to-hitler-made-me-feel/132337; on Stone, see "Jewish Group Slams Oliver Stone's Hitler Remark," YNet News.com, January 18, 2010, www.ynetnews.com/articles/0,7340,L-3835486,00.html; on London Mayor Boris Johnson's comparison of George Clooney to Hitler, see http://uk.news.yahoo.com/london-mayor-boris-johnson-compares-george-clooney-hitler-172419546.html#WLbAfKP; Lars von Trier reaped criticism for saying that he understood Hitler and "sympathize[d] with him a little bit," "Lars von Trier Kicks Ups a Cannes Controversy," *New York Times*, May 18, 2011; "Galliano fired after reportedly praising Hitler in rant," March 1, 2011, http://today.msnbc.msn.com/id/41848694/ns/today-style/t/galliano-fired-after-reportedly-praising-hitler-rant/#.UD4fI5TNiE.

7. Erk, *So viel Hitler war selten*, chapter 3.

8. See "Dobson Likened Embryonic Stem Cell Research to Nazi Experiments," Media Matters, August 3, 2005, http://mediamatters.org/video/2005/08/03/dobson-likened-embryonic-stem-cell-research-to/133587; David Postman, "Distorting Nazi History to Attack Environmentalists," *Seattle Times*, April 3, 2008; "Paul LePage Compares IRS to Nazis, Again," Media Matters, July 12, 2012, www.politico.com/news/stories/0712/78451.html; "Beck Links Health Care Reform to Nazis," *Media Matters*, August 6, 2009, http://mediamatters.org/video/2009/08/06/beck-links-health-care-reform-to-nazis-suggests/152971; "Ben Stein's Anti-Evolution Film Raises Hackles," *Jewish Telegraphic Agency*, April 22, 2008, http://blogs.jta.org/telegraph/article/2008/04/22/999918/ben-steins-anti-evolution-film-raises-hackles; "Let's Settle the Facts about Nazi Gun Control," September 10, 2009, www.dailykos.com/story/2009/09/10/780010/-Let-s-settle-the-facts-about-Nazi-gun-control; "Pope Criticized by German Jews for Comparing Abortion to Holocaust," February 19, 2005, www.lifenews.com/2005/02/19/nat-1202/; "Smoking Ban Like Yellow Stars Nazis Forced on Jews: GOP Pol," *New York Daily News*, April 19, 2012; "GOP Candidate: Hitler Invented Separation of Church and State," *The Raw Story*, September 17, 2010, www.rawstory.com/rs/2010/09/17/gop-candidate-hitler-church-state/; on the filibuster see www.adl.org/PresRele/HolNa_52/4719_52.htm; "Patriot Act vs. German Enabling Act," www.illuminati-news.com/patriot-act-vs-german-enabling-act.htm; "Durbin Defends Guantanamo Comments," *Washington Post*, June 17, 2005.

9. "North Korea calls Japanese PM 'Asian Hitler,'" www.telegraph.co.uk/news/worldnews/asia/northkorea/10616018/North-Korea-calls-Japanese-PM-Asian-

Hitler.html; "Modi's Fascism Is No Different from Hitler's Nazi Germany: Jairam," www.firstpost.com/politics/modis-fascism-is-no-different-from-hitlers-nazi-germany-jairam-1212145.html; "Ousted from Power, Ukraine's Yanukovych Invokes Hitler's Rise," www.jpost.com/International/Ukraine-protesters-seize-President-Yanukovichs-Kiev-compound-342208; "Rivals Are 'Heirs to Hitler': Venezuela's Maduro," www.israelnationalnews.com/News/News.aspx/166672#.Uwzv1ygaCnY; "South African Politician Julius Malema Likened to Hitler and Mussolini," www.theguardian.com/world/2013/aug/07/south-africa-julius-malema-politician-mamphela-ramphele.

10. Erk, *So viel Hitler war selten*, pp. 10–11.

11. It is notable that the main scholars who have challenged the concept of uniqueness in the most recent phase of the debate hail from this younger generation: Donald Bloxham (born in 1973), Timothy Snyder (1969), and Dirk Moses (1967). The most recent defenders of uniqueness, meanwhile – Doris Bergen (1961) and Omer Bartov (1954) – are somewhat older. This pattern is less apparent among the revisionist critics of the "good war." Although one of the most prominent hails from this generation – Niall Ferguson (born in 1963) – others are older: Nicholson Baker (1957), Michael Bess (1954), Jacques Pauwels (1946), Norman Davies (1939), and Patrick Buchanan (1938). Generational identity is thus only one factor among others in determining scholars' historiographical positions.

12. Determining the precise significance of these events requires more research, but they have generally made this generation less Eurocentric and more focused on global issues than their predecessors, who were more concerned with the problems of Cold War era Europe.

13. The birth years of some of the major figures who have produced works of alternate history and directed recent films about Hitler are as follows (in descending order): Rory Patrick McHenry (1987), Edward Alexander McHenry (1983), Owen Sheers (1974), Guy Saville (1973), Siegfried Langer (1966), Jo Walton (1964), Michael Chabon (1963), Quentin Tarantino (1963), Alan Glenn/Brendan Dubois (1959), Dani Levy (1957), Urs Odermatt (1955), Menno Meyes (1954), Wolfgang Brenner (1954), C. J. Sansom (1952), Harry Turtledove (1949), Bernd Eichinger (1949), Alexander Demandt (1937), Dieter Kühn (1935), Walter Laqueur (1921).

14. Erk, *So viel Hitler war selten*, p. 19.

15. This quotation has been attributed to such varied comedians as Steve Allen, Carol Burnett, and Woody Allen, http://quoteinvestigator.com/2013/06/25/comedy-plus/

16. These comic works, by focusing attention on Hitler, also shift attention away from the German people's responsibility for Nazism.

17. Brockmann, "'Normalization': Has Helmut Kohl's Vision Been Realized?" in Taberner and Cooke, eds., *German Culture, Politics, and Literature into the Twenty-First Century: Beyond Normalization*, p. 20.
18. Ignatz Bubis observed in 1999 that what made Germany abnormal was "its constant debates on the desire for normality." Quoted in Pearce, *Contemporary Germany and the Nazi Legacy*, p. 53
19. Quoted in Joachim Güntner, "Der Führer als Spassfaktor," *Neue Zürchner Zeitung*, January 27, 2007.
20. Thomas Nipperdey once observed that "the demands of the therapists who demand that the past be confronted [*Bewältigungstherapeuten*] make the neurosis [of an unmastered past] permanent (as well as the necessity of having therapists)." Quoted in Hermann Lübbe, "Der Nationalsozialismus im politischen Bewusstsein der Gegenwart," in Martin Broszat, ed., *Deutschlands Weg in die Diktatur* (Berlin, 1983), p. 369.
21. Quoted in Güntner, "Der Führer als Spassfaktor."

BIBLIOGRAPHY

Adams, Michael C. C., *The Best War Ever: America and World War II* (Baltimore, 1994).

Adorno, Theodor W., *Negative Dialectics* (London, 2004).

Alexander, Edward, "Stealing the Holocaust," *Midstream*, November, 1980, pp. 46–50.

Alexander, Jeffrey, *Remembering the Holocaust: A Debate* (Oxford, 2009).

Ambrose, Stephen and Günter Bischof, eds., *Eisenhower and the German POWs: Facts against Falsehood* (Baton Rouge, LA, 1992).

Amouroux, Henri, *La grande histoire des français sous l'occupation* (*The Full History of the French under the Occupation*) (8 volumes, Paris, 1976–1988).

Anderson, Perry, "On Emplotment: Two Kinds of Ruin," in Saul Friedlander, ed., *Probing the Limits of Representation: Nazism and the "Final Solution"* (Cambridge, MA, 1992), pp. 54–65.

Anonymous, *Eine Frau in Berlin, Tagebuch-Aufzeichnungen vom 20. April bis 22. Juni 1945* (Munich, 2005).

Arendt, Hannah, *Eichmann in Jerusalem: A Report on the Banality of Evil* (New York, 1963).

Aron, Robert and Georgette Elgey, *Histoire de Vichy* (Paris, 1956).

Aronson, Shlomo, *Hitler, the Allies, and the Jews* (Cambridge, UK, 2004).

Arpaci, Annette Seidel, "Lost in Translation? The Discourse of 'German Suffering' and W. G. Sebald's *Luftkrieg und Literatur*," in Schmitz, ed., *A Nation of Victims: Representations of German Wartime Suffering from 1945 to the Present* (Amsterdam, 2007), pp. 164–65.

Assmann, Aleida, *Das neue Unbehagen an der Erinnerungskultur: Eine Intervention* (Munich, 2013).

Assmann, Aleida, and Ute Frevert, *Geschichtsvergessenheit, Geschichtsversessenheit:. vom Umgang mit deutschen Vergangenheiten nach 1945* (Stuttgart, 1999).

Assmann, Jan, "Kollektives Gedächtnis und kulturelle Identität," in Jan Assmann and Tonio Holscher, eds., *Kultur und Gedächtnis* (Frankfurt am Main, 1988).

Assmann, Jan, and Tonio Holscher, eds., *Kultur und Gedächtnis* (Frankfurt am Main, 1988).

Avishai, Bernard, *The Tragedy of Zionism: How Its Revolutionary Past Haunts Israeli Democracy* (New York, 2002).

Backes, Uwe, Eckhard Jesse, and Rainer Zitelmann, eds., *Die Schatten der Vergangenheit: Impulse zur Historisierung des Nationalsozialismus* (Berlin, 1990).

Bacque, James, *Other Losses: An Investigation into the Mass Deaths of German Prisoners at the Hands of the French and Americans After World War II* (Toronto, 1989).

Baker, Nicholson, *Human Smoke* (New York, 2008).

Bankier, David and Dan Michman, *Holocaust Historiography in Context: Emergence, Challenges, Polemics, and Achievements* (Jerusalem, 2008).

Barkan, Elazar, *The Guilt of Nations: Restitution and Negotiating Historical Injustices* (Baltimore, 2000).

Barnes, Harry Elmer, ed., *Perpetual War for Perpetual Peace: A Critical Examination of the Foreign Policy of Franklin D. Roosevelt and Its Aftermath* (Caldwell, ID, 1953).

Barnett, Correlli, *The Audit of War* (London, 1986).

Bartov, Omer, "Genocide and the Holocaust: What Are We Arguing About?" reprinted in Uffa Jenesen et al., eds., *Gewalt und Gesellschaft: Klassiker modernen Denkens neu gelesen* (Göttingen, 2011).

"Locating the Holocaust," *Journal of Genocide Research*, March–June, 2011, pp. 121–29.

Bathrick, David, "Whose Hi/story Is It? The U. S. Reception of *Downfall*," *New German Critique*, Fall, 2007, pp. 1–16.

Bauer, Yehuda, *American Jewry and the Holocaust: the American Jewish Joint Distribution* Committee (Detroit, 1981).

Jews for Sale? Nazi-Jewish Negotiations, 1933–1945 (New Haven, 1994).

Rethinking the Holocaust (New Haven, 2001).

"Whose Holocaust?" *Midstream*, November, 1980, pp. 42–46.

Bauman, Zygmunt, *Modernity and the Holocaust* (New York, 1989).

Bavendamm, Dirk, *Roosevelts Krieg, 1937–45* (Munich, 1993).

Roosevelts Weg zum Krieg: amerikanischer Politik, 1914–1939 (Frankfurt, 1983).

Beard, Charles A., *President Roosevelt and the Coming of the War, 1941* (New Haven, 1948).

Beattie, Andrew, "The Victims of Totalitarianism and the Centrality of Nazi Genocide: Continuity and Change in German Commemorative Politics," in Bill Niven, ed., *Germans as Victims: Remembering the Past in Contemporary Germany* (Houndmills, UK, 2006), pp. 147–63.

Beevor, Antony, *The Second World War* (New York, 2012).

Behrens, Laurence and Leonard Rosen, eds., *Writing and Reading Across the Curriculum*, 3rd edn (Glenview, IL, 1988).

Bendix, John, "Facing Hitler: German Responses to *Downfall*," *German Politics and Society*, 1:2007, pp. 70–89.

Benz, Wolfgang, *Der Ort des Terrors: Geschichte der nationalsozialistischen Konzentrationslager* (Munich, 2009).

Bergen, Doris, "An Easy Target?" in Marrus, Rittner and Roth, eds., *Pope Pius XII and the Holocaust*, pp. 105–19.

"Challenging Uniqueness: Decentring and Recentring the Holocaust," *Journal of Genocide Research*, March–June 2011, pp. 129–34.

War and Genocide: A Concise History of the Holocaust (Lanham, MD, 2009).

Berger, Stefan, *The Search for Normalcy: National Identity and Historical Consciousness in Germany Since 1800* (Providence, 1997).

Berghahn, Klaus L. and Jost Hermand, eds., *Unmasking Hitler: Cultural Representations of Hitler from the Weimar Republic to the Present* (Bern, 2005).

Bess, Michael, *Choices Under Fire: Moral Dimensions of World War II* (New York, 2008).

The Light-Green Society: Ecology and Technological Modernity in France, 1960–2000 (Chicago, 2003).

Realism, Utopia, and the Mushroom Cloud: Four Activist Intellectuals and their Strategies for Peace, 1945–1989 (Chicago, 1993).

Bessel, Richard, *Germany, 1945: From War to Peace* (New York, 2010).

Black, Edwin, *Farhud: Roots of the Arab–Nazi Alliance in the Holocaust* (New York, 2010).

Blet, Pierre, *Pius XII and the Second World War* (Mahwah, NJ, 1999).

Bloxham, Donald, *The Final Solution: A Genocide* (Oxford, 2010).

"Response – Discussing Genocide: Two Moralities and Some Obstacles," *Journal of Genocide Research*, March–June, 2011, pp. 135–48.

Bloxham, Donald, and Tony Kushner, *The Holocaust: Critical Historical Approaches* (Manchester, 2005).

Bodemann, Y. Michal, *In den Wogen der Erinnerung: Jüdische Existenz in Deutschland* (Berlin, 2002).

Bodnar, John, *The "Good War" in American Memory* (Baltimore, 2010).

Bracher, Karl-Dietrich, *The German Dictatorship* (New York, 1970).

Braham, Randolph L., ed., *Perspectives on the Holocaust* (Boston, 1983).

Brenner, Wolfgang, *Führerlos* (Berlin, 2008).

Brochhagen, Ulrich, *Nach Nürnberg: Vergangenheitsbewältigung und Westinteg-ration in der Ära Adenauer* (Hamburg, 1994).

Broszat, Martin, *The Hitler State* (London, 1981).

Broszat, Martin, ed., *Deutschlands Weg in die Diktatur* (Berlin, 1983).

Browning, Christopher, *The Path to Genocide* (Cambridge, UK, 1992).

Buchanan, Patrick, *Churchill, Hitler, and "The Unnecessary War"* (New York, 2008).

Bulhof, Johannes, "What If? Modality and History," *History and Theory*, 2, 1999, pp. 145–68.

Bullock, Alan, *Hitler: A Study in Tyranny* (London, 1952).

Bunting, Madeline, *The Model Occupation: The Channel Islands under German Rule* (New York, 1995).

Burg, Avraham, *The Holocaust Is Over: We Must Rise from Its Ashes* (New York, 2008).

Burleigh, Michael, *Moral Combat: Good and Evil in World War II* (New York, 2011).

Burrin, Philippe, *Hitler and the Jews: The Genesis of the Holocaust* (New York, 1994).

Buruma, Ian, *The Wages of Guilt: Memories of War in Germany and Japan* (New York, 1994).

Calder, Angus, *The Myth of the Blitz* (London, 1995).

Carr, Nicholas, *The Shallows: What the Internet is Doing to Our Brains* (New York, 2011).

Carroll, James, *Constantine's Sword: The Church and the Jews* (New York, 2001).

Chabon, Michael, *The Yiddish Policemen's Union* (New York, 2007).

Chamberlin, William Henry, *America's Second Crusade* (Chicago, 1950).

Chaplin, Charles, *My Autobiography* (New York, 1992).

Charmley, John, *Churchill: The End of Glory: A Political Biography* (New York, 1993).

Churchill, Ward, *A Little Matter of Genocide: Holocaust and Denial in the Americas, 1492 to the Present* (San Francisco, 1997).

Churchill, Winston, *The Second World War: Vol. I, The Gathering Storm and Vol. II, Their Finest Hour* (Boston, 1949).

Clay, Lucius, *Decision in Germany* (Garden City, NY, 1950).

Clendinnen, Inga, *Reading the Holocaust* (Cambridge, UK, 2002).

Cohen, Warren I., *The American Revisionists: The Lessons of Intervention in World War I* (Chicago, 1967).

Confino, Alon, "Collective Memory and Cultural History: Problems of Method," *American Historical Review*, December 1997, pp. 1386–403.

Foundational Pasts: The Holocaust as Historical Understanding (Cambridge, UK, 2012).

Connelly, John, "Nazis and Slavs: From Racial Theory to Racist Practice," *Central European History*, 1, 1999, pp. 1–33.

Connelly, Mark, *We Can Take It! Britain and the Memory of the Second World War* (Harlow, UK, 2005).

Cornwell, John, *Hitler's Pope* (New York, 1999).

Courtois, Stéphane et al., eds., *The Black Book of Communism: Crimes, Terror, Repression* (Cambridge, MA, 1999).

Cowley, Robert, ed., *What Ifs? of American History* (New York, 2003).

What If? 2: Eminent Historians Imagine What Might Have Been (New York, 2001).

What If? The World's Foremost Military Historians Imagine What Might Have Been (New York, 1999).

Cowling, Maurice, *The Impact of Hitler: British Politics and British Policy, 1933–1940* (Cambridge, UK, 1975).

Dahmash-Jarrah, Samar, and Kirt M. Dressler, *Arab Voices Speak to American Hearts* (Charles City, VA, 2005).

Dahrendorf, Ralf, *Society and Democracy in Germany* (New York, 1967).

Dalin, David G., *The Myth of Hitler's Pope: How Pope Pius XII Rescued Jews from the Nazis* (Washington, DC, 2005).

Dalin, David G., and John Rothmann, *Icon of Evil: Hitler's Mufti and the Rise of Radical Islam* (New York, 2008).

Davies, Norman, *The Isles: A History* (Oxford, 2000).

No Simple Victory: World War II in Europe, 1939–45 (New York, 2007).

Dawidowicz, Lucy, *The Holocaust and the Historians* (Boston, 1981).

A Holocaust Reader (New York, 1976).

The War Against the Jews (New York, 1976).

What is the Use of Jewish History? (New York, 1992).

De Gaulle, Charles, *Mémoires de guerre: L'Appel 1940–1942* (Paris, 1954).

De Zayas, Alfred-Maurice, *Nemesis at Potsdam: The Anglo-Americans and the Expulsion of the Germans. Background, Execution, Consequences* (Boston, 1977).

A Terrible Revenge: The Ethnic Cleansing of the East European Germans, 1944–1950 (New York, 1994).

Dean, Carolyn J., *Aversion and Erasure: The Fate of the Victim After the Holocaust* (Ithaca, 2010).

Demandt, Alexander, *Es hätte auch anders kommen können* (Berlin, 2010).

History That Never Happened: A Treatise on the Question, What Would Have Happened If…? (Jefferson, NC, 1993).

Diner, Hasia, *We Remember With Love and Reverence: American Jews and the Myth of Silence after the Holocaust, 1945–62* (New York, 2009).

Doenecke, Justus, "U. S. Policy and the European War, 1939–1941," *Diplomatic History*, 4, Fall 1995, pp. 669–98.

Dreyfuss, Richard, and Harry Turtledove, *The Two Georges* (New York, 1996).

Dubiel, Helmut, *Niemand ist frei von der Geschichte* (Munich, 1999).

Durkheim, Emile, *The Rules of Sociological Method* (New York, 1982).

Echternkamp, Jörg, and Stefan Martens, eds., *Experience and Memory: The Second World War in Europe* (New York, 2010).

Egbert, Donald Drew, *Social Radicalism and the Arts* (New York, 1970).

Eisenhower, Dwight D., *Crusade in Europe* (Garden City, NY, 1948).

Eley, Geoff, "Finding the People's War: Film, British Collective Memory, and World War II," *AHR*, June, 2001, pp. 818–38.

Epstein, Catherine, *Model Nazi: Arthur Greiser and the Occupation of Western Poland* (Oxford, 2010).

Erk, Daniel, *So viel Hitler war selten: Die Banalisierung des Bösen, oder warum der Mann mit dem kleinen Bart nicht totzukriegen ist* (Munich, 2012).

Evans, Richard, *Altered Pasts: Counterfactuals in History* (Waltham, MA, 2014) "Telling It Like It Wasn't," in Donald A. Yerxa, ed., *Recent Themes in Historical Thinking: Historians in Conversation* (Columbia, SC, 2008), pp. 77–84.

The Third Reich at War (New York, 2008).

Falconi, Carlo, *The Silence of Pius XII* (Boston, 1970).

Faulenbach, Bernd, Markus Meckel, and Hermann Weber, eds., *Die Partei hatte immer Recht: Aufarbeitung von Geschichte und Folgen der SED-Diktatur* (Essen, 1994).

Feingold, Henry, *The Politics of Rescue: The Roosevelt Administration and the Holocaust, 1938–1945* (New York, 1970).

Ferguson, Niall, *The Pity of War* (New York, 1999).

Empire: The Rise and Demise of the British World Order and the Lessons for Global Power (New York, 2004).

The War of the World: Twentieth-Century Conflict and the Descent of the West (New York, 2006).

Ferguson, Niall, ed., *Virtual History: Alternatives and Counterfactuals* (New York, 1999).

Fermaglich, Kirsten, *American Dreams and Nazi Nightmares: Early Holocaust Consciousness and Liberal America, 1957–1965* (Waltham, MA, 2007).

Fest, Joachim, *Hitler* (New York, 1973).

Finkelstein, Norman, and Ruth Bettina Birn, *A Nation on Trial: The Goldhagen Thesis and Historical Truth* (New York, 1998).

Finkelstein, Norman, *The Holocaust Industry: Reflections on the Exploitation of Jewish Suffering* (London, 2000).

Finney, Patrick, *Remembering the Road to World War Two: International History, National Identity, and Collective Memory* (London, 2011).

Foucault, Michel, *Language, Counter-memory, Practice: Selected Essays and Interviews* (Ithaca, 1977).

Fox, Jo, *Film Propaganda in Britain and Nazi Germany* (Oxford, 2007).

Frankel, Jonathan, *The Fate of the European Jews, 1939–1945: Continuity or Contingency?* (New York, 1997).

Frei, Norbert, *1945 und Wir: Das Dritte Reich im Bewußtsein der Deutschen* (Munich, 2005).

Adenauer's Germany and the Nazi Past (New York, 2002).

Friedlander, Saul, *Pius XII and the Third Reich: A Documentation* (New York, 1966).

Friedlander, Saul, ed., *Probing the Limits of Representation: Nazism and the 'Final Solution'* (Cambridge, MA, 1992).

Friedman, Philip, *Roads to Extinction: Essays on the Holocaust* (New York, 1980).

Friedman, Saul S., *No Haven for the Oppressed: United States Policy Toward Jewish Refugees, 1938–1945* (Detroit, 1973).

Friedrich, Jörg, *Der Brand: Deutschland im Bombenkrieg, 1940–1945* (Berlin, 2002).

Fussell, Paul, *Wartime: Understanding and Behavior in the Second World War* (New York, 1989).

Gavanski, Igor, Paula M. Niedenthal, and June Price Tangney, "'If Only I Weren't' Versus 'If Only I Hadn't': Distinguishing Shame and Guilt in Counterfactual Thinking," *Journal of Personality and Social Psychology*, October, 1994, pp. 585–95.

Glenn, Alan, *Amerikan Eagle* (New York, 2011).

Goldhagen, Daniel J., *A Moral Reckoning: The Role of the Catholic Church in the Holocaust and Its Unfulfilled Duty of Repair* (New York, 2002).

Worse Than War: Genocide, Eliminationism, and the Ongoing Assault on Humanity (New York, 2009).

Grass, Günter, *Im Krebsgang* (Göttingen, 2002).

Gross, Jan, *Neighbors: The Destruction of the Jewish Community in Jedwabne, Poland* (New York, 2002).

Grynberg, Henryk, "Appropriating the Holocaust," *Commentary*, November 1982, pp. 54–57.

Habermas, Jürgen, *The Past as Future* (Lincoln, NE, 1994).

Haffner, Sebastian, *The Ailing Empire: Germany from Bismarck to Hitler* (New York, 1989).

The Meaning of Hitler (Cambridge, MA, 1983).

Hake, Sabine, *Screen Nazis: Cinema, History, and Democracy* (Madison, 2012).

Halbwachs, Maurice, *The Collective Memory* (New York, 1980).

Hastings, Max, *All Hell Let Loose: The World at War, 1939–1945* (London, 2011).

Heer, Hannes, *Hitler war's: Die Befreiung der Deutschen von ihrer Vergangenheit* (Berlin, 2005).

Hellekson, Karen, *The Alternate History: Refiguring Historical Time* (Kent, OH, 2001).

Herf, Jeffrey, *Divided Memory: The Nazi Past in the Two Germanys* (Cambridge, MA, 1997).

Nazi Propaganda for the Arab World (New Haven, 2009).

Hilberg, Raul, *The Destruction of the European Jews* (New York, 1961).

Hildebrand, Klaus, *The Foreign Policy of the Third Reich* (Oakland, CA, 1973).

Hillgruber, Andreas, *Hitlers Strategie: Politik und Kriegführung, 1940–1941* (Bonn, 1975).

Zweierlei Untergang: Die Zerschlagung des Deutschen Reiches und das Ende des europäischen Judentums (Berlin, 1986).

Himka, John-Paul, and Joanna Beata Michlic, eds., *Bringing the Dark Past to Light: The Reception of the Holocaust in Postcommunist Europe* (Lincoln, NE, 2013).

Himmelfarb, Milton, "No Hitler, No Holocaust," *Commentary*, March 1984, pp. 37–43.

Hitchcock, William, *The Bitter Road to Freedom: A New History of the Liberation of Europe* (New York, 2008).

Hofmann, Wilhelm, and Anna Baumert, "Hitler als Figur der psychologischen Medienforschung," in Rainer Rother and Karin Herbst-Meßlinger, eds., *Hitler darstellen: Zur Entwicklung und Bedeutung einer filmischen Figur* (Munich, 2008)

Hoggan, David, *Der erzwungene Krieg: Die Ursachen und Urheber des 2. Weltkrieges* (Tübingen, 1977).

Hylton, Stuart, *Their Darkest Hour: The Hidden History of the Home Front 1939–1945* (London, 2001).

Insdorf, Annette, *Indelible Shadows: Film and the Holocaust* (Cambridge, UK, 2003).

Jäckel, Eberhard, *Hitler's Weltanschauung* (Middletown, CT, 1972).

Jenkins, Philip, *The New Anti-Catholicism: The Last Acceptable Prejudice* (Oxford, 2004).

Jones, Adam, *Genocide: A Comprehensive Introduction* (New York, 2007).

Judt, Tony, "Goodbye to All That," *The Nation*, January 3, 2005.

"The Morbid Truth," *New Republic*, July 19–26, 1999, pp. 36–40.

"The Past Is Another Country: Myth and Memory in Postwar Europe," *Daedalus*, Fall 1992, pp. 83–118.

"The 'Problem of Evil' in Postwar Europe," *New York Review of Books*, February 14, 2008.

Kaes, Anton, *From Hitler to Heimat: The Return of History as Film* (Cambridge, MA, 1989).

Kansteiner, Wulf, *In Pursuit of German Memory: History, Television, and Politics after Auschwitz* (Athens, OH, 2006).

Kantor, MacKinlay, "If the South Had Won the Civil War," *Look Magazine*, November 22, 1960, pp. 30–62.

Karsh, Efraim, *Israel: The First Hundred Years, Volume 1* (New York, 2001).

Katz, Steven T., "The 'Unique' Intentionality of the Holocaust," *Modern Judaism*, 1:2, 1981, pp. 161–83.

Kershaw, Ian, "Hitler and the Uniqueness of Nazism," *Journal of Contemporary History*, 2, 2004, pp. 239–54.

  The "Hitler Myth": Image and Reality in the Third Reich (Oxford, UK, 1987).

  The Nazi Dictatorship: Problems and Perspectives of Interpretation (London, 2000).

Kiernan, Ben, *Blood and Soil: A World History of Genocide and Extermination from Sparta to Darfur* (New Haven, 2007).

Kift, Dagmar, "Neither Here nor There? The Memorialization of the Expulsion of Ethnic Germans," in Bill Niven and Chloe Paver, eds., *Memorialization in Germany since 1945* (New York, 2010), pp. 78–90.

Kittel, Manfred, *Die Legende von der zweiten Schuld: Vergangenheitsbewältigung in der Ära Adenauer* (Berlin, 1993).

Klemperer, Victor, *Language of the Third Reich: LTI: Lingua Tertii Imperii* (New York, 2006).

Kogon, Eugen, *The Theory and Practice of Hell* (New York, 1964).

Korn, Salomon, *Geteilte Erinnerung* (Berlin, 1999).

Kudryashov, Sergei, "Remembering and Researching the War: The Soviet and Russian Experience," in Jörg Echternkamp and Stefan Martens, eds., *Experience and Memory: The Second World War in Europe* (New York, 2010), pp. 86–115.

Kühn, Dieter, *Ich war Hitlers Schutzengel* (Frankfurt, 2010).

Kundnani, Hans, *Utopia or Auschwitz? Germany's 1968 Generation and the Holocaust* (New York, 2009).

Landman, Janet, *Regret: The Persistence of the Possible* (New York, 1993).

Lang, Berel, *The Future of the Holocaust* (Ithaca, 1999).

Langenbacher, Eric, "Changing Memory Regimes in Contemporary Germany?" *German Politics and Society*, Summer, 2003, pp. 46–68.

Langenbacher, Eric, Bill Niven, and Ruth Wittlinger, eds., *Dynamics of Memory and Identity in Contemporary Europe* (New York, 2012).

Langer, Siegfried, *Alles bleibt anders* (Stolberg, 2008).

Laqueur, Walter, "Disraelia: A Counterfactual History, 1848–2008," *Middle East Papers: Middle East Strategy at Harvard*, April 1, 2008, pp. 1–21.

  A History of Zionism (New York, 1972).

Harvest of a Decade: Disraelia and Other Essays (New York, 2011).

The Last Days of Europe: Epitaph for an Old Continent (New York, 2007).

The Terrible Secret: Suppression of the Truth about Hitler's "Final Solution" (Boston, 1980).

Lebow, Richard Ned, "Counterfactuals, History and Fiction," in *Historical Social Research*, 2, 2009, pp. 57–73.

"Counterfactual Thought Experiments: A Necessary Teaching Tool," *The History Teacher*, February, 2007.

Forbidden Fruit: Counterfactuals and International Relations (Princeton, NJ, 2010).

Lebow, Richard Ned, Wulf Kansteiner, and Claudio Fogu, eds., *The Politics of Memory in Postwar Europe* (Durham, NC, 2006).

Leiser, Erwin, *Nazi Cinema* (London, 1974).

Lesnor, Carl, "The 'Good' War," *The Philosophical Forum*, Spring 2005, pp. 77–85.

Levene, Mark, *Genocide in the Age of the Nation State: The Meaning of Genocide* (London, 2005).

Levy, Daniel, and Natan Sznaider, "Memory Unbound: The Holocaust and the Formation of Cosmopolitan Memory," *European Journal of Social Theory*, 5 1, 2002, pp. 87–106.

Levy, Daniel, and Natan Sznaider, *The Holocaust and Memory in the Global Age* (Philadelphia, 2006).

Lewy, Gunter, *The Catholic Church and Nazi Germany* (New York, 1964).

Linenthal, Edward, *Preserving Memory: The Struggle to Create America's Holocaust Museum* (New York, 1995).

Lipstadt, Deborah, *Beyond Belief: The American Press and the Coming of the Holocaust, 1933–1945* (New York, 1986).

Denying the Holocaust: The Growing Assault on Truth and Memory (New York, 1993).

"The Failure to Rescue and Contemporary American Jewish Historiography of the Holocaust: Judging from a Distance," in Michael J. Neufeld and Michael Berenbaum, eds., *The Bombing of Auschwitz: Should the Allies Have Attempted It?*(Lawrence, KS, 2003), pp. 227–37.

Longerich, Peter, *Holocaust: The Nazi Persecution and Murder of the Jews* (Oxford, 2010).

The Unwritten Order: Hitler's Role in the Final Solution (Charleston, SC, 2001).

Lookstein, Haskell, *Were We Our Brothers' Keepers? The Public Response of American Jews to the Holocaust, 1938–1944* (New York, 1985).

Louis, William Roger, ed., *The Origins of the Second World War: A. J. P. Taylor and His Critics* (New York, 1972).

Lowe, Keith, *Savage Continent: Europe in the Aftermath of World War II* (New York, 2012).

Lübbe, Hermann, "Der Nationalsozialismus im politischen Bewusstsein der Gegenwart," in Martin Broszat, ed., *Deutschlands Weg in die Diktatur* (Berlin, 1983), pp. 329–49.

Lukacs, John, *The Legacy of the Second World War* (New Haven, 2010).

Lutomski, Pawel, "The Debate about a Center against Expulsions: An Unexpected Crisis in German–Polish Relations?" *German Studies Review*, 3, October, 2004, pp. 449–68.

Maccoby, Hyam, "Theologian of the Holocaust," *Commentary*, December 1982, pp. 33–37.

MacDonald, David B., *Identity Politics in the Age of Genocide: The Holocaust and Historical Representation* (London, 2008).

MacDonogh, Giles, *After the Reich: The Brutal History of the Allied Occupation* (New York, 2007).

Machtans, Karolin, and Martin A. Ruehl, eds., *Hitler Films from Germany: History, Cinema and Politics since 1945* (New York, 2012).

Mackenzie, S. P., "Essay and Reflection: On the 'Other Losses' Debate," *International History Review*, 14:4 (Nov., 1992), pp. 717–31.

Madajczyk, Czesław, "General Plan Ost," *Polish Western Affairs*, 2, 1962, pp. 391–442.

Maier, Charles, *The Unmasterable Past: History, Holocaust, and German National Identity* (Cambridge, MA, 1988).

Mallmann, Klaus-Michael, and Martin Cüppers, *Nazi Palestine: The Plans for the Extermination of the Jews in Palestine* (New York, 2010).

Mann, Michael, *The Dark Side of Democracy: Explaining Ethnic Cleansing* (Cambridge, UK, 2004).

Manvell, Roger, *Films and the Second World War* (New York, 1974).

Marchione, Margherita, *Pope Pius XII: Architect for Peace* (New York, 2000).

Margalit, Avishai, *On Compromise and Rotten Compromises* (Princeton, NJ, 2009).

Marrus, Michael, "Eichmann in Jerusalem: Justice and History," in Steven Aschheim, ed., *Hannah Arendt in Jerusalem* (Berkeley, 2001).

The Holocaust in History (New York, 1987).

Marrus, Michael, Carol Rittner, and John K. Roth, eds., *Pope Pius XII and the Holocaust* (Leicester, 2002).

Martel, Gordon, *The Origins of the Second World War Reconsidered* (London, 1986).

Martin, Rod A., *The Psychology of Humor: An Integrative Approach* (Burlington, MA, 2007).

Maser, Werner, *Hitler: Legend, Myth, and Reality* (New York, 1973).

Matthäus, Jürgen, and Martin Shaw, *Journal of Genocide Research*, March–June, 2011, pp. 115–120.

Matthäus, Jürgen, "The Precision of the Indefinite," *Journal of Genocide Research*, March–June, 2011, pp. 107–15.

Mazower, Mark, *Hitler's Empire: How the Nazis Ruled Europe* (New York, 2008).

McKale, Donald, *Hitler: The Survival Myth* (New York, 1981).

Medoff, Rafael, *The Deafening Silence: American Jewish Leaders and the Holocaust* (New York, 1986).

  FDR and the Holocaust: A Breach of Faith (Washington, DC, 2013).

Meinecke, Friedrich, *The German Catastrophe* (Cambridge, MA, 1950).

Miles, William F.S., "Third World Views of the Holocaust," *Journal of Genocide Research*, September 2004, pp. 371–93.

Minow, Martha, *Between Vengeance and Forgiveness: Facing History after Genocide and Mass Violence* (Boston, 1999).

Mitchell, Charles, *The Hitler Filmography: Worldwide Feature Film and Television Miniseries Portrayals, 1940 through 2000* (Jefferson, NC, 2002).

Moeller, Robert, *War Stories: The Search for a Usable Past in the Federal Republic of Germany* (Berkeley, 2003).

Monro, D.H., "Theories of Humor," in Laurence Behrens and Leonard Rosen, eds., *Writing and Reading Across the Curriculum*, 3rd edn (Glenview, IL, 1988), pp. 349–55.

Moore, Ward, *Bring the Jubilee* (New York, 1953).

Morse, Arthur, *While Six Million Died: A Chronicle of American Apathy* (New York, 1968).

Moses, A. Dirk, "Conceptual Blockages and Definitional Dilemmas in the 'Racial Century': Genocides of Indigenous Peoples and the Holocaust," *Patterns of Prejudice*, Nr. 4, 2002, pp. 7–36.

  "The Fate of Blacks and Jews: A Response to Jeffrey Herf," *Journal of Genocide Research*, June, 2008, pp. 269–87.

  "Genocide and the Terror of History," *Parallax*, 4, 2011, pp. 90–108.

  "Paranoia and Partisanship: Genocide Studies, Holocaust Historiography, and the 'Apocalyptic Conjuncture,'" *The Historical Journal*, 2, 2011, pp. 553–83.

  "Revisiting a Founding Assumption of Genocide Studies," *Genocide Studies and Prevention*, December, 2011, pp. 287–300

Moses, A. Dirk, ed., *Genocide and Settler Society: Frontier Violence and Stolen Indigenous Children in Australian History* (New York, 2004).

Moses, A. Dirk and Dan Stone, eds., *Colonialism and Genocide* (London, 2006).

Namier, Lewis, *In the Nazi Era* (New York, 1952).

Neufeld, Michael J., and Michael Berenbaum, eds., *The Bombing of Auschwitz: Should the Allies Have Attempted It?*(Lawrence, KS, 2003).

Niven, Bill, *Facing the Nazi Past: United Germany and the Legacy of the Third Reich* (London, 2002).

"Introduction: German Victimhood at the Turn of the Millennium," in Bill Niven, ed., *Germans as Victims: Remembering the Past in Contemporary Germany* (Houndmills, UK, 2006).

Niven, Bill, ed., *Germans as Victims: Remembering the Past in Contemporary Germany* (Houndmills, UK, 2006).

Nolte, Ernst, *Three Faces of Fascism* (New York, 1966).

Noon, David Hoogland, "Operation Enduring Analogy: World War II, the War on Terror, and the Uses of Historical Memory," *Rhetoric & Public Affairs*, 3, Fall 2004, pp. 339–64.

Nora, Pierre, "Between Memory and History: *Les lieux de mémoire*," *Representations*, 26, Spring 1989, pp. 7–25.

Nossack, Hans Erich, *Der Untergang* (Frankfurt, 1996).

Novick, Peter, *That Noble Dream: The 'Objectivity Question' and the American Historical Profession* (Cambridge, UK, 1988).

The Holocaust in American Life (Boston, 1999).

O'Carroll, Michael, *Pius XII, Greatness Dishonored* (Chicago, 1980).

Olick, Jeffrey K., "What Does It Mean to Normalize the Past?" *Social Science History*, Winter 1998, pp. 547–71.

Onken, Eva-Clarita, "The Politics of Finding Historical Truth: Reviewing Baltic History Commissions and Their Work," *Journal of Baltic Studies*, March 2001, pp. 109–16.

Pakier, Małgorzata, and Bo Stråth, eds., *A European Memory? Contested Histories and Politics of Remembrance* (New York, 2010).

Pauwels, Jacques, *The Myth of the Good War: America in the Second World War* (London, 2003).

Paxton, Robert, *The Anatomy of Fascism* (New York, 2004).

Pearce, Caroline, *Contemporary Germany and the Nazi Legacy: Remembrance, Politics and the Dialectic of Normality* (London, 2008).

Phayer, Michael, *The Catholic Church and the Holocaust, 1930–1965* (Bloomington, IN, 2001).

Piper, Ernst, ed., *Gibt es wirklich eine Holocaust-Industrie? Zur Auseinandersetzung um Norman Finkelstein* (Zurich, 2001).

Poliakov, Leon, *Harvest of Hate: The Nazi Program for the Destruction of the Jews of Europe* (New York, 1951).

Polonsky, Antony, *The Neighbors Respond: The Controversy over the Jedwabne Massacre in Poland* (Princeton, NJ, 2003).

Ponting, Clive, *1940: Myth and Reality* (London, 1990).

Power, Samantha, "To *Suffer* by Comparison?" *Daedalus*, 2, Spring 1999, pp. 31–66.

Prinz, Michael, and Rainer Zitelmann, eds., *Nationalsozialismus und Modernisierung* (Darmstadt, 1991).

Radonic, Ljiljana, "Transformation of Memory in Croatia," in Eric Langenbacher, Bill Niven, and Ruth Wittlinger, eds., *Dynamics of Memory and Identity in Contemporary Europe* (New York, 2012), pp. 166–79.

Reitlinger, Gerald, *The Final Solution* (London, 1953).

Rich, Norman, *Hitler's War Aims* (New York, 1973).

Robbins, Keith, *Appeasement* (Oxford, 2001).

Roberts, Andrew, *The Storm of War: A New History of the Second World* War (New York, 2010).

Robinson, Jacob, *And the Crooked Shall Be Made Straight: The Eichmann Trial, the Jewish Catastrophe, and Hannah Arendt's Narrative* (New York, 1965).

Rosenfeld, Alvin H., "The Assault on Holocaust Memory," *American Jewish Year Book*, 2001, pp. 3–20.

"Feeling Alone, Again: The Growing Unease of Germany's Jews," *American Jewish Committee: Global Jewish Advocacy*, 2002.

Rosenfeld, Gavriel D., "A Looming Crash or a Soft Landing? Forecasting the Future of the Memory 'Industry,'" *The Journal of Modern History*, March 2009, pp. 122–58.

Munich and Memory: Architecture, Monuments, and the Legacy of the Third Reich in Postwar Munich (Berkeley, 2000).

"The Politics of Uniqueness: Reflections on the Recent Polemical Turn in Holocaust and Genocide Scholarship," *Holocaust and Genocide Studies*, 1, Spring 1999, pp. 28–61.

The World Hitler Never Made: Alternate History and the Memory of Nazism (Cambridge, UK, 2005).

Rosenstone, Robert, *History on Film, Film on History* (Harlow, UK, 2012).

Rossino, Alexander B., *Hitler Strikes Poland: Blitzkrieg, Ideology, and Atrocity* (Lawrence, KS, 2005).

Roth, John K., *Holocaust Politics* (Atlanta, 2001).

Rothberg, Michael, *Multidirectional Memory: Remembering the Holocaust in the Age of Decolonization* (Palo Alto, CA, 2009).

Rousso, Henry, *The Vichy Syndrome: History and Memory in France since 1944* (Cambridge, MA, 1991).

Rubenstein, Richard L., and John K. Roth, *Approaches to Auschwitz: The Holocaust and its Legacy* (Atlanta, 1987).

Rubinstein, William D., *Genocide: A History* (Harlow, UK, 2004).

The Myth of Rescue: Why the Democracies Could Not Have Saved More Jews From the Nazis (New York, 1997).

Russett, Bruce M., *No Clear and Present Danger: A Skeptical View of the U.S. Entry into World War II* (New York, 1972).

Rutherford, Phillip T., *Prelude to the Final Solution: The Nazi Program for Deporting Ethnic Poles, 1939–1941* (Lawrence, KS, 2007).

Ryan, Johnny, *A History of the Internet and the Digital Future* (London, 2010).

Rychlak, Ronald J., *Hitler, the War, and the Pope* (Columbus, MS, 2000).

Salzborn, Samuel, "The German Myth of a Victim Nation: (Re-)presenting Germans as Victims in the New Debate on their Flight and Expulsion from Eastern Europe," in Helmut Schmitz, ed., *A Nation of Victims? Representations of German Wartime Suffering from 1945 to the Present* (Amsterdam, 2007), pp. 87–104.

Sanchez, José M., *Pius XII and the Holocaust: Understanding the Controversy* (Washington, DC, 2002).

Sansom, C. J., *Dominion* (London, 2012).

Saville, Guy, *The Afrika Reich* (London, 2011).

Schmitz, Helmut, ed., *A Nation of Victims? Representations of German Wartime Suffering from 1945 to the Present* (Amsterdam, 2007).

Schoenbaum, David, *Hitler's Social Revolution: Class and Status in Nazi Germany, 1933–1939* (New York, 1967).

Sebald, W. G., *Luftkrieg und Literatur* (Munich, 1999).

Segev, Tom, *One Palestine, Complete: Jews and Arabs Under the British Mandate* (New York, 2001).

The Seventh Million: The Israelis and the Holocaust (New York, 1993).

Selfa, Lance, *The Struggle for Palestine* (Chicago, 2002).

Shandler, Jeffrey, *While America Watches: Televising the Holocaust* (New York, 1999).

Shaw, Martin, "Shifting the Foundations of Genocide Research," *Journal of Genocide Research*, March–June, 2011, pp. 115–20.

What is Genocide? (Cambridge, UK, 2007).

Sheers, Owen, *Resistance* (New York, 2007).

Shermer, Michael and Alex Grobman, *Denying History: Who Says the Holocaust Never Happened and Why Do They Say It?* (Berkeley, 2009).

Shirer, William, *The Rise and Fall of the Third Reich* (1960).

Small, Melvin, *Was War Necessary? National Security and U. S. Entry into War* (Beverly Hills, CA, 1980).

Smith, Ashley, "World War II: The Good War?" *International Socialist Review*, 10, Winter 2000.

Smith, Malcolm, *Britain and 1940: History, Myth and Popular Memory* (London, 2001).

Snyder, Timothy, *Bloodlands: Europe Between Hitler and Stalin* (New York, 2010).

"The Causes of the Holocaust," *Contemporary European History*, 21:2, 2012, pp. 149–68.

Sobel, Robert, *For Want of a Nail: If Burgoyne Had Won at Saratoga* (London, 1997).

Speer, Albert, *Inside the Third Reich* (New York, 1970).

Stannard, David, "Uniqueness as Denial: The Politics of Genocide Scholarship," in Alan Rosenbaum, *Is the Holocaust Unique? Perspectives in Comparative Genocide* (Boulder, 1996), pp. 163–208.

Stedman, Andrew David, *Alternatives to Appeasement: Neville Chamberlain and Hitler's Germany* (New York, 2011).

Steiner, George, *Language and Silence: Essays on Language, Literature, and the Inhuman* (New York, 1967).

Steinweis, Alan, "The Auschwitz Analogy: Holocaust Memory and American Debates over Intervention in Bosnia and Kosovo in the 1990s," *Holocaust and Genocide Studies*, Fall 2005, pp. 276–89.

Stern, J. P., *Hitler: The Führer and the People* (Berkeley, 1975).

Stolzfus, Nathan, *Resistance of the Heart: Intermarriage and the Rosenstrasse Protest in Nazi Germany* (New York, 1996), p. 248.

Stone, Dan, "Beyond the Auschwitz Syndrome: Holocaust Historiography after the Cold War," *Patterns of Prejudice*, 44:5, 2010, pp. 454–68.

Histories of the Holocaust (Oxford, 2010).

Sutherland, John, "Mainstreaming Neo-Nazism," *Dimensions: A Journal of Holocaust Studies*, 13:1, 1999.

Taberner, Stuart, and Paul Cooke, eds., *German Culture, Politics, and Literature into the Twenty-First Century: Beyond Normalization* (Rochester, NY, 2006).

Taylor, A. J. P., *The Origins of the Second World War* (London, 1961).

Terkel, Studs, *"The Good War": An Oral History of World War II* (New York, 1984).

Tetlock, Philip E., Richard Ned Lebow, and Geoffrey Parker, eds., *Unmaking the West: 'What-If?' Scenarios That Rewrite World History* (Ann Arbor, MI, 2006).

Tooze, Adam, *The Wages of Destruction: The Making and Breaking of the Nazi Economy* (New York, 2008).

Torpey, John, "Making Whole What Has Been Smashed: Reflections on Reparations," *The Journal of Modern History*, June 2001, pp. 333–58.

Torpey, John, ed., *Politics and the Past: On Repairing Historical Injustices* (Lanham, MD, 2003).

Trunk, Isaiah, *Judenrat: The Jewish Councils in Eastern Europe under Nazi Occupation* (New York, 1972).

Tumarkin, Nina, *The Living and the Dead: The Rise and Fall of the Cult of World War II in Russia* (New York, 1995).

Turner, Henry, "Hitler's Impact on History," in David Wetzel, ed., *From the Berlin Museum to the Berlin Wall: Essays on the Cultural and Political History of Modern Germany* (Westport, CT, 1996), pp. 109–26.

Turtledove, Harry, *The Man With the Iron Heart* (New York, 2009).

Uldricks, Teddy J., "War, Politics and Memory: Russian Historians Reevaluate the Origins of World War II," *History & Memory*, 2, Fall/Winter 2009, pp. 60–82.

Vermes, Timur, *Er ist wieder da* (Cologne, 2012).

Walton, Jo, *Farthing* (New York, 2006).

  Ha'Penny (New York, 2007).

  Half a Crown (New York, 2008).

Weinberg, Gerhard L., *The Foreign Policy of Hitler's Germany: Diplomatic Revolution in Europe, 1933–36* (Chicago, 1971).

  The Foreign Policy of Hitler's Germany: Starting World War II, 1937–1939 (Chicago, 1980).

  "Two Separate Issues? Historiography of World War II and the Holocaust," in David Bankier and Dan Michman, *Holocaust Historiography in Context: Emergence, Challenges, Polemics, and Achievements* (Jerusalem, 2008), pp. 379–401.

Weiss, John, *Ideology of Death: Why the Holocaust Happened in Germany* (Chicago, 1997).

Weitz, Eric, *A Century of Genocide: Utopias of Race and Nation* (Princeton, NJ, 2005).

Welch, David, *Propaganda and the German Cinema, 1933–1945* (Oxford, 1983).

Wheeler-Bennett, John, *Munich: Prologue to Tragedy* (New York, 1948).

White, Hayden, *Content of the Form: Narrative Discourse and Historical Representation* (Baltimore, 1987).

  "Historical Emplotment and the Problem of Truth," in Saul Friedlander, ed., *Probing the Limits of Representation: Nazism and the 'Final Solution'* (Cambridge, MA, 1992), pp. 37–53.

Wilds, Karl, "Identity Creation and the Culture of Contrition: Recasting 'Normality' in the Berlin Republic," *German Politics*, April 2000, pp. 83–102.

Wills, Garry, *Papal Sin: Structures of Deceit* (New York, 2001).

Wittlinger, Ruth, "British–German Relations and Collective Memory," *German Politics and Society*, Autumn 2007, pp. 46–48.

  "The Merkel Government's Politics of the Past," *German Politics and Society*, 4, Winter, 2008, pp. 9–27.

Wittlinger, Ruth, and Martin Larose, "No Future for Germany's Past: Collective Memory and German Foreign Policy," *German Politics*, 4, 2007, pp. 481–95.

Wittlinger, Ruth, and Steffi Boothroyd, "A 'Usable' Past at Last? The Politics of the Past in United Germany," *German Studies Review*, 3, 2010, pp. 489–502.

Wolf, Christopher, "Hate on the Internet Leads to Hate Crime: What Is Society's Best Response?" in Barbara Perry et al., eds., *Hate Crimes: Volume 5, Responding to Hate Crimes* (Westport, CT, 2009), pp. 213–24.

Wolffsohn, Michael, *Eternal Guilt: Forty Years of German–Jewish–Israeli Relations* (New York, 1993).

Wood, Elizabeth, "Performing Memory: Vladimir Putin and the Celebration of WWII in Russia," *The Soviet and Post-Soviet Review*, 38, 2011, pp. 179–85.

Wyden, Peter, *The Hitler Virus: The Insidious Legacy of Adolf Hitler* (New York, 2001).

Wyman, David, *The Abandonment of the Jews: America and the Holocaust* (New York, 1984).

Paper Walls: America and the Refugee Crisis, 1938–1941 (New York, 1985).

Yakira, Elhanan, *Post-Zionism, Post-Holocaust: Three Essays on Denial, Forgetting, and the Delegitimation of Israel* (Cambridge, UK, 2010).

Young, James E., *The Texture of Memory: Holocaust Memorials and Meaning* (New Haven, 1993).

Youngblood, Denise, *Russian War Films: On the Cinema Front, 1914–2005* (Lawrence, KS, 2006).

Zertal, Idith, *Israel's Holocaust and the Politics of Nationhood* (Cambridge, UK, 2005).

Ziv, Avner, "Humor as a Social Corrective," in Laurence Behrens and Leonard J. Rosen, eds., *Writing and Reading Across the Curriculum* 3rd edn (Glenview, IL, 1988), pp. 356–60.

Zuccotti, Susan, *Under His Very Windows: The Vatican and the Holocaust in Italy* (New Haven, 2002).

Films

Downfall

Dresden

Die Flucht

Hitler – The Rise of Evil

Inglourious Basterds

Iron Sky

Jackboots on Whitehall

Max

Mein Führer

Mein Kampf

Unsere Mütter, unsere Väter

INDEX